THE ENDURING QUESTIONS
Main Problems of Philosophy

THE ENDURING QUESTIONS
Main Problems of Philosophy

FIFTH EDITION

MELVIN RADER
University of Washington

JERRY H. GILL
College of Saint Rose

Holt, Rinehart and Winston, Inc.

Fort Worth   Chicago   San Francisco   Philadelphia
Montreal   Toronto   London   Sydney   Tokyo

Publisher: Ted Buchholz
Acquisitions Editor: Jo-Anne Weaver
Senior Project Editor: Dawn Youngblood
Production Manager: Annette Dudley Wiggins
Art & Design Supervisor: Guy Jacobs
Text Designer: Barbara Bert/North 7 Atelier Ltd.
Cover Designer: George Rigg
Cover Illustration: Ron Lusk

Library of Congress Cataloging-in-Publication Data

Rader, Melvin Miller, 1903-1981
   The enduring questions : main problems of philosophy / Melvin
Rader, Jerry Gill. —5th ed.
     p. cm.
   Includes bibliographical references.
   ISBN 0-03-032949-3
   1. Philosophy—Introductions.   I. Gill, Jerry H., 1903-
II. Title
BD21.R28 1990
100—dc20   90-4088
                                              CIP

Address Editorial Correspondence To: 301 Commerce Street, Suite 3700, Fort Worth, TX 76102

Address Orders To: 6277 Sea Harbor Drive, Orlando, FL 32887
1-800-782-4479, or 1-800-433-0001 (in Florida)

Printed in the United States of America

1 2 3 4   0 9 0   9 8 7 6 5 4 3 2 1

Holt, Rinehart and Winston, Inc.
The Dryden Press
Saunders College Publishing

To the memory of
Melvin M. Rader
1903-1981

Philosopher
Teacher
Friend

Preface
to the Fifth Edition

I have been greatly honored to participate in the process of keeping Professor Rader's *The Enduring Questions* available as an introductory text. It has a long and fruitful history of opening the minds of literally thousands of students to the joys and difficulties of philosophy. I studied with Professor Rader briefly during my days as a graduate student and have used his texts repeatedly in various courses over the years. His students all remember warmly the Friday afternoon tea hour at the Rader home, as well as the broad sweep and deep sincerity of his philosophical interests. Today his written works are appreciated, as much as his person is missed, by those who knew him.

In revising Professor Rader's text, I have sought as much as possible to stick to the issues and perspectives he himself selected. Thus, I have re-introduced several readings from previous editions and returned to structural format of the first edition. Also, I have endeavored to continue the policy he stated in his preface to the fourth edition of including fewer readings overall. In addition, I have added a few selections at what seemed to be appropriate places.

Specifically, I have expanded the introduction with some general remarks on the various subdivisions within philosophy and the inclusion of Plato's *Euthyphro* as an example of Socrates at work. Along this line, I have also added Plato's *Meno* as a companion to Descartes on rationalism (Chapter One). Also in Part One I have introduced a selection from Thomas Reid on commonsense (Chapter Three) and added Gabriel Marcel's "Problems and Mystery" to the section on existentialism (Chapter Six).

In Part Two, in addition to re-introducing Montague's essay on the problem of evil (Chapter Seven), I have added a chapter on the pantheism of Spinoza (Chapter Ten) and one on the relationalism of A.N. Whitehead (Chapter Twelve). Part Three now includes a selection from Epicurus (Chapter Fourteen), as well as the return of Marcus Aurelius (Chapter Fifteen) and Friedrich Nietzsche (Chapter Eighteen). In Part Four I have introduced a selection from John Locke on the social contract (Chapter Twenty-two) and re-introduced the selections from Thomas Hobbes (Chapter Twenty-one), Henry David Thoreau (Chapter Twenty-three), and Martin Buber (Chapter Twenty-five).

Finally, I am especially happy to acknowledge the help and encouragement I received on this project from my wife Mari Sorri, my typist Tricia Saville, and the editorial staff at Holt, Rinehart and Winston, Jo-Anne Weaver, Wendy Ludgewait, Timothy Westmoreland, and Dawn Youngblood. The suggestions made by the following reviewers were also of valuable assistance: Robert Hollinger, Iowa State University; Michael Washburn, Indiana University–South Bend; Dolores Miller, University of Missouri–Kansas City; Virginia Ringer, California State University–Long Beach; John Utzinger, Central Washington University; and Richard Becka, Texas A&M University.

J.H.G.
Albany, NY
Feb. 1990

Contents

PART IV   SOCIAL IDEALS   511

INTRODUCTION:

THE NATURE
OF PHILOSOPHY

"Philosophy is an effort to give unity to human art and sciences by a critical examination of the grounds of our meanings, values, and beliefs."
Melvin Rader

THE GENERAL INTERPRETATION OF
EXPERIENCE

If the philosopher can be called a "specialist," he or she is a specialist in the general. Socrates (in Plato's *Republic*) defines the philosopher as "the spectator of all time and all existence"; and William James declares that philosophy deals "with the principles of explanation that underlie all things without exception, the elements common to gods and men and animals and stones, the first *whence* and the last *whither* of the whole cosmic procession, the conditions of all knowing, and the most general rules of human conduct."[1]

[1]*Some Problems of Philosophy* (New York: Longmans, Green, 1911), p. 5.

1

C. D. Broad similarly characterizes philosophy. He distinguishes between *critical* and *speculative* philosophy, both of which deal with what is general. The task of critical philosophy is to analyze and define our most fundamental and general concepts, such as "goodness," "truth," "reality," and "causation." The object of speculative philosophy is "to take over the results of the various sciences, to add to them the results of the religious and ethical experiences of mankind, and then to reflect upon the whole" in an attempt "to reach some general conclusions as to the nature of the Universe, and as to our position and prospects in it."[2]

These characterizations seem to fit the problems that philosophers most often discuss: What is a good life? What is the relation between mind and body? Do we have free will? Is there a God? Is the world fundamentally material or spiritual? Can we know the ultimate nature of reality? These are basic questions involved in a general interpretation of the world. Accordingly, Herbert Spencer defines philosophy as "knowledge of the highest degree of generality."[3]

There are certain difficulties in this view. First, science is sometimes *very* general. Newton's theory of gravitation, for example, characterizes the nearest and the most remote, the least and the greatest of objects — the pin in one's bedroom as well as the most distant galaxy. Similarly, modern atomic physics is applicable to every material entity in the universe; and the theory of evolution, summarizing the whole history of life from the first germs in the primordial sea to the highest stages of human life, is also exceedingly wide in scope. Second, the synthesis of all the sciences, or the interpretation of the whole of reality, is a pretty big order. A person would need to be a kind of god, or at least a universal genius, to succeed at so prodigious an undertaking. But philosophy is not the peculiar business of the gods or of rare geniuses; it is everyone's business.

THE PURSUIT OF MEANING

Such considerations have led many philosophers to define their field in a more restricted way. One of the most widely accepted definitions is that philosophy is the analysis, or systematic study, of meanings. This definition would in effect limit the field to what C. D. Broad calls critical philosophy.

Those who adopt this interpretation sometimes cite Socrates as an example of a philosopher. In employing his favorite conversational

[2]*Scientific Thought* (New York: Harcourt, Brace & World, 1923). p. 152.
[3]*First Principles* (New York: Burt, 1880), p. 111.

method of giving and receiving questions and answers, he is usually trying to analyze the meaning of some basic concept, such as "knowledge," "justice," "courage," "friendship," or "beauty."

One of the most influential philosophers of modern times, Moritz Schlick (1882 – 1936), has said,

> . . . Socrates' philosophy consists of what we may call "The Pursuit of Meaning." He tried to clarify thought by analyzing the meaning of our expressions and the real sense of our propositions. Here then we find a definite contrast between this philosophic method, which has for its object the discovery of meaning, and the method of the sciences, which have for their object the discovery of truth. . . . Science should be defined as the "pursuit of truth" and philosophy as the "pursuit of meaning." Socrates has set the example of the true philosophic method for all times.[4]

I do not believe that this is an adequate characterization of the method of Socrates or the nature of philosophy. Socrates was engaged not only in the pursuit of meaning but also in the pursuit of truth, and the former was largely instrumental to the latter. His definitions were intended not as arbitrary or merely verbal: They were what philosophers call "real" definitions — that is, they sought to characterize actually existent things. When Socrates asserted that justice or friendship or beauty was this or that, he implied that justice or friendship or beauty really existed and actually bore the character marked off and fixed in the definition. Consequently, he kept referring to the facts of experience so as to make his definitions truthful. Also, he was interested in fitting together the various insights thus gained into a critical interpretation of man's nature, his destiny, and his values.

To define philosophy as the pursuit of meaning is at once too broad and too narrow. It is too broad because scientists as well as philosophers seek to clarify meanings. As C. J. Ducasse has said,

> To mention but a few, such concepts as salt, acid, gas, liquid, solid, water, air, iron, etc. are concepts the exact meaning of which is investigated and discovered not by metaphysicians, logicians, or mathematicians, but by chemists and physicists; and the same is true of such even more basic physical concepts as light, electricity, matter, mass, etc. Moreover, although physicians do give us precise accounts of the meaning of these and

[4]"The Future of Philosophy," in D. J. Bronstein, Y. H. Krikorian, and P. P. Wiener, *Basic Problems of Philosophy* (Englewood Cliffs, NJ: Prentice-Hall, 1947), p. 739.

numerous other concepts, they do so in their capacity as natural scientists, *i.e.,* on the basis, ultimately, of observations and experiments. . . . [5]

In another sense, Schlick's definition of philosophy is too narrow. If Plato, Aristotle, Aquinas, Descartes, Spinoza, and Kant, for example, are to be considered philosophers — and no one has a better claim — it would appear that their field includes what Broad calls "speculative philosophy." Schlick seeks to dismiss the problems of speculative philosophy as either nonsensical or nonphilosophical. "Some of them will disappear by being shown to be mistakes and misunderstandings of our language," he declares, "and the others will be found to be ordinary scientific questions in disguise."[6] But it is unlikely that all the problems of speculative philosophy will either vanish when they are stated clearly or will turn out to be nonphilosophical problems, more appropriately treated by science. Moreover, the sharp distinction between the pursuit of meaning and the pursuit of truth is artificial, for the clarification of meaning and the discovery of truth go hand in hand. Broad rightly includes under "critical philosophy" not only the clarification of concepts but also the resolute criticism of our fundamental beliefs.

THE CULTIVATION OF WISDOM

Philosophy, we conclude, involves both the analysis of meanings and the search for generic truths. To complete our definition, we need to distinguish the kinds of meanings and generic truths that are essentially philosophical from the kinds that are scientific.

It will help us to consider the original meaning of *philosophy*. Etymologically, *philosophy* means "the love of wisdom" (from the Greek *philein*, "to love," and *sophia*, "wisdom"). The word has ordinarily been used to designate an activity rather than an emotion — the activity of pursuing wisdom rather than the emotion motivating that pursuit. The essential question that we need to consider is what, exactly, is the wisdom that the philosopher seeks.

Wisdom has been used in two senses. First, it is contrasted with ignorance. The wise person is one who knows and therefore is not ignorant. This meaning, however, does not help us to distinguish philosophy from science since the scientist also, of course, is trying to replace ignorance by knowledge. In the second sense, wisdom is contrasted with foolishness.

---

[5]*Philosophy as a Science* (New York: Oskar Piest, 1941), pp. 77–78.
[6]Ibid., p. 745.

The wise person is one who has good judgment and therefore is not foolish. Fools may have a great deal of knowledge about ordinary matters of fact, but they lack the balance and maturity and ripe insight that make it possible not only to live but also to live well.

If philosophy is the pursuit of wisdom as contrasted with foolishness, it *is* marked off from ordinary science. The subject matter of science is facts, and science attempts to discover verifiable laws — regularities — among these facts. These laws give a *description* of the facts. It is obvious that the physicist does not talk about wicked atoms or beneficent motions, and even the sociologist, in a purely scientific role, tries to *describe* rather than to *evaluate* the behavior of social groups. If philosophy, on the other hand, seeks wisdom as the opposite of foolishness, it must be a kind of critical activity concerned with appraisals. Matthew Arnold has defined poetry as "the criticism of life," but this definition fits philosophy better than poetry. It is similar to the definition of Ducasse, who maintains that "philosophy is the general theory of criticism,"[7] and the definition of John Dewey, who declares that "philosophy is inherently criticism, having its distinctive position among various modes of criticism in its generality: a criticism of criticisms, as it were"[8]

It is characteristic of criticism that it is yea-saying or nay-saying — a favoring or a disfavoring. The ways of saying *yea* or *nay* are quite various, and they correspond to different pairs of adjectives. In logic, for example, we speak of *valid* or *fallacious*; in epistemology, of *true* or *false*; in metaphysics, of *real* or *unreal*; in theology, of *holy* or *unholy*; in esthetics, of *beautiful* or *ugly*; in ethics, of *right* or *wrong*. In using these adjectives, we are making judgments. The function of philosophy is to provide the intellectual bases of sound judgments about the great issues of life.

Even when philosophy wears the garb of science, it is distinctive. For example, Lucretius was not primarily concerned with the hypotheses of atoms and evolution as scientific descriptions of the nature of things: He was concerned with the right way to think and live in the sort of universe that he regarded as real. Metaphysics should not be interpreted — as it often is — as potential or generalized natural science; rather, it should be regarded as the attempt to achieve a true understanding of humankind and our place in the cosmos so that we can distinguish the deep and permanent from the superficial and temporary, the important from the unimportant. Thus to distinguish is to *judge*, and metaphysics, like other branches of philosophy, provides a basis for judgment.

Philosophy resembles science not so much in its aim as in its method. Both employ reason and evidence as means to the discovery of truth and the clarification of meaning. Both are forms of inquiry — science being an

[7]*The Philosophy of Art* (New York: Dial, 1929), p. 3.
[8]*Experience and Nature* (Chicago: Open Court, 1925), p. 398.

inquiry into the laws of nature; philosophy, into the norms of criticism. The faith of the philosopher, like that of the scientist, is that inquiry is worthwhile. In the *Apology*, Socrates expresses the fundamental conviction of all true philosophers: "The unexamined life," he declares, "is not worth living." Likewise, in the *Meno*, his faith rings out sharp and clear:

> Some things I have said of which I am not altogether confident. But that we shall be better and braver and less helpless if we think that we ought to inquire, than we should have been if we indulged in the idle fancy that there was no knowing and no use in seeking to know what we do not know; — that is a theme upon which I am ready to fight, in word and deed, to the utmost of my power.[9]

We can fully appreciate the brave words of Socrates only if we too engage in the quest for wisdom. The proof of the pudding is in the eating — we can best judge the value of philosophy after we have philosophized. Each person must oneself taste of the pudding; no one else can do it. Of course, it is immensely helpful to study the great thinkers, such as Plato, Aristotle, Hume, and Kant, or nearer to us, William James, Santayana, and Russell. As Descartes declares in the opening chapter of his *Discourse on Method*, "The reading of good books is, as it were, to engage in talk with their authors, the finest minds of past ages, artfully contrived talk in which they give us none but the best and most select of their thoughts."[10] But like all the very good things of life, wisdom is something that cannot be given and that each must attain for himself.

In thumbing through some old lecture notes, I have found a definition of philosophy that sums up much that I have said: "Philosophy is an effort to give unity to human arts and sciences by a critical examination of the grounds of our meanings, values, and beliefs."

The foregoing discussion of the analytic and speculative modes of philosophizing serves to distinguish philosophy from two other major areas of human cognitive activity, namely science and religion. Science seeks general truth about the behavior of the natural, animal, and human aspects of reality. Unlike philosophy, it is limited to "factual" truth based on sensory observation and empirical verification. Ideally, scientific hypotheses arise from such observations and are confirmed or discredited by them. On the other hand, religion is concerned about beliefs as they bear on human meaning and destiny. Religion seeks to develop liturgical and

[9]*The Dialogues of Plato*, trans. Benjamin Jowett (London: Oxford, 1924), II, p. 47.
[10]*Discourse on Method*, in *Descartes' Philosophical Writings* (London: Macmillan, 1952), p. 119.

ethical practices that will enhance human well-being both now and for eternity. While science aims at theories that *explain* natural events and human behavior, religion constructs theories in order to *guide* human thought and life.

Philosophy, in its analytic mode, may be seen as overlapping with science, while its speculative mode has something in common with religion. In each case, however, philosophy is best understood as a "second-order" activity. That is to say, during and after scientists and theologians engage in their respective endeavors, philosophers engage in theirs: probing and seeking to clarify the meaning, implications, and presuppositions of the various methods employed by scientists and theologians. Indeed, some philosophers suggest that the primary function of philosophy is this process of "conceptual clarification," of exploring and charting the crucial moves made by theoreticians in other disciplines.

Generally speaking, philosophy may be subdivided into five main areas of interest: logic, epistemology, metaphysics, ethics, and social or political philosophy. *Logic* has been defined as the "study of the standards of rational thought." As such, it is to be distinguished from psychology, which studies the ways various people actually *do* think, not how they are *supposed* to think. Logic focuses on the relationships within and among various assertions, such as what follows from what (implication), what is presupposed by what (entailment), or whether an argument is rational (valid). Logic itself is usually divided into two parts: deductive (including symbolic logic) and inductive (pertaining to scientific reasoning and probability). Although all of these specific considerations come into play in this volume, the actual principles of logic are not specifically discussed here since the study of logic is a course all its own.

The second main area of philosophy is that of *epistemology*, or the "study of the basis and nature of knowledge". Once again, it is important to distinguish this branch of philosophy from a parallel field, cognitive psychology. Epistemology is concerned with how knowledge and truth are *defined* and *established*, not with how they are acquired. In Part One of this edition, the main schools of thought in this dimension of philosophy are presented, along with interrelated issues.

A third area of philosophy is usually termed *metaphysics* or *ontology* and may be defined as the "study of the nature of reality." Here, too, a cautionary distinction is in order. In popular discourse the term *metaphysics* has come to designate anything that transcends the normal, whatever is mystical, occult, or supernatural. In philosophy, by contrast, metaphysics refers to theories about what constitutes "the real"; what makes the world what it is and what makes it work the way it does. Part Two is comprised of chapters representing major points of view in metaphysical theory, including many relevant issues.

Fourth, there is *ethics*, the area of philosophy dealing with the "study of the standards of right conduct." As before, this aspect of philosophy must not be confused with sociology, which studies how people do, in fact, conduct themselves in relation to one another. Ethics explores the various standards for judging the moral worth of human behavior: what constitutes the Good, and what comprises the "good life". At the same time, philosophical ethics is to be distinguished from religious ethics, which represents one type of moral standard. Part Three of this book presents several of the more important approaches to the question of the proper criterion by means of which human behavior is to be judged.

A subdivision of ethics, one that has recently become a field of study in its own right, is social or *political philosophy*. Here the central questions and issues have to do with how human beings should organize and govern themselves. This area of philosophy is treated under the heading of "Social Ideals" and makes up Part Four of this text. Although closely related to questions of morality and virtue, the issues discussed in these chapters are broader and more complex. Here one must be careful to distinguish between this area of philosophy and political science, which considers how people actually do organize and govern themselves but does not try to say how they *should* do so.

A further area of philosophy, one that is too large and specialized for inclusion in a text of this sort, is *aesthetics*. Here the focus is generally on the "study of the standards of artistic value." Such questions as what makes a work of art beautiful, how aesthetic value is related to taste, and even what is art, are at the center of philosophical discussions of aesthetic meaning. Those interested in pursuing such issues may wish to consult *A Modern Book of Aesthetics* by Melvin M. Rader (Holt, Rinehart and Winston, 1979).

Finally, a few words about how to "do" philosophy. Although it is very valuable and interesting to study what the great philosophers have thought about "the enduring questions," it should be remembered that philosophy — like business, art, science, and religion — is an *activity* that people actively engage in. Thus, the content of the following chapters is no more important than the process they represent. This means that an introduction to philosophy should challenge students to learn to think philosophically themselves while exposing them to the ideas of other thinkers. To achieve this purpose, readers of the following pages will need to discuss and write both *empathetically* and *assertively*.

Empathetic skills are not highly regarded in our culture, and thus are likely to be more difficult for us to acquire. The term *empathy* is used here to designate the process of placing oneself in another person's position in order to understand and appreciate the person's perspective more fairly and thoroughly. Obviously, this process involves giving the thinker in question—whether a philosopher included in this book, your professor, or a fellow student—the benefit of the doubt at the outset. It involves learning to *listen* to what is actually being said without trying to evaluate it too quickly. This process of empathetic understanding can even be applied to one's own ideas by asking how someone coming from a different perspective might think.

Being assertive means not being passive in relation to what is being read or discussed. Three questions that may help one focus upon this assertive attitude are: (1) What exactly is being said here?, (2) What are its ramifications (presuppositions and implications)? and (3) What are its strong points and potential difficulties? It is, of course, important not to confuse being assertive with being aggressive. The goal of philosophy is, after all, increased clarity and understanding, not winning arguments. With these suggestions in mind, and recalling Socrates' confidence about the importance and value of continually asking questions, the reader is in a good position to begin his or her own quest for wisdom. We shall begin with Socrates' own defense of his philosophical activity and then move on to an example of his particular technique.

THE SOCRATIC QUEST

Socrates (470? – 399 B.C.)

We have been considering the meaning of philosophy and its relation to the sciences. But to understand the nature of philosophy we must have in mind more than a set of definitions and abstract distinctions. *Philosophy*, as we have said, means literally "the love of wisdom," and this is what philosophy at its best has always meant. As Thoreau put it, to be a philosopher means so to love wisdom as to live according to its dictates.

There is no better way in which to grasp the personal import of philosophy than to study the life and character of Socrates. More than anyone else in the history of thought, he represents the very type and ideal of the philosopher. His portrait, drawn by the genius of Plato, has for more than two thousand years been the standard by which all philosophy and philosophers have been measured. No one has loved wisdom more fervently than Socrates, and no one has lived more truly according to its dictates. In him, philosophy is not merely a way of thinking but a way of living.

Born about 470 B.C., Socrates grew up during the time of Athens' greatest power and achievement—the half century following the victories over the Persians—and he lived through the supreme crisis of Athenian history—the bitter, protracted, and catastrophic war with

Sparta. He was a contemporary of many of the greatest figures in the history of culture, among them Sophocles, Herodotus, Phidias, and Pericles. Thus he knew the city both in the height of its glory and in the depths of its crisis and defeat.

His father was a sculptor or stonemason and his mother a midwife. The family was apparently of good standing and aristocratic connections. Socrates, perhaps in jest, declared that the family pedigree could be traced back to Daedalus, a legendary maker of wooden images. Whatever his background, he moved with ease in the best and most select circles of Athenian society.

It was inevitable that a man of Socrates's bent should display a penchant for philosophy. He is said to have studied under Archelaus, the first native Athenian philosopher, and he was also familiar with the teachings of the Sophists — humanistic philosophers and paid educators who traveled from city to city. But, preferring intellectual leisure to lucrative employment, he was too poor to take formal instruction from the Sophists, whose "wisdom," moreover, he regarded as somewhat hollow. He also studied science, becoming familiar with the doctrines of the Sicilian Empedocles about biological evolution, the theories of the Italian Alcmaeon about the brain as the organ of mental life, the mathematical doctrines of Pythagoras and Zeno, and the theory of Diogenes of Apollonia that everything consists of "air." But he soon became disillusioned by the flat contradictions of such rival tenets; and when one day he read in the book of Anaxagoras (the first important philosopher to live in Athens) that "mind" is the cause of the natural order, the concept struck him with the force of revelation. Reading on, he discovered that Anaxagoras introduced a cosmic mind to explain only the initial impetus given to matter and then employed mechanical principles to explain the general structure of reality. Socrates, in contrast, vowed that he would try really to understand mind and its place in the cosmos. Thenceforth his main endeavor was to search his own mind and the minds of his fellow citizens in an attempt to discover the essence of humankind and of goodness.

In pursuing his "mission," Socrates was trying to explore the human mind and to reach the truth by dint of question and answer, dialogue, and debate. This give-and-take method of investigation by discussion is called "dialectic" or "the Socratic method" — and it is still the essential method of the philosopher. It may be carried on between two or more persons or within the mind of a single inquirer, as one puts questions to oneself and wrestles with one's answers. Usually its objective is to establish a definition, to fix in mind the essential reality of some basic value or property. Each proposed definition is tested by a process of critical examination. Is it internally consistent? Does it fit the facts? Does it agree with what we already know? In formulating and testing the definition, the philosopher continually refers to the particular data of experience; but he or she examines the particulars as instances of a type and defines the type — the "idea," "form," or "universal" — by establishing its significance in the particulars.

The years of Socrates' mission and the last thirty years of his life fell mainly in the period of the war with Sparta, when Athens was fighting for its existence. As we gather from the pages of the great historian Thucydides, it was a period of intense crisis and civil strife. Toward the close of this difficult time, it became apparent that Athens was losing the war, and revolutions were taking place within the city. Socrates, by his independence, his critical spirit, and his refusal to adopt unjust methods, offended both the democratic and aristocratic parties.

In 404 B.C. the city was finally compelled to surrender. After a short and bloody interval of oligarchical dictatorship, the old democratic form of government was restored. But the political situation remained tense, and the ruling democrats were fearful of counterrevolution. It was Socrates' misfortune that a number of his former close associates had proved themselves traitors or vicious enemies of the democratic cause. Alcibiades, Socrates' young friend, had been a brilliant general of the Athenian army, but when he was accused of religious sacrilege and ordered to stand trial, he deserted to Sparta and became a most formidable enemy of the Athenian state. Similarly, Critias and Charmides, two associates of Socrates, had been leaders of the violent oligarchical dictatorship that was established at the conclusion of the war. Inevitably, Socrates, who had long been known as a vigorous critic of democratic follies, was suspected of subversive activities. Political motives, combined with their intense dislike of Socrates' unconventional teachings, prompted Anytus, a prominent democratic politician, and two lesser associates, Meletus and Lycon, to bring charges against Socrates in 399 B.C., about four years after the war's end. The indictment, as recorded by the later historian Diogenes Laertius, read, "Socrates is guilty of not worshipping the gods whom the State worships, but introducing new and unfamiliar religious practices; and, further, of corrupting the young. The prosecutor demands the death penalty."

The main "offense," not specified in the indictment or at the trial, was that Socrates had fostered the antidemocratic spirit that had inspired the oligarchical revolutions. According to an amnesty that had been officially declared in the year 404 – 403 B.C., no one could be prosecuted for political offences committed before that date. Hence the accusations in the formal indictment were, to some extent, trumpery charges, designed to bring Socrates to trial for an offense that, perforce, remained unspecified. Yet the charges were not merely manufactured: There was widespread hostility against Socrates for his critical spirit and his unremitting search for a new rationale and norm for life. In the eyes of conservatives, he *had* blasphemed and corrupted youth. Indeed, he had questioned the very foundation of the social order, and the guardians of the status quo, hurt to the quick, retaliated by seeking to impose the ultimate penalty — death.

Tried before five hundred jurors selected by lot, Socrates spoke with such uncompromising independence that he angered the jury and provoked the death penalty. Some of his friends made a last-minute attempt to effect his escape, but he would brook no such disgraceful tactics. After a serene philosophical conversation with a group of intimates in his prison cell, he drank the fatal hemlock.

The following dialogues of Plato are two that scholars generally acknowledge as presenting the most genuine portrait of Socrates and his method of *philosophizing*. In the *Apology* Socrates defends himself and his *calling* against the charges of the state, and in the *Euthyphro* he displays his commitment to the search for truth by relentlessly pressing for the definition of a concept that nearly everyone else takes for granted. It is this commitment, rather than particular answers, that exemplifies the true philosophic spirit.

The Apology

CHARACTERS

SOCRATES
MELETUS

SCENE: The Court of Justice.

SOCRATES. I cannot tell what impression my accusers have made upon you, Athenians: for my own part, I know that they nearly made me forget who I was, so plausible were they; and yet they have scarcely uttered one single word of truth. But

The following dialogues of Plato are from the translation by F. J. Church, first published by Macmillan and Company, London, 1880.

of all their many falsehoods, the one which astonished me most, was when they said that I was a clever speaker, and that you must be careful not to let me mislead you. I thought that it was most impudent of them not to be ashamed to talk in that way; for as soon as I open my mouth the lie will be exposed, and I shall prove that I am not a clever speaker in any way at all: unless, indeed, by a clever speaker they mean a man who speaks the truth. If that is their meaning, I agree with them that I am a much greater orator than they. My accusers, then I repeat, have said little or nothing that is true; but from me you shall hear the whole truth. Certainly you will not hear an elaborate speech, Athenians, drest up, like theirs, with words and phrases. I will say to you what I have to say, without preparation, and in the words which come first, for I believe that my cause is just; so let none of you expect anything else. Indeed, my friends, it would hardly be seemly for me, at my age, to come before you like a young man with his specious falsehoods. But there is one thing, Athenians, which I do most earnestly beg and entreat of you. Do not be surprised and do not interrupt, if in my defence I speak in the same way that I am accustomed to speak in the market-place, at the tables of the money-changers, where many of you have heard me, and elsewhere. The truth is this. I am more than seventy years old, and this is the first time that I have ever come before a Court of Law; so your manner of speech here is quite strange to me. If I had been really a stranger, you would have forgiven me for speaking in the language and the fashion of my native country: and so now I ask you to grant me what I think I have a right to claim. Never mind the style of my speech —it may be better or it may be worse—give your whole attention to the question, Is what I say just, or is it not? That is what makes a good judge, as speaking the truth makes a good advocate.

I have to defend myself. Athenians, first against the old false charges of my old accusers, and then against the later ones of my present accusers. For many men have been accusing me to you, and for very many years, who have not uttered a word of truth: and I fear them more than I fear Anytus and his companions, formidable as they are. But, my friends, those others are still more formidable; for they got hold of most of you when you were children, and they have been more persistent in accusing me with lies, and in trying to persuade you that there is one Socrates, a wise man, who speculates about the heavens, and who examines into all things that are beneath the earth, and who can "make the worse appear the better reason." These men, Athenians, who spread abroad this report, are the accusers whom I fear; for their hearers think that persons who pursue such inquiries never believe in the gods. And then they are many, and their attacks have been going on for a long time: and they spoke to you when you were at the age most readily to believe them: for you were all young, and many of you were children: and there was no one to answer them when they attacked me. And the most unreasonable thing of all is that commonly I do not even know their names: I cannot tell you who they are, except in the case of the comic poets. But all the rest who have been trying to prejudice you against me, from motives of spite and jealousy, and sometimes, it may be, from conviction, are the enemies whom it is hardest to meet. For I cannot call any one of them forward in Court, to cross-examine him: I have, as it were, simply to fight with shadows in my defence, and to put questions which there is no one to answer. I ask you, therefore, to believe that, as I say, I have been attacked by two classes of accusers— first by Meletus and his friends, and then by those older ones of whom I have spoken. And, with your leave, I will defend myself first against my old enemies; for you heard their accusations first, and they were much more persistent than my present accusers are.

Well, I must make my defence, Athenians, and try in the short time allowed me to remove the prejudice which you have had against me for a long time. I hope that I may manage to do this, if it be good for you and for me, and that my defence may be successful; but I am quite aware of the nature of my task, and I know that it is a difficult one. Be the issue, however, as God wills, I must obey the law, and make my defence.

Let us begin again, then, and see what is the charge which has given rise to the prejudice against me, which was what Meletus relied on when he drew his indictment. What is the calumny which my enemies have been spreading about me? I must assume that they are formally accusing me, and read their indictment. It would run somewhat in this fashion: "Socrates is an evil-doer, who meddles with inquiries into things beneath the earth, and in heaven, and who 'makes the worse appear the better reason,' and who teaches others these same things." That is what they say; and in the Comdey of Aristophanes [*The Clouds*] you yourselves saw a man called Socrates swinging round in a basket, and saying that he walked the air, and talking a great deal of nonsense about matters of which I understand nothing, either more or less. I do not mean to disparage that kind of knowledge, if there is any man who possesses it. I trust Meletus may never be able to prosecute me for that. But, the truth is, Athenians, I have nothing to do with these matters, and almost all of you are yourselves my witnesses of this. I beg all of you who have ever heard me converse, and they are many, to inform your neighbors and tell them if any of you have ever heard me conversing about such matters, either more or less. That will show you that the other common stories about me are as false as this one.

But, the fact is, that not one of these stories is true; and if you have heard that I undertake to educate men, and exact money from them for so doing, that is not true either; though I think that it would be a fine thing to be able to educate men, as Gorgias of Leontini, and Prodicus of Ceos, and Hippias of Elis do. For each of them, my friends, can go into any city, and persuade the young men to leave the society of their fellow-citizens, with any of whom they might associate for nothing, and to be only too glad to be allowed to pay money for the privilege of associating with themselves. And I believe that there is another wise man from Paros residing in Athens at this moment. I happened to meet Callias, the son of Hipponicus, a man who has spent more money on the So-

phists than every one else put together. So I said to him — he has two
sons — Callias, if your two sons had
been foals or calves, we could have
hired a trainer for them who would
have made them perfect in the excellence which belongs to their nature.
He would have been either a groom
or a farmer. But whom do you intend to take to train them, seeing
that they are men? Who understands
the excellence which belongs to men
and to citizens? I suppose that you
must have thought of this, because
of your sons. Is there such a person,
said I, or not? Certainly there is, he
replied. Who is he, said I, and where
does he come from, and what is his
fee? His name is Evenus, Socrates, he
replied: he comes from Paros, and
his fee is five minæ. Then I thought
that Evenus was a fortunate person
if he really understood this art and
could teach so cleverly. If I had possessed knowledge of that kind, I
should have given myself airs and
prided myself on it. But, Athenians,
the truth is that I do not possess it.

Perhaps some of you may reply:
But, Socrates, what is this pursuit of
yours? Whence come these calumnies against you? You must have
been engaged in some pursuit out of
the common. All these stories and
reports of you would never have
gone about, if you had not been in
some way different from other men.
So tell us what your pursuits are,
that we may not give our verdict in
the dark. I think that that is a fair
question, and I will try to explain to
you what it is that has raised these
calumnies against me, and given me

this name. Listen, then: some of you
perhaps will think that I am jesting;
but I assure you that I will tell you
the whole truth. I have gained this
name, Athenians, simply by reason
of a certain wisdom. But by what
kind of wisdom? It is by just that
wisdom which is, I believe, possible
to men. In that, it may be, I am
really wise. But the men of whom I
was speaking just now must be wise
in a wisdom which is greater than
human wisdom, or in some way
which I cannot describe, for certainly I know nothing of it myself,
and if any man says that I do, he lies
and wants to slander me. Do not interrupt me, Athenians, even if you
think that I am speaking arrogantly.
What I am going to say is not my
own: I will tell you who says it, and
he is worthy of your credit. I will
bring the god of Delphi to be the
witness of the fact of my wisdom
and of its nature. You remember
Chærephon. From youth upwards he
was my comrade; and he went into
exile with the people,[1] and with the
people he returned. And you remember, too, Chærephon's character; how vehement he was in carrying through whatever he took in
hand. Once he went to Delphi and
ventured to put this question to the
oracle — I entreat you again, my
friends, not to cry out — he asked if
there was any man who was wiser
than I: and the priestess answered
that there was no man. Chærephon

---

[1]Chærephon was forced into exile during the
antidemocratic dictatorship of the Thirty in
404 B.C.

himself is dead, but his brother here will confirm what I say.

Now see why I tell you this. I am going to explain to you the origin of my unpopularity. When I heard of the oracle I began to reflect: What can God mean by this dark saying? I know very well that I am not wise, even in the smallest degree. Then what can he mean by saying that I am the wisest of men? It cannot be that he is speaking falsely, for he is a god and cannot lie. And for a long time I was at a loss to understand his meaning: then, very reluctantly, I turned to seek for it in this manner. I went to a man who was reputed to be wise, thinking that there, if anywhere, I should prove the answer wrong, and meaning to point out to the oracle its mistake, and to say, "You said that I was the wisest of men, but this man is wiser than I am." So I examined the man—I need not tell you his name, he was a politician—but this was the result, Athenians. When I conversed with him I came to see that, though a great many persons, and most of all he himself, thought that he was wise, yet he was not wise. And then I tried to prove to him that he was not wise, though he fancied that he was: and by so doing I made him, and many of the bystanders, my enemies. So when I went away, I thought to myself, "I am wiser than this man: neither of us probably knows anything that is really good, but he thinks that he has knowledge, when he has not, while I, having no knowledge, do not think that I have. I seem, at any rate, to be a little wiser than he is on this point: I do not think that I know what I do not know." Next I went to another man who was reputed to be still wiser than the last, with exactly the same result. And there again I made him, and many other men, my enemies.

Then I went on to one man after another, seeing that I was making enemies every day, which caused me much unhappiness and anxiety: still I thought that I must set God's command above everything. So I had to go to every man who seemed to possess any knowledge, and search for the meaning of the oracle: and, Athenians, I must tell you the truth; verily, by the dog of Egypt, this was the result of the search which I made at God's bidding. I found that the men, whose reputation for wisdom stood highest, were nearly the most lacking in it; while others, who were looked down on as common people, were much better fitted to learn. Now, I must describe to you the wanderings which I undertook, like a series of Heraclean labors, to make full proof of the oracle. After the politicians, I went to the poets, tragic, dithyrambic, and others, thinking that there I should find myself manifestly more ignorant than they. So I took up the poems on which I thought that they had spent most pains, and asked them what they meant, hoping at the same time to learn something from them. I am ashamed to tell you the truth, my friends, but I must say it. Almost any one of the bystanders could have talked about the works of these poets better than the poets themselves. So I soon found that it is not by wisdom that the poets create their works, but by a certain natural power and by inspiration, like soothsayers and prophets, who say many fine things, but who understand nothing of what they say. The poets seemed to me to be in a similar case. And at the same time I perceived that, because of their poetry, they thought that they were the wisest of men in other matters too, which they were not. So I went away again, thinking that I had the same advantage over the poets that I had over the politicians.

Finally, I went to the artisans, for I knew very well that I possessed no knowledge at all, worth speaking of, and I was sure that I should find that they knew many fine things. And in that I was not mistaken. They knew what I did not know, and so far they were wiser than I. But, Athenians, it seemed to me that the skilled artisans made the same mistake as the poets. Each of them believed himself to be extremely wise in matters of the greatest importance, because he was skillful in his own art: and this mistake of theirs threw their real wisdom into the shade. So I asked myself, on behalf of the oracle, whether I would choose to remain as I was, without either wisdom or their ignorance, or to possess both, as they did. And I made answer to myself and to the oracle that it was better for me to remain as I was.

By reason of this examination, Athenians, I have made many enemies of a very fierce and bitter kind, who have spread abroad a great number of calumnies about me, and people say that I am "a wise man." For the bystanders always think that I am wise myself in any matter wherein I convict another man of ignorance. But, my friends, I believe that only God is really wise: and that by this oracle he meant that men's wisdom is worth little or nothing. I do not think that he meant that Socrates was wise. He only made use of my name, and took me as an example, as though he would say to men, "He among you is the wisest, who, like Socrates, knows that in very truth his wisdom is worth nothing at all." And therefore I still go about testing and examining every man whom I think wise, whether he be a citizen or a stranger, as God has commanded me; and whenever I find that he is not wise, I point out to him on the part of God that he is not wise. And I am so busy in this pursuit that I have never had leisure to take any part worth mentioning in public matters, or to look after my private affairs. I am in very great poverty by reason of my service to God.

And besides this, the young men who follow me about, who are the sons of wealthy persons and have a great deal of spare time, take a natural pleasure in hearing men cross-examined: and they often imitate me among themselves: then they try their hands at cross-examining other people. And, I imagine, they find a great abundance of men who think that they know a great deal, when in fact they know little or nothing. And then the persons who are cross-examined, get angry with me instead of with themselves, and say that Socrates is an abominable fellow who corrupts young men. And when they are asked, "Why, what does he do? what does he teach?" they do not know what to say; but, not to seem at a loss, they repeat the stock charges against all philosophers, and allege that he investigates things in the air and under the earth, and that he teaches people to disbelieve in the gods, and "to make the worse appear the better reason." For, I fancy, they would not like to confess the truth, which is that they are shown up as ignorant pretenders to knowledge that they do not possess. And so they have been filling your ears with their bitter calumnies for a long time, for they are zealous and numerous and bitter against me; and they are well disciplined and plausible in speech. On these grounds Meletus and Anytus and Lycon have attacked me. Meletus is indignant with me on the part of the poets, and Anytus on the part of the artisans and politicians, and Lycon on the part of the orators. And so, as I said at the beginning, I shall be surprised if I am able, in the short time allowed me for my defence, to remove from your minds this prejudice which has grown so strong. What I have told you, Athenians, is the truth: I neither conceal, nor do I suppress anything, small or great. And yet I know that it is just this plainness of speech which makes me enemies. But that is only a proof that my words are true, and that the prejudice against me, and the causes of it, are what I have said.

And whether you look for them now or hereafter, you will find that they are so.

What I have said must suffice as my defence against the charges of my first accusers. I will try next to defend myself against that "good patriot" Meletus, as he calls himself, and my later accusers. Let us assume that they are a new set of accusers, and read their indictment, as we did in the case of the others. It runs thus. He says that Socrates is an evildoer who corrupts the youth, and who does not believe in the gods whom the city believes in, but in other new divinities. Such is the charge. Let us examine each point in it separately. Meletus says that I do wrong by corrupting the youth: but I say, Athenians, that he is doing wrong; for he is playing off a solemn jest by bringing men lightly to trial, and pretending to have a great zeal and interest in matters to which he has never given a moment's thought. And now I will try to prove to you that it is so.

Come here, Meletus. Is it not a fact that you think it very important that the younger men should be as excellent as possible?

MELETUS. It is.

SOCR. Come then: tell the judges, who is it who improves them? You take so much interest in the matter that of course you know that. You are accusing me, and bringing me to trial, because, as you say, you have discovered that I am the corrupter of the youth. Come now, reveal to the judges who improves them. You see,

Meletus, you have nothing to say; you are silent. But don't you think that this is a scandalous thing? Is not your silence a conclusive proof of what I say, that you have never given a moment's thought to the matter? Come, tell us, my good sir, who makes the young men better citizens?

MEL.   The laws.

SOCR.   My excellent sir, that is not my question. What man improves the young, who starts with a knowledge of the laws?

MEL.   The judges here, Socrates.

SOCR.   What do you mean, Meletus? Can they educate the young and improve them?

MEL.   Certainly . . .

SOCR.   All of them? or only some of them?

MEL.   All of them.

SOCR.   By Hera that is good news! There is a great abundance of benefactors. And do the listeners here improve them, or not?

MEL.   They do.

SOCR.   And do the senators?

MEL.   Yes.

SOCR.   Well then, Meletus; do the members of the Assembly corrupt the younger men? or do they again all improve them?

MEL.   They too improve them.

SOCR.   Then all the Athenians, apparently, make the young into fine fellows except me, and I alone corrupt them. Is that your meaning?

MEL.   Most certainly; that is my meaning.

SOCR.   You have discovered me to be a most unfortunate man. Now tell me: do you think that the same holds good in the case of horses? Does one man do them harm and every one else improve them? On the contrary, is it not one man only, or a very few —namely, those who are skilled in horses—who can improve them; while the majority of men harm them, if they use them, and have to do with them? Is it not so, Meletus, both with horses and with every other animal? Of course it is, whether you and Anytus say yes or no. And young men would certainly be very fortunate persons if only one man corrupted them, and every one else did them good. The truth is, Meletus, you prove conclusively that you have never thought about the youth in your life. It is quite clear, on your own showing, that you take no interest at all in the matters about which you are prosecuting me.

Now, be so good as to tell us, Meletus, is it better to live among good citizens or bad ones? Answer, my friend: I am not asking you at all a difficult question. Do not bad citizens do harm to their neighbors and good citizens good?

MEL.   Yes.

SOCR.   Is there any man who would rather be injured than benefited by his companions? Answer, my good sir: you are obliged by the law to answer. Does any one like to be injured?

MEL. Certainly not.

SOCR. Well then, are you prosecuting me for corrupting the young, and making them worse men, intentionally or unintentionally?

MEL. For doing it intentionally.

SOCR. What, Meletus? Do you mean to say that you, who are so much younger than I, are yet so much wiser than I, that you know that bad citizens always do evil, and that good citizens always do good, to those with whom they come in contact, while I am so extraordinarily stupid as not to know that if I make any of my companions a rogue, he will probably injure me in some way, and as to commit this great crime, as you allege, intentionally? You will not make me believe that, nor any one else either, I should think. Either I do not corrupt the young at all, or if I do, I do so unintentionally: so that you are a liar in either case. And if I corrupt them unintentionally, the law does not call upon you to prosecute me for a fault like that, which is an involuntary one: you should take me aside and admonish and instruct me: for of course I shall cease from doing wrong involuntarily, as soon as I know that I have been doing wrong. But you declined to instruct me: you would have nothing to do with me: instead of that, you bring me up before the Court, where the law sends persons, not for instruction, but for punishment.

The truth is, Athenians, as I said, it is quite clear that Meletus has never paid the slightest attention to these matters. However, now tell us, Meletus, how do you say that I corrupt the younger men? Clearly, according to your indictment, by teaching them not to believe in the gods of the city, but in other new divinities instead. You mean that I corrupt young men by that teaching, do you not?

MEL. Yes: most certainly, I mean that.

SOCR. Then in the name of these gods of whom we are speaking, explain yourself a little more clearly to me and to the judges here. I cannot understand what you mean. Do you mean that I teach young men to believe in some gods, but not in the gods of the city? Do you accuse me of teaching them to believe in strange gods? If that is your meaning, I myself believe in some gods, and my crime is not that of absolute atheism. Or do you mean that I do not believe in the gods at all myself, and that I teach other people not to believe in them either?

MEL. I mean that you do not believe in the gods in any way whatever.

SOCR. Wonderful, Meletus! Why do you say that? Do you mean that I believe neither the sun nor the moon to be gods, like other men?

MEL. I swear he does not, judges: he says that the sun is a stone, and the moon earth.

SOCR. My dear Meletus, do you think that you are prosecuting Anaxagoras? You must have a very poor opinion of the judges, and think them very unlettered men, if you imagine that they do not know that the works of Anaxagoras of Clazomenæ are full of these doctrines. And so young men learn these things from me, when they can often buy places in the theater[2] for a drachma at most, and laugh Socrates to scorn, were he to pretend that these doctrines, which are very peculiar doctrines, too, were his. But please tell me, do you really think that I do not believe in the gods at all?

MEL.   Most certainly I do. You are a complete atheist.

SOCR.   No one believes that, Meletus, and I think that you know it to be a lie yourself. It seems to me, Athenians, that Meletus is a very insolent and wanton man, and that he is prosecuting me simply in the insolence and wantonness of youth. He is like a man trying an experiment on me, by asking me a riddle that has no answer. "Will this wise Socrates," he says to himself, "see that I am jesting and contradicting myself? or shall I outwit him and every one else who hears me?" Meletus seems to me to contradict himself in his indictment: it is as if he were to say, "Socrates is a wicked man who does not believe in the gods, but who believes in the gods." But that is mere trifling.

Now, my friends, let us see why I think that this is his meaning. Do you answer me, Meletus: and do you, Athenians, remember the request which I made to you at starting, and do not interrupt me if I talk in my usual way.

Is there any man, Meletus, who believes in the existence of things pertaining to men and not in the existence of men? Make him answer the question, my friends, without these absurd interruptions. Is there any man who believes in the existence of horsemanship and not in the existence of horses? or in flute-playing and not in flute-players? There is not, my excellent sir. If you will not answer, I will tell both you and the judges that. But you must answer my next question. Is there any man who believes in the existence of divine things and not in the existence of divinities?

MEL.   There is not.

SOCR.   I am very glad that the judges have managed to extract an answer from you. Well then, you say that I believe in divine beings, whether they be old or new ones, and that I teach others to believe in them; at any rate, according to your statement, I believe in divine beings. That you have sworn in your deposition. But if I believe in divine beings, I suppose it follows necessarily that I believe in divinities. Is it not so? It is. I assume that you grant that, as you do not answer. But do we not believe that divinities are either gods themselves or the children of the gods? Do you admit that?

MEL.   I do.

SOCR.   Then you admit that I believe

[2]Socrates here alludes to the references to Anaxagoras by Aristophanes, Euripides, and other Greek dramatists. Anaxagoras' doctrine that the sun is a stone is mentioned in the *Orestes* of Euripedes.

in divinities: now, if these divinities are gods, then, as I say, you are jesting and asking a riddle, and asserting that I do not believe in the gods, and at the same time that I do, since I believe in divinities. But if these divinities are the illegitimate children of the gods, either by the nymphs or by other mothers, as they are said to be, then, I ask, what man could believe in the existence of the children of the gods and not in the existence of the gods? That would be as strange as believing in the existence of the offspring of horses and asses, and not in the existence of horses and asses. You must have indicted me in this manner, Meletus, either to test my skill, or because you could not find any crime that you could accuse me of with truth. But you will never contrive to persuade any man, even of the smallest understanding, that a belief in divine things and things of the gods does not necessarily involve a belief in divinities, and in the gods, and in heroes.

But in truth, Athenians, I do not think that I need say very much to prove that I have not committed the crime for which Meletus is prosecuting me. What I have said is enough to prove that. But, I repeat, it is certainly true, as I have already told you, that I have incurred much unpopularity and made many enemies. And that is what will cause my condemnation, if I am condemned; not Meletus, nor Anytus either, but the prejudice and suspicion of the multitude. They have been the destruction of many good men before me,

and I think that they will be so again. There is no fear that I shall be their last victim.

Perhaps some one will say: "Are you not ashamed, Socrates, of following pursuits which are very likely now to cause your death?" I should answer him with justice, and say: My friend, if you think that a man of any worth at all ought to reckon the chances of life and death when he acts, or that he ought to think of anything but whether he is acting rightly or wrongly, and as a good or a bad man would act, you are grievously mistaken. According to you, the demigods who died at Troy would be men of no great worth, and among them the son of Thetis, who thought nothing of danger when the alternative was disgrace. For when his mother, a goddess, addressed him, as he was burning to slay Hector, I suppose in this fashion, "My son, if thou avengest the death of thy comrade Patroclus, and slayest Hector, thou wilt die thyself, for 'fate awaits thee straightway after Hector's death,'" he heard what she said, but he scorned danger and death; he feared much more to live a coward, and not to avenge his friend. "Let me punish the evil-doer and straightway die," he said, "that I may not remain here by the beaked ships, a scorn of men, encumbering the earth." Do you suppose that he thought of danger or of death? For this, Athenians, I believe to be the truth. Wherever a man's post is, whether he has chosen it of his own will, or whether he has been placed at it by his commander, there it is his duty to remain and face the danger, without thinking of death, or of any other thing, except dishonor.

When the generals whom you chose to command me, Athenians, placed me at my post at Potidæa, and at Amphipolis, and at Delium, I remained where they placed me, and ran the risk of death, like other men: and it would be very strange conduct on my part if I were to desert my post now from fear of death or of any other thing, when God has commanded me, as I am persuaded that he has done, to spend my life in searching for wisdom, and in examining myself and others. That would indeed be a very strange thing: and then certainly I might with justice be brought to trial for not believing in the gods: for I should be disobeying the oracle, and fearing death, and thinking myself wise, when I was not wise. For to fear death, my friends, is only to think ourselves wise, without being wise: for it is to think that we know what we do not know. For anything that men can tell, death may be the greatest good that can happen to them: but they fear it as if they knew quite well that it was the greatest of evils. And what is this but that shameful ignorance of thinking that we know what we do not know? In this matter too, my friends, perhaps I am different from the mass of mankind: and if I were to claim to be at all wiser than others, it would be because I do not think that I have any clear knowledge about the other world, when, in fact, I have none. But I do know very well that it is evil and base to do wrong, and to disobey my superior, whether he be man or god. And I will never do what I know to be evil, and shrink in fear from what, for all that I can tell, may be a good. And so, even if you acquit me now, and do not listen to Anytus' argument that, if I am to be acquitted, I ought never to have been brought to trial at all; and that, as it is, you are bound to put me to death, because, as he said, if I escape, all your children will forthwith be utterly corrupted by practising what Socrates teaches; if you were therefore to say to me, "Socrates, this time we will not listen to Anytus: we will let you go; but on this condition, that you cease from carrying on this search of yours, and from philosophy; if you are found following those pursuits again, you shall die": I say, if you offered to let me go on these terms, I should reply:—Athenians, I hold you in the highest regard and love; but I will obey God rather than you: and as long as I have breath and strength I will not cease from philosophy, and from exhorting you, and declaring the truth to every one of you whom I meet, saying, as I am wont: "My excellent friend, you are a citizen of Athens, a city which is very great and very famous for wisdom and power of mind; are you not ashamed of caring so much for the making of money, and for reputation, and for honor? Will you not think or care about wisdom and truth, and the perfection of your soul?" And if he disputes my words, and says that he does care about these things, I shall not forthwith release him and go away: I shall question him and cross-examine him and test him: and if I think that he has not virtue, though he says that he has, I shall reproach him for setting the lower value on the most important things, and a higher value on those that are of less account. This I shall do to every one whom I meet, young or old, citizen or stranger: but more especially to the citizens, for they are more nearly akin to me. For, know well, God has commanded me to do so. And I think that no better piece of fortune has every befallen you in Athens than my service to God. For I spend my whole life in going about and persuading you all to give your first and chiefest care to the perfection of your souls, and not till you have done that to think of your bodies, or your wealth; and telling you that virtue does not come from wealth, but that wealth, and every other good thing which men have, whether in public, or in private, comes from virtue. If then I corrupt the youth by this teaching, the mischief is great: but if any man says that I teach anything else, he speaks falsely. And therefore, Athenians, I say, either listen to Anytus, or do not listen to him: either acquit me, or do not acquit me: but be sure that I shall not alter my way of life; no, not if I have to die for it many times.

Do not interrupt me, Athenians. Remember the request which I made to you, and listen to my words. I think that it will profit you to hear them. I am going to say something more to you, at which you may be inclined to cry out: but do not do that. Be sure that if you put me to death, who am what I have told you that I am, you will do yourselves more harm than me. Meletus and Anytus can do me no harm: that is impossible: for I am sure that God will not allow a good man to be injured by a bad one. They may indeed kill me, or drive me into exile, or deprive me of my civil rights; and perhaps Meletus and others think those things great evils. But I do not think so: I think that it is a much greater evil to do what he is doing now, and to try to put a man to death unjustly. And now, Athenians, I am not arguing in my own defence at all, as you might expect me to do: I am trying to persuade you not to sin against God, by condemning me, and rejecting his gift to you. For if you put me to death, you will not easily find another man to fill my place. God has sent me to attack the city, as if it were a great and noble horse, to use a quaint simile, which was rather sluggish from its size, and which needed to be aroused by a gadfly: and I think that I am the gadfly that God has sent to the city to attack it; for I never cease from settling upon you, as it were, at every point, and rousing, and exhorting, and reproaching each man of you all day long. You will not easily find any one else, my friends, to fill my place: and if you take my advice, you will spare my life. You are vexed, as drowsy persons are, when they are awakened, and of course, if you listened to Anytus, you could easily kill me with a single blow, and then sleep on undisturbed for the rest of your lives, unless God were to care for you enough to send another man to arouse you. And you may easily see that it is God who has given me to your city: a mere human impulse would never have led me to neglect all my own interests, or to endure seeing my private affairs neglected now for so many years, while it made me busy myself unceasingly in your interests, and go to each man of you by himself, like a father, or an elder brother, trying to persuade him to care for virtue. There would have been a reason for it, if I had gained any advantage by this conduct, or if I had been paid for my exhortations; but you see yourselves that my accusers, though they accuse me of everything else without blushing, have not had the effrontery to say that I ever either exacted or demanded payment. They could bring no evidence of that. And I think that I have sufficient evidence of the truth of what I say in my poverty.

Perhaps it may seem strange to you that, though I am so busy in going about in private with my counsel, yet I do not venture to come forward in the assembly, and take part in the public councils. You have often heard me speak of my reason for this, and in many places: it is that I have a certain divine sign from God, which is the divinity that Meletus has caricatured in his indictment. I have had it from childhood: it is a kind of voice, which whenever I hear it, always turns me back from something which I was going to do, but never urges me to act. It is this which forbids me to take part in politics. And I think that it does well to forbid me. For, Athenians, it is quite certain that if I had attempted to take part in politics, I should have perished at once and long ago, without doing any good either to you or to myself. And do not be vexed with me for telling the truth. There is no man who will preserve his life for long, either in Athens or elsewhere, if he firmly opposes the wishes of the people, and tries to prevent the commission of much injustice and illegality in the State. He who would really fight for injustice, must do so as a private man, not in public, if he means to preserve his life, even for a short time.

I will prove to you that this is so by very strong evidence, not by mere words, but by what you value highly, actions. Listen then to what has happened to me, that you may know that there is no man who could make me consent to do wrong from the fear of death; but that I would perish at once rather than give way. What I am going to tell you may be a commonplace in the Courts of Law; nevertheless it is true. The only office that I ever held in the State, Athenians, was that of Senator. When you wished to try the ten generals, who did not rescue their men after the battle of Arginusæ, in a body, which was illegal, as you all came to think afterwards, the tribe Antiochis, to which I belong, held the presidency. On that occasion I alone of all the presidents opposed your illegal action, and gave my vote against you. The speakers were ready to suspend me and arrest me; and you were clamoring against me, and crying out to me to submit. But I thought that I ought to face the danger out in the cause of law and justice, rather than join with you in your unjust proposal, from fear of imprisonment or death. That was before the destruction of the democracy. When the oligarchy came, the Thirty sent for me, with four others, to the Council-Chamber, and ordered us to bring over Leon the Salaminian from Salamis, that they might put him to death. They were in the habit of frequently giving similar orders to many others, wishing to implicate as many men as possible in their crimes. But then I again proved, not by mere words, but by my actions, that, if I may use a vulgar expression, I do not care a straw for death; but that I do care very much indeed about not doing anything against the laws of God or man. That government with all its power did not terrify me into doing anything wrong; but when we left the Council-Chamber, the other four went over to Salamis, and brought Leon across to Athens; and I went away home: and if the rule of the Thirty had not been destroyed soon afterwards, I should very likely have been put to death for what I did then. Many of you will be my witnesses in this matter.

Now do you think that I should have remained alive all these years, if I had taken part in public affairs, and had always maintained the cause of justice like an honest man, and

had held it a paramount duty, as it is, to do so? Certainly not, Athenians, nor any other man either. But throughout my whole life, both in private, and in public, whenever I have had to take part in public affairs, you will find that I have never yielded a single point in a question of right and wrong to any man; no, not to those whom my enemies falsely assert to have been my pupils.[3] But I was never any man's teacher. I have never withheld myself from any one, young or old, who was anxious to hear me converse while I was about my mission; neither do I converse for payment, and refuse to converse without payment: I am ready to ask questions of rich and poor alike, and if any man wishes to answer me, and then listen to what I have to say, he may. And I cannot justly be charged with causing these men to turn out good or bad citizens: for I never either taught, or professed to teach any of them any knowledge whatever. And if any man asserts that he ever learnt or heard any thing from me in private, which every one else did not hear as well as he, be sure that he does not speak the truth.

Why is it, then, that people delight in spending so much time in my company? You have heard why, Athenians. I told you the whole truth when I said that they delight in hearing me examine persons who think that they are wise when they are not wise. It is certainly very amusing to listen to that. And, I say,

[3]For example, Critias and Alcibiades.

God has commanded me to examine men in oracles, and in dreams, and in every way in which the divine will was ever declared to man. This is the truth, Athenians, and if it were not the truth, it would be easily refuted. For if it were really the case that I have already corrupted some of the young men, and am now corrupting others, surely some of them, finding as they grew older that I had given them evil counsel in their youth, would have come forward today to accuse me and take their revenge. Or if they were unwilling to do so themselves, surely their kinsmen, their fathers, or brothers, or other relatives, would, if I had done them any harm, have remembered it, and taken their revenge. Certainly I see many of them in Court. Here is Crito, of my own deme and of my own age, the father of Critobulus; here is Lysanias of Sphettus, the father of Æschinus: here is also Antiphon of Cephisus, the father of Epigenes. Then here are others, whose brothers have spent their time in my company; Nicostratus, the son of Theozotides, and brother of Theodotus — and Theodotus is dead, so he at least cannot entreat his brother to be silent: here is Paralus, the son of Demodocus, and the brother of Theages: here is Adeimantus, the son of Ariston, whose brother is Plato here: and Æantodorus, whose brother is Aristodorus. And I can name many others to you, some of whom Meletus ought to have called as witnesses in the course of his own speech: but if he forgot to call them then, let him call them now — I will stand aside while he does so — and tell us if he has any such evidence. No, on the contrary, my friends, you will find all these men ready to support me, the corrupter, the injurer of their kindred, as Meletus and Anytus call me. Those of them who have been already corrupted might perhaps have some reason for supporting me: but what reason can their relatives, who are grown up, and who are uncorrupted, have, except the reason of truth and justice, that they know very well that Meletus is a liar, and that I am speaking the truth?

Well, my friends, this, together it may be with other things of the same nature, is pretty much what I have to say in my defence. There may be some one among you who will be vexed when he remembers how, even in a less important trial than this, he prayed and entreated the judges to acquit him with many tears, and brought forward his children and many of his friends and relatives in Court, in order to appeal to your feelings; and then finds that I shall do none of these things, though I am in what he would think the supreme danger. Perhaps he will harden himself against me when he notices this: it may make him angry, and he may give his vote in anger. If it is so with any of you — I do not suppose that it is, but in case it should be so — I think that I should answer him reasonably if I said: "My friend, I have kinsmen too, for, in the words of Homer, 'I am not born of stocks and stones,' but of woman"; and so, Athenians, I have kinsmen, and I have three sons, one of them a lad, and the other two still children. Yet I will not bring any of them forward before you, and implore you to acquit me. And why will I do none of these things? It is not from arrogance, Athenians, nor because I hold you cheap: whether or no I can face death bravely is another question: but for my own credit, and for your credit, and for the credit of our city, I do not think it well, at my age, and with my name, to do anything of that kind. Rightly or wrongly, men have made up their minds that in some way Socrates is different from the mass of mankind. And it will be a shameful thing if those of you who are thought to excel in wisdom, or in bravery, or in any other virtue, are going to act in this fashion. I have often seen men with a reputation behaving in a strange way at their trial, as if they thought it a terrible fate to be killed, and as though they expected to live for ever, if you did not put them to death. Such men seem to me to bring discredit on the city: for any stranger would suppose that the best and most eminent Athenians, who are selected by their fellow-citizens to hold office, and for other honors, are no better than women. Those of you, Athenians, who have any reputation at all, ought not to do these things: and you ought not to allow us to do them: you should show that you will be much more merciless to men who make the city ridiculous by these pitiful pieces of acting, than to men who remain quiet.

But apart from the quesion of credit, my friends, I do not think that it is right to entreat the judge to acquit us, or to escape condemnation in that way. It is our duty to convince his mind by reason. He does not sit to give away justice to his friends, but to pronounce judgment: and he has sworn not to favor any man whom he would like to favor, but to decide questions according to law. And therefore we ought not to teach you to forswear yourselves; and you ought not to allow yourselves to be taught, for then neither you nor we would be acting righteously. Therefore, Athenians, do not require me to do these things, for I believe them to be neither good nor just nor holy; and, more especially do not ask me to do them today, when Meletus is prosecuting me for impiety. For were I to be successful, and to prevail on you by my prayers to break your oaths, I should be clearly teaching you to believe that there are no gods; and I should be simply accusing myself by my defence of not believing in them. But, Athenians, that is very far from the truth. I do believe in the gods as no one of my accusers believes in them: and to you and to God I commit my cause to be decided as is best for you and for me.

[*He is found guilty by 281 votes to 220.*]

I am not vexed at the verdict which you have given, Athenians, for many reasons. I expected that you would find me guilty; and I am not so much surprised at that, as at the numbers of the votes. I, certainly, never thought that the majority against me would have been so narrow. But now it seems that if only thirty votes had changed sides, I should have escaped. So I think that I have escaped Meletus, as it is: and not only have I escaped him; for it is perfectly clear that if Anytus and Lycon had not come forward to accuse me too, he would not have obtained the fifth part of the votes, and would have had to pay a fine of a thousand drachmæ.

So he proposes death as the penalty. Be it so. And what counter-penalty shall I propose to you, Athenians? What I deserve, of course, must I not? What then do I deserve to pay or to suffer for having determined not to spend my life in ease? I neglected the things which most men value, such as wealth, and family interests, and military commands, and popular oratory, and all the political appointments, and clubs, and factions, that there are in Athens; for I thought that I was really too conscientious a man to preserve my life if I engage in these matters. So I did not go where I should have done no good either to you or to myself. I went instead to each one of you by himself, to do him, as I say, the greatest of services, and strove to persuade him not to think of his affairs, until he had thought of himself, and tried to make himself as perfect and wise as possible; nor to think of the affairs of Athens, until he had thought of Athens herself; and in all cases to bestow his thoughts on things in the same manner. Then what do I de-

serve for such a life? Something good, Athenians, if I am really to propose what I deserve; and something good which it would be suitable to me to receive. Then what is a suitable reward to be given to a poor benefactor, who requires leisure to exhort you? There is no reward, Athenians, so suitable for him as a public maintenance in the Prytaneum. It is a much more suitable reward for him than for any of you who has won a victory at the Olympic games with his horse or his chariots. Such a man only makes you seem happy, but I make you really happy: and he is not in want, and I am. So if I am to propose the penalty which I really deserve, I propose this, a public maintenance in the Prytaneum.

Perhaps you think me stubborn and arrogant in what I am saying now, as in what I said about the entreaties and tears. It is not so, Athenians; it is rather than I am convinced that I never wronged any man intentionally, though I cannot persuade you of that, for we have conversed together only a little time. If there were a law at Athens, as there is elsewhere, not to finish a trial of life and death in a single day, I think that I could have convinced you of it: but now it is not easy in so short a time to clear myself of the gross calumnies of my enemies. But when I am convinced that I have never wronged any man, I shall certainly not wrong myself, or admit that I deserve to suffer any evil, or propose any evil for myself as a penalty. Why should I? Lest I should suffer the penalty which Meletus proposes, when I say that I do not know whether it is a good or an evil? Shall I choose instead of it something which I know to be an evil, and propose that as a penalty? Shall I propose imprisonment? And why should I pass the rest of my days in prison, the slave of successive officials? Or shall I propose a fine, with imprisonment until it is paid? I have told you why I will not do that. I should have to remain in prison for I have no money to pay a fine with. Shall I then propose exile? Perhaps you would agree to that. Life would indeed be very dear to me, if I were unreasonable enough to expect that strangers would cheerfully tolerate my discussions and reasonings, when you who are my fellow-citizens cannot endure them, and have found them so burdensome and odious to you, that you are seeking now to be released from them. No, indeed, Athenians, that is not likely. A fine life I should lead for an old man, if I were to withdraw from Athens, and pass the rest of my days in wandering from city to city, and continually being expelled. For I know very well that the young men will listen to me, wherever I go, as they do here; and if I drive them away, they will persuade their elders to expel me: and if I do not drive them away, their fathers and kinsmen will expel me for their sakes.

Perhaps some one will say, "Why cannot you withdraw from Athens, Socrates, and hold your peace?" It is the most difficult thing in the world to make you understand why I cannot do that. If I say that I cannot hold my peace, because that would be to disobey God, you will think that I am not in earnest and will not believe me. And if I tell you that no better thing can happen to a man than to converse every day about virtue and the other matters about which you have heard me conversing and examining myself and others, and that an unexamined life is not worth living, then you will believe me still less. But that is the truth, my friends, though it is not easy to convince you of it. And, what is more, I am not accustomed to think that I deserve any punishment. If I had been rich, I would have proposed as large a fine as I could pay: that would have done me no harm. But I am not rich enough to pay a fine, unless you are willing to fix it at a sum within my means. Perhaps I could pay you a mina: so I propose that. Plato here, Athenians, and Crito, and Critobulus, and Apollodorus bid me propose thirty minæ, and they will be sureties for me. So I propose thirty minæ. They will be sufficient sureties to you for the money.

[*He is condemned to death.*]

You have not gained very much time, Athenians, and, as the price of it, you will have an evil name from all who wish to revile the city, and they will cast in your teeth that you put Socrates, a wise man, to death. For they will certainly call me wise, whether I am wise or not, when they want to reproach you. If you would have waited for a little while, your wishes would have been fulfilled in the course of nature; for you see that I am an old man, far advanced in years, and near to death. I am speaking not to all of you, only to those who have voted for my death. And now I am speaking to them still. Perhaps, my friends, you think that I have been defeated because I was wanting in the arguments by which I could have persuaded you to acquit me, if, that is, I had thought it right to do or to say anything to escape punishment. It is not so. I have been defeated because I was wanting, not in arguments, but in overboldness and effrontery: because I would not plead before you as you would have liked to hear me plead, or appeal to you with weeping and wailing, or say and do many other things, which I maintain are unworthy of me, but which you have been accustomed to from other men. But when I was defending myself, I thought that I ought not to do anything unmanly because of the danger which I ran, and I have not changed my mind now. I would very much rather defend myself as I did, and die, than as you would have had me do, and live. Both in a law suit, and in war, there are some things which neither I nor any other man may do in order to escape from death. In battle a man often sees that he may at least escape from death by throwing down his arms and falling on his knees before the pursuer to beg for his life. And there are many other ways of avoiding death in every danger, if a man

will not scruple to say and to do anything. But, my friends, I think that it is a much harder thing to escape from wickedness than from death; for wickedness is swifter than death. And now I, who am old and slow, have been overtaken by the slower pursuer: and my accusers, who are clever and swift, have been overtaken by the swifter pursuer, which is wickedness. And now I shall go hence, sentenced by you to death; and they will go hence, sentenced by truth to receive the penalty of wickedness and evil. And I abide by this award as well as they. Perhaps it was right for these things to be so: and I think that they are fairly measured.

And now I wish to prophesy to you, Athenians who have condemned me. For I am going to die, and that is the time when men have most prophetic power. And I prophesy to you who have sentenced me to death, that a far severer punishment than you have inflicted on me, will surely overtake you as soon as I am dead. You have done this thing, thinking that you will be relieved from having to give an account of your lives. But I say that the result will be very different from that. There will be more men who will call you to account, whom I have held back, and whom you did not see. And they will be harder masters to you than I have been, for they will be younger, and you will be more angry with them. For if you think that you will restrain men from reproaching you for your evil lives by putting them to death, you are very much mistaken. That way of escape is hardly possible, and it is not a good one. It is much better, and much easier, not to silence reproaches, but to make yourselves as perfect as you can. This is my parting prophecy to you who have condemned me.

With you who have acquitted me I should like to converse touching this thing that has come to pass, while the authorities are busy, and before I go to the place where I have to die. So, I pray you, remain with me until I go hence: there is no reason why we should not converse with each other while it is possible. I wish to explain to you, as my friends, the meaning of what has befallen me. A wonderful thing has happened to me, judges — for you I am right in calling judges. The prophetic sign, which I am wont to receive from the divine voice, has been constantly with me all through my life till now, opposing me in quite small matters if I were not going to act rightly. And now you yourselves see what has happened to me; a thing which might be thought, and which is sometimes actually reckoned, the supreme evil. But the sign of God did not withstand me when I was leaving my house in the morning, nor when I was coming up hither to the Court, nor at any point in my speech, when I was going to say anything: though at other times it has often stopped me in the very act of speaking. But now, in this matter, it has never once withstood me, either in my words or my actions. I will tell you what I believe to be the reason of that. This thing that has come

upon me must be a good: and those of us who think that death is an evil must needs be mistaken. I have a clear proof that that is so; for my accustomed sign would certainly have opposed me, if I had not been going to fare well.

And if we reflect in another way we shall see that we may well hope that death is a good. For the state of death is one of two things: either the dead man wholly ceases to be, and loses all sensation; or, according to the common belief, it is a change and a migration of the soul unto another place. And if death is the absence of all sensation, and like the sleep of one whose slumbers are unbroken by any dreams, it will be a wonderful gain. For if a man had to select that night in which he slept so soundly that he did not even see any dreams, and had to compare with it all the other nights and days of his life, and then had to say how many days and nights in his life he had spent better and more pleasantly than this night, I think that a private person, nay, even the great King [of Persia] himself, would find them easy to count, compared with the others. If that is the nature of death, I for one count it a gain. For then it appears that eternity is nothing more than a single night. But if death is a journey to another place, and the common belief be true, that there are all who have died, what good could be greater than this, my judges? Would a journey not be worth taking, at the end of which, in the other world, we should be released from the self-styled judges who are here, and should find the true judges, who are said to sit in judgment below, such as Minos, and Rhadamanthus, and Æacus, and Triptolemus, and the other demi-gods who were just in their lives? Or what would you not give to converse with Orpheus and Musæus and Hesiod and Homer? I am willing to die many times, if this be true. And for my own part I should have a wonderful interest in meeting there Palamedes, and Ajax the son of Telamon, and the other men of old who have died through an unjust judgment, and in comparing my experiences with theirs. That I think would be no small pleasure. And, above all, I could spend my time in examining those who are there, as I examine men here, and in finding out which of them is wise, and which of them thinks himself wise, when he is not wise. What would we not give, my judges, to be able to examine the leader of the great expedition against Troy, or Odysseus, or Sisyphus, or countless other men and women whom we could name? It would be an infinite happiness to converse with them, and to live with them, and to examine them. Assuredly there they do not put men to death for doing that. For besides the other ways in which they are happier than we are, they are immortal, at least if the common belief be true.

And you too, judges, must face death with a good courage, and believe this as a truth, that no evil can happen to a good man, either in life, or after death. His fortunes are not neglected by the gods; and what has come to me today has not come by chance. I am persuaded that it was better for me to die now, and to be released from trouble: and that was the reason why the sign never turned me back. And so I am hardly angry with my accusers, or with those who have condemned me to die. Yet it was not with this mind that they accused me and condemned me, but meaning to do me an injury. So far I may find fault with them.

Yet I have one request to make of them. When my sons grow up, visit them with punishment, my friends, and vex them in the same way that I have vexed you, if they seem to you to care for riches, or for any other thing, before virtue: and if they think that they are something, when they are nothing at all, reproach them, as I have reproached you, for not caring for what they should, and for thinking that they are great men when in fact they are worthless. And if you will do this, I myself and my sons will have received our deserts at your hands.

But now the time has come, and we must go hence; I to die, and you to live. Whether life or death is better is known to God, and to God only.

Euthyphro*

EUTHYPHRO, SOCRATES

EUTHYPHRO. What strange thing has happened, Socrates, that you have left your accustomed haunts in the Lyceum and are now haunting the portico where the king archon sits? For it cannot be that you have an action before the king, as I have.

SOCRATES. Our Athenians, Euthyphro, do not call it an action, but an indictment.

EUTHYPHRO. What? Somebody has, it seems, brought an indictment against you; for I don't accuse you of having brought one against anyone else.

SOCRATES. Certainly not.

EUTHYPHRO. But someone else against you?

SOCRATES. Quite so.

EUTHYPHRO. Who is he?

SOCRATES. I don't know the man very well myself, Euthyphro, for he seems to be a young and unknown person. His name, however, is Meletus, I believe. And he is of the deme of Pitthus, if you remember any Pitthian Meletus, with long hair

and only a little beard, but with a hooked nose.

EUTHYPHRO. I don't remember him, Socrates. But what sort of an indictment has he brought against you?

SOCRATES. What sort? No mean one, it seems to me; for the fact that, young as he is, he has apprehended so important a matter reflects no small credit upon him. For he says he knows how the youth are corrupted and who those are who corrupt them. He must be a wise man; who, seeing my lack of wisdom and that I am corrupting his fellows, comes to the State, as a boy runs to his mother, to accuse me. And he seems to me to be the only one of the public men who begins in the right way; for the right way is to take care of the young men first, to make them as good as possible, just as a good husbandman will naturally take care of the young plants first and afterwards of the rest. And so Meletus, perhaps, is first clearing away us who corrupt the young plants, as he says; then after this, when he has turned his attention to the older men, he will bring countless most precious blessings upon the State,— at least, that is the natural outcome of the beginning he has made.

EUTHYPHRO. I hope it may be so, Socrates; but I fear the opposite may result. For it seems to me that he

*Reprinted by permission of the publishers from Loeb Classical Library, H. N. Fowler, trans., Plato, *Euthyphro*, Cambridge, MA.: Harvard University Press, 1947.

begins by injuring the State at its very heart, when he undertakes to harm you. Now tell me, what does he say you do that corrupts the young?

SOCRATES. Absurd things, my friend, at first hearing. For he says I am a maker of gods; and because I make new gods and do not believe in the old ones, he indicted me for the sake of these old ones, as he says.

EUTHYPHRO. I understand, Socrates; it is because you say the divine monitor keeps coming to you. So he has brought the indictment against you for making innovations in religion, and he is going into court to slander you, knowing that slanders on such subjects are readily accepted by the people. Why, they even laugh at me and say I am crazy when I say anything in the assembly about divine things and fortell the future to them. And yet there is not one of the things I have foretold that is not true; but they are jealous of all such men as you and I are. However, we must not be disturbed, but must come to close quarters with them.

SOCRATES. My dear Euthyphro, their ridicule is perhaps of no consequence. For the Athenians, I fancy, are not much concerned, if they think a man is clever, provided he does not impart his clever notions to others; but when they think he makes others to be like himself, they are angry with him, either through jealousy, as you say, or for some other reason.

EUTHYPHRO. I don't much desire to test their sentiments toward me in this matter.

SOCRATES. No, for perhaps they think that you are reserved and unwilling to impart your wisdom. But I fear that because of my love of men they think that I not only pour myself out copiously to anyone and everyone without payment, but that I would even pay something myself, if anyone would listen to me. Now if, as I was saying just now, they were to laugh at me, as you say they do at you, it would not be at all unpleasant to pass the time in the court with jests and laughter; but if they are in earnest, then only soothsayers like you can tell how this will end.

EUTHYPHRO. Well, Socrates, perhaps it won't amount to much, and you will bring your case to a satisfactory ending, as I think I shall mine.

SOCRATES. What is your case, Euthyphro? Are you defending or prosecuting?

EUTHYPHRO. Prosecuting.

SOCRATES. Whom?

EUTHYPHRO. Such a man that they think I am insane because I am prosecuting[1] him.

SOCRATES. Why? Are you prosecuting one who has wings to fly away with?

[1]The Greek word has much the same meaning as the Latin *prosequor*, from which the English 'prosecute' is derived, 'follow,' 'pursue,' and is at the same time the technical term for 'prosecute.'

EUTHYPHRO. No flying for him at his ripe old age.

SOCRATES. Who is he?

EUTHYPHRO. My father.

SOCRATES. Your father, my dear man?

EUTHYPHRO. Certainly.

SOCRATES. But what is the charge, and what is the suit about?

EUTHYPHRO. Murder, Socrates.

SOCRATES. Heracles! Surely, Euthyphro, most people do not know where the right lies; for I fancy it is not everyone who can rightly do what you are doing, but only one who is already very far advanced in wisdom.

EUTHYPHRO. Very far, indeed, Socrates, by Zeus.

SOCRATES. Is the one who was killed by your father a relative? But of course he was; for you would not bring a charge of murder against him on a stranger's account.

EUTHYPHRO. It is ridiculous, Socrates, that you think it matters whether the man who was killed was a stranger or a relative, and do not see that the only thing to consider is whether the action of the slayer was justified or not, and that if it was justified one ought to let him alone, and if not, one ought to proceed against him, even if he share one's hearth and eat at one's table. For the pollution is the same if you associate knowingly with such a man and do not purify yourself and him by proceeding against him. In this case, the man who was killed was a hired workman of mine, and when we were farming at Naxos, he was working there on our land. Now he got drunk, got angry with one of our house slaves, and butchered him. So my father bound him hand and foot, threw him into a ditch, and sent a man here to Athens to ask the religious adviser what he ought to do. In the meantime he paid no attention to the man as he lay there bound, and neglected him, thinking that he was a murderer and it did not matter if he were to die. And that is just what happened to him. For he died of hunger and cold and his bonds before the messenger came back from the adviser. Now my father and the rest of my relatives are angry with me, because for the sake of this murderer I am prosecuting my father for murder. For they say he did not kill him, and if he had killed him never so much, yet since the dead man was a murderer, I ought not to trouble myself about such a fellow, because it is unholy for a son to prosecute his father for murder. Which shows how little they know what the divine law is in regard to holiness and unholiness.

SOCRATES. But, in the name of Zeus, Euthyphro, do you think your knowledge about divine laws and holiness and unholiness is so exact that, when the facts are as you say, you are not afraid of doing something unholy yourself in prosecuting your father for murder?

EUTHYPHRO. I should be of no use, Socrates, and Euthyphro would be in no way different from other men, if I did not have exact knowledge about all such things.

SOCRATES. Then the best thing for me, my admirable Euthyphro, is to become your pupil and, before the suit with Meletus comes on, to challenge him and say that I always thought it very important before to know about divine matters and that now, since he says I am doing wrong by acting carelessly and making innovations in matters of religion, I have become your pupil. And "Meletus," I should say, "if you acknowledge that Euthyphro is wise in such matters, then believe that I also hold correct opinions, and do not bring me to trial; and if you do not acknowledge that, then bring a suit against him, my teacher, rather than against me, and charge him with corrupting the old, namely, his father and me, which he does by teaching me and by correcting and punishing his father." And if he does not do as I ask and does not release me from the indictment or bring it against you in my stead, I could say in the court the same things I said in my challenge to him, could I not?

EUTHYPHRO. By Zeus, Socrates, if he should undertake to indict me, I fancy I should find his weak spot, and it would be much more a question about him in court than about me.

SOCRATES. And I, my dear friend, perceiving this, wish to become your pupil; for I know that neither this fellow Meletus, nor anyone else,

seems to notice you at all, but he has seen through me so sharply and so easily that he has indicted me for impiety. Now in the name of Zeus, tell me what you just now asserted that you knew so well. What do you say is the nature of piety and impiety, both in relation to murder and to other things? Is not holiness always the same with itself in every action, and, on the other hand, is not unholiness the opposite of all holiness, always the same with itself and whatever is to be unholy possessing some one characteristic quality?

EUTHYPHRO. Certainly, Socrates.

SOCRATES. Tell me then, what do you say holiness is, and what unholiness?

EUTHYPHRO. Well then, I say that holiness is doing what I am doing now, prosecuting the wrongdoer who commits murder or steals from the temples or does any such thing, whether he be your father or your mother or anyone else, and not prosecuting him is unholy. And, Socrates, see what a sure proof I offer you,—a proof I have already given to others,—that this is established and right and that we ought not to let him who acts impiously go unpunished, no matter who he may be. Men believe that Zeus is the best and most just of the gods, and they acknowledge that he put his father in bonds because he wickedly devoured his children, and he in turn had mutilated his father for similar reasons; but they are incensed against me because I proceed against my father when he has done wrong, and so they are inconsistent in what they say about the gods and about me.

SOCRATES. Is not this, Euthyphro, the reason why I am being prosecuted, because when people tell such stories about the gods I find it hard to accept them? And therefore, probably, people will say I am wrong. Now if you, who know so much about such things, accept these tales, I suppose I too must give way. For what am I to say, who confess frankly that I know nothing about them? But tell me, in the name of Zeus, the god of friendship, do you really believe these things happened?

EUTHYPHRO. Yes, and still more wonderful things than these, Socrates, which most people do not know.

SOCRATES. And so you believe that there was really war between the gods, and fearful enmities and battles and other things of the sort, such as are told of by the poets and represented in varied designs by the great artists in our sacred places and especially on the robe which is carried up to the Acropolis at the great Panathenaea? for this is covered with such representations. Shall we agree that these things are true, Euthyphro?

EUTHYPHRO. Not only these things, Socrates; but, as I said just now, I will, if you like, tell you many other things about the gods, which I am sure will amaze you when you hear them.

SOCRATES. I dare say. But you can tell me those things at your leisure some other time. At present try to tell more clearly what I asked you just now. For, my friend, you did not give me sufficient information before, when I asked what holiness was, but you told me that this was holy which you are now doing, prosecuting your father for murder.

EUTHYPHRO. Well, what I said was true, Socrates.

SOCRATES. Perhaps. But, Euthyphro, you say that many other things are holy, do you not?

EUTHYPHRO. Why, so they are.

SOCRATES. Now call to mind that this is not what I asked you, to tell me one or two of the many holy acts, but to tell the essential aspect, by which all holy acts are holy; for you said that all unholy acts were unholy and all holy ones holy by one aspect. Or don't you remember?

EUTHYPHRO. I remember.

SOCRATES. Tell me then what this aspect is, that I may keep my eye fixed upon it and employ it as a model and, if anything you or anyone else does agrees with it, may say that the act is holy, and if not, that it is unholy.

EUTHYPHRO. If you wish me to explain in that way, I will do so.

SOCRATES. I do wish it.

EUTHYPHRO. Well then, what is dear to the gods is holy, and what is not dear to them is unholy.

SOCRATES. Excellent, Euthyphro; now you have answered as I asked you to answer. However, whether it is true,

I am not yet sure; but you will, of course, show that what you say is true.

EUTHYPHRO. Certainly.

SOCRATES. Come then, let us examine our words. The thing and the person that are dear to the gods are holy, and the thing and the person that are hateful to the gods are unholy; and the two are not the same, but the holy and the unholy are the exact opposites of each other. Is not this what we have said?

EUTHYPHRO. Yes, just this.

SOCRATES. And it seems to be correct?

EUTHYPHRO. I think so, Socrates.

SOCRATES. Well then, have we said this also, that the gods, Euthyphro, quarrel and disagree with each other, and that there is enmity between them?

EUTHYPHRO. Yes, we have said that.

SOCRATES. But what things is the disagreement about, which causes enmity and anger? Let us look at it in this way. If you and I were to disagree about number, for instance, which of two numbers were the greater, would the disagreement about these matters make us enemies and make us angry with each other, or should we not quickly settle it by resorting to arithmetic?

EUTHYPHRO. Of course we should.

SOCRATES. Then, too, if we were to disagree about the relative size of things, we should quickly put an end to the disagreement by measuring?

EUTHYPHRO. Yes.

SOCRATES. And we should, I suppose, come to terms about relative weights by weighing?

EUTHYPHRO. Of course.

SOCRATES. But about what would a disagreement be, which we could not settle and which would cause us to be enemies and be angry with each other? Perhaps you cannot give an answer offhand; but let me suggest it. Is it not about right and wrong, and noble and disgraceful, and good and bad? Are not these the questions about which you and I and other people become enemies, when we do become enemies, because we differ about them and cannot reach any satisfactory agreement?

EUTHYPHRO. Yes, Socrates, these are the questions about which we should become enemies.

SOCRATES. And how about the gods, Euthyphro? If they disagree, would they not disagree about these questions?

EUTHYPHRO. Necessarily.

SOCRATES. Then, my noble Euthyphro, according to what you say, some of the gods too think some things are right or wrong and noble or disgraceful, and good or bad, and others disagree; for they would not quarrel with each other if they did not disagree about these matters. Is that the case?

EUTHYPHRO. You are right.

SOCRATES. Then the gods in each

group love the things which they consider good and right and hate the opposites of these things?

EUTHYPHRO.   Certainly.

SOCRATES.   But you say that the same things are considered right by some of them and wrong by others; and it is because they disagree about these things that they quarrel and wage war with each other. Is not this what you said?

EUTHYPHRO.   It is.

SOCRATES.   Then, as it seems, the same things are hated and loved by the gods, and the same things would be dear and hateful to the gods.

EUTHYPHRO.   So it seems.

SOCRATES.   And then the same things would be both holy and unholy, Euthyphro, according to this statement.

EUTHYPHRO.   I suppose so.

SOCRATES.   Then you did not answer my question, my friend. For I did not ask you what is at once holy and unholy; but, judging from your reply, what is dear to the gods is also hateful to the gods. And so, Euthyphro, it would not be surprising if, in punishing your father as you are doing, you were performing an act that is pleasing to Zeus, but hateful to Cronus and Uranus, and pleasing to Hephaestus, but hateful to Hera, and so forth in respect to the other gods, if any disagree with any other about it.

EUTHYPHRO.   But I think, Socrates, that none of the gods disagrees with any other about this, or holds that he who kills anyone wrongfully ought not to pay the penalty.

SOCRATES.   Well, Euthyphro, to return to men, did you ever hear anybody arguing that he who had killed anyone wrongfully, or had done anything else whatever wrongfully, ought not to pay the penalty?

EUTHYPHRO.   Why, they are always arguing these points, especially in the law courts. For they do very many wrong things; and then there is nothing they will not do or say, in defending themselves, to avoid the penalty.

SOCRATES.   Yes, but do they acknowledge, Euthyphro, that they have done wrong and, although they acknowledge it, nevertheless say that they ought not to pay the penalty?

EUTHYPHRO.   Oh, no, they don't do that.

SOCRATES.   Then there is something they do not do and say. For they do not, I fancy, dare to say and argue that, if they have really done wrong, they ought not to pay the penalty; but, I think, they say they have not done wrong; do they not?

EUTHYPHRO.   You are right.

SOCRATES.   Then they do not argue this point, that the wrongdoer must not pay the penalty; but perhaps they argue about this, who is a wrongdoer, and what he did, and when.

EUTHYPHRO.   That is true.

SOCRATES.   Then is not the same thing

true of the gods, if they quarrel about right and wrong, as you say, and some say others have done wrong, and some say they have not? For surely, my friend, no one, either of gods or men, has the face to say that he who does wrong ought not to pay the penalty.

EUTHYPHRO. Yes, you are right about this, Socrates, in the main.

SOCRATES. But I think, Euthyphro, those who dispute, both men and gods, if the gods do dispute, dispute about each separate act. When they differ with one another about any act, some say it was right and others that it was wrong. Is it not so?

EUTHYPHRO. Certainly.

SOCRATES. Come now, my dear Euthyphro, inform me, that I may be made wiser, what proof you have that all the gods think that the man lost his life wrongfully, who, when he was a servant, committed a murder, was bound by the master of the man he killed, and died as a result of his bonds before the master who had bound him found out from the advisers what he ought to do with him, and that it is right on account of such a man for a son to proceed against his father and accuse him of murder. Come, try to show me clearly about this, that the gods surely believe that this conduct is right; and if you show it to my satisfaction, I will glorify your wisdom as long as I live.

EUTHYPHRO. But perhaps this is no small task, Socrates; though I could show you quite clearly.

SOCRATES. I understand; it is because you think I am slower to understand than the judges; since it is plain that you will show them that such acts are wrong and that all the gods hate them.

EUTHYPHRO. Quite clearly, Socrates; that is, if they listen to me.

SOCRATES. They will listen, if they find that you are a good speaker. But this occurred to me while you were talking, and I said to myself: "If Euthyphro should prove to me no matter how clearly that all the gods think such a death is wrongful, what have I learned from Euthyphro about the question, What is holiness and what is unholiness? For this act would, as it seems, be hateful to the gods; but we saw just now that holiness and its opposite are not defined in this way; for we saw that what is hateful to the gods is also dear to them; and so I let you off any discussion of this point, Euthyphro. If you like, all the gods may think it wrong and may hate it. But shall we now emend our definition and say that whatever all the gods hate is unholy and whatever they all love is holy, and what some love and others hate is neither or both? Do you wish this now to be our definition of holiness and unholiness?

EUTHYPHRO. What is to hinder, Socrates?

SOCRATES. Nothing, so far as I am concerned, Euthyphro, but consider your own position, whether by adopting this definition you will most easily teach me what you promised.

EUTHYPHRO. Well, I should say that what all the gods love is holy and, on the other hand, what they all hate is unholy.

SOCRATES. Then shall we examine this again, Euthyphro, to see if it is correct, or shall we let it go and accept our own statement, and those of others, agreeing that it is so, if anyone merely says that it is? Or ought we to inquire into the correctness of the statement?

EUTHYPHRO. We ought to inquire. However, I think this is now correct.

SOCRATES. We shall soon know more about this, my friend. Just consider this question:— Is that which is holy loved by the gods because it is holy, or is it holy because it is loved by the gods?

EUTHYPHRO. I don't know what you mean, Socrates.

SOCRATES. Then I will try to speak more clearly. We speak of being carried and of carrying, of being led and of leading, of being seen and seeing; and you understand—do you not? —that in all such expressions the two parts differ one from the other in meaning, and how they differ.

EUTHYPHRO. I think I understand.

SOCRATES. Then, too, we conceive of a thing being loved and of a thing loving, and the two are different?

EUTHYPHRO. Of course.

SOCRATES. Now tell me, is a thing which is carried a carried thing because one carries it, or for some other reason?

EUTHYPHRO. No, for that reason.

SOCRATES. And a thing which is led because one leads it, and a thing which is seen is so because one sees it?

EUTHYPHRO. Certainly.

EUTHYPHRO. Then one does not see it because it is a seen thing, but, on the contrary, it is a seen thing because one sees it; and one does not lead it because it is a led thing, but it is a led thing because one leads it; and one does not carry it because it is a carried thing, but it is a carried thing because one carries it. Is it clear, Euthyphro, what I am trying to say? I am trying to say this, that if anything becomes or undergoes, it does not become because it is in a state of becoming, but it is in a state of becoming because it becomes, and it does not undergo because it is a thing which undergoes, but because it undergoes it is a thing which undergoes; or do you not agree to this?

EUTHYPHRO. I agree.

SOCRATES. Is not that which is beloved a thing which is either becoming or undergoing something?

EUTHYPHRO. Certainly.

SOCRATES. And is this case like the former ones: those who love it do not love it because it is a beloved thing, but it is a beloved thing because they love it?

EUTHYPHRO. Obviously.

SOCRATES. Now what do you say about that which is holy, Euthyphro?

It is loved by all the gods, is it not, according to what you said?

EUTHYPHRO. Yes.

SOCRATES. For this reason, because it is holy, or for some other reason?

EUTHYPHRO. No, for this reason.

SOCRATES. It is loved because it is holy, not holy because it is loved?

EUTHYPHRO. I think so.

SOCRATES. But that which is dear to the gods is dear to them and beloved by them because they love it.

EUTHYPHRO. Of course.

SOCRATES. Then that which is dear to the gods and that which is holy are not identical, but differ one from the other.

EUTHYPHRO. How so, Socrates?

SOCRATES. Because we are agreed that the holy is loved because it is holy and that it is not holy because it is loved; are we not?

EUTHYPHRO. Yes.

SOCRATES. But we are agreed that what is dear to the gods is dear to them because they love it, that is, by reason of this love, not that they love it because it is dear.

EUTHYPHRO. Very true.

SOCRATES. But if that which is dear to the gods and that which is holy were identical, my dear Euthyphro, then if the holy were loved because it is holy, that which is dear to the gods would be loved because it is dear, and if that which is dear to the gods is dear because it is loved, then that which is holy would be holy because it is loved; but now you see that the opposite is the case, showing that the two are entirely different from each other. For the one becomes lovable from the fact that it is loved, whereas the other is loved because it is in itself lovable. And, Euthyphro, it seems that when you were asked what holiness is you were unwilling to make plain its essence, but you mentioned something that has happened to this holiness, namely, that it is loved by the gods. But you did not tell as yet what it really is. So, if you please, do not hide it from me, but begin over again and tell me what holiness is, no matter whether it is loved by the gods or anything else happens to it; for we shall not quarrel about that. But tell me frankly, What is holiness, and what is unholiness?

EUTHYPHRO. But, Socrates, I do not know how to say what I mean. For whatever statement we advance, somehow or other it moves about and won't stay where we put it.

SOCRATES. Your statements, Euthyphro, are like works of my ancestor Daedalus, and if I were the one who made or advanced them, you might laugh at me and say that on account of my relationship to him my works in words run away and won't stay where they are put. But now — well, the statements are yours; so some other jest is demanded; for they won't stay fixed, as you yourself see.

EUTHYPHRO. I think the jest does very well as it is; for I am not the one who makes these statements move about and not stay in the same place, but you are the Daedalus; for they would have stayed, so far as I am concerned.

SOCRATES. Apparently then, my friend, I am a more clever artist than Daedalus, inasmuch as he made only his own works move, whereas I, as it seems, give motion to the works of others as well as to my own. And the most exquisite thing about my art is that I am clever against my will; for I would rather have my words stay fixed and stable than possess the wisdom of Daedalus and the wealth of Tantalus besides. But enough of this. Since you seem to be indolent, I will aid you myself, so that you may instruct me about holiness. And do not give it up beforehand. Just see whether you do not think that everything that is holy is right.

EUTHYPHRO. I do.

SOCRATES. But is everything that is right also holy? Or is all which is holy right, and not all which is right holy, but part of it holy and part something else?

EUTHYPHRO. I can't follow you, Socrates.

SOCRATES. And yet you are as much younger than I as you are wiser; but, as I said, you are indolent on account of your wealth of wisdom. But exert yourself, my friend; for it is not hard to understand what I mean. What I mean is the opposite of what the poet said, who wrote: "Zeus the creator, him who made all things, thou wilt not name; for where fear is, there also is reverence." Now I disagree with the poet. Shall I tell you how?

EUTHYPHRO. By all means.

SOCRATES. It does not seem to me true that where fear is, there also is reverence; for many who fear diseases and poverty and other such things seem to me to fear, but not to reverence at all these things which they fear. Don't you think so, too?

EUTHYPHRO. Certainly.

SOCRATES. But I think that where reverence is, there also is fear; for does not everyone who has a feeling of reverence and shame about any act also dread and fear the reputation for wickedness?

EUTHYPHRO. Yes, he does fear.

SOCRATES. Then it is not correct to say "where fear is, there also is reverence." On the contrary, where reverence is, there also is fear; but reverence is not everywhere where fear is, since, as I think, fear is more comprehensive than reverence; for reverence is a part of fear, just as the odd is a part of number, so that it is not true that where number is, there also is the odd, but that where the odd is, there also is number. Perhaps you follow me now?

EUTHYPHRO. Perfectly.

SOCRATES. It was something of this sort that I meant before, when I asked whether where the right is, there also is holiness, or where holiness is, there also is the right; but holiness is not everywhere where the right is, for holiness is a part of the right. Do we agree to this, or do you dissent?

EUTHYPHRO. No, I agree; for I think the statement is correct.

SOCRATES. Now observe the next point. If holiness is a part of the right, we must, apparently, find out what part of the right holiness is. Now if you asked me about one of the things I just mentioned, as, for example, what part of number the even was, and what kind of a number it was I should say, "that which is not indivisible by two, but divisible by two"; or don't you agree?

EUTHYPHRO. I agree.

SOCRATES. Now try in your turn to teach me what part of the right holiness is, that I may tell Meletus not to wrong me any more or bring suits against me for impiety, since I have now been duly instructed by you about what is, and what is not, pious and holy.

EUTHYPHRO. This then is my opinion, Socrates, that the part of the right which has to do with attention to the gods constitutes piety and holiness, and that the remaining part of the right is that which has to do with the service of men.

SOCRATES. I think you are correct, Euthyphro; but there is one little point about which I still want information, for I do not yet understand what you mean by "attention." I don't suppose you mean the same kind of attention to the gods which is paid to other things. We say, for example, that not everyone knows how to attend to horses, but only he who is skilled in horsemanship, do we not?

EUTHYPHRO. Certainly.

SOCRATES. Then horsemanship is the art of attending to horses?

EUTHYPHRO. Yes.

SOCRATES. And not everyone knows how to attend to dogs, but only the huntsman?

EUTHYPHRO. That is so.

SOCRATES. Then the huntsman's art is the art of attending to dogs?

EUTHYPHRO. Yes.

SOCRATES. And the oxherd's art is that of attending to oxen?

EUTHYPHRO. Certainly.

SOCRATES. And holiness and piety is the art of attending to the gods? Is that what you mean, Euthyphro?

EUTHYPHRO. Yes.

SOCRATES. Now does attention always aim to accomplish the same end? I mean something like this: It aims at some good or benefit to the one to whom it is given, as you see that horses, when attended to by the horseman's art are benefited and made better; or don't you think so?

EUTHYPHRO. Yes, I do.

SOCRATES. And dogs are benefited by the huntsman's art and oxen by the oxherd's and everything else in the same way? Or do you think care and attention are ever meant for the injury of that which is cared for?

EUTHYPHRO. No, by Zeus, I do not.

SOCRATES. But for its benefit?

EUTHYPHRO. Of course.

SOCRATES. Then holiness, since it is the art of attending to the gods, is a benefit to the gods, and makes them better? And you would agree that when you do a holy or pious act you are making one of the gods better?

EUTHYPHRO. No, by Zeus, not I.

SOCRATES. Nor do I, Euthyphro, think that is what you meant. Far from it. But I asked what you meant by "attention to the gods" just because I did not think you meant anything like that.

EUTHYPHRO. You are right, Socrates; that is not what I mean.

SOCRATES. Well, what kind of attention to the gods is holiness?

EUTHYPHRO. The kind, Socrates, that servants pay to their masters.

SOCRATES. I understand. It is, you mean, a kind of service to the gods?

EUTHYPHRO. Exactly.

SOCRATES. Now can you tell me what result the art that serves the physician serves to produce? Is it not health?

EUTHYPHRO. Yes.

SOCRATES. Well then; what is it which the art that serves shipbuilders serves to produce?

EUTHYPHRO. Evidently, Socrates, a ship.

SOCRATES. And that which serves housebuilders serves to build a house?

EUTHYPHRO. Yes.

SOCRATES. Then tell me, my friend; what would the art which serves the gods serve to accomplish? For it is evident that you know, since you say you know more than any other man about matters which have to do with the gods.

EUTHYPHRO. And what I say is true, Socrates.

SOCRATES. Then, in the name of Zeus, tell me, what is that glorious result which the gods accomplish by using us as servants?

EUTHYPHRO. They accomplish many fine results, Socrates.

SOCRATES. Yes, and so do generals, my friend; but nevertheless, you could easily tell the chief of them, namely, that they bring about victory in war. Is that not the case?

EUTHYPHRO. Of course.

SOCRATES. And farmers also, I think, accomplish many fine results; but still the chief result of their work is food from the land?

EUTHYPHRO. Certainly.

SOCRATES. But how about the many fine results the gods accomplish? What is the chief result of their work?

EUTHYPHRO. I told you a while ago, Socrates, that it is a long task to learn accurately all about these things. However, I say simply that when one knows how to say and do what is gratifying to the gods, in praying and sacrificing, that is holiness, and such things bring salvation to individual families and to states; and the opposite of what is gratifying to the gods is impious, and that overturns and destroys everything.

SOCRATES. You might, if you wished, Euthyphro have answered much more briefly the chief part of my question. But it is plain that you do not care to instruct me. For now, when you were close upon it you turned aside; and if you had answered it, I should already have obtained from you all the instruction I need about holiness. But, as things are, the questioner must follow the one questioned wherever he leads. What do you say the holy, or holiness, is? Do you not say that it is a kind of science of sacrificing and praying?

EUTHYPHRO. Yes.

SOCRATES. And sacrificing is making gifts to the gods and praying is asking from them?

EUTHYPHRO. Exactly, Socrates.

SOCRATES. Then holiness, according to this definition, would be a science of giving and asking.

EUTHYPHRO. You understand perfectly what I said, Socrates.

SOCRATES. Yes, my friend, for I am eager for your wisdom, and give my mind to it, so that nothing you say shall fall to the ground. But tell me, what is this service of the gods? Do you say that it consists in asking from them and giving to them?

EUTHYPHRO. Yes.

SOCRATES. Would not the right way of asking be to ask of them what we need from them?

EUTHYPHRO. What else?

SOCRATES. And the right way of giving, to present them with what they need from us? For it would not be scientific giving to give anyone what he does not need.

EUTHYPHRO. You are right, Socrates.

SOCRATES. Then holiness would be an art of barter between gods and men?

EUTHYPHRO. Yes, of barter, if you like to call it so.

SOCRATES. I don't like to call it so, if it is not true. But tell me, what advantage accrues to the gods from the gifts they get from us? For everybody knows what they give, since we have nothing good which they do not give. But what advantage do they derive from what they get from us? Or have we so much the better of them in our bartering that we get all good things from them and they nothing from us?

EUTHYPHRO. Why you don't suppose, Socrates, that the gods gain any advantage from what they get from us, do you?

SOCRATES. Well then, what would those gifts of ours to the gods be?

EUTHYPHRO. What else than honour and praise, and, as I said before, gratitude?

SOCRATES. Then, Euthyphro, holiness

is grateful to the gods, but not advantageous or precious to the gods?

EUTHYPHRO. I think it is precious, above all things.

SOCRATES. Then again, it seems, holiness is that which is precious to the gods.

EUTHYPHRO. Certainly.

SOCRATES. Then will you be surprised, since you say this, if your words do not remain fixed but walk about, and will you accuse me of being the Daedalus who makes them walk, when you are yourself much more skillful than Daedalus and make them go round in a circle? Or do you not see that our definition has come round to the point from which it started? For you remember, I suppose, that a while ago we found that holiness and what is dear to the gods were not the same, but different from each other; or do you not remember?

EUTHYPHRO. Yes, I remember.

SOCRATES. Then don't you see that now you say that what is precious to the gods is holy? And is not this what is dear to the gods?

EUTHYPHRO. Certainly.

SOCRATES. Then either our agreement a while ago was wrong, or if that was right, we are wrong now.

EUTHYPHRO. So it seems.

SOCRATES. Then we must begin again at the beginning and ask what holiness is. Since I shall not willingly give up until I learn. And do not scorn me, but by all means apply your mind now to the utmost and tell me the truth; for you know, if any one does, and like Proteus, you must be held until you speak. For if you had not clear knowledge of holiness and unholiness, you would surely not have undertaken to prosecute your aged father for murder for the sake of a servant. You would have been afraid to risk the anger of the gods, in case your conduct should be wrong, and would have been ashamed in the sight of men. But now I am sure you think you know what is holy and what is not. So tell me, most excellent Euthyphro, and do not conceal your thought.

EUTHYPHRO. Some other time, Socrates. Now I am in a hurry and it is time for me to go.

SOCRATES. Oh my friend, what are you doing? You go away and leave me cast down from the high hope I had that I should learn from you what is holy, and what is not, and should get rid of Meletus' indictment by showing him that I have been made wise by Euthyphro about divine matters and am no longer through ignorance acting carelessly and making innovations in respect to them, and that I shall live a better life henceforth.

PART I

THE WAYS OF UNDERSTANDING

One of the main divisions of philosophy is epistemology, or the theory of knowledge. Epistemology asks such fundamental questions as: How much do we know? How do we know? How can we distinguish between appearance and reality? What is the nature of truth and how can we separate it from falsehood? In addition it asks questions concerning the nature of philosophy: What is its scope and function? Is its method the same as that of science or is it distinctive in method? We shall be dealing with questions such as these in Part One.

The plan of our discussion will be as follows: First, we shall examine rationalism, with its emphasis on pure reason, using the philosophy of Descartes as our example. Second, we shall take up David Hume's empiricism, with its stress on sensory experience, together with Immanuel Kant's critique. Third, we shall consider the commonsense philosophy of Thomas Reid, who was critical of both Hume and Kant. Next, we shall ponder the contribution of direct insight, both the "intuitionism" of Henri-Louis Bergson and Bertrand Russell's "knowledge by acquaintance". Then we shall turn to the ideas of the great American philosopher, Charles Peirce. In the same chapter we shall consider William James and John Dewey as advocates of pragmatism, a movement closely related to the philosophy of Peirce. Finally, in the concluding chapter of Part One, we shall examine the sharply contrasting movement of "existentialism" as represented by its most notable figure, Søren Kierkegaard, and his twentieth century counterpart, Gabriel Marcel.

Rationalism

"Knowledge is the result of rational analysis alone, and is achieved completely independently of sensory experience."

Melvin Rader

PLATO (428/7-348/7 B.C.)

As a member of one of the most distinguished families in Athens, Plato was in touch with political and social developments from his early childhood. He grew to manhood during the long, turbulent period of the Peloponnesian War, and his mind must have been deeply disturbed by war and revolution. Athens was finally defeated by Sparta when Plato was twenty-three, and he watched the ensuing oligarchical dictatorship, of which his uncle Charmides and his cousin Critias were leaders, with great hope. It soon turned to horror and anger, however, when his old friend Socrates was eventually tried and executed by the restored democratic faction. The shock of this event, occurring when he was just twenty-eight, was the decisive influence on his entire career. He concluded that good government depends on the rare union of power and wisdom, and he resolved to emulate and as far as possible complete the work of Socrates. Retiring from Athens to Megara, he began to write his famous dialogues, which lovingly portray his old master.

He is said to have spent the next ten years traveling in Greece, Italy, Egypt, and Asia Minor. For a time he lived at the court of Dionysius I, the tyrant of Syracuse, whose son-in-law, Dion, became Plato's friend and ardent admirer. At the age of forty he returned to Athens to found the Academy, a school for philosophers, mathematicians, and statesmen. This

51

school was the main center of his interest for the remainder of his long life. In addition to teaching, he continued to write dialogues, which became more technical as he grew older. This quiet, academic life was interrupted in 367 B.C., when he was close to sixty. Dion, his old friend, persuaded him to return to Syracuse as tutor to Dionysius II, a young man of thirty, who had succeeded to the throne. The venture turned out badly. Dionysius and Dion eventually quarreled and Plato went back to Athens. Not easily dismayed, he returned to Syracuse six years later in the hope of remedying the situation — and once again met with broken promises and barely escaped with his life. Then he settled down in the Academy to spend the last years of his life teaching and writing. He died at the age of eighty or eighty-one and, according to Cicero, was hard at work at the very end. Generally considered the greatest of the Greek philosophers, he has exercised an immense influence on the thought and literature of the world to this day.

Meno

SOCRATES. Then begin again and answer: What is virtue, according to you and your friend?

MENON. Well now, my dear Socrates, you are just like what I always heard before I met you: always puzzled yourself and puzzling everybody else. And now you seem to me to be a regular wizard, you dose me with drugs and bewitch me with charms and spells, and drown me in puzzledom. I'll tell you just what you are like, if you will forgive a little jest: your looks and the rest of you are exactly like a flatfish and you sting like this stingray — only go near and touch one of those fish and you go numb, and that is the sort of thing you seem to have done to me. Really and truly, my soul is numb and my mouth is numb, and what to answer you I do not know. Yet I have a thousand times made long speeches about virtue, before many a large audience, and good speeches, too, as I was convinced; but now I have not a word to say at all as to what it is. I must say you are wise not to sail away or travel abroad; for if you did this as a foreigner in a foreign city, you would probably be run in for a wizard.

SOCRATES. You are a young rogue, Menon, and you almost took me in.

MENON. How Socrates?

SOCRATES. I know why you made that comparison of me.

MENON. Why, do you think?

SOCRATES. That I might make another of *you*.[1] I know this — that all

[1] A favorite game in society.

the famous beauties love being put into comparisons; it pays them, you see, for comparisons of the beautiful are beautiful, I think; but I will not do it with you in return. Well, if this stingray is numb itself as well as making others numb, I am like it; if not, I am not. For I am not clear-headed myself when I make others puzzled, but I am as puzzled as puzzled can be, and thus I make others puzzled too. So now, what virtue is I do not know; but you knew, perhaps, before you touched me, although now you resemble one who does not know. All the same, I wish to investigate, with your help, that we may both try to find out what it is.

MENON. And how will you try to find out something, Socrates, when you have no notion at all what it is? Will you lay out before us a thing you don't know, and then try to find it? Or, if at best you meet it by chance, how will you know this is that which you did not know?

SOCRATES. I understand what you wish to say, Menon. You look on this as a piece of chop-logic, don't you see, as if a man cannot try to find either what he knows or what he does not know. Of course he would never try to find what he knows, because he knows it, and in that case he needs no trying to find; or what he does not know, because he does not know what he will try to find.

MENON. Then you don't think that is a good argument, Socrates?

SOCRATES. Not I.

MENON. Can you tell me why?

SOCRATES. Oh yes. I have heard wise men and women on the subject of things divine—

MENON. And what did they say?

SOCRATES. True things and fine things, to my thinking.

MENON. What things, and who were the speakers?

SOCRATES. The speakers were some priests and priestesses who have paid careful attention to the things of their ministry, so as to be able to give a reasoned explanation of them; also inspired poets have something to say, Pindar and many others. What they say I will tell you; pray consider, if they seem to you to be speaking truth. They say that the soul of man is immortal, and sometimes it comes to an end—which they call death—and sometimes it is born again, but it is never destroyed; therefore we must live our lives as much as we can in holiness: for from whomsoever

Persephone shall accept payment for
  ancient wrong,
She gives up again their souls to the
  upper sun in the ninth year;
From these grow lordly kings, and
  men of power and might,
And those who are chief in wisdom;
  these for time to come
Are known among men for holy
  heroes.[1]

Then, since the soul is immortal and often born, having seen what is on

---

[1]From Pindar. Persephone was Pluto's consort in Hades.

earth and what is in the house of Hades, and everything, there is nothing it has not learnt; so there is no wonder it can remember about virtue and other things, because it knew about these before. For since all nature is akin, and the soul has learnt everything, there is nothing to hinder a man, remembering one thing only — which men call learning[2] — from himself finding out all else, if he is brave and does not weary in seeking; for seeking and learning is all remembrance. Then we must not be guided by this chop-logic argument; for this would make us idle, and it is pleasant for soft people to hear, but our way makes them active and enquiring. I have faith that this is true, and I wish with your help to try to find out what virtue is.

MENON. Yes, Socrates. But what do you mean by saying that we do not learn, but what we call learning is remembering? Can you teach me how this is?

SOCRATES. You are a young rogue, as I said a moment ago, Menon, and now you ask me if I can teach you, when I tell you there is no such thing as teaching, only remembering. I see you want to show me up at once as contradicting myself.

MENON. I swear that isn't true, my dear Socrates; I never thought of that, it was just habit. But if you know any way to show me how this can be as you say, show away!

SOCRATES. That is not easy, but still I want to do my best for your sake. Here, just call up one of your own men from all this crowd of servants, any one you like, and I'll prove my case in him.

MENON. All right. (To a boy) Come here.

SOCRATES. Is he Greek, can he speak our language?

MENON. Rather! Born in my house.

SOCRATES. Now, kindly attend and see whether he seems to be learning from me, or remembering.

MENON. All right, I will attend.

SOCRATES. Now my boy, tell me: Do you know that a four-cornered space is like this? [Diagram 1][1]

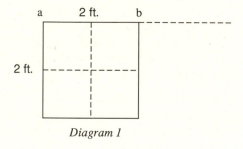

Diagram 1

BOY. I do.

SOCRATES. Is this a four-cornered space having all these lines[2] equal, all four?

BOY. Surely.

---

[2]I.e., the one thing needed to remember is how to learn; also remembering is learning. Both statements are covered here.

[1]There are no diagrams in the Greek text; they and the lettering have been added to assist the reader.
[2]I.e., sides.

SOCRATES. And these across the middle, are they not equal too?

BOY. Yes.

SOCRATES. Such a space might be larger or smaller?

BOY. Oh yes.

SOCRATES. Then if this side is two feet long and this two, how many feet would the whole be? Or look at it this way: if it were two feet this way, and only one the other, would not the space[3] be once two feet?

BOY. Yes.

SOCRATES. But as it is two feet this way also, isn't it twice two feet?

BOY. Yes, so it is.

SOCRATES. So the space is twice two feet?

BOY. Yes.

SOCRATES. Then how many are twice two feet? Count and tell me.

BOY. Four, Socrates.

SOCRATES. Well, could there be another such space, twice as big, but of the same shape, with all the lines equal like this one?

BOY. Yes.

SOCRATES. How many feet will there be in that, then?

BOY. Eight.

SOCRATES. Very well, now try to tell me how long will be each line of that one. The line of this one is two feet;

how long would the line of the double one be?

BOY. The line would be double, Socrates, that is clear.

SOCRATES. (*aside to* MENON): You see, Menon, that I am not teaching this boy anything: I ask him everything; and now he thinks he knows what the line is from which the eight-[square] foot space is to be made. Don't you agree?

MENON. Yes, I agree.

SOCRATES. Does he know then?

MENON. Not at all.

SOCRATES. He *thinks* he knows, from the double size which is wanted?

MENON. Yes.

SOCRATES. Well, observe him while he remembers bit by bit, as he ought to remember.

Now, boy, answer me. You say the double space is made from the double line. You know what I mean; not long this way and short this way, it must be equal every way like this, but double this — eight [*square*] feet. Just look and see if you think it will be made from the double line.

BOY. Yes, I do.

SOCRATES. Then this line [*ac*][1] is double this [*ab*], if we add as much [*bc*] to it on this side.

BOY. Of course!

SOCRATES. Then if we put four like this [*ac*], you say we shall get the eight-foot space.

[3]I.e., area.

[1]In Diagram 1.

BOY. Yes.

SOCRATES. Then let us draw these four equal lines [*ac, cd, de, ea*].[1] Is that the space which you say will be eight feet?

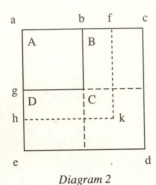

Diagram 2

BOY. Of course.

SOCRATES. Can't you see in it these four spaces here [*A, B, C, D*] each of them equal to the one we began with, the four-foot space?

BOY. Yes.

SOCRATES. Well, how big is the new one? Is it not four times the old one?

BOY. Surely it is!

SOCRATES. Is four times the old one, double?

BOY. Why no, upon my word!

SOCRATES. How big, then?

BOY. Four times as big!

SOCRATES. Then, my boy, from a double line we get a space four times as big, not double.

BOY. That's true.

[1]In Diagram 2.

SOCRATES. Four times four is sixteen, isn't it?

BOY. Yes.

SOCRATES. But what line will make an eight-foot space? This line makes one four times as big, sixteen, doesn't it?

BOY. That's what I say.

SOCRATES. And this four-foot space [*A*] comes from this line [*ab*], half the length of the long one?

BOY. Yes.

SOCRATES. Good. The eight-foot space will be double this [*double A*] and half this [*half A, B, C, D*].

BOY. Yes.

SOCRATES. Then its line must be longer than this [*ab*], and shorter than this [*ac*]. What do you think?

BOY. That's what I think.

SOCRATES. That's right, just answer what you think. Tell me also: Was not this line [*ab*] two feet, and this [*ac*] four?

BOY. Yes.

SOCRATES. Then the line of the eight-foot space must be longer than this line of two feet, and shorter than the line of four feet.

BOY. Yes, it must.

SOCRATES. Try to tell me, then, how long you say it must be.

BOY. Three feet.

SOCRATES. Three feet, very well: If we take half this bit [*half of bc*] and add it on, that makes three feet [*af*], doesn't it? For here we have two [*ab*], and here one [*bf*], the added bit; and, on the other side, in the same way, here are two [*ag*], here one [*gh*]; and that makes the space you say [*afkh*].

BOY.   Yes.

SOCRATES.   Then if the space is three feet this way and three feet that way, the whole space will be three times three feet?

BOY.   It looks like it.

SOCRATES.   How much is three times three feet?

BOY.   Nine.

SOCRATES.   How many feet was the double to be?

BOY.   Eight.

SOCRATES.   So we have not got the eight-foot space from the three-feet line after all.

BOY.   No, we haven't.

SOCRATES.   Then how long ought the line to be? Try to tell us exactly, or if you don't want to give it in numbers, show it if you can.

BOY.   Indeed, Socrates, on my word I don't know.

SOCRATES.   Now, Menon, do you notice how this boy is getting on in his remembering? At first he did not know what line made the eight-foot space, and he does not know yet; but he thought he knew then, and boldly answered as if he did know, and did not think there was any doubt; now he thinks there is a doubt, and as he

does not know, so he does not think he does know.

MENON.   Quite true.

SOCRATES.   Then he is better off as regards the matter he did not know?

MENON.   Yes, I think so too.

SOCRATES.   So now we have put him into a difficulty, and like the stingray we have made him numb, have we done him any harm?

MENON.   I don't think so.

SOCRATES.   At least we have brought him a step onwards, as it seems, to find out how he stands. For now he would go on contentedly seeking, since he does not know; but then he could easily have thought he would be talking well about the double space, even before any number of people again and again, saying how it must have a line of double length.

MENON.   It seems so.

SOCRATES.   Then do you think he would have tried to find out or to learn what he thought he knew, not knowing, until he tumbled into a difficulty by thinking he did not know, and longed to know?

MENON.   I do not think he would, Socrates.

SOCRATES.   So he gained by being numbed?

MENON.   I think so.

SOCRATES.   Just notice now that after this difficulty he will find out by seeking along with me, while I do nothing but ask questions and give no instruction. Look out if you find me teaching and explaining to him, instead of asking for his opinions. Now, boy, answer me. Is not this our four-foot space [A]?[1] Do you understand?

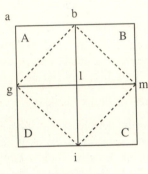

Diagram 3

BOY. I do.

SOCRATES. Shall we add another equal to it, thus [B]?

BOY. Yes.

SOCRATES. And a third equal to either of them, thus [C]?

BOY. Yes.

SOCRATES. Now shall we not also fill in this space in the corner [D]?

BOY. Certainly.

SOCRATES. Won't these be four equal spaces?

BOY. Yes.

SOCRATES. Very well. How many times the small one is this whole space?

BOY. Four times.

[1]In Diagram 3.

SOCRATES. But we wanted a double space; don't you remember?

BOY. Oh yes, I remember.

SOCRATES. Then here is a line running from corner to corner, cutting each of these spaces in two parts [*draws lines bm, mi, ig, gb*].

BOY. Yes.

SOCRATES. Are not these four lines equal, and don't they contain this space within them [bmig]?

BOY. Yes, that is right.

SOCRATES. Just consider: How big is the space?

BOY. I don't understand.

SOCRATES. Does not each of these lines cut each of the spaces, four spaces, in half? Is that right?

BOY. Yes.

SOCRATES. How many spaces as big as that [blg] are in this middle space?

BOY. Four.

SOCRATES. How many in this one [A]?

BOY. Two.

SOCRATES. How many times two is four?

BOY. Twice.

SOCRATES. Then how many [square] feet big is this middle space?

BOY. Eight [square] feet.

SOCRATES. Made from what line?

BOY. This one [gb].

SOCRATES. From the line drawn from

corner to corner of the four-foot space?

BOY. Yes.

SOCRATES. The professors[1] call this a diameter [diagonal]: so if this is a diagonal, the double space would be made from the diagonal, as you say, Menon's boy!

BOY. Certainly, Socrates.

SOCRATES. Now then, Menon, what do you think? Was there one single opinion which the boy did not give as his own?

MENON. No, they were all his own opinions.

SOCRATES. Yet he did not know, as we agreed shortly before.

MENON. Quite true, indeed.

SOCRATES. Were these opinions in him, or not?

MENON. They were.

SOCRATES. Then in one who does not know, about things he does not know, there are true opinions about the things which he does not know?

MENON. So it appears.

SOCRATES. And now these opinions have been stirred up in him as in a dream; and if someone will keep asking him these same questions often and in various forms, you can be sure that in the end he will know about them as accurately as anybody.

[1]Sophists, experts in some subject who gave lessons for a fee.

MENON. It seems so.

SOCRATES. And no one having taught him, only asked questions, yet he will know, having got the knowledge out of himself?

MENON. Yes.

SOCRATES. But to get knowledge out of yourself is to remember, isn't it?

MENON. Certainly it is.

SOCRATES. Well then: This knowledge which he now has—he either got it sometime, or he had it always?

MENON. Yes.

SOCRATES. Then if he had it always, he was also always one who knew; but if he got it sometime, he could not have got it in this present life. Or has someone taught him geometry? For he will do just these same things in all matters of geometry, and so with all other sciences. Then is there anyone who has taught him everything? You are sure to know that, I suppose, especially since he was born and brought up in your house.

MENON. Well, I indeed know that no one has ever taught him.

SOCRATES. Has he all these opinions, or not?

MENON. He has, Socrates, it must be so.

SOCRATES. Then if he did not get them in this life, is it not clear now that he had them and had learnt at some other time?

MENON. So it seems.

RENÉ DESCARTES (1596–1650)

Descartes' father was councillor of the Parliament of Brittany and owner of a fair amount of landed property. His mother, apparently consumptive, died during his infancy and left him with enfeebled health. Anxious to surround the delicate boy with every care, his father entrusted Descartes' education to the Jesuits. It was at the newly established Jesuit college at La Flèche that the young Descartes fell in love with geometry.

Leaving school at seventeen, Descartes spent the next four years in Paris studying law. Thereafter for several years, he lived as a traveler and a soldier, serving as a volunteer in three European armies, in the Netherlands, Bavaria, and Hungary. During this period, when he had a good deal of time to reflect, he came to doubt the value of everything he had learned with the single exception of mathematics.

On November 10, 1619, he had the remarkable experience to which he refers at the beginning of Part II of the *Discourse on Method*. He spent this cold November day in a stove-heated room, meditating about the mathematical and scientific ideas that had been tumbling through his mind for several days. Nervously exhausted, he finally fell asleep and had three strange dreams, which he interpreted as pointing to a life of philosophical reflection. As a result of these dreams, which he thought were inspired by God, and the intense intellectual activity that preceded them, he saw himself at the parting of the ways, and he resolved thenceforth to follow the path of philosophy and scientific research.

Although Descartes has not given us a detailed account of "the foundations of a wonderful science" that he discovered at this time, we know he had the conviction that the method of mathematics could be generalized to apply to all the sciences and that thereby certainty could be gained. Moreover, he conceived the method of applying algebraic symbolism to geometry and of using coordinates to describe geometrical figures; in other words, he founded analytical geometry. Finally, he was convinced that science and philosophy should form one whole, subject to a single method.

He vowed that no ties of marriage or society should deter him from a life of intellectual research devoted to the development of these insights. Although he continued to travel and to study "the great book of the world" for the next nine years (1619–1628), he still found time to work on various problems of mathematics and science. Growing tired of his wanderings at last, in 1628 he sold his inherited estates in France and settled in a quiet country house in Holland. With abundant leisure and a few servants to take care of his material needs, he formed the habit of staying in bed until about noon, reading, writing, or meditating. He soon acquired a wide reputation and was visited by, or corresponded with, many notable scientists and philosophers of the age. During this sojourn in Holland, he had what was apparently his only love affair. The daughter who was the product of this alliance died at the age of five, much to her father's sorrow.

In the autumn of 1649, Descartes accepted an invitation from Queen Christina of Sweden to spend a winter at her court. An imperious though learned monarch, Christina thought that she had the right to command his services at any hour she chose. Daily at five in the morning throughout the bitterly cold winter, Descartes was ushered into the presence of the Queen, where he discoursed to her about philosophy while he stood shivering on the marble floor. Unused to the biting climate and the rigors of such early rising, he caught pneumonia and died in March 1650, a few days before his fifty-fifth birthday.

Rules for the Direction of the Mind

RULE I

The end of study should be to direct the mind towards the enunciation of sound and correct judgments on all matters that come before it.

Whenever men notice some similarity between two things, they are wont to ascribe to each, even in those respects in which the two differ, what they have found to be true of the other. Thus they erroneously compare the sciences, which entirely consist in the cognitive exercise of the mind, with the arts, which depend upon an exercise and disposition of the body. They see that not all the arts can be acquired by the same

The following excerpts from the *Rules* are from *The Philosophical Works of Descartes*, translated by Elizabeth S. Haldane and G. R. T. Ross. Copyright 1911 by the Cambridge University Press. Reprinted by permission.

man, but that he who restricts himself to one, most readily becomes the best executant, since it is not so easy for the same hand to adapt itself both to agricultural operations and to harp-playing, or to the performance of several such tasks as to one alone. Hence they have held the same to be true of the sciences also, and distinguishing them from one another according to their subject matter, they have imagined that they ought to be studied separately, each in isolation from all the rest. But this is certainly wrong. For since the sciences taken all together are identical with human wisdom, which always remains one and the same, however applied to different subjects, and suffers no more differentiation proceeding from them than the light of the sun experiences from the variety of the things which it illumines, there is no need for minds to be confined at all within limits; for neither does the knowing of one truth have an effect like that of the acquisition of one art and prevent us from finding out another, it rather aids us to do so. . . . Hence we must believe that all the sciences are so inter-connected, that it is much easier to study them all together than to isolate one from all the others. . . .

RULE II

Only those objects should engage our attention, to the sure and indubitable knowledge of which our mental powers seem to be adequate.

Science in its entirety is true and evident cognition. He is no more learned who has doubts on many matters than the man who has never thought of them; nay he appears to be less learned if he has formed wrong opinions on any particulars. Hence it were better not to study at all than to occupy one's self with objects of such difficulty, that, owing to our inability to distinguish true from false, we are forced to regard the doubtful as certain; for in those matters any hope of augmenting our knowledge is exceeded by the risk of diminishing it. Thus in accordance with the above maxim we reject all such merely probable knowledge and make it a rule to trust only what is completely known and incapable of being doubted. . . .

But if we adhere closely to this rule we shall find left but few objects of legitimate study. For there is scarce any question occurring in the sciences about which talented men have not disagreed. But whenever two men come to opposite decisions about the same matter one of them at least must certainly be in the wrong, and apparently there is not even one of them in the right; for if the reasoning of the second was sound and clear he would be able so to lay it before the other as finally to succeed in convincing *his* understanding also. Hence apparently we cannot attain to a perfect knowledge in any such case of probable opinion, for it would be rashness to hope for more than others have attained to. Consequently if we reckon correctly, of the sciences already discovered, Arithmetic and Geometry alone are left, to which the observance of this rule reduces us. . . .

Now let us proceed to explain more carefully our reasons for saying that of all the sciences known as yet, Arithmetic and Geometry alone are free from any taint of falsity or uncertainty. We must note then that there are two ways by which we arrive at the knowledge of facts, viz., by experience and by deduction. We must further observe that while our inferences from experience are frequently fallacious, deduction, or the pure illation of one thing from another, though it may be passed over, if it is not seen through, cannot be erroneous when performed by an understanding that is in the least degree rational. . . . My reason for saying so is that none of the mistakes which men can make (men, I say, not beasts) are due to faulty inference; they are caused merely by the fact that we base inferences upon poorly comprehended experiences, or that propositions are posited which are hasty and groundless.

This furnishes us with an evident explanation of the great superiority in certitude of Arithmetic and Geometry to other sciences. The former alone deal with an object so pure and uncomplicated, that they need make no assumptions at all which experience renders uncertain, but wholly consist in the rational deduction of consequences. They are on that account much the easiest and clearest of all, and possess an object such as we require, for in-them it is scarce humanly possible for anyone to err except by inadvertence. And yet we should not be surprised to find that plenty of people of their own accord prefer to apply their intelligence to other studies. The reason for this is that every person permits himself the liberty of making guesses in the matter of an obscure subject with more confidence than in one which is clear, and that it is much easier to have some vague notion about any subject, no matter what, than to arrive at the real truth about a single question however simple that may be.

But one conclusion now emerges out of these considerations, viz. not, indeed, that Arithmetic and Geometry are the sole sciences to be studied, but only that in our search for the direct road towards truth we should busy ourselves with no object about which we cannot attain a certitude equal to that of the demonstrations of Arithmetic and Geometry.

RULE III

In the subjects we propose to investigate, our inquiries should be directed, not to what others have thought, nor to what we ourselves conjecture, but to what we can clearly and perspicuously behold and with certainty deduce; for knowledge is not won in any other way.

To study the writings of the ancients is right, because it is a great boon for us to be able to make use of the labours of so many men; and we should do so, both in order to discover what they have correctly made out in previous ages, and also that we may inform ourselves as to what in the various sciences is still left for investigation. But yet there is a great danger lest in a too absorbed study of these works we should become infected with their errors, guard against them as we may. For it is the way of writers, whenever they have allowed themselves rashly and credulously to take up a position in any controverted matter, to try with the subtlest of arguments to compel us to go along with them. But when, on the contrary, they have happily come upon something certain and evident, in displaying it they never fail to surround it with ambiguities, fearing, it would seem, lest the simplicity of their explanation should make us respect their discovery less, or because they grudge us an open vision of the truth.

Further, supposing now that all were wholly open and candid, and never thrust upon us doubtful opinions as true, but expounded every matter in good faith, yet since scarce anything has been asserted by any one man the contrary of which has not been alleged by another, we should be eternally uncertain which of the two to believe. It would be no use to total up the testimonies in favour of each, meaning to follow that opinion which was supported by the greater number of authors; for if it is a question of difficulty that is in dispute, it is more likely that the truth would have been discovered by few than by many. But even though all these men agreed among themselves, what they teach us would not suffice for us. For we shall not, e.g., all turn out to be mathematicians though we know by heart all the proofs that others have elaborated, unless we have an intellectual talent that fits us to resolve difficulties of any kind. Neither, though we have mastered all the arguments of Plato and Aristotle, if yet we have not the capacity for passing a solid judgment on these matters, shall we become Philosophers; we should have acquired the knowledge not of a science, but of history.

I lay down the rule also, that we must wholly refrain from ever mixing up conjectures with our pronouncements on the truth of things. This warning is of no little importance. There is no stronger reason for our finding nothing in the current Philosophy which is so evident and certain as not to be capable of being controverted, than the fact that the learned, not content with the recognition of what is clear and certain, in the first instance hazard the assertion of obscure and ill-comprehended theories, at which they have arrived merely by probable conjecture. Then afterwards they gradually attach complete credence to them, and mingling them promiscuously with what is true and evident, they finish by being unable to deduce any conclusion which does not appear to depend upon some proposition of the doubtful sort, and hence is not uncertain.

But lest we in turn should slip into the same error, we shall here take note of all those mental operations by which we are able, wholly without fear of illusion, to arrive at the knowledge of things. Now I admit only two, viz., intuition and deduction.

By *intuition* I understand, not the fluctuating testimony of the senses, nor the misleading judgment that proceeds from the blundering constructions of imagination, but the conception which an unclouded and attentive mind gives us so readily and distinctly that we are wholly freed from doubt about that which we understand. Or, what comes to the same thing, *intuition* is the undoubting conception of an unclouded and attentive mind, and springs from the light of reason alone; it is more certain than deduction itself, in that it is simpler, though deduction, as we have noted above, cannot by us be erroneously conducted. Thus each individual can mentally have intuition of the fact that he exists, and that he thinks; that the triangle is bounded by three lines only, the sphere by a single superficies, and so on. Facts of such a kind are far more numerous than many people think, disdaining as they do . . . to direct their attention upon such simple matters. . . .

This evidence and certitude, however, which belongs to intuition, is required not only in the enunciation of propositions, but also in discursive reasoning of whatever sort. For example consider this consequence: 2 and 2 amount to the same as 3 and 1. Now we need to see intuitively not only that 2 and 2 make 4, and likewise 3 and 1 make 4, but further that the third of the above statements is a necessary conclusion from these two.

Hence now we are in a position to raise the question as to why we have, besides intuition, given this supplementary method of knowing, viz., knowing by *deduction*, by which we understand all necessary inference from other facts that are known with certainty. This, however, we could not avoid, because many things are known with certainty, though not by themselves evident, but only deduced from true and known principles by the continuous and uninterrupted action of a mind that has a clear vision of each step in the process. It is in a similar way that we know that the last link in a long chain is connected with the first, even though we do not take in by means of one and the same act of vision all the intermediate links on which that connection depends, but only remember that we have taken them successively under review and that each single one is united to its neighbour, from the first even to the last. Hence we distinguish this mental intuition from deduction by the fact that into the conception of the latter there enters a certain movement or succession, into that of the former there does not. Further deduction does not require an immediately presented evidence such as intuition possesses; its certitude is rather conferred upon it in some way by memory. The upshot of the matter is that it is possible to say that those propositions indeed which are immediately deduced from first principles are known now by intuition, now by deduction, i.e., in a way that differs according to our point of view. But the first principles themselves are given by intuition alone, while, on the contrary, the remote conclusions are furnished only by deduction.

These two methods are the most certain routes to knowledge, and the mind should admit no others. All the rest should be rejected as suspect of error and dangerous. . . .

RULE IV

There is need of a method for finding out the truth.

So blind is the curiosity by which mortals are possessed, that they often conduct their minds along unexplored routes, having no reason to hope for success, but merely being willing to risk the experiment of finding whether the truth they seek lies there. As well might a man burning with an unintelligent desire to find treasure, continuously roam the streets, seeking to find something that a passerby might have chanced to drop. This is the way in which most Chemists, many Geometricians, and Philosophers not a few prosecute their studies. I do not deny that sometimes in these wanderings they are lucky enough to find something true. But I do not allow that this argues greater industry on their part, but only better luck. But, however that may be, it were far better never to think of investigating truth at all, than to do so without a method. For it is very certain that unregulated inquiries and confused reflections of this kind only confound the natural light and blind our mental powers. Those who so become accustomed to walk in darkness weaken their eye-sight so much that afterwards they cannot bear the light of day. This is confirmed by experience; for how often do we not see that those who have never taken to letters, give a sounder and clearer decision about obvious matters than those who have spent all their time in the schools? Moreover by a method I mean certain and simple rules, such that, if a man observe them accurately, he shall never assume what is false as true, and will never spend his mental efforts to no purpose, but will always gradually increase his knowledge and so arrive at a true understanding of all that does not surpass his powers. . . .

RULE V

Method consists entirely in the order and disposition of the objects towards which our mental vision must be directed if we would find out any truth. We shall comply with it exactly if we reduce involved and obscure propositions step by step to those that are simpler, and then starting with the intuitive apprehension of all those that are absolutely simple, attempt to ascend to the knowledge of all others by precisely similar steps.

In this alone lies the sum of all human endeavour, and he who would approach the investigation of truth must hold to this rule as closely as he who enters the labyrinth must follow the thread which guided Theseus. But many people either do not reflect on the precept at all, or ignore it altogether, or presume not to need it. Consequently they often investigate the most difficult questions with so little regard to order, that, to my mind, they act like a man who should attempt to leap with one bound from the base to the summit of a house, either making no account of the ladders provided for his ascent or not noticing them. It is thus that all Astrologers behave, who, though in ignorance of the nature of the heavens, and even without having made proper observations of the movements of the heavenly bodies, expect to be able to indicate their effects. This is also what many do who study Mechanics apart from Physics, and readily set about devising new instruments for producing motion. Along with them go also those Philosophers who, neglecting experience, imagine that truth will spring from their brain like Pallas from the head of Zeus.

Now it is obvious that all such people violate the present rule. But since the order here required is often so obscure and intricate that not everyone can make it out, they can scarcely avoid error unless they diligently observe what is laid down in the following proposition.

RULE VI

In order to separate out what is quite simple from what is complex, and to arrange these matters methodically, we ought, in the case of every series in which we have deduced certain facts the one from the other, to notice which fact is simple, and to mark the interval, greater, less or equal, which separates all the others from this.

Although this proposition seems to teach nothing very new, it contains, nevertheless, the chief secret of method, and none in the whole of this treatise is of greater utility. For it tells us that all facts can be arranged in certain series, not indeed in the sense of being referred to some ontological genus such as the categories employed by Philosophers in their classification, but in so far as certain truths can be known from others; and thus, whenever a difficulty occurs we are able at once to perceive whether it will be profitable to examine certain others first, and which, and in what order.

Further, in order to do that correctly, we must note first that for the purpose of our procedure, which does not regard things as isolated realities, but compares them with one another in order to discover the dependence in knowledge of one upon the other, all things can be said to be either absolute or relative.

I call that absolute which contains within itself the pure and simple essence of which we are in quest. Thus the term will be applicable to whatever is considered as being independent, or a cause, or simple, universal, one, equal, like, straight, and so forth; and the absolute I call the simplest and the easiest of all, so that we can make use of it in the solution of questions.

But the relative is that which, while participating in the same nature, or at least sharing in it to some degree which enables us to relate it to the absolute and to deduce it from that by a chain of operations, involves in addition something else in its concept which I call relativity. Examples of this are found in whatever is said to be dependent, or an effect, composite, particular, many, unequal, unlike, oblique, etc. These relatives are the further removed from the absolute, in proportion as they contain more elements of relativity subordinate the one to the other. We state in this rule that these should all be distinguished and their correlative connection and natural order so observed, that we may be able by traversing all the intermediate steps to proceed from the most remote to that which is in the highest degree absolute. . . .

Finally we must note that our inquiry ought not to start with the investigation of difficult matters. Rather, before setting out to attack any definite problem, it behooves us first, without making any selection, to assemble those truths that are obvious as they present themselves to us, and afterwards, proceeding step by step, to inquire whether any others can be deduced from these, and again any others from these conclusions and so on, in order. This done, we should attentively think over the truths we have discovered and mark with diligence the reasons why we have been able to detect some more easily than others, and which these are. Thus, when we come to attack some definite problem we shall be able to judge what previous questions it were best to settle first. For example, if it comes into my thought that the number 6 is twice 3, I may then ask what is twice 6, viz., 12; again, perhaps I seek for the double of this, viz., 24, and again of this, viz., 48. Thus I may deduce that there is the same proportion between 3 and 6, as between 6 and 12, and likewise 12 and 24, and so on, and hence that the numbers 3, 6, 12, 24, 48, etc., are in continued proportion. But though these facts are all so clear as to seem almost childish, I am now able by attentive reflection to understand what is the form involved by all questions that can be propounded about the proportions or relations of things, and the order in which they should be investigated; and this discovery embraces the sum of the entire science of Pure Mathematics.

RULE VII

If we wish our science to be complete, those matters which promote the end we have in view must one and all be scrutinized by a movement of thought which is continuous and nowhere interrupted; they must also be included in an enumeration which is both adequate and methodical.

It is necessary to obey the injunctions of this rule if we hope to gain admission among the certain truths for those which, we have declared above, are not immediate deductions from primary and self-evident principles. For this deduction frequently involves such a long series of transitions from ground to consequent that when we come to the conclusion we have difficulty in recalling the whole of the route by which we have arrived at it. This is why I say that there must be a continuous movement of thought to make good this weakness of the memory. Thus, e.g., if I have first found out by separate mental operations what the relation is between the magnitudes A and B, then

what between B and C, between C and D, and finally between D and E, that does not entail my seeing what the relation is between A and E, nor can the truths previously learnt give me a precise knowledge of it unless I recall them all. To remedy this I would run them over from time to time, keeping the imagination moving continuously in such a way that while it is intuitively perceiving each fact it simultaneously passes on to the next; and this I would do until I had learned to pass from the first to the last so quickly, that no stage in the process was left to the care of the memory, but I seemed to have the whole in intuition before me at the same time. This method will both relieve the memory, diminish the sluggishness of our thinking, and definitely enlarge our mental capacity.

But we must add that this movement should nowhere be interrupted. Often people who attempt to deduce a conclusion too quickly and from remote principles do not trace the whole chain of intermediate conclusions with sufficient accuracy to prevent them from passing over many steps without due consideration. But it is certain that wherever the smallest link is left out the chain is broken and the whole of the certainty of the conclusion falls to the ground. . . .

RULE VIII

If in the matters to be examined we come to a step in the series of which our understanding is not sufficiently well able to have an intuitive cognition, we must stop short there. We must make no attempt to examine what follows; thus we shall spare ourselves superfluous labour.

. . . If a man proposes to himself the problem of examining all the truths for the knowledge of which human reason suffices — and I think that this is a task which should be undertaken once at least in his life by every person who seriously endeavors to attain equilibrium of thought — he will, by the rules given above, certainly discover that nothing can be known prior to the understanding, since the knowledge of all things else depends upon this and not conversely. Then, when he has clearly grasped all those things which follow proximately on the knowledge of the naked understanding, he will enumerate among other things whatever instruments of thought we have other than the understanding; and these are only two, viz., imagination and sense. He will therefore devote all his energies to the distinguishing and examining of these three modes of cognition, and seeing that in the strict sense truth and falsity can be a matter of the understanding alone, though often it derives its origin from the other two faculties, he will attend carefully to every source of deception in order that he may be on his guard. He will also enumerate exactly all the ways leading to truth which lie open to us, in order that he may follow the right way. They are not so many that they cannot all be easily discovered and embraced in an adequate enumeration. And though this will seem marvellous and incredible to the inexpert, as soon as in each matter he has distinguished those cognitions which only fill and embellish the memory, from those which cause one to be deemed really more instructed, which it will be easy for him to do, he will feel assured that any absence of further knowledge is not due to lack of intelligence or of skill, and that nothing at all can be known by anyone else which he is not capable of knowing, provided only that he gives to it his utmost mental application.

COMMENT

Plato's *Meno*

Classical rationalism differed from its modern version in many respects, as a comparison of these readings from Plato and Descartes clearly reveals. Nonetheless, both versions argue that knowledge is the result of rational analysis alone and is achieved completely independently of sensory experience. In addition, both Plato and Descartes take geometric reasoning as the paradigm of cognitive activity since it is strictly a function of intellectual processes and leaves no margin for error.

Plato's *Meno* begins, as most of his works do, with a good deal of verbal byplay, followed by the admission of both Socrates and his interlocutor that they do not know how to define the key concept in question, in this case "virtue." We pick up the conversation at the point where a fresh and more serious start is made. Meno expresses their problem in the form of a paradoxical dilemma: Knowledge of any truth would seem to be impossible since *either* one already knows it and thus cannot learn it, *or* one does not know it and thus would not recognize it when confronted with it.

After rehearsing a common belief of the day concerning the immortality of the soul, including the mind, Socrates suggests the possibility that all human knowledge is merely a remembering or recollecting of that which was known by the soul in its previous existence. If this is the case, all that is necessary to prove it is to draw some seemingly fresh knowledge out of an uneducated young person without relying in any way on sensory input. This Socrates proceeds to do with the help of Meno's slave boy. Simply by means of pure logic, aided by a diagram, he leads the slave, step by step, to a "discovery" of the truth of what has come to be called the "Pythagorean Theorem."

The results of such analysis, according to the rationalist approach to knowledge, clearly establish the conceptual rather than the perceptual basis of all truth. Thus, even the knowledge of such abstract notions as "virtue" can be obtained through the rational, albeit arduous, analysis of their implicit and essential meanings. By beginning with simple, undefined yet unquestionable concepts and axioms, and then moving by the laws of logic to conclusions entailed by them, anyone with sufficient intellectual ability will be able to arrive at knowledge.

The heart of the rationalist claim is that apart from the activity of the mind, which enables a person to grasp the connection or similarity between various experiential objects or qualities, our sensory encounters would remain mere "exposures," with no pattern or coherence. It is the mind, what Plato called "the eye of the soul," which enables one to *see* what things have in common and what follows from what and why. Other animals have sensory exposure to trees, sounds, and fears, for instance, but only humans *understand* the concept of a "tree," the meaning of sounds, and how to alleviate fears—or so claims the rationalist.

The critics of rationalism, however, question whether Socrates actually drew the knowledge of geometry out of the slave's mind. The use of the diagram is itself a *perceptual* device, and throughout their conversation, Socrates is said to be relying on the boy's sensory experience with other aspects of life. At best, this is another version of the famous "chicken or egg" controversy: How is it possible to prove or know anything until you already know something else? Every idea seems to be dependent on another idea; both mental activity and sensory experience would seem to be necessary for knowledge to exist.

Another, more modern criticism of the rationalist approach to knowledge focuses on the nature of mathematical reasoning. Many thinkers suggest that the reason Socrates is able to help the boy pull the rabbit out of the logical hat is that it was already in the hat, rather than in the boy's mind, at the outset. That is, the very concepts with which Socrates began, such as "four-corned space," "equal," "larger or smaller," "twice two," and so on are defined and used in such a way as to necessitate certain conclusions. In other words, many modern thinkers believe that mathematical "knowledge" is empty of any factual information about the world, that it is strictly a matter of setting up certain definitions and axioms and then squeezing them to see what is entailed by them, because the information was built into them at the beginning. Such knowledge can only be a priori, or independent of experience, because it is "analytic" in the sense that its meaning and truth are, strictly speaking, obtainable only by analyzing the original terms used at the outset. Such knowledge is absolutely certain, but the price for certainty is, according to these critics, emptiness.

Descartes' Method

The question of method became a matter of keen and widespread interest with the great flowering of science in the seventeenth and eighteenth centuries. The discoveries of such great scientists as Kepler, Galileo, Newton, Gilbert, and Harvey and the rapid development of mathematics and natural science forced people to reflect on the nature of scientific knowledge and the means to its attainment.

The principal cleavage among the philosophers was between the *rationalists* and the *empiricists*. The rationalists, among them Descartes, Spinoza, and Leibniz, relied chiefly on reason as the source of genuine knowledge, taking the methods of mathematics, especially geometry, as their model. The empiricists, among them Locke, Berkeley, and Hume, depended mainly on experience, regarding the methods of hypothesis, observation, and experiment as the principal foundations of knowledge. Actually, the differences between the two groups were not so sharp as they are often represented. Both groups recognized the necessity of a combination of experience and reason, but they veered toward opposite sides in their emphasis.

Of primary significance in considering Descartes' philosophy as an example of rationalism is his intense desire for certainty: "I always had an excessive desire to learn to distinguish the true from the false, in order to see clearly in my actions and to walk with confidence in this life."[1] He

---

[1]*Discourse on Method*, in *The Philosophical Works of Descartes*, trans. Elizabeth S. Haldane and G. R. T. Ross (Cambridge: Cambridge University Press, 1931), I, p. 87.

believed that the key to certainty, the way in which to dispel his innumerable doubts, lay in a sound and logical method of reasoning. The proper employment of reason, he believed, would make vast provinces accessible to human knowledge.

Descartes asserted that all certain knowledge is based on two mental operations: *intuition* — which he also called "the natural light of reason" — and *deduction*. His definitions of these terms are contained in his *Rules for the Direction of the Mind*:

> By *intuition* I understand, not the fluctuating testimony of the senses, nor the misleading judgment that proceeds from the blundering constructions of imagination, but the conception which an unclouded and attentive mind gives us so readily and distinctly that we are wholly freed from doubt about that which we understand. Or, what comes to the same thing, *intuition* is the undoubting conception of an unclouded and attentive mind, and springs from the light of reason alone. . . .
>
> By *deduction* . . . we understand all necessary inference from other facts that are known with certainty. . . . Many things are known with certainty, though not by themselves evident, but only deduced from true and known principles by the continuous and uninterrupted action of a mind that has a clear vision of each step in the process. It is in a similar way that we know that the last link in a long chain is connected with the first, even though we do not take in by means of one and the same act of vision all the intermediate links on which that connection depends, but only remember that we have taken them successively under review and that each single one is united to its neighbor, from the first even to the last.[2]

In formulating these definitions, Descartes was thinking specifically of the method of mathematics, particularly geometry. The certainty of rigorous mathematical reasoning, he believed, consists in starting with meanings and insights so clear and distinct that they cannot be doubted, and then accepting nothing as true unless it follows no less evidently from these foundations. An intuited truth is such that reason has only to understand its meaning fully to see that it *must* be true. Examples of intuitions are the insights that five is more than four, that a triangle is bounded by only three lines, and that things equal to the same thing are equal to each other. Given such manifest and self-evident premises, our conclusion will be certain provided that it is *necessarily* implied by what

[2]*Rules for the Direction of the Mind*, in ibid., pp. 7–8.

precedes and that nothing is admitted in the steps of reasoning that does not thus necessarily follow. Thus, in a chain of reasoning symbolized by letters, if *p* implies *q*, and *q* implies *r*, and *r* implies *s*, then *s* is certain provided that *p* is certain and that each subsequent step leading to *s* is also certain. Descartes believed that thinkers have succeeded in the past and will succeed in the future to the extent that they have rigorously employed, or will employ, intuition and deduction.

With this conception of reasoning in mind, he summed up his method in four rules, which are stated in Part II of the *Discourse:*

1. *The rule of certainty.* This rule is (1) to accept nothing as true that we do not unquestionably recognize to be such, and (2) carefully to avoid all precipitation and prejudice so as to reach judgments so clear and distinct that they cannot be doubted. Only what we *know* to be true is to be admitted into the sphere of belief: Thus Descartes aimed not at mere probability but at absolute certainty. This rule compelled him to reject all beliefs that are at all dubious.

He recognized two causes as chiefly responsible for error: precipitate judgment, due to insufficient care, and prejudiced judgment, due to habit or emotional bias. Many beliefs are tenaciously held not because they are seen with clearness and distinctness to be true but because, in our haste or bias, we feel a very strong inclination to believe them. "I term that clear," he declared, "which is present and apparent to an attentive mind. . . . But the distinct is that which is so precise and different from all other objects that it contains within itself nothing but what is clear."[3] A judgment is worthy of belief only if all the ideas in it and the judgment as a whole are thus clear and distinct.

2. *The rule of division.* We should analyze each of the difficulties involved in our problem into its smallest and simplest parts. If we then attack each of the subordinate parts separately, we shall find it easier to understand and deal with the simple than the complex. When we have thus discovered elements so simple, so clear, and so distinct that the mind cannot break them down into still more simple parts, we can know these elements by a direct awareness exempt from illusion and error; and after this analysis, reason can more surely reconstruct the complex objects of thought.

3. *The rule of order.* We should carry on our reflections in due order, starting with the simplest ideas and proceeding, step by step, to the more and more complex. Descartes had in mind a deductive chain of reasoning in which each stage follows necessarily from the preceding stage, reason always being careful to follow the one and only order. Every step in this

[3]*The Principles of Philosophy,* in ibid., I, p. 237.

process must command certainty since it is guaranteed by *intuition*, that "undoubting conception of an unclouded and attentive mind."

4. *The rule of enumeration and review.* In a long chain of reasoning, we are apt to make a slip—to think that we grasp something clearly and distinctly, when in fact we do not, or to remember incorrectly some earlier stage in the reasoning. Whenever the smallest link is thus impaired, the chain of reasoning is broken, and all certainty is lost. Hence, it is necessary to recount and review the steps again and again to be absolutely sure that there has been no trick of memory or mistake in reasoning. Certainty is attained only when every link is so firmly grasped, and every connection has been so often reviewed, that the mind finally gathers together the links into an indissoluble, self-evident whole, which it views, as it were, all at the same time. Intuition then can grasp this whole as certain, just as it has grasped the initial premises and each successive step as certain.

Systematic Doubt

The success of the Cartesian method depends on having a sure foundation on which to build and thereafter on successfully applying the first rule—to admit nothing that is uncertain. Therefore Descartes resolved to doubt everything that he could possibly doubt, provisionally retaining only those ordinary maxims of conduct that are necessary in order to live decently. To doubt in this methodical way is not to consider something false or improbable but to recognize that it is not *absolutely* certain. The function of systematic doubt is to find a solid foundation for science and philosophy and thus to dispel scepticism.

The kind of indubitable foundation for which Descartes was searching is not any formal principle of logic or mathematics, such as the principle that one and the same proposition cannot be both true and false. Such a principle, although a necessary foundation of reasoning, tells us nothing about *what exists* and hence cannot provide the necessary basis for a philosophy or science of *reality*. The kind of premise that he sought, therefore, must be such that its truth cannot be doubted, it must be self-evident and not deduced from something else, and it must refer to something actually existing.

In resolutely admitting nothing except what is certain, Descartes was forced to doubt almost everything that he had ever believed: sensory experience, memory, expectation, the existence of other people, his body, the external physical world, and even simple mathematical truths such as two plus two equals four. His argument is so lucid that the reader should have no difficulty in understanding it.

It would seem that nothing at all is left to believe; but something remains even when doubt has done its worst. "I suppose myself to be deceived," Descartes exclaimed; "doubtless, then, I exist, since I am deceived." My very act of doubting proves something that I cannot doubt, "I think, therefore I am."

Here is the first principle — the absolute and indubitable certainty — for which Descartes was searching, and here also is the main point of departure of modern epistemology. The certainty of self-consciousness had been proclaimed earlier by St. Augustine (354 – 430) and St. Thomas Aquinas (1225? – 1274). But Descartes gave the idea wide currency, backing it up with systematic doubt, and without admitting the element of faith essential to Augustine and Aquinas. No one before him had so deliberately adopted doubt as a method of procedure or employed it so boldly and sweepingly.

Empiricism and Its Limits

"A thorough empiricist, Hume traced all knowledge back to some original basis in experience . . . to this reduction of the mind to a succession of awarenesses, Kant opposes the mind's awareness of succession, which he says is unaccountable without more synthesis and continuity than Hume recognized."

Melvin Rader

DAVID HUME (1711–1776)

Born in Edinburgh, Hume was the youngest son of a gentleman landowner. His father died when he was an infant, and he was reared by his mother, who, somewhat critical of his bookish tendencies, is said to have remarked that "oor Davie's a fine good-natured crater but uncommon wake-minded." Hume's studies at the University of Edinburgh instilled in him a love of literature and philosophy, which kept him from settling down to a legal or business career. He decided to devote his life to scholarly pursuits, and at the age of twenty-three crossed the Channel to live in France, studying at La Flèche, where Descartes had gone to school.

There he completed, before he reached the age of twenty-five, his greatest philosophical work, the *Treatise of Human Nature*. In his brief autobiography he remarked that the book "fell dead-born from the press." Although this remark is an exaggeration, it suggest Hume's great disap-

76

pointment that his ideas did not find a wider public. His *An Enquiry Concerning Human Understanding* (1748) and *An Enquiry Concerning the Principles of Morals* (1751), which restated principal parts of the *Treatise*, were somewhat more popular, but his literary reputation was based mainly on his *Political Discourses* (1752) and his *History of England*, published in 1755 and following years. He also wrote *Dialogues Concerning Natural Religion*, which he regarded as a bit too shocking to publish during his own lifetime.

Although the income from his books gradually increased and he remained a frugal bachelor, he had to find other means of livelihood. Early in his career, he applied first to the University of Edinburgh and then to the University of Glasgow for a teaching position, but both universities rejected him because of the heterodoxy of his views. For a short time he was tutor to a lunatic, the Marquis of Annandale, and then secretary to General St. Clair. Thereafter he secured a six-year post as keeper of Advocates' Library in Edinburgh, and from 1763 to 1765 served as secretary to the British Embassy in Paris. His French acquaintances included the most famous intellectuals of the period — D'Alembert, Diderot, Holbach, and Rousseau. After his sojourn in France, he spent two years in London (1767–1769) as under secretary of state for Scotland. In Great Britain as in France, he was a friend of distinguished wits, such as Burke, Gibbon, and Adam Smith. Having received a moderate pension, he finally retired to Edinburgh, where he lived quietly with his sister until his death in 1776.

In a self-obituary, he describes himself as follows: "I was a man of mild disposition, of command of temper, of an open, social and cheerful humor, capable of attachment but little susceptible of enmity, and of great moderation in all my passions. Even my love of literary fame, my ruling passion, never soured my temper, notwithstanding my frequent disappointments." This characterization appears to be entirely accurate. Hume was a canny Scot, with a kindly, humorous, equable disposition.

Knowledge and Causality

1. [Impressions and Ideas]

Everyone will readily allow, that there is a considerable difference between the perceptions of the mind, when a man feels the pain of excessive heat, or the pleasure of moderate warmth, and when he afterwards recalls to his memory this sensation, or anticipates it by his imagination. These faculties may mimic or copy the perceptions of the senses; but they never can entirely reach the force and vivacity of the original sentiment. The utmost we say of them, even when they operate with greatest vigor, is, that they represent their object in so lively a manner, that we could *almost* say we feel or see it: But, except the mind be disordered by disease or madness, they never can arrive at such a pitch of vivacity, as to render these perceptions altogether undistinguishable. All the colors of poetry, however splendid, can never paint natural objects in such a manner as to make the description be taken for a real landskip. The most lively thought is still inferior to the dullest sensation.

We may observe a like distinction to run through all the other perceptions of the mind. A man in a fit of anger, is actuated in a very different manner from one who only thinks of that emotion. If you tell me, that any person is in love, I easily understand your meaning, and form a just conception of his situation; but never can mistake that conception for the real disorders and agitations of the passion. When we reflect on our past sentiments and affections, our thought is a faithful mirror, and copies its objects truly; but the colors which it employs are faint and dull, in comparison of those in which our original perceptions were clothed. It requires no nice discernment or metaphysical head to mark the distinction between them.

Here therefore we may divide all the perceptions of the mind into two classes or species, which are distinguished by their different degrees of force and vivacity. The less forcible and lively are commonly denominated *Thoughts* or *Ideas*. The other species want a name in our language, and in most others; I suppose, because it was not requisite for any, but philosophical purposes, to rank them under a general term or appellation. Let us, therefore, use a little freedom, and call them *Impressions*; employing that word in a sense somewhat different from the usual. By the term *impression*, then, I mean all our more lively perceptions, when we hear, or see, or feel, or love, or hate, or desire, or will. And impressions are distinguished from ideas, which are the less lively perceptions, of which we are conscious, when we reflect on any of those sensations or movements above mentioned. . . .

Section 1 combines excerpts from the *Treatise* and the *Enquiry*; sections 2, 4, 5, 6, and 8 are from the *Enquiry*; sections 3 and 7 are from the *Treatise*. The *Treatise* was published in 1739; the *Enquiry* in 1748.

Impressions may be divided into two kinds, those of *sensation*, and those of *reflection*. The first kind arises in the soul originally, from unknown causes. The second is derived, in a great measure, from our ideas, and that in the following order. An impression first strikes upon the senses, and makes us perceive heat or cold, thirst or hunger, pleasure or pain, of some kind or other. Of this impression there is a copy taken by the mind, which remains after the impression ceases; and this we call an idea. This idea of pleasure or pain, when it returns upon the soul, produces the new impressions of desire and aversion, hope and fear, which may properly be called impressions of reflection, because derived from it. These again are copied by the memory and imagination, and become ideas; which, perhaps, in their turn, give rise to other impressions and ideas; so that the impressions of reflection, are not only antecedent to their correspondent ideas, but posterior to those of sensation, and derived from them. . . .

We find, by experience, that when any impression has been present with the mind, it again makes its appearance there as an idea; and this it may do after two different ways: either when, in its new appearance, it retains a considerable degree of its first vivacity, and is somewhat intermediate betwixt an impression and an idea; or when it entirely loses that vivacity, and is a perfect idea. The faculty by which we repeat our impressions in the first manner, is called the *memory*, and the other the *imagination*. It is evident, at first sight, that the ideas of the memory are much more lively and strong than those of the imagination, and that the former faculty paints its objects in more distinct colors than any which are employed by the latter. When we remember any past event, the idea of it flows in upon the mind in a forcible manner; whereas, in the imagination, the perception is faint and languid, and cannot, without difficulty, be preserved by the mind steady and uniform for any considerable time. Here, then, is a sensible difference betwixt one species of ideas and another.

There is another difference betwixt these two kinds of ideas, which is no less evident, namely, that though neither the ideas of the memory nor imagination, neither the lively nor faint ideas, can make their appearance in the mind, unless their correspondent impressions have gone before to prepare the way for them, yet the imagination is not restrained to the same order and form with the original impressions; while the memory is in a manner tied down in that respect, without any power of variation.

Nothing, at first view, may seem more unbounded than the thought of man, which not only escapes all human power and authority, but is not even restrained within the limits of nature and reality. To form monsters, and join incongruous shapes and appearances, costs the imagination no more trouble than to conceive the most natural and familiar objects. And while the body is confined to one planet, along which it creeps with pain and difficulty; the thought can in an instant transport us into the most distant regions of the universe; or even beyond the universe, into the unbounded chaos, where nature is supposed to lie in total confusion. What never was seen, or heard of, may yet be conceived; nor is anything beyond the power of thought, except what implies an absolute contradiction.

But though our thought seems to possess this unbounded liberty, we shall find, upon a nearer examination, that it is really confined within very narrow limits, and that all this creative power of the mind amounts to no more than the faculty of compounding, transposing, augmenting, or diminishing the materials afforded us by the senses and experience. When we think of a golden mountain, we only join two consistent ideas, *gold*, and *mountain*, with which we were formerly acquainted. A virtuous horse we can conceive; because, from our own feeling, we can conceive virtue; and this we may unite to the figure and shape of a horse, which is an animal familiar to us. In short, all the materials of thinking are derived either from our outward or inward sentiment: the mixture and composition of these belongs alone to the mind and will. Or, to express myself in philosophical language, all our ideas or more feeble perceptions are copies of our impressions or more lively ones. . . .

Here, therefore, is a proposition, which not only seems, in itself, simple and intelligible; but, if a proper use were made of it, might render every dispute equally intelligible, and banish all that jargon, which has so long taken possession of metaphysical reasonings, and drawn disgrace upon them. All ideas, especially abstract ones, are naturally faint and obscure: the mind has but a slender hold of them: they are apt to be confounded with other resembling ideas; and when we have often employed any term, though without a distinct meaning, we are apt to imagine it has a determinate idea annexed to it. On the contrary, all impressions, that is, all sensations, either outward or inward, are strong and vivid: the limits between them are more exactly determined: nor is it easy to fall into any error or mistake with regard to them. When we entertain, therefore, any suspicion that a philosophical term is employed without any meaning or idea (as is but too frequent), we need but enquire, *from what impression is that supposed idea derived?* And if it be impossible to assign any, this will serve to confirm our suspicion. By bringing ideas into so clear a light we may reasonably hope to remove all dispute, which may arise, concerning their nature and reality.

2. [The Forms of Reasoning]

All the objects of human reason or enquiry may naturally be divided into two kinds, to wit, *Relations of Ideas*, and *Matters of Fact*. Of the first kind are the sciences of Geometry, Algebra, and Arithmetic; and in short, every affirmation which is either intuitively or demonstratively certain. *That the square of the hypothenuse is equal to the square of the two sides*, is a proposition which expresses a relation between these figures. *That three times five is equal to the half of thirty*, expresses a relation between these numbers. Propositions of this kind are discoverable by the mere operation of thought, without dependence on what is anywhere existent in the universe. Though there never were a circle or triangle in nature, the truths demonstrated by Euclid would for ever retain their certainty and evidence.

Matters of fact, which are the second objects of human reason, are not ascertained in the same manner; nor is our evidence of their truth, however great, of a like nature with the foregoing. The contrary of every matter of fact is still possible; bcause it can never imply a contradiction, and is conceived by the mind with the same facility and distinctness, as if ever so comfortable to reality. *That the sun will not rise tomorrow* is no less intelligible a proposition, and implies no more contradiction than the affirmation, *that it will rise*. We should in vain, therefore, attempt to demonstrate its falsehood. Were it demonstratively false, it would imply a contradiction, and could never be distinctly conceived by the mind.

It may, therefore, be a subject worthy of curiosity, to enquire what is the nature of that evidence which assures us of any real existence and matter of fact, beyond the present testimony of our senses, or the records of our memory. This part of philosophy, it is observable, has been little cultivated, either by the ancients or moderns; and therefore our doubts and errors, in the prosecution of so important an enquiry, may be the more excusable; while we march through such difficult paths without any guide or direction. They may even prove useful, by exciting curiosity, and destroying that implicit faith and security, which is the bane of all reasoning and free enquiry. The discovery of defects in the com-

mon philosophy, if any such there be, will not, I presume, be a discouragement, but rather an incitement, as is usual, to attempt something more full and satisfactory than has yet been proposed to the public.

All reasonings concerning matter of fact seem to be founded on the relation of *Cause and Effect*. By means of that relation alone we can go beyond the evidence of our memory and senses. If you were to ask a man, why he believes any matter of fact, which is absent; for instance, that his friend is in the country, or in France; he would give you a reason; and this reason would be some other fact; as a letter received from him, or the knowledge of his former resolutions and promises. A man finding a watch or any other machine in a desert island, would conclude that there had once been men in that island. All our reasonings concerning fact are of the same nature. And here it is constantly supposed that there is a connection between the present fact and that which is inferred from it. Were there nothing to bind them together, the inference would be entirely precarious. The hearing of an articulate voice and rational discourse in the dark assures us of the presence of some person: Why? because these are the effects of the human make and fabric, and closely connected with it. If we anatomize all the other reasonings of this nature, we shall find that they are founded on the relation of cause and effect, and that this relation is either near or remote, direct or collateral. Heat and light are collateral effects of fire, and the one effect may justly be inferred from the other.

If we would satisfy ourselves, therefore, concerning the nature of that evidence, which assures us of matters of fact, we must enquire how we arrive at the knowledge of cause and effect.

I shall venture to affirm, as a general proposition, which admits of no exception, that the knowledge of this relation is not, in any instance, attained by reasonings *a priori*; but arises entirely from experience, when we find that any particular objects are constantly conjoined with each other. Let an object be presented to a man of ever so strong natural reason and abilities; if that object be entirely new to him, he will not be able, by the most accurate examination of its sensible qualities, to discover any of its causes or effects. Adam, though his rational faculties be supposed, at the very first, entirely perfect, could not have inferred from the fluidity and transparency of water that it would suffocate him, or from the light and warmth of fire that it would consume him. No object ever discovers, by the qualities which appear to the senses, either the causes which produced it, or the effects which will arise from it; nor can our reason, unassisted by experience, ever draw any inference concerning real existence and matter of fact.

This proposition, *that causes and effects are discoverable, not by reason but by experience*, will readily be admitted with regard to such objects, as we remember to have once been altogether unknown to us; since we must be conscious of the utter inability, which we then lay under, of foretelling what would arise from them. Present two smooth pieces of marble to a man who has no tincture of natural philosophy; he will never discover that they will adhere together in such a manner as to require great force to separate them in a direct line, while they make so small a resistance to a lateral pressure. Such events, as bear little analogy to the common course of nature, are also readily confessed to be known only by experience; nor does any man imagine that the explosion of gunpowder, or the attraction of a loadstone, could ever be discovered by arguments *a priori*. In like manner, when an effect is supposed to depend upon an intricate machinery or secret structure of parts, we make no difficulty in attributing all our knowledge of it to experience. Who will assert that he can give the ultimate reason, why milk or bread is proper nourishment for a man, not for a lion or a tiger? . . .

3. [The Idea of Causation]

We must consider the idea of *causation*, and see from what origin it is derived. It is impossible to reason justly, without understanding perfectly the idea concerning which we reason; and it is impossible perfectly to understand any idea, without tracing it up to its origin, and examining that primary impression, from which it arises. The examination of the impression bestows a clearness on the idea; and the examination of the idea bestows a like clearness on all our reasoning.

Let us therefore cast our eye on any two objects, which we call cause and effect, and turn them on all sides, in order to find that impression, which produces an idea of such prodigious consequence. At first sight I perceive, that I must not search for it in any of the particular *qualities* of the objects; since, whichever of these qualities I pitch on, I find some object that is not possessed of it, and yet falls under the denomination of cause or effect. And indeed there is nothing existent, either externally or internally, which is not to be considered either as a cause or an effect; though it is plain there is no one quality which universally belongs to all beings, and gives them a title to that denomination.

The idea then of causation must be derived from some *relation* among objects; and that relation we must now endeavor to discover. I find in the first place, that whatever objects are considered as causes or effects, are *contiguous*; and that nothing can operate in a time or place, which is ever so little removed from those of its existence. Though distant objects may sometimes seem productive of each other, they are commonly found upon examination to be linked by a chain of causes, which are contiguous among themselves, and to the distant objects; and when in any particular instance we cannot discover this connection, we still presume it to exist. We may therefore consider the relation of *contiguity* as essential to that of causation. . . .

The second relation I shall observe as essential to causes and effects, is . . . that of *priority* of time in the cause before the effect. . . .

[A third] relation betwixt cause and effect . . . is their *constant conjunction*. Contiguity and succession are not sufficient to make us pronounce any two objects to be cause and effect, un-less we perceive that these two relations are preserved in several instances. . . . Thus we remember to have seen that species of object we call *flame*, and to have felt that species of sensation we call *heat*. We likewise call to mind their constant conjunction in all past instances. Without any farther ceremony, we call the one *cause* and the other *effect*, and infer the existence of the one from that of the other. . . .

There is [also] a *necessary connection* to be taken into consideration; and that relation is of much greater importance. . . .

What is our idea of necessity, when we say that two objects are necessarily connected together? Upon this head I repeat, what I have often had occasion to observe, that as we have no idea that is not derived from an impression, we must find some impression that gives rise to this idea of necessity, if we assert we have really such an idea. In order to this, I consider in what objects necessity is commonly supposed to lie; and, finding that it is always ascribed to causes and effects, I turn my eye to two objects supposed to be placed in that relation, and examine them in all the situations of which they are susceptible. I immediately perceive that they are *contiguous* in time and place, and that the object we call cause *precedes* the other we call effect. In no one instance can I go any further, nor is it possible for me to discover any third relation betwixt these objects. I therefore enlarge my view to comprehend several instances, where I find like objects always existing in like relations of contiguity and succession. At first sight this seems to serve but little to my purpose. The reflection on several instances only repeats the same objects; and therefore can never give rise to a new idea. But upon further enquiry I find, that the repetition is not in every particular the same, but produces a new impression, and by that means the idea which I at present examine. For after a frequent repetition I find, that upon the appearance of one of the objects, the mind is *determined* by custom to consider its usual attendant, and to consider it in a stronger light upon account of its relation to the first object. It is this impression, then, or *determination*, which affords me the idea of necessity. . . .

Suppose two objects to be presented to us, of which the one is the cause and the other the effect; it is plain that, from the simple consideration of one, or both these objects, we never shall perceive the tie by which they are united, or be able certainly to pronounce, that there is a connection betwixt them. It is not, therefore, from any one instance, that we arrive at the idea of cause and effect, of a necessary connection of power, of force, of energy, and of efficacy. Did we never see any but particular conjunctions of objects, entirely different from each other, we should never be able to form any such ideas [as cause and effect].

But, again, suppose we observe several instances in which the same objects are always conjoined together, we immediately conceive a connection betwixt them, and begin to draw an inference from one to another. This multiplicity of resembling instances, therefore, constitutes the very essence of power or connection, and is the

source from which the idea of it arises. . . .

Though the several resembling instances, which give rise to the idea of power, have no influence on each other, and can never produce any new quality *in the object*, which can be the model of that idea, yet the *observation* of this resemblance produces a new impression *in the mind*, which is its real model. For after we have observed the resemblance in a sufficient number of instances, we immediately feel a determination of the mind to pass from one object to its usual attendant, and to conceive it in a stronger light upon account of that relation. This determination is the only effect of the resemblance; and, therefore, must be the same with power or efficacy, whose idea is derived from the resemblance. The several instances of resembling conjunctions lead us into the notion of power and necessity. These instances are in themselves totally distinct from each other, and have no union but in the mind, which observes them, and collects their ideas. Necessity, then, is the effect of this observation, and is nothing but an internal impression of the mind, or a determination to carry our thoughts from one object to another. Without considering it in this view, we can never arrive at the most distant notion of it, or be able to attribute it either to external or internal objects, to spirit or body, to causes or effects. . . .

The idea of necessity arises from some impression. There is no impression conveyed by our senses, which can give rise to that idea. It must, therefore, be derived from some internal impression, or impression of reflection. There is no internal impression which has any relation to the present business, but that propensity, which custom produces, to pass from an object to the idea of its usual attendant. This, therefore, is the essence of necessity. Upon the whole, necessity is something that exists in the mind, not in objects; nor is it possible for us ever to form the most distant idea of it, considered as a quality in bodies. Either we have no idea of necessity, or necessity is nothing but that determination of the thought to pass from causes to effects, and from effects to causes, according to their experienced union.

Thus, as the necessity, which makes two times two equal to four, or three angles of a triangle equal to two right ones, lies only in the act of the understanding, by which we consider and compare these ideas; in like manner, the necessity of power, which unites causes and effects, lies in the determination of the mind to pass from the one to the other. The efficacy or energy of causes is neither placed in the causes themselves, nor in the Deity, nor in the concurrence of these two principles; but belongs entirely to the soul, which considers the union of two or more objects in all past instances. It is here that the real power of causes is placed, along with their connection and necessity. . . .

4. [Of Liberty and Necessity]

I hope . . . to make it appear that all men have ever agreed in the doctrine both of necessity and of liberty, according to any reasonable sense, which can be put on these terms; and that the whole controversy has hitherto turned merely upon words. We shall begin with examining the doctrine of necessity.

It is universally allowed that matter, in all its operations, is actuated by a necessary force, and that every natural effect is so precisely determined by the energy of its cause that no other effect, in such particular circumstances, could possibly have resulted from it. The degree and direction of every motion is, by the laws of nature, prescribed with such exactness that a living creature may as soon arise from the shock of two bodies as motion in any other degree or direction than what is actually produced by it. Would we, therefore, form a just and precise idea of *necessity*, we must consider whence that idea arises when we apply it to the operation of bodies.

It seems evident that, if all the scenes of nature were continually shifted in such a manner that no two events bore any resemblance to each other, but every object was entirely new, without any similitude to whatever had been seen before, we should never, in that case, have attained the least idea of necessity, or of a connexion among these objects. We might say, upon such a supposition, that one object or event has followed another; not that one was produced by the other. The relation of cause and effect must be utterly unknown to mankind. Inference and reasoning concerning the operations of nature would, from that moment, be at an end; and the memory and senses remain the only canals, by which the knowledge of any real existence could possibly have access to the mind. Our idea, therefore, of necessity and causation arises entirely from the uniformity observable in the operations of nature, where similar objects are constantly conjoined together, and the mind is determined by custom to infer the one from the appearance of the other. These two circumstances form the whole of that necessity, which we ascribe to matter. Beyond the constant *conjunction* of similar objects, and the consequent *inference* from one to the other, we have no notion of any necessity or connexion.

If it appear, therefore, that all mankind have ever allowed, without any doubt or hesitation, that these two circumstances take place in the voluntary actions of men, and in the operations of mind; it must follow, that all mankind have ever agreed in the doctrine of necessity, and that they have hitherto disputed, merely for not understanding each other.

As to the first circumstance, the constant and regular conjunction of similar events, we may possibly satisfy ourselves by the following considerations. It is universally acknowledged that there is a great uniformity among the actions of men, in all nations and ages, and that human nature remains still the same, in its principles and operations. The same motives always produce the same actions: The same events follow from the same causes. Ambition, avarice, self-love, vanity, friendship, generosity, public spirit: these passions, mixed in various degrees, and distributed through society, have been, from the beginning of the world, and still are, the source of all the actions and enterprises, which have ever been observed among mankind. . . .

We must not, however, expect that this uniformity of human actions should be carried to such a length as that all men, in the same circumstances, will always act precisely in the same manner, without making any allowance for the diversity of characters, prejudices, and opinions. Such a uniformity in every particular, is found in no part of nature. On the contrary, from observing the variety of conduct in different men, we are enabled to form a greater variety of maxims, which still suppose a degree of uniformity and regularity.

Are the manners of men different in different ages and countries? We learn thence the great force of custom and education, which mould the human mind from its infancy and form it into a fixed and established character. Is the behaviour and conduct of the one sex very unlike that of the other? Is it thence we become acquainted with the different characters which nature has impressed upon the sexes, and which she preserves with constancy and regularity? Are the actions of the same person much diversified in the different periods of his life, from infancy to old age? This affords room for many general observations concerning the gradual change of our sentiments and inclinations, and the different maxims which prevail in the different ages of human creatures. Even the characters, which are peculiar to each individual, have a uniformity in their influence; otherwise our acquaintance with the persons and our observation of their conduct could never teach us their dispositions, or serve to direct our behaviour with regard to them.

I grant it possible to find some actions, which seem to have no regular connexion with any known motives, and are exceptions to all the measures of conduct which have ever been established for the government of men. But if we would willingly know what judgment should be formed of such irregular and extraordinary actions, we may consider the sentiments commonly entertained with regard to those irregular events which appear in the course of nature, and the operations of external objects. All causes are not conjoined to their usual effects with like uniformity. An artificer, who handles only dead matter, may be disappointed of his aim as well as the politician, who directs the conduct of sensible and intelligent agents.

The vulgar, who take things according to their first appearance, attribute the uncertainty of events to such an uncertainty in the causes as makes the latter often fail of their usual influence; though they meet with no impediment in their operation. But philosophers, observing that, almost in every part of nature, there is contained a vast variety of springs and principles, which are hid, by reason of their minuteness or remoteness, find, that it is at least possible the contrariety of events may not proceed from any contingency in the cause, but from the secret operation of contrary causes. This possibility is converted into certainty by farther observation, when they remark that, upon an exact scrutiny, a contrariety of effects always betrays a contrariety of causes, and proceeds from their mutual opposi-

tion. A peasant can give no better reason for the stopping of any clock or watch than to say that it does not commonly go right: But an artist easily perceives that the same force in the spring or pendulum has always the same influence on the wheels; but fails of its usual effect, perhaps by reason of a grain of dust, which puts a stop to the whole movement. From the observation of several parallel instances, philosophers form a maxim that the connexion between all causes and effects is equally necessary, and that its seeming uncertainty in some instances proceeds from the secret opposition of contrary causes.

Thus, for instance, in the human body, when the usual symptoms of health or sickness disappoint our expectation; when medicines operate not with their wonted powers; when irregular events follow from any particular cause; the philosopher and physician are not surprised at the matter, nor are ever tempted to deny, in general, the necessity and uniformity of those principles by which the animal economy is conducted. They know that a human body is a mighty complicated machine: That many secret powers lurk in it, which are altogether beyond our comprehension: That to us it must often appear very uncertain in its operations: And that therefore the irregular events, which outwardly discover themselves, can be no proof that the laws of nature are not observed with the greatest regularity in its internal operations and government.

The philosopher, if he be consistent, must apply the same reasoning to the actions and volitions of intelligent agents. The most irregular and unexpected resolutions of men may frequently be accounted for by those who know every particular circumstance of their character and situation. A person of an obliging disposition gives a peevish answer: But he has the toothache, or has not dined. A stupid fellow discovers an uncommon alacrity in his carriage: But he has met with a sudden piece of good fortune. Or even when an action, as sometimes happens, cannot be particularly accounted for, either by the person himself or by others; we know, in general, that the characters of men are, to a certain degree, inconstant and irregular. This is, in a manner, the constant character of human nature; though it be applicable, in a more particular manner, to some persons who have no fixed rule for their conduct, but proceed in a continued course of caprice and inconstancy. The internal principles and motives may operate in a uniform manner, notwithstanding these seeming irregularities; in the same manner as the winds, rain, clouds, and other variations of the weather are supposed to be governed by steady principles; though not easily discoverable by human sagacity and enquiry.

Thus it appears, not only that the conjunction between motives and voluntary actions is as regular and uniform as that between the cause and effect in any part of nature; but also that this regular conjunction has been universally acknowledged among mankind, and has never been the subject of dispute, either in philosophy or common life. Now, as it is from past experience that we draw all inferences concerning the future, and as we conclude that ob-

jects will always be conjoined together which we find to have always been conjoined; it may seem superfluous to prove that this experienced uniformity in human actions is a source whence we draw *inferences* concerning them. But in order to throw the argument into a greater variety of lights we shall also insist, though briefly, on this latter topic.

The mutual dependence of men is so great in all societies that scarce any human action is entirely complete in itself, or is performed without some reference to the actions of others, which are requisite to make it answer fully the intention of the agent. The poorest artificer, who labours alone, expects at least the protection of the magistrate, to ensure him the enjoyment of the fruits of his labour. He also expects that, when he carries his goods to market, and offers them at a reasonable price, he shall find purchasers, and shall be able, by the money he acquires, to engage others to supply him with those commodities which are requisite for his subsistence. In proportion as men extend their dealings, and render their intercourse with others more complicated, they always comprehend, in their schemes of life, a greater variety of voluntary actions, which they expect, from the proper motives, to cooperate with their own. In all these conclusions they take their measures from past experience, in the same manner as in their reasonings concerning external objects; and firmly believe that men, as well as all the elements, are to continue, in their operations, the same that they have ever found them. A manufacturer reckons upon the labour of his servants for the execution of any work as much as upon the tools which he employs, and would be equally surprised were his expectations disappointed. In short, this experimental inference and reasoning concerning the actions of others enters so much into human life that no man, while awake, is ever a moment without employing it. Have we not reason, therefore, to affirm that all mankind have always agreed in the doctrine of necessity according to the foregoing definition and explication of it? . . .

I have frequently considered, what could possibly be the reason why all mankind, though they have ever, without hesitation, acknowledged the doctrine of necessity in their whole practice and reasoning, have yet discovered such a reluctance to acknowledge it in words, and have rather shown a propensity, in all ages, to profess the contrary opinion. The matter, I think, may be accounted for after the following manner. If we examine the operations of body, and the production of effects from their causes, we shall find that all our faculties can never carry us farther in our knowledge of this relation than barely to observe that particular objects are *constantly conjoined* together, and that the mind is carried, by a *customary transition*, from the appearance of one to the belief of the other. But though this conclusion concerning human ignorance be the result of the strictest scrutiny of this subject, men still entertain a strong propensity to believe that they penetrate farther into the powers of nature, and perceive something like a necessary connexion between the cause and the effect. When again they turn their reflections towards the operations of their own minds, and *feel* no such connexion of the motive and the action; they are thence apt to suppose, that there is a difference between the effects which result from material force, and those which arise from thought and intelligence. But being once convinced that we know nothing farther of causation of any kind than merely the *constant conjunction* of objects, and the consequent *inference* of the mind from one to another, and finding that these two circumstances are universally allowed to have place in voluntary actions; we may be more easily led to own the same necessity common to all causes. . . .

It would seem, indeed, that men begin at the wrong end of this question concerning liberty and necessity, when they enter upon it by examining the faculties of the soul, the influence of the understanding, and the operations of the will. Let them first discuss a more simple question, namely, the operations of body and of brute unintelligent matter; and try whether they can there form any idea of causation and necessity, except that of a constant conjunction of objects, and subsequent inference of the mind from one to another. If these circumstances form, in reality, the whole of that necessity, which we conceive in matter, and if these circumstances be also universally acknowledged to take place in the operations of the mind, the dispute is at an end; at least, must be owned to be thenceforth merely verbal. But as long as we will rashly suppose, that we have some farther idea of necessity and causation in the operations of external objects; at the same time, that we can find nothing farther in the voluntary actions of the mind; there is no possibility of bringing the question to any determinate issue, while we proceed upon so erroneous a supposition. The only method of undeceiving us is to mount up higher; to examine the narrow extent of science when applied to material causes; and to convince ourselves that all we know of them is the constant conjunction and inference above mentioned. We may, perhaps, find that it is with difficulty we are induced to fix such narrow limits to human understanding: But we can afterwards find no difficulty when we come to apply this doctrine to the actions of the will. For as it is evident that these have a regular conjunction with motives and circumstances and characters, and as we always draw inferences from one to the other, we must be obliged to acknowledge in words that necessity, which we have already avowed, in every deliberation of our lives, and in every step of our conduct and behaviour. . . .

But to proceed in this reconciling project with regard to the question of liberty and necessity; the most contentious question of metaphysics, the most contentious science; it will not require many words to prove, that all mankind have ever agreed in the doctrine of liberty as well as in that of necessity, and that the whole dispute, in this respect also, has been hitherto merely verbal. For what is meant by liberty, when applied to voluntary actions? We cannot surely mean that actions have so little connexion with motives, inclinations, and circumstances, that one does not follow with a certain degree of uni-

formity from the other, and that one affords no inference by which we can conclude the existence of the other. For these are plain and acknowledged matters of fact. By liberty, then, we can only mean *a power of acting or not acting, according to the determinations of the will;* that is, if we choose to remain at rest, we may; if we choose to move, we also may. Now this hypothetical liberty is universally allowed to belong to every one who is not a prisoner and in chains. Here, then, is no subject of dispute.

Whatever definition we may give of liberty, we should be careful to observe two requisite circumstances; *first,* that it be consistent with plain matter of fact; *secondly,* that it be consistent with itself. If we observe these circumstances, and render our definition intelligible, I am persuaded that all mankind will be found of one opinion with regard to it.

It is universally allowed that nothing exists without a cause of its existence, and that chance, when strictly examined, is a mere negative word, and means not any real power which has anywhere a being in nature. But it is pretended that some causes are necessary, some not necessary. Here then is the advantage of definitions. Let any one *define* a cause, without comprehending, as a part of the definition, a *necessary connexion* with its effect; and let him show distinctly the origin of the idea, expressed by the definition; and I shall readily give up the whole controversy. But if the foregoing explication of the matter be received, this must be absolutely impracticable. Had not objects a regular conjunction with each other, we should never have entertained any notion of cause and effect; and this regular conjunction produces that inference of the understanding, which is the only connexion, that we can have any comprehension of. Whoever attempts a definition of cause, exclusive of these circumstances, will be obliged either to employ unintelligible terms or such as are synonymous to the term which he endeavours to define. And if the definition above mentioned be admitted; liberty, when opposed to necessity, not to constraint, is the same thing with chance; which is universally allowed to have no existence.

5. [Will the Future Resemble the Past?]

It must certainly be allowed, that nature has kept us at a great distance from all her secrets, and has afforded us only the knowledge of a few superficial qualities of objects; while she conceals from us those powers and principles on which the influence of those objects entirely depends. Our senses inform us of the color, weight, and consistence of bread; but neither sense nor reason can ever inform us of those qualities which fit it for the nourishment and support of a human body. Sight or feeling conveys an idea of the actual motion of bodies; but as to that wonderful force or power, which would carry on a moving body for ever in a continued change of place, and which bodies never lose but by communicating it to others; of this we cannot form the most distant conception. But notwithstanding this ignorance of natural powers and principles, we always presume, when we see like sensible qualities, that they have

like secret powers, and expect that effects, similar to those which we have experienced, will follow from them. If a body of like color and consistence with that bread, which we have formerly eat, be presented to us, we make no scruple of repeating the experiment, and foresee, with certainty, like nourishment and support. Now this is a process of the mind or thought, of which I would willingly know the foundation. It is allowed on all hands that there is no known connexion between the sensible qualities and the secret powers; and consequently, that the mind is not led to form such a conclusion concerning their constant and regular conjunction, by anything which it knows of their nature. As to past *Experience*, it can be allowed to give *direct* and *certain* information of those precise objects only, and that precise period of time, which fell under its cognizance: but why this experience should be extended to future times, and to other objects, which for aught we know, may be only in appearance similar; this is the main question on which I would insist. The bread, which I formerly eat, nourished me; that is, a body of such sensible qualities was, at that time, endued with such secret powers: but does it follow, that other bread must also nourish me at another time, and that like sensible qualities must always be attended with like secret powers? The consequence seems nowise necessary. At least, it must be acknowledged that there is here a consequence drawn by the mind; that there is a certain step taken; a process of thought, and an inference, which wants to be explained. These two propositions are far from being the same, *I have found that such an object has always been attended with such an effect*, and *I foresee, that other objects, which are, in appearance, similar, will be attended with similar effects*. I shall allow, if you please, that the one proposition may justly be inferred from the other: I know, in fact, that it always is inferred. But if you insist that the inference is made by a chain of reasoning, I desire you to produce that reasoning. . . .

All reasonings may be divided into two kinds, namely, demonstrative reasoning, or that concerning relations of ideas, and moral reasoning, or that concerning matter of fact and existence. That there are no demonstrative arguments in the case seems evident; since it implies no contradiction that the cause of nature may change, and that an object, seemingly like those which we have experienced, may be attended with different or contrary effects. May I not clearly and distinctly conceive that a body, falling from the clouds, and which, in all other respects, resembles snow, has yet the taste of salt or feeling of fire? Is there any more intelligible proposition than to affirm, that all the trees will flourish in December and January, and decay in May and June? Now whatever is intelligible, and can be distinctly conceived, implies no contradiction, and can never be proved false by any demonstrative argument or abstract reasoning *a priori*.

If we be, therefore, engaged by arguments to put trust in past experience, and make it the standard of our future judgment, these arguments must be probable only, or such as regard matter of fact and real existence, according to the division above mentioned. But that there is no argument of this kind, must appear, if our explication of that species of reasoning be admitted as solid and satisfactory. We have said that all arguments concerning existence are founded on the relation of cause and effect; that our knowledge of that relation is derived entirely from experience; and that all our experimental conclusions proceed upon the supposition that the future will be conformable to the past. To endeavor, therefore, the proof of this last supposition by probable arguments, or arguments regarding existence, must be evidently going in a circle, and taking that for granted, which is the very point in question. . . .

Should it be said that, from a number of uniform experiments, we *infer* a connexion between the sensible qualities and the secret powers; this, I must confess, seems the same difficulty, couched in different terms. The question still recurs, on what process of argument this *inference* is founded? Where is the medium, the interposing ideas, which join propositions so very wide of each other? It is confessed that the color, consistence, and other sensible qualities of bread appear not, of themselves, to have any connection with the secret powers of nourishment and support. For otherwise we could infer these secret powers from the first appearance of these sensible qualities, without the aid of experience; contrary to the sentiment of all philosophers, and contrary to plain matter of fact. Here, then, is our natural state of ignorance with regard to the powers and influence of all objects. How is this remedied by experience? It only shows us a number of uniform effects, resulting from certain objects, and teaches us that those particular objects, at that particular time, were endowed with such powers and forces. When a new object, endowed with similar sensible qualities, is produced, we expect similar powers and forces, and look for a like effect. From a body of like color and consistence with bread we expect like nourishment and support. But this surely is a step or progress of the mind, which wants to be explained. When a man says, *I have found in all past instances, such sensible qualities conjoined with such secret powers:* And when he says, *Similar sensible qualities will always be conjoined with similar secret powers*, he is not guilty of a tautology, nor are these propositions in any respect the same. You say that the one proposition is an inference from the other. But you must confess that the inference is not intuitive; neither is it demonstrative: Of what nature is it, then? To say it is experimental is begging the question. For all inferences from experience suppose, as their foundation, that the future will resemble the past, and that similar powers will be conjoined with similar sensible qualities. If there be any suspicion that the course of nature may change, and that the past may be no rule for the future, all experience becomes useless, and can give rise to no inference or conclusion. It is impossible, therefore, that any arguments from experience can prove this resemblance of the past to the future; since all these arguments are founded on the supposition of that resemblance. Let the course of things be allowed hitherto ever so regular; that alone, without some new argument or inference, proves not that, for the future, it will continue so. In vain do you pretend to have learned the nature of bodies from your past experience. Their secret nature, and consequently all their effects and influence, may change, without any change in their sensible qualities. This happens sometimes, and with regards to some objects: Why may it not happen always, and with regard to all objects? What logic, what process of argument secures you against this supposition? My practice, you say, refutes my doubts. But you mistake the purport of my question. As an agent, I am quite satisfied in the point; but as a philosopher, who has some share of curiosity, I will not say scepticism, I want to learn the foundation of this inference. No reading, no enquiry has yet been able to remove my difficulty, or give me satisfaction in a matter of such importance. Can I do better than propose the difficulty to the public, even though, perhaps, I have small hopes of obtaining a solution? We shall at least, by this means, be sensible of our ignorance, if we do not augment our knowledge.

6. [Can We Know External Objects?]

It seems evident, that men are carried, by a natural instinct or prepossession, to repose faith in their senses; and that, without any reasoning, or even almost before the use of reason, we always suppose an external universe, which depends not on our perception, but would exist, though we and every sensible creature were absent or annihilated.

Even the animal creation are governed by a like opinion, and preserve this belief of external objects, in all their thoughts, designs, and actions.

It seems also evident, that, when men follow this blind and powerful instinct of nature, they always suppose the very images, presented by the senses, to be the external objects, and never entertain any suspicion, that the one are nothing but representations of the other. This very table, which we see white, and which we feel hard, is believed to exist, independent of our perception, and to be something external to our mind, which perceives it. Our presence bestows not being on it: our absence does not annihilate it. It preserves its existence uniform and entire, independent of the situation of intelligent beings, who perceive or contemplate it.

But this universal and primary opinion of all men is soon destroyed by the slightest philosophy, which teaches us, that nothing can ever be present to the mind but an image or perception, and that the senses are only the inlets, through which these images are conveyed, without being able to produce any immediate intercourse between the mind and the object. The table, which we see, seems to diminish, as we remove farther from it: but the real table, which exists independent of us, suffers no alteration: it was, therefore, nothing but its image, which was present to the mind. These are the obvious dictates of reason; and no man, who reflects, ever doubted, that the existences, which we consider, when we say, *this house* and *that tree*, are nothing but perceptions in the mind, and fleeting copies or representations of other existences, which remain uniform and independent.

So far, then, we are necessitated by reasoning to contradict or depart from the primary instincts of nature, and to embrace a new system with regard to the evidence of our senses. But here philosophy finds herself extremely embarrassed, when she would justify this new system, and obviate the cavils and objections of the sceptics. She can no longer plead the infallible and irresistible instinct of nature: for that led us to a quite different system, which is acknowledged fallible and even erroneous. And to justify this pretended philosophical system, by a chain of clear and convincing argument, or even any appearance of argument, exceeds the power of all human capacity.

By what argument can it be proved, that the perceptions of the mind must be caused by external objects, entirely different from them, though resembling them (if that be possible) and could not arise either from the energy of the mind itself, or from the suggestion of some invisible and unknown spirit, or from some other cause still more unknown to us? It is acknowledged, that, in fact, many of these perceptions arise not from anything external, as in dreams, madness, and other diseases. And nothing can be more inexplicable than the manner, in which body should so operate upon mind as ever to convey an image of itself to a substance, supposed of so different, and even contrary a nature.

It is a question of fact, whether the perceptions of the senses be produced by external objects, resembling them: how shall this question be determined? By experience surely; as all other questions of a like nature. But here experience is, and must be entirely silent. The mind has never anything present to it but the perceptions, and cannot possibly reach any experience of their connection with objects. The supposition of such a connexion is, therefore, without any foundation in reasoning.

To have recourse to the veracity of the Supreme Being, in order to prove the veracity of our senses, is surely making a very unexpected circuit. If his veracity were at all concerned in this matter, our senses would be entirely infallible; because it is not possible that he can ever deceive. Not to mention, that, if the external world be once called in question, we shall be at a loss to find arguments, by which we may prove the existence of that Being or any of his attributes.

This is a topic, therefore, in which the profounder and more philosophical sceptics will always triumph, when they endeavor to introduce an universal doubt into all subjects of human knowledge and enquiry. Do you follow the instincts and propensities of nature, may they say, in assenting to the veracity of sense? But these lead you to believe that the very perception or sensible image is the external object. Do you disclaim this principle, in order to embrace a more rational opinion, that the perceptions are only representations of something external? You here depart from your natural propensities and more obvious sentiments; and yet are not able to satisfy your reason, which can never find any convincing argument from experience to prove, that the perceptions are connected with any external objects. . . .

It is universally allowed by modern enquirers, that all the sensible qualities of objects, such as hard, soft, hot, cold, white, black, &c. are merely secondary, and exist not in the objects themselves, but are perceptions of the mind, without any external archetype or model, which they represent. If this be allowed, with regard to secondary qualities, it must also follow, with regard to the supposed primary qualities of extension and solidity; nor can the latter be any more entitled to that denomination than the former. The idea of extension is entirely acquired from the senses of sight and feeling; and if all the qualities, perceived by the senses, be in the mind, not in the object, the same conclusion must reach the idea of extension, which is wholly dependent on the sensible ideas or the ideas of secondary qualities. . . .

Thus the first philosophical objection to the evidence of sense or to the opinion of external existence consists in this, that such an opinion, if rested on natural instinct, is contrary to reason, and if referred to reason, is contrary to natural instinct, and at the same time carries no rational evidence with it, to convince an impartial enquirer. The second objection goes farther, and represents this opinion as contrary to reason: at least, if it be a principle of reason, that all sensible qualities are in the mind, not in the object. Bereave matter of all its intelligible qualities, both primary and secondary, you in a manner annihilate it, and leave only a certain unknown, inexplicable *something*, as the cause of our perceptions; a notion so imperfect, that no sceptic will think it worth while to contend against it.

7. [The Idea of Self]

There are some philosophers, who imagine we are every moment intimately conscious of what we call our *self*; that we feel its existence and its continuance in existence; and are certain, beyond the evidence of a demonstration, both of its perfect identity and simplicity. The strongest sensation, the most violent passion, say they, instead of distracting us from this view, only fix it the more intensely, and make us consider their influence on *self* either by their pain or pleasure. To attempt a further proof of this were to weaken its evidence; since no proof can be derived from any fact of which we are so intimately conscious; nor is there any thing of which we can be certain, if we doubt of this.

Unluckily all these positive assertions are contrary to that very experience which is pleaded for them; nor have we any idea of *self*, after the manner it is here explained. For, from what impression could this idea be derived? This question it is impossible to answer without a manifest contradiction and absurdity; and yet it is a question which must necessarily be answered, if we would have the idea of self pass for clear and intelligible. It must be some one impression that gives rise to every real idea. But self or person is not any one impression, but that to which our

several impressions and ideas are supposed to have a reference. If any impression gives rise to the idea of self, that impression must continue invariably the same, through the whole course of our lives; since self is supposed to exist after that manner. But there is no impression constant and invariable. Pain and pleasure, grief and joy, passions and sensations succeed each other, and never all exist at the same time. It cannot therefore be from any of these impressions, or from any other, that the idea of self is derived; and consequently there is no such idea.

But further, what must become of all our particular perceptions upon this hypothesis? All these are different, and distinguishable, and separable from each other, and may be separately considered, and may exist separately, and have no need of any thing to support their existence. After what manner therefore do they belong to self, and how are they connected with it? For my part, when I enter most intimately into what I call *myself*, I always stumble on some particular perception or other, of heat or cold, light or shade, love or hatred, pain or pleasure. I never can catch *myself* at any time without a perception, and never can observe any thing but the perception. When my perceptions are removed for any time, as by sound sleep, so long am I insensible of *myself*, and may truly be said not to exist. And were all my perceptions removed by death, and could I neither think, nor feel, nor see, nor love, nor hate, after the dissolution of my body, I should be entirely annihilated, nor do I conceive what is further requisite to make me a perfect nonentity. If any one, upon serious and unprejudiced reflection, thinks he has a different notion of *himself*, I must confess I can reason no longer with him. All I can allow him is, that he may be in the right as well as I, and that we are essentially different in this particular. He may, perhaps, perceive something simple and continued, which he calls *himself*; though I am certain there is no such principle in me.

But setting aside some metaphysicians of this kind, I may venture to affirm of the rest of mankind, that they are nothing but a bundle or collection of different perceptions, which succeed each other with an inconceivable rapidity, and are in a perpetual flux and movement. Our eyes cannot turn in their sockets without varying our perceptions. Our thought is still more variable than our sight; and all our other senses and faculties contribute to this change; nor is there any single power of the soul, which remains unalterably the same, perhaps for one moment. The mind is a kind of theater, where several perceptions successively make their appearance; pass, repass, glide away, and mingle in an infinite variety of postures and situations. There is properly no *simplicity* in it at one time, nor identity in different, whatever natural propension we may have to imagine that simplicity and identity. The comparison of the theater must not mislead us. They are the successive perceptions only, that constitute the mind; nor have we the most distant notion of the place where these scenes are represented, or of the materials of which it is composed.

8. [On the Proper Limits of Enquiry]

The *imagination* of man is naturally sublime, delighted with whatever is remote and extraordinary, and running, without control, into the most distant parts of space and time in order to avoid the objects, which custom has rendered too familiar to it. A correct *Judgment* observes a contrary method, and avoiding all distant and high enquiries, confines itself to common life and to such subjects as fall under daily practice and experience; leaving the more sublime topics to the embellishment of poets and orators, or to the arts of priests and politicians. . . . Those who have a propensity to philosophy, will still continue their researches; because they reflect, that, besides the immediate pleasure, attending such an occupation, philosophical decisions are nothing but the reflections of common life, methodized and corrected. But they will never be tempted to go beyond common life, so long as they consider the imperfection of those faculties which they employ, their narrow reach, and their inaccurate operations. While we cannot give a satisfactory reason, why we believe, after a thousand experiments, that a stone will fall, or fire burn; can we ever satisfy ourselves concerning any determination, which we may form, with regard to the origin of worlds, and the situation of nature, from, and to eternity?

This narrow limitation; indeed, of our enquiries, is, in every respect, so reasonable that it suffices to make the slightest examination into the natural powers of the human mind and to compare them with their objects, in order to recommend it to us. We shall then find what are the proper subjects of science and enquiry.

It seems to me, that the only objects of the abstract science or of demonstration are quantity and number, and that all attempts to extend this more perfect species of knowledge beyond these bounds are mere sophistry and illusion. As the component parts of quantity and number are entirely similar, their relations become intricate and involved; and nothing can be more curious, as well as useful, than to trace, by a variety of mediums, their equality or inequality, through their different appearances. But as all other ideas are clearly distinct and different from each other, we can never advance farther, by our utmost scrutiny, than to observe this diversity, and, by an obvious reflection, pronounce one thing not to be another. Or if there be any difficulty in these decisions, it proceeds entirely from the undeterminate meaning of words, which is corrected by juster definitions. That *the square of the hypothenuse is equal to the squares of the other two sides*, cannot be known, let the terms be ever so exactly defined, without a train of reasoning and enquiry. But to convince us of this proposition, *that where there is no property, there can be no injustice*, it is only necessary to define the terms, and explain injustice, to be a violation of property. This proposition is, indeed, nothing but a more imperfect definition. It is the same case with all those pretended syllogistical reasonings, which may be found in every other branch of learning, except the sciences of quantity and number; and these may safely, I think,

be pronounced the only proper objects of knowledge and demonstration.

All other enquiries of men regard only matter of fact and existence; and these are evidently incapable of demonstration. Whatever *is* may *not be*. No negation of a fact can involve a contradiction. The nonexistence of any being, without exception, is as clear and distinct an idea as its existence. The proposition, which affirms it not to be, however false, is no less conceivable and intelligible, than that which affirms it to be. The case is different with the sciences, properly so called. Every proposition, which is not true, is there confused and unintelligible. That the cube root of 64 is equal to the half of 10, is a false proposition, and can never be distinctly conceived. But that Cæsar, or the angel Gabriel, or any being never existed, may be a false proposition, but still is perfectly conceivable, and implies no contradiction.

The existence, therefore, of any being can only be proved by arguments from its cause or its effect; and these arguments are founded entirely on experience. If we reason *a priori*, anything may appear able to produce anything. The falling of a pebble may, for aught we know, extinguish the sun; or the wish of a man control the planets in their orbits. It is only experience, which teaches us the nature and bounds of cause and effect, and enables us to infer the existence of one object from that of another. . . .

When we run over libraries, persuaded of these principles, what havoc must we make? If we take in our hand any volume; of divinity or school metaphysics, for instance; let us ask, *Does it contain any abstract reasoning concerning quantity or number?* No. *Does it contain any experimental reasoning concerning matter of fact and existence?* No. Commit it then to the flames: for it can contain nothing but sophistry and illusion.

IMMANUEL KANT (1724–1804)

The fourth child of an humble saddle maker, Kant was born in Königsberg, East Prussia. His parents belonged to the Pietists, a revivalist sect within the Lutheran Church, and their family life was characterized by simple religious devotion. Kant detested the mechanical discipline and narrow range of ideas of the Pietist school to which he was sent. At sixteen, he enrolled in the University of Königsberg, supporting himself mainly by tutoring well-to-do students. There his intellectual interests turned to physics and astronomy. After six years at the University, Kant became a private tutor in several homes in East Prussia, a profession that he followed for some nine years. Returning to the university in 1755, he obtained a higher degree and a subordinate post on the faculty. For the next fifteen years he lived in academic poverty, until in 1770 he was finally appointed a full professor. In his lectures, he enthralled his student audiences with his knowledge, eloquence, and wit. The popular form of his teaching was in marked contrast to the difficult and technical style of his writing.

He never married, and the clocklike regularity of his bachelor ways became proverbial. His servant awakened him at 4:45 every morning; he spent the next hour drinking tea, smoking his pipe, and planning the day's work; from 6:00 to 7:00 he prepared his lectures; from 7:00 to 9:00 or 10:00 he taught; then he wrote until 11:30; at 12:00 he ate a hearty dinner; in the afternoon, rain or shine, he took a regular walk; after that, he read or wrote until, at 10:00, he went to bed. The rigidity of his routine did not prevent him from enjoying the society of women and enlivening many social gatherings with his dry wit. He had many friends in the town, and until he was old, he always dined with friends. His gallantry never deserted him; even when he was so old and feeble that he lost his footing and fell in the street, he courteously presented one of the two unknown women who helped him to his feet with the rose that he happened to be carrying.

Although he never traveled far from Königsberg, he was fond of travel books and sympathetic with intellectual and political emancipation the world over. "Have the courage to use your own intelligence!" he advised. He applauded the American and French revolutions, but not the Reign of

Terror. "It was a time in Königsberg," wrote one of his colleagues, "when anyone who judged the Revolution even mildly, let alone favorably, was put on a black list as a Jacobin. Kant did not allow himself by that fact to be deterred from speaking up for the Revolution even at the table of noblemen."

Except for a remarkable astronomical treatise (1755), in which he anticipated Laplace's nebular hypothesis, all of his more important works were published late in his life, after he was awakened by Hume from his "dogmatic slumber." In an amazing decade, from 1780 to 1790, there appeared a series of epoch-making books: *The Critique of Pure Reason* (1781), *The Prolegomena to All Future Metaphysics* (1783), *The Foundations of the Metaphysic of Morals* (1785), *The Critique of Practical Reason* (1788), and *The Critique of Judgment* (1790). He subsequently published works on politics and religion, but his main task was done. After 1796, his health gradually declined, and he died in 1804, aged nearly eighty.

The Limits of Knowledge

1. [Kant's Indebtedness to Hume]

Since the essays of Locke and Leibniz were written, or better, since the beginning of metaphysics, as history records it, no event has been more decisive for this science than the attack of David Hume. He shed no light but he did strike a spark from which a light might be kindled in receptive tinder, if its glow were carefully tended.

The following excerpts are from *An Immanuel Kant Reader*, ed. and trans. Raymond B. Blakney (New York: Harper & Row, 1960). Reprinted by permission of the publishers. The first section is from *The Prolegomena to All Future Metaphysics* and the final section is from *The Critique of Judgment*. All else is from *The Critique of Pure Reason*.

Hume began with one important metaphysical idea. It was the supposed connection of cause and effect. He challenged the claim that this connection was conceived in the mind itself. He wanted to know how anyone could think anything so constituted that its mere existence necessarily called for the existence of something else; for this is what the notion of cause means. He proved conclusively that it is quite impossible to conceive the connection of cause and effect abstractly, solely by means of thought, because it involves the idea of <u>necessity</u>. We do not see that if one thing exists, another has to exist in consequence, and we do not know how an abstract idea of this relation could occur to anyone.

Hume concluded that the idea of

cause constitutes a delusion which seems to be a human brain child but is just the bastard of imagination sired by experience. Thus, certain perceptions are joined together as the law of association provides. Then habit, which is a psychological necessity, is passed off as objective and as being discovered through insight. He then inferred that we cannot conceive a causal connection between events, even in general; for if we did, our ideas would be fictional and knowledge, which is supposed to be abstract and necessary, would be nothing but common experience under a false label. This, plainly, means that there is not and cannot be such a thing as metaphysics.

However hasty and mistaken Hume's conclusion may be, it was at least based on investigation. This made it worthwhile for the bright people of the day to co-operate in finding a happier solution to the problem as he explained it. The outcome might well have been a complete reform of the science, but the unhappy genius of metaphysicians caused him not to be understood.

I frankly confess that many years ago it was the memory of David Hume that first interrupted my dogmatic slumber and gave new direction to my studies in the field of speculative philosophy.

I tried first to see if Hume's objection could be put in a general form. I soon found that the idea of a connection between cause and effect was by no means the only idea we conceive abstractly of relations between things. Metaphysics consists first and last of such ideas. I tried to count them and

when I had succeeded as I wished, taking first one and then another, I went on to explain them. I was now certain that they are not derived from experience, as Hume has asserted, but that they spring from the mind alone. These explanations had seemed impossible to my smart predecessor and had not even occurred to anyone else, although everyone used such ideas without asking what the security behind them might be. This, I say, was the most difficult work ever undertaken on behalf of metaphysics. The worst of it was that no help at all could be had from metaphysics itself because the very possibility of metaphysics depends on this kind of explanation.

Having now succeeded in the solution of Hume's problem, not only in special cases but with a view to the whole reasoning function of mind, I could proceed safely, if slowly, to survey the field of pure reasoning, its boundaries as well as its contents, and I could do this working from general principles. This is exactly what metaphysics needs to build a system which is securely planned.

2. [A New Way of Thinking]

In metaphysics, thought is continually coming to a dead end, even when laws which common experience supports are under examination, purely as laws. Times without number it is necessary to go back to the fork because the road does not take us where we want to go. As for unanimity among the practitioners of metaphysics, there is so little of it that the discipline seems more like an arena, a ring constructed for those who like to exercise their skills in mock combat. At any rate, no contestant has yet succeeded in getting and holding a spot of his own. It appears, then, that to date, the procedure in metaphysics has just been to grope and worse than that, to grope among ideas.

How can it be explained that in this field, scientific certainty has not yet been found? Can it be impossible? If it is, why has nature visited our minds with a restless drive for certainty, as if this were the most important business of all? Not only that but there would be little reason ever to trust the powers of thought, if they fail in one of the most important projects of human curiosity, proffering illusions and giving at last betrayal. Perhaps it is only that up to now we have failed to read the road signs correctly. If we renew the search, may we hope to have better luck than has been the lot of those who preceded us?

It seems to me that the examples of mathematics and physics, having become what they are by sudden revolution, are remarkable enough to warrant attention to the essential element of their change, the change that proved so beneficial. It may be worth our while also to make the experiment of imitating them, to the degree the analogy between these two rational disciplines and metaphysics permits.

Hitherto it has been assumed that knowledge must conform to the things known; but on this basis all attempts to find out about the world of things by abstract thought, and thus to permit an extension of human knowledge, have come to nothing. Let us then experiment to see whether or not we do better

with the problems of metaphysics if we assume that things to be known must conform in advance to our knowing process. This would appear to lead to what we want, namely, knowledge that tells us something about an object of thought before it becomes a part of our experience.

If my perception of an object has to conform to the object, I do not see how there could be any abstract knowledge of it; but if the objects of my perceptions conform to the laws by which I know them, it is easy to conceive of abstract knowledge, for all experience is a kind of knowledge involving the mind, the laws of which I must suppose were a part of me before I ever saw anything. Those laws get expressed in abstract terms but all my experience must agree with them.

This experiment succeeds as well as could be desired. It promises scientific certainty for the part of metaphysics that deals in abstract ideas, the corresponding objects of which may be checked off in experience. It involves a new way of thinking which enables us to explain perfectly how abstract knowledge, knowledge prior to experience, is possible. It also furnishes satisfactory proofs of the laws which form the mental framework of the natural world. Both of these achievements had been impossible heretofore.

3. [Empirical and A Priori Knowledge]

There is no doubt that knowledge begins with experience. How else could mental powers be awakened to action, if not by the objects that excite our senses, in part arousing images and in part stimulating the mental activity by which the images are compared? Images must then be combined or separated and the raw material of sense impressions worked over into the knowledge of things called experience. In the order of time, life begins with experience; there is no knowledge before that.

But if knowledge begins with experience, it does not follow that all of it is derived from experience. It may well be that whatever knowledge we do get from experience is already a combination of impressions and mental activity, the sense impressions being merely the occasion. It may be that the mental additive cannot be distinguished from the basic stuff until long practice makes one alert to it and skilled to pick it out.

This then is a question that needs close study and for which no offhand answer will do: Is there knowledge apart from both experience and sense impressions? This kind of knowledge is called abstract and prior (a priori) in contrast to knowledge derived from experience, which is empirical (a posteriori).

The word "a priori" is not yet definite enough to indicate the full meaning of the question at hand. It is often said of knowledge derived from experience that it is abstract because it does not come immediately from experience, but from some general rule borrowed from experience. Of a man who undermines the foundations of his house, we might say that he might have known a priori, that is, abstractly and beforehand, that the house would fall. He need not have waited for the actual experience of seeing it go down. He could not, however, have known about the house falling, from abstract principles only. He needs first to learn that bodies are heavy and that they fall when supports are removed; this would have to be learned from experience.

In what follows, by *abstract* knowledge we do not mean knowledge independent of this or that experience but knowledge utterly independent of all experience. In contrast, there is empirical, or *a posteriori* knowledge which we get only through experience. Abstract knowledge is called *pure* when it contains no trace of experience. So, for example, the proposition, "Every change has its cause," is abstract but not pure because *change* is an idea drawn only from experience.

We need now a criterion by which to distinguish pure from empirical knowledge. Experience teaches one that an object is what it is, but not that it could not be otherwise. So, first, if a proposition cannot be conceived without thinking it *necessary*, it is *abstract*. Secondly, a judgment based on experience is never truly or strictly universal but only relatively so. But if a judgment is strictly *universal* and there is no possible exception to this, then it is not derived from experience and is valid, absolutely *abstract, pure.*

We need also to distinguish between two kinds of judgments, or statements: *analytic*, in which the predicate merely analyzes the subject; and *synthetic*, or *amplifying* in which the predicate adds something to the subject. If A is the subject of a statement and B is the predicate, there are two choices. If B is contained in A, the statement is analytic; if B is not contained in A but is related to it otherwise, the statement is synthetic, or amplifying.

For example, if I say, "All bodies are extended," this is an analytic statement of judgment. I need not go beyond the very idea of "body" to find the idea of "extension." On the other hand when I say, "All bodies are heavy," the predicate is quite different from what I think in the idea of "body" as such, and the addition of this kind of predicate to the subject makes the statement synthetic. Statements of experience always amplify the subject.

In abstract, amplifying judgments, no help can be had from experience. If I go beyond idea A and find idea B related to it, on what could such an amplification be based? Take, for example, the proposition: Everything that happens has a cause. In the idea of "something that happens," I can think of a time before the event and from it derive analytic judgments. But the idea of "cause" is something else; it does not fall within the idea of "something that happens." How then can I say something about this subject that is entirely unrelated to it? How do I know that cause belongs necessarily to that "something that happens," even when that something does not contain any notion of it? What is the unknown X on which one depends when he discovers a predicate B, foreign to A, which is, nevertheless, connected with it?

The unknown X cannot be experience because the principle just discussed adds a second conception (cause) to the first (existence), not only with wider generalization than experience can proffer but with an assertion of necessity. It is therefore wholly abstract

and unrelated to experience. The whole aim of our speculative, abstract knowledge depends on synthetic, or amplifying propositions of this kind. Analytic judgments are of the highest importance and necessary, but only to clarify conception. This, in turn, is required for the secure and broader amplification by which something really new may be added to the matter of knowledge.

Examples from science. Mathematical judgments always amplify. One might think at first that $7 + 5 = 12$ is a straight analytic proposition. On closer inspection, it appears that the sum $7 + 5$ contains nothing more than the combination of these two numbers. There is nothing to indicate what number embraces both. Arithmetical propositions always amplify.

Nor are geometric propositions analytic. That a straight line is the shortest distance between two points is an amplifying conception. Straightness has nothing to do with quantity, but only with quality. The idea of shortness is thus additive, and intuition is necessary at this point. Without it, amplification would be impossible.

The science of physics also contains principles which are abstract and amplifying. For example, there is the proposition that in all the changes of the physical world, the total quantity of matter remains unchanged. But in the idea of matter, I do not imagine its permanency. I think only of its presence in the space it fills. So I really have to go beyond the idea of matter itself and attribute something to it abstractly, something I never thought it involved. The proposition is thus not analytic but synthetic, or amplifying and yet it is abstractly conceived.

There must be amplifying and abstract knowledge in metaphysics too, even if metaphysics is regarded only as a pseudo science, necessary to human nature. It is not the duty of metaphysicians merely to dissect subjects and so, analytically, to illustrate abstract ideas. It is their duty to extend abstract knowledge and for this purpose they use principles which add to their ideas matter not originally contained in them. By means of abstract, amplifying judgments they may even go where experience cannot follow, as, for example, in the statement that "the world must have a beginning," and the like. So, metaphysics, at least by aim, consists of pure, amplifying propositions.

The characteristic problem then of pure reason is: How are abstract, amplifying judgments possible? That metaphysics has so far remained in the state of vacillating uncertainty and contradiction, is due to the fact that this problem was not recognized sooner, nor, perhaps, was the difference between analytic and amplifying judgment made clear.

4. [The Matter and Form of Intuition]

Of the varied processes by which things become known, there is one from which all thought stems. It is awareness (intuition), and it alone is direct or immediate. Ultimately all food for thought comes from the outside world through our awareness of it, but among humans this occurs only when mind is involved.

The property of mind by which external things are recognized may be called sensitivity. Objects appear to mind because of its sensitivity, and this is the only way awareness can occur. In functioning mind, then, awareness gives rise to thoughts and finally to concepts. Directly or indirectly, all thought goes back to awareness and so to sensitivity, because there is no other way to know external things. Sensation is the effect an object has on the sensitive mind. If awareness comes through sensation, it is said to be empirical; and the object so revealed, whatever it may be, is called "phenomenon," or simply "thing."

By matter, I mean the substance of a thing, to which sensations are traceable; by form, I refer to my awareness that the substance of something is arranged in a given order.

It is clear that sensations are not put in form by other sensations. The matter of which things are composed may be known through sensation but their form is provided by the mind, and form is therefore separate from sensation.

I call awareness (intuition) which does not participate in sensation, *pure* (that is, belonging only to mind). The pure form which sense impressions take on, the form or order in which the many elements of things are arranged by the mind, must be in mind beforehand. The pure form of sensitivity may be called pure awareness.

If, from your awareness of a body, you subtract the contribution of thought processes such as substance, forces, divisibility, etc., and then take away all that pertains to sensation, such as impenetrability, color, etc., there will still remain extension and form. These belong to pure awareness and exist only in mind, as forms for sense impressions, even if there were present no external objects or sensations from them.

5. [The Pure Forms of Intuition — Space and Time]

There is a sense or sensitivity of mind, by which we reach out to things and see them located in external space. Within this space their form, size, and relative positions are or can be fixed.

There is an internal sense by which the mind is aware of itself or its internal states. This sense does not present the soul as an object to be observed. It is, however, a fixed function without which an awareness of internal states of mind would be impossible. Its operations pertain to the relationships of time. Time cannot appear as an external matter any more than space can appear to be something within.

What then are space and time? Are they real entities? Or if not, are they the delimitations of things or relations between things which exist whether anyone observes them or not? Or are they delimitations and relations which are inherent in one's awareness of the world and thus in the subjective character of the mind? If so, then without these properties of mind, predicates like space and time would never appear anywhere.

To understand this matter more clearly, let us first consider space.

1. Space is not an idea derived from experience of the external world. If my sensations are to be referred to things outside me, i.e., to things located at some point of space other than where I am, or if I am to be able to refer my sensations to differing objects located at several points, the idea of space must be present in advance. My conception of space therefore cannot be the product of experience or borrowed from the relations of things to each other. On the contrary, it is only by means of the idea of space that external experience becomes possible at all.

2. Space is the visualization which is necessary to the mind, and the basis of all external perceptions. One might imagine space with no objects to fill it, but it is impossible to imagine that there should be no space. Space is therefore a condition of the possibility of phenomena and not a form required by them. It is subjective, a visualization which precedes all external experience.

3. The demonstrable certainty of geometric propositions depends on the necessity of this mental visualization of space. If space were a conception gained empirically or borrowed from general external experience, the first principles of mathematical definition would be merely perceptions. They would be subject to all the accidents of perception and there would be no necessity that there should be only one straight line between two points. A theorem would be something to be learned in each case by experience. Whatever is derived from experience possesses only relative generality, based on reasoning from observations. We should accordingly be able to say only that so far as anyone can see, there is no space having more than three dimensions.

4. Space is not a discursive or general

idea of the relations between things. It is pure awareness or mental visualization. First of all, only one space is imaginable, and if many spaces are mentioned, they are all parts of the one space. They are not to be considered as leading up to the one all-embracing space, or the component parts from which an aggregate of space is formed.

Space is essentially one. The general idea of a multiplicity of spaces is the result of imposing limitations on space. Hence, it follows that the foundation of all ideas of space is a mental awareness, and it is thus not derived from experience. So geometrical principles, such as "The sum of two sides of a triangle is greater than the third," may never be derived from the general conception of sides and triangles but from an awareness of visualization which is purely mental and which is derived thence with demonstrable certainty.

5. Space is visualized as an infinite quantity. The general idea of space, which is to be found in a foot as well as a yard, would furnish no information about the quantity of the space involved if there were not infinity in the reach of awareness. Without this, no conception of relations in space could ever contain the principle of infinity.

Space is not in any sense a property of things or the relation between them. It is nothing but the form the appearances of things take to man's outer senses. It is the mental basis of sensitivity and makes possible one's awareness of the external world.

One may speak of space, extension, etc., only from the human point of view. Apart from one's awareness of the outer world, the idea of space means nothing at all. The space predicate is attributed to things only as they are sensed.

The rule that "things are juxtaposed in space" is valid within the limitation that "things" are taken only as objects of awareness. Add one condition and say that "things as they appear externally are juxtaposed in space," and the rule is universally valid.

This exposition therefore teaches the *reality* (objective validity) of space. Space is as real as anything else in the world. At the same time, it teaches the *ideality* of space, when things are viewed as only the mind can view them, as they are by themselves, apart from the activity of human sense. We also assert the reality of space as verifiable fact in human experience of the external world.

The *formal* idea of phenomena in space is a critical reminder that there is nothing of which one is aware that is a thing-itself (that is, something apart from man's perception of it). Space is not the form of things-themselves. The phenomena of which we are aware tell us nothing about things as they are apart from us, and in experience nobody ever asks about them as such.

[Kant's treatment of time parallels that of space, and need not be quoted. Time, like space, is a form of perception, not a thing perceived. Just as phenomena are spread out in space, above or below, near or far, to the right or the left, so likewise are they ordered in time, before, after, or simultaneous with other events. Anything experienced as spatial is thought of as belonging to the outer world, but temporal order applies to one's psychological *acts of apprehension. Hence time is "the form of inner sense, that is, of our awareness of ourselves and our own inner states." But both space and time are necessary forms of human perception, and cannot be ascribed to objects in themselves apart from experience.*]

6. [How the Categories of the Understanding Unify and Organize Our Experience]

Among the many strands from which the complicated web of human knowledge is woven there are some which are destined from the start to be used abstractly and to continue independent of experience. The claims made for these ideas generally require special demonstration (deduction). Their legitimacy is not established by a deduction based on experience, even though we do want to know how these ideas can refer to objects within one's experience, and yet be derived apart from it. The explanation of the way abstract and prior ideas refer to objects is to be called *formal deduction*. This is distinguished from *empirical deduction*, which shows how an idea is derived by reflection from experience. *Empirical deduction* applies not to the legitimacy of the use of the ideas but to the facts from which they arise.

Without doubt an investigation of the functioning of man's power to know, beginning with single perceptions and climbing to general ideas, is useful. We have to thank the celebrated John Locke for opening up this avenue. The deduction of pure ideas is not, however, to be achieved along these lines; it is to be worked out in another direction. Their future use, indepen-

dent of experience, requires for them a very particular birth certificate, in which descent from experience is denied. Locke's attempted psychological derivation is not deduction at all, because it depends on matters of fact. It is rather an explanation of the possession of pure knowledge. It is clear, therefore, that only a formal deduction of pure ideas is usable and that empirical deductions will not do.

Our entire investigation of the formal deduction of pure ideas should be based on this principle: Pure ideas are the abstract and prior conditions of experience. They supply the objective ground of experience and are, accordingly, necessary. To know how they occur, the abstract and prior conditions necessary to experience must be discovered and kept separate from knowledge derived from experience. The categories are pure ideas which express the formal and objective conditions of experience with sufficient generality and which contain the pure thought involved in every experience. It is really a sufficient deduction of the categories and a justification of their objective validity to prove that no object is conceivable without them.

The famous John Locke, lacking these considerations and having come across pure ideas in the course of experience, proceeded to derive them from experience itself. Then, inconsistently, he went far beyond the bounds of experience in studies of knowledge. David Hume saw that to do this, ideas from pure origins are needed. He could not explain, however, how it was that ideas, disconnected in one's mind, came together in some object of thought. It never occurred to him that mind itself might be the author of the experience of its object.

So he, too, was led to derive pure ideas from experience, or habit, i.e., from a subjective necessity begotten of frequent associations of experiences. This finally came to be accepted as objective, but falsely so. Subsequently Hume explained, and quite consistently this time, that with ideas so derived and with their attendant principles, it is not possible to get beyond personal experience. The deduction of pure ideas from experience, as practiced by Locke and Hume, cannot be reconciled with the abstract and prior knowledge encountered in pure mathematics and natural science. It is therefore refuted by the facts.

The first of these men left the door wide open to fantasy. It is hard to keep reasoning within due bounds once it has had unlimited prestige. The second gave in entirely to skepticism because he believed he had found in the knowing process an illusion which generally passed as reasonable. We now turn to study whether or not reasoning can be steered between these two cliffs, its limits indicated, and still keep its proper field of function open.

If every perception or idea were isolated from every other, there could be no knowledge as we know it, because knowledge consists of perceptions and ideas conjoined and compared to each other. Since the senses cover a whole field of awareness, they need a synopsis corresponding to the organization that makes knowledge possible when mind spontaneously comprehends sense data. Spontaneity is the be-

ginning of a threefold organization which is necessary to every kind of knowledge. It consists of (1) *comprehension*, in which awareness is made into perceptions by ideas; (2) imagination in the *recollection* of the various elements necessary to knowledge; (3) *recognition* of the resultant ideas. Thus we have three inner sources of knowledge which make understanding and its empirical product, experience, possible.

However ideas or images arise, whether from the influence of external things or inner causes, or abstractly, or empirically as phenomena, they belong to man's inner sense because they are simply modifications of mind. All knowledge is, accordingly, subject to the formal condition of inner sense, namely, time. Everything is arranged, connected, and related by time. This general remark is fundamental to all subsequent discussion.

Generally speaking, awareness means being aware of many things at once, and this could not be imagined if time were not marked in the mind by a succession of impressions. In any given instant each impression is an absolute unity by itself; so, in order to get unity in awareness (as the idea of space requires), it is first necessary to let the various elements of awareness run in succession through the mind and then pull them together. This is the act which I call the organization of apprehension, or understanding. It is applied directly to awareness, which actually is multiple and so requires organization if it is to be unified or comprehended by means of a single idea.

The synthesis, or organization of understanding must be carried out abstractly and in advance, since ideas which are not empirical are involved. The ideas of space and time would be impossible without it; the many elements of sense data must be organized before they appear. This is how the pure organization of understanding is accomplished.

Again, it is apparent that if I draw an imaginary line, or consider the time lapse from one noon to the next, or even think of a certain number, I must begin by getting a general idea of the aggregates or sets of perceptions involved. If I were to lose from thought the antecedent part of either of them, say the first part of the line, the first hours of the day, or the digits preceding my number, and if I were unable to reproduce the lost parts as I went on, then no general idea of either of these sets would be possible to me. Neither could I, in that case, have the foregoing thoughts of even the first and purest ideas of space and time.

The organization of understanding is inseparably connected with recollection. Since the former is the formal basis of all knowledge, both empirical and pure, the organization of recollection by imagination belongs to the formal activity of mind and is here to be called *formal imagination*.

Again, if I were not aware that what I now think is the same as what I was thinking a moment ago, recollection of a lost step in a series of perceptions would be useless. Each perception in its place would be new, and not part of the action that made the series. A series of experiences could never be complete because it would lack the unity which only consciousness can give it. When I

count, if I forget how the series of numbers now in my thought has been added up, one by one, I can never understand how the final sum is produced. The sum is a concept which depends on my consciousness of the organized unity of the number series.

The very word "idea" could have been the occasion of these remarks; consciousness gathers up the items in a series or a field, one by one, then recollection pulls them all together in a single idea. The consciousness involved may be so weak that it is felt, not in the act or process of production but only in the final idea. Nevertheless, even though it is not very clear, consciousness must always be there. Without it, ideas and all knowledge of objects would be impossible. . . .

If it is desired to follow up the inward connections among perceptions to their point of convergence, where they are unified as experience requires, we must begin with pure self-consciousness. Awareness amounts to nothing until it merges into consciousness, directly or indirectly. If this did not happen there would be no knowledge. Among all the perceptions of a given moment, we are conscious, abstractly and in advance, of our own identity. This is how any perception becomes possible, and it is a firm principle which may be called the formal principle of unity in one's perception of a field of sense data.

This unity, however, presupposes or involves an organization which is as necessary to knowledge and as prior and abstract as the unity itself. Unification depends on pure imagination to organize a field of perceptions into knowledge. Such an organization is said to be formal if, ignoring differences of awareness, it effects only the necessary unification of the field. The unity involved is also formal when it refers only to the original unity of self and thus becomes prior and necessary. Formal and organizing imagination is thus the pure form of knowledge by means of which—both abstractly and in advance—objects of experience become known.

Understanding is the self at work in imagination, unifying and organizing experience; pure understanding is the self at work when imagination effects a formal organization. Understanding, therefore, involves pure, abstract forms for knowledge, which carry the unity the imagination uses to organize the data or experience into phenomena. These forms are the categories; that is, they are the mind's pure conceptions, or ideas. This then is how man learns from experience: Mind focuses on objects of sense by its own necessity, via awareness and by means of an organizing imagination; then phenomena, the data of experience, conform to mind; by means of the categories, pure mind constitutes a formal and organizing principle of experience, and this shows how, necessarily, phenomena are related to mind. . . .

Imagination, therefore, is man's prior and necessary capacity to organize things, and this makes us call it *productive imagination*. If imagination effects only necessary unity in the organization of phenomena, it can be called formal. The foregoing may appear strange, but it must be clear by now that the affinity, the association of phenomena and their recollection according to law, which is to say the whole of human experience, is made possible by formal imagination. Without this, ideas of objects could never foregather in a single experience.

It is the permanent and unchanging "I" (pure apperception) that correlates perceptions when we become conscious of them. All consciousness belongs to one all-embracing pure apperception, "I," as sense awareness belongs to one pure inner awareness, namely, time. So that this "I" may function mentally, imagination is added and the organization effected by imagination, though of itself prior and necessary, is carried out in the senses. Phenomena are connected in a field of impressions only as they appear in awareness: for example, a triangle. When the field is once related to the "I," ideas of it fit into the mind, and imagination relates them to sense awareness.

Pure imagination is therefore a fundamental operation of the soul, and abstractly, in advance, all knowledge depends on it. It connects all that one is aware of with the unitary "I." It brings the two extremes of sense and mind together. Without it, the senses might report phenomena but not empirical knowledge, and so experience would be impossible. Real experience comes of apprehension, association, and recognition of phenomena and contains the ultimate and highest ideas, the ideas that formally unify experience and validate empirical knowledge objectively. These ideas constitute the basis on which a field of sense data is recognized. If they concern only the form of experience, they are, accordingly, categories. The whole formal unity of recognition by means of imagination depends on the categories, and in turn the whole empirical use of the categories (in recognition, recollection, association, and apprehension), even down to phenomena, depends on imagination. These four elements of knowing make it possible for a phenomenon to belong to our consciousness and so to ourselves.

It is we who bring order and regularity to phenomena and call the result "nature." These properties would not be discovered in nature if our own minds had not first put them there; for unity in nature means a prior, necessary, and certain connection of phenomena. How indeed could organized unity in nature be conceived in advance, if the original source of knowledge, the inner core of our minds, did not first contain it? What would there be to see if this mental condition of ours were not objectively valid, valid because it is the condition by which objects become part of experience?

7. [Phenomena and Noumena]

We have now explored the land of pure reasoning and carefully surveyed every part of it. We have measured its extent and put everything in its right place. It is an island, by nature enclosed within unchangeable limits. It is the land of truth (enchanting name!), surrounded by a wide and stormy ocean, the native home of illusion, where cloud banks and icebergs falsely prophesy new lands and incessantly deceive adventurous seafarers with empty hopes, engaging them in romantic pursuits which they can neither abandon nor fulfill. Before we venture on this sea, we ought to glance at the map of the island and consider whether or not to be satisfied with it, lest there be no other territory on which to settle. We should know what title we have to it, by which we may be secure against opposing claims.

We have seen that the produce of mind is not borrowed from experience but is for use only in experience. The mind's principles may be either abstract and constitutive, like mathematical principles, or merely regulative, like dynamic principles. In either case they contain nothing but the pure schema of possible experience. Unity comes into experience from the organizing unity of mind, which the mind confers on self-consciousness via imagination; and phenomena, as the data of possible experience, must fit into that unity abstractly and in advance. These rules of mind not only are true but also are the source of all truth, the reason for the agreement of our knowledge with objects. They contain the basis on which experience is possible, that is, experience viewed as the sum of one's knowledge of objects. We are not, however, satisfied with an exposition merely of what is true; we want also to know what mankind otherwise wants to know. This long, critical inquiry would hardly seem worthwhile if at the end of it, we have learned only what would have gone on anyway in everyday mental operations.

Even if our minds do work satisfactorily without such an inquiry as this, the inquiry has one advantage. The mind that is in us is unable to determine for itself the limits of its own uses. That is why the deep inquiry we have set up is required. If we cannot decide whether certain questions lie within our mental horizon, we must be prepared for getting lost among the delusions that result from overstepping our limitations.

If we can know certainly whether the mind can use its principles only within experience and never purely formally, this knowledge will have important consequences. The formal use of an idea is its application to things in general and to entities for which we have no sense data; the empirical use of an idea is its application to phenomena, or to objects of possible experience. It is evident that only the latter application is practicable. For example, consider the ideas of mathematics, first as pure awareness: space has three dimensions; there can be but one straight line between two points; etc. Although these principles are generated abstractly in the mind, they would mean nothing if their meaning could not be demonstrated in phenomena. It is therefore required that a pure idea be made sensible, that is, that one should or can be aware of an object corresponding to it. Otherwise, the idea, we say, would make no sense, i.e., it would be meaningless.

The mathematician meets this need by the construction of a figure which is, to the senses, a phenomenon, even though abstractly produced. In the same science, the idea of size finds its meaning and support in number, whether by fingers, or abacus beads, or in strokes and points on the printed page. The idea is always abstractly conceived, as are the amplifying principles and formulas derived from them; but finally, their use and their relation to their indicated objects appear only in experience, even though they contain the formal conditions of the possibility of that experience.

That this is the case with all the categories and the principles spun out of them, appears as follows. We cannot really define the categories, or make the possibility of their objects intelligible, without descending at once to the conditions of sense and the forms of phenomena, to which, as their only objects, the categories must be limited. If this condition is removed, all meaning, all relation to an object disappears, and no example will make the meaning of such an idea comprehensible. . . .

If *noumenon* means something which is not an object of sense and so is abstracted from awareness, this is the negative sense of the term. If, however, it means an object of nonsensible awareness, we presuppose a special kind of awareness, which is purely mental, not part of our equipment, and of which we cannot imagine even the possibility. That would be *noumenon* in the positive sense of the word. . . .

The division of objects into phenomena and noumena, and the world into a world of the senses and a world of mind, is not admissible in the positive sense, even though the division of ideas as sensible and mental is legitimate. For we cannot conceive a mind which knows objects, not discursively or through categories, but by a nonsensible awareness. What mind acquires through the idea of noumenon is a negative extension. It is not then limited by sense but rather, it limits sense by applying the term "noumena" to things-themselves, which are not phenomena. It also limits itself, since noumena are not to be known by means of categories. They can be thought of only as unknown somethings.

8. [God, Freedom, and Immortality]

God, freedom, and the immortality of the soul are the problems to the solution of which all the labors of metaphysics are directed. It used to be believed that the doctrine of freedom was necessary only as a negative condition of practical philosophy, and that the ideas of God and the soul belonged to theoretical philosophy; they had to be demonstrated separately. Religion was achieved subsequently by adding morality to these ideas.

It soon appears, however, that such an attempt must miscarry. It is absolutely impossible to conceive an original Being whose characteristics make him experienceable, and therefore knowable, if one starts with only simple, abstract, ontological ideas. Neither would an idea based on the experience of physical appropriateness in nature adequately demonstrate morality or acquaintance with God. Just as little would knowledge of the soul, acquired from experience in this life, provide an idea of the soul's spiritual, immortal nature, adequate to morality. Neither theology nor spiritualism can be established by empirical data. They deal with matters that transcend human knowledge. Ideas of God and the immortal soul can be defined only by predicates drawn from supersensible sources, predicates whose reality is demonstrated by experience. This is the only way a supersensible Being can be known.

The freedom of man under moral law conjoined with the final end which freedom prescribes by means of the moral law compose the only predicate of this kind. This combination of ideas contains the conditions necessary to the possibility of both God and man. An inference can then be made to the actuality and the nature of God and the soul, both of which would otherwise be entirely hidden from us.

Theoretical proofs of God and immortality fail because natural ideas tell us nothing about supersensible matters. Proofs via morality and freedom do succeed because there is causality in these ideas and their roots are supersensible. The causal law of freedom here establishes its own actuality by the way men behave. It also provides means of knowing other supersensible objects, such as the final moral end and its practicability. The conception of freedom's causality is, of course, based on practical considerations, but that happens to be all religion needs.

It is remarkable that of the three pure, rational ideas—God, freedom, and immortality—whose objects are supersensible, freedom alone proves its objective reality in the world of nature by what it can effect there. Freedom, therefore, makes possible the connection of the other two ideas with nature and of all three with religion. We may thus conceive the supersensible realm within man and around him, so that it becomes practical knowledge. Speculative philosophy, which offers only a negative idea even of freedom itself, can never accomplish anything like this. The idea of freedom, fundamental to unconditioned practical law, reaches beyond the limits within which natural, theoretical ideas remain hopelessly restricted.

COMMENT

Impressions and Ideas

The supreme advocate of the skeptical spirit is David Hume. He is a member of the sequence of classic British empiricists, which includes such great figures as Bacon, Hobbes, Locke, Berkeley, and Mill. More consistent in his empiricism than his predecessors, Hume pushed the skeptical implications of this approach to its logical extreme. Many philosophers have tried to refute his arguments, but his influence continues to be immense.

A thorough empiricist, Hume traced all knowledge back to some original basis in experience. The stream of experience, he pointed out, is made up of *perceptions*, a term he employed to designate any mental content whatever. He divided perceptions into *impressions*, the original sensations or feelings, and *ideas*, the images, copies, or representations of these originals. It is important to note that Hume, unlike Locke and Berkeley, reserved the word *idea* for mental copies or representations of original data.

Hume's practice of tracing ideas back to their original impressions becomes a *logical test* of the soundness of concepts. If a concept, such as that of substance, cannot be traced back to some reliable basis in impressions, it immediately becomes suspect. A fertile source of confusion in our thinking is the tendency to impute to outer things the qualities that belong to internal impressions. Thus an internal feeling of necessity may be falsely imputed to some outer chain of events. The human mind, if it does not carefully analyze the sources of its ideas, is prone to fall into such errors. Hume's philosophy consists largely in exposing these pitfalls in our thinking.

Criticism of the Idea of Causation

The most famous example of this critical method is Hume's analysis of the idea of causation. He began by pointing out that this idea is extremely crucial in our thinking. "The only connection or relation of objects," he declared, "which can lead us beyond the immediate impressions of our memory and senses, is that of cause and effect; and that because it is the only one on which we can found a just inference from one object to another."[1] We infer external objects only because we suppose them to be the causes of the immediate data of experience. The idea of causation is thus the basis of empirical science and the ultimate ground for belief in an external world. For Hume, scientific knowledge as a whole stands or falls according to whether causation can be validated as a principle of reasoning.

Upon analysis, the idea of causation breaks up into four notions: (1) *succession*, (2) *contiguity*, (3) *constant conjunction*, and (4) *necessary connection*. Hume maintained that the first three notions can be defended — we can verify them by recalling the original sensory impressions from which they are derived. But *necessity* cannot thus be verified — try as we may, we cannot trace it back to any sensory impressions. It turns out, therefore, to be a confused and illegitimate notion. I shall not analyze the details of his argument since this exercise in analysis is excellent practice for students.

Skeptical Implications

Hume was quick to draw the consequences from his theory of causation. One implication is that our commonsense idea that the future will resemble the past is merely an assumption, an expectation begotten by habit, not a rational conviction. Since we never discover an objective necessity binding effect to cause, we have no reason to assume that this cause-and-effect relation must continue to hold. The sun has risen many times, but this does not mean that it will rise tomorrow. There is no "law" that the sun must rise: There is only inexplicable repetition.

One of the most significant applications of Hume's analysis of causation is his attack on the arguments for an external world. Both Locke and Berkeley, whose arguments Hume had primarily in mind, inferred the existence of an external world on the basis of a theory of causation. They reasoned that the regular character of experience, which is largely determined for us independently of our wills, must have some external cause. Locke found the cause in material substances and primary qualities; Berkeley, in God and the ideas that God imprints on our minds. Now Hume, in attack, went to the nerve of the argument and maintained that we are not justified in employing the idea of cause in this way.

[1] *An Enquiry Concerning Human Understanding,* ed. L. A. Selby-Bigge (Oxford: Clarendon Press, 1902), p. 89.

> The only conclusion we can draw from the existence of one thing to that of another is by means of the relation of cause and effort, which shows that there is a connection betwixt them, and that the existence of one is dependent on that of the other. . . . But as no beings are ever present to the mind but perceptions, it follows that we may observe a conjunction or a relation of cause and effort between different perceptions, but can never observe it between perceptions and objects. 'Tis impossible, therefore, that from the existence of any of the qualities of the former, we can ever form any conclusion concerning the existence of the latter. . . .[2]

What emerges from this devastating criticism? If we are resolved thus to stay within the closed circle of experience, we can either accept our perceptions as the ultimate character of existence or say that there may be something more — *some* kind of external world — but that we cannot know what that something more is. There is little basis here for positive belief.

A final twist to Hume's skepticism is his denial of a substantial self. Just as Berkeley rejected Locke's doctrine of material substance, so Hume for similar reasons rejected Berkeley's doctrine of a mental substance. He denied that we ever have an *impression* of a self, and in the absence of any such impression, he saw no way of proving that a self exists. All the content of experience is fleeting, evanescent, whereas the self is supposed to be identical through succeeding states. Impressions, being variable and evanescent, are incapable of revealing a permanent self; and to *infer* an unexperienced self as the necessary cause of our mental states is to project illegitimately the relation of cause and effect, which is through and through experiential, beyond the circle of experience.

Hume thus reduced reality, as far as it can be verified, to a stream of "perceptions" neither caused nor sustained by any mental or material substance. Existence is made up of mental facts, perceptions, with no selves to which the perceptions belong and no material world in which they reside.

How Kant Differed from Hume

Kant was struck, as Hume himself had been struck, by the largely negative results of Hume's inquiry. "I am . . . affrighted and confounded with the forlorn solitude in which I am placed by my philosophy," Hume

---

[2]*A Treatise of Human Nature*, ed. L. A. Selby-Bigge (Oxford: Clarendon Press, 1896), p. 212.

confessed, "and fancy myself some strange uncouth monster, utterly abandoned and disconsolate." The effect of Hume's skepticism on Kant was different—not to fill his mind with fright and confusion, but to awaken him from his "dogmatic slumbers." Hume convinced Kant that traditional metaphysics was bankrupt and that a new start was necessary. But Kant was also convinced that there must be something fundamentally wrong with an empiricism that led to such devastating conclusions. He was not content to fall back on "natural instinct" but sought some kind of rationale for his trust in science and his moral and religious convictions. The task that he set himself, in the words of one of his contemporaries, was "to limit Hume's scepticism on the one hand, and the old dogmatism on the other, and to refute and destroy materialism, fatalism, atheism, as well as sentimentalism and superstition."

In the *Critique of Pure Reason*, Kant undertook to prove that all genuine scientific knowledge, whether in mathematics or in the natural sciences, is universally valid, but that speculative metaphysics, which seeks to go beyond experience to determine the ultimate and absolute nature of things, cannot be established on any sound and dependable basis. Science is reliable because it deals with *phenomena*—things as they *appear* in human experiences—but metaphysics is unreliable because it tries to interpret *noumena*—things as they are in themselves, apart from experience. The world of ultimate reality, in contrast to the world of appearance, can never be known to reason. The noumenal realities must be interpreted, if at all, by moral conviction and religious faith—not by science or pure theoretical philosophy.

The phenomena, Kant insisted, exhibit spatial and temporal forms of rational connections, such as cause and effect. In grasping these forms and connections, consciousness is an awareness of meanings—not passive contemplation but active judgment, not mere perception but synthetic interpretation. We can never know things as they are apart from these synthetic modes of apprehension and judgment, which are the necessary conditions of all human experience. To interpret *ultimate* reality as either finite or infinite, one or many, mechanistic or teleological, mental or material, is to attempt to probe the supersensible nature of existence—and this human reason can never do. But if the positive claims of transcendent metaphysics are thus overthrown, so are its negative claims. The metaphysician is as powerless to *disprove* the existence of God as to prove His existence, or to *disprove* an idealistic account of reality as to prove it. When the overweening claims of "pure reason" are thus refuted, our "practical reason" is no longer inhibited by atheism, materialism, or mechanistic determinism.

Let me sum up Kant's answer to Hume's skepticism. He tries to make secure the foundations of natural science by demonstrating that the order and regularity necessary to science — the sensory forms of space and time and the intelligible order of substance, causation, and the other "categories" — inhere necessarily in phenomena because they are contributed by the mind in the very act of knowing (knowledge being a joint product of mind and things-in-themselves). To Hume's reduction of the mind to a succession of awarenesses, Kant opposes the mind's awareness of succession, which he says is unaccountable without more synthesis and continuity than Hume recognized. Although he agrees with Hume that the doctrines of speculative metaphysics cannot be demonstrated, he tries to justify the ideas of God, freedom, and immortality on moral grounds.

3

Common Sense

"According to Reid, our anticipation that the future will be like the past is preinferential or 'instinctive'; it can neither be given a rational justification nor be in need of one."

J. H. Gill

THOMAS REID (1710–1796)

Thomas Reid was born and raised in Scotland to a family with a strong religious heritage. His father was a Presbyterian minister and Reid himself became a minister as well. During his youth he was a librarian while studying mathematics and physics. After serving as a pastor for fifteen years, during which time he studied philosophy on his own, he was appointed to a professorship at Kings College in Aberdeen. Reid began as a follower of Bishop (of Cloyne) Berkeley's philosophy, but like Kant was jolted by his reading of David Hume's *Treatise of Human Nature*. In 1764 Reid succeeded Adam Smith as professor of moral philosophy at the University of Glasgow and published his own *Inquiry* in which he attacks both rationalism and empiricism in the name of common sense. During the last years of his life he published several important essays. After having been nearly eclipsed by the philosophies of Descartes, Hume, and Kant, as well as their twentieth century followers, Reid's thought has recently undergone something of a revival.

An Inquiry into the Human Mind*

. . . Upon the whole, it appears that our philosophers have imposed upon themselves and upon us, in pretending to deduce from sensation the first origin of our notions of external existences, of space, motion, and extension, and all the primary qualities of body — that is, the qualities whereof we have the most clear and distinct conception. These qualities do not at all tally with any system of the human faculties that hath been advanced. They have no resemblance to any sensation, or to any operation of our minds; and, therefore, they cannot be ideas either of sensation or of reflection. The very conception of them is irreconcilable to the principles of all our philosophic systems of the understanding. The belief of them is no less so.

SECTION VII: OF THE EXISTENCE OF A MATERIAL WORLD

It is beyond our power to say when, or in what order, we came by our notions of these qualities. When we trace the operations of our minds as far back as memory and reflection can carry us, we find them already in possession of our imagination and belief, and quite familiar to the mind: but how they came first into its acquaintance, or what has given them so strong a hold of our belief, and what regard they deserve, are, no doubt, very important questions in the philosophy of human nature.

Shall we, with the Bishop of Cloyne, serve them with a *quo warranto*, and have them tried at the bar of philosophy, upon the statute of the ideal system? Indeed, in this trial they seem to have come off very pitifully; for, although they had very able counsel, learned in the law — viz., Des Cartes, Malebranche, and Locke, who said everything they could for their clients — the Bishop of Cloyne, believing them to be aiders and abetters of heresy and schism, prosecuted them with great vigour, fully answered all that had been pleaded in their defense, and silenced their ablest advocates, who seem, for half a century past, to decline the argument, and to trust to the favour of the jury rather than to the strength of their pleadings.

Thus, the wisdom of *philosophy* is set in opposition to the *common sense* of mankind. The first pretends to demonstrate, *a priori*, that there can be no such thing as a material world; that sun, moon, stars, and earth, vegetable and animal bodies, are, and can be nothing else, but sensations in the mind, or images of those sensations in the memory and imagination; that, like pain and joy, they can have no existence when they are not thought of. The last can

*Reprinted by permission of the publishers from *Thomas Reid's Inquiry and Essays*, edited by Ronald Beanblossom and Keith Lehrer (Indianapolis, Hackett Publishing Company, 1983).

conceive no otherwise of this opinion, than as a kind of metaphysical lunacy, and concludes that too much learning is apt to make men mad; and that the man who seriously entertains this belief, though in other respects he may be a very good man, as a man may be who believes that he is made of glass; yet, surely he hath a soft place in his understanding, and hath been hurt by much thinking.

This opposition betwixt philosophy and common sense, is apt to have a very unhappy influence upon the philosopher himself. He sees human nature in an odd, unamiable, and mortifying light. He considers himself, and the rest of his species, as born under a necessity of believing ten thousand absurdities and contradictions, and endowed with such a pittance of reason as is just sufficient to make this unhappy discovery: and this is all the fruit of his profound speculations. Such notions of human nature tend to slacken every nerve of the soul, to put every noble purpose and sentiment out of countenance, and spread a melancholy gloom over the whole face of things.

If this is wisdom, let me be deluded with the vulgar. I find something within me that recoils against it, and inspires more reverent sentiments of the human kind, and of the universal administration. Common Sense and Reason have both one author; that Almighty Author in all whose other works we observe a consistency, uniformity, and beauty which charm and delight the understanding: there must, therefore, be some order and consistency in the human faculties, as well as

in other parts of his workmanship. A man that thinks reverently of his own kind, and esteems true wisdom and philosophy, will not be fond, nay, will be very suspicious, of such strange and paradoxical opinions. If they are false, they disgrace philosophy; and, if they are true, they degrade the human species, and make us justly ashamed of our frame.

To what purpose is it for philosophy to decide against common sense in this or any other matter? The belief of a material world is older, and of more authority, than any principles of philosophy. It declines the tribunal of reason, and laughs at all the artillery of the logician. It retains its sovereign authority in spite of all the edicts of philosophy, and reason itself must stoop to its orders. Even those philosophers who have disowned the authority of our notions of an external material world, confess that they find themselves under a necessity of submitting to their power.

Methinks, therefore, it were better to make a virtue of necessity; and, since we cannot get rid of the vulgar notion and belief of an external world, to reconcile our reason to it as well as we can; for, if Reason should stomach and fret ever so much at this yoke, she cannot throw it off; if she will not be the servant of Common Sense, she must be her slave.

In order, therefore, to reconcile Reason to Common Sense in this matter, I beg leave to offer to the consideration of philosophers these two observations. First, that, in all this debate about the existence of a material world, it hath been taken for granted on both sides, that this same material world, if any such there be, must be the express image of our sensations; that we can have no conception of any material thing which is not like some sensation in our minds; and particularly that the sensations of touch are images of extension, hardness, figure, and motion. Every argument brought again: the existence of a material world, either by the Bishop of Cloyne, or by the author of the "Treatise of Human Nature," supposeth this. If this is true, their arguments are conclusive and unanswerable; but, on the other hand, if it is not true, there is no shadow of argument left. Have those philosophers, then, given any solid proof of this hypothesis, upon which the whole weight of so strange a system rests? No. They have not so much as attempted to do it. But, because ancient and modern philosophers have agreed in this opinion, they have taken it for granted. But let us, as becomes philosophers, lay aside authority; we need not, surely, consult Aristotle or Locke, to know whether pain be like the point of a sword. I have as clear a conception of extension, hardness, and motion, as I have of the point of a sword; and, with some pains and practice, I can form as clear a notion of the other sensations of touch as I have of pain. When I do so, and compare them together, it appears to me clear as daylight, that the former are not of kin to the latter, not resemble them in any one feature. They are as unlike, yea as certainly and manifestly unlike, as pain is to the point of a sword. It may be true, that those sensations first introduced

the material world to our acquaintance; it may be true that it seldom or never appears without their company; but, for all that, they are as unlike as the passion of anger is to those features of the countenance which attend it.

So that, in the sentence those philosophers have passed against the material world, there is an *error personae*. Their proof touches not matter, or any of its qualities; but strikes directly against an idol of their own imagination, a material world made of ideas and sensations, which never had, nor can have an existence.

Secondly, the very existence of our conceptions of extension, figure, and motion, since they are neither ideas of sensation nor reflection, overturns the whole ideal system, by which the material world hath been tried and condemned; so that there hath been likewise in this sentence an *error juris*.

It is a very fine and a just observation of Locke, that, as no human art can create a single particle of matter, and the whole extent of our power over the material world consists in compounding, combining, and disjoining the matter made to our hands; so, in the world of thought, the materials are all made by nature, and can only be variously combined and disjoined by us. So that it is impossible for reason or prejudice, true or false philosophy, to produce one simple notion or conception, which is not the work of nature, and the result of our constitution. The conception of extension, motion, and the other attributes of matter, cannot be the effect of error or prejudice; it must be the work of nature. And the power or faculty by which we acquire those conceptions, must be something different from any power of the human mind that hath been explained, since it is neither sensation nor reflection.

This I would, therefore, humbly propose, as an *experimentum crucis*, by which the ideal system must stand or fall; and it brings the matter to a short issue: Extension, figure, motion, may any one, or all of them, be taken for the subject of this experiment. Either they are ideas of sensation, or they are not. If any one of them can be shewn to be an idea of sensation, or to have the least resemblance to any sensation, I lay my hand upon my mouth, and give up all pretence to reconcile reason to common sense in this matter, and must suffer the ideal scepticism to triumph. But if, on the other hand, they are not ideas of sensation, nor like to any sensation, then the ideal system is a rope of sand, and all the laboured arguments of the sceptical philosophy against a material world, and against the existence of every thing but impressions and ideas, proceed upon a false hypothesis. . . .

Bishop Berkeley hath proved, beyond the possibility of reply, that we cannot by reasoning infer the existence of matter from our sensations: and the author of the "Treatise of Human Nature" hath proved no less clearly, that we cannot by reasoning infer the existence of our own or other minds from our sensations. But are we to admit nothing but what can be proved by reasoning? Then we must be sceptics indeed, and believe nothing at all. The author of the "Treatise of Human Nature" appears to me to be but a half-

sceptic. He hath not followed his principles so far as they lead him; but, after having, with unparalleled intrepidity and success, combated vulgar prejudices, when he had but one blow to strike, his courage fails him, he fairly lays down his arms, and yields himself a captive to the most common of all vulgar prejudices — I mean the belief of the existence of his own impressions and ideas.

I beg, therefore, to have the honour of making an addition to the sceptical system, without which I conceive it cannot hang together. I affirm, that the belief of the existence of impressions and ideas, is as little supported by reason, as that of the existence of minds and bodies. No man ever did or could offer any reason for this belief. Des Cartes took it for granted, that he thought, and had sensations and ideas; so have all his followers done. Even the hero of scepticism hath yielded this point, I crave leave to say, weakly and imprudently. I say so, because I am persuaded that there is no principle of his philosophy that obliged him to make this concession. And what is there in impressions and ideas so formidable, that this all-conquering philosophy, after triumphing over every other existence, should pay homage to them? Besides, the concession is dangerous: for belief is of such a nature, that, if you leave any root, it will spread; and you may more easily pull it up altogether, than say, Hitherto shalt thou go and no further: the existence of impressions and ideas I give up to thee; but see thou pretend to nothing more. A thorough and consistent sceptic will never, therefore, yield this point; and while he holds it, you can never oblige him to yield anything else.

To such a sceptic I have nothing to say; but of the semisceptics, I should beg to know, why they believe the existence of their impressions and ideas. The true reason I take to be, because they cannot help it; and the same reason will lead them to believe many other things.

All reasoning must be from first principles; and for first principles no other reason can be given but this, that, by the constitution of our nature, we are under a necessity of assenting to them. Such principles are parts of our constitution, no less than the power of thinking: reason can neither make nor destroy them; nor can it do anything without them: it is like a telescope, which may help a man to see farther, who hath eyes; but, without eyes, a telescope shews nothing at all. A mathematician cannot prove the truth of his axioms, nor can he prove anything, unless he takes them for granted. We cannot prove the existence of our minds, nor even of our thoughts and sensations. A historian, or a witness, can prove nothing, unless it is taken for granted that the memory and senses may be trusted. A natural philosopher can prove nothing, unless it is taken for granted that the course of nature is steady and uniform.

How or when I got such first principles, upon which I build all my reasoning, I know not; for I had them before I can remember: but I am sure they are parts of my constitution, and that I cannot throw them off. That our thoughts and sensations must have a subject, which we call *ourself* is not therefore an opinion got by reasoning, but a natural principle. That our sensations of touch indicate something external, extended, figured, hard or soft, is not a deduction of reason, but a natural principle. The belief of it, and the very conception of it, are equally parts of our constitution. If we are deceived in it, we are deceived by Him that made us, and there is no remedy.

I do not mean to affirm, that the sensations of touch do, from the very first, suggest the same notions of body and its qualities which they do when we are grown up. Perhaps Nature is frugal in this, as in her other operations. The passion of love, with all its concomitant sentiments and desires, is naturally suggested by the perception of beauty in the other sex; yet the same perception does not suggest the tender passion till a certain period of life. A blow given to an infant, raises grief and lamentation; but when he grows up, it as naturally stirs resentment, and prompts him to resistance. Perhaps a child in the womb, or for some short period of its existence, is merely a sentient being; the faculties by which it perceives an external world, by which it reflects on its own thoughts, and existence, and relation to other things, as well as its reasoning and moral faculties, unfold themselves by degrees so that it is inspired with the various principles of common sense, as with the passions of love and resentment, when it has occasion for them.

SECTION VIII: OF THE SYSTEMS OF PHILOSOPHERS CONCERNING THE SENSES

All the systems of philosophers about our senses and their objects have split upon this rock, of not distinguishing properly sensations which can have no existence but when they are felt, from the things suggested by them. Aristotle —with as distinguishing a head as ever applied to philosophical disquisitions —confounds these two; and makes every sensation to be the form, without the matter, of the thing perceived by it. As the impression of a seal upon wax has the form of the seal but nothing of the matter of it, so he conceived our sensations to be impressions upon the mind, which bear the image, likeness, or form of the external thing perceived, without the matter of it. Colour, sound, and smell, as well as extension, figure, and hardness, are, according to him, various forms of matter: our sensations are the same forms imprinted on the mind, and perceived in its own intellect. It is evident from this, that Aristotle made no distinction between primary and secondary qualities of bodies, although that distinction was made by Democritus, Epicurus, and others of the ancients.

Des Cartes, Malebranche, and Locke, revived the distinction between primary and secondary qualities; but they made the secondary qualities mere sensations, and the primary ones resemblances of our sensations. . . .

Bishop Berkeley gave new light to this subject, by shewing that the qualities of an inanimate thing, such as matter is conceived to be, cannot resemble any sensation; that it is impossible to conceive anything like the sensations of our minds, but the sensations of other minds. Every one that attends properly to his sensations must assent to this; yet it had escaped all the philosophers that came before Berkeley. . . .

But let us observe what use the Bishop makes of this important discovery. Why, he concludes, that we can have no conception of an inanimate substance, such as matter is conceived to be, or of any of its qualities; and that there is the strongest ground to believe that there is no existence in nature but minds, sensations, and ideas: if there is any other kind of existence, it must be what we neither have nor can have any conception of. But how does this follow? Why, thus: We can have no conception of anything but what resembles some sensation or idea in our minds; but the sensations and ideas in our minds can resemble nothing but the sensations and ideas in other minds; therefore, the conclusion is evident. This argument, we see, leans upon two propositions. The last of them the ingenious author hath, indeed, made evident to all that understand his reasoning, and can attend to their own sensations: but the first proposition he never attempts to prove; it is taken from the doctrine of ideas, which hath been so universally received by philosophers, that it was thought to need no proof.

We may here again observe, that this acute writer argues from a hypothesis against fact, and against the common sense of mankind. That we can have no conception of anything, unless there is some impression, sensation, or idea, in our minds which resembles it, is indeed an opinion which hath been very generally received among philosophers; but it is neither self-evident, nor hath it been clearly proved; and therefore it hath been more reasonable to call in question this doctrine of philosophers, than to discard the material world, and by that means expose philosophy to the ridicule of all men who will not offer up common sense as a sacrifice to metaphysics.

We ought, however, to do this justice both to the Bishop of Cloyne and to the author of the "Treatise of Human Nature," to acknowledge, that their conclusions are justly drawn from the doctrine of ideas, which has been so universally received. On the other hand, from the character of Bishop Berkeley, and of his predecessors, Des Cartes, Locke, and Malebranche, we may venture to say, that, if they had seen all the consequences of this doctrine, as clearly as the author before mentioned did, they would have suspected it vehemently, and examined it more carefully than they appear to have done.

The theory of ideas, like the Trojan horse, had a specious appearance both of innocence and beauty; but if those philosophers had known that it carried in its belly death and destruction to all science and common sense, they would not have broken down their walls to give it admittance.

That we have clear and distinct conceptions of extension, figure, motion, and other attributes of body, which are neither sensations, nor like any sensation, is a fact of which we may be as certain as that we have sensations. And

that all mankind have a fixed belief of an external material world—a belief which is neither got by reasoning nor education, and a belief which we cannot shake off, even when we seem to have strong arguments against it and no shadow of argument for it—is likewise a fact, for which we have all the evidence that the nature of the thing admits. These facts are phaenomena of human nature, from which we may justly argue against any hypothesis, however generally received. But to argue from a hypothesis against facts, is contrary to the rules of true philosophy. . . .

SECTION XX: OF PERCEPTION IN GENERAL

Sensation, and the perception of external objects by the senses, though very different in their nature, have commonly been considered as one and the same thing. The purposes of common life do not make it necessary to distinguish them, and the received opinions of philosophers tend rather to confound them; but, without attending carefully to this distinction, it is impossible to have any just conception of the operations of our senses. The most simple operations of the mind, admit not of a logical definition: all we can do is to describe them, so as to lead those who are conscious of them in themselves, to attend to them, and reflect upon them; and it is often very difficult to describe them so as to answer this intention.

The same mode of expression is used to denote sensation and perception:

and, therefore, we are apt to look upon them as things of the same nature. Thus, *I feel a pain; I see a tree:* the first denoteth a sensation, the last a perception. The grammatical analysis of both expressions is the same: for both consist of an active verb and an object. But, if we attend to the things signified by these expressions, we shall find that, in the first, the distinction between the act and the object is not real but grammatical: in the second, the distinction is not only grammatical but real.

The form of the expression, *I feel pain*, might seem to imply that the feeling is something distinct from the pain felt; yet, in reality, there is no distinction. As *thinking a thought* is an expression which could signify no more than *thinking*, so *feeling a pain* signifies no more than *being pained*. What we have said of pain is applicable to every other mere sensation. It is difficult to give instances, very few of our sensations having names; and, where they have, the name being common to the sensation, and to something else which is associated with it. But, when we attend to the sensation by itself, and separate it from other things which are conjoined with it in the imagination, it appears to be something which can have no existence but in a sentient mind, no distinction from the act of the mind by which it is felt.

Perception, as we here understand it, hath always an object distinct from the act by which it is perceived; an object which may exist whether it be perceived or not. I perceive a tree that grows before my window; there is here an object which is perceived, and an act

of the mind by which it is perceived; and these two are not only distinguishable, but they are extremely unlike in their natures. The object is made up of a trunk, branches, and leaves; but the act of the mind by which it is perceived hath neither trunk, branches, nor leaves. I am conscious of this act of my mind, and I can reflect upon it; but it is too simple to admit of an analysis, and I cannot find proper words to describe it. I find nothing that resembles it so much as the remembrance of the tree, or the imagination of it. Yet both these differ essentially from perception; they differ likewise one from another. It is in vain that a philosopher assures me, that the imagination of the tree, the remembrance of it, and the perception of it, are all one, and differ only in degree of vivacity. I know the contrary; for I am as well acquainted with all the three as I am with the apartments of my own house. I know this also, that the perception of an object implies both a conception of its form, and a belief of its present existence. I know, moreover, that this belief is not the effect of argumentation and reasoning; it is the immediate effect of my constitution.

I am aware that this belief which I have in perception stands exposed to the strongest batteries of scepticism. But they make no great impression upon it. The sceptic asks me, Why do you believe the existence of the external object which you perceive? This belief, sir, is none of my manufacture; it came from the mint of Nature; it bears her image and superscription; and, if it is not right, the fault is not mine: I even took it upon trust, and without suspicion. Reason, says the sceptic, is the only judge of truth, and you ought to throw off every opinion and every belief that is not grounded on reason. Why, sir, should I believe the faculty of reason more than that of perception? — they came both out of the same shop, and were made by the same artist; and if he puts one piece of false ware into my hands, what should hinder him from putting another?

Perhaps the sceptic will agree to distrust reason, rather than give any credit to perception. For, says he, since, by your own concession, the object which you perceive, and that act of your mind by which you perceive it, are quite different things, the one may exist without the other; and, as the object may exist without being perceived, so the perception may exist without an object. There is nothing so shameful in a philosopher as to be deceived and deluded; and, therefore, you ought to resolve firmly to withhold assent, and to throw off this belief of external objects, which may be all delusion. For my part, I will never attempt to throw it off; and, although the sober part of mankind will not be very anxious to know my reasons, yet, if they can be of use to any sceptic, they are these: —

First, because it is not in my power: why, then, should I make a vain attempt? It would be agreeable to fly to the moon, and to make a visit to Jupiter and Saturn; but, when I know that Nature has bound me down by the law of gravitation to this planet which I inhabit, I rest contented, and quietly suffer myself to be carried along in its orbit. My belief is carried along by perception, as irresistibly as my body by the earth. And the greatest sceptic will find himself to be in the same condition. He may struggle hard to disbelieve the informations of his senses, as a man does to swim against a torrent; but, ah! it is in vain. It is in vain that he strains every nerve, and wrestles with nature, and with every object that strikes upon his senses. For, after all, when his strength is spent in the fruitless attempt, he will be carried down the torrent with the common herd of believers.

Secondly, I think it would not be prudent to throw off this belief, if it were in my power. If Nature intended to deceive me, and impose upon me by false appearances, and I, by my great cunning and profound logic, have discovered the imposture, prudence would dictate to me, in this case, even to put up [with] this indignity done me, as quietly as I could, and not to call her an impostor to her face, lest she should be even with me in another way. For what do I gain by resenting this injury? You ought at least not to believe what she says. This indeed seems reasonable, if she intends to impose upon me. But what is the consequence? I resolve not to believe my senses. I break my nose against a post that comes in my way; I step into a dirty kennel; and, after twenty such wise rational actions, I am taken up and clapped into a mad-house. Now, I confess I would rather make one of the credulous fools whom Nature imposes upon, than of those wise and rational philosophers who resolve to withhold assent at all this expense. If a man pretends to be a sceptic with regard to the informations of sense, and yet prudently keeps out of harm's way as other men do, he must excuse my suspicion, that he either acts the hypocrite, or imposes upon himself. For, if the scale of his belief were so evenly poised as to lean no more to one side than to the contrary, it is impossible that his actions could be directed by any rules of common prudence.

Thirdly, although the two reasons already mentioned are perhaps two more than enough, I shall offer a third. I gave implicit belief to the informations of Nature by my senses, for a considerable part of my life, before I had learned so much logic as to be able to start a doubt concerning them. And now, when I reflect upon what is past, I do not find that I have been imposed upon by this belief. I find that without it I must have perished by a thousand accidents. I find that without it I should have been no wiser now than when I was born. I should not even have been able to acquire that logic which suggests these sceptical doubts with regard to my senses. Therefore, I consider this instinctive belief as one of the best gifts of Nature. I thank the Author of my being, who bestowed it upon me before the eyes of my reason were opened, and still bestows it upon me, to be my guide where reason leaves me in the dark. And now I yield to the direction of my senses, not from instinct only, but from confidence and trust in a faithful and beneficent Monitor, grounded upon the experience of his paternal care and goodness.

In all this, I deal with the Author of my being, no otherwise than I thought it reasonable to deal with my parents and tutors, I believed by instinct whatever they told me, long before I had the idea of a lie, or thought of the possibility of their deceiving me. Afterwards, upon reflection, I found they had acted like fair and honest people, who wished me well. I found that, if I had not believed what they told me, before I could give a reason of my belief, I had to this day been little better than a changeling. And although this natural credulity hath sometimes occasioned my being imposed upon by deceivers, yet it hath been of infinite advantage to me upon the whole; therefore, I consider it as another good gift of Nature. And I continue to give that credit, from reflection, to those of whose integrity and veracity I have had experience, which before I gave from instinct.

There is a much greater similitude than is commonly imagined, between the testimony of nature given by our senses, and the testimony of men given by language. The credit we give to both is at first the effect of instinct only. When we grow up, and begin to reason about them, the credit given to human testimony is restrained and weakened, by the experience we have of deceit. But the credit given to the testimony of our senses, is established and confirmed by the uniformity and constancy of the laws of nature.

Our perceptions are of two kinds: some are natural and original; others acquired, and the fruit of experience. When I perceive that this is the taste of cyder, that of brandy; that this is the smell of an apple, that of an orange; that this is the noise of thunder, that the ringing of bells; this the sound of a coach passing, that the voice of such a friend; these perceptions, and others of the same kind, are not original — they are acquired. But the perception which I have, by touch, of the hardness and softness of bodies, of their extension, figure, and motion, is not acquired — it is original.

In all our senses, the acquired perceptions are many more than the original, especially in sight. By this sense we perceive originally the visible figure and colour of bodies only, and their visible place; but we learn to perceive by the eye, almost everything which we can perceive by touch. The original perceptions of this sense serve only as signs to introduce the acquired.

The signs by which objects are presented to us in perception, are the language of Nature to man: and as, in many respects, it hath great affinity with the language of man to man, so particularly in this, that both are partly natural and original, partly acquired by custom. Our original or natural perceptions are analogous to the natural language of man to man, of which we took notice in the fourth chapter; and our acquired perceptions are analogous to artificial language, which, in our mother tongue, is got very much in the same manner with our acquired perceptions — as we shall afterwards more fully explain. . . .

Perception ought not only to be distinguished from sensation, but likewise from that knowledge of the objects of sense which is got by reasoning. There is no reasoning in perception, as hath been observed. The belief which is implied in it, is the effect of instinct. But there are many things, with regard to sensible objects, which we can infer from what we perceive; and such conclusions of reason ought to be distinguished from what is merely perceived. When I look at the moon, I perceive her to be sometimes circular, sometimes horned, and sometimes gibbous. This is simple perception, and is the same in the philosopher and in the clown: but from these various appearances of her enlightened part, I infer that she is really of a spherical figure. This conclusion is not obtained by simple perception, but by reasoning. Simple perception has the same relation to the conclusions of reason drawn from our perceptions, as the axioms in mathematics have to the propositions. I cannot demonstrate that two quantities which are equal to the same quantity, are equal to each other; neither can I demonstrate that the tree which I perceive, exists. But, by the constitution of my nature, my belief is irresistibly carried along by my apprehension of the axiom; and, by the constitution of my nature, my belief is no less irresistibly carried along by my perception of the tree. All reasoning is from principles. The first principles of mathematical reasoning are mathematical axioms and definitions; and the first principles of all our reasoning about existences, are our perceptions. The first principles of every kind of reasoning are given us by Nature, and are of equal authority with the faculty of reason itself, which is also the gift of Nature. The conclusions of reason are all built upon first principles, and can have no other foundation.

Most justly, therefore, do such principles disdain to be tried by reason, and
laugh at all the artillery of the logician,
when it is directed against them.

When a long train of reasoning is
necessary in demonstrating a mathematical proposition, it is easily distinguished from an axiom; and they seem
to be things of a very different nature.
But there are some propositions which
lie so near to axioms, that it is difficult
to say whether they ought to be held as
axioms, or demonstrated as propositions. The same thing holds with regard
to perception, and the conclusions
drawn from it. Some of these conclusions follow our perceptions so easily,
and are so immediately connected with
them, that it is difficult to fix the limit
which divides the one from the
other. . . .

SECTION XXIV: OF THE ANALOGY BETWEEN PERCEPTION AND THE CREDIT WE GIVE TO HUMAN TESTIMONY

The objects of human knowledge are
innumerable; but the channels by
which it is conveyed to the mind are
few. Among these, the perception of
external things by our senses, and the
informations which we receive upon
human testimony, are not the least considerable; and so remarkable is the analogy between these two, and the analogy
between the principles of the mind
which are subservient to the one and
those which are subservient to the

other, that, without further apology,
we shall consider them together.

In the testimony of Nature given by
the senses, as well as in human testimony given by language, things are signified to us by signs: and in one as well
as the other, the mind, either by original principles or by custom, passes
from the sign to the conception and belief of the things signified.

We have distinguished our perceptions into original and acquired; and
language, into natural and artificial. Between acquired perception and artificial language, there is a great analogy;
but still a greater between original perception and natural language.

The signs in original perception are
sensations, of which Nature hath given
us a great variety, suited to the variety
of the things signified by them. Nature
hath established a real connection between the signs and the things signified; and Nature hath also taught us the
interpretation of the signs—so that,
previous to experience, the sign suggests the thing signified, and creates the
belief of it.

The signs in natural language are
features of the face, gestures of the
body, and modulations of the voice; the
variety of which is suited to the variety
of the things signified by them. Nature
hath established a real connection between these signs, and the thoughts and
dispositions of the mind which are signified by them; and Nature hath taught
us the interpretation of these signs; so
that, previous to experience, the signs
suggest the thing signified, and create
the belief of it.

A man in company, without doing

good or evil, without uttering an articulate sound, may behave himself gracefully, civilly, politely; or, on the contrary, meanly, rudely, and impertinently. We see the dispositions of his mind by their natural signs in his countenance and behaviour, in the same manner as we perceive the figure and other qualities of bodies by the sensations which nature hath connected with them.

The signs in the natural language of the human countenance and behavior, as well as the signs in our original perceptions, have the same signification in all climates and in all nations; and the skill of interpreting them is not acquired, but innate.

In acquired perception the signs are either sensations, or things which we perceive by means of sensations. The connection between the sign and the thing signified, is established by nature; and we discover this connection by experience; but not without the aid of our original perceptions, or of those which we have already acquired. After this connection is discovered, the sign, in like manner as in original perception, always suggests the things signified, and creates the belief of it.

In artificial language, the signs are articulate sounds, whose connection with the things signified by them, is established by the will of men; and, in learning our mother tongue, we discover this connection by experience; but not without the aid of natural language, or of what we had before attained of artificial language. And, after this connection is discovered, the sign, as in natural language, always suggests the thing signified, and creates the belief of it.

Our original perceptions are few, compared with the acquired; but, without the former, we could not possibly attain the latter. In like manner, natural language is scanty, compared with artificial; but, without the former, we could not possibly attain the latter.

Our original perceptions, as well as the natural language of human features and gestures, must be resolved into particular principles of the human constitution. Thus, it is by one particular principle of our constitution that certain features express anger; and, by another particular principle, that certain features express benevolence. It is, in like manner, by one particular principle of our constitution that a certain sensation signifies hardness in the body which I handle; and it is by another particular principle that a certain sensation signifies motion in that body.

But our acquired perceptions, and the information we receive by means of artificial language, must be resolved into general principles of the human constitution. When a painter perceives that this picture is the work of Raphael, that the work of Titian; a jeweller, that this is a true diamond, that a counterfeit; a sailor, that this is a ship of five hundred ton, that of four hundred; these different acquired perceptions are produced by the same general principles of the human mind, which have a different operation in the same person according as they are variously applied, and in different persons according to the diversity of their education and manner of life. In like manner, when certain articulate sounds convey to my mind the knowledge of the battle of Pharsalia, and others, the knowledge of the battle of Poltowa — when a Frenchman and an Englishman receive the same information by different articulate sounds — the signs used in these different cases, produce the knowledge and belief of the things signified, by means of the same general principles of the human constitution.

Now, if we compare the general principles of our constitution, which fit us for receiving information from our fellow-creatures by language, with the general principles which fit us for acquiring the perception of things by our senses, we shall find them to be very similar in their nature and manner of operation.

When we begin to learn our mother tongue, we perceive, by the help of natural language, that they who speak to us use certain sounds to express certain things. We imitate the same sounds when we would express the same things; and find that we are understood.

But here a difficulty occurs which merits our attention, because the solution of it leads to some original principles of the human mind, which are of great importance, and of very extensive influence. We know by experience that men *have* used such words to express such things; but all experience is of the *past*, and can, of itself, give no notion or belief of what is *future*. How come we, then, to believe, and to rely upon it with assurance, that men, who have it in their power to do otherwise, will continue to use the same words when they think the same things? Whence

comes this knowledge and belief — this foresight, we ought rather to call it — of the future and voluntary actions of our fellow-creatures? Have they promised that they will never impose upon us by equivocation or falsehood? No, they have not. And, if they had, this would not solve the difficulty; for such promise must be expressed by words or by other signs; and, before we can rely upon it, we must be assured that they put the usual meaning upon the signs which express that promise. No man of common sense ever thought of taking a man's own word for his honesty; and it is evident that we take his veracity for granted when we lay any stress upon his word or promise. I might add, that this reliance upon the declarations and testimony of men is found in children long before they know what a promise is.

There is, therefore, in the human mind an early anticipation, neither derived from experience, nor from reason, nor from any compact or promise, that our fellow-creatures will use the same signs in language, when they have the same sentiments.

This is, in reality, a kind of prescience of human actions; and it seems to me to be an original principle of the human constitution, without which we should be incapable of language, and consequently incapable of instruction.

The wise and beneficent Author of Nature, who intended that we should be social creatures, and that we should receive the greatest and most important part of our knowledge by the information of others, hath, for these purposes, implanted in our natures two principles that tally with each other.

The first of these principles is, a propensity to speak truth, and to use the signs of language so as to convey our real sentiments. This principle has a powerful operation, even in the greatest liars; for where they lie once, they speak truth a hundred times. Truth is always uppermost, and is the natural issue of the mind. It requires no art or training, no inducement or temptation, but only that we yield to a natural impulse. Lying, on the contrary, is doing violence to our nature; and is never practised, even by the worst men, without some temptation. Speaking truth is like using our natural food, which we would do from appetite, although it answered no end; but lying is like taking physic, which is nauseous to the taste, and which no man takes but for some end which he cannot otherwise attain.

If it should be objected, That men may be influenced by moral or political considerations to speak truth, and, therefore, that their doing so is no proof of such an original principle as we have mentioned—I answer, First, That moral or political considerations can have no influence until we arrive at years of understanding and reflection; and it is certain, from experience, that children keep to truth invariably, before they are capable of being influenced by such considerations. Secondly, When we are influenced by moral or political considerations, we must be conscious of that influence, and capable of perceiving it upon reflection. Now, when I reflect upon my actions most attentively, I am not conscious that, in speaking truth, I am influenced on ordinary occasions by any motive, moral or political. I find that

truth is always at the door of my lips, and goes forth spontaneously, if not held back. It requires neither good nor bad intention to bring it forth, but only that I be artless and undesigning. There may indeed be temptations to falsehood, which would be too strong for the natural principle of veracity, unaided by principles of honour or virtue; but where there is no such temptation, we speak truth by instinct—and this instinct is the principle I have been explaining.

By this instinct, a real connection is formed between our words and our thoughts, and thereby the former become fit to be signs of the latter, which they could not otherwise be. And although this connection is broken in every instance of lying and equivocation, yet these instances being comparatively few, the authority of human testimony is only weakened by them but not destroyed.

Another original principle implanted in us by the Supreme Being, is a disposition to confide in the veracity of others, and to believe what they tell us. This is the counterpart to the former; and, as that may be called *the principle of veracity*, we shall, for want of a more proper name, call this *the principle of credulity*. It is unlimited in children, until they meet with instances of deceit and falsehood; and it retains a very considerable degree of strength through life.

If Nature had left the mind of the speaker *in aequilibrio*, without any inclination to the side of truth more than to that of falsehood, children would lie as often as they speak truth, until reason was so far ripened as to suggest the imprudence of lying, or conscience, as to suggest its immorality. And if Nature had left the mind of the hearer *in aequilibrio*, without any inclination to the side of belief more than to that of disbelief, we should take no man's word until we had positive evidence that he spoke truth. His testimony would, in this case, have no more authority than his dreams; which may be true or false, but no man is disposed to believe them, on this account, that they were dreamed. It is evident that, in the matter of testimony, the balance of human judgment is by nature inclined to the side of belief; and turns to that side of itself, when there is nothing put into the opposite scale. If it was not so, no proposition that is uttered in discourse would be believed, until it was examined and tried by reason; and most men would be unable to find reasons for believing the thousandth part of what is told them. Such distrust and incredulity would deprive us of the greatest benefits of society, and place us in a worse condition than that of savages.

Children, on this supposition, would be absolutely incredulous, and, therefore, absolutely incapable of instruction: those who had little knowledge of human life, and of the manners and characters of men, would be in the next degree incredulous: and the most credulous men would be those of greatest experience, and of the deepest penetration: because, in many cases, they would be able to find good reasons for believing testimony, which the weak and the ignorant could not discover.

In a word, if credulity were the effect of reasoning and experience, it must grow up and gather strength, in the same proportion as reason and experience do. But, if it is the gift of Nature, it will be strongest in childhood, and limited and restrained by experience; and the most superficial view of human life shews, that the last is really the case, and not the first.

It is the intention of Nature, that we should be carried in arms before we are able to walk upon our legs; and it is likewise the intention of Nature, that our belief should be guided by the authority and reason of others, before it can be guided by our own reason. The weakness of the infant, and the natural affection of the mother, plainly indicate the former; and the natural credulity of youth, and authority of age, as plainly indicate the latter. The infant, by proper nursing, and care, acquires strength to walk without support. Reason hath likewise her infancy, when she must be carried in arms: then she leans entirely upon authority, by natural instinct, as if she was conscious of her own weakness; and, without this support, she becomes vertiginous. When brought to maturity by proper culture, she begins to feel her own strength, and leans less upon the reason of others; she learns to suspect testimony in some cases, and to disbelieve it in others; and sets bounds to that authority to which she was at first entirely subject. But still, to the end of life, she finds a necessity of borrowing light from testimony, where she has none within herself, and of leaning, in some degree, upon the reason of others, where she is conscious of her own imbecility.

And as, in many instances, Reason, even in her maturity, borrows aid from testimony, so in others she mutually gives aid to it, and strengthens its authority. For, as we find good reason to reject testimony in some cases, so in others we find good reason to rely upon it with perfect security, in our most important concerns. The character, the number, and the disinterestedness of witnesses, the impossibility of collusion, and the incredibility of their concurring in their testimony without collusion, may give an irresistible strength to testimony, compared to which its native and intrinsic authority is very inconsiderable.

Having now considered the general principles of the human mind which fit us for receiving information from our fellow-creatures, by the means of language, let us next consider the general principles which fit us for receiving the information of Nature by our acquired perceptions.

It is undeniable, and indeed is acknowledged by all, that when we have found two things to have been constantly conjoined in the course of nature, the appearance of one of them is immediately followed by the conception and belief of the other. The former becomes a natural sign of the latter; and the knowledge of their constant conjunction in time past, whether got by experience or otherwise, is sufficient to make us rely with assurance upon the continuance of that conjunction.

This process of the human mind is so familiar that we never think of inquiring into the principles upon which it is founded. We are apt to conceive it as a self-evident truth, that what is to come must be similar to what is past. Thus, if a certain degree of cold freezes water to-day, and has been known to do so in all time past, we have no doubt but the same degree of cold will freeze water to-morrow, or a year hence. That this is a truth which all men believe as soon as they understand it, I readily admit; but the question is, Whence does its evidence arise? Not from comparing the ideas, surely. For, when I compare the idea of cold with that of water hardened into a transparent solid body, I can perceive no connection between them: no man can shew the one to be the necessary effect of the other; no man can give a shadow of reason why Nature hath conjoined them. But do we not learn their conjunction from experience? True; experience informs us that they have been conjoined in time *past*; but no man ever had any experience of what is *future*: and this is the very question to be resolved. How we come to believe that the *future* will be like the *past*? Hath the Author of nature promised this? Or were we admitted to his council, when he established the present laws of nature, and determined the time of their continuance. No, surely. Indeed, if we believe that there is a wise and good Author of nature, we may see a good reason why he should continue the same laws of nature, and the same connections of things, for a long time: because, if he did otherwise, we could learn nothing from what is past, and all our experience would be of no use to us. But, though this consideration, when we come to the use of reason, may confirm our belief of the continuance of the present course of nature, it is certain that it did not give rise to this belief; for children and idiots have this belief as soon as they know that fire will burn them. It must, therefore, be the effect of instinct, not of reason.

The wise Author of our nature intended, that a great and necessary part of our knowledge should be derived from experience, before we are capable of reasoning, and he hath provided means perfectly adequate to this intention. For, First, He governs nature by fixed laws, so that we find innumerable connections of things which continue from age to age. Without this stability of the course of nature, there could be no experience; or, it would be a false guide, and lead us into error and mischief. If there were not a principle of veracity in the human mind, men's words would not be signs of their thoughts: and if there were no regularity in the course of nature, no one thing could be a natural sign of another. Secondly, He hath implanted in human minds an original principle by which we believe and expect the continuance of the course of nature, and the continuance of those connections which we have observed in time past. It is by this general principle of our nature, that, when two things have been found connected in time past, the appearance of the one produces the belief of the other.

I think the ingenious author of the "Treatise of Human Nature" first observed, That our belief of the continuance of the laws of nature cannot be founded either upon knowledge or probability: but, far from conceiving it to be an original principle of the mind, he endeavours to account for it from his favourite hypothesis, That belief is nothing but a certain degree of vivacity in the idea of the thing believed. I made a remark upon this curious hypothesis in the second chapter, and shall now make another.

The belief which we have in perception, is a belief of the present existence of the object; that which we have in memory, is a belief of its past existence; the belief of which we are now speaking is a belief of its future existence; and in imagination there is no belief at all. Now, I would gladly know of this author, how one degree of vivacity fixes the existence of the object to the present moment; another carries it back to time past; a third, taking a contrary direction, carries it into futurity; and a fourth carries it out of existence altogether. Suppose, for instance, that I see the sun rising out of the sea: I remember to have seen him rise yesterday; I believe he will rise to-morrow near the same place; I can likewise imagine him rising in that place, without any belief at all. Now, according to this sceptical hypothesis, this perception, this memory, this foreknowledge, and this imagination, are all the same idea, diversified only by different degrees of vivacity. The perception of the sun rising is the most lively idea; the memory of his rising yesterday is the same idea a little more faint; the belief of his rising to-morrow is the same idea yet fainter; and the imagination of his rising is still the same idea, but faintest of all. One is apt to think, that this idea might gradually pass through all possible degrees of vivacity without stirring out of its place. But, if we think so, we deceive ourselves; for no sooner does it begin to grow languid than it moves backward into time past. Supposing this to be granted, we expect, at least, that, as it moves backward by the decay of its vivacity, the more that vivacity decays it will go back the farther, until it remove quite out of sight. But here we are deceived again; for there is a certain period of this declining vivacity, when, as if it had met an elastic obstacle in its motion backward, it suddenly rebounds from the past to the future, without taking the present in its way. And now, having got into the regions of futurity, we are apt to think that it has room enough to spend all its remaining vigour: but still we are deceived; for, by another sprightly bound, it mounts up into the airy region of imagination. So that ideas, in the gradual declension of their vivacity, seem to imitate the inflection of verbs in grammar. They begin with the present, and proceed in order to the preterite, the future, and the indefinite. This article of the sceptical creed is indeed so full of mystery, on whatever side we view it, that they who hold that creed are very injuriously charged with incredulity; for, to me, it appears to require as much faith as that of St Athanasius.

However, we agree with the author of the "Treatise of Human Nature," in this, That our belief of the continuance of nature's laws is not derived from reason. It is an instinctive prescience of the operations of nature, very like to that prescience of human actions which makes us rely upon the testimony of our fellow-creatures; and as, without the latter, we should be incapable of receiving information from men by language, so, without the former, we should be incapable of receiving the information of nature by means of experience.

All our knowledge of nature beyond our original perceptions, is got by experience, and consists in the interpretation of natural signs. The constancy of nature's laws connects the sign with the thing signified; and, by the natural principle just now explained, we rely upon the continuance of the connections which experience hath discovered; and thus the appearance of the sign is followed by the belief of the thing signified. Upon this principle of our constitution, not only acquired perception, but all inductive reasoning, and all our reasoning from analogy, is grounded; and, therefore, for want of another name, we shall beg leave to call it *the inductive principle*. It is from the force of this principle that we immediately assent to that axiom upon which all our knowledge of nature is built. That effects of the same kind must have the same cause; for *effects* and *causes*, in the operations of nature, mean nothing but signs and the things signified by them. We perceive no proper causality or efficiency in any natural cause; but only a connection established by the course of nature between it and what is called its effect. Antecedently to all reasoning, we have, by our constitution, an anticipation that there is a fixed and steady course of nature: and we have an eager desire to discover this course of nature. We attend to every conjunction of things which presents itself, and expect the continuance of that conjunction. And, when such a conjunction has been often observed, we conceive the things to be naturally connected, and the appearance of one, without any reasoning or reflection, carries along with it the belief of the other.

If any reader should imagine that the inductive principle may be resolved into what philosophers usually call the *association of ideas*, let him observe, that, by this principle, natural signs are not associated with the idea only, but with the belief of the things signified. Now, this can with no propriety be called an association of ideas, unless ideas and belief be one and the same thing. A child has found the prick of a pin conjoined with pain; hence he believes, and knows, that these things are naturally connected; he knows that the one will always follow the other. If any man will call this only an association of ideas, I dispute not about words, but I think he speaks very improperly. For, if we express it in plain English, it is a prescience that things which he hath found conjoined in time past, will be conjoined in time to come. And this prescience is not the effect of reasoning, but of an original principle of human nature, which I have called *the inductive principle*.

This principle, like that of credulity, is unlimited in infancy, and gradually restrained and regulated as we grow up. It leads us often into mistakes; but is of infinite advantage upon the whole. By it, the child once burnt shuns the fire; by it, he likewise runs away from the surgeon by whom he was inoculated. It is better that he should do the last, than he should not do the first.

But the mistakes we are led into by these two natural principles, are of a different kind. Men sometimes lead us into mistakes, when we perfectly understand their language, by speaking lies. But Nature never misleads us in this way: her language is always true; and it is only by misinterpreting it that we fall into error. There must be many accidental conjunctions of things, as well as natural connections; and the former are apt to be mistaken for the latter. Thus, in the instance above mentioned, the child connected the pain of inoculation with the surgeon; whereas it was really connected with the incision only. Philosophers, and men of science, are not exempted from such mistakes; indeed, all false reasoning in philosophy is owing to them; it is drawn from experience and analogy, as well as just reasoning, otherwise it could have no verisimilitude; but the one is an unskillful and rash, the other a just and legitimate interpretation of natural signs. If a child, or a man of common understanding, were put to interpret a book of science, written in his mother-tongue, how many blunders and mistakes would he be apt to fall into? Yet he knows as much of this language as is necessary for his manner of life.

The language of Nature is the universal study; and the students are of different classes. Brutes, idiots, and children employ themselves in this study, and owe to it all their acquired perceptions. Men of common understanding make a greater progress, and learn, by a small degree of reflection, many things of which children are ignorant. . . .

From the time that children begin to

use their hands, Nature directs them to handle everything over and over, to look at it while they handle it, and to put it in various positions, and at various distances from the eye. We are apt to excuse this as a childish diversion, because they must be doing something, and have not reason to entertain themselves in a more manly way. But, if we think more justly, we shall find, that they are engaged in the most serious and important study; and, if they had all the reason of a philosopher, they could not be more properly employed. For it is this childish employment that enables them to make the proper use of their eyes. They are thereby every day acquiring habits of perception, which are of greater importance than anything we can teach them. The original perceptions which Nature gave them are few, and insufficient for the purposes of life; and, therefore, she made them capable of acquiring many more perceptions by habit. And, to complete her work, she hath given them an unwearied assiduity in applying to the exercises by which those perceptions are acquired. . . .

We have shewn, on the contrary, that every operation of the senses, in its very nature, implies judgment or belief, as well as simple apprehension. Thus, when I feel the pain of the gout in my toe, I have not only a notion of pain, but a belief of its existence, and a belief of some disorder in my toe which occasions it; and this belief is not produced by comparing ideas, and perceiving their agreements and disagreements; it is included in the very nature of the sensation. When I perceive a tree before me, my faculty of seeing gives me

not only a notion or simple apprehension of the tree, but a belief of its existence, and of its figure, distance, and magnitude; and this judgment or belief is not got by comparing ideas, it is included in the very nature of the perception. We have taken notice of several original principles of belief in the course of this inquiry; and when other faculties of the mind are examined, we shall find more, which have not occurred in the examination of the five senses.

Such original and natural judgments are, therefore, a part of that furniture which Nature hath given to the human understanding. They are the inspiration of the Almighty, no less than our notions or simple apprehensions. They serve to direct us in the common affairs of life, where our reasoning faculty would leave us in the dark. They are a part of our constitution; and all the discoveries of our reason are grounded upon them. They make up what is called *the common sense of mankind*; and, what is manifestly contrary to any of those first principles, is what we call *absurd*. The strength of them is *good sense*, which is often found in those who are not acute in reasoning. A remarkable deviation from them, arising from a disorder in the constitution, is what we call *lunacy*; as when a man believes that he is made of glass. When a man suffers himself to be reasoned out of the principles of common sense, by metaphysical arguments, we may call this *metaphysical lunacy*; which differs from other species of the distemper in this, that it is not continued, but intermittent: it is apt to seize the patient in solitary and speculative moments; but, when he enters into society, Common Sense recovers her authority. A clear explication and enumeration of the principles of common sense, is one of the chief *desiderata* in logic. We have only considered such of them as occurred in the examination of the five senses.

5. The last observation that I shall make upon the new system is, that, although it professes to set out in the way of reflection, and not of analogy, it hath retained some of the old analogical notions concerning the operations of the mind; particularly, that things which do not now exist in the mind itself, can only be perceived, remembered or imagined, by means of ideas or images of them in the mind, which are the immediate objects of perception, remembrance, and imagination. This doctrine appears evidently to be borrowed from the old system; which taught that external things make impressions upon the mind, like the impressions of a seal upon wax; that it is by means of those impressions that we perceive, remember, or imagine them; and that those impressions must resemble the things from which they are taken. When we form our notions of the operations of the mind by analogy, this way of conceiving them seems to be very natural, and offers itself to our thoughts; for, as everything which is felt must make some impression upon the body, we are apt to think that everything which is understood must make some impression upon the mind.

From such analogical reasoning, this opinion of the existence of ideas or images of things in the mind, seems to have taken its rise, and to have been so universally received among philosophers. It was observed already, that Berkeley, in one instance, apostatizes from this principle of the new system, by affirming that we have no ideas of spirits, and that we can think of them immediately, without ideas. But I know not whether in this he has had any followers. There is some difference, likewise, among modern philosophers with regard to the ideas or images by which we perceive, remember, or imagine sensible things. For, though all agree in the existence of such images they differ about their place; some placing them in a particular part of the brain, where the soul is thought to have her residence, and others placing them in the mind itself. Des Cartes held the first of these opinions; to which Newton seems likewise to have inclined. . . . But Locke seems to place the ideas of sensible things in the mind; and that Berkeley, and the author of the "Treatise of Human Nature," were of the same opinion, is evident. The last makes a very curious application of this doctrine, by endeavouring to prove from it, That the mind either is no substance, or that it is an extended and divisible substance; because the ideas of extension cannot be in a subject which is indivisible and unextended.

I confess I think his reasoning in this, as in most cases, is clear and strong. For whether the idea of extension be only another name for extension itself, as Berkeley and this author assert; or whether the idea of extension be an image and resemblance of extension, as Locke conceived; I appeal to any man of common sense, whether extension, or any image of extension, can be in an unextended and indivisible subject. But while I agree with him in his reasoning, I would make a different application of it. He takes it for granted, that there are ideas of extension in the mind; and thence infers, that, if it is at all a substance, it must be an extended and divisible substance. On the contrary, I take it for granted, upon the testimony of common sense, that my mind is a substance — that is, a permanent subject of thought; and my reason convinces me that it is an unextended and indivisible substance; and hence I infer that there cannot be in it anything that resembles extension. If this reasoning had occurred to Berkeley, it would probably have led him to acknowledge that we may think and reason concerning bodies, without having ideas of them in the mind, as well as concerning spirits.

I intended to have examined more particularly and fully this doctrine of the existence of ideas or images of things in the mind; and likewise another doctrine, which is founded upon it — to wit, That judgment or belief is nothing but a perception of the agreement or disagreement of our ideas; but, having already shewn, through the course of this inquiry, that the operations of the mind which we have examined, give no countenance to either of these doctrines, and in many things contradict them, I have thought it proper to drop this part of my design. It may be executed with more advantage, if it is at all necessary, after inquiring into some other powers of the human understanding.

COMMENT

Reid's complaint against the dominant philosophies of his time — rationalism and empiricism — in the name of common sense must not be misunderstood as a criticism of philosophy itself. He well knew that to claim that philosophy is useless or harmful is *itself* a philosophical point of view, which in turn needs examination and evaluation. Rather, Reid argues that the basis or starting point for all thought, including philosophy, must be the commonsense beliefs we have all acquired as part of our enculturation as human beings. Thus, for Reid, to question the existence of material objects, or the "external world," is technically impossible since the questioner is *simultaneously* taking the material world for granted. Consider Descartes seated in a chair, writing with a pen on paper, which is resting on a table, asking whether or not such objects are real!

Reid's answer to skepticism does not involve arriving at different conclusions by inferring from similar observational premises. Rather, he insists that we must begin our reasonings from certain "first principles," the truth of which can neither be established by deductive nor by inductive inference. These first principles must simply be "taken for granted." Otherwise no living, let alone reasoning, can take place. The first principles of common sense, according to Reid, are given by God to enable us to live in the world. Nature and our senses are bound together by a kind of "language" that can only be questioned at the cost of self-contradiction or fantasy.

The sort of thing Reid has in mind here is, as he says, the predisposition to believe that other people speak the truth. A moment's reflection will make it clear that without this "assumption," language would be impossible. Lying and pretending are parasitic on truth telling; otherwise we could never get started in language, let alone survive as families and societies. Another propensity, one that speaks directly to causation — the central difficulty encountered by Hume and Kant — is that of induction. According to Reid, our anticipation that the future will be like the past is preinferential, or "instinctive"; it can neither be given a rational justification nor be in need of one. All reasoning, even Hume's critique of inductive inference, is based on and makes use of the inferential process. After all, Hume himself gives a "causal explanation" of the psychological basis of the inferential process.

There are two highly influential philosophers in the twentieth century who take up a position quite similar to that of Reid. One is Ludwig Wittgenstein,[1] who in his later philosophy sought to undermine the "foundationalist" posture of nearly all modern thought; to wit that some things must simply be accepted as "bedrock" or taken as "certain" in order for any language and thought to be possible. The other is Michael Polanyi,[2] whose notion of "tacit knowledge," whereby we accredit our cognitive powers as reliable (even when raising skeptical questions) suggests that we always "know more than we can say." Space will not permit a further discussion of these two thinkers here, but the interested reader is encouraged to consult their major works.

There are, to be sure, certain difficulties that arise in connection with Reid's appeal to common sense as the basis and ultimate test for knowledge. Cultural anthropology has taught us to ask whether what is taken for granted in one culture is necessarily taken as such in others. Also, there is something somewhat "rationalistic" about Reid's position, something that smacks of Descartes' "self-evident axioms" or innate ideas. On the surface, at least, it would seem that some sort of justification for these "first principles" must be given. Reid, of course, could reply, with Wittgenstein, that justifications "must come to an end, otherwise they would

[1]See *Philosophical Investigations* (New York: Macmillan, 1953).
[2]See *Personal Knowledge* (Chicago: University of Chicago Press, 1958).

not be justifications." However, not all philosophers agree with this anti-foundationalist posture and at the very least more work needs to be done to clarify the nature of any supposed "truths" that are claimed to be beyond scrutiny.

Finally, it can be asked whether Reid's approach is all that different from that of Kant. Kant, too, argues that our belief in causation, among other first principles, is the result of the very structure of the human mind. Thus both he and Reid assert that to believe in and practice inductive inference is part of what it means to have a mind in the first place and that there is nothing "irrational" about such beliefs and practices. In fact, it would be irrational not to so believe and act. It would be worthwhile to ask what differences there are between Reid's view and that of Kant. It would also be valuable to construct the reply to them that Hume might have given had he been able or so inclined. The reader is encouraged to follow up on these suggestions, both in private and in class discussion, as they will serve as an excellent bridge to the next chapters in this epistemological unit.

4

Intuition and Acquaintance

*"For Bergson . . . intuition is the direct appre-
hension by a knowing subject of himself, of his
mental states, or of anything with which he is immediately acquainted . . . For Russell, we have
acquaintance with anything of which we are directly aware, without the intermediary of any process of inference."*

Melvin Rader

HENRI BERGSON (1859–1941)

Bergson was born in Paris of an English mother and a Polish father. From
his father, an accomplished musician, he may have inherited the artistic
temperament that is reflected throughout his work. Although interested
in literature and science, he devoted himself to philosophy, which he
taught in various lycées and, from 1900 to 1921, at the Collège de France.

In 1888 he published his first major work, *Time and Free Will*, but it
was not until 1908, with the appearance of his *Creative Evolution*, that he
suddenly became the most popular figure in the philosophic world. The
audience gathered in the lecture hall an hour in advance to secure seats,
and people from many countries flocked to his lectures. Among his
honors were election to the Council of the Legion of Honor, the French
Academy, and the Academy of Sciences, and the award of the Nobel Prize
in literature.

After World I, he devoted himself to the cause of peace, presiding over the International Commission for Intellectual Cooperation of the League of Nations. When the Vichy government introduced anti-Semitic measures during the Nazi occupation, it proposed to exempt Bergson despite his Jewish extraction. As a protest against the infamy of the regime, he refused exemption and renounced his various honors. Finally, at the age of eighty-one, he rose from his sickbed and waited in line to register as a Jew. He died a few days later.

Intuition

A comparison of the definitions of metaphysics and the various concepts of the absolute leads to the discovery that philosophers, in spite of their apparent divergencies, agree in distinguishing two profoundly different ways of knowing a thing. The first implies that we move round the object; the second, that we enter into it. The first depends on the point of view at which we are placed and on the symbols by which we express ourselves. The second neither depends on a point of view nor relies on any symbol. The first kind of knowledge may be said to stop at the *relative*; the second, in those cases where it is possible, to attain the *absolute*.

Consider, for example, the movement of an object in space. My perception of the motion will vary with the point of view, moving or stationary, from which I observe it. My expression of it will vary with the systems of axes, or the points or reference, to which I relate it; that is, with the symbols by which I translate it. For this double reason I call such motion *relative*: in the one case, as in the other, I am placed outside the object itself. But when I speak of an *absolute* movement, I am attributing to the moving object an interior and, so to speak, states of mind; I also imply that I am in sympathy with those states, and that I insert myself in them by an effort of imagination. Then, according as the object is moving or stationary, according as it adopts one movement or another, what I experience will vary. And what I experience will depend neither on the point of view I may take up in regard to the object, since I am inside the object itself, nor on the symbols by which I may translate the motion, since I have rejected all translations in order to possess the original. In short, I shall no longer grasp the movement from without, remaining where I am, but from where it is, from within, as it is in itself. I shall possess an absolute.

Consider, again, a character whose adventures are related to me in a novel.

From *An Introduction to Metaphysics*, trans. T. E. Hulme. Copyright 1912 by G. P. Putnam's Sons.

The author may multiply the traits of his hero's character, may make him speak and act as much as he pleases, but all this can never be equivalent to the simple and indivisible feeling which I should experience if I were able for an instant to identify myself with the person of the hero himself. Out of that indivisible feeling, as from a spring, all the words, gestures, and actions of the man would appear to me to flow naturally. They would no longer be accidents which, added to the idea I had already formed of the character, continually enriched that idea, without ever completing it. The character would be given to me all at once, in its entirety, and the thousand incidents which manifest it, instead of adding themselves to the idea and so enriching it, would seem to me, on the contrary, to detach themselves from it, without, however, exhausting it or impoverishing its essence. All the things I am told about the man provide me with so many points of view from which I can observe him. All the traits which describe him, and which can make him known to me only by so many comparisons with persons or things I know already, are signs by which he is expressed more or less symbolically. Symbols and points of view, therefore, place me outside him; they give me only what he has in common with others, and not what belongs to him and to him alone. But that which is properly himself, that which constitutes his essence, cannot be perceived from without, being internal by definition, nor be expressed by symbols, being incommensurable with everything else. Description, history, and analysis leave me here in the relative.

Coincidence with the person himself would alone give me the absolute.

It is in this sense, and in this sense only, that *absolute* is synonymous with *perfection*. Were all the photographs of a town, taken from all possible points of view, to go on indefinitely completing one another, they would never be equivalent to the solid town in which we talk about. Were all the translations of a poem into all possible languages to add together their various shades of meaning and, correcting each other by a kind of mutual retouching, to give a more and more faithful image of the poem they translate, they would yet never succeed in rendering the inner meaning of the original. A representation taken from a certain point of view, a translation made with certain symbols, will always remain imperfect in comparison with the object of which a view has been taken, or which the symbols seek to express. But the absolute, which is the object and not its representation, the original and not its translation, is perfect, by being perfectly what it is.

It is doubtless for this reason that the *absolute* has often been identified with the *infinite*. Suppose that I wished to communicate to some one who did not know Greek the extraordinarily simple impression that a passage in Homer makes upon me; I should first give a translation of the lines, I should then comment on my translation, and then develop the commentary; in this way, by piling up explanation on explanation, I might approach nearer and nearer to what I wanted to express; but I should never quite reach it. When you raise your arm, you accomplish a movement of which you have, from within, a simple perception; but for me, watching it from the outside, your arm passes through one point, then through another, and between these two there will be still other points; so that, if I began to count, the operation would go on forever. Viewed from the inside, then, an absolute is a simple thing; but looked at from the outside, that is to say, relatively to other things, it becomes, in relation to these signs which express it, the gold coin for which we never seem able to finish giving small change. Now, that which lends itself at the same time both to an indivisible apprehension and to an inexhaustible enumeration is, by the very definition of the word, an infinite.

It follows from this that an absolute could only be given in an *intuition*, whilst everything else falls within the province of *analysis*. By intuition is meant the kind of *intellectual sympathy* by which one places oneself within an object in order to coincide with what is unique in it and consequently inexpressible. Analysis, on the contrary, is the operation which reduces the object to elements already known, that is, to elements common both to it and other objects. To analyze, therefore, is to express a thing as a function of something other than itself. All analysis is thus a translation, a development into symbols, a representation taken from successive points of view from which we note as many resemblances as possible between the new object which we are studying and others which we believe we know already. In its eternally unsatisfied desire to embrace the object around which it is compelled to turn, analysis multiplies without end the number of its points of view in order to complete its always incomplete representation, and ceaselessly varies its symbols that it may perfect the always imperfect translation. It goes on, therefore, to infinity. But intuition, if intuition is possible, is a simple act.

Now it is easy to see that the ordinary function of positive science is analysis. Positive science works, then, above all, with symbols. Even the most concrete of the natural sciences, those concerned with life, confine themselves to the visible form of living beings, their organs and anatomical elements. They make comparisons between these forms, they reduce the more complex to the more simple; in short, they study the workings of life in what is, so to speak, only its visual symbol. If there exists any means of possessing a reality absolutely instead of knowing it relatively, of placing oneself within it instead of looking at it from outside points of view, of having the intuition instead of making the analysis: in short, of seizing it without any expression, translation, or symbolic representation —metaphysics is that means. *Metaphysics, then, is the science which claims to dispense with symbols.*

There is one reality, at least, which we all seize from within, by intuition and not by simple analysis. It is our own personality in its flowing through time — our self which endures. We may sympathize intellectually with nothing else, but we certainly sympathize with our own selves.

When I direct my attention inward to contemplate my own self (supposed for the moment to be inactive), I perceive at first, as a crust solidified on the surface, all the perceptions which come to it from the material world. These perceptions are clear, distinct, juxtaposed or juxtaposable one with another; they tend to group themselves into objects. Next, I notice the memories which more or less adhere to these perceptions and which serve to interpret them. These memories have been detached, as it were, from the depth of my personality, drawn to the surface by the perceptions which resemble them; they rest on the surface of my mind without being absolutely myself. Lastly, I feel the stir of tendencies and motor habits — a crowd of virtual actions, more or less firmly bound to these perceptions and memories. All these clearly defined elements appear more distinct from me, the more distinct they are from each other. Radiating, as they do, from within outwards, they form, collectively, the surface of a sphere which tends to grow larger and lose itself in the exterior world. But if I draw myself in from the periphery towards the center, if I search in the depth of my being that which is most uniformly, most constantly, and most enduringly myself, I find an altogether different thing.

There is, beneath these sharply cut crystals and this frozen surface, a continuous flux which is not comparable to any flux I have ever seen. There is a succession of states, each of which announces that which follows and contains that which precedes it. They can, properly speaking, only be said to form multiple states when I have already passed them and turn back to observe their track. Whilst I was experiencing them they were so solidly organized, so profoundly animated with a common life, that I could not have said where any one of them finished or where another commenced. In reality no one of them begins or ends, but all extend into each other.

This inner life may be compared to the unrolling of a coil, for there is no living being who does not feel himself coming gradually to the end of his rôle; and to live is to grow old. But it may just as well be compared to a continual rolling up, like that of a thread on a ball, for our past follows us, it swells incessantly with the present that it picks up on its way; and consciousness means memory.

But actually it is neither an unrolling nor a rolling up, for these two similes evoke the idea of lines and surfaces whose parts are homogeneous and superposable on one another. Now, there are no two identical moments in the life of the same conscious being. Take the simplest sensation, suppose it constant, absorb in it the entire personality: the consciousness which will accompany this sensation cannot remain identical with itself for two consecutive moments, because the second moment always contains, over and above the first, the memory that the first has bequeathed to it. A consciousness which could experience two identical moments would be a consciousness without memory. It would die and be born again continually. In what other way could one represent unconsciousness?

It would be better, then, to use as a comparison the myriad-tinted spectrum, with its insensible gradations leading from one shade to another. A current of feeling which passed along the spectrum, assuming in turn the tint of each of its shades, would experience a series of gradual changes, each of which would announce the one to follow and would sum up those which preceded it. Yet even here the successive shades of the spectrum always remain external one to another. They are juxtaposed; they occupy space. But pure duration, on the contrary, excludes all idea of juxtaposition, reciprocal externality, and extension

Let us, then, rather, imagine an infinitely small elastic body, contracted, if it were possible, to a mathematical point. Let this be drawn out gradually in such a manner that from the point comes a constantly lengthening line. Let us fix our attention not on the line as a line, but on the action by which it is traced. Let us bear in mind that this action, in spite of its duration, is indivisible if accomplished without stopping, that if a stopping-point is inserted, we have two actions instead of one, that each of these separate actions is then the indivisible operation of which we speak, and that it is not the moving action itself which is divisible, but, rather, the stationary line it leaves behind it as its track in space. Finally, let us free ourselves from the space which underlies the movement in order to consider only the movement itself, the act of tension or extension; in short, pure mobility. We shall have this time a more faithful image of the development of our self in duration.

However, even this image is incomplete, and, indeed, every comparison will be insufficient, because the unrolling of our duration resembles in some of its aspects the unity of an advancing movement and in others the multiplicity of expanding states; and, clearly, no metaphor can express one of these two aspects without sacrificing the other. If I use the comparison of the spectrum with its thousand shades, I have before me a thing already made, whilst duration is continually in the making. If I think of an elastic which is being stretched, or of a spring which is extended or relaxed, I forget the richness of color, characteristic of duration that is lived, to see only the simple movement by which consciousness passes from one shade to another. The inner life is all this at once: variety of qualities, continuity of progress, and unity of direction. It cannot be represented by images.

But it is even less possible to represent it by *concepts*, that is by abstract, general, or simple ideas. It is true that no image can reproduce exactly the original feeling I have of the flow of my own conscious life. But it is not even necessary that I should attempt to render it. If a man is incapable of getting for himself the intuition of the constitutive duration of his own being, nothing will ever give it to him, concepts no more than images. Here the single aim of the philosopher should be to promote a certain effort, which in most men is usually fettered by habits of mind more useful to life. Now the image has at least this advantage, that it keeps us in the concrete. No image can replace the intuition of duration, but many diverse images, borrowed from very different orders of things, may, by the convergence of their action, direct consciousness to the precise point where there is a certain intuition to be seized. By choosing images as dissimilar as possible, we shall prevent any one of them from usurping the place of the intuition it is intended to call up, since it would then be driven away at once by its rivals. By providing that, in spite of their differences of aspect, they all require from the mind the same kind of attention, and in some sort the same degree of tension, we shall gradually accustom consciousness to a particular and clearly-defined disposition — that precisely which it must adopt in order to appear to itself as it really is, without any veil. But, then, consciousness must at least consent to make the effort. For it will have been shown nothing: It will simply have been placed in the attitude it must take up in order to make the desired effort, and so come by itself to the intuition. Concepts on the contrary —especially if they are simple — have the disadvantage of being in reality symbols substituted for the object they symbolize, and demand no effort on our part. Examined closely, each of them, it would be seen, retains only that part of the object which is common to it and to others, and expresses, still more than the image does, a *comparison* between the object and others which resemble it. But as the comparison has made manifest a resemblance, as the resemblance is a property of the object, and as a property has every appearance of being a *part* of the object which possesses it, we easily persuade ourselves that by setting concept beside concept we are reconstructing the whole of the object with its parts, thus

obtaining, so to speak, its intellectual equivalent. In this way we believe that we can form a faithful representation of duration by setting in line the concepts of unity, multiplicity, continuity, finite or infinite divisibility, etc. There precisely is the illusion. There also is the danger. Just in so far as abstract ideas can render service to analysis, that is, to the scientific study of the object in its relations to other objects, so far are they incapable of replacing intuition, that is, the metaphysical investigation of what is essential and unique in the object. For on the one hand these concepts, laid side by side, never actually give us more than an artificial reconstruction of the object, of which they can only symbolize certain general, and, in a way, impersonal aspects; it is therefore useless to believe that with them we can seize a reality of which they present to us the shadow alone. And, on the other hand, besides the illusion there is also a very serious danger. For the concept generalizes at the same time as it abstracts. The concept can only symbolize a particular property by making it common to an infinity of things. It therefore always more or less deforms the property by the extension it gives to it. Replaced in the metaphysical object to which it belongs, a property coincides with the object, or at least moulds itself on it, and adopts the same outline. Extracted from the metaphysical object, and presented in a concept, it grows indefinitely larger, and goes beyond the object itself, since henceforth it has to contain it, along with a number of other objects. Thus the different concepts that we form of the properties of a thing inscribe round it so many circles, each much too large and none of them fitting it exactly. And yet, in the thing itself the properties coincided with the thing, and coincided consequently with one another. So that if we are bent on reconstructing the object with concepts, some artifice must be sought whereby this coincidence of the object and its properties can be brought about. For example, we may choose one of the concepts and try, starting from it, to get round to the others. But we shall then soon discover that according as we start from one concept or another, the meeting and combination of the concepts will take place in an altogether different way. According as we start, for example, from unity or from multiplicity, we shall have to conceive differently the multiple unity of duration. Everything will depend on the weight we attribute to this or that concept, and this weight will always be arbitrary, since the concept extracted from the object has no weight, being only the shadow of a body. In this way, as many different *systems* will spring up as there are external points of view from which the reality can be examined, or larger circles in which it can be enclosed. Simple concepts have, then, not only the inconvenience of dividing the concrete unity of the object into so many symbolical expressions; they also divide philosophy into distinct schools, each of which takes its seat, chooses its counters, and carries on with the others a game that will never end. Either metaphysics is only this play of ideas, or else, if it is a serious occupation of the mind, if it is a science and not simply an exercise, it must transcend concepts in order to reach intuition. Certainly, concepts are necessary to it, for all the other sciences work as a rule with concepts, and metaphysics cannot dispense with the other sciences. But it is only truly itself when it goes beyond the concept, or at least when it frees itself from rigid and ready-made concepts in order to create a kind very different from those which we habitually use; I mean supple, mobile, and almost fluid representations, always ready to mould themselves on the fleeting forms of intuition. We shall return later to this important point. Let it suffice us for the moment to have shown that our duration can be presented to us directly in an intuition, that it can be suggested to us indirectly by images, but that it can never — if we confine the word *concept* to its proper meaning — be enclosed in a conceptual representation. . . .

Thinking usually consists in passing from concepts to things, and not from things to concepts. To know a reality, in the usual sense of the word "know," is to take ready-made concepts, to portion them out and to mix them together until a practical equivalent of the reality is obtained. But it must be remembered that the normal work of the intellect is far from being disinterested. We do not aim generally at knowledge for the sake of knowledge, but in order to take sides, to draw profit — in short, to satisfy an interest. We inquire up to what point the object we seek to know is *this* or *that*, to what known class it belongs, and what kind of action, bearing, or attitude it should suggest to us. These different possible actions and attitudes are so many *conceptual directions* of our thought, determined once for all; it remains only to follow them: in that precisely consists the application of concepts to things. To try to fit a concept on an object is simply to ask what we can do with the object, and what it can do for us. To label an object with a certain concept is to mark in precise terms the kind of action or attitude the object should suggest to us. All knowledge, properly so called, is then oriented in a certain direction, or taken from a certain point of view. It is true that our interest is often complex. This is why it happens that our knowledge of the same object may face several successive directions and may be taken from various points of view. It is this which constitutes, in the usual meaning of the terms, a "broad" and "comprehensive" knowledge of the object; the object is then brought not under one single concept, but under several in which it is supposed to "participate." How does it participate in all these concepts at the same time? This is a question which does not concern our practical action and about which we need not trouble. It is, therefore, natural and legitimate in daily life to proceed by the juxtaposition and portioning out of concepts; no philosophical difficulty will arise from this procedure, since by a tacit agreement we shall abstain from philosophizing. But to carry this *modus operandi* into philosophy, to pass here also from concepts to the thing, to use in order to obtain a disinterested knowledge of an object (that this time we desire to grasp as it is in itself) a manner of knowing inspired by a determinate interest, consisting by definition in an externally-taken view of the object, is to go against the end that we

have chosen, to condemn philosophy to an eternal skirmishing between the schools and to install contradiction in the very heart of the object and of the method. Either there is no philosophy possible, and all knowledge of things is a practical knowledge aimed at the profit to be drawn from them, or else philosophy consists in placing oneself within the object itself by an effort of intuition.

. . . Analysis operates always on the immobile, whilst intuition places itself in mobility, or, what comes to the same thing, in duration. There lies the very distinct line of demarcation between intuition and analysis. The real, the experienced, and the concrete are recognized by the fact that they are variability itself, the element by the fact that it is invariable. And the element is invariable by definition, being a diagram, a simplified reconstruction, often a mere symbol, in any case a motionless view of the moving reality.

But the error consists in believing that we can reconstruct the real with these diagrams. As we have already said and may as well repeat here — from intuition one can pass to analysis, but not from analysis to intuition.

Out of variability we can make as many variations, qualities and modifications as we please, since these are so many static views, taken by analysis, of the mobility given to intuition. But these modifications, put end to end, will produce nothing which resembles variability, since they are not parts of it, but elements, which is quite a different thing.

Consider, for example, the variability which is nearest to homogeneity, that of movement in space. Along the whole of this movement we can imagine possible stoppages; these are what we call the positions of the moving body, or the points by which it passes. But with these positions, even with an infinite number of them, we shall never make movement. They are not parts of the movement, they are so many snapshots of it; they are, one might say, only supposed stopping-places. The moving body is never really *in* any of the points; the most we can say is that it passes through them. But passage, which is movement, has nothing in common with stoppage, which is immobility. A movement cannot be superposed on an immobility, or it would then coincide with it, which would be a contradiction. The points are not *in* the movement, as parts, nor even *beneath* it, as positions occupied by the moving body. They are simply projected by us under the movement, as so many places where a moving body, which by hypothesis does not stop, would be it if were to stop. They are not, therefore, properly speaking, positions, but "suppositions," aspects, or points of view of the mind. But how could we construct a thing with points of view?

Nevertheless, this is what we try to do whenever we reason about movement, and also about time, for which movement serves as a means of representation. As a result of an illusion deeply rooted in our mind, and because we cannot prevent ourselves from considering analysis as the equivalent of intuition, we begin by distinguishing along the whole extent of the movement, a certain number of possible stoppages or points, which we make, whether they like it or no, parts of the movement. Faced with our impotence to reconstruct the movement with these points, we insert other points, believing that we can in this way get nearer to the essential mobility in the movement. Then, as this mobility still escapes us, we substitute for a fixed and finite number of points an "indefinitely increasing" number—thus vainly trying to counterfeit, by the movement of a thought that goes on indefinitely adding points to points, the real and undivided motion of the moving body. Finally, we say that movement is composed of points, but that it comprises, in addition, the obscure and mysterious passage from one position to the next. As if the obscurity was not due entirely to the fact that we have supposed immobility to be clearer than mobility and rest anterior to movement! As if the mystery did not follow entirely from our attempting to pass from stoppages to movement by way of addition, which is impossible, when it is so easy to pass, by simple diminution, from movement to the slackening of movement, and so to immobility! It is movement that we must accustom ourselves to look upon as simplest and clearest, immobility being only the extreme limit of the slowing down of movement, a limit reached only, perhaps, in thought and never realized in nature. What we have done is to seek for the meaning of the poem in the form of the letters of which it is composed; we have believed that by considering an increasing number of letters we would grasp at last the ever-escaping meaning, and in desperation, seeing that it was useless to seek for a part of the sense in each of the letters, we have supposed that it was between each letter and the next that this long-sought fragment of the mysterious sense was lodged! But the letters, it must be pointed out once again, are not parts of the thing, but elements of the symbol. Again, the positions of the moving body are not parts of the movement; they are points of the space which is supposed to underlie the movement. This empty and immobile space which is merely conceived, never perceived, has the value of a symbol only. How could you ever manufacture reality by manipulating symbols?

But the symbol in this case responds to the most inveterate habits of our thought. We place ourselves as a rule in immobility, in which we find a point of support for practical purposes, and with this immobility we try to reconstruct motion. We only obtain in this way a clumsy imitation, a counterfeit of real movement, but this imitation is much more useful in life than the intuition of the thing itself would be. Now our mind has an irresistible tendency to consider that idea clearest which is most often useful to it. That is why immobility seems to it clearer than mobility, and rest anterior to movement.

The difficulties to which the problem of movement has given rise from the earliest antiquity have originated in this way. They result always from the fact that we insist on passing from space to movement, from the trajectory to the flight, from immobile positions to mobility, and on passing from one to the other by way of addition. But it is movement which is anterior to immobility, and the relation between positions and a displacement is not that of parts to a whole, but that of the diversity of possible points of view to the real indivisibility of the object.

Many other problems are born of the same illusion. What stationary points are to the movement of a moving body, concepts of different qualities are to the qualitative change of an object. The various concepts into which a change can be analyzed are therefore so many stable views of the instability of the real. And to think of an object — in the usual meaning of the word "think" — is to take one or more of these immobile views of its mobility. It consists, in short, in asking from time to time where the object is, in order that we may know what to do with it. Nothing could be more legitimate, moreover, than this method of procedure, so long as we are concerned only with a practical knowledge of reality. Knowledge, in so far as it is directed to practical matters, has only to enumerate the principal possible attitudes of the thing towards us, as well as our best possible attitude towards it. Therein lies the ordinary function of ready-made concepts, those stations with which we mark out the path of becoming. But to seek to penetrate with them into the inmost nature of things, is to apply to the mobility of the real a method created in order to give stationary points of observation on it. It is to forget that, if metaphysic is possible, it can only be a laborious, and even painful, effort to remount the natural slope of the work of thought, in order to place oneself directly, by a kind of intellectual expansion, within the thing studied: in short, a passage from reality to concepts and no longer from concepts to reality. Is it astonishing that, like children trying to catch smoke by closing their hands, philosophers so often see the object they would grasp fly before them? It is in this way that many of the quarrels between the schools are perpetuated, each of them reproaching the others with having allowed the real to slip away.

. . . The inherent difficulties of metaphysic, the antinomies which it gives rise to, and the contradictions into which it falls, the division into antagonistic schools, and the irreducible opposition between systems are largely the result of our applying, to the disinterested knowledge of the real, processes which we generally employ for practical ends. They arise from the fact that we place ourselves in the immobile in order to lie in wait for the moving thing as it passes, instead of replacing ourselves in the moving thing itself, in order to traverse with it the immobile positions. They arise from our professing to reconstruct reality — which is tendency and consequently mobility — with percepts and concepts whose function it is to make it stationary. With stoppages, however numerous they may be, we shall never make mobility; whereas, if mobility is given, we can, by means of diminution, obtain from it by thought as many stoppages as we desire. In other words, *it is clear that fixed concepts may be extracted by our thought from mobile reality; but there are no means of reconstructing the mobility of the real with fixed concepts.* Dogmatism, however, in so far as it has been a builder of systems, has always attempted this reconstruction.

In this it was bound to fail. It is on this impotence and on this impotence only that the sceptical, idealist, critical doctrines really dwell: in fact, all doctrines that deny to our intelligence the power of attaining the absolute. But because we fail to reconstruct the living reality with stiff and ready-made concepts, it does not allow that we cannot grasp it in some other way. *The demonstrations which have been given of the relativity of our knowledge are therefore tainted with an original vice; they imply, like the dogmatism they attack, that all knowledge must necessarily start from concepts with fixed outlines, in order to clasp with them the reality which flows.*

But the truth is that our intelligence can follow the opposite method. It can place itself within the mobile reality, and adopt its ceaselessly changing direction; in short, can grasp it by means of that *intellectual sympathy* which we call intuition. This is extremely difficult. The mind has to do violence to itself, has to reverse the direction of the operation by which it habitually thinks, has perpetually to revise, or rather to recast, all its categories. But in this way it will attain to fluid concepts, capable of following reality in all its sinuosities and of adopting the very movement of the inward life of things. Only thus will a progressive philosophy be built up, freed from the disputes which arise between the various schools, and able to solve its problems naturally, because it will be released from the artificial expression in terms of which such problems are posited. *To philosophize, therefore, is to invert the habitual direction of the work of thought.*

This inversion has never been practised in a methodical manner; but a profoundly considered history of human thought would show that we owe to it all that is greatest in the sciences, as well as all that is permanent in metaphysics. The most powerful of the methods of investigation at the disposal of the human mind, the infinitesimal calculus, originated from this very inversion. Modern mathematics is precisely an effort to substitute the *being made* for the *ready made*, to follow the generation of magnitudes, to grasp motion no longer from without and in its displayed result, but from within and in its tendency to change; in short, to adopt the mobile continuity of the outlines of things. It is true that it is confined to the outline, being only the science of magnitudes. It is true also that it has only been able to achieve its marvelous applications by the invention of certain symbols, and that if the intuition of which we have just spoken lies at the origin of invention, it is the symbol alone which is concerned in the application. But metaphysics, which aims at no application, can and usually must abstain from converting intuition into symbols. Liberated from the obligation of working for practically useful results, it will indefinitely enlarge the domain of its investigations. What it may lose in comparison with science in utility and exactitude, it will regain in range and extension. Though mathematics is only the science of magnitudes, though mathematical processes are applicable only to quantities, it must not be forgotten that quantity is always quality in a nascent state; it is, we might say, the limiting case of equality. It is natural, then, that metaphysics should adopt the generative idea of our mathematics in order to extend it to all qualities; that is, to reality in general. It will not, by doing this, in any way be moving towards universal mathematics, that chimera of modern philosophy. On the contrary, the farther it goes, the more untranslatable into symbols will be the objects it encounters. But it will at least have begun by getting into contact with the continuity and mobility of the real, just where this contact can be most marvelously utilized. It will have contemplated itself in a mirror which reflects an image of itself, much shrunken, no doubt, but for that reason very luminous. It will have seen with greater clearness what the mathematical processes borrow from concrete reality, and it will continue in the direction of concrete reality, and not in that of mathematical processes. Having then discounted beforehand what is too modest, and at the same time too ambitious, in the following formula, we may say that *the object of metaphysics is to perform* qualitative *differentiations and integrations.*

The reason why this object has been lost sight of, and why science itself has been mistaken in the origin of the processes it employs, is that intuition, once attained, must find a mode of expression and of application which conforms to the habits of our thought, and one which furnishes us, in the shape of well-defined concepts, with the solid points of support which we so greatly need. In that lies the condition of what we call exactitude and precision, and also the condition of the unlimited extension of a general method to particular cases. Now this extension and this work of logical improvement can be continued for centuries, whilst the act which creates the method lasts but for a moment. That is why we so often take the logical equipment of science for science itself, forgetting the metaphysical intuition from which all the rest has sprung.

From the overlooking of this intuition proceeds all that has been said by philosophers and by men of science themselves about the "relativity" of scientific knowledge. *What is relative is the symbolic knowledge by pre-existing concepts, which proceeds from the fixed to the moving, and not the intuitive knowledge which installs itself in that which is moving and adopts the very life of things.* This intuition attains the absolute.

Science and metaphysics therefore come together in intuition. A truly intuitive philosophy would realize the much-desired union of science and metaphysics. While it would make of metaphysics a positive science — that is, a progressive and indefinitely perfectible one — it would at the same time lead the positive sciences, properly so-called, to become conscious of their true scope, often far greater than they imagine. It would put more science into metaphysics, and more metaphysics into science. It would result in restoring the continuity between the intuitions which the various sciences have obtained here and there in the course of their history, and which they have obtained only by strokes of genius.

BERTRAND RUSSELL (1872–1970)

The second son of Viscount Amberly and grandson of Lord John Russell, a famous liberal prime minister, Bertrand Russell was born on May 18, 1872, in the lovely valley of the Wye (described in Wordsworth's *Tintern Abbey*). His mother died when he was two years old and his father when he was three, so the boy was brought up in the home of his grandfather. Until he went to Cambridge University, at the age of eighteen, he lived a solitary life, supervised by German and Swiss governesses and English tutors and seeing little of other children. But Cambridge opened to him "a new world of infinite delight." Here he found mathematics and philosophy extremely exciting and formed warm friendships with a number of brilliant young men, including the philosophers McTaggart, Moore, and Whitehead.

After leaving Cambridge in 1894, Russell spent time abroad, at first as attaché at the British Embassy in Paris. He married at the end of a year's service in the embassy — he was then twenty-two — and went to Germany to study economics and politics. His wife, the sister of Logan Pearsall

Smith, well-known essayist, and a Philadelphia Quaker, persuaded him to spend three months in America in 1896. After these travels, the young couple settled down in a workman's cottage in Sussex, where Russell, with enough income to support his family without other remuneration, devoted himself intensively to philosophy and mathematics.

The next two decades were the most intellectually productive in his long career. During this period he wrote a series of important books, including *A Critical Exposition of the Philosophy of Leibniz* (1900), *The Principles of Mathematics* (1903), *Principia Mathematica* (with Whitehead, 1910–1913), and *Our Knowledge of the External World* (1914). These books, especially *Principia Mathematica*, which was the result of twelve years of intense labor, firmly established Russell's reputation as one of the great figures in modern thought.

Always interested in politics, Russell was profoundly disturbed by the outbreak of World War I and was quite unsatisfied with the melodramatic pronouncements of the belligerent governments. His bold defense of conscientious objectors and his antiwar publications brought him fines and imprisonment, as well as loss of his position as fellow at Trinity College, Cambridge. He emerged from the war a changed man, aware of great social perils and pathological evil in human nature that he had never suspected. He subsequently devoted a large part of his time and energy to writing about political, educational, and moral affairs.

In 1921, after seventeen years of married life, his first marriage was dissolved, and he then wed Dora Winifred Black, who bore him a daughter and son, and from whom he was later divorced. Upon the death of his elder brother in 1931, he succeeded to the family earldom; and in 1934 he remarried, thus making Helen Patricia Spence, a young and beautiful woman, the Countess Russell. In 1950 he received the Nobel Prize for literature, the same honor that Bergson had been awarded. Despite his advanced age, he continued to live a busy and adventurous life, writing prolifically and espousing the cause of peace, until his death in 1970.

Knowledge by Acquaintance and Knowledge by Description

It is often said, as though it were a self-evident truism, that we cannot know that anything exists which we do not know. It is inferred that whatever can in any way be relevant to our experience must be at least capable of being known by us; whence it follows that if matter were essentially something with which we could not become acquainted, matter would be something which we could not know to exist, and which could have for us no importance whatever. It is generally also implied, for reasons which remain obscure, that what can have no importance for us cannot be real, and that therefore matter, if it is not composed of minds or of mental ideas, is impossible and a mere chimaera.

To go into this argument fully at our present stage would be impossible, since it raises points requiring a considerable preliminary discussion; but certain reasons for rejecting the argument may be noticed at once. To begin at the end: there is no reason why what cannot have any *practical* importance for us should not be real. It is true that, if *theoretical* importance is included, everything real is of *some* importance to us, since, as persons desirous of knowing the truth about the universe, we have some interest in everything that the universe contains. But if this sort of interest is included, it is not the case that matter has no importance for us, provided it exists, even if we cannot know that it exists. We can, obviously, suspect that it may exist, and wonder whether it does; hence it is connected with our desire for knowledge, and has the importance of either satisfying or thwarting this desire.

Again, it is by no means a truism, and is in fact false, that we cannot know that anything exists which we do not know. The word 'know' is here used in two different senses. (1) In its first use it is applicable to the sort of knowledge which is opposed to error, the sense in which what we know is *true*, the sense which applies to our beliefs and convictions, i.e. to what are called *judgements*. In this sense of the word we know *that* something is the case. This sort of knowledge may be described as knowledge of *truths*. (2) In the second use of the word 'know' above, the word applies to our knowledge of *things*, which we may call *acquaintance*. This is the sense in which we know sense-data. (The distinction involved is roughly that between *savoir* and *connaître* in French, or between *wissen* and *kennen* in German).

Thus the statement which seemed like a truism becomes, when re-stated, the following: 'We can never truly judge that something with which we are not acquainted exists.' This is by no

From *The Problems of Philosophy* (London, New York, and Toronto: Oxford University Press, 1912). Reprinted by permission.

means a truism, but on the contrary a palpable falsehood. I have not the honour to be acquainted with the Emperor of China, but I truly judge that he exists. It may be said, of course, that I judge this because of other people's acquaintance with him. This, however, would be an irrelevant retort, since, if the principle were true, I could not know that any one else is acquainted with him. But further: there is no reason why I should not know of the existence of something with which *nobody* is acquainted. This point is important, and demands elucidation.

If I am acquainted with a thing which exists, my acquaintance gives me the knowledge that it exists. But it is not true that, conversely, whenever I can know that a thing of a certain sort exists, I or some one else must be acquainted with the thing. What happens, in cases where I have true judgement without acquaintance, is that the thing is known to me by *description*, and that, in virtue of some general principle, the existence of a thing answering to this description can be inferred from the existence of something with which I am acquainted. In order to understand this point fully, it will be well first to deal with the difference between knowledge by acquaintance and knowledge by description, and then to consider what knowledge of general principles, if any, has the same kind of certainty as our knowledge of the existence of our own experiences.

. . . We saw that there are two sorts of knowledge: knowledge of things, and knowledge of truths. . . . We shall be concerned exclusively with knowledge of things, of which in turn we shall have to distinguish two kinds. Knowledge of things, when it is of the kind we call knowledge by *acquaintance*, is essentially simpler than any knowledge of truths, and logically independent of knowledge of truths, though it would be rash to assume that human beings ever, in fact, have acquaintance with things without at the same time knowing some truth about them. Knowledge of things by *description*, on the contrary, always involves, as we shall find in the course of the present chapter, some knowledge of truths as its source and ground. But first of all we must make clear what we mean by 'acquaintance' and what we mean by 'description'.

We shall say that we have *acquaintance* with anything of which we are directly aware, without the intermediary of any process of inference or any knowledge of truths. Thus in the presence of my table I am acquainted with the sense-data that make up the appearance of my table — its colour, shape, hardness, smoothness, etc.; all these are things of which I am immediately conscious when I am seeing and touching my table. The particular shade of colour that I am seeing may have many things said about it — I may say that it is brown, that it is rather dark, and so on. But such statements, though they make me know truths *about* the colour, do not make me know the colour itself any better than I did before: so far as concerns knowledge of the colour itself, as opposed to knowledge of truths about it, I know the colour perfectly and completely when I see it, and no further knowledge of it itself is even theoretically possible. Thus the sense-data which make up the appearance of my table are things with which I have acquaintance, things immediately known to me just as they are.

My knowledge of the table as a physical object, on the contrary, is not direct knowledge. Such as it is, it is obtained through acquaintance with the sense-data that make up the appearance of the table. We have seen that it is possible, without absurdity, to doubt whether there is a table at all, whereas it is not possible to doubt the sense-data. My knowledge of the table is of the kind which we shall call 'knowledge by description'. The table is 'the physical object which causes such-and-such sense-data.' This *describes* the table by means of the sense-data. In order to know anything at all about the table, we must know truths connecting it with things with which we have acquaintance: we must know that 'such-and-such sense-data are caused by a physical object.' There is no state of mind in which we are directly aware of the table; all our knowledge of the table is really knowledge of *truths*, and the actual thing which is the table is not, strictly speaking, known to us at all. We know a description, and we know that there is just one object to which this description applies, though the object itself is not directly known to us. In such a case, we say that our knowledge of the object is knowledge by description.

All our knowledge, both knowledge of things and knowledge of truths, rests upon acquaintance as its foundation. It is therefore important to consider what kinds of things there are with which we have acquaintance.

Sense-data, as we have already seen, are among the things with which we are acquainted; in fact, they supply the most obvious and striking example of knowledge by acquaintance. But if they were the sole example, our knowledge would be very much more restricted than it is. We should only know what is now present to our senses: we could not know anything about the past—not even that there was a past—nor could we know any truths about our sense-data, for all knowledge of truths, as we shall show, demands acquaintance with things which are of an essentially different character from sense-data, the things which are sometimes called 'abstract ideas', but which we shall call 'universals'. We have therefore to consider acquaintance with other things besides sense-data if we are to obtain any tolerably adequate analysis of our knowledge.

The first extension beyond sense-data to be considered is acquaintance by *memory*. It is obvious that we often remember what we have seen or heard or had otherwise present to our senses, and that in such cases we are still immediately aware of what we remember, in spite of the fact that it appears as past and not as present. This immediate knowledge by memory is the source of all our knowledge concerning the past: without it, there could be no knowledge of the past by inference, since we should never know that there was anything past to be inferred.

The next extension to be considered is acquaintance by *introspection*. We are not only aware of being aware of things, but we are often aware of being aware of them. When I see the sun, I am often aware of my seeing the sun;

thus 'my seeing the sun' is an object with which I have acquaintance. When I desire food, I may be aware of my desire for food; thus 'my desiring food' is an object with which I am acquainted. Similarly we may be aware of our feeling pleasure or pain, and generally of the events which happen in our minds. This kind of acquaintance, which may be called self-consciousness, is the source of all our knowledge of mental things. It is obvious that it is only what goes on in our own minds that can be thus known immediately. What goes on in the minds of others is known to us through our perception of their bodies, that is, through the sense-data in us which are associated with their bodies. But for our acquaintance with the contents of our own minds, we should be unable to imagine the minds of others, and therefore we could never arrive at the knowledge that they have minds. It seems natural to suppose that self-consciousness is one of the things that distinguish men from animals: animals, we may suppose, though they have acquaintance with sense-data, never become aware of this acquaintance. I do not mean that they *doubt* whether they exist, but that they have never become conscious of the fact that they have sensations and feelings, nor therefore of the fact that they, the subjects of their sensations and feelings, exist.

We have spoken of acquaintance with the contents of our minds as *self*-consciousness, but it is not, of course, consciousness of our *self*: it is consciousness of particular thoughts and feelings. The question whether we are also acquainted with our bare selves, as

opposed to particular thoughts and feelings, is a very difficult one, upon which it would be rash to speak positively. When we try to look into ourselves we always seem to come upon some particular thought or feeling, and not upon the 'I' which has the thought or feeling. Nevertheless there are some reasons for thinking that we are acquainted with 'I', though the acquaintance is hard to disentangle from other things. To make clear what sort of reason there is, let us consider for a moment what our acquaintance with particular thoughts really involves.

When I am acquainted with 'my seeing the sun,' it seems plain that I am acquainted with two different things in relation to each other. On the one hand there is the sense-datum which represents the sun to me, on the other hand there is that which sees this sense-datum. All acquaintance, such as my acquaintance with the sense-datum which represents the sun, seems obviously a relation between the person acquainted and the object with which the person is acquainted. When a case of acquaintance is one with which I can be acquainted (as I am acquainted with my acquaintance with the sense-datum representing the sun), it is plain that the person acquainted is myself. Thus, when I am acquainted with my seeing the sun, the whole fact with which I am acquainted is 'Self-acquainted-with-sense-datum'.

Further, we know the truth 'I am acquainted with this sense-datum.' It is hard to see how we could know this truth, or even understand what is meant by it, unless we were acquainted with something which we call 'I'. It does not seem necessary to suppose that we are acquainted with a more or less permanent person, the same to-day as yesterday, but it does seem as though we must be acquainted with that thing, whatever its nature, which sees the sun and has acquaintance with sense-data. Thus, in some sense it would seem we must be acquainted with Selves as opposed to our particular experiences. But the question is difficult, and complicated arguments can be adduced on either side. Hence, although acquaintance with ourselves seems *probably* to occur, it is not wise to assert that it undoubtedly does occur.

We may therefore sum up as follows what has been said concerning acquaintance with things that exist. We have acquaintance in sensation with the data of the outer senses, and in introspection with the data of what may be called the inner sense — thoughts, feelings, desires, etc.; we have acquaintance in memory with things which have been data either of the outer senses or of the inner sense. Further, it is probable, though not certain, that we have acquaintance with Self, as that which is aware of things or has desires towards things.

In addition to our acquaintance with particular existing things, we also have acquaintance with what we shall call *universals*, that is to say, general ideas, such as *whiteness*, *diversity*, *brotherhood*, and so on. Every complete sentence must contain at least one word which stands for a universal, since all verbs have a meaning which is universal. . . . For the present, it is only necessary to guard against the supposition that whatever we can be acquainted with must be something particular and existent. Awareness of universals is called *conceiving*, and a universal of which we are aware is called a *concept*.

It will be seen that among the objects with which we are acquainted are not included physical objects (as opposed to sense-data), nor other people's minds. These things are known to us by what I call 'knowledge by description', which we must now consider.

By a 'description' I mean any phrase of the form 'a so-and-so' or 'the so-and-so'. A phrase of the form 'a so-and-so' shall call an 'ambiguous' description; a phrase of the form 'the so-and-so' (in the singular) I shall call a 'definite' description. Thus 'a man' is an ambiguous description, and 'the man with the iron mask' is a definite description. There are various problems connected with ambiguous descriptions, but I pass them by, since they do not directly concern the matter we are discussing, which is the nature of our knowledge concerning objects in cases where we know that there is an object answering to a definite description, though we are not *acquainted* with any such object. This is a matter which is concerned exclusively with *definite* descriptions. I shall therefore, in the sequel, speak simply of 'descriptions' when I mean 'definite descriptions'. Thus a description will mean any phrase of the form 'the so-and-so' in the singular.

We shall say that an object is 'known by description' when we know that it is 'the so-and-so', i.e. when we know that there is one object, and no more, having a certain property; and it will generally be implied that we do not have knowledge of the same object by acquaintance. We know that the man with the iron mask existed, and many propositions are known about him; but we do not know who he was. We know that the candidate who gets the most votes will be elected, and in this case we are very likely also acquainted (in the only sense in which one can be acquainted with some one else) with the man who is, in fact, the candidate who will get most votes; but we do not know which of the candidates he is, i.e. we do not know any proposition of the form 'A is the candidate who will get most votes where A is one of the candidates by name. We shall say that we have 'merely descriptive knowledge' of the so-and-so when, although we know that the so-and-so exists, and although we may possibly be acquainted with the object which is, in fact, the so-and-so, yet we do not know any proposition '*a* is the so-and-so', where *a* is something with which we are acquainted.

When we say 'the so-and-so exists,' we mean that there is just one object which is the so-and-so. The proposition '*a* is the so-and-so' means that *a* has the property so-and-so, and nothing else has. 'Mr. A. is the Unionist candidate for this constituency' means 'Mr. A. is the Unionist candidate for this constituency, and no one else is.' 'The Unionist candidate for this constituency exists' means 'some one is a Unionist candidate for this constituency, and no one else is'. Thus, when we are acquainted with an object which is the so-and-so, we know that the so-and-so exists; but we may know that the so-and-so exists when we are not acquainted with any object which we

know to be the so-and-so, and even when we are not acquainted with any object which, in fact, is the so-and-so.

Common words, even proper names, are usually really descriptions. That is to say, the thought in the mind of a person using a proper name correctly can generally only be expressed explicitly if we replace the proper name by a description. Moreover, the description required to express the thought will vary for different people, or for the same person at different times. The only thing constant (so long as the name is rightly used) is the object to which the name applies. But so long as this remains constant, the particular description involved usually makes no difference to the truth or falsehood of the proposition in which the name appears.

Let us take some illustrations. Suppose some statement made about Bismarck. Assuming that there is such a thing as direct acquaintance with oneself, Bismarck himself might have used his name directly to designate the particular person with whom he was acquainted. In this case, if he made a judgement about himself, he himself might be constituent of the judgement. Here the proper name has the direct use which it always wishes to have, as simply standing for a certain object, and not for a description of the object. But if a person who knew Bismarck made a judgement about him, the case is different. What this person was acquainted with were certain sense-data which he connected (rightly, we will suppose) with Bismarck's body. His body, as a physical object, and still more his mind, were only known as the body and the mind connected with these sense-data. That is, they were known by description. It is, of course, very much a matter of chance which characteristics of a man's appearance will come into a friend's mind when he thinks of him; thus the description actually in the friend's mind is accidental. The essential point is that he knows that the various descriptions all apply to the same entity, in spite of not being acquainted with the entity in question.

When we, who did not know Bismarck, make a judgement about him, the description in our minds will probably be some more or less vague mass of historical knowledge — far more, in most cases, than is required to identify him. But, for the sake of illustration, let us assume that we think of him as 'the first Chancellor of the German Empire'. Here all the words are abstract except 'German'. The word 'German' will, again, have different meanings for different people. To some it will recall travels in Germany, to some the look of Germany on the map, and so on. But if we are to obtain a description which we know to be applicable, we shall be compelled, at some point, to bring in a reference to a particular with which we are acquainted. Such reference is involved in any mention of past, present, and future (as opposed to definite dates), or of here and there, or of what others have told us. Thus it would seem that, in some way or other, a description known to be applicable to a particular must involve some reference to a particular with which we are acquainted, if our knowledge about the thing described is not to be merely what follows *logically* from the description. For example, 'the most long-lived of men' is a description involving only universals, which must apply to some man, but we can make no judgements concerning this man which involve knowledge about him beyond what the description gives. If, however, we say, 'The first Chancellor of the German Empire was an astute diplomatist,' we can only be assured of the truth of our judgement in virtue of something with which we are acquainted — usually a testimony heard or read. Apart from the information we convey to others, apart from the fact about the actual Bismarck, which gives importance to our judgement, the thought we really have contains the one or more particulars involved, and otherwise consists wholly of concepts.

All names of places — London, England, Europe, the Earth, the Solar System — similarly involve, when used, descriptions which start from some one or more particulars with which we are acquainted. I suspect that even the Universe, as considered by metaphysics, involves such a connexion with particulars. In logic, on the contrary, where we are concerned not merely with what does exist, but with whatever might or could exist or be, no reference to actual particulars is involved.

It would seem that, when we make a statement about something only known by description, we often *intend* to make our statement, not in the form involving the description, but about the actual thing described. That is to say, when we say anything about Bismarck, we should like, if we could, to make the judgement which Bismarck alone can make, namely, the judgement of which he himself is a constituent. In this we are necessarily defeated, since the actual Bismarck is unknown to us. But we know that there is an object B, called Bismarck, and that B was an astute diplomatist. We can thus *describe* the proposition we should like to affirm, namely, 'B was an astute diplomatist,' where B is the object which was Bismarck. If we are describing Bismarck as 'the first Chancellor of the German Empire,' the proposition we should like to affirm may be described as 'the proposition asserting, concerning the actual object which was the first Chancellor of the German Empire, that this object was an astute diplomatist.' What enables us to communicate in spite of the varying descriptions we employ is that we know there is a true proposition concerning the actual Bismarck, and that however we may vary the description (so long as the description is correct) the proposition described is still the same. This proposition, which is described and is known to be true, is what interests us; but we are not acquainted with the proposition itself, and do not know *it*, though we know it is true.

It will be seen that there are various stages in the removal from acquaintance with particulars: there is Bismarck to people who knew him; Bismarck to those who only know of him through history; the man with the iron mask; the longest-lived of men. These are progressively further removed from acquaintance with particulars; the first comes as near to acquaintance as is possible in regard to another person; in the second, we shall still be said to know 'who Bismarck was'; in the third, we do not know who was the man with the iron mask, though we can know many propositions about him which are not logically deducible from the fact that he wore an iron mask; in the fourth, finally, we know nothing beyond what is logically deducible from the definition of the man. There is a similar hierarchy in the region of universals. Many universals, like many particulars, are only known to us by description. But here, as in the case of particulars, knowledge concerning what is known by description is ultimately reducible to knowledge concerning what is known by acquaintance.

The fundamental principle in the analysis of propositions containing descriptions is this: *Every proposition which we can understand must be composed wholly of constituents with which we are acquainted.*

We shall not at this stage attempt to answer all the objects which may be urged against this fundamental principle. For the present, we shall merely point out that, in some way or other, it must be possible to meet these objections, for it is scarcely conceivable that we can make a judgement or entertain a supposition without knowing what it is that we are judging or supposing about. We must attach *some* meaning to the words we use, if we are to speak significantly and not utter mere noise; and the meaning we attach to words must be something with which we are acquainted. Thus when, for example, we make a statement about Julius Caesar, it is plain that Julius Caesar himself is not before our minds, since we are not acquainted with him. We have in mind some *description* of Julius Caesar: 'the man who was assassinated on the Ides of March,' 'the founder of the Roman Empire,' or, perhaps, merely 'the man whose name was *Julius Caesar.*' (In this last description, *Julius Caesar* is a noise or shape with which we are acquainted.) Thus our statement does not mean quite what it seems to mean, but means something involving, instead of Julius Caesar, some description of him which is composed wholly of particulars and universals with which we are acquainted.

The chief importance of knowledge by description is that it enables us to pass beyond the limits of our private experience. In spite of the fact that we can only know truths which are wholly composed of terms which we have experienced in acquaintance, we can yet have knowledge by description of things which we have never experienced. In view of the very narrow range of our immediate experience, this result is vital, and until it is understood much of our knowledge must remain mysterious and therefore doubtful.

COMMENT

The word *intuition* is derived from the Latin *intuere* — "to look at." The looking or directness of the insight, is its fundamental mark. In intuitive knowledge, as John Locke wrote, "the mind . . . perceives the truth as the eye doth the light, only by being directed towards it."[1] Intuition can be defined as the direct apprehension that a proposition is true, or that something is the case.

Both Descartes and Bergson regard intuition as basic to philosophic method, but each differs in his conception of intuitive insight. For Descartes it is the immediate grasp of truths, for example, that six is more than five. As the source of axiomatic truths, it provides the premises from which deduction draws forth, by a process of logical inference, the conclusions that necessarily follow. For Bergson, in contrast, intuition is the direct apprehension by a knowing subject of oneself, of one's mental states, or of anything with which one is immediately acquainted. It is more akin to sympathetic imagination than to abstract reasoning, and valued more for its own sake than as a foundation for deductive inference. It is an imaginative realization of the real rather than the fictitious.

The Bergsonian type of intuition is vividly illustrated by a number of passages in the letters of John Keats. Consider, for example, his characterization of a poet's grasp of things:

As to the poetical Character itself . . . it is not itself — it has no self — it is every thing and nothing — It has no character — it

[1] *An Essay Concerning Human Understanding*, Book IV, Chap. 2.

enjoys light and shade; it lives in gusto, be it foul or fair, high or low, rich or poor, mean or elevated — It has as much delight in conceiving an Iago as an Imogen. What shocks the virtuous philosopher, delights the camelion Poet. It does not harm from its relish of the dark side of things any more than from its taste for the bright one; because they both end in speculation. A Poet is the most unpoetical of any thing in existence; because he has no Identity — he is continually in for [ming?] — and filling some other Body — The Sun, the Moon, the Sea and Men and Women who are creatures of impulse are poetical and have about them an unchangeable attribute — the poet has none; no identity — he is certainly the most unpoetical of all God's Creatures. . . . It is a wretched thing to confess; but is a very fact that not one word I ever utter can be taken for granted as an opinion growing out of my identical nature — how can it, when I have no nature? When I am in a room with People if I ever am free from speculating on creations of my own brain, then not myself goes home to myself: but the identity of every one in the room begins to press upon me [so] that I am in a very little time an[ni]hilated — not only among Men; it would be the same in a Nursery of children.

Keats was aware in his keen, intuitive way not only of human beings but also of animals and even inanimate things. "I go among the Fields," he wrote, "and catch a glimpse of a Stoat or a fieldmouse peeping out of the withered grass — the creature hath a purpose and its eyes are bright with it." In another letter he remarked, ". . . If a Sparrow come before my window I take part in its existence and pick about the Gravel." Keats claimed that he could imaginatively project himself into a moving billiard ball, and conceive, as though its qualities were his own, the "roundness, smoothness and volubility and the rapidity of its motion."

According to Bergson, all humans have the ability to intuit but only genius exhibits it to a high degree. "Between nature and ourselves," he declares, "nay, between ourselves and our own consciousness a veil is interposed: a veil that is dense and opaque for the common herd — thin, almost transparent, for the artist and the poet." The ordinary man moves about amid "generalities and symbols," but the intuitive person, whether called an artist or not, brushes aside "the utilitarian symbols, the conventional and socially accepted generalities, in short everything that veils reality from us, in order to bring us face to face with reality itself."[2] In its innermost character, this reality is *duration* — the ceaseless, undivided

[2]*Laughter* (London: Macmillan, 1921), pp. 151, 157.

flow of time, not clock time, with its mathematical abstractness, but *living* time, in its qualitative richness, fullness, and density.

Bergson distinguishes between *intellect*, the analytical faculty whose function is to facilitate action by dissecting and classifying, and *intuition*, the synthetic faculty whose function is to grasp the wholeness and concrete individuality of things. On the basis of these distinctions, he rejects the claims of mechanistic and materialistic philosophy and espouses a theory of free will and creative evolution. There is an irreducible life force, or *élan vital*, moving not toward any fixed or final goal but thrusting upward toward new and higher forms of existence. The downward movement of usable matter governed by the law of entropy is counter to this vital impetus.

There is much in this metaphysics and methodology with which Russell disagrees. Superficially, at least, he and Bergson could scarcely be farther apart. "I prefer sharp outlines and definite separations,"[3] he has remarked, deploring the opposite tendency of Bergson. Whereas the latter leans toward art and mysticism, Russell clings tenaciously to logic, mathematics, and science. "He seems very early to have felt, with justice," G. J. Warnock writes, "that by contrast with his own work and that of a few others in logic and the philosophy of mathematics, the writings of most contemporary philosophers were exceedingly loose, amateurish, and obscure. He was fond of saying that philosophy ought to be, as it had never yet been, 'scientific'—not only not less rigorous and exact, but more so, than mathematics and the physical sciences."[4] Judged by this standard, Bergson's "irrationalism" seemed to him deplorable.

During the very long period in which Russell had been writing, he had continued to develop, modify, and change his ideas. The views we are here considering are those expressed in *The Problems of Philosophy* (1912)—an early work. It is here that he develops, in the excerpt reprinted in this book, the distinction between "knowledge by acquaintance" and "knowledge by description," the latter being ultimately based on the former. But it is unnecessary for me to summarize an argument that is so lucid. To refute those who would exaggerate the opposition between Bergson and Russell, it is sufficient to point out the similarity of "intuition" and "acquaintance." On the basis of this link, the two men stand together in contrast to such rationalists as Descartes, Spinoza, and Leibniz.

[3]*Portraits from Memory* (London: Allen & Unwin, 1956), p. 38.
[4]*English Philosophy Since 1900* (New York: Oxford University Press, 1966), p. 21.

5

Pragmatism

"Pragmatism is the attitude of looking away from first things, principles, 'categories,' supposed necessities; and of looking towards last things, fruits, consequences, facts."

William James

CHARLES SANDERS PEIRCE (1839–1914)

Charles Peirce was born in Cambridge, Massachusetts, the second son of Benjamin Peirce, a professor at Harvard and one of America's foremost mathematicians. At the time of Peirce's birth, Cambridge was one of the main centers of American culture, and the Peirce home was a principal gathering place of celebrities. Such famous scientists as Louis Agassiz and Asa Gray and such great literary figures as Longfellow, Emerson, and Oliver Wendell Holmes were frequent guests. Peirce's father, himself remarkable, gave his son Charles an impressive education in logic, mathematics, philosophy, and experimental science. At the age of twelve, Charles set up a chemical laboratory in which he undertook some rather advanced experiments. At Harvard, which he attended from the age of sixteen until he was twenty, he did not buckle down to a strict routine of study but roamed over a vast philosophical and scientific literature. After graduation, he continued his studies at Harvard, receiving a master's degree in mathematics and an additional degree in chemistry.

This wide reading and scientific training was supplemented by a great deal of practical experience in scientific research. He was an assistant for three years in the Harvard astronomical observatory, where he carried out the investigations published in *Photometric Researches* (1878), the only one of his books to appear during his lifetime. He also conducted extensive scientific research for the U.S. Coastal and Geodetic Survey, with which he was associated from 1861 to 1891. His researches led to important original contributions in chemistry, astronomy, optics, the theory of gravity and pendulum movement, and the determination of weights and measures.

During the 1860s he found time to give a number of lecture courses at Harvard on logic and the history of science, and from 1879 to 1884, he was a lecturer in logic at Johns Hopkins University. He never received a permanent university appointment, however, largely because his ideas were too bold and original and his personality was too eccentric. Publishers showed themselves indifferent to an author who had no official university backing, and consequently a great deal of his writing was never presented to the public during his own lifetime. His reputation at Harvard also suffered as a result of his divorce from his first wife, who belonged to a very respectable family and was popular in Cambridge. Although he contracted a happy second marriage to a French woman, he never quite regained his status in the eyes of the community.

In his younger days, Peirce was a member, along with William James and Oliver Wendell Holmes, Jr., of an intimate circle of brilliant thinkers in Cambridge, but as he grew older he became more isolated. In 1881, at the age of forty-eight, he retired to Milford, Pennsylvania, where he lived in seclusion with his French wife. Here he waged a gradually losing battle against poverty, eking out a small income by writing articles for popular scientific magazines. Dogged by his creditors and seeking intellectual refuge, he would retire to his attic, pulling up a rope ladder after him so that no one could follow. To make matters worse, in the last years of his life, he suffered from a slow-growing cancer. When he finally became too ill to do any sustained work, he was supported mainly by the charity of William James and a few other friends.

During these final years of illness and poverty, he heroically persevered in his philosophical labors, often writing the whole night through. Nothing daunted him — not physical pain, the lack of a publisher, the isolation from friends, the failure to achieve public recognition. He continued to write even when he trembled so much that he was compelled to steady one hand against the other. Only death, at the age of seventy-five, could quell his spirit.

How to Make Our Ideas Clear

I

Whoever has looked into a modern treatise on logic of the common sort, will doubtless remember the two distinctions between *clear* and *obscure* conceptions, and between *distinct* and *confused* conceptions. They have lain in the books now for nigh two centuries, unimproved and unmodified, and are generally reckoned by logicians as among the gems of their doctrine.

A clear idea is defined as one which is so apprehended that it will be recognized wherever it is met with, and so that no other will be mistaken for it. If it fails of this clearness, it is said to be obscure.

This is rather a neat bit of philosophical terminology; yet, since it is clearness that they were defining, I wish the logicians had made their definition a little more plain. Never to fail to recognize an idea, and under no circumstances to mistake another for it, let it come in how recondite a form it may, would indeed imply such prodigious force and clearness of intellect as is seldom met with in this world. On the other hand, merely to have such an acquaintance with the idea as to have become familiar with it, and to have lost all hesitancy in recognizing it in ordinary cases, hardly seems to deserve the name of clearness of apprehension, since after all it only amounts to a subjective feeling of mastery which may be entirely mistaken. I take it, however, that when the logicians speak of "clearness," they mean nothing more than such a familiarity with an idea, since they regard the quality as but a small merit, which needs to be supplemented by another, which they call *distinctness*.

A distinct idea is defined as one which contains nothing which is not clear. This is technical language; by the *contents* of an idea logicians understand whatever is contained in its definition. So that an idea is *distinctly* apprehended, according to them, when we can give a precise definition of it, in abstract terms. Here the professional logicians leave the subject; and I would not have troubled the reader with what they have to say, if it were not such a striking example of how they have been slumbering through ages of intellectual activity, listlessly disregarding the enginery of modern thought, and never dreaming of applying its lessons to the improvement of logic. It is easy to show that the doctrine that familiar use and abstract distinctness make the perfection of apprehension has its only true place in philosophies which have long been extinct; and it is now time to formulate the method of attaining to a more perfect clearness of thought, such as we see and admire in the thinkers of our own time.

This essay is a sequel to "The Fixation of Belief." Reprinted from *Popular Science Monthly*, 1878, with some omissions.

When Descartes set about the reconstruction of philosophy, his first step was to (theoretically) permit scepticism and to discard the practice of the schoolmen of looking to authority as the ultimate source of truth. That done, he sought a more natural fountain of true principles, and professed to find it in the human mind; thus passing, in the directest way, from the method of authority to that of a priority, as described in my first paper. Self-consciousness was to furnish us with our fundamental truths, and to decide what was agreeable to reason. But since, evidently, not all ideas are true, he was led to note, as the first condition of infallibility, that they must be clear. The distinction between an idea *seeming* clear and really being so, never occurred to him. Trusting to introspection, as he did, even for a knowledge of external things, why should he question its testimony in respect to the contents of our own minds? But then, I suppose, seeing men, who seemed to be quite clear and positive, holding opposite opinions upon fundamental principles, he was further led to say that clearness of ideas is not sufficient, but that they need also to be distinct, *i.e.*, to have nothing unclear about them. What he probably meant by this (for he did not explain himself with precision) was, that they must sustain the test of dialectical examination; that they must not only seem clear at the outset, but that discussion must never be able to bring to light points of obscurity connected with them.

Such was the distinction of Descartes, and one sees that it was precisely on the level of his philosophy. It was somewhat developed by Leibnitz. This great and singular genius was as remarkable for what he failed to see as for what he saw. That a piece of mechanism could not do work perpetually without being fed with power in some form, was a thing perfectly apparent to him; yet he did not understand that the machinery of the mind can only transform knowledge, but never originate it, unless it be fed with facts of observation. He thus missed the most essential point of the Cartesian philosophy, which is, that to accept propositions which seem perfectly evident to us is a thing which, whether it be logical or illogical, we cannot help doing. Instead of regarding the matter in this way, he sought to reduce the first principles of science to formulas which cannot be denied without self-contradiction, and was apparently unaware of the great difference between his position and that of Descartes. So he reverted to the old formalities of logic, and, above all, abstract definitions played a great part in his philosophy. It was quite natural, therefore, that on observing that the method of Descartes labored under the difficulty that we may seem to ourselves to have clear apprehensions of ideas which in truth are very hazy, no better remedy occurred to him than to require an abstract definition of every important term. Accordingly, in adopting the distinction of *clear* and *distinct* notions, he described the latter quality as the clear apprehension of everything contained in the definition; and the books have ever since copied his words. There is no danger that his chimerical scheme will ever again be overvalued. Nothing new can ever be learned by analyzing definitions. Nevertheless, our existing beliefs can be set in order by this process, and order is an essential element of intellectual economy, as of every other. It may be acknowledged, therefore, that the books are right in making familiarity with a notion the first step toward clearness of apprehension, and the defining of it the second. But in omitting all mention of any higher perspicuity of thought, they simply mirror a philosophy which was exploded a hundred years ago. That much-admired "ornament of logic"— the doctrine of clearness and distinctness—may be pretty enough, but it is high time to relegate to our cabinet of curiosities the antique *bijou*, and to wear about us something better adapted to modern uses.

The very first lesson that we have a right to demand that logic shall teach us is, how to make our ideas clear; and a most important one it is, depreciated only by minds who stand in need of it. To know what we think, to be masters of our own meaning, will make a solid foundation for great and weighty thought. It is most easily learned by those whose ideas are meager and restricted; and far happier they than such as wallow helplessly in a rich mud of conceptions. A nation, it is true, may, in the course of generations, overcome the disadvantage of an excessive wealth of language and its natural concomitant, a vast, unfathomable deep of ideas. We may see it in history, slowly perfecting its literary forms, sloughing at length its metaphysics, and, by virtue of the untirable patience which is often a compensation, attaining great excellence in every branch of mental ac-

quirement. The page of history is not yet unrolled which is to tell us whether such a people will or will not in the long run prevail over one whose ideas (like the words of their language) are few, but which possesses a wonderful mastery over those which it has. For an individual, however, there can be no question that a few clear ideas are worth more than many confused ones. A young man would hardly be persuaded to sacrifice the greater part of his thoughts to save the rest; and the muddled head is the least apt to see the necessity of such a sacrifice. Him we can usually only commiserate, as a person with a congenital defect. Time will help him, but intellectual maturity with regard to clearness comes rather late, an unfortunate arrangement of Nature, inasmuch as clearness is of less use to a man settled in life, whose errors have in great measure had their effect, than it would be to one whose path lies before him. It is terrible to see how a single unclear idea, a single formula without meaning, lurking in a young man's head, will sometimes act like an obstruction of inert matter in an artery, hindering the nutrition of the brain, and condemning its victim to pine away in the fullness of his intellectual vigor and in the midst of intellectual plenty. Many a man has cherished for years as his hobby some vague shadow of an idea, too meaningless to be positively false; he has, nevertheless, passionately loved it, has made it his companion by day and by night, and has given to it his strength and his life, leaving all other occupations for its sake, and in short has lived with it and for it, until it has become, as it were, flesh of his flesh and bone of his bone; and then he has waked up some bright morning to find it gone, clean vanished away like the beautiful Melusina of the fable, and the essence of his life gone with it. I have myself known such a man; and who can tell how many histories of circle-squarers, metaphysicians, astrologers, and what not, may not be told in the old German story?

II

The principles set forth in the first of these papers lead, at once, to a method of reaching a clearness of thought of a far higher grade than the "distinctness" of the logicians. We have there found that the action of thought is excited by the irritation of doubt, and ceases when belief is attained; so that the production of belief is the sole function of thought. All these words, however, are too strong for my purpose. It is as if I had described the phenomena as they appear under a mental microscope. Doubt and Belief, as the words are commonly employed, relate to religious or other grave discussions. But here I use them to designate the starting of any question, no matter how small or how great, and the resolution of it. If, for instance, in a horse-car, I pull out my purse and find a five-cent nickel and five coppers, I decide, while my hand is going to the purse, in which way I will pay my fare. To call such a question Doubt, and my decision Belief, is certainly to use words very disproportionate to the occasion. To speak of such a doubt as causing an irritation which needs to be appeased, suggests a temper which is uncomfortable to the verge of insanity. Yet, looking at the matter minutely, it must be admitted that, if there is the least hesitation as to whether I shall pay the five coppers or the nickel (as there will be sure to be, unless I act from some previously contracted habit in the matter), though irritation is too strong a word, yet I am excited to such small mental activity as may be necessary to deciding how I shall act. Most frequently doubts arise from some indecision, however momentary, in our action. Sometimes it is not so. I have, for example, to wait in a railway-station, and to pass the time I read the advertisements on the walls, I compare the advantages of different trains and different routes which I never expect to take, merely fancying myself to be in a state of hesitancy, because I am bored with having nothing to trouble me. Feigned hesitancy, whether feigned for mere amusement or with a lofty purpose, plays a great part in the production of scientific inquiry. However the doubt may originate, it stimulates the mind to an activity which may be slight or energetic, calm or turbulent. Images pass rapidly through consciousness, one incessantly melting into another, until at last, when all is over — it may be in a fraction of a second, in an hour, or after long years — we find ourselves decided as to how we should act under such circumstances as those which occasioned our hesitation. In other words, we have attained belief.

In this process we observe two sorts of elements of consciousness, the distinction between which may best be made clear by means of an illustration. In a piece of music there are the separate notes, and there is the air. A single tone may be prolonged for an hour or a day, and it exists as perfectly in each second of that time as in the whole taken together; so that, as long as it is sounding, it might be present to a sense from which everything in the past was as completely absent as the future itself. But it is different with the air, the performance of which occupies a certain time, during the portions of which only portions of it are played. It consists in an orderliness in the succession of sounds which strike the ear at different times; and to perceive it there must be some continuity of consciousness which makes the events of a lapse of time present to us. We certainly only perceive the air by hearing the separate notes; yet we cannot be said to directly hear it, for we hear only what is present at the instant, and an orderliness of succession cannot exist in an instant. These two sorts of objects, what we are *immediately* conscious of and what we are *mediately* conscious of, are found in all consciousness. Some elements (the sensations) are completely present at every instant so long as they last, while others (like thought) are actions having the beginning, middle, and end, and consist in a congruence in the succession of sensations which flow through the mind. They cannot be immediately present to us, but must cover some portion of the past or future. Thought is a thread of melody running through the succession of our sensations.

We may add that just as a piece of music may be written in parts, each part having its own air, so various systems of relationship of succession subsist together between the same sensations. These different systems are distinguished by having different motives, ideas, or functions. Thought is only one such system, for its sole motive, idea, and function, is to produce belief, and whatever does not concern that purpose belongs to some other system of relations. The action of thinking may incidentally have other results; it may serve to amuse us, for example, and among *dillettanti* it is not rare to find those who have so perverted thought to the purposes of pleasure that it seems to vex them to think that the questions upon which they delight to exercise it may ever get finally settled; and a positive discovery which takes a favorite subject out of the arena of literary debate is met with ill-concealed dislike. This disposition is the very debauchery of thought. But the soul and meaning of thought, abstracted from the other elements which accompany it, though it may be voluntarily thwarted, can never be made to direct itself toward anything but the production of belief. Thought in action has for its only possible motive the attainment of thought at rest; and whatever does not refer to belief is no part of the thought itself.

And what, then, is belief? It is the demicadence which closes a musical phrase in the symphony of our intellectual life. We have seen that it has just three properties: First, it is something that we are aware of; second, it appeases the irritation of doubt; and, third, it involves the establishment in our nature of a rule of action, or, say, for short, a *habit*. As it appeases the irritation of doubt, which is the motives for thinking, thought relaxes, and comes to rest for a moment when belief is reached. But, since belief is a rule for action, the application of which involves further doubt and further thought, at the same time that it is a stopping-place, it is also a new starting-place for thought. That is why I have permitted myself to call it thought at rest, although thought is essentially an action. The *final* upshot of thinking is the exercise of volition, and of this thought no longer forms a part; but belief is only a stadium of mental action, an effect upon our nature due to thought, which will influence future thinking.

The essence of belief is the establishment of a habit, and different beliefs are distinguished by the different modes of action to which they give rise. If beliefs do not differ in this respect, if they appease the same doubt by producing the same rule of action, then no mere differences in the manner of consciousness of them can make them different beliefs, any more than playing a tune in different keys is playing different tunes. Imaginary distinctions are often drawn between beliefs which differ only in their mode of expression; —the wrangling which ensues is real enough, however. To believe that any objects are arranged as in Fig. 1, and to believe that they are arranged [as] in Fig. 2, are one and the same belief; yet it is conceivable that a man should assert one proposition and deny the other. Such false distinctions do as much harm as the confusion of beliefs really different, and are among the pitfalls of which we ought constantly to beware, especially when we are upon metaphysical ground. One singular deception of this sort, which often occurs, is to mistake the sensation produced by our own unclearness of thought for a character of the object we are thinking. Instead of perceiving that the obscurity is purely subjective, we fancy that we contemplate a quality of the object which is essentially mysterious; and if our conception be afterward presented to us in a clear form we do not recognize it as the same, owing to the absence of the feeling of unintelligibility. So long as this deception lasts, it obviously puts an impassable barrier in the way of perspicuous thinking; so that it equally interests the opponent of

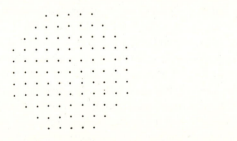

Figure 1

Figure 2

rational thought to perpetuate it, and its adherents to guard against it.

Another such deception is to mistake a mere difference in the grammatical construction of two words for a distinction between the ideas they express. In this pedantic age, when the general mob of writers attend so much more to words than to things, this error is common enough. When I just said that thought is an *action*, and that it consists in a relation, although a person performs an action but not a relation, which can only be the result of an action, yet there was no inconsistency in what I said, but only a grammatical vagueness.

From all these sophisms we shall be perfectly safe so long as we reflect that the whole function of thought is to produce habits of action; and that whatever there is connected with a thought, but irrelevant to its purpose, is an accretion to it, but no part of it. If there be a unity among our sensations which has no reference to how we shall act on a given occasion, as when we listen to a piece of music, why, we do not call that thinking. To develop its meaning, we have, therefore, simply to determine what habits it produces, for what a thing means is simply what habits it involves. Now the identity of a habit depends on how it might lead us to act, not merely under such circumstances as are likely to arise, but under such as might possibly occur, no matter how improbable they may be. What the habit is depends on *when* and *how* it causes us to act. As for the *when*, every stimulus to action is derived from perception; as for the how, every purpose of action is to produce some sensible result. Thus, we come down to what is tangible and conceivably practical, as the root of every real distinction of thought, no matter how subtile it may be; and there is no distinction of meaning so fine as to consist in anything but a possible difference of practice.

To see what this principle leads to, consider in the light of it such a doctrine as that of transubstantiation. The Protestant churches generally hold that the elements of the sacrament are flesh and blood only in a tropical sense; they nourish our souls as meat and the juice of it would our bodies. But the Catholics maintain that they are literally just that; although they possess all the sensible qualities of wafer-cakes and diluted wine. But we can have no conception of wine except what may enter into a belief, either—

1. That this, that, or the other, is wine; or,

2. That wine possesses certain properties.

Such beliefs are nothing but self-notification that we should, upon occasion, act in regard to such things as we believe to be wine according to the qualities which we believe wine to possess. The occasion of such an action would be some sensible perception, the motive of it to produce some sensible result. Thus our action has exclusive reference to what affects the senses, our habit has the same bearing as our action, our belief the same as our habit, our conception the same as our belief; and we can consequently mean nothing by wine but what has certain effects, direct or indirect, upon our senses; and to talk of something as having all the sensible characters of wine, yet being in reality blood, is senseless jargon. Now, it is not my object to pursue the theological question; and having used it as a logical example I drop it, without caring to anticipate the theologian's reply. I only desire to point out how impossible it is that we should have an idea in our minds which relates to anything but conceived sensible effects of things. Our idea of anything *is* our idea of its sensible effects; and if we fancy that we have any other we deceive ourselves, and mistake a mere sensation accompanying the thought for a part of the thought itself. It is absurd to say that thought has any meaning unrelated to its only function. It is foolish for Catholics and Protestants to fancy themselves in disagreement about the elements of the sacrament, if they agree in regard to all their sensible effects, here or hereafter.

It appears, then, that the rule for attaining the third grade of clearness of apprehension is as follows: Consider what effects, which might conceivably have practical bearings, we conceive the object of our conception to have. Then, our conception of these effects is the whole of our conception of the object.

III

Let us illustrate this rule by some examples; and, to begin with the simplest one possible, let us ask what we mean by calling a thing *hard*. Evidently that it will not be scratched by many other substances. The whole conception of this quality, as of every other, lies in its conceived effects. There is absolutely no difference between a hard thing and a soft thing so long as they are not brought to the test. Suppose, then, that a diamond could be crystallized in the midst of a cushion of soft cotton, and should remain there until it was finally burned up. Would it be false to say that that diamond was soft? This seems a foolish question, and would be so, in fact, except in the realm of logic. There such questions are often of the greatest utility as serving to bring logical principles into sharper relief than real discussions ever could. In studying logic we must not put them aside with hasty answers, but must consider them with attentive care, in order to make out the principles involved. We may, in the present case, modify our question, and ask what prevents us from saying that all hard bodies remain perfectly soft until they are touched, when their hardness increases with the pressure until they are scratched. Reflection will show that the reply is this: there would be no *falsity* in such modes of speech. They would involve a modification of our present usage of speech with regard to the words hard and soft, but not of their meanings. For they represent no fact to be different from what it is; only they involve arrangements of facts which would be exceedingly maladroit. This leads us to remark that the question of what would occur under circumstances which do not actually arise is not a question of fact, but only of the most perspicuous arrangement of them. For example, the question of free-will and fate in its simplest form, stripped of verbiage, is something like this: I have done something of which I am ashamed; could I, by an effort of the will, have resisted the temptation, and done otherwise? The philosophical reply is, that this is not a question of fact, but only of the arrangement of facts. Arranging them so as to exhibit what is particularly pertinent to my question—namely, that I ought to blame myself for having done wrong—it is perfectly true to say that, if I had willed to do otherwise than I did, I should have done otherwise. On the other hand, arranging the facts so as to exhibit another important consideration, it is equally true that, when a temptation has once been allowed to work, it will, if it has a certain force, produce its effect, let me struggle how I may. There is no objection to a contradiction in what would result from a false supposition. The *reductio ad absurdum* consists in showing that contradictory results would follow from a hypothesis which is consequently judged to be false. Many questions are involved in the free-will discussion, and I am far from desiring to say that both sides are equally right. On the contrary, I am of opinion that one side denies important facts, and that the other does not. But what I do say is, that the above single question was the origin of the whole doubt; that, had it not been for this question, the controversy would never have arisen; and that this question is perfectly solved in the manner which I have indicated.

Let us next seek a clear idea of weight. This is another very easy case. To say that a body is heavy means simply that, in the absence of opposing force, it will fall. This (neglecting certain specifications of how it will fall,

etc., which exist in the mind of the physicist who uses the word) is evidently the whole conception of weight. It is a fair question whether some particular facts may not *account* for gravity; but what we mean by the force itself is completely involved in its effects. . . .

IV

Let us now approach the subject of logic, and consider a conception which particularly concerns it, that of *reality*. Taking clearness in the sense of familiarity, no idea could be clearer than this. Every child uses it with perfect confidence, never dreaming that he does not understand it. As for clearness in its second grade, however, it would probably puzzle most men, even among those of a reflective turn of mind, to give an abstract definition of the real. Yet such a definition may perhaps be reached by considering the points of difference between reality and its opposite, fiction. A figment is a product of somebody's imagination; it has such characters as his thought impresses upon it. That whose characters are independent of how you or I think is an external reality. There are, however, phenomena within our own minds, dependent upon our thought, which are at the same time real in the sense that we really think them. But though their characters depend on how we think, they do not depend on what we think those characters to be. Thus, a dream has a real existence as a mental phenomenon, if somebody has really dreamt it; that he dreamt so and so, does not depend on what anybody thinks was dreamt, but is completely independent of all opinion on the subject. On the other hand, considering, not the fact of dreaming but the thing dreamt, it retains its peculiarities by virtue of no other fact than that it was dreamt to possess them. Thus we may define the real as that whose characters are independent of what anybody may think them to be.

But, however satisfactory such a definition may be found, it would be a great mistake to suppose that it makes the idea of reality perfectly clear. Here, then, let us apply our rules. According to them, reality, like every other quality, consists in the peculiar sensible effects which things partaking of it produce. The only effect which real things have is to cause belief, for all the sensations which they excite emerge into consciousness in the form of beliefs. The question therefore is, how is true belief (or belief in the real) distinguished from false belief (or belief in fiction). Now, as we have seen in the former paper, the ideas of truth and falsehood, in their full development, appertain exclusively to the scientific method of settling opinion. A person who arbitrarily chooses the propositions which he will adopt can use the word truth only to emphasize the expression of his determination to hold on to his choice. Of course, the method of tenacity never prevailed exclusively; reason is too natural to men for that. But in the literature of the dark ages we find some fine examples of it. When Scotus Erigena is commenting upon a poetical passage in which hellebore is spoken of as having caused the death of Socrates, he does not hesitate to inform the inquiring reader that Helleborus and Socrates were two eminent Greek philosophers, and that the latter having been overcome in argument by the former took the matter to heart and died of it! What sort of an idea of truth could a man have who could adopt and teach, without the qualification of a perhaps, an opinion taken so entirely at random? The real spirit of Socrates, who I hope would have been delighted to have been "overcome in argument," because he would have learned something by it, is in curious contrast with the naïve idea of the glossist, for whom discussion would seem to have been simply a struggle. When philosophy began to awake from its long slumber, and before theology completely dominated it, the practice seems to have been for each professor to seize upon any philosophical position he found unoccupied and which seemed a strong one, to intrench himself in it, and to sally forth from time to time to give battle to the others. Thus, even the scanty records we possess of those disputes enable us to make out a dozen or more opinions held by different teachers at one time concerning the question of nominalism and realism. Read the opening part of the "Historia Calamitatum" of Abelard, who was certainly as philosophical as any of his contemporaries, and see the spirit of combat which it breathes. For him, the truth is simply his particular stronghold. When the method of authority prevailed, the truth meant little more than the Catholic faith. All the efforts of the scholastic doctors are directed toward harmonizing their faith in Aristotle and their faith in the Church, and one may search their ponderous folios through without finding an argument which goes any further. It is noticeable that where different faiths flourish side by side, renegades are looked upon with contempt even by the party whose belief they adopt; so completely has the idea of loyalty replaced that of truth-seeking. Since the time of Descartes, the defect in the conception of truth has been less apparent. Still, it will sometimes strike a scientific man that the philosophers have been less intent on finding out what the facts are, than on inquiring what belief is most in harmony with their system. It is hard to convince a follower of the *a priori* method by adducing facts; but show him that an opinion he is defending is inconsistent with what he has laid down elsewhere, and he will be very apt to retract it. These minds do not seem to believe that disputation is ever to cease; they seem to think that the opinion which is natural for one man is not so for another, and that belief will, consequently, never be settled. In contenting themselves with fixing their own opinions by a method which would lead another man to a different result, they betray their feeble hold of the conception of what truth is.

On the other hand, all the followers of science are fully persuaded that the processes of investigation, if only pushed far enough, will give one certain solution to every question to which they can be applied. One man may investigate the velocity of light by studying the transits of Venus and the aberration of the stars; another by the oppositions of Mars and the eclipses of Jupiter's satellites; a third by the method of Fizeau; a fourth by that of Foucault; a fifth by the motions of the curves of Lissajous; a sixth, a seventh, an eighth, and a ninth, may follow the different methods of comparing the measures of statical and dynamical electricity. They may at first obtain different results, but, as each perfects his method and his processes, the results will move steadily together toward a destined center. So with all scientific research. Different minds may set out with the most antagonistic views, but the progress of investigation carries them by a force outside of themselves to one and the same conclusion. This activity of thought by which we are carried, not where we wish, but to a foreordained goal, is like the operation of destiny. No modification of the point of view taken, no selection of other facts for study, no natural bent of mind even, can enable a man to escape the predestinate opinion. This great law is embodied in the conception of truth and reality. The opinion which is fated[1] to be ultimately agreed to by all who investigate, is what we mean by the truth, and the object represented in this opinion is the real. That is the way I would explain reality.

But it may be said that this view is directly opposed to the abstract definition which we have given of reality, inasmuch as it makes the characters of

---

[1]Fate means merely that which is sure to come true, and can nohow be avoided. It is a superstition to suppose that a certain sort of events are ever fated, and it is another to suppose that the word fate can never be freed from its superstitious taint. We are all fated to die. [Footnote added in later reprinting.]

the real to depend on what is ultimately thought about them. But the answer to this is that, on the one hand, reality is independent, not necessarily of thought in general, but only of what you or I or any finite number of men may think about it; and that, on the other hand, though the object of the final opinion depends on what that opinion is, yet what that opinion is does not depend on what you or I or any man thinks. Our perversity and that of others may indefinitely postpone the settlement of opinion; it might even conceivably cause an arbitrary proposition to be universally accepted as long as the human race should last. Yet even that would not change the nature of the belief, which alone could be the result of investigation carried sufficiently far; and if, after the extinction of our race, another should arise with faculties and disposition for investigation, that true opinion must be the one which they would ultimately come to. "Truth crushed to earth shall rise again," and the opinion which would finally result from investigation does not depend on how anybody may actually think. But the reality of that which is real does depend on the real fact that investigation is destined to lead, at last, if continued long enough, to a belief in it.

But I may be asked what I have to say to all the minute facts of history, forgotten never to be recovered, to the lost books of the ancients, to the buried secrets.

Full many a gem of purest ray serene
  The dark, unfathomed caves of ocean bear;

Full many a flower is born to blush unseen,
  And waste its sweetness on the desert air.

Do these things not really exist because they are hopelessly beyond the reach of our knowledge? And then, after the universe is dead (according to the prediction of some scientists), and all life has ceased forever, will not the shock of atoms continue though there will be no mind to know it? To this I reply that, though in no possible state of knowledge can any number be great enough to express the relation between the amount of what rests unknown and the amount of the known, yet it is unphilosophical to suppose that, with regard to any given question (which has any clear meaning), investigation would not bring forth a solution of it, if it were carried far enough. Who would have said, a few years ago, that we could ever know of what substances stars are made whose light may have been longer in reaching us than the human race has existed? Who can be sure of what we shall not know in a few hundred years? Who can guess what would be the result of continuing the pursuit of science for ten thousand years, with the activity of the last hundred? And if it were to go on for a million, or a billion, or any number of years you please, how is it possible to say that there is any question which might not ultimately be solved?

But it may be objected, "Why make so much of these remote considerations, especially when it is your principle that only practical distinctions have a meaning?" Well, I must confess that it makes very little difference whether we say that a stone on the bottom of the ocean, in complete darkness, is brilliant or not — that is to say, that it *probably* makes no difference, remembering always that that stone *may* be fished up tomorrow. But that there are gems at the bottom of the sea, flowers in the untraveled desert, etc., are propositions which, like that about a diamond being hard when it is not pressed, concern much more the arrangement of our language than they do the meaning of our ideas.

We have, hitherto, not crossed the threshold of scientific logic. It is certainly important to know how to make our ideas clear, but they may be ever so clear without being true. . . . How to give birth to those vital and procreative ideas which multiply into a thousand forms and diffuse themselves everywhere, advancing civilization and making the dignity of man, is an art not yet reduced to rules, but of the secret of which the history of science affords some hints.

WILLIAM JAMES (1842–1910)

Born in New York City in 1842, William James grew up in a family remarkable for its high spirits, intelligence, and congeniality. His father, Henry James, Senior, a man of intense religious and philosophical disposition, used his considerable inherited fortune to surround his five children with an atmosphere of culture. The family traveled a great deal, and William, like his sister and three brothers, was educated in various schools in the United States, England, France, Germany, and Switzerland. Thus he acquired the cosmopolitanism and *savoir faire* that distinguished him throughout his life. Uncertain of the choice of a career, he dabbled in painting, then studied chemistry, physiology, and medicine at Harvard. Still unable to reach a decision, he accompanied Louis Agassiz, the great naturalist, on a field trip up the Amazon, and spent the next two years studying in Europe, mainly Germany. During this period and the subsequent three years spent in America, he suffered from a profound mental depression, at times even considering suicide.

Although he completed the work for his doctor's degree at the Harvard Medical School in 1869, it was not until 1872, when he was appointed to the post of instructor in physiology at Harvard, that he found regular employment. This appointment, which he called " a perfect God-send to me," contributed to a happier outlook. The last traces of his morbid mental state had apparently disappeared by 1878, when he married Alice Gibbens.

By this time, aged 36, he was an established teacher of physiology and psychology at Harvard. In 1880, he became assistant professor of philosophy and before long, professor. During his tenure, the Department of Philosophy attained a high point of distinction, including among its faculty Josiah Royce, Hugo Münsterberg, and George Santayana. James's own importance as an original thinker was established with the publication, in 1890, of his master work, *Principles of Psychology*, the product of eleven years of labor. Although he finally won great acclaim as a philosopher, he never succeeded in writing a philosophical work as substantial and comprehensive as this great treatise in psychology.

Among his favorite recreations was mountain climbing. In June 1899, while climbing alone in the Adirondacks, he lost his way and overstrained his heart in a desperate thirteen-hour scramble. The result was an irreparable lesion, which forced him to curtail his intellectual activities. Finally, in 1910, his heart trouble became very serious, and he died in his New Hampshire home in August of that year.

Witty, kindly, urbane, but restless and neurasthenic, James was a remarkably complex and attractive character—"a being," to quote his sister, "who would bring life and charm to a treadmill." This charm he communicated in his writing, which often lends a rollicking sprightliness to the most abstruse subjects. Despite his artistic flair, he had the scientist's keen sense of fact and the moralist's high seriousness. But his seriousness was never stuffy—he was always opposed to the snobs, the dogmatists, the dry-as-dusts, and the goody-goodies that would fence in the human spirit.

What Pragmatism Means

Some years ago, being with a camping party in the mountains, I returned from a solitary ramble to find every one engaged in a ferocious metaphysical dispute. The *corpus* of the dispute was a squirrel—a live squirrel supposed to be clinging to one side of a tree-trunk; while over against the tree's opposite side a human being was imagined to stand. This human witness tries to get sight of the squirrel by moving rapidly round the tree, but no matter how fast he goes, the squirrel moves as fast in the opposite direction, and always keeps the tree between himself and the man, so that never a glimpse of him is caught. The resultant metaphysical problem now is this: *Does the man go round the squirrel or not?* He goes round the tree, sure enough, and the squirrel is on the tree; but does he go

From *Pragmatism: A New Name for Some Old Ways of Thinking*. Lectures II and VI (New York: Longmans, Green, 1907). Reprinted by permission.

round the squirrel? In the unlimited leisure of the wilderness, discussion had been worn threadbare. Every one had taken sides, and was obstinate; and the numbers on both sides were even. Each side, when I appeared, therefore appealed to me to make it a majority. Mindful of the scholastic adage that whenever you meet a contradiction you must make a distinction, I immediately sought and found one, as follows: "Which party is right," I said, "depends on what you *practically mean* by 'going round' the squirrel. If you mean passing from the north of him to the east, then to the south, then to the west, and then to the north of him again, obviously the man does go round him, for he occupies these successive positions. But if on the contrary you mean being first in front of him, then on the right of him, then behind him, then on his left, and finally in front again, it is quite as obvious that the man fails to go round him, for by the compensating movements the squirrel makes, he keeps his belly turned towards the man all the time, and his back turned away. Make the distinction, and there is no occasion for any further dispute. You are both right and both wrong according as you conceive the verb 'to go round' in one practical fashion or the other."

Although one or two of the hotter disputants called my speech a shuffling evasion, saying they wanted no quibbling or scholastic hair-splitting, but meant just plain honest English "round," the majority seemed to think that the distinction had assuaged the dispute.

I tell this trivial anecdote because it is a peculiarly simple example of what I wish now to speak of as *the pragmatic method.* The pragmatic method is primarily a method of settling metaphysical disputes that otherwise might be interminable. Is the world one or many? — fated or free? — material or spiritual? — here are notions either of which may or may not hold good of the world; and disputes over such notions are unending. The pragmatic method in such cases is to try to interpret each notion by tracing its respective practical consequences. What difference would it practically make to any one if this notion rather than that notion were true? If no practical difference whatever can be traced, then the alternatives mean practically the same thing, and all dispute is idle. Whenever a dispute is serious, we ought to be able to show some practical difference that must follow from one side or the other's being right.

A glance at the history of the idea will show you still better what pragmatism means. The term is derived from the same Greek word πράγμα, meaning action, from which our words "practice" and "practical" come. It was first introduced into philosophy by Mr. Charles Peirce in 1878. In an article entitled "How to Make Our Ideas Clear," in the *Popular Science Monthly* for January of that year Mr. Peirce, after pointing out that our beliefs are really rules for action, said that, to develop a thought's meaning, we need only determine what conduct it is fitted to produce: that conduct is for us its sole significance. And the tangible fact at the root of all our thought-distinctions, however subtle, is that there is no one of them so fine as to consist in anything but a possible difference of practice. To attain perfect clearness in our thoughts of an object, then, we need only consider what conceivable effects of a practical kind the object may involve — what sensations we are to expect from it, and what reactions we must prepare. Our conception of these effects, whether immediate or remote, is then for us the whole of our conception of the object, so far as that conception has positive significance at all.

This is the principle of Peirce, the principle of pragmatism. It lay entirely unnoticed by any one for twenty years, until I, in an address before Professor Howison's Philosophical Union at the University of California, brought it forward again and made a special application of it to religion. By that date (1898) the time seemed ripe for its reception. The word "pragmatism" spread, and at present it fairly spots the pages of the philosophic journals. On all hands we find the "pragmatic movement" spoken of, sometimes with respect, sometimes with contumely, seldom with clear understanding. It is evident that the term applies itself conveniently to a number of tendencies that hitherto have lacked a collective name, and that it has "come to stay."

To take in the importance of Peirce's principle, one must get accustomed to applying it to concrete cases. I found a few years ago that Ostwald, the illustrious Leipzig chemist, had been making perfectly distinct use of the principle of pragmatism in his lectures on the philosophy of science, though he had not called it by that name.

"All realities influence our practice," he wrote me, "and that influence is their meaning for us. I am accustomed to put questions to my classes in this way: In what respects would the world be different if this alternative or that were true? If I can find nothing that would become different, then the alternative has no sense."

That is, the rival views mean practically the same thing, and meaning, other than practical, there is for us none. Ostwald in a published lecture gives this example of what he means. Chemists have long wrangled over the inner constitution of certain bodies called "tautomerous." Their properties seemed equally consistent with the notion that an instable hydrogen atom oscillates inside of them, or that they are instable mixtures of two bodies. Controversy raged, but never was decided. "It would never have begun," says Ostwald, "if the combatants had asked themselves what particular experimental fact could have been made different by one or the other view being correct. For it would then have appeared that no difference of fact could possibly ensue; and the quarrel was as unreal as if, theorizing in primitive times about the raising of dough by yeast, one party should have invoked a 'brownie,' while another insisted on an 'elf' as the true cause of the phenomenon."[1]

---

[1]"Theorie und Praxis," *Zeitschrift des Oesterreichischen Ingenieur-u. Architecten-Vereines;* 1905, Nr. 4 u. 6. I find a still more radical pragmatism than Ostwald's in an address by Professor W. S. Franklin: "I think that the sickliest notion of physics, even if a student gets it, is that it is 'the science of masses, molecules, and the ether.' And I think that the healthiest notion, even if a student does not wholly get it, is that physics is the science of the ways of taking hold of bodies and pushing them!" (*Science,* January 2, 1903.)

It is astonishing to see how many philosophical disputes collapse into insignificance the moment you subject them to this simple test of tracing a concrete consequence. There can *be* no difference anywhere that doesn't *make* a difference elsewhere — no difference in abstract truth that doesn't express itself in a difference in concrete fact and in conduct consequent upon that fact, imposed on somebody, somehow, somewhere, and somewhen. The whole function of philosophy ought to find out what definite difference it will make to you and me, at definite instants of our life, if this world-formula or that world-formula be the true one.

There is absolutely nothing new in the pragmatic method. Socrates was an adept at it. Aristotle used it methodically. Locke, Berkeley, and Hume made momentous contributions to truth by its means. Shadworth Hodgson keeps insisting that realities are only what they are "known as." But these forerunners of pragmatism used it in fragments: they were preluders only. Not until in our time has it generalized itself, become conscious of a universal mission, pretended to a conquering destiny. I believe in that destiny, and I hope I may end by inspiring you with my belief.

Pragmatism represents a perfectly familiar attitude in philosophy, the empiricist attitude, but it represents it, as it seems to me, both in a more radical and in a less objectionable form than it has ever yet assumed. A pragmatist turns his back resolutely and once for all upon a lot of inveterate habits dear to professional philosophers. He turns away from abstraction and insufficiency, from verbal solutions, from bad *a priori* reasons, from fixed principles, closed systems, and pretended absolutes and origins. He turns towards concreteness and adequacy, towards fact, towards action and towards power. That means the empiricist temper regnant and the rationalist temper sincerely given up. It means the open air and possibilities of nature, as against dogma, artificiality, and the pretence of finality in truth.

At the same time it does not stand for any special results. It is a method only. But the general triumph of that method would mean an enormous change in . . . the "temperament" of philosophy. Teachers of the ultra-rationalistic type would be frozen out, much as the courtier type is frozen out in republics, as the ultramontane type of priest is frozen out in protestant lands. Science and metaphysics would come much nearer together, would in fact work absolutely hand in hand.

Metaphysics has usually followed a very primitive kind of quest. You know how men have always hankered after unlawful magic, and you know what a great part in magic *words* have always played. If you have his name, or the formula of incantation that binds him, you can control the spirit, genie, afrite, or whatever the power may be. Solomon knew the names of all the spirits, and having their names, he held them subject to his will. So the universe has always appeared to the natural mind as a kind of enigma, of which the key must be sought in the shape of some illuminating or power-bringing word or name. That word names the universe's *principle*, and to possess it is after a fashion to possess the universe itself. "God," "Matter," "Reason," "the Absolute," "Energy," are so many solving names. You can rest when you have them. You are at the end of your metaphysical quest.

But if you follow the pragmatic method, you cannot look on any such word as closing your quest. You must bring out of each word its practical cash-value, set it at work within the stream of your experience. It appears less as a solution, then, than as a program for more work, and more particularly as an indication of the ways in which existing realities may be *changed*.

Theories thus become instruments, not answers to engimas, in which we can rest. We don't like back upon them, we move forward, and, on occasion, make nature over again by their aid. Pragmatism unstiffens all our theories, limbers them up and sets each one at work. Being nothing essentially new, it harmonizes with many ancient philosophic tendencies. It agrees with nominalism, for instance, in always appealing to particulars; with utilitarianism in emphasizing practical aspects; with positivism in its disdain for verbal solutions, useless questions and metaphysical abstractions.

All these, you see, are *anti-intellectualist* tendencies. Against rationalism as a pretension and a method pragmatism is fully armed and militant. But, at the outset, at least, it stands for no particular results. It has no dogmas, and no doctrines save its method. As the young Italian pragmatist Papini has well said, it lies in the midst of our theories, like a corridor in a hotel. Innumerable chambers open out of it. In one you may find a man writing an atheistic volume; in the next some one on his knees praying for faith and strength; in a third a chemist investigating a body's properties. In a fourth a system of idealistic metaphysics is excogitated; in a fifth the impossibility of metaphysics is being shown. But they all own the corridor, and all must pass through it if they want a practicable way of getting into or out of their respective rooms.

No particular results then, so far, but only an attitude of orientation, is what the pragmatic method means. *The attitude of looking away from first things, principles, "categories," supposed necessities; and of looking towards last things, fruits, consequences, facts.*

So much for the pragmatic method! . . . Meanwhile the word pragmatism has come to be used in a still wider sense, as meaning also a certain *theory of truth*. . . .

Truth, as any dictionary will tell you, is a property of certain of our ideas. It means their "agreement," as falsity means their "disagreement," with "reality." Pragmatists and intellectualists both accept this definition as a matter of course. They begin to quarrel only after the question is raised as to what may precisely be meant by the term "agreement," and what by the term "reality," when reality is taken as something for our ideas to agree with.

In answering these questions the pragmatists are more analytic and painstaking, the intellectualists more offhand and irreflective. The popular notion is that a true idea must copy its reality. Like other popular views, this one follows the analogy of the most usual experience. Our true ideas of sensible things do indeed copy them. Shut your eyes and think of yonder clock on the wall, and you get just such a true picture or copy of its dial. But your idea of its "works" (unless you are a clock-maker) is much less of a copy, yet it passes muster, for it in no way clashes with the reality. Even though it should shrink to the mere word "works," that word still serves you truly; and when you speak of the "time-keeping function" of the clock, or of its spring's "elasticity," it is hard to see exactly what your ideas can copy.

You perceive that there is a problem here. Where our ideas cannot copy definitely their object, what does agreement with that object mean? Some idealists seem to say that they are true whenever they are what God means that we ought to think about that subject. Others hold the copy-view all through, and speak as if our ideas possessed truth just in proportion as they approach to being copies of the Absolute's eternal way of thinking.

These views, you see, invite pragmatistic discussion. But the great assumption of the intellectualists is that truth means essentially an inert static relation. When you've got your true idea of anything, there's an end of the matter. You're in possession; you *know*; you have fulfilled your thinking destiny. You are where you ought to be mentally; you have obeyed your categorical imperative; and nothing more need follow on that climax of your rational destiny. Epistemologically you are in stable equilibrium.

Pragmatism, on the other hand, asks its usual question. "Grant an idea or belief to be true," it says, "what concrete difference will its being true make in any one's actual life? How will the truth be realized? What experiences will be different from those which would obtain if the belief were false? What, in short, is the truth's cash-value in experiential terms?"

The moment pragmatism asks this question, it sees the answer: *True ideas are those that we can assimilate, validate, corroborate and verify. False ideas are those that we cannot.* That is the practical difference it makes to us to have true ideas; that, therefore, is the meaning of truth, for it is all that truth is known-as.

This thesis is what I have to defend. The truth of an idea is not a stagnant property inherent in it. Truth *happens* to an idea. It *becomes* true, is *made* true by events. Its verity *is* in fact an event, a process: the process namely of its verifying itself, its veri-*fication*. Its validity is the process of its valid-*ation*.

But what do the words verification and validation themselves pragmatically mean? They again signify certain practical consequences of the verified and validated idea. It is hard to find any one phrase that characterizes these consequences better than the ordinary agreement-formula—just such consequences being what we have in mind whenever we say that our ideas "agree" with reality. They lead us, namely, through the acts and other ideas which they instigate, into or up to, or towards, other parts of experience with which we feel all the while—such feeling being among our potentialities—that the original ideas remain in agreement.

The connections and transitions come to us from point to point as being progressive, harmonious, satisfactory. This function of agreeable leading is what we mean by an idea's verification.

To "agree" in the widest sense with a reality *can only mean to be guided either straight up to it or into its surroundings, or to be put into such working touch with it as to handle either it or something connected with it better than if we disagreed.* Better either intellectually or practically! And often agreement will only mean the negative fact that nothing contradictory from the quarter of that reality comes to interfere with the way in which our ideas guide us elsewhere. To copy a reality is, indeed, one very important way of agreeing with it, but it is far from being essential. The essential thing is the process of being guided. Any idea that helps us to deal, whether practically or intellectually, with either the reality or its belongings, that doesn't entangle our progress in frustrations, that *fits*, in fact, and adapts our life to the reality's whole setting, will agree sufficiently to meet the requirement. It will hold true of that reality.

Thus, *names* are just as "true" or "false" as definite mental pictures are. They set up similar verification-processes, and lead to fully equivalent practical results. . . .

The overwhelming majority of our true ideas admit of no direct or face-to-face verification—those of past history, for example, as of Cain and Abel. The stream of time can be remounted only verbally, or verified indirectly by the present prolongations or effects of what the past harbored. Yet if they agree with these verbalities and effects, we can know that our ideas of the past are true. *As true as past time itself was*, so true was Julius Caesar, so true were antediluvian monsters, all in their proper dates and settings. That past time itself was, is guaranteed by its coherence with everything that's present. True as the present *is*, the past *was* also.

Agreement thus turns out to be essentially an affair of leading—leading that is useful because it is into quarters that contain objects that are important. True ideas lead us into useful verbal and conceptual quarters as well as directly up to useful sensible termini. They lead to consistency, stability and flowing human intercourse. They lead away from eccentricity and isolation, from foiled and barren thinking. The untrammeled flowing of the leading-process, its general freedom from clash and contradiction, passes for its indirect verification; but all roads lead to Rome, and in the end and eventually, all true processes must lead to the face of directly verifying sensible experiences *somewhere*, which somebody's ideas have copied.

Such is the large loose way in which the pragmatist interprets the word agreement. He treats it altogether practically. He lets it cover any process of conduction from a present idea to a future terminus, provided only it run prosperously. It is only thus that "scientific" ideas, flying as they do beyond common sense, can be said to agree with their realities. It is, as I have already said, *as if* reality were made of ether, atoms or electrons, but we mustn't think so literally. The term "energy" doesn't even pretend to stand for anything "objective." It is only a way of measuring the surface of phenomena so as to string their changes on a simple formula.

Yet in the choice of these man-made formulas we cannot be capricious with impunity any more than we can be capricious on the common-sense practical level. We must find a theory that will *work*; and that means something extremely difficult; for our theory must mediate between all previous truths and certain new experiences. It must derange common sense and previous belief as little as possible, and it must lead to some sensible terminus or other that can be verified exactly. To "work" means both these things; and the squeeze is so tight that there is little loose play for any hypothesis. Our theories are wedged and controlled as nothing else is. Yet sometimes alternative theoretic formulas are equally compatible with all the truths we know, and then we choose between them for subjective reasons. We choose the kind of theory to which we are already partial; we follow "elegance" or "economy." Clerk-Maxwell somewhere says it would be "poor scientific taste" to choose the more complicated of two equally well-evidenced conceptions; and you will all agree with him. Truth in science is what gives us the maximum possible sum of satisfactions, taste included, but consistency both with previous truth and with novel fact is always the most imperious claimant. . . .

Our account of truth is an account of truths in the plural, of processes of leading, realized *in rebus* [in things], and having only this quality in common, that they *pay*. They pay by guiding us into or towards some part of a system that dips at numerous points into sense-percepts, which we may copy mentally or not, but with which at any rate we are now in the kind of commerce vaguely designated as verification. Truth for us is simply a collective name for verification-processes, just as health, wealth, strength, etc., are names for other processes connected with life, and also pursued because it pays to pursue them. Truth is *made*, just as health, wealth and strength are made, in the course of experience. . . .

"The true," to put it very briefly, is only the expedient in the way of our thinking, just as "the right" is only the expedient in the way of our behaving. Expedient in almost any fashion; and expedient in the long run and on the whole of course; for what meets expediently all the experience in sight won't necessarily meet all further experiences equally satisfactorily. Experience, as we know, has ways of *boiling over*, and making us correct our present formulas.

The "absolutely" true, meaning what no further experience will ever alter, is that ideal vanishing-point towards which we imagine that all our temporary truths will some day converge. It runs on all fours with the perfectly wise man, and with the absolutely complete experience; and, if these ideals are ever realized, they will all be realized together. Meanwhile we have to live today by what truth we can get today, and be ready tomorrow to call it falsehood. Ptolemaic astronomy, Euclidean space, Aristotelian logic, Scholastic metaphysics, were expedient for centuries, but human experience has boiled over those limits, and we now call these things only relatively true, or true within those borders of experience. "Absolutely" they are false: for we know that those limits were casual, and might have been transcended by past theorists just as they are by present thinkers. . . .

The trail of the human serpent is thus over everything. Truth independent; truth that we *find* merely; truth no longer malleable to human need; truth incorrigible, in a word; such truth exists indeed superabundantly — or is supposed to exist by rationalistically minded thinkers; but then it means only the dead heart of the living tree, and its being there means only that truth also has its paleontology, and its "prescription," and may grow stiff with years of veteran service and petrified in men's regard by sheer antiquity. But how plastic even the oldest truths nevertheless really are has been vividly shown in our day by the transformation of logical and mathematical ideas, a transformation which seems even to be invading physics. The ancient formulas are reinterpreted as special expressions of much wider principles, principles that our ancestors never got a glimpse of in their present shape and formulation. . . .

Such then would be the scope of pragmatism — first, a method; and second, a genetic theory of what is meant by truth.

JOHN DEWEY (1859 – 1952)

John Dewey was born in the beautiful New England town of Burlington, Vermont. "All my forefathers," he has said, "earned an honest living as farmers, wheelwrights, coopers. I was absolutely the first one in seven generations to fall from grace."[1] But his father, a grocer, loved to recite from Shakespeare and Milton, and his parents gave their four sons the advantages of a college education and of a liberal moral and religious outlook. John took his undergraduate degree at the University of Vermont and his doctor's degree in philosophy at Johns Hopkins in 1884.

He taught at the University of Michigan from 1884 to 1894 (except for one year at the University of Minnesota) and then, for an additional ten-year period, at the University of Chicago. During these years, he gradually shifted from Hegelian idealism to his own version of pragmatism, or as he preferred to call it, "instrumentalism." His ideas had begun to cause some controversy even before he went to Chicago, but this was mild compared with the storm that broke out when he began to apply his pragmatic ideals as director of the "Laboratory School" for children at the

Edwin E. Slosson, *Six Major Prophets* (Boston: Little, Brown, 1917), p. 268. (From a letter of Dewey to Slosson.)

University of Chicago. Aided by his wife, for seven and a half years Dewey conducted a bold educational experiment based on the concepts of "learning by doing" and "education for democracy." Whereas traditional education had sought to instill obedience and receptivity, he sought to cultivate activity, initiative, diversity, and voluntary cooperation; and in so doing, he wrought a veritable revolution in educational theory and practice. The volume in which he explained what he was trying to do, *School and Society*, was first published in 1899 and has since been translated into a dozen European and Oriental languages and reprinted many times.

Having achieved fame both as an educator and as a philosopher, Dewey in 1904 was called to Columbia University, where he remained until his retirement in 1929. With prodigious energy, he poured forth an immense volume of publications and engaged in many educational, political, and civic activities. In 1919 he lectured at the Imperial University of Japan in Tokyo, and during the next two years at the National universities at Peking and at Nanking, where he made a profound impression on Chinese students and intellectuals. For briefer periods he visited Turkey in 1924, Mexico in 1926, and Soviet Russia in 1928. Later he served as a member of the international Commission of Inquiry into the charges made against Leon Trotsky at the famous Moscow trial of Trotsky's alleged confederates. This commission, which met in Mexico City, finally issued a report *Not Guilty* (1937), which became the object of heated political controversy.

During the later years of his life, Dewey's interests continued to broaden, as indicated by the wide range of his writings — on education, religion, art, politics, ethics, logic, epistemology, and metaphysics. His many social and intellectual activities, however, did not prevent him from rearing a large family and forming many warm personal friendships. When he died at the age of ninety-two, he had had a more comprehensive and profound impact on the modern world than any other American philosopher.

His personality was not as vivid as James', and his literary style is not as readable. Modest, unobtrusive, somewhat halting in speech, and ultra-democratic in manner, Dewey the human being has sometimes seemed to be quite different from Dewey the bold and independent thinker. This contrast has led many people to misinterpret and vulgarize his ideas and to underestimate his native radicalism. But if, as has been claimed, Dewey is more representative of democratic America than any other thinker, it is an intellectually adventurous and daring America that he represents.

Scientific Philosophy

I

That the publication of *The Origin of Species* marked an epoch in the development of the natural sciences is well known to the layman. That the combination of the very words origin and species embodied an intellectual revolt and introduced a new intellectual temper is easily overlooked by the expert. The conceptions that had reigned in the philosophy of nature and knowledge for two thousand years, the conceptions that had become the familiar furniture of the mind, rested on the assumption of the superiority of the fixed and final; they rested upon treating change and origin as signs of defect and unreality. In laying hands upon the sacred ark of absolute permanency, in treating the forms that had been regarded as types of fixity and perfection as originating and passing away, *The Origin of Species* introduced a mode of thinking that in the end was bound to transform the logic of knowledge, and hence the treatment of morals, politics, and religion.

No wonder, then, that the publication of Darwin's book, a half century ago, precipitated a crisis. The true nature of the controversy is easily concealed from us, however, by the theo-

From *The Influence of Darwin on Philosophy and Other Essays in Contemporary Thought* (New York: Henry Holt and Company, 1910). Reprinted by permission.

logical clamor that attended it. The vivid and popular features of the anti-Darwinian row tended to leave the impression that the issue was between science on one side and theology on the other. Such was not the case — the issue lay primarily within science itself, as Darwin himself early recognized. The theological outcry he discounted from the start, hardly noticing it save as it bore upon the "feelings of his female relatives." But for two decades before final publication he contemplated the possibility of being put down by his scientific peers as a fool or as crazy; and he set, as the measure of his success, the degree in which he should affect three men of science: Lyell in geology, Hooker in botany, and Huxley in zoölogy.

Religious considerations lent fervor to the controversy, but they did not provoke it. Intellectually, religious emotions are not creative but conservative. They attach themselves readily to the current view of the world and consecrate it. They steep and dye intellectual fabrics in the seething vat of emotions; they do not form their warp and woof. There is not, I think, an instance of any large idea about the world being independently generated by religion. Although the ideas that rose up like armed men against Darwinism owed their intensity to religious associations, their origin and meaning are to be sought in science and philosophy, not in religion.

II

Few words in our language foreshorten intellectual history as much as does the word species. The Greeks, in initiating the intellectual life of Europe, were impressed by characteristic traits of the life of plants and animals; so impressed indeed that they made these traits the key to defining nature and to explaining mind and society. And truly, life is so wonderful that a seemingly successful reading of its mystery might well lead men to believe that the key to the secrets of heaven and earth was in their hands. The Greek rendering of this mystery, the Greek formulation of the aim and standard of knowledge, was in the course of time embodied in the word species, and it controlled philosophy for two thousand years. To understand the intellectual face-about expressed in the phrase "Origin of Species," we must, then, understand the long dominant idea against which it is a protest.

Consider how men were impressed by the facts of life. Their eyes fell upon certain things slight in bulk, and frail in structure. To every appearance, these perceived things were inert and passive. Suddenly, under certain circumstances, these things—henceforth known as seeds or eggs or germs—begin to change, to change rapidly in size, form, and qualities. Rapid and extensive changes occur, however, in many things—as when wood is touched by fire. But the changes in the living thing are orderly; they are cumulative; they tend constantly in one direction; they do not, like other changes, destroy or consume, or pass fruitless into wandering flux; they realize and fulfil. Each successive stage, no matter how unlike its predecessor, preserves its net effect and also prepares the way for a fuller activity on the part of its successor. In living beings, changes do not happen as they seem to happen elsewhere, any which way; the earlier changes are regulated in view of later results. This progressive organization does not cease till there is achieved a true final term, a *telos*, a completed, perfected end. This final form exercises in turn a plenitude of functions, not the least noteworthy of which is production of germs like those from which it took its own origin, germs capable of the same cycle of self-fulfilling activity.

But the whole miraculous tale is not yet told. The same drama is enacted to the same destiny in countless myriads of individuals so sundered in time, so severed in space, that they have no opportunity for mutual consultation and no means of interaction. As an old writer quaintly said, "things of the same kind go through the same formalities"—celebrate, as it were, the same ceremonial rites.

This formal activity which operates throughout a series of changes and holds them to a single course; which subordinates their aimless flux to its own perfect manifestation; which, leaping the boundaries of space and time, keeps individuals distant in space and remote in time to a uniform type of structure and function: this principle seemed to give insight into the very nature of reality itself. To it Aristotle gave the name, *eidos*. This term the scholastics translated as *species*.

The force of this term was deepened

by its application to everything in the universe that observes order in flux and manifests constancy through change. From the casual drift of daily weather, through the uneven recurrence of seasons and unequal return of seed time and harvest, up to the majestic sweep of the heavens — the image of eternity in time — and from this to the unchanging pure and contemplative intelligence beyond nature lies one unbroken fulfilment of ends. Nature as a whole is a progressive realization of purpose strictly comparable to the realization of purpose in any single plant or animal.

The conception of *edios*, species, a fixed form and final cause, was the central principle of knowledge as well as of nature. Upon it rested the logic of science. Change as change is mere flux and lapse; it insults intelligence. Genuinely to know is to grasp a permanent end that realizes itself through changes, holding them thereby within the metes and bounds of fixed truth. Completely to know is to relate all special forms to their one single end and good: pure contemplative intelligence. Since, however, the scene of nature which directly confronts us is in change, nature as directly and practically experienced does not satisfy the conditions of knowledge. Human experience is in flux, and hence the instrumentalities of sense-perception and of inference based upon observation are condemned in advance. Science is compelled to aim at realities lying behind and beyond the processes of nature, and to carry on its search for these realities by means of rational forms transcending ordinary modes of perception and inference.

There are, indeed, but two alternative courses. We must either find the appropriate objects and organs of knowledge in the mutual interactions of changing things; or else, to escape the infection of change, we *must* seek them in some transcendent and supernal region. The human mind, deliberately as it were, exhausted the logic of the changeless, the final, and the transcendent, before it essayed adventure on the pathless wastes of generation and transformation. We dispose all too easily of the efforts of the schoolmen to interpret nature and mind in terms of real essences, hidden forms, and occult faculties, forgetful of the seriousness and dignity of the ideas that lay behind. We dispose of them by laughing at the famous gentleman who accounted for the fact that opium put people to sleep on the ground it had a dormitive faculty. But the doctrine, held in our own day, that knowledge of the plant that yields the poppy consists in referring the peculiarities of an individual to a type, to a universal form, a doctrine so firmly established that any other method of knowing was conceived to be unphilosophical and unscientific, is a survival of precisely the same logic. This identity of conception in the scholastic and anti-Darwinian theory may well suggest greater sympathy for what has become unfamiliar as well as greater humility regarding the further unfamiliarities that history has in store.

Darwin was not, of course, the first to question the classic philosophy of nature and of knowledge. The beginnings of the revolution are in the physical science of the sixteenth and seventeenth centuries. When Galileo said: "It is my opinion that the earth is very noble and admirable by reason of so many and so different alterations and generations which are incessantly made therein," he expressed the changed temper that was coming over the world; the transfer of interest from the permanent to the changing. When Descartes said: "The nature of physical things is much more easily conceived when they are beheld coming gradually into existence, than when they are only considered as produced at once in a finished and perfect state," the modern world became self-conscious of the logic that was henceforth to control it, the logic of which Darwin's *Origin of Species* is the latest scientific achievement. Without the methods of Copernicus, Kepler, Galileo, and their successors in astronomy, physics, and chemistry, Darwin would have been helpless in the organic sciences. But prior to Darwin the impact of the new scientific method upon life, mind, and politics, had been arrested, because between these ideal or moral interests and the inorganic world intervened the kingdom of plants and animals. The gates of the garden of life were barred to the new ideas; and only through this garden was there access to mind and politics. The influence of Darwin upon philosophy resides in his having conquered the phenomena of life for the principle of transition, and thereby freed the new logic for application to mind and morals and life. When he said of species what Galileo had said of the earth, *eppur si muove* [and yet it does move], he emancipated, once for all, genetic and experimental ideas as an organon of asking questions and looking for explanations.

III

The exact bearings upon philosophy of the new logical outlook are, of course, as yet uncertain and inchoate. We live in the twilight of intellectual transition. One must add the rashness of the prophet to the stubbornness of the partizan to venture a systematic exposition of the influence upon philosophy of the Darwinian method. At best, we can but inquire as to its general bearing—the effect upon mental temper and complexion, upon that body of half-conscious, half-instinctive intellectual aversions and preferences which determine, after all, our more deliberate intellectual enterprises. In this vague inquiry there happens to exist as a kind of touchstone a problem of long historic currency that has also been much discussed in Darwinian literature. I refer to the old problem of design *versus* chance, mind *versus* matter, as the causal explanation, first or final, of things.

As we have already seen, the classic notion of species carried with it the idea of purpose. In all living forms, a specific type is present directing the earlier stages of growth to the realization of its own perfection. Since this purposive regulative principle is not visible to the senses, it follows that it must be an ideal or rational force. Since, however, the perfect form is gradually approximated through the sensible changes, it also follows that in and through a sensible realm a rational ideal force is working out its own ultimate manifestation. These inferences were extended to nature: (*a*) She does nothing in vain, but all for ulterior purpose. (b) Within natural sensible events there is therefore contained a spiritual causal force, which as spiritual escapes perception, but is apprehended by an enlightened reason. (c) The manifestation of this principle brings about a subordination of matter and sense to its own realization, and this ultimate fulfilment is the goal of nature and man. The design argument thus operated in two directions. Purposefulness accounted for the intelligibility of nature and the possibility of science, while the absolute or cosmic character of this purposefulness gave sanction and worth to the moral and religious endeavors of man. Science was underpinned and morals authorized by one and the same principle, and their mutual agreement was eternally guaranteed.

This philosophy remained, in spite of sceptical and polemic outbursts, the official and the regnant philosophy of Europe for over two thousand years. The expulsion of fixed first and final causes from astronomy, physics, and chemistry had indeed given the doctrine something of a shock. But, on the other hand, increased acquaintance with the details of plant and animal life operated as a counterbalance and perhaps even strengthened the argument from design. The marvelous adaptations of organisms to their environment, of organs to the organism, of unlike parts of a complex organ — like the eye — to the organ itself; the foreshadowing by lower forms of the higher; the preparation in earlier stages of growth for organs that only later had

their functioning — these things were increasingly recognized with the progress of botany, zoölogy, paleontology, and embryology. Together, they added such prestige to the design argument that by the late eighteenth century it was, as approved by the sciences of organic life, the central point of theistic and idealistic philosophy.

The Darwinian principle of natural selection cut straight under this philosophy. If all organic adaptations are due simply to constant variation and the elimination of those variations which are harmful in the struggle for existence that is brought about by excessive reproduction, there is no call for a prior intelligent causal force to plan and preordain them. Hostile critics charged Darwin with materialism and with making chance the cause of the universe.

Some naturalists, like Asa Gray, favored the Darwinian principle and attempted to reconcile it with design. Gray held to what may be called design on the installment plan. If we conceive the "stream of variations" to be itself intended, we may suppose that each successive variation was designed from the first to be selected. In that case, variation, struggle and selection simply define the mechanism of "secondary causes" through which the "first cause" acts; and the doctrine of design is none the worse off because we know more of its *modus operandi.*

Darwin could not accept this mediating proposal. He admits or rather he asserts that it is "impossible to conceive this immense and wonderful universe including man with his capacity of looking far backwards and far into futurity as the results of blind chance or necessity."[1] But nevertheless he holds that since variations are in useless as well as useful directions, and since the latter are sifted out simply by the stress of the conditions of struggle for existence, the design argument as applied to living beings is unjustifiable; and its lack of support there deprives it of scientific value as applied to nature in general. If the variations of the pigeon, which under artificial selection give the pouter pigeon, are not preordained for the sake of the breeder, by what logic do we argue that variations resulting in natural species are predesigned?[2]

IV

So much for some of the more obvious facts of the discussion of design *versus* chance, as causal principles of nature and of life as a whole. We brought up this discussion, you recall, as a crucial instance. What does our touchstone indicate as to the bearing of Darwinian ideas upon philosophy? In the first place, the new logic outlaws, flanks, dismisses — what you will — one type of problems and substitutes for it another type. Philosophy forswears inquiry after absolute origins and absolute finalities in order to explore specific values and the specific conditions that generate them.

Darwin concluded that the impossibility of assigning the world to chance as a whole and to design in its parts indicated the insolubility of the question. Two radically different reasons, however, may be given as to why a problem is insoluble. One reason is that the problem is too high for intelligence; the other is that the question in its very asking makes assumptions that render the question meaningless. The latter alternative is unerringly pointed to in the celebrated case of design *versus* chance. Once admit that the sole verifiable or fruitful object of knowledge is the particular set of changes that generate the object of study together with the consequences that then flow from it, and no intelligible question can be asked about what, by assumption, lies outside. To assert — as is often asserted — that specific values of particular truth, social bonds and forms of beauty, if they can be shown to be generated by concretely knowable conditions, are meaningless and in vain; to assert that they are justified only when they and their particular causes and effects have all at once been gathered up into some inclusive first cause and some exhaustive final goal, is intellectual atavism. Such argumentation is reversion to the logic that explained the extinction of fire by water through the formal essence of aqueousness and the quenching of thirst by water through the final cause of aqueousness. Whether used in the case of the special event or that of life as a whole, such logic only abstracts some aspect of the existing course of events in order to reduplicate it as a petrified eternal principle by which to explain the very changes of which it is the formalization.

[1]*Life and Letters*, Vol. I, p. 282, cf. 285.
[2]*Life and Letters*, Vol. II, pp. 146, 170, 245; Vol. I, pp. 283–284. See also the closing portion of his *Variations of Animals and Plants Under Domestication.*

When Henry Sidgwick casually re-marked in a letter that as he grew older his interest in what or who made the world was altering into interest in what kind of a world it is anyway, his voicing of a common experience of our own day illustrates also the nature of that intellectual transformation effected by the Darwinian logic. Interest shifts from the wholesale essence back of special changes to the question of how special changes serve and defeat concrete purposes; shifts from an intelligence that shaped things once for all to the particular intelligences which things are even now shaping; shifts from an ultimate goal of good to the direct increments of justice and happiness that intelligent administration of existent conditions may beget and that present carelessness or stupidity will destroy or forego.

In the second place, the classic type of logic inevitably set philosophy upon proving that life *must* have certain qualities and values — no matter how experience presents the matter — because of some remote cause and eventual goal. The duty of wholesale justification inevitably accompanies all thinking that makes the meaning of special occurrences depend upon something that once and for all lies behind them. The habit of derogating from present meanings and uses prevents our looking the facts of experience in the face; it prevents serious acknowledgement of the evils they present and serious concern with the goods they promise but do not as yet fulfill. It turns thought to the business of finding a wholesale transcendent remedy for the one and guarantee for the other. One is reminded of the way many moralists and theologians greeted Herbert Spencer's recognition of an unknowable energy from which welled up the phenomenal physical processes without and the conscious operations within. Merely because Spencer labeled his unknowable energy "God," this faded piece of metaphysical goods was greeted as an important and grateful concession to the reality of the spiritual realm. Were it not for the deep hold of the habit of seeking justification for ideal values in the remote and transcendent, surely this reference of them to an unknowable absolute would be despised in comparison with the demonstrations of experience that knowable energies are daily generating about us precious values.

The displacing of this wholesale type of philosophy will doubtless not arrive by sheer logical disproof, but rather by growing recognition of its futility. Were it a thousand times true that opium produces sleep because of its dormitive energy, yet the inducing of sleep in the tired, and the recovery of waking life of the poisoned, would not be thereby one least step forwarded. And were it a thousand times dialectically demonstrated that life as a whole is regulated by a transcendent principle to a final inclusive goal, none the less truth and error, health and disease, good and evil, hope and fear in the concrete, would remain just what and where they now are. To improve our education, to ameliorate our manners, to advance our politics, we must have recourse to specific conditions of generation.

Finally, the new logic introduces responsibility into the intellectual life. To idealize and rationalize the universe at large is after all a confession of inability to master the courses of things that specifically concern us. As long as mankind suffered from this impotency, it naturally shifted a burden of responsibility that it could not carry over to the more competent shoulders of the transcendent cause. But if insight into specific conditions of value and into specific consequences of ideas is possible, philosophy must in time become a method of locating and interpreting the more serious of the conflicts that occur in life, and a method of projecting ways for dealing with them: a method of moral and political diagnosis and prognosis.

The claim to formulate *a priori* the legislative constitution of the universe is by its nature a claim that may lead to elaborate dialectic developments. But it is also one that removes these very conclusions from subjection to experimental test, for, by definition, these results make no differences in the detailed course of events. But a philosophy that humbles its pretentions to the work of projecting hypotheses for the education and conduct of mind, individual and social, is thereby subjected to test by the way in which the ideas it propounds work out in practice. In having modesty forced upon it, philosophy also acquires responsibility.

Doubtless I seem to have violated the implied promise of my earlier remarks and to have turned both prophet and partizan. But in anticipating the direction of the transformations in philosophy to be wrought by the Darwinian genetic and experimental logic, I do not profess to speak for any save those who yield themselves consciously or unconsciously to this logic. No one can fairly deny that at present there are two effects of the Darwinian mode of thinking. On the one hand there are many making sincere and vital efforts to revise our traditional philosophic conceptions in accordance with its demands. On the other hand, there is as definitely a recrudescence of absolutistic philosophies; an assertion of a type of philosophic knowing distinct from that of the sciences, one which opens to us another kind of reality from that to which the sciences give access; an appeal through experience to something that essentially goes beyond experience. This reaction affects popular creeds and religious movements as well as technical philosophies. The very conquest of the biological sciences by the new ideas has led many to proclaim an explicit and rigid separation of philosophy from science.

Old ideas give way slowly; for they are more than abstract logical forms and categories. They are habits, predispositions, deeply engrained attitudes of aversion and preference. Moreover, the conviction persists—though history shows it to be a hallucination—that all the questions that the human mind has asked are questions that can be answered in terms of the alternatives that the questions themselves present. But in fact intellectual progress usually occurs through sheer abandonment of questions together with both of the alternatives they assume—an abandonment that results from their decreasing vitality and a change of urgent interest. We do not solve them: we get over

them. Old questions are solved by disappearing, evaporating, while new
questions corresponding to the changed
attitude of endeavor and preference
take their place. Doubtless the greater
dissolvent in contemporary thought to

old questions, the greatest precipitant
of new methods, new intentions, new
problems, is the one affected by the scientific revolution that found its climax
in *The Origin of Species.*

COMMENT

The Origin and Development of Pragmatism

The word *pragmatism* was introduced into modern philosophy by Charles
Peirce to designate the "method of ascertaining the meaning of hard
words and abstract conceptions," which he had advocated in "How to
Make Our Ideas Clear" (1878). Even before he wrote this essay, Peirce had
expressed the basic principle of his pragmatism in a review (1871) of
Fraser's edition of Berkeley's *Works*, in which he offered the following
"rule for avoiding the deceits of language": "Do things fulfill the same
function practically? Then let them be signified by the same word. Do
they not? Then let them be distinguished." In neither of these early
statements did Peirce use the word *pragmatism*. But in 1898, at the
University of California, William James delivered a lecture entitled "Philosophical Conceptions and Practical Results," in which he hailed Peirce
not only as the founder of pragmatism but also as the originator of the
term. It appears that Peirce used the word orally for some time before he
first committed it to print in 1902, when he contributed an article on the
subject to Baldwin's *Philosophical Dictionary*.

The terms *pragmatic* and *pragmatism* were suggested to Peirce by his
study of Kant. In *The Metaphysic of Morals*, Kant distinguished between
pragmatic and *practical.* The former term, deriving from the Greek
pragma ("things done"), applies to the rules of art or technique based on
experience; the latter term applies to moral rules, which Kant regarded as
a priori. Hence Peirce, wishing to emphasize an experimental and non-a
priori type of reasoning, chose the word *pragmatic* to designate his way of
clarifying meanings.

The pragmatic movement first sprang to life in the early 1870s in the
Metaphysical Club, a philosophical discussion group founded by Peirce,
which included among its members William James and Oliver Wendell
Holmes, Jr. Two of the brilliant young members of the club, Chauncey
Wright and Nicholas St. John Green, emphasized the practical bearing and
function of ideas. They thus suggested to Peirce the criterion of clarity,

which he expressed in "How to Make Our Ideas Clear." But this essay lay unnoticed for twenty years, until James, in his address of 1898, pointed to Peirce as the founder of an important new philosophical movement.

As Peirce initially used the term, *pragmatism* referred to a maxim for the clarification of ideas and hypotheses, not for their verification; it was a theory of meaning, not of truth. Later he also used the term to designate the rule that only hypotheses that are *clear* should be admitted in scientific or philosophical inquiry. As interpreted and amplified by James, pragmatism became a theory of truth and so changed into something alien to Peirce's way of thinking. "The modern movement known as pragmatism," Ralph Barton Perry has remarked, "is largely the result of James' misunderstanding of Peirce."[1]

While James was developing his own version of pragmatism, John Dewey was working along similar lines at the University of Michigan and later at the University of Chicago. As early as 1886, he and James began to exchange letters, and in 1903, in the Preface to *Studies in Logical Theory*, Dewey acknowledged "a preëminent obligation" to James. In certain ways, however, Dewey shows a closer affinity to Peirce — for example, in his close study of the experimental methods of natural science, in his rejection of James's criterion of emotional satisfaction as a test of truth, in his emphasis on the *social* bearing of ideas, and in his opposition to all "intuitionist" theories of knowledge.

However much he differed in some respects from James, Dewey fully agreed with the forward-looking and empirical temper of James's pragmatism — "the attitude of looking away from first things, principles, 'categories,' supposed necessities; and of looking toward last things, fruits, consequences, facts." He also agreed that thinking is essentially instrumental to the attainment of human purposes, although the purposes of the scientist are to be distinguished from the purposes of the practical man of affairs. Like James, moreover, he vehemently rejected a dualism of experience and nature: The stuff of the word is natural events such as we directly experience. His interpretation of inquiry, however, was more akin to Peirce's experimentalism than to James' ethical pragmatism. The result is a constellation of ideas that can be described as "experimental naturalism." Perhaps the best brief expression of this naturalistic philosophy is to be found in Dewey's essay "The Influence of Darwinism Upon Philosophy."

In this essay, Dewey argues that the Darwinian revolution in science necessitates a comparable revolution in philosophy. The philosopher, using a method like that of the biologist, should forswear "inquiry after

---

[1]*The Thought and Character of William James*, Briefer Version (Cambridge, MA: Harvard University Press, 1935), p. 281.

absolute origins and absolute finalities in order to explore specific values and the specific conditions that generate them." First and final causes, as allegedly lying behind and beyond nature, are beyond the reach of science, and the philosopher should turn away from such illusory objects. For him as for the scientist, things should be understood in terms of their origins and functions, and inquiry should be empirical in method and practical in motivation.

Conceiving philosophical and scientific method in this way, Dewey regards fruitful inquiry as essentially active and prospective rather than passive and retrospective:

> Intelligence develops within the sphere of action for the sake of possibilities not yet given. . . . Intelligence *as* intelligence is inherently forward-looking. . . . A pragmatic intelligence is a creative intelligence, not a routine mechanic. . . . Intelligence is . . . instrumental *through* action to the determination of the qualities of future experience.[2]

Accordingly, Dewey proposes to determine meanings and test beliefs by examining the *consequences* that flow from them. What can the idea or belief promise for the future? How can it help us in resolving our perplexities? What predictions are implied by the hypothesis and how can they be verified?

Such questions apply even to propositions about the past, and even these propositions must be verified in terms of future consequences: "The past event has left effects, consequences, that are present and that will continue in the future. Our belief about it, if genuine, must also modify action in *some* way and so have objective effects. If these two sets of effects interlock harmoniously, then the judgment is true."[3] For example, the assassination of Lincoln *had* consequences, such as records of the event. My belief about it *has* consequences, such as expectations that the records will be so-and-so. If the two sets of consequences harmoniously coincide so that my expectations are fulfilled, the statement is true.

Dewey regarded this emphasis on consequences as the essential characteristic of pragmatism. "The term 'pragmatic,'" he declared, "means only the rule of referring all thinking, all reflective considerations, to *consequences* for final meaning and test."[4] This insistence on consequent rather than antecedent phenomena is, as we have noted, like the pragmatism of James except that it does not define truth in terms of emotional

[2]*Creative Intelligence* (New York: Henry Holt, 1917), p. 65.
[3]*The Influence of Darwin on Philosophy and Other Essays* (New York: Henry Holt, 1910), p. 160.
[4]*Essays in Experimental Logic* (Chicago: University of Chicago Press, 1916), p. 330.

satisfactions and the play of desires, as James did in his more extreme statements.

There were other important contributors to pragmatism, such as George Herbert Mead (1863 – 1931) in America and F. C. S. Schiller (1864 – 1937) in England; but Peirce, James, and Dewey are the towering figures.

We would be making a mistake to conclude that pragmatism is only a false and outmoded way of thinking. It contains many insights that are both important and salutary. Perhaps its value can be suggested by the following description by John Jay Chapman of a social gathering at the home of a friend, Mrs. Henry Whitman, in Boston:

> I remember a curious Bostonian cockfight at her studio, where Professor Royce and Judge Oliver Wendell Holmes were pitted against each other to talk about the Infinite. Royce won, of course . . . by involving the subject in such adamantine cobwebs of voluminous rolling speculation that no one could regain his senses thereafter. He not only cut the ground from under everyone's feet; but he pulled down the sun and moon, and raised up the ocean, and everyone was shipwrecked and took to small planks and cups of tea.[5]

Holmes, the friend of James and Peirce, was a pragmatist, whereas Royce was of the old-fashioned school of metaphysics. Holmes lost the argument, but he had a greater humility, a keener sense of reality, and a firmer hold on the perennially human point of view than Royce did. If homely realism and practical concern for humanity's lot have tended to supersede the daring flights of metaphysicians, the pragmatists, such as James, Dewey, and Holmes, are in large measure responsible. This change one may count as either a loss or a gain.

---

[5]*Memories and Milestones* (New York: Moffatt, Yard, 1915), p. 106. Cited by Max H. Fisch, *Classic American Philosophers* (New York: Appleton-Crofts, 1951), p. 7.

6

Existentialism

"An objective uncertainty held fast in an appropriation-process of the most passionate inwardness is the truth, the highest truth attainable for an existing individual."

Søren Kierkegaard

SØREN KIERKEGAARD (1813–1855)

The youngest son of rather elderly parents, Kierkegaard was born in Copenhagen and reared in a pious Lutheran family. His father was a wealthy and retired merchant with a strong sense of sin, which he impressed on his children. As a young university student, Søren lived a Bohemian life in revolt against his father and religious pietism. After a moral conversion, he returned to his studies and passed his theological examinations at the University of Copenhagen in 1840. The next year he went to Berlin to attend Schelling's lectures, which confirmed his dislike of Hegel's philosophy. The abstractions of Hegelianism did not supply what he demanded — "a truth which is true *for me*, to find the *idea for which I can live and die*" (*Journal*, Aug. 1, 1935).

Thenceforth the driving force of his life was to "become a Christian," a task that, in his opinion, would not be easy. Although he was in love with seventeen-year-old Regine Olsen, he broke the engagement because it seemed incompatible with his religious commitment. This break not only hurt his fiancée's pride but also had a profoundly traumatic effect on him. He thereafter searched his tormented soul for self-knowledge in book after book.

During his later years Kierkegaard was involved in intense controversy with the Danish State Church, which he accused of being pseudo-Christian. On the point of death he refused the sacrament. "Pastors are royal officials," he explained. "Royal officials have nothing to do with Christianity." The epitaph that he composed for himself was simply "That individual."

Individuality and Subjective Truth

The Single Individual and the Crowd[1]

This that follows is in part the expression of a way of thinking and feeling characteristic of my nature, which possibly is in need of revision (which I myself would welcome), and as it does not claim to be more than that, it is at the farthest remove from claiming the reader's adherence and is rather inclined to concessions. In part, however, it is a well-thought-out view of 'the Life', of 'the Truth', of 'the Way'.[2]

There is a view of life which conceives that where the crowd is, there also is the truth, and that in truth itself there is need of having the crowd on its side. There is another view of life which conceives that wherever there is a crowd there is untruth, so that (to consider for a moment the extreme case), even if every individual, each for himself in private, were to be in possession of the truth, yet in case they were all to get together in a crowd—a crowd to which any sort of *decisive* significance is attributed, a voting, noisy, audible crowd—untruth would at once be in evidence.[3]

For a 'crowd' is the untruth. In a godly sense it is true, eternally, Christianly, as St. Paul says, that 'only one

---

[1]From *The Point of View* by Søren Kierkegaard, translated and edited by Dr. Walter Lowrie (London, New York, and Toronto: Oxford University Press, 1939). Reprinted by permission. Footnotes followed by (K) are by Kierkegaard.

[2]Perhaps it may be well to note here once and for all a thing that goes without saying and which I never have denied, that in relation to all temporal, earthly, worldly matters the crowd may have competency, and even decisive competency as a court of last resort. But it is not of such matters I am speaking, nor have I ever concerned myself with such things. I am speaking about the ethical, about the ethico-religious, about 'the truth', and I am affirming the untruth of the crowd, ethico-religiously regarded, when it is treated as a criterion for what 'truth' is. (K)

[3]Perhaps it may be well to note here, although it seems to me almost superfluous, that it naturally could not occur to me to object to the fact, for example, that preaching is done or that the truth is proclaimed, even though it were to an assemblage of hundreds of thousands. Not at all; but if there were an assemblage even of only ten —and if they should put the truth to the ballot, that is to say, if the assemblage should be regarded as the authority, if it is the crowd which turns the scale—then there *is* untruth. (K)

attains the goal'—which is not meant in a comparative sense, for comparison takes others into account. It means that every man can be that one, God helping him therein—but only one attains the goal. And again this means that every man should be chary about having to do with 'the others', and essentially should talk only with God and with himself—for only one attains the goal. And again this means that man, or to be a man, is akin to deity.—In a worldly and temporal sense, it will be said by the man of bustle, sociability, and amicableness, 'How unreasonable that only one attains the goal; for it is far more likely that many, by the strength of united effort, should attain the goal; and when we are many success is more certain and it is easier for each man severally.' True enough, it is far more *likely*; and it is true also with respect to all earthly and material goods. If it is allowed to have its way, this becomes the only true point of view, for it does away with God and eternity and with man's kinship with deity. It does away with it or transforms it into a fable, and puts in its place the modern (or, we might rather say, the old pagan) notion that to be a man is to belong to a race endowed with reason, to belong to it as a specimen, so that the race or species is higher than the individual, which is to say that there are no more individuals but only specimens. But eternity which arches over and high above the temporal, tranquil as the starry vault at night, and God in heaven who in the bliss of that sublime tranquility holds in survey, without the least sense of dizziness at such a height, these countless multitudes of men and knows each

single individual by name—He, the great Examiner, says that only one attains the goal. That means, every one can and every one should be this *one*—but only one attains the goal. Hence where there is a multitude, a crowd, or where decisive significance is attached to the fact that there is a multitude, *there* it is sure that no one is working, living, striving for the highest aim, but only for one or another earthly aim; since to work for the eternal decisive aim is possible only where there is one, and to be this one which all can be is to let God be the helper—the 'crowd' is the untruth.

A crowd—not this crowd or that, the crowd now living or the crowd long deceased, a crowd of humble people or of superior people, of rich or of poor, &c.—a crowd in its very concept[4] is the untruth, by reason of the fact that it renders the individual completely impenitent and irresponsible, or at least weakens his sense of responsibility by reducing it to a fraction. Observe that there was not one single soldier that dared lay hands upon Caius Marius —this was an instance of truth. But given merely three or four women with the consciousness or the impression

---

[4]The reader will also remember that here the word 'crowd' is understood in a purely formal sense, not in the sense one commonly attaches to 'the crowd' when it is meant as an invidious qualification, the distinction which human selfishness irreligiously erects between 'the crowd' and superior persons, &c. Good God! How could a religious man hit upon such an inhuman equality! No, 'crowd' stands for number, the numerical, a number of noblemen, millionaires, high dignitaries, &c.—as soon as the numerical is involved it is 'crowd', 'the crowd'. (K)

that they were a crowd, and with hope of a sort in the possibility that no one could say definitely who was doing it or who began it — then they had courage for it. What a falsehood! The falsehood first of all is the notion that the crowd does what in fact only the *individual* in the crowd does, though it be every *individual*. For 'crowd' is an abstraction and has no hands: but each individual has ordinarily two hands, and so when an individual lays his two hands upon Caius Marius they are the two hands of the individual, certainly not those of his neighbour, and still less those of the . . . crowd which has no hands. In the next place, the falsehood is that the crowd had the 'courage' for it, for no one of the individuals was ever so cowardly as the crowd always is. For every individual who flees for refuge into the crowd, and so flees in cowardice from being an individual (who had not the courage to lay his hands upon Caius Marius, nor even to admit that he had it not), such a man contributes his share of cowardliness to the cowardliness which we know as the 'crowd'. — Take the highest example, think of Christ —and the whole human race, all the men that ever were born or are to be born. But let the situation be one that challenges the individual, requiring each one for himself to be alone with Him in a solitary place and as an individual to step up to Him and spit upon Him — the man never was born and never will be born with courage or insolence enough to do such a thing. This is untruth.

The crowd is untruth. Hence none has more contempt for what it is to be a man than they who make it their profession to lead the crowd. Let some one approach a person of this sort, some individual — that is an affair far too small for his attention, and he proudly repels him. There must be hundreds at the least. And when there are thousands, he defers to the crowd, bowing and scraping to them. What untruth! No, when it is a question of a single individual man, then is the time to give expression to the truth by showing one's respect for what it is to be a man; and if perhaps it was, as it is cruelly said, a poor wretch of a man, then the thing to do is to invite him into the best room, and one who possesses several voices should use the kindest and most friendly. That is truth. If on the other hand there were an assemblage of thousands or more and the truth was to be decided by ballot, then this is what one should do (unless one were to prefer to utter silently the petition of the Lord's Prayer, 'Deliver us from evil'): one should in godly fear give expression to the fact that the crowd, regarded as a judge over ethical and religious matters, is untruth, whereas it is eternally true that every man can be the *one*. This is truth.

The crowd is untruth. Therefore was Christ crucified, because, although He addressed himself to all, He would have no dealings with the crowd, because He would not permit the crowd to aid him in any way, because in this regard He repelled people absolutely, would not found a party, did not permit balloting, but would be what He is, the Truth, which relates itself to the individual. — And hence every one who truly would serve the truth is *eo ipso*, in one way or another, a martyr. If it were possible for a person in his mother's womb to make the decision to will to serve the truth truly, then, whatever his martyrdom turns out to be, he is *eo ipso* from his mother's womb a martyr. For it is not so great a trick to win the crowd. All that is needed is some talent, a certain dose of falsehood, a little acquaintance with human passions. But no witness for the truth (ah! and that is what every man should be, including you and me) — no witness for the truth dare become engaged with the crowd. The witness for the truth — who naturally has nothing to do with politics and must above everything else be most vigilantly on the watch not to be confounded with the politician — the God-fearing work of the witness to the truth is to engage himself if possible with all, but always individually, talking to every one severally on the streets and lanes . . . in order to disintegrate the crowd, or to talk even to the crowd, though not with the intent of educating the crowd as such, but rather with the hope that one or another individual might return from this assemblage and become a single individual. On the other hand the 'crowd', when it is treated as an authority and its judgement regarded as the final judgement, is detested by the witness for the truth more heartily than a maiden of good morals detests the public dance-floor; and he who addresses the crowd as the supreme authority is regarded by him as the tool of the untruth. For (to repeat what I have said) that which in politics or in similar fields may be justifiable, wholly or in part, becomes untruth when it is transferred to the intellectual, the spiritual, the religious fields.

And one thing more I would say, perhaps with a cautiousness which is exaggerated. By 'truth' I mean always 'eternal truth'. But politics, &c., have nothing to do with 'eternal truth'. A policy which in the proper sense of 'eternal truth' were to make serious work of introducing 'eternal truth' into real life would show itself in that very same second to be in the most eminent degree the most 'impolitic' thing that can be imagined.

A crowd is untruth. And I could weep, or at least I could learn to long for eternity, at thinking of the misery of our age, in comparison even with the greatest misery of bygone ages, owing to the fact that the daily press with its anonymity makes the situation madder still with the help of the public, this abstraction which claims to be the judge in matters of 'truth'. For in reality assemblies which make this claim do not now take place. The fact that an anonymous author by the help of the press can day by day find occasion to say (even about intellectual, moral, and religious matters) whatever he pleases to say, and what perhaps he would be very far from having the courage to say as an individual; that every time he opens his mouth (or shall we say his abysmal gullet?) he at once is addressing thousands of thousands; that he can get ten thousand times ten thousand to repeat after him what he has said — and with all this nobody has any responsibility, so that it is not as in ancient times the relatively unrepentant crowd which possesses omnipotence, but the absolutely unrepentant thing, a nobody, an anonymity, who is the producer (*auctor*), and another anonymity, the public, sometimes even anonymous subscribers, and with all this, nobody, nobody! Good God! And yet our states call themselves Christian states! Let no one say that in this case it is possible for 'truth' in its turn by the help of the press to get the better of lies and errors. O thou who speakest thus, dost thou venture to maintain that men regarded as a crowd are just as quick to seize upon truth which is not always palatable as upon falsehood which always is prepared delicately to give delight?— not to mention the fact that acceptance of the truth is made the more difficult by the necessity of admitting that one has been deceived! Or dost thou venture even to maintain that 'truth' can just as quickly be understood as falsehood, which requires no preliminary knowledge, no schooling, no discipline, no abstinence, no self-denial, no honest concern about oneself, no patient labour?

Nay, truth—which abhors also this untruth of aspiring after broad dissemination as the one aim—is not nimble on its feet. In the first place it cannot work by means of the fantastical means of the press, which is the untruth; the communicator of the truth can only be a single individual. And again the communication of it can only be addressed to the individual; for the truth consists precisely in that conception of life which is expressed by the individual. The truth can neither be communicated nor be received except as it were under God's eyes, not without God's help, not without God's being involved as the middle term, He himself being the Truth. It can therefore only be communicated by and received by 'the individ-

ual', which as a matter of fact can be every living man. The mark which distinguishes such a man is merely that of the truth, in contrast to the abstract, the fantastical, the impersonal, the crowd—the public which excludes God as the middle term (for the *personal* God cannot be a middle term in an *impersonal* relationship), and thereby excludes also the truth, for God is at once the Truth and the middle term which renders it intelligible.

And to honour every man, absolutely every man, is the truth, and this is what it is to fear God and love one's neighbour'. But from an ethico-religious point of view, to recognize the 'crowd' as the court of last resort is to deny God, and it cannot exactly mean to love the 'neighbour'. And the 'neighbour is the absolutely true expression for human equality. In case every one were in truth to love his neighbour as himself, complete human equality would be attained. Every one who loves his neighbour in truth, expresses unconditionally human equality. Every one who, like me, admits that his effort is weak and imperfect, yet is aware that the task is to love one's neighbour, is also aware of what human equality is. But never have I read in Holy Scripture the commandment, Thou shalt love the crowd—and still less, Thou shalt recognize, ethico-religiously, in the crowd the supreme authority in matters of 'truth'. But the thing is simple enough: this thing of loving one's neighbour is self-denial; that of loving the crowd, or of pretending to love it, of making it the authority in matters of truth, is the way to material power, the way to temporal and earthly advantages of all sorts—at the same time it is the untruth, for a crowd is the untruth.

But he who acknowledges the truth of this view, which is seldom presented (for it often happens that a man thinks that the crowd is the untruth, but when it—the crowd—accepts his opinion *en masse*, everything is all right again), admits for himself that he is weak and impotent; for how could it be possible for an individual to make a stand against the crowd which possesses the power! And he could not wish to get the crowd on his side for the sake of ensuring that his view would prevail, the crowd, ethico-religiously regarded, being the untruth—that would be mocking himself. But although from the first this view involves an admission of weakness and impotence, and seems therefore far from inviting, and for this reason perhaps is so seldom heard, yet it has the good feature that it is even-handed, that it offends no one, not a single person, that it makes no invidious distinctions, not the least in the world. The crowd, in fact, is composed of individuals; it must therefore be in every man's power to become what he is, an individual. From becoming an individual no one, no one at all, is excluded, except he who excludes himself by becoming a crowd. To become a crowd, to collect a crowd about one, is on the contrary to affirm the distinctions of human life. The most well-meaning person who talks about these distinctions can easily offend an individual. But then it is not the crowd which possesses power, influence, repute, and mastery over men, but it is the invidious distinctions of human life which despotically ignore the single individual as the weak and impotent, which in a temporal and worldly interest ignore the eternal truth—the single individual.

HOW JOHANNES CLIMACUS BECAME AN AUTHOR[5]

It is now about four years since I got the notion of wanting to try my hand as an author. I remember it quite clearly; it was on a Sunday, yes, that's it, a Sunday afternoon. As usual I was sitting out-of-doors at the café in the Frederiksberg Garden, that wonderful garden which for the child was fairyland, where the King dwelt with his Queen, that delightful garden which afforded the youth happy diversion in the merriment of the populace, that friendly garden where now for the man of riper years there is such a homely feeling of sad exaltation above the world and all that is of the world, where even the invidious glory of royal dignity is what it is now out there—a queen's remembrance of her deceased lord.[6] There I sat as usual and smoked my cigar. . . .

I had been a student for ten years.

---

[5]This and the following excerpt on "The Subjective Truth: Inwardness" are from *Concluding Unscientific Postscript*, trans. David F. Swenson, Lillian Marvin Swenson, and Walter Lowrie, in *A Kierkegaard Anthology*, ed. Robert Bretall. Copyright 1946 by Princeton University Press. Reprinted by permission.

[6]Referring to the widow of Frederick VI, who continued to reside there a great part of the year. [Note by Lowrie. The remaining notes are by Kierkegaard.]

Although never lazy, all my activity nevertheless was like a glittering inactivity, a kind of occupation for which I still have a strong predilection, and perhaps even a little talent. I read much, spent the rest of the day idling and thinking, or thinking and idling, but that was all it came to; the earliest sproutings of my productivity barely sufficed for my daily use and were consumed in their first greening. An inexplicable and overwhelming might constantly held me back, by strength as well as by artifice. This might was my indolence. It is not like the vehement aspiration of love, nor like the strong incentive of enthusiasm, it is rather like a housekeeper who holds one back, and with whom one is very well off, so well off that it never occurs to one to get married. This much is sure: though with the comforts of life I am not on the whole unacquainted, of all, indolence is the most comfortable.

So there I sat and smoked my cigar until I lapsed into reverie. Among other thoughts I remember this: "You are now," I said to myself, "on the way to becoming an old man, without being anything, and without really undertaking to do anything. On the other hand, wherever you look about you, in literature and in life, you see the celebrated names and figures, the precious and much heralded men who are coming into prominence and are much talked about, the many benefactors of the age who know how to benefit mankind by making life easier and easier, some by railways, others by omnibuses and steamboats, others by telegraph, others by easily apprehended compendiums and short recitals of everything worth knowing, and finally the true benefac-

tors of the age who by virtue of thought make spiritual existence systematically easier and easier, and yet more and more significant. And what are you doing?"

Here my self-communion was interrupted, for my cigar was burned out and a new one had to be lit. So I smoked again, and then suddenly there flashed through my mind this thought: "You must do something, but inasmuch as with your limited capacities it will be impossible to make anything easier than it has become, you must, with the same humanitarian enthusiasm as the others, undertake to make something harder." This notion pleased me immensely, and at the same time it flattered me to think that I, like the rest of them, would be loved and esteemed by the whole community. For when all combine in every way to make everything easier and easier, there remains only one possible danger, namely, that the easiness might become so great that it would be too great; then only one want is left, though not yet a felt want —that people will want difficulty. Out of love for mankind, and out of despair at my embarrassing situation, seeing that I had accomplished nothing and was unable to make anything easier than it had already been made, and moved by a genuine interest in those who make everything easy, I conceived it my task to create difficulties everywhere. I was struck also by the strange reflection that, after all, I might have to thank my indolence for the fact that this task became mine. For far from having found it, as Aladdin did the lamp, I must rather suppose that my indolence, by hindering me from intervening at an opportune time to make things easy, had forced upon me the only task that was left. . . .

THE SUBJECTIVE TRUTH: INWARDNESS TRUTH IS SUBJECTIVITY

When *the question of truth is raised in an objective manner, reflection is directed objectively to the truth, as an object to which the knower is related. Reflection is not focused upon the relationship, however, but upon the question of whether it is the truth to which the knower is related. If only the object to which he is related is the truth, the subject is accounted to be in the truth. When the question of the truth is raised subjectively, reflection is directed subjectively to the nature of the individual's relationship: if only the mode of this relationship is in the truth, the individual is in the truth, even if he should happen to be thus related to what is not true.*[7] Let us take as an example the knowledge of God. Objectively, reflection is directed to the problem of whether this object is the true God; subjectively, reflection is directed to the question whether the individual is related to a something *in such a manner* that his relationship is in truth a God-relationship. On which side is the truth now to be found? Ah, may we not here resort to a mediation, and say: It is on neither side, but in the mediation of both? Excellently well said, provided we might have it explained how an existing individual manages to be in a state of mediation. For to be in a state of mediation is to be finished, while to exist is to become. Nor can an existing individual be in two places at the same time—he cannot be an identity of subject and object. When he is nearest to being in two places at the same time he is in passion; but passion is merely momentary, and passion is also the highest expression of subjectivity.

The existing individual who chooses to pursue the objective way enters upon the entire approximation-process by which it is proposed to bring God to light objectively. But this is in all eternity impossible, because God is a subject, and therefore exists only for subjectivity in inwardness. The existing individual who chooses the subjective way apprehends instantly the entire dialectical difficulty involved in having to use some time, perhaps a long time, in finding God objectively; and he feels this dialectical difficulty in all its painfulness, because he must use God at that very moment, since every moment is wasted in which he does not have God.[8] That very instant he has God, not

[7] The reader will observe that the question here is about essential truth, or about the truth which is essentially related to existence, and that it is precisely for the sake of clarifying it as inwardness or as subjectivity that this contrast is drawn. (K)

[8] In this manner God certainly becomes a postulate, but not in the otiose manner in which this word is commonly understood. It becomes clear rather that the only way in which an existing individual comes into relation with God is when the dialectical contradiction brings his passion to the point of despair, and helps him to embrace God with the "category of despair" (faith). Then the postulate is so far from being arbitrary that it is precisely a life-necessity. It is then not so much that God is a postulate as that the existing individual's postulation of God is a necessity. (K)

by virtue of any objective deliberation but by virtue of the infinite passion of inwardness. The objective inquirer, on the other hand, is not embarrassed by such dialectical difficulties as are involved in devoting an entire period of investigation to finding God — since it is possible that the inquirer may die tomorrow; and if he lives he can scarcely regard God as something to be taken along if convenient, since God is precisely that which one takes *a tout prix*, which in the understanding of passion constitutes the true inward relationship to God.

It is at this point, so difficult dialectically, that the way swings off for everyone who knows what it means to think, and to think existentially; which is something very different from sitting at a desk like a fantastical being and writing about what one has never done, something very different from writing *de omnibus dubitandum*, and at the same time being as existentially credulous as the most sensuous of men. Here is where the way swings off, and the change is marked by the fact that, while objective knowledge rambles comfortably on by way of the long road of approximation without being impelled by the urge of passion, subjective knowledge counts every delay a deadly peril, and the decision so infinitely important and so instantly pressing that it is as if the opportunity had already passed unutilized.

Now when the problem is to reckon up on which side there is most truth, whether on the side of one who seeks the true God objectively, and pursues the approximate truth of the God-idea; or on the side of one who, driven by the infinite passion of his need of God, feels an infinite concern for his own relationship to God in truth (and to be at one and the same time on both sides equally is, as we have noted, not possible for an existing individual, but is merely the happy delusion of an imaginary I-am-I): the answer cannot be in doubt for anyone who has not been demoralized with the aid of science. If one who lives in the midst of Christianity goes up to the house of God, the house of the true God, with the true conception of God in his knowledge, and prays, but prays in a false spirit; and one who lives in an idolatrous community prays with the entire passion of the infinite, although his eyes rest upon the image of an idol: where is there most truth? The one prays in truth to God though he worships an idol; the other prays falsely to the true God, and hence worships in fact an idol.

When one man investigates objectively the problem of immortality, and another embraces an uncertainty with the passion of the infinite: where is there most truth, and who has the greater certainty? The one has entered upon a never-ending approximation, for the certainty of immortality lies precisely in the subjectivity of the individual; the other is immortal, and fights for his immortality by struggling with the uncertainty. Let us consider Socrates. Nowadays everyone dabbles in a few proofs; some have several such proofs, others fewer. But Socrates! He puts the question objectively in a problematic manner: *if* there is an immortality. Must he therefore be accounted a doubter in comparison with one of our modern thinkers with the three proofs? By no means. On this "if" he risks his entire life, he has the courage to meet death, and he has with the passion of the infinite so determined the pattern of his life that it must be found acceptable — *if* there is an immortality. Can any better proof be given for the immortality of the soul? But those who have the three proofs do not at all determine their lives in conformity therewith; if there is an immortality, it must feel disgust over their manner of life: can any better refutation be given of the three proofs? The "bit" of uncertainty that Socrates had helped him, because he himself contributed the passion of the infinite; the three proofs that the others have do not profit them at all, because they are and remain dead to spirit and enthusiasm, and their three proofs, in lieu of proving anything else, prove just this. A young girl may enjoy all the sweetness of love on the basis of what is merely a weak hope; but she is beloved, because she rests everything on this weak hope; but many a wedded matron more than once subjected to the strongest expressions of love has in so far indeed had proofs, but strangely enough has not enjoyed *quod erat demonstrandum*. The Socratic ignorance, which Socrates held fast with the entire passion of his inwardness, was thus an expression for the principle that the eternal truth is related to an existing individual, and that this truth must therefore be a paradox for him as long as he exists; and yet it is possible that there was more truth in the Socratic ignorance as it was in him, than in the entire objective truth of the System, which flirts with what the times demand and accommodates itself to *Privatdocents*.

The objective accent falls on WHAT is said, the subjective accent on HOW it is said. This distinction holds even in the aesthetic realm, and receives definite expression in the principle that what is in itself true may in the mouth of such and such a person become untrue. In these times this distinction is particularly worthy of notice for, if we wish to express in a single sentence the difference between ancient times and our own, we should doubtless have to say: "In ancient times only an individual here and there knew the truth; now all know it, but the inwardness of its appropriation stands in an inverse relationship to the extent of its dissemination. Aesthetically the contradiction that truth becomes untruth in this or that person's mouth is best construed comically. In the ethico-religious sphere, the accent is again on the "how." But this is not to be understood as referring to demeanor, expression, delivery, or the like; rather it refers to the relationship sustained by the existing individual, in his own existence, to the content of his utterance. Objectively the interest is focused merely on the thought-content, subjectively on the inwardness. At its maximum this inward "how" is the passion of the infinite, and the passion of the infinite is the truth. But the passion of the infinite is precisely subjectivity, and thus subjectivity becomes the truth. Objectively there is no infinite decision, and hence it is objectively in order to annul the difference between good and evil, together with the principle of contradiction, and therewith also the infinite difference between the true and the false. Only in subjectivity is there decision, to seek objectivity is to be in error. It is the passion of the infinite that is the decisive factor and not its content, for its content is precisely it-self. In this manner subjectivity and the subjective "how" constitute the truth.

But the "how" which is thus subjectively accentuated, precisely because the subject is an existing individual, is also subject to a dialectic with respect to time. In the passionate moment of decision, where the road swings away from objective knowledge, it seems as if the infinite decision were thereby realized. But in the same moment the existing individual finds himself in the temporal order, and the subjective "how" is transformed into a striving, a striving which receives indeed its impulse and a repeated renewal from the decisive passion of the infinite, but is nevertheless a striving.

When subjectivity is the truth, the conceptual determination of the truth must include an expression for the antithesis to objectivity, a memento of the fork in the road where the way swings off; this expression will also indicate the tension of the subjective inwardness. Here is such a definition of truth: *An objective uncertainty held fast in an appropriation-process of the most passionate inwardness is the truth*, the highest truth attainable for an *existing individual*. At the point where the way swings off (and where this is cannot be specified objectively, since it is a matter of subjectivity), there objective knowledge is placed in abeyance. Thus the subject merely has, objectively, the uncertainty; but it is this which precisely increases the tension of that infinite passion which constitutes his inwardness. The truth is precisely the venture which chooses an objective uncertainty with the passion of the infinite. I contemplate nature in the hope of finding God, and I see omnipotence and wisdom; but I also see much else that disturbs my mind and excites anxiety. The sum of all this is an objective uncertainty. But it is for this very reason that the inwardness becomes as intense as it is, for it embraces this objective uncertainty with the entire passion of the infinite. In the case of a mathematical proposition the objectivity is given, but for this reason the truth of such a proposition is also an indifferent truth.

But the above definition of truth is an equivalent expression for faith. Without risk there is no faith. Faith is precisely the contradiction between the infinite passion of the individual's inwardness and the objective uncertainty. If I am capable of grasping God objectively, I do not believe, but precisely because I cannot do this I must believe. If I wish to preserve myself in faith I must constantly be intent upon holding fast the objective uncertainty, so that in the objective uncertainty I am out "upon the seventy thousand fathoms of water," and yet believe. . . .

GABRIEL MARCEL (1889–1973)

Gabriel Marcel was born and raised in France and is generally regarded as a twentieth-century exponent of "religious existentialism." He began his life as a highly cultured, liberal idealist, but he was shocked into seeking a more "realistic" philosophy by the horrors he saw while working for the Red Cross during World War I. Marcel converted to Catholicism in 1929 but seems never to have considered himself a religious philosopher. In fact, although his thought bears strong resemblance to that of Søren Kierkegaard, Martin Heidegger, and Martin Buber, Marcel is known to have raised frequently the question of whether or not he was an existentialist thinker.

Nonetheless, like other existentialists, Marcel exhibited a strong interest in the arts. He wrote plays and experimented with music. In all his work he sought to avoid the empty theoretic abstractions often associated with traditional philosophy. Instead he strove to develop an approach that would provide a concrete analysis of thought, faith, and being as they are actually experienced by human beings, while at the same time preserving their mysterious quality.

Marcel's main philosophical works include *Creative Fidelity* (1940), *The Philosophy of Existence* (1949), *The Mystery of Being* (1950), and *Man Against Humanity* (1952). His plays include *The Lantern* (1958), *A Man of God* (1958), *Ariadne* (1965), and *The Funeral Pyre* (1965). The following selection is taken from the book *The Mystery of Being*.

Problems and Mystery

ON THE ONTOLOGICAL MYSTERY

The title of this essay is likely to annoy the philosopher as much as to startle the layman, since philosophers are inclined to leave mystery either to the theologians or else to the vulgarisers, whether of mysticism or of occultism, such as Maeterlinck. Moreover, the term *ontological*, which has only the vaguest meaning for the layman, has become discredited in the eyes of Idealist philosophers; while the term *mystery* is reserved by those thinkers who are imbued with the ideas of Scholasticism for the revealed mysteries of religion.

Thus my terminology is clearly open to criticism from all sides. But I can find no other which is adequate to the body of ideas which I intend to put forward and on which my whole outlook is based. Readers of my *Journal Méta-*

Reprinted by permission from Marcel's *The Philosophy of Existentialism* 1956, translated by Manya Harari. Published by arrangement with Carol Publishing Group.

physique will see that they represent the term of the whole spiritual and philosophical evolution which I have described in that book.

Rather than to begin with abstract definitions and dialectical arguments which may be discouraging at the outset, I should like to start with a sort of global and intuitive characterisation of the man in whom the sense of the ontological—the sense of being—is lacking, or, to speak more correctly, of the man who has lost the awareness of this sense. Generally speaking, modern man is in this condition; if ontological demands worry him at all, it is only dully, as an obscure impulse. Indeed I wonder if a psychoanalytical method, deeper and more discerning than any that has been evolved until now, would not reveal the morbid effects of the repression of this sense and of the ignoring of this need.

The characteristic feature of our age seems to me to be what might be called the misplacement of the idea of function, taking function in its current sense which includes both the vital and the social functions.

The individual tends to appear both to himself and to others as an agglomeration of functions. As a result of deep historical causes, which can as yet be understood only in part, he has been led to see himself more and more as a mere assemblage of functions, the hierarchical interrelation of which seems to him questionable or at least subject to conflicting interpretations.

To take the vital functions first. It is hardly necessary to point out the role which historical materialism on the one hand, and Freudian doctrines on the other, have played in restricting the concept of man.

Then there are the social functions —those of the consumer, the producer, the citizen, etc.

Between these two there is, in theory, room for the psychological functions as well; but it is easy to see how these will tend to be interpreted in relation either to the social or the vital functions, so that their independence will be threatened and their specific character put in doubt. In this sense, Comte, served by his total incomprehension of psychical reality, displayed an almost prophetic instinct when he excluded psychology from his classification of sciences.

So far we are still dealing only with abstractions, but nothing is easier than to find concrete illustrations in this field.

Travelling on the Underground, I often wonder with a kind of dread what can be the inward reality of the life of this or that man employed on the railway—the man who opens the doors, for instance, or the one who punches the tickets. Surely everything both within him and outside him conspires to identify this man with his functions—meaning not only with his functions as worker, as trade union member or as voter, but with his vital functions as well. The rather horrible expression "time table" perfectly describes his life. So many hours for each function. Sleep too is a function which must be discharged so that the other functions may be exercised in their turn. The same with pleasure, with relaxation; it is logical that the weekly allowance of recreation should be determined by an expert on hygiene; recreation is a psycho-organic function which must not be neglected any more than, for instance, the function of sex. We need go no further; this sketch is sufficient to suggest the emergence of a kind of vital schedule; the details will vary with the country, the climate, the profession, etc., but what matters is that there is a schedule.

It is true that certain disorderly elements — sickness, accidents of every sort — will break in on the smooth working of the system. It is therefore natural that the individual should be overhauled at regular intervals like a watch (this is often done in America). The hospital plays the part of the inspection bench or the repair shop. And it is from this same standpoint of function that such essential problems as birth control will be examined.

As for death, it becomes, objectively and functionally, the scrapping of what has ceased to be of use and must be written off as total loss.

I need hardly insist on the stifling impression of sadness produced by this functionalised world. It is sufficient to recall the dreary image of the retired official, or those urban Sundays when the passers-by look like people who have retired from life. In such a world, there is something mocking and sinister even in the tolerance awarded to the man who has retired from his work.

But besides the sadness felt by the onlooker, there is the dull, intolerable unease of the actor himself who is reduced to living as though he were in fact submerged by his functions. This uneasiness is enough to show that there is in all this some appalling mistake,

some ghastly misinterpretation, implanted in defenceless minds by an increasingly inhuman social order and an equally inhuman philosophy (for if the philosophy has prepared the way for the order, the order has also shaped the philosophy).

I have written on another occasion that, provided it is taken in its metaphysical and not its physical sense, the distinction between the *full* and the *empty* seems to me more fundamental than that between the *one* and the *many*. This is particularly applicable to the case in point. Life in a world centered on function is liable to despair because in reality this world is *empty*, it rings hollow; and if it resists this temptation it is only to the extent that there come into play from within it and in its favour certain hidden forces which are beyond its power to conceive or to recognise.

It should be noted that this world is, on the one hand, riddled with problems and, on the other, determined to allow no room for mystery. I shall come back to this distinction between problem and mystery which I believe to be fundamental. For the moment I shall only point out that to eliminate or to try to eliminate mystery is (in this functionalist world) to bring into play in the face of events which break in on the course of existence — such as birth, love and death — that psychological and pseudo-scientific category of the "purely natural" which deserves a study to itself. In reality, this is nothing more than the remains of a degraded rationalism from whose standpoint cause explains effect and accounts for it exhaustively. There exists in such a world, nevertheless, an infinity of problems, since the causes are not known to us in detail and thus leave room for unlimited research. And in addition to these theoretical puzzles there are innumerable technical problems, bound up with the difficulty of knowing how the various functions, once they have been inventoried and labelled, can be made to work together without doing one another harm. These theoretical and technical questions are interdependent, for the theoretical problems arise out of the different techniques while the technical problems can not be solved without a measure of pre-established theoretical knowledge.

In such a world the ontological need, the need of being, is exhausted in exact proportion to the breaking up of personality on the one hand and, on the other, to the triumph of the category of the "purely natural" and the consequent atrophy of the faculty of *wonder*.

But to come at last to the ontological need itself; can we not approach it directly and attempt to define it? In reality this can only be done to a limited extent. For reasons which I shall develop later, I suspect that the characteristic of this need is that it can never be wholly clear to itself.

To try to describe it without distorting it we shall have to say something like this:

Being is — or should be — necessary. It is impossible that everything should be reduced to a play of successive appearances which are inconsistent with each other ("inconsistent" is essential), or, in the words of Shakespeare, to "a tale told by an idiot." I aspire to participate in this being, in this reality — and perhaps this aspiration is already a degree of participation, however rudimentary.

Such a need, it may be noted, is to be found at the heart of the most inveterate pessimism. Pessimism has no meaning unless it signifies: it would surely be well if there were being, but there is no being, and I, who observe this fact, am therefore nothing.

As for defining the word "being," let us admit that it is extremely difficult. I would merely suggest this method of approach: being is what withstands — or what would withstand — an exhaustive analysis bearing on the data of experience and aiming to reduce them step by step to elements increasingly devoid of intrinsic or significant value. (An analysis of this kind is attempted in the theoretical works of Freud.)

When the pessimist Besme says in *La Ville* that *nothing is*, he means precisely this, that there is no experience that withstands this analytical test. And it is always towards death regarded as the manifestation, the proof of this ultimate nothingness that the kind of inverted apologetic which arises out of absolute pessimism will inevitably gravitate.

A philosophy which refuses to endorse the ontological need is, nevertheless, possible; indeed, generally speaking, contemporary thought tends towards this abstention. But at this point a distinction must be made between two different attitudes which are sometimes confused: one which consists in a systematic reserve (it is that of agnosticism in all its forms), and the other, bolder and more coherent, which regards the ontological need as the expression of an outworn body of dogma liquidated once and for all by the Idealist critique.

The former appears to me to be purely negative: it is merely the expression of an intellectual policy of "not raising the question."

The latter, on the contrary, claims to be based on a positive theory of thought. This is not the place for a detailed critical study of this philosophy. I shall only note that it seems to me to tend towards an unconscious relativism, or else towards a monism which ignores the personal in all its form, ignores the tragic and denies the transcendent, seeking to reduce it to its caricatural expressions which distort its essential character. I shall also point out that, just because this philosophy continually stresses the activity of verification, it ends by ignoring *presence* —that inward realisation of presence through love which infinitely transcends all possible verification because it exists in an immediacy beyond all conceivable mediation. This will be clearer to some extent from what follows.

Thus I believe for my part that the ontological need cannot be silenced by an arbitrary dictatorial act which mutilates the life of the spirit at its roots. It remains true, nevertheless, that such an act is possible, and the conditions of our life are such that we can well believe that we are carrying it out; this must never be forgotten.

These preliminary reflections on the ontological need are sufficient to bring out its indeterminate character and to reveal a fundamental paradox. To formulate this need is to raise a host of questions: Is there such a thing as being? What is it? etc. Yet immediately an abyss opens under my feet: I who ask these questions about being, how can I be sure that I exist?

Yet surely I, who formulate this *problem*, should be able to remain *outside* it —*before* or *beyond* it? Clearly this is not so. The more I consider it the more I find that this problem tends inevitably to invade the proscenium from which it is excluded in theory: it is only by means of a fiction that Idealism in its traditional form seeks to maintain on the margin of being the consciousness which asserts it or denies it.

So I am inevitably forced to ask: Who am I—I who question being? How am I qualified to begin this investigation? If I do not exist, how can I succeed in it? And if I do exist, how can I be sure of this fact?

Contrary to the opinion which suggests itself at this point, I believe that on this plane the *cogito* cannot help us at all. Whatever Descartes may have thought of it himself, the only certainty with which it provides us concerns only the epistemological subject as organ of objective cognition. As I have written elsewhere, the *cogito* merely guards the threshold of objective validity, and that is strictly all; this is proved by the indeterminate character of the *I*. The *I am* is, to my mind, a global statement which it is impossible to break down into its component parts.

There remains a possible objection; it might be said: Either the being designated in the question "What am I?" concerns the subject of cognition, and in this case we are on the plane of the *cogito*; or else that which you call the ontological need is merely the extreme point (or perhaps only the fallacious transposition) of a need which is, in reality, vital and with which the metaphysician is not concerned.

But is it not a mistake arbitrarily to divide the question, *Who am I?* from the ontological "problem" taken as a whole? The truth is that neither of the two can be dealt with separately, but that when they are taken together, they cancel one another out *as problems.*

It should be added that the Cartesian position is inseparable from a form of dualism which I, for my part, would unhesitatingly reject. To raise the ontological problem is to raise the question of being as a whole and of oneself seen as a totality.

But should we not ask ourselves if we must not reject this dissociation between the intellectual and the vital, with its resultant over- or under-estimation of the one or the other? Doubtless it is legitimate to establish certain distinctions within the unity of the being who thinks and who endeavours to *think himself*; but it is only beyond such distinctions that the ontological problem can arise and it must relate to that being seen in his all-comprehensive unity.

To sum up our reflections at this point, we find that we are dealing with an urge towards an affirmation — yet an affirmation which it seems impossible to make, since it is not until it has been made that I can regard myself as qualified to make it.

It should be noted that this difficulty never arises at a time when I am actually faced with a problem to be solved. In such a case I work on the data, but everything leads me to believe that I

need not take into account the *I* who is at work — it is a factor which is presupposed and nothing more.

Here, on the contrary, which I would call the ontological status of the investigator assumes a decisive importance. Yet so long as I am concerned with thought itself I seem to follow an endless regression. But by the very fact of recognising it as endless I transcend it in a certain way: I see that this process takes place within an affirmation of being — an affirmation which I *am* rather than an affirmation which I *utter*: by uttering it I break, I divide it, I am on the point of betraying it.

It might be said, by way of an approximation, that my inquiry into being presupposes an affirmation in regard to which I am, in a sense, passive, *and of which I am the stage rather than the subject.* But this is only at the extreme limit of thought, a limit which I cannot reach without falling into contradiction. I am therefore led to assume or to recognise a form of participation which has the reality of a subject; this participation cannot be, by definition, an *object* of thought; it cannot serve as a solution — it appears beyond the realm of problems: it is meta-problematical.

Conversely, it will be seen that, if the meta-problematical can be asserted at all, it must be conceived as transcending the opposition between the subject who asserts the existence of being, on the one hand, and being *as asserted by that subject*, on the other, and as underlying it in a given sense. To postulate the meta-problematical is to postulate the primacy of being over knowledge (not of being as *asserted,* but of being as *asserting itself*); it is to recognise that knowledge is, as it were, environed by being, that it is interior to it in a certain sense—a sense perhaps analogous to that which Paul Claudel tried to define in his *Art Poètique*. From this standpoint, contrary to what epistemology seeks vainly to establish, there exists well and truly a mystery of cognition; knowledge is contingent on a participation in being for which no epistemology can account because it continually presupposes it.

At this point we can begin to define the distinction between mystery and problem. A mystery is a problem which encroaches upon its own data, invading them, as it were, and thereby transcending itself as a simple problem. A set of examples will help us to grasp the content of this definition.

It is evident that there exists a mystery of the union of the body and the soul. The indivisible unity always inadequately expressed by such phrases as *I have a body, I make use of my body, I feel my body,* etc., can be neither analysed nor reconstituted out of precedent elements. It is not only data, I would say that it is the basis of data, in the sense of being my own presence to myself, a presence of which the act of self-consciousness is, in the last analysis, only an inadequate symbol.

It will be seen at once that there is no hope of establishing an exact frontier between problem and mystery. For in reflecting on a mystery we tend inevitably to degrade it to the level of a problem. This is particularly clear in the case of the problem of evil.

In reflecting upon evil, I tend, almost inevitably, to regard it as a disorder which I view from outside and of which I seek to discover the causes or the secret aims. Why is it that the "mechanism" functions so defectively? Or is the defect merely apparent and due to a real defect of my vision? In this case the defect is in myself, yet it remains objective in relation to my thought, which discovers it and observes it. But evil which is only stated or observed is no longer evil which is suffered: in fact, it ceases to be evil. In reality, I can only grasp it as evil in the measure in which it *touches* me—that is to say, in the measure in which I am *involved*, as one is involved in a lawsuit. Being "involved" is the fundamental fact; I cannot leave it out of account except by an unjustifiable fiction, for in doing so, I proceed as though I were God, and a God who is an onlooker at that.

This brings out how the distinction between what is *in me* and what is only *before me* can break down. This distinction falls under the blow of a certain kind of thought: thought at one remove.

But it is, of course, in love that the obliteration of this frontier can best be seen. It might perhaps even be shown that the domain of the meta-problematical coincides with that of love, and that love is the only starting point for the understanding of such mysteries as that of a body and soul, which, in some manner, is its expression.

Actually, it is inevitable that, in being brought to bear on love, thought which has not thought itself—unreflected reflection—should tend to dissolve its meta-problematical character and interpret it in terms of abstract concepts, such as the will to live, the will to power, the *libido*, etc. On the other hand, since the domain of the problematical is that of the objectively valid, it will be extremely difficult—if not impossible—to refute these interpretations without changing to a new ground: a ground on which, to tell the truth, they lose their meaning. Yet I have the assurance, the certainty—and it envelops me like a protective cloak—that for as much as I really love I must not be concerned with these attempts at devaluation.

It will be asked: What is the criterion of true love? It must be answered that there is no criteriology except in the order of the objective and the problematical; but we can already see at a distance the eminent ontological value to be assigned to fidelity.

Let us take another illustration, more immediate and more particular, which may shed some light on the distinction between problem and mystery.

Say that I have made an encounter which has left a deep and lasting trace on all my life. It may happen to anyone to experience the deep spiritual significance of such a meeting—yet this is something which philosophers have commonly ignored or disdained, doubtless because it effects only the particular person as person—it cannot be universalised, it does not concern rational being in general.

It is clear that such a meeting raises, if you will, a problem; but it is equally clear that the solution of this problem will always fall short of the only question that matters. Suppose that I am told, for instance: "The reason you have met this person in this place is

that you both like the same kind of scenery, or that you both need the same kind of treatment for your health"—the explanation means nothing. Crowds of people who apparently share my tastes were in the Engadine or in Florence at the time I was there; and there are always numbers of patients suffering from the same disease as myself at the health resort I frequent. But neither this supposed identity of tastes nor this common affliction has brought us together in any real sense; it has nothing to do with that intimate and unique affinity with which we are dealing. At the same time, it would be transgression of this valid reasoning to treat this affinity as if it were itself the cause and to say: "It is precisely this which has determined our meeting."

Hence I am in the presence of a mystery. That is to say, of a reality rooted in what is beyond the domain of the problematical properly so called. Shall we avoid the difficulty by saying that it was after all nothing but a coincidence, a lucky chance? But the whole of me immediately protests against this empty formula, this vain negation of what I apprehend with the deepest of my being. Once again we are brought back to our first definition of a mystery as a problem which encroaches upon its own data: I who inquire into the meaning and the possibility of this meeting, I cannot place myself outside it or before it; I am engaged in this encounter, I depend upon it, I am inside it in a certain sense, it envelops me and it comprehends me—even if it is not comprehended by me. Thus it is only by a kind of betrayal or denial that I can say: "After all, it might not have happened,

I would still have been what I was, and what I am to-day." Nor must it be said: I have been changed by it as by an outward cause. No, it has developed me from within, it has acted in me as an inward principle.

But this is very difficult to grasp without distortion. I shall be inevitably tempted to react against this sense of the inwardness of the encounter, tempted by my probity itself, by what from a certain standpoint I must judge to be the best — or at least the safest — of myself.

There is a danger that these explanations may strengthen in the minds of my readers a preliminary objection which must be stated at once.

It will be said: The meta-problematical of which you speak is after all a content of thought; how then should we not ask ourselves what is its mode of existence? What assures us of its existence at all? Is it not itself problematical in the highest degree?

My answer is categorical: To think, or, rather, to assert, the meta-problematical is to assert it as indubitably real, as a thing of which I cannot doubt without falling into contradiction. We are in a sphere where it is no longer possible to dissociate the idea itself from the certainty or the degree of certainty which pertains to it. Because this idea *is* certainty, it *is* the assurance of itself; it is, in this sense, something other and something more than an idea. As for the term *content of thought* which figured in the objection, it is deceptive in the highest degree. For content is, when all is said and done, derived from experience; whereas it is only by a way of liberation and detach-ment from experience that we can possibly rise to the level of the meta-prob-lematical and of mystery. This liberation must be *real*; this detach-ment must be *real*; they must not be an abstraction, that is to say a fiction re-cognised as such.

And this at last brings us to recollec-tion, for it is in recollection and in this alone that this detachment is accom-plished. I am convinced, for my part, that no ontology — that is to say, no apprehension of ontological mystery in whatever degree — is possible except to a being who is capable of recollecting himself, and of thus proving that he is not a living creature pure and simple, a creature, that is to say, which is at the mercy of its life and without a hold upon it.

It should be noted that recollection, which has received little enough atten-tion from pure philosophers, is very difficult to define — if only because it transcends the dualism of being and ac-tion or, more correctly, because it rec-onciles in itself these two aspects of the antinomy. The word means what it says — the act whereby I re-collect my-self as a unity; but this hold, this grasp upon myself, is also relaxation and abandon. *Abandon to . . . relaxation in the presence of . . .* — yet there is no noun for these prepositions to gov-ern. The way stops at the threshold.

Here, as in every other sphere, prob-lems will be raised, and it is the psy-chologist who will raise them. All that must be noted is that the psychologist is no more in a position to shed light on the metaphysical bearing of recollec-tion than on the noetic value of knowledge.

It is within recollection that I take up my position — or, rather, I become capable of taking up my position — in regard to my life; I withdraw from it in a certain way, but not as the pure subject of cognition; *in this withdrawal I carry with me that which I am and which perhaps my life is not.* This brings out the gap between by being and my life. I am not my life; and if I can judge my life — a fact I cannot deny without falling into a radical scepticism which is nothing other than despair — it is only on condition that I encounter myself within recollection beyond all possible judgment and, I would add, beyond all representation. Recollection is doubtless what is least spectacular in the soul; it does not consist in looking at something, it is an inward hold, an inward reflection, and it might be asked in passing whether it should not be seen as the ontological basis of memory — that principle of effective and non-representational unity on which the possibility of remembrance rests. The double meaning of "recollection" in English is revealing.

It may be asked: is not recollection identical with that dialectical moment of the turning to oneself (*retour sur soi*) or else with the *fuer sich sein* which is the central theme of German Idealism?

I do not think so. To withdraw into oneself is not to be for oneself nor to mirror oneself in the intelligible unity of subject and object. On the contrary. I would say that here we come up against the paradox of that actual mystery whereby the I into which I withdraw ceases, for as much, to belong to itself. "You are not your own" — this great saying of St. Paul assumes in this connection its full concrete and ontological significance; it is the nearest approach to the reality for which we are groping. It will be asked: is not this reality an object of intuition? Is not that which you term "recollection" the same as what others have termed "intuition"?

But this again seems to me to call for the utmost prudence. If intuition can be mentioned in this content at all, it is not an intuition which is, or can be, given as such.

The more an intuition is central and basic in the being whom it illuminates, the less it is capable of turning back and apprehending itself.

Moreover, if we reflect on what an intuitive knowledge of being could possibly be, we see that it could never figure in a collection, a procession of simple experiences or *Erlebnisse*, which all have this characteristic that they can be at times absorbed and at others isolated and, as it were, uncovered. Hence, any effort to remember such an intuition, to represent it to oneself, is inevitably fruitless. From this point of view, to be told of an intuitive knowledge of being is like being invited to play on a soundless piano. Such an intuition cannot be brought out into the light of day, for the simple reason that we do not possess it.

We are here at the most difficult point of our whole discussion. Rather than to speak of intuition in this context, we should say that we are dealing with an assurance which underlies the entire development of thought, even of discursive thought; it can therefore be approached only by a second reflection

—a reflection whereby I ask myself how and from what starting point I was able to proceed in my initial reflection, which itself postulated the ontological, but without knowing it. This second reflection is recollection in the measure in which recollection can be self-conscious.

COMMENT

Kierkegaard and Existentialism

The present century has witnessed crises of unparalleled scope and intensity: two world wars, a very severe economic depression, revolutionary movements of tremendous magnitude and fury, the threat of nuclear holocaust. Philosophers have reacted with different degrees of intensity to these world-shaking events. Apart from the Marxists, the existentialists have been the philosophers most responsive. Existentialism, in fact, is a philosophy of crisis — its popularity can be explained largely in these terms. Although Sartre and Camus in France, Heidegger and Jaspers in Germany and the other existentialist philosophers have been able to agree on almost nothing else, they are alike in reflecting a time out of joint, when people have been hungry for meaning, for identity, for some roots in existence, for some structure of purpose in human experience, for some protection against anxieties and frustrations.

Certainly the "existentialists" are a strange assortment of figures. Jaspers, for example, is a Protestant, Marcel a Catholic, Buber a religious Jew, Heidegger an agnostic, Sartre an atheist. Their political convictions are no less diverse. As a result, "existentialism" has come to mean so many things that, by itself, it would seem to mean nothing. Nevertheless the existentialists exhibit, as Wittgenstein would say, a "family resemblance." We can best understand this resemblance if we trace the family tree back to its roots in such forerunners as Kierkegaard and Nietzsche. It is Søren Kierkegaard, above all, who is the fountainhead of our contemporary existentialism. His influence, which rapidly increased in the period between the two world wars, has spread beyond the boundaries of the Scandinavian countries and has largely molded the philosophy of existentialism in Germany, France, Spain, Latin America, and to a lesser degree, the United States.

In the foregoing readings from Kierkegaard there are several themes that are typical of the existentialist movement:

1. EMPHASIS ON CONCRETE INDIVIDUAL EXISTENCE. Kierkegaard was convinced that his religious and philosophical mission could be fulfilled

only through his own personal experience and not through abstract mental processes. He is an existentialist in the sense that his stress is on the sheer factual existence of the individual. As Master Eckhart, the German mystic, has said, "That I am a man, this I share with other men. That I see and hear and that I eat and drink is what all animals do likewise. But that I am I is only mine and belongs to me and to nobody else; to no other man nor to an angel nor to God—except inasmuch as I am one with him."[1] Every man is an individual. He is "man" in the singular; he is not the abstraction "mankind." He shares many characteristics with other animals and with other men; but there is always a peculiar temperament, a unique blend of talents, a separate and distinctive consciousness. There is always something about me that is never common to you and me. Respect for a person is respect for this core of individuality. It is appreciation of the real person of flesh and blood—the unique *me*.

Individuality for Kierkegaard is opposed to both the stereotypes of mass society and the abstractness of philosophical systems. He detested the anonymity of "the crowd" and every kind of dehumanizing collectivism. "The crowd is untruth," he said again and again. The kind of "truth" that Kierkegaard valued most is realized inwardly in the life of the individual. Hence he had a profound distaste for all *systems* of thought, such as Hegelianism. To exist as an individual is to suffer and to struggle, to develop, to be open to new possibilities, to be incomplete and inconsistent—whereas a system by its very nature is closed, static, dead, complete. "A logical system is possible," he said, but "an existential system is impossible."[2]

The very titles of Kierkegaard's major works—*Philosophical Fragments* and *Concluding Unscientific Postscript*—suggest the deliberately untidy and fragmentary character of his reflections. He issued a number of his books under pseudonyms, different from book to book, so that he was free to attack his own work under a different pseudonym. He thus avoided even the appearance of trying to construct a single, consistent, systematic body of thought.

2. The Need to Make Things Difficult. "With everyone engaged everywhere in making things easier," the pseudonymous author Johannes Climacus remarks, "someone was needed to make them difficult again." The passage from which this sentence is taken is a witty piece of fiction, but there is an underlying seriousness about it. The modern world, with

---

[1]Master Eckhart, *Fragments*, as quoted by Erich Fromm, *Man for Himself* (New York: Holt, Rinehart & Winston, 1947), p. 38.
[2]*Concluding Unscientific Postscript*, in Robert Bretall, *A Kierkegaard Anthology* (Princeton, NJ: Princeton University Press, 1946), p. 196.

its labor-saving devices and painkillers, its mass stereotypes and oversimplified explanations, has made things too easy. One should face up to the
tragic conflicts, paradoxes, and complexities of human existence. Where a
rigid scientific rationalism has postulated only one kind of truth—
objective scientific truth—and only one kind of good—the value of
scientific and technological mastery—someone is needed to stress the
truths and values of other modes of experience. Few men have explored
more deeply than Kierkegaard the meaning of dread, anguish, alienation,
and self-estrangement, "sickness unto death," and the kind of wisdom
that can be gleaned from such experiences.

In the "pregnant moment" of crisis, existence and thought are fused
into unity, and a person attains, if ever, authentic existence. The individual in a crisis may make dramatic and irrevocable choices for which he or
she must assume sole responsibility. One of the persistent themes of
existentialism, from Pascal to Sartre, is the need and reality of choice.
Sartre speaks as if every action expresses an individual choice, whereas
Kierkegaard speaks more often of the choice of a way of life, aesthetic or
moral or religious. This transition from one way of life to another is
conceived as a kind of conversion, dramatic and sometimes catastrophic.
But both Kierkegaard and Sartre agree that people do not have fixed
natures or predetermined roles.

3. THE CLAIM THAT TRUTH IS SUBJECTIVITY. Kierkegaard's view of
truth is based on the distinction between what we believe and how we
believe. Objectively the interest is focused on the object of belief, subjectively on the attitude of the believer. When it comes to matters of scientific truth, it is the object as verifiable that is of primary concern. But
Kierkegaard is not much interested in objective truth in this sense. He is
primarily concerned with an existential relationship of the individual
with God. When it comes to this, what is most important is an intense
spirituality. Through faith the individual appropriates in passionate inwardness the eternal truth of God's existence. What is sought is not
scientific verification or rational understanding, which in this instance is
impossible, but something that passes understanding, namely, a faith so
intense that it amounts to salvation. With this kind of "truth" in mind,
Kierkegaard proclaims his thesis: Truth is subjectivity.

The reader may feel that such a conception of truth is highly paradoxical if not downright contradictory. To call "true" the existential status of
the individual in believing may seem to be an abuse of language. In a
revealing passage Kierkegaard declares, "It is impossible to express with
more intensive inwardness the principle that subjectivity is truth, than
when subjectivity is in the first instance untruth, and yet subjectivity is

the truth."[3] In other words, a superstition believed in a certain manner is subjectively "true," regardless of its objective falsity.

Almost everything that Kierkegaard has written is highly controversial. Before committing oneself pro or con the reader might ponder such questions as these: Is Kierkegaard's emphasis on will and feeling, rather than reason or the scientific method, exaggerated? In his preference for passionate participation and commitment, does he undervalue a disinterested analytical attitude? Does he argue inconsistently both that ultimate choice is criterionless and that the choice of a religious way of life is more correct than any other? Is he a one-sided romanticist, and in that sense a reductionist, despite his proposal to "make things difficult"? In his preference for "existence" over "essence," is he begging the question as to what is "really real"? Does he undervalue the ability to sense the essential and to formulate it in something like a definition? These questions can best be answered if the point of view of Kierkegaard is critically compared with the views of the philosophers studied in the preceding chapters.

We have said that Kierkegaard has little use for the "crowd" or the "public" and that his emphasis is almost invariably on the "single one." In this respect he has struck a note that has reverberated throughout the present century. Human beings have been threatened or abused to a shocking degree by dehumanizing bureaucracies and all-powerful totalitarian states. All of the existentialists join in protest against this mass degradation. But here too there is ground for question or criticism of Kierkegaard's extreme individualism. "If ever a person was self-centered, it was Kierkegaard," H. J. Paton has declared: "He hardly ever thinks of anyone but himself."[4] — of himself in relation to God, we might add. This preoccupation with individual religious salvation can be challenged by an attack on either theism or individualism. Existentialists such as Nietzsche and Sartre have attacked the theism; existentialists such as Marcel and Buber have attacked the individualism.

Marcel and Self-Knowledge

Gabriel Marcel begins by pointing out the inherent circularity involved in Descartes' efforts to establish his own existence. No matter which way we come at this issue, we seem to find it necessary in some sense to assume what we are seeking to prove. Surely the act of proving something to be the case must be performed by an agent who would presumably be a self. Thus, when a self engages in proving its own existence, the argument

[3]*Concluding Unscientific Postscript* p. 191.
[4]*The Modern Predicament* (London: George Allen & Unwin, 1955), p. 120.

becomes confused. To put it another way, the first "I" in Descartes's famous *Cogito*, "I think, therefore I am," already makes use of and thus presupposes the conclusion.

This difficulty leads Marcel to distinguish between a "problem" and a "mystery". Problems can be separated from the person who is seeking to solve them, whereas mysteries cannot be objectified in this way since "they encroach on their own data." Marcel clearly thinks that the question of self-knowledge is more of a mystery than a problem. In other contexts, he includes our knowledge of other persons and God in this category as well. In a sense, such questions are so "close" to us, so involve our basic commitments and values, that we are inextricably connected with what is being examined, are as much a part of the problem as of the solution.

If this is the case, it is hardly surprising that according to Marcel, whenever we try to apply to a mystery our analytic or strictly intellectual capacities — which are designed for and appropriate to the solving of problems — we turn it into a problem and thereby miss its essence. In other words, Marcel contends, along with Kierkegaard, that not all knowledge is the result of objectifying cognitive activity. Questions that bear on the meaning of human existence, the ultimate nature of reality, the meaning of love, and so on can only be treated "inwardly" because they are mysteries rather than problems.

This inward reflection is termed *recollection* by Marcel. He does not use this term in the sense that Plato used it, as a remembrance of knowledge acquired in a previous existence. Rather, he seems to mean a form of reflective self-consciousness, a kind of self-transcendence in which one is both the knower and the known. Our knowledge of mysteries is, then, *reciprocal* in character: We both know ourselves and are the ones who do the knowing. Although this argument sounds very similar to Bergsonian intuition, Marcel is careful to distinguish his notion of recollection from that of Bergson. What is known with respect to mysteries is not a "datum" in the sense that Bergson or even Russell would speak of it. Rather, it is more like the "assurance which underlies the entire development of thought," the confidence with which we participate in the various dimensions of human existence.

Perhaps the most troubling question regarding this way of thinking about knowledge pertains to verification. The same problems that arose with Kierkegaard's notion of "subjectivity" would seem to plague Marcel's concept of "inwardness". If the knowledge supposedly appropriate to mystery cannot be articulated and tested in the manner appropriate to problems, how can we establish that it is knowledge? Is not one person's inward "knowledge" the same as another's inward "error"? How are conflicting claims to such knowledge adjudicated?

There is one significant difference between Kierkegaard's view and that of Marcel. Whereas the former stresses the individual character of truth, the latter appeals to the common cognitive experience of all humans. Marcel claims that the sort of knowledge he is speaking of, this interaction between the knower and the known, is shared by everyone at various level of life and in various contexts. We all know ourselves, each other, the world around us, and even the divine presence, in a way that, although not reducible to observation and inferential reasoning, is nonetheless absolutely certain. Indeed, he would say that we must draw on our knowledge of such mysteries even to explore and examine them, as well as to engage in the whole problem-solving procedure itself. Needless to say, not everyone agrees with Marcel's approach. As the British philosopher John Wisdom once said, "In philosophy someone always objects."

THE NATURE
OF REALITY

In Part One we have been concerned mainly with epistemology, or the theory of knowledge — especially with the meaning of truth and the methods of its attainment. In Part Two we shall be concerned primarily with metaphysics, or the theory of reality. It is impossible, however, to separate sharply epistemology and metaphysics. For example, in Part One, we studied the philosophy of Descartes, which is as important for metaphysics as for epistemology; and in Part Two we shall examine the philosophies of Berkeley, Hume, and Kant, which have contributed as greatly to epistemology as to metaphysics. The difference between Part One and Part Two, therefore, is not an absolute difference in subject matter but a relative difference in emphasis.

We shall consider the question "What is the fundamental nature of humanity and the surrounding universe?" This question directs attention to "the metaphysics of the microcosm" — of the "I," or self, as a small part of the whole scheme of things — and to "metaphysics of the macrocosm" — of the great, all-enveloping system of reality. We shall not attempt to separate these two inquiries, and indeed, any sharp separation would be artificial. However, each of the theories that we shall consider will throw light on the nature of the human being and the nature of the total environment. We shall discuss five answers, not all mutually exclusive:

1. *The answer of the theist.* The view of the theist may be combined with teleology, dualism, idealism, or vitalism, but it is incompatible with a complete materialism or an absolute skepticism. It conceives of human beings and animals as the creatures of God and of nature as God's handiwork.

2. *The answer of the materialist.* As opposed to the teleologist, the materialist tries to explain the present and the future in terms of past or antecedent causes, and these causes are conceived to be material, such as the movement of physical atoms.

3. *The answer of the idealist.* Like the materialist, the idealist denies ultimate dualism, but unlike the materialist, the idealist regards mind rather than matter as the basic stuff.

4. *The answer of the pantheist.* Pantheism is the view that all (*pan*), or everything, is God (*theos*) and God is all. In other words, the world and God are the same reality, albeit a reality that exhibits diverse attributes.

5. *The answer of the dualist.* The dualist recognizes two distinct and irreducible kinds of being—mind and matter—and regards a human being as a combination of the two. Although Descartes defined the essence of the mind as thought and the essence of the body as extension, he maintained that the two substances, the physical and the mental, interact within the pineal gland of the human brain.

6. *The answer of the relationalist.* A relationalist believes that the interaction and interconnectedness among all of the particular things constituting reality is more fundamental than the particulars themselves. Events and relationships are thought to be the essential qualities of reality.

The Existence of God

*"Why, then, has the fool said in his heart, there is
no God, since it is so evident, to a rational mind,
that thou dost exist in the highest degree of all?"*
                                        Saint Anselm

SAINT ANSELM (1033?–1109)

Although Italian by birth, Saint Anslem ended his career as archbishop of
Canterbury. He is famous not only for his philosophical works but also
for his interpretation of Christian theology. As abbot of a monastery in
Normandy and as archbishop in England, he was a zealous defender of the
Church against the expansion of secular power.

The Ontological Argument

. . . I do not seek to understand that I
may believe, but I believe in order to
understand. For this also I believe, —
that unless I believed, I should not
understand.

And so, Lord, do thou, who dost give

Translated by Sidney Norton Deane, Open
Court Publishing Co., 1903. Reprinted by
permission.

understanding to faith, give me, so far
as thou knowest it to be profitable, to
understand that thou art as we believe;
and that thou art that which we believe.
And, indeed, we believe that thou art a
being than which nothing greater can
be conceived. Or is there no such nature, since the fool hath said in his
heart, there is no God? (Psalms xiv. 1).
But, at any rate, this very fool, when he

hears of this being of which I speak — a being than which nothing greater can be conceived — understands what he hears, and what he understands is in his understanding; although he does not understand it to exist.

For, it is one thing for an object to be in the understanding, and another to understand that the object exists. When a painter first conceives of what he will afterwards perform, he has it in his understanding, but he does not yet understand it to be, because he has not yet performed it. But after he has made the painting, he both has it in his understanding, and he understands that it exists, because he has made it.

Hence, even the fool is convinced that something exists in the understanding, at least, than which nothing greater can be conceived. For, when he hears of this, he understands it. And whatever is understood, exists in the understanding. And assuredly that, than which nothing greater can be conceived, cannot exist in the understanding alone. For, suppose it exists in the understanding alone: then it can be conceived to exist in reality; which is greater.

Therefore, if that, than which nothing greater can be conceived, exists in the understanding alone, the very being, than which nothing greater can be conceived, is one, than which a greater can be conceived. But obviously this is impossible. Hence, there is no doubt that there exists a being, than which nothing greater can be conceived, and it exists both in the understanding and in reality.

And it assuredly exists so truly, that it cannot be conceived not to exist. For, it is possible to conceive of a being which cannot be conceived not to exist; and this is greater than one which can be conceived not to exist. Hence, if that, than which nothing greater can be conceived, can be conceived not to exist, it is not that, than which nothing greater can be conceived. But this is an irreconcilable contradiction. There is, then, so truly a being than which nothing greater can be conceived to exist, that it cannot even be conceived not to exist; and this being thou art, O Lord, our God.

So truly, therefore, dost thou exist, O Lord, my God, that thou canst not be conceived not to exist; and rightly. For, if a mind could conceive of a being better than thee, the creature would rise above the Creator; and this is most absurd. And, indeed, whatever else there is, except thee alone, can be conceived not to exist. To thee alone, therefore, it belongs to exist more truly than all other beings, and hence in a higher degree than all others. For, whatever else exists does not exist so truly, and hence in a less degree it belongs to it to exist. Why, then, has the fool said in his heart, there is no God, since it is so evident, to a rational mind, that thou dost exist in the highest degree of all? Why, except that he is dull and a fool?

SAINT THOMAS AQUINAS (1255?–1274)

Thomas, the son of Count Landolfo, of Aquino, was born at the ancestral castle near Naples. At the age of five, he was sent to the Benedictine monastery of Monte Cassino to be educated. When ten years old, he entered the University of Naples, where he remained for six years. He then joined the Dominican Order, very much against the will of his parents and so much to the disgust of his brothers that they kidnapped and imprisoned him in the family stronghold for two years. At last he escaped and continued his education at Paris and Cologne. In 1256 he became a master of theology, and thereafter taught at the University of Paris and elsewhere. During his career, he succeeded in constructing the greatest of all systems of Catholic philosophy. He died at the age of forty-nine. Three years after his death he was censured by the bishop of Paris for his alleged heterodoxy, but in 1323 he was canonized by Pope John XXII.

Five Proofs of God's Existence

1. [The Argument from Change]

[In his first argument, St. Thomas argues from the fact of change to an Unmoved Mover; in his second argument, from the fact of causation to an Uncaused Cause; in his third argument, from the fact of non-necessary being to a Necessary Being. In each case the reasoning is an inference from something dependent (change, causation, or contingent being) to something independent and self-sufficient—namely, God. Motion, movement, and change, as employed in the first argument, are synonymous. Note that the argument is not restricted to change of place (motion as we ordinarily use the term), but refers to all change whatsoever.]

The first and most open way is presented by change or motion. It is evident to our senses and certain that in the whole some things are in motion.

Whatever is in motion is set in motion by another. For nothing is in motion unless it be potential to that to which it is in motion; whereas a thing sets in motion inasmuch as it is actual, because to set in motion is naught else than to bring a thing from potentiality to actuality, and from potentiality a subject cannot be brought except by a being that is actual; actually hot makes potentially hot become actually hot, as when fire changes and alters wood. Now for the same thing to be simulta-

From St. Thomas Aquinas, *Philosophical Texts*, trans. Thomas Gilby, (London, New York, Toronto: Oxford University Press, 1951). Reprinted by permission.

neously and identically actual and potential is not possible, though it is possible under different respects; what is actually hot cannot simultaneously be potentially hot, though it may be potentially cold. It is impossible, therefore, for a thing both to exert and to suffer motion in the same respect and according to the same motion.

If that which sets in motion is itself in motion then it also must be set in motion by another, and that in its turn by another again. But here we cannot proceed to infinity, otherwise there would be no first mover, and consequently no other mover, seeing that subsequent movers do not initiate motion unless they be moved by a former mover, as stick by hand.

Therefore we are bound to arrive at the first mover set in motion by no other, and this everyone understands to be God.

Summa Theologica, Ia. ii. 3

Having indicated that the attempt to prove God's existence is not hopeless from the outset, we proceed now to fix on the arguments of philosophers and theologians alike, beginning with Aristotle who sets off from the concept of change. His argument takes two directions, of which the first is as follows.

Everything in a process of change is set in motion by another. Our senses tell us that things are in motion, the sun for instance. Therefore they are set in motion by another. Now this setter-in-motion is either itself in motion or it is not. If not, then we have our conclusion, namely the necessity of inferring a motionless mover which we term God. But if it is itself in motion then

it must be set in motion by another. Either we have an infinite series or we arrive as a changeless mover. But we cannot go back infinitely. Therefore we must infer a first changeless mover.

There are two propositions to be proved; first, that everything in motion is set in motion by another; second, that an infinite series of things setting and set in motion is impossible.

Summa Contra Gentiles, I, 13

2. [The Argument from Efficient Causality]

The second approach starts from the nature of efficient causality. Among phenomena we discover an order of efficient causes. But we never come across, nor ever shall, anything that is an efficient cause of itself; such a thing would be prior to itself, which is impossible. It is also impossible to go on to infinity with efficient causes, for in an ordered series the first is the cause of the intermediate and the intermediate is the cause of the last. Whether or not the intermediate causes be one or many is irrelevant. Take away the cause and the effect also goes. Therefore if there were not a first among efficient causes —which would be the case in an infinite series— there would be no intermediate causes nor an ultimate effect. This plainly is not the case. A first cause, generally termed God, must therefore be inferred.

Summa Theologica, Ia. ii. 3

An infinite series of efficient causes in essential subordination is impossible. Causes essentially required for the production of a determinate effect cannot consequently be infinitely multiplied, as if a block could be shifted by a crowbar, which in turn is levered by a hand, and so on to infinity.

But an infinite series of causes in accidental subordination is not reputed impossible, so long as all the causes thus multiplied are grouped as one cause and their multiplication is incidental to the causality at work. For instance a blacksmith may work with many hammers because one after another breaks in his hand, but that one particular hammer is used after another particular one is incidental. Similarly that in begetting a child a man was himself begotten by another man; for he is father as man, not as son. In a genealogy of efficient causes all men have the same status of particular generator. Hence, for such a line to stretch back to infinity is not unthinkable.

Summa Theologica, Ia. xlvi. 2, ad 7

3. [The Argument from Contingent Being]

We observe in our environment how things are born and die away; they may or may not exist; to be or not to be — they are open to either alternative. All things cannot be so contingent, for what is able not to be may be reckoned as once a non-being, and were everything like that once there would have been nothing at all. Now were this true, nothing would ever have begun, for what is does not begin to be except because of something which is, and so there would be nothing even now. This is clearly hollow. Therefore all things cannot be might-not-have-beens;

among them must be being whose existence is necessary.

Summa Theologica, Ia. ii. 3

Everything that is a possible-to-be has a cause, since its essence as such is equally uncommitted to the alternatives of existing and not existing. If it be credited with existence, then this must be from some cause. Causality, however, is not an infinite process. Therefore a necessary being is the conclusion. The principle of its necessity is either from outside or not. If not, then the being is inwardly necessary. If necessity comes from without, we must still propose a first being necessary of itself, since we cannot have an endless series of derivatively necessary beings.

Summa Contra Gentiles, I, 15

4. [The Argument from Degrees of Excellence]

The fourth argument is taken from the degrees of reality we discover in things. Some are truer and better and nobler than others, so also with other perfections. But more or less are attributed to different things in proportion as they variously approach something which is the maximum. Hence, there is something truest, and best, and noblest, and in consequence the superlative being, for the greatest truths are the greatest beings. Now the maximum in any order is the cause of all the other realities of that order. Therefore there is a real cause of being and goodness and all perfections whatsoever in everything; and this we term God.

Summa Theologica, Ia, ii. 3

The argument can be gathered from words let fall by Aristotle in the *Metaphysics*. He says that the truest things are also the most real; and again, that there is a superlative truth. One piece of architecture is more sham than another, one more genuine; throughout a comparison is implied with what is true without qualification and most of all. We can go farther and conclude that there is something most real, and this we call God.

Summa Contra Gentiles, I, 13

5. [The Argument from Purpose or Design]

Contrary and discordant elements . . . cannot always, or nearly always, work harmoniously together unless they be directed by something providing each and all with their tendencies to a definite end. Now in the universe we see things of diverse natures conspiring together in one scheme, not rarely or haphazardly, but approximately always or for the most part. There must be something, therefore, whose providence directs the universe.

Summa Contra Gentiles, I, 13

We observe that things without consciousness, such as physical bodies, operate with a purpose, as appears from their co-operating invariably, or almost so, in the same way in order to obtain the best result. Clearly then they reach this end by intention and not by chance. Things lacking knowledge move towards an end only when directed by someone who knows and understands, as an arrow by an archer. There is consequently an intelligent being who directs all natural things to their ends; and this being we call God.

Summa Theologica, Ia. ii. 3

When diverse things are co-ordinated the scheme depends on their directed unification, as the order of battle of a whole army hangs on the plan of the commander-in-chief. The arrangement of diverse things cannot be dictated by their own private and divergent natures; of themselves they are diverse and exhibit no tendency to make a pattern. It follows that the order of many among themselves is either a matter of chance or it must be resolved into one first planner who has a purpose in mind. What comes about always, or in the great majority of cases, is not the result of accident. Therefore the whole of this world has but one planner or governor.

Summa Contra Gentiles, I, 42

DAVID HUME (1711–1776)

For a biographical note, see page 76–77.

A Critique of Natural Theology

1. [The Argument for a First Cause]

The argument, replied Demea, which I would insist on is the common one. Whatever exists must have a cause or reason of its existence, it being absolutely impossible for anything to produce itself or be the cause of its own existence. In mounting up, therefore, from effects to causes, we must either go on in tracing an infinite succession, without any ultimate cause at all, or must at last have recourse to some ultimate cause that is *necessarily* existent. Now that the first supposition is absurd may be thus proved. In the infinite chain or succession of causes and effects, each single effect is determined to exist by the power and efficacy of that cause which immediately preceded; but the whole eternal chain or succession, taken together, is not determined or cause by anything, and yet it is evident that it requires a cause or reason, as much as any particular object which begins to exist in time. The question is still reasonable why this particular succession of causes existed from eternity, and not any other succession or no succession at all. If there be no necessarily existent being, any supposition which can be formed is equally possible; nor is there any more absurdity in *nothing's* having existed from eternity than there is in that succession of causes which constitutes the universe. What was it, then, which determined *something* to exist rather than *nothing*, and bestowed being on a particular possibility, exclusive of the rest? *External causes*, there are supposed to be none. *Chance* is a word without a meaning. Was it *nothing*? But that can never produce anything. We must, therefore, have recourse to a necessarily existent Being who carries the *reason* of his existence in himself, and who cannot be supposed not to exist, without an express contradiction. There is, consequently, such a Being—that is, there is a Deity.

I shall not leave it to Philo, said Cleànthes, though I know that the starting objections is his chief delight, to point out the weakness of this metaphysical reasoning. It seems to me so obviously ill-grounded, and at the same time of so little consequence to the cause of true piety and religion, that I shall myself venture to show the fallacy of it.

I shall begin with observing that there is an evident absurdity in pre-

Published in London, 1779. Critical edition by Norman Kemp Smith (Oxford: Oxford University Press, 1935).

tending to demonstrate a matter of fact, or to prove it by any arguments *a priori*. Nothing is demonstrable unless the contrary implies a contradiction. Nothing that is distinctly conceivable implies a contradiction. Whatever we conceive as existent, we can also conceive as non-existent. There is no being, therefore, whose non-existence implies a contradiction. Consequently there is no being whose existence is demonstrable. I propose this argument as entirely decisive, and am willing to rest the whole controversy upon it.

It is pretended that the Deity is a necessarily existent being; and this necessity of his existence is attempted to be explained by asserting that, if we knew his whole essence or nature, we should perceive it to be as impossible for him not to exist, as for twice two not to be four. But it is evident that this can never happen, while our faculties remain the same as at present. It will still be possible for us, at any time, to conceive the non-existence of what we formerly conceived to exist; nor can the mind ever lie under a necessity of supposing any object to remain always in being; in the same manner as we lie under a necessity of always conceiving twice two to be four. The words, therefore, *necessary existence* have no meaning or, which is the same thing, none that is consistent.

But further, why may not the material universe be the necessarily existent Being, according to this pretended explication of necessity? We dare not affirm that we know all the qualities of matter; and, for aught we can determine, it may contain some qualities which, were they known, would make its non-existence appear as great a contradiction as that twice two is five. I find only one argument employed to prove that the material world is not the necessarily existent Being; and this argument is derived from the contingency both of the matter and the form of the world. "Any particle of matter," it is said, "may be *conceived* to be annihilated, and any form may be *conceived* to be altered. Such an annihilation or alteration, therefore, is not impossible."[1] But it seems a great partiality not to perceive that the same argument extends equally to the Deity, so far as we have any conception of him, and that the mind can at least imagine him to be non-existent or his attributes to be altered. It must be some unknown, inconceivable qualities which can make his non-existence appear impossible or his attributes unalterable; and no reason can be assigned why these qualities may not belong to matter. As they are altogether unknown and inconceivable, they can never be proved incompatible with it.

Add to this that in tracing an eternal succession of objects it seems absurd to inquire for a general cause or first author. How can anything that exists from eternity have a cause, since that relation implies a priority in time and a beginning of existence?

In such a chain, too, or succession of objects, each part is caused by that which preceded it, and causes that which succeeds it. Where then is the difficulty? But the *whole*, you say, wants a cause. I answer that the uniting of these parts into a whole, like the

[1] Dr. Clarke.

uniting of several distinct countries into one kingdom, or several distinct members into one body, is performed merely by an arbitrary act of the mind, and has no influence on the nature of things. Did I show you the particular causes of each individual in a collection of twenty particles of matter, I should think it very unreasonable should you afterwards ask me what was the cause of the whole twenty. This is sufficiently explained in explaining the cause of the parts.

Though the reasonings which you have urged, Cleanthes, may well excuse me, said Philo, from starting any further difficulties, yet I cannot forbear insisting still upon another topic. It is observed by arithmeticians that the products of 9 compose always either 9 or some lesser product of 9 if you add together all the characters of which any of the former products is composed. Thus, of 18, 27, 36, which are products of 9, you make 9 by adding 1 to 8, 2 to 7, 3 to 6. Thus 369 is a product also of 9; and if you add 3, 6, and 9, you make 18, a lesser product of 9. To a superficial observer so wonderful a regularity may be admired as the effect either of chance or design; but a skilful algebraist immediately concludes it to be the work of necessity, and demonstrates that it must for ever result from the nature of these numbers. Is it not probable, I ask, that the whole economy of the universe is conducted by a like necessity, though no human algebra can furnish a key which solves the difficulty? And instead of admiring the order of natural beings, may it not happen that, could we penetrate into the intimate nature of bodies, we should

clearly see why it was absolutely impossible they could ever admit of any other disposition? So dangerous is to introduce this idea of necessity into the present question! and so naturally does it afford an inference directly opposite to the religious hypothesis!

2. [The Argument from Design]

Not to lose any time in circumlocutions, said Cleanthes . . . I shall briefly explain how I conceive this matter. Look round the world, contemplate the whole and every part of it: you will find it to be nothing but one great machine, subdivided into an infinite number of lesser machines, which again admit of subdivisions to a degree beyond what human senses and faculties can trace and explain. All these various machines, and even their most minute parts, are adjusted to each other with an accuracy which ravishes into admiration all men who have ever contemplated them. The curious adapting of means to ends, throughout all nature, resembles exactly, though it much exceeds, the productions of human contrivance — of human design, thought, wisdom, and intelligence. Since therefore the effects resemble each other, we are led to infer, by all the rules of analogy, that the causes also resemble, and that the Author of nature is somewhat similar to the mind of man, though possessed of much larger faculties, proportioned to the grandeur of the work which he has executed. By this argument a posteriori, and by this argument alone, do we prove at once the existence of a Deity and his similarity to human mind and intelligence.

I shall be free, Cleanthes, said Demea, as to tell you that from the beginning I could not approve of your conclusion concerning the similarity of the Deity to men, still less can I approve of the mediums by which you endeavor to establish it. What! No demonstration of the Being of God! No abstract arguments! No proofs *a priori!* Are these which have hitherto been so much insisted on by philosophers all fallacy, all sophism? Can we reach no farther in this subject than experience and probability? I will not say that this is betraying the cause of a Deity; but surely, by this affected candor, you give advantages to atheists which they never could obtain by the mere dint of argument and reasoning.

What I chiefly scruple in this subject, said Philo, is not so much that all religious arguments are by Cleanthes reduced to experience, as that they appear not to be even the most certain and irrefragable of that inferior kind. That a stone will fall, that fire will burn, that the earth has solidity, we have observed a thousand and a thousand times; and when any new instance of this nature is presented, we draw without hesitation the accustomed inference. The exact similarity of the cases gives us a perfect assurance of a similar event, and a stronger evidence is never desired nor sought after. But wherever you depart, in the least, from the similarity of the cases, you diminish proportionably the evidence, and may at last bring it to a very weak *analogy,* which is confessedly liable to error and uncertainty. After having experienced the circulation of the blood in human creatures, we make no doubt that it takes place in Titius and Maevius; but from its circulation in frogs and fishes it is only a presumption, though a strong one, from analogy that it takes place in men and other animals. The analogical reasoning is much weaker when we infer the circulation of the sap in vegetables from our experience that the blood circulates in animals; and those who hastily followed that imperfect analogy are found, by more accurate experiments, to have been mistaken.

If we see a house, Cleanthes, we conclude, with the greatest certainty, that it had an architect or builder because this is precisely that species of effect which we have experienced to proceed from that species of cause. But surely you will not affirm that the universe bears such a resemblance to a house that we can with the same certainty infer a similar cause, or that the analogy is here entire and perfect. The dissimilitude is so striking that the utmost you can here pretend to is a guess, a conjecture, a presumption concerning a similar cause; and how that pretension will be received in the world, I leave you to consider. . . .

That all inferences, Cleanthes, concerning fact are founded on experience, and that all experimental reasonings are founded on the supposition that similar causes prove similar effects, and similar effects similar causes, I shall not at present much dispute with you. But observe, I entreat you, with what extreme caution all just reasoners proceed in the transferring of experiments to similar cases. Unless the cases be exactly similar, they repose no perfect confidence in applying their past observation to any particular phenomenon. Every alteration of circumstances occasions a doubt concerning the event; and it requires new experiments to prove certainly that the new circumstances are of no moment or importance. A change in bulk, situation, arrangement, age, disposition of the air, or surrounding bodies — any of these particulars may be attended with the most unexpected consequences. And unless the objects be quite familiar to us, it is the highest temerity to expect with assurance, after any of these changes, an event similar to that which before fell under our observation. The slow and deliberate steps of philosophers here, if anywhere, are distinguished from the precipitate march of the vulgar, who, hurried on by the smallest similitude, are incapable of all discernment or consideration.

But can you think, Cleanthes, that your usual phlegm and philosophy have been preserved in so wide a step as you have taken when you compared to the universe houses, ships, furniture, machines, and, from their similarity in some circumstances, inferred a similarity in their causes? Thought, design, intelligence, such as we discover in men and other animals, is no more than one of the springs and principles of the universe, as well as heat or cold, attraction or repulsion, and a hundred others which fall under daily observation. It is an active cause by which some particular parts of nature, we find, produce alterations on other parts. But can a conclusion, with any propriety, be transferred from parts to the whole? Does not the great disproportion bar all comparison and inference? From observing the growth of a hair, can we learn anything concerning the genera-

tion of a man? Would the manner of a leaf's blowing, even though perfectly known, afford us any instruction concerning the vegetation of a tree?

But allowing that we were to take the *operations* of one part of nature upon another for the foundation of our judgment concerning the *origin* of the whole (which never can be admitted), yet why select so minute, so weak, so bounded a principle as the reason and design of animals is found to be upon this planet? What peculiar privilege has this little agitation of the brain which we call *thought*, that we must thus make it the model of the whole universe? Our partiality in our own favor does indeed present it on all occasions, but sound philosophy ought carefully to guard against so natural an illusion.

So far from admitting, continued Philo, that the operations of a part can afford us any just conclusion concerning the origin of the whole, I will not allow any one part to form a rule for another part if the latter be very remote from the former. Is there any reasonable ground to conclude that the inhabitants of other planets possess thought, intelligence, reason, or anything similar to these faculties in men? When nature has so extremely diversified her manner of operation in this small globe, can we imagine that she incessantly copies herself throughout so immense a universe? And if thought, as we may well suppose, be confined merely to this narrow corner and has even there so limited a sphere of action, with what propriety can we assign it for the original cause of all things? The narrow views of a peasant who makes his domestic economy the rule for the government of kingdoms is in comparison a pardonable sophism.

But were we ever so much assured that a thought and reason resembling the human were to be found throughout the whole universe, and were its activity elsewhere vastly greater and more commanding than it appears in this globe, yet I cannot see why the operations of a world constituted, arranged, adjusted, can with any propriety be extended to a world which is in its embryo state, and is advancing towards that constitution and arrangement. By observation we know somewhat of the economy, action, and nourishment of a finished animal, but we must transfer with great caution that observation to the growth of a foetus in the womb, and still more to the formation of an animalcule in the loins of its male parent. Nature, we find, even from our limited experience, possesses an infinite number of springs and principles which incessantly discover themselves on every change of her position and situation. And what new and unknown principles would actuate her in so new and unknown a situation as that of the formation of a universe, we cannot, without the utmost temerity, pretend to determine.

A very small part of this great system, during a very short time, is very imperfectly discovered to us; and do we thence pronounce decisively concerning the origin of the whole?

Admirable conclusion! Stone, wood, brick, iron, brass, have not, at this time, in this minute globe of earth, an order or arrangement without human art and contrivance; therefore, the universe could not originally attain its order and arrangement without something similar to human art. But is a part of nature a rule for another part very wide of the former? Is it a rule for the whole? Is a very small part a rule for the universe? Is nature in one situation a certain rule for nature in another situation vastly different from the former?

And can you blame me, Cleanthes, if I here imitate the prudent reserve of Simonides, who, according to the noted story, being asked by Hiero, *What God was?* desired a day to think of it, and then two days more; and after that manner continually prolonged the term, without ever bringing in his definition or description? Could you even blame me if I had answered, at first, *that I did not know*, and was sensible that this subject lay vastly beyond the reach of my faculties? You might cry out sceptic and rallier, as much as you pleased; but, having found in so many other subjects much more familiar the imperfections and even contradictions of human reason, I never should expect any success from its feeble conjectures in a subject so sublime and so remote from the sphere of our observation. When two *species* of objects have always been observed to be conjoined together, I can *infer*, by custom, the existence of one whenever I *see* the existence of the other; and this I call an argument from experience. But how this argument can have place where the objects, as in the present case, are single, individual, without parallel or specific resemblance, may be difficult to explain. And will any man tell me with a serious countenance that an orderly universe must arise from some thought and art like the human because we have experience of it? To ascertain this reasoning it were requisite that we had experience of the origin of worlds; and it is not sufficient, surely, that we have seen ships and cities arise from human art and contrivance. . . .

. . . I shall endeavor to show you, a little more distinctly, the inconveniences of that anthropomorphism which you have embraced, and shall prove that there is no ground to suppose a plan of the world to be formed in the Divine mind, consisting of distinct ideas, differently arranged, in the same manner as an architect forms in his head the plan of a house which he intends to execute.

It is not easy, I own, to see what is gained by this supposition, whether we judge of the matter by *reason* or by *experience*. We are still obliged to mount higher in order to find the cause of this cause which you had assigned as satisfactory and conclusive.

If *reason* (I mean abstract reason derived from inquiries *a priori*) be not alike mute with regard to all questions concerning cause and effect, this sentence at least it will venture to pronounce: that a mental world or universe of ideas requires a cause as much as does a material world or universe of objects, and, if similar in its arrangement, must require a similar cause. For what is there in this subject which should occasion a different conclusion or inference? In an abstract view, they are entirely alike; and no difficulty attends the one supposition which is not common to both of them.

Again, when we will needs force *experience* to pronounce some sentence, even on these subjects which lie beyond her sphere, neither can she perceive any material difference in this particular between these two kinds of worlds, but finds them to be governed by similar principles, and to depend upon an equal variety of causes in their operations. We have specimens in miniature of both of them. Our own mind resembles the one; a vegetable or animal body the other. Let experience, therefore, judge from these samples. Nothing seems more delicate, with regard to its causes, than thought; and as these causes never operate in two persons after the same manner, so we never find two persons who think exactly alike. Nor indeed does the same person think exactly alike at any two different periods of time. A difference of age, of the disposition of his body, of weather, of food, of company, of books, of passions — any of these particulars, or others more minute, are sufficient to alter the curious machinery of thought and communicate to it very different movements and operations. As far as we can judge, vegetables and animal bodies are not more delicate in their motions, nor depend upon a greater variety or more curious adjustment of springs and principles.

How, therefore, shall we satisfy ourselves concerning the cause of that Being whom you suppose the Author of nature, or, according to your system of anthropomorphism, the ideal world into which you trace the material? Have we not the same reason to trace that ideal world into another ideal world or new intelligent principle? But if we stop and go no farther, why go so far? why not stop at the material world? How can we satisfy ourselves without going on *in infinitum*? And, after all, what satisfaction is there in that infinite progression? Let us remember the story of the Indian philosopher and his elephant. It was never more applicable than to the present subject. If the material world rests upon a similar ideal world, this ideal world must rest upon some other, and so on without end. It were better, therefore, never to look beyond the present material world. By supposing it to contain the principle of its order within itself, we really assert it to be God; and the sooner we arrive at that Divine Being, so much the better. When you go one step beyond the mundane system, you only excite an inquisitive humor which it is impossible ever to satisfy.

To say that the different ideas which compose the reason of the Supreme Being fall into order of themselves and by their own nature is really to talk without any precise meaning. If it has a meaning, I would fain know why it is not as good sense to say that the parts of the material world fall into order of themselves and by their own nature. Can the one opinion be intelligible, while the other is not so?

We have, indeed, experience of ideas which fall into order of themselves and without any *known* cause. But, I am sure, we have a much larger experience of matter which does the same, as in all instances of generation and vegetation where the accurate analysis of the cause exceeds all human comprehension. We have also experience of particular systems of thought and of matter which have no order; of the first in madness, of the second in corruption. Why, then, should we think that order is more es-

sential to one than the other? And if it requires a cause in both, what do we gain by your system, in tracing the universe of objects into a similar universe of ideas? The first step which we make leads us on for ever. It were, therefore, wise in us to limit all our inquiries to the present world, without looking father. No satisfaction can ever be attained by these speculations which so far exceed the narrow bounds of human understanding. . . .

But to show you still more inconveniences, continued Philo, in your anthropomorphism, please to take a new survey of your principles. *Like effects prove like causes.* This is the experimental argument; and this, you say too, is the sole theological argument. . . .

Now, Cleanthes, said Philo, with an air of alacrity and triumph, mark the consequences. *First*, by this method of reasoning you renounce all claim to infinity in any of the attributes of the Deity. For, as the cause ought only to be proportioned to the effect, and the effect, so far as if falls under our cognizance, is not infinite, what pretensions have we, upon your suppositions, to ascribe that attribute to the Divine Being? You will still insist that, by removing him so much from all similarity to human creatures, we give in to the most arbitrary hypothesis, and at the same time weaken all proofs of his existence.

Secondly, you have no reason, on your theory, for ascribing perfection to the Deity, even in his finite capacity, or for supposing him free from every error, mistake, or incoherence, in his undertakings. There are many inexplicable difficulties in the works of nature which, if we allow a perfect author to be proved *a priori*, are easily solved, and become only seeming difficulties from the narrow capacity of man, who cannot trace infinite relations. But according to your method of reasoning, these difficulties become all real, and, perhaps, will be insisted on as new instances of likeness to human art and contrivance. At least, you must acknowledge that it is impossible for us to tell, from our limited views, whether this system contains any great faults or deserves any considerable praise if compared to other possible and even real systems. Could a peasant, if the *Aeneid* were read to him, pronounce that poem to be absolutely faultless, or even assign to its proper rank among the productions of human wit, he who had never seen any other production?

But were this world ever so perfect a production, it must still remain uncertain whether all the excellences of the work can justly be ascribed to the workman. If we survey a ship, what an exalted idea must we form of the ingenuity of the carpenter who framed so complicated, useful, and beautiful a machine? And what surprise must we feel when we find him a stupid mechanic who imitated others, and copied an art which, through a long succession of ages, after multiplied trials, mistakes, corrections, deliberations, and controversies, had been gradually improving? Many worlds might have been botched and bungled, throughout an eternity, ere this system was struck out; much labor lost, many fruitless trials made, and a slow but continued improvement carried on during infinite ages in the art of world-making. In such subjects, who can determine where the truth, nay, who can conjecture where the probability lies, amidst a great number of hypotheses which may be proposed and a still greater which may be imagined?

And what shadow of an argument, continued Philo, can you produce from your hypothesis to prove the unity of the Deity? A great number of men join in building a house or ship, in rearing a city, in framing a commonwealth; why may not several deities combine in contriving and framing a world? This is only so much greater similarity to human affairs. By sharing the work among several, we may so much further limit the attributes of each, and get rid of that extensive power and knowledge which must be supposed in one deity, and which, according to you, can only serve to weaken the proof of his existence. And if such foolish, such vicious creatures as man can yet often unite in framing and executing one plan, how much more those deities or demons, whom we may suppose several degrees more perfect! . . .

It must be a slight fabric, indeed, said Demea, which can be erected on so tottering a foundation. While we are uncertain whether there is one deity or many, whether the deity or deities, to whom we owe our existence, be perfect or imperfect, subordinate or supreme, dead or alive, what trust or confidence can we repose in them? What devotion or worship address to them? What veneration or obedience pay them? To all the purposes of life the theory of religion becomes altogether useless; and even with regard to speculative consequences its uncertainty, according to you, must render it totally precarious and unsatisfactory.

To render it still more unsatisfactory, said Philo, there occurs to me another hypothesis which must acquire an air of probability from the method of reasoning so much insisted on by Cleanthes. That like effects arise from like causes—this principle he supposes the foundation of all religion. But there is another principle of the same kind, no less certain and derived from the same source of experience, that, where several known circumstances are observed to be similar, the unknown will also be found similar. Thus, if we see the limbs of a human body, we conclude that it is also attended with a human head, though hid from us. Thus, if we see, through a chink in a wall, a small part of the sun, we conclude that were the wall removed we should see the whole body. In short, this method of reasoning is so obvious and familiar that no scruple can ever be made with regard to its solidity.

Now, if we survey the universe, so far as it falls under our knowledge, it bears a great resemblance to an animal or organized body, and seems actuated with a like principle of life and motion. A continual circulation of matter in it produces no disorder; a continual waste in every part is incessantly repaired; the closest sympathy is perceived throughout the entire system; and each part or member, in performing its proper offices, operates both to its own preservation and to that of the whole. The world, therefore, I infer, is an animal; and the Deity is the *soul* of the world, actuating it, and actuated by it.

You have too much learning, Cleanthes, to be at all surprised at this opinion which, you know, was maintained by almost all the theists of antiquity, and chiefly prevails in their discourses and reasonings. For though, sometimes, the ancient philosophers reason from final causes, as if they thought the world the workmanship of God, yet it appears rather their favorite notion to consider it as his body whose organization renders it subservient to him. And it must be confessed that, as the universe resembles more a human body than it does the works of human art and contrivance, if our limited analogy could ever, with any propriety, be extended to the whole of nature, the inference seems juster in favor of the ancient than the modern theory.

There are many other advantages, too, in the former theory which recommended it to the ancient theologians. Nothing more repugnant to all their notions, because nothing more repugnant to common experience, than mind without body, a mere spiritual substance which fell not under their senses nor comprehension, and of which they had not observed one single instance throughout all nature. Mind and body they knew because they felt both; an order, arrangement, organization, or internal machinery, in both they likewise knew, after the same manner; and it could not but seem reasonable to transfer this experience to the universe, and to suppose the divine mind and body to be also coeval and to have, both of them, order and arrangement naturally inherent in them and inseparable from them.

Here, therefore, is a new species of anthropomorphism, Cleanthes, on which you may deliberate, and a theory which seems not liable to any considerable difficulties. You are too much superior, surely, to systematical prejudices to find any more difficulty in supposing an animal body to be, originally, of itself or from unknown causes, possessed of order and organization, than in supposing a similar order to belong to mind. But the vulgar prejudice that body and mind ought always to accompany each other ought not, one should think, to be entirely neglected; since it is founded on vulgar experience, the only guide which you profess to follow in all these theological inquiries. And if you assert that our limited experience is an unequal standard by which to judge of the unlimited extent of nature, you entirely abandon your own hypothesis, and must thenceforward adopt our mysticism, as you call it, and admit of the absolute incomprehensibility of the Divine Nature.

This theory, I own, replied Cleanthes, has never before occurred to me, though a pretty natural one; and I cannot readily, upon so short an examination and reflection, deliver any opinion with regard to it. You are very scrupulous, indeed, said Philo; were I to examine any system of yours, I should not have acted with half that caution and reserve, in stating objections and difficulties to it. However, if anything occur to you, you will oblige us by proposing it.

Why then, replied Cleanthes, it seems to me that, though the world does, in many circumstances, resemble an animal body, yet is the analogy also defective in many circumstances the most material: no organs of sense; no seat of thought or reason; no one precise origin of motion and action. In short, it seems to bear a stronger resemblance to a vegetable than to an animal, and your inference would be so far inconclusive in favor of the soul of the world. . . .

But here, continued Philo, in examining the ancient system of the soul of the world there strikes me, all on a sudden, a new idea which, if just, must go near to subvert all your reasoning, and destroy even your first inferences on which you repose such confidence. If the universe bears a greater likeness to animal bodies and to vegetables than to the works of human art, it is more probable that its cause resembles the cause of the former than that of the latter, and its origin ought rather to be ascribed to generation or vegetation than to reason or design. Your conclusion, even according to your own principles, is therefore lame and defective.

Pray open up this argument a little further, said Demea, for I do not rightly apprehend it in that concise manner in which you have expressed it.

Our friend Cleanthes, replied Philo, as you have heard, asserts that, since no question of fact can be proved otherwise than by experience, the existence of a Deity admits not of proof from any other medium. The world, says he, resembles the works of human contrivance; therefore its cause must also resemble that of the other. Here we may remark that the operation of one very small part of nature, to wit, man, upon another very small part, to wit, that inanimate matter lying within his reach, is the rule by which Cleanthes judges of the origin of the whole; and he measures objects, so widely disproportioned, by the same individual standard. But to waive all objections drawn from this topic, I affirm that there are other parts of the universe (besides the machines of human invention) which bear still a greater resemblance to the fabric of the world, and which, therefore, afford a better conjecture concerning the universal origin of this system. These parts are animals and vegetables. The world plainly resembles more an animal or a vegetable than it does a watch or a knitting-loom. Its cause, therefore, it is more probable, resembles the cause of the former. The cause of the former is generation or vegetation. The cause, therefore, of the world we may infer to be something similar or analogous to generation or vegetation.

. . . In this little corner of the world alone, there are four principles, *reason, instinct, generation, vegetation*, which are similar to each other, and are the causes of similar effects. What a number of other principles may we naturally suppose in the immense extent and variety of the universe could we travel from planet to planet, and from system to system, in order to examine each part of this mighty fabric? Any one of these four principles above mentioned (and a hundred others which lie open to our conjecture) may afford us a theory by which to judge of the origin of the world; and it is a palpable and egregious partiality to confine our view entirely to that principle by which our own minds operate. Were this principle more intelligible on that account, such a partiality might be somewhat excusable; but reason, in its internal fabric and structure, is really as little known to us as instinct or vegetation; and per-

haps, even that vague, undeterminate word *nature* to which the vulgar refer everything is not at the bottom more inexplicable. The effects of these principles are all known to us from experience; but the principles themselves and their manner of operation are totally unknown; nor is it less intelligible or less conformable to experience to say that the world arose by vegetation, from a seed shed by another world, than to say that it arose from a divine reason or contrivance, according to the sense in which Cleanthes understands it.

But methinks, said Demea, if the world had a vegetative quality and could sow the seeds of new worlds into the infinite chaos, this power would be still an additional argument for design in its author. For whence could arise so wonderful a faculty but from design? Or how can order spring from anything which perceives not that order which it bestows?

You need only look around you, replied Philo, to satisfy yourself with regard to this question. A tree bestows order and organization on that tree which springs from it, without knowing the order; an animal in the same manner on its offspring; a bird on its nest; and instances of this kind are even more frequent in the world than those of order which arise from reason and contrivance. To say that all this order in animals and vegetables proceeds ultimately from design is begging the question; nor can that great point be ascertained otherwise than by proving, *a priori*, both that order is, from its nature, inseparably attached to thought and that it can never of itself or from original unknown principles belong to matter. . . .

I must confess, Philo, replied Cleanthes, that, of all men living, the task which you have undertaken, of raising doubts and objections, suits you best and seems, in a manner, natural and unavoidable to you. So great is your fertility of invention that I am not ashamed to acknowledge myself unable, on a sudden, to solve regularly such out-of-the-way difficulties as you incessantly start upon me, though I clearly see, in general, their fallacy and error. And I question not, but you are yourself, at present, in the same case, and have not the solution so ready as the objection, while you must be sensible that common sense and reason are entirely against you, and that such whimsies as you have delivered may puzzle but never can convince us.

What you ascribe to the fertility of my invention, replied Philo, is entirely owing to the nature of the subject. In subjects adapted to the narrow compass of human reason there is commonly but one determination which carries probability or conviction with it; and to a man of sound judgment all other suppositions but that one appear entirely absurd and chimerical. But in such questions as the present, a hundred contradictory views may preserve a kind of imperfect analogy, and invention has here full scope to exert itself. Without any great effort of thought, I believe that I could, in an instant, propose other systems of cosmogony which would have some faint appearance of truth, though it is a thousand, a million to one if either yours or any one of mine be the true system.

For instance, what if I should revive the old Epicurean hypothesis? This is commonly, and I believe justly, esteemed the most absurd system that has yet been proposed; yet I know not whether, with a few alterations, it might not be brought to bear a faint appearance of probability. Instead of supposing matter infinite, as Epicurus did, let us suppose it finite. A finite number of particles is only susceptible of finite transpositions; and it must happen, in an eternal duration, that every possible order or position must be tried an infinite number of times. This world, therefore, with all its events, even the most minute, has before been produced and destroyed, and will again be produced and destroyed, without any bounds and limitations. No one who has a conception of the powers of infinite, in comparison of finite, will ever scruple this determination.

But this supposes, said Demea, that matter can acquire motion without any voluntary agent or first mover.

And where is the difficulty, replied Philo, of that supposition? Every event, before experience, is equally difficult and incomprehensible; and every event, after experience, is equally easy and intelligible. Motion, in many instances, from gravity, from elasticity, from electricity, begins in matter, without any known voluntary agent; and to suppose always, in these cases, an unknown voluntary agent is mere hypothesis and hypothesis attended with no advantages. The beginning of motion in matter itself is as conceivable *a priori* as its communication from mind and intelligence.

Besides, why may not motion have been propagated by impulse through all eternity, and the same stock of it, or nearly the same, be still upheld in the universe? As much as is lost by the composition of motion, as much is gained by its resolution. And whatever the causes are, the fact is certain that matter is and always has been in continual agitation, as far as human experience or tradition reaches. There is not probably, at present, in the whole universe, one particle of matter at absolute rest.

And this very consideration, too, continued Philo, which we have stumbled on in the course of the argument suggests a new hypothesis of cosmogony that is not absolutely absurd and improbable. Is there a system, an order, an economy of things, by which matter can preserve that perpetual agitation which seems essential to it, and yet maintain a constancy in the forms which it produces? There certainly is such an economy, for this is actually the case with the present world. The continual motion of matter, therefore, in less than infinite transpositions, must produce this economy or order, and, by its very nature, that order, when once established, supports itself for many ages if not to eternity. But wherever matter is so poised, arranged, and adjusted, as to continue in perpetual motion, and yet preserve a constancy in the forms, its situation must, of necessity, have all the same appearance of art and contrivance which we observe at present. All the parts of each form must have a relation to each other and to the whole; and the whole itself must have a relation to the other parts

of the universe, to the element in which the form subsists, to the materials with which it repairs its waste and decay, and to every other form which is hostile or friendly. A defect in any of these particulars destroys the form, and the matter of which it is composed is again set loose, and is thrown into irregular motions and fermentations till it unite itself to some other regular form. If no such form be prepared to receive it, and if there be a great quantity of this corrupted matter in the universe, the universe itself is entirely disordered, whether it be the feeble embryo of a world in its first beginnings that is thus destroyed or the rotten carcass of one languishing in old age and infirmity. In either case, a chaos ensues till finite though innumerable revolutions produce, at last, some forms whose parts and organs are so adjusted as to support the forms amidst a continued succession of matter.

Suppose (for we shall endeavor to vary the expression) that matter were thrown into any position by a blind, unguided force; it is evident that this first position must, in all probability, be the most confused and most disorderly imaginable, without any resemblance to those works of human contrivance which, along with a symmetry of parts, discover an adjustment of means to ends and a tendency to self-preservation. If the actuating force cease after this operation, matter must remain for ever in disorder and continue an immense chaos, without any proportion or activity. But suppose that the actuating force, whatever it be, still continues in matter, this first position will immediately give place to a second which will likewise, in all probability, be as disorderly as the first, and so on through many successions of changes and revolutions. No particular order or position ever continues a moment unaltered. The original force, still remaining in activity, gives a perpetual restlessness to matter. Every possible situation is produced, and instantly destroyed. If a glimpse or dawn of order appears for a moment, it is instantly hurried away and confounded by that never-ceasing force which actuates every part of matter.

Thus the universe goes on for many ages in a continued succession of chaos and disorder. But is it not possible that it may settle at last, so as not to lose its motion and active force (for that we have supposed inherent in it), yet so as to preserve an uniformity of appearance, amidst the continual motion and fluctuation of its parts? This we find to be the case with the universe at present. Every individual is perpetually changing, and every part of every individual; and yet the whole remains, in appearance, the same. May we not hope for such a position or rather be assured of it from the eternal revolutions of unguided matter; and may not this account for all the appearing wisdom and contrivance which is in the universe? Let us contemplate the subject a little, and we shall find that this adjustment, if attained by matter, of a seeming stability in the forms, with a real and perpetual revolution or motion of parts, affords a plausible, if not a true, solution of the difficulty.

It is in vain, therefore, to insist upon the uses of the parts in animals or vegetables, and their curious adjustment to each other. I would fain know how an animal could subsist unless its parts were so adjusted? Do we not find that it immediately perishes whenever this adjustment ceases, and that is matter, corrupting, tries some new form? It happens indeed that the parts of the world are so well adjusted that some regular form immediately lays claim to this corrupted matter; and if it were not so, could the world subsist? Must it not dissolve, as well as the animal, and pass through new positions and situations till in great but finite succession it fall, at last, into the present or some such order?

It is well, replied Cleanthes, you told us that this hypothesis was suggested on a sudden, in the course of the argument. Had you had leisure to examine it, you would soon have perceived the insuperable objections to which it is exposed. No form, you say, can subsist unless it possess those powers and organs requisite for its subsistence; some new order or economy must be tried, and so on, without intermission, till at last some order which can support and maintain itself is fallen upon. But according to this hypothesis, whence arise the many conveniences and advantages which men and all animals possess? Two eyes, two ears are not absolutely necessary for the subsistence of the species. Human race might have been propagated and preserved without horses, dogs, cows, sheep, and those innumerable fruits and products which serve to our satisfaction and enjoyment. If no camels had been created for the use of man in the sandy deserts of Africa and Arabia, would the world have been dissolved? If no loadstone had been framed to give that wonderful and useful direction to the needle, would human society and the human kind have been immediately extinguished? Though the maxims of nature be in general very frugal, yet instances of this kind are far from being rare; and any one of them is a sufficient proof of design — and of a benevolent design — which gave rise to the order and arrangement of the universe.

At least, you may safely infer, said Philo, that the foregoing hypothesis is so far incomplete and imperfect, which I shall not scruple to allow. But can we ever reasonably expect greater success in any attempts of this nature? Or can we ever hope to erect a system of cosmogony that will be liable to no exceptions, and will contain no circumstance repugnant to our limited and imperfect experience of the analogy of nature? Your theory itself cannot surely pretend to any such advantage, even though you have run into *anthropomorphism*, the better to preserve a conformity to common experience. Let us once more put it to trial. In all instances which we have ever seen, ideas are copied from real objects, and are ectypal, not archetypal, to express myself in learned terms. You reverse this order and give thought the precedence. In all instances which we have ever seen, thought has no influence upon matter except where that matter is so conjoined with it as to have an equal reciprocal influence upon it. No animal can move immediately anything but the members of its own body; and, indeed, the equality of action and reaction seems to be an universal law of nature; but your theory implies a contradiction to this experience. These instances, with many more which it were easy to collect (particularly the supposition of a mind or system of thought that is eternal or, in other words, an animal ingenerable and immortal) — these instances, I say, may teach all of us sobriety in condemning each other, and let us see that as no system of this kind ought ever to be received from a slight analogy, so neither ought any to be rejected on account of a small incongruity. For that is an inconvenience from which we can justly pronounce no one to be exempted.

All religious systems, it is confessed, are subject to great and insuperable difficulties. Each disputant triumphs in his turn, while he carries on an offensive war, and exposes the absurdities, barbarities, and pernicious tenets of his antagonist. But all of them, on the whole, prepare a complete triumph for the *sceptic*, who tells them that no system ought ever to be embraced with regard to such subjects: for this plain reason than no absurdity ought ever to be assented to with regard to any subject. A total suspense of judgment is here our only reasonable resource. And if every attack, as is commonly observed, and no defense among theologians is successful, how complete must be *his* victory who remains always, with all mankind, on the offensive, and has himself no fixed station or abiding city which he is ever, on any occasion, obliged to defend?

WILLIAM PEPPERELL MONTAGUE
(1873–1953)

Montague was educated at Harvard during the golden years of its philosophy department. After receiving his Ph.D. degree in 1898, he taught briefly at Radcliffe, Harvard, and the University of California, and from 1903 until his retirement in 1947, at Barnard College and Columbia University. He also lectured at various other American universities, as well as in Japan, Czechoslovakia, and Italy. The reader can glean something of the daring of his philosophical vision and the charm of his personality by reading his "Confessions of an Animistic Materialist" in *The Ways of Things*.

The Problem of Good and Evil

In our opening discussion we defined religion as the belief in a power greater than ourselves that makes for good. We defended this definition on the ground that it left religion free from the proven falsities, ethical and physical, embodied in traditional creeds, while at the same time it avoided the emptiness and platitude of those schools of ultra-modernism which cling to the word "religion," but use it to mean only the recognition of some sort of unity and mystery in the universe, plus a praiseworthy devotion to whatever is praiseworthy, as, for example, the perfecting of humanity. Taking religion as we took it, we see at once that it is neither certainly and obviously true nor certainly and obviously false, but possibly true, and, if true, tremendously exciting. The question of its truth is exciting and momentous because it is a question, not of the validity of this or that theory as to the nature of the physical world or as to the origin and destiny of the human race, but because it is the question whether the things we care for most are at the mercy of the things we care for least. If God is not, then the existence of all that is beautiful and in any sense good, is but the accidental and ineffective by-product of blindly swirling atoms, or of the equally unpurposeful, though more conceptually complicated, mechanisms of present-day physics. A man may well believe that this dreadful thing is true. But only the fool will say in his heart that he is glad that it is true. For to wish there should be no God is to wish that the things which we love and strive to realize and make permanent, should be only temporary and doomed to frustration and destruction. If life and its fulfilments are good, why should one rejoice at the news that God is dead and that there is nothing in the whole world except our frail and perishable selves that is concerned with anything that matters? Not that such a prospect would diminish the duty to make the best of what we have while we have it. Goodness is not made less good by a lack of cosmic support for it. Morality is sanctionless, and an ideal can never derive its validity from what is external to itself and to the life whose fulfilment it is. Atheism leads not to badness but only to an incurable sadness and loneliness. For it is the nature of life everywhere to outgrow its present and its past, and, in the life of man, the spirit has outgrown the body on which it depends and seeks an expansion which no finite fulfiment can satisfy. It is this yearning for the infinite and the sense of desolation attending the prospect of its frustration that constitutes the motive to seek religion and to make wistful and diligent inquiry as to the possibility of its truth. . . .

There are two great problems which, taken together, comprise the prolegomena to every possible theology or atheology. They are the Problem of Evil and the Problem of Good.

How can the amount of evil and purposelessness in the world be compatible with the existence of a God? And how can the amount of goodness and purposefulness in the world be compatible with nonexistence of a God?

1. THE PROBLEM OF EVIL

The first of these problems has already been touched upon, but its importance justifies us in considering it again. Of one thing we can be certain, since the existing world contains evil, God's alleged attributes of infinite power and perfect goodness can be reconciled only by altering the one or the other of those attributes. For surely it would seem that since God does not abolish evil it must be either because he can't or because he won't, which means that he is limited either in his power or in his goodness. The line more commonly adopted by theological apologetics is to preserve the infinite power of God at any cost and do what one can with the goodness. Since evil occurs, God must be willing that it should occur. Why? Well, perhaps evil is a mere negation or illusion; perhaps it is good in disguise, a necessary ingredient of divine satisfaction; or a desirable and natural punishment of human sin; or a lesson and opportunity for human good. Or God's ideal of goodness may be quite different from ours, etc. To each and all of these suggestions there are two answers, one theoretical, the other practical. In the theoretical retort we ask, if evil is only a negation or illusion or disguise, then why would we and all other creatures suffer the failure to realize this? The experience of what is alleged to be unreal evil becomes itself the real evil. As for the portion of the world's evil that serves as a wholesome punishment or wholesome lesson for anybody, it is but an infinitesimal fraction of the total of the world's misery.

Finally, if God's purposes are other than what we call good, then his nature is other than what we mean by good, while to go further and assume, as some absolute idealists have assumed, that our sin and agony actually contribute to God's enjoyment, would be to make him not merely lacking in good, but a demon of evil. In short, the explanations do not explain. But if they did (and this is the practical retort that follows and clinches the theoretical), the case of the theologians would be still worse; for if evil is really nothing, it is nothing to avoid; while if it is some disguised or indirect form of good, it is a duty to abet it, not oppose it. If the Vessels of Wrath, like the Vessels of Grace, contribute to the divine happiness, why should we care which sort of Vessels our brothers and ourselves become? We should not only be *"willing to be damned for the glory of God,"* we should strive for it. Surely no such vicious nonsense as that perpetrated by these defenders of God's unlimited power would ever have blackened the history of religious apologetics had it not been for man's ignoble and masochistic craving to have at any price a monarch or master, no matter how evil in the light of his own conscience such a master might be.

If our analysis of the Problem of Evil is valid, there can exist no omnipotent God. Possibly an omnipotent It, conceivably an omnipotent Demon, but not an omnipotent Goodness.

2. THE PROBLEM OF GOOD

The world that we know contains a quantity of good which, though limited, is still far in excess of what could be expected in a purely mechanistic system.

If the Universe were composed entirely of a vast number of elementary entities, particles of matter or electricity, or pulses of radiant energy, which preserved themselves and pushed and pulled one another about according to merely physical laws, we should expect that they would occasionally agglutinate into unified structures, which in turn, though far less frequently, might combine to form structures still more complex, and so on. But that any considerable number of these higher aggregates would come about by mere chance would itself be a chance almost infinitely small. Moreover, there would be a steady tendency for such aggregates, as soon as they were formed, to break down and dissipate the matter and energy that had been concentrated in them. This increase of leveling, scattering, and disorganization to which all differentiated, concentrated, and organized aggregates are subject in our world, and in any world in which there is random motion alone, or random motion supplemented by such reciprocal *ab extra* determinations as are formulated in the laws of physics, is named the Increase of Entropy. This principle is exemplified in many familiar ways. The intense and concentrated waves caused by the stone dropped in the pool spread out and become less intense as their extensity increases. The hot stove in the cool room dissipates its differentiated and concentrated heat until a uniform level of temperature is reached. Stars radiate their energy and their mass into space, heavy and complex atoms break down into their simpler and lighter atomic constituents. Even the electrons and protons themselves are supposed to amalgamate and by so doing dissipate into space as short pulses of energy the very stuff of which they were made. And living organisms, with their minds, their societies, and their cultures, grow old, degenerate, and die, which is not merely the way of all flesh, but the way of all things.

And yet within this world that is forever dying, there have been born or somehow come to be, protons and electrons, atoms of hydrogen and helium, and the whole series of increasingly complex chemical elements culminating in radium and uranium. And these atoms not only gather loosely into nebulae, but in the course of time combine tightly into molecules, which in turn combine into the various complicated crystals and colloids that our senses can perceive. And on the only planet we really know, certain of the compounds of carbon gain the power of building themselves up by assimilation, and so growing and reproducing. Life thus started "evolves," as we say, into higher and higher forms, such as fishes, reptiles, and birds, mammals, primates, men, and, among men, sages and heroes.

Now the serious atheist must take his world seriously and seriously ask: What is the chance that all this ascent is, in a universe of descent, the result of chance? And of course by chance, as here used, we mean not absence of any causality, but absence of any causality except that recognized in physics. Thus it would be "chance" if a bunch of little cards, each with a letter printed on it, when thrown up into the breeze, should fall so as to make a meaningful sentence like "See the cat." Each movement of each letter would be mechanically caused, but it would be a chance and a real chance, though a small one, that they would so fall. And if a sufficiently large bundle of letters were thrown into the air there would also be a chance that they would fall back so as to spell out the entire play of Hamlet. The chance of this happening would be real enough, but it would be so small that, if properly expressed as a fraction, $1/n$, the string of digits contained in the denominator would, I suspect, reach from here to one of the fixed stars. And as for the probability that the atoms composing the brain of the author of *Hamlet*, if left to the mercy of merely mechanistic breezes, would fall into the combinations which that brain embodied — well, that is a chance that is smaller still. Surely we need not pursue the game further. Let the atheist lay the wager and name the odds that he will demand of us. Given the number of corpuscles, waves, or what not, that compose the universe, he is to bet that with only the types of mechanistic causality (or, if you are modern and fussy about the word "cause" you can call them "functional correlations") that are recognized in physics, there would result, I will not say the cosmos that we actually have, but any cosmos with an equal quantity of significant structures and processes. He certainly will not bet with us on even terms, and I am afraid that the odds that he will feel bound to ask of us will be so heavy that they will make him sheepish, because it is, after all, the truth of his own theory on which he is betting.

But what is the alternative to all this? Nothing so very terrible; merely the hypothesis that the kind of causality that we know best, the kind that we find in the only part of matter that we can experience directly and from within, the causality, in short, that operates in our lives and minds, is not an alien accident but an essential ingredient of the world that spawns us. The alternative to mere mechanistic determination is not some unknown thing concocted *ad hoc* to help us out of a difficulty. Surely, mind is a *vera causa* if ever there was one, and we merely suggest that the kind of anabolic and anti-entropic factor of whose existence we are certain in ourselves, is present and operative in varying degree in all nature. If we are right, we escape the universe of perpetual miracle, on which the atheist sets his heart. The organized structures and currents of ascent and evolution, from the atoms themselves to the lives of men, cease to be outrageously improbable runs of luck and become the normal expression of something akin to us. Material nature makes altogether too many winning throws for us not to suspect that she is playing with dice that are loaded, loaded with life and mind and purpose. This is the solution that seems to me almost inevitable of the problem which, for want of a better name, I have called the Problem of Good.

And so we are confronted with a God, or something very like a God, that exists, not as an omnipotent monarch, a giver of laws and punishments, but as an ascending force, a nisus, a thrust toward concentration, organization, and life. This power appears to labor slowly and under difficulties. We can liken it to a year that, through the aeons, pervades the chaos of matter and slowly leavens it with spirit.

COMMENT

The Meaning of Theism

For the theist, the key to reality lies in God and his design. This belief does not exclude several positions that we have already examined, since a theist can be a teleologist, a dualist, or an idealist; but cannot be a complete materialist or an absolute sceptic.

God has been defined as "a being who is personal, supreme, and good." This definition is in accord with what most people mean when they use the word "God." They think of Him as personal — that is, as conscious mind or spirit. Of course, God's mind is conceived as much larger or greater than any human mind, but still somewhat like mind or spirit as we know it. God is also thought of as supreme — if not omnipotent, at least immensely great and powerful — so powerful, indeed, that He can profoundly affect the whole world. Finally, a personal and supreme being would not be called God if He were not also good—perhaps not perfect, but at least good in a measure that far surpasses our poor human capacities.

If it be granted that the concept of God should be so defined, the question arises whether the belief in God is mature and defensible—whether it is consistent with the life of reason, which Socrates declared is alone worth living. Is faith in God, as Freud maintained, a mere illusory compensation for fear, repression, and catastrophe? Or is it an inalienable possession of man's spiritual life, as rational as it is emotionally satisfying? Can this faith withstand the criticism of philosophy? What *reasons* are there for believing in the existence of God, and how valid are these reasons?

The main arguments *pro* and *con* are contained in this chapter. The ontological proof ("ontological" means "pertaining to the nature of being") as stated by St. Anselm is an *a priori* argument. From his definition of God as "that being than which no greater can be conceived," he reasons that we cannot, without contradiction, assert that God does not exist. St. Thomas rejected this form of proof, his five arguments all being *a posteriori*. They start with some fact given in experience—change, causality, nonnecessary being, degrees of excellence, or design—and they proceed to reason from this fact to the conclusion that God exists. The arguments of both St. Anselm and St. Thomas are intended to prove the existence of a perfect and omnipotent God. The argument of Montague resembles the fifth proof of St. Thomas but concludes that God must be limited in power.

Hume's *Dialogues Concerning Natural Religion* are conversations (sometimes long speeches) between three characters: Demea, a partisan of "the argument for a first cause," Cleanthes, a defender of "the argument from design," and Philo, who is sceptical of both arguments. Demea's argument resembles the first three proofs of St. Thomas, but Demea also falls back upon St. Anselm's contention that the nonexistence of God would be a logical contradiction. Cleanthes' argument is like the fifth proof of St. Thomas.

I shall not restate the arguments because the reader, perhaps with help from his instructor, should be able to understand them, but I will say something about the criticisms that have been brought to bear against these arguments.

Criticism of the Ontological Argument

The ontological argument has had a chequered history. It was immediately criticized by an aged monk, Gaunilo, and was rejected by the greatest medieval philosopher, St. Thomas Aquinas. Then it was revived by

Descartes, restated by Spinoza and Leibniz, and sharply criticized by Locke, Hume, and Kant. Relatively few philosophers in more recent times have accepted it.

The import of the argument is clarified by Gaunilo's objection and Anselm's reply. As interpreted by Gaunilo, the argument can be restated as follows: God is thought of as perfect; existence is necessary to perfection; therefore, God exists. This argument, said Gaunilo, is fallacious because by the same kind of reasoning I could "prove" the existence of a perfect island, to wit: If the island did not exist it would lack one of the elements of perfection, namely, real existence, and hence it would not be a perfect island. But the conclusion that a perfect island must exist is obviously absurd, and hence this type of argument is fallacious.

Anselm promptly replied to this attempted *reductio ad absurdum* by pointing out that a "perfect island" is perfect only in a weak and limited sense. By its very nature, an island is finite, and hence can be "perfect" only in a relative or inaccurate manner of speaking—it cannot be *infinitely* perfect. God, and not the hypothetical island, is that being than which no greater can be conceived—a being perfect in the sense of being incomparably greatest. Such absolute and infinite perfection applies to God and to God alone, and only such perfection requires existence.

Another objection was advanced by St. Thomas Aquinas. Going to the root of the argument, he questioned whether we really have in mind the concept of an utterly infinite or perfect being. He pointed out that we finite human beings have only an inadequate and indirect knowledge of God. Because of the infirmity of our understanding, we cannot discern God as He is in Himself, but only by the effects that He produces. If we could know God's essence absolutely, we would surely see that His essence involves His existence. But since we know God only relatively, His existence is not self-evident to us. We cannot leap from our imperfect idea of God to the conclusion that an absolutely perfect being exists.

Perhaps the most profound criticism of the ontological argument was advanced by Kant, whose objection turns on the meaning of the word "exists." Suppose I say that God exists. Am I making the same sort of statement as when I say that God is omnipotent? Kant would say no. The first statement asserts nothing about the *characteristics* of God; it merely tells me that God, whatever He is, exists, just as a rabbit, a cabbage, a stone, or a planet exists. This statement can be denied in only one way—namely, by denying that God exists. The second statement, that God is omnipotent, does tell me something about the *character* of God, and this statement, unlike the first, can be denied in *two* ways—either by denying that there is a God or by denying that God is omnipotent.

Since the question of a thing's existence is thus *additional* to the question of its characteristics, we can grasp its characteristics without knowing whether it exists. Take the following illustration. As I sit at my desk I wonder whether there is a dollar bill in my pocket. Before I reach into my pocket to find out, I have in mind what the dollar bill would be like. The characteristics of the dollar bill which I have in mind are the same whether or not there really is a dollar bill in my pocket. Hence, I can grasp the characteristics of a dollar bill without knowing that it exists. Can we likewise grasp God's characteristics without knowing whether He exists? Yes, declares Kant. It is logically possible to think of an infinite and perfect Being without knowing that there *is* such a Being. But suppose we *mean* by God a necessarily existent God. It would still not follow that there really is such a Being. It would merely follow that *if* there is a God, then He is a necessarily existent Being—because that is what we mean. At best, Anselm's argument shows only that the thought of God implies the *thought* of God's existence. The thought of perfection implies the thought of existence, and real perfection implies real existence. But the *thought* of perfection does imply *real* existence. This is the tenor of Kant's criticism.

I shall leave to the reader the evaluation of the original argument and these criticisms. Regardless of the criticisms, Anselm's distinction between "essence" and "existence" has had a very stimulating influence on later philosophical thought. Existentialism, which we shall examine in Chapter 10, is based in large measure on this distinction. The ontological proof, moreover, still fascinates both students and philosophers. Two very able American philosophers, Norman Malcolm and Charles Hartshorne, have reformulated and defended the argument. If the reader wishes to pursue the matter, he will find references to their discussions in my suggestions for further reading at the end of this chapter.

Criticism of the Cosmological Proof

The term "cosmological proof" has been used in a blanket way to cover arguments like the first three of St. Thomas. These arguments are alike in maintaining that the insufficiency of nature requires the self-sufficiency of God to explain it. *Change* ("motion" in the sense of actualization of potentialities) cannot explain itself but requires an Unchanged Changer ("Unmoved Mover"—a fully actualized being) for its explanation. *Causation* (in the sense of bringing something into existence) cannot explain itself but requires an Uncaused Cause. *Contingent being* cannot explain itself but requires a Necessary Being for its explanation. Because these proofs are parallel they can be grouped together. It is the third that we shall take as the most instructive and consider in some detail.

Fundamental to the third argument is the contention that we cannot explain one dependent event merely by another or yet another dependent event, even if we push back the regress indefinitely. St. Thomas is prepared to admit, apart from Revelation, that contingent events may be causally linked to one another in a never-ending regress. What he denies is that we can have a *sufficient* explanation in terms of such an infinite regress of *dependent* causes.

So long as we have merely series of causes of causes, however infinitely extended, we are explaining one dependent event by another dependent event by still another dependent event, and so on and on. This is unsatisfactory for two reasons. First, each event is dependent upon its antecedents, and hence no event is more than *conditionally* necessary. If everything is dependent upon something else, the whole process hangs on nothing. An explanation that thus never gives us an *ultimate* necessity is incomplete, and hence is not a full and satisfactory explanation. Secondly, even if there is an infinite regress of causes, we can always ask why this chain occurs rather than some other chain. Or even if we consider the sum total of nature, we can ask why we have *this* totality rather than some quite different totality. The only *sufficient* explanation is that natural events, and even the whole of nature, must ultimately depend upon a necessary Being. Such a Being cannot have had an external cause, because it is an infinite and eternal Being — namely, God — whose essence is to exist. The argument arrives at the same conclusion as the ontological proof but via a different route.

This argument can be criticized in a number of ways. First, we can ask what is meant by saying that God is a necessary Being. The word "necessity" applies to *propositions* whose denial would be contradictory. "Two plus two equals four" is a necessary proposition, since it would be contradictory to deny it. But does "necessity" apply to *things* as well as to propositions? The character Cleanthes, in Hume's dialogue, answers: "Nothing is demonstrable unless the contrary implies a contradiction. Nothing that is distinctly conceivable implies a contradiction. Whatever we conceive as existent, we can also conceive as nonexistent. There is no being, therefore, whose nonexistence implies a contradiction." If necessity thus applies to logically necessitated propositions and not to things, nothing, not even God, is a necessary Being.

If, in some mysterious way, a Being can be necessary, why might not the natural universe be this necessarily existent Being? If you reply that every natural event is seen to be non-necessary (in the sense that its absence involves no contradiction), it does not follow that the whole of nature is non-necessary. A whole need not have the character of its parts. It does not follow from the fact that every note in a musical composition is short that the whole composition is short. Similarly, it does not follow from the fact that every natural thing or event is non-necessary that the whole of nature is non-necessary. If we are to insist upon a necessity that we do not understand, this necessity would seem as applicable to nature as to supernature.

But should we demand such an ultimate necessity? Why not simply suppose that the causal series of linked events stretches back infinitely and that there is no other explanation? If each part is determined by its antecedents, is not the whole sufficiently determined? It would seem to be absurd to demand an external cause for an infinite regress without beginning, since the causal relation implies priority in time and hence a beginning of existence. Our whole experience of causal connections, moreover, lies *within* nature, and we have no sufficient basis for projecting this relation *outside* of nature. Can we assume that what is true of particular things in the world — namely, that *they* are caused — is true of the universe in its totality? Must the universe have a cause outside its own nature? Or must it have any cause at all? To a consistent empiricist, such as Hume, the extension of the concept of causation beyond the field of all actual or possible experience offers special difficulties. On the other hand, if we understand the "necessity" of a necessary Being as logical rather than causal, we are faced by the difficulty already mentioned — that the necessity here involved is mysterious and seems applicable to the whole of nature no less than to supernature.

Despite these objections of Hume, most Catholic and some non-Catholic philosophers believe that the argument retains its cogency. It seems to them that the evident self-insufficiency of natural events requires an ultimate self-sufficient foundation. Nature as a composite whole, moreover, seems *not* self-sufficient, because any composite *could* be composed in a different way. Why should there be this total natural constellation rather than some other? Does not the existence of such dependent and conditioned being require existence of independent and unconditioned Being? Only an infinite, eternal, completely actualized, and noncomposite Being — a pure spirit — could be thus independent and unconditioned, the guarantor of its own existence and all else besides. We may have to fall back upon other arguments to establish some of the attributes of God, but the cosmological argument at least proves that nature is dependent upon supernature, and this conclusion carries us a long way — or so the believer in the cosmological argument would continue to maintain.

Criticism of the Teleological Argument

The teleological argument, or argument from design, is very ancient but still popular. It was first expressly formulated by Plato, in the *Laws*, and has been restated by innumerable philosophers, among them St. Augustine, St. Thomas (in his Fifth Proof), Locke, and Rousseau. It was especially popular in the seventeenth and eighteenth centuries, when the astronomy and physics of Newton were interpreted as the disclosure of a wonderful natural order requiring God as its source.

The criticisms of Hume, as set forth by the character Philo in the *Dialogues Concerning Natural Religion*, constitute a powerful attack upon the design argument. Are these criticisms conclusive? Evidently Hume did not think so. The criticisms are not presented as his but are put in the mouth of Philo, one of the three characters in the *Dialogues.* Hume abstains from indicating his own sympathies except at the very end of the book, where he suggests that "the opinions" of Cleanthes, the proponent of the design argument, are nearer to the truth than those of Philo. In a letter to a friend, George Elliot (dated March 10, 1751), Hume refers to Cleanthes as the "hero" of the dialogues, and asks for any suggestions that will strengthen that side of the dispute. Even Philo, in a final passage not quoted here, is made to remark that the apparent design in nature proves that its cause bears an analogy, though somewhat remote, to the human mind. Probably Hume felt that Philo's criticisms were weighty but by no means decisive.

One thing to note about most of these criticisms is that they do not tend to prove the *absence* of a designing agency or agencies. They indicate limitations rather than fatal defects in the design argument. They show that the finite order and goodness of nature are an insufficient basis for inferring an infinite, perfect, unitary, external, and conscious designer. Kant later pointed out an additional limitation — that the design argument can prove only a kind of architect, but it cannot prove a creator who makes the world out of nothing. Just as a watchmaker uses materials already in existence to make a watch, so the designer of a natural order may use pre-existing materials to compose his design. But these considerations are consistent with some kind of teleological explanation of the goodness and higher levels of order to be found in nature. It is true that Philo's final point, that the natural order may be the result of mere natural selection, is opposed to a teleological hypothesis, but the further course of the dialogue suggests that neither Cleanthes nor Philo regarded natural selection as sufficient, in itself, to explain the whole order of nature. It is also noteworthy that John Stuart Mill and William James could not bring themselves to the view that the Darwinian hypothesis of natural selection was alone sufficient to explain the higher levels of evolution. They preferred to believe in a finite God, struggling against evil but not wholly able to eliminate it. Moreover, this finite God need not be thought of as an external, transcendent Deity but can be construed as the total society of natural forces that are pushing on toward the good. Admittedly, this concept alters the usual meaning of "God," but some modern philosophers nevertheless prefer it.

Among arguments of this type none is more eloquent than the passage from W. P. Montague's *Belief Unbound* reproduced in this chapter. Montague refers to "the problem of evil" to refute the belief in a perfect and omnipotent God, and to "the problem of good" to refute an atheistic interpretation. He remarks, "Material nature makes altogether too many winning throws for us not to suspect that she is playing with dice that are loaded, loaded with life and mind and purpose." I will leave my readers to judge the strength of his argument.

I shall not discuss St. Thomas' Fourth Proof except to remark that it appears to me inconclusive. That there are degrees of excellence I do not doubt, but I see no reason to suppose that there must be Perfection at the top of the scale or that lower degrees of excellence must depend for their existence upon the highest degree.

8

Materialism

"All nature as it is in itself consists of two things —bodies and the vacant space in which the bodies are situated and through which they move."

Titus Lucretius Carus

TITUS LUCRETIUS CARUS (95?–52? B.C.)

We know nothing certain about the life of Lucretius. St. Jerome, a hostile critic, declared that he had fits of madness, composed his poem during intervals of sanity, and killed himself in his forty-fourth year. This report, as George Santayana has remarked, must be taken with a large grain of salt. From his book we discover that he revered Epicurus, detested religious superstition, and delighted in the bounty of nature.

On the Nature of the Universe

1. [Prayer to the Creative Force of Nature (personified as Venus) to Inspire the Poet, to Bless His Patron Memmius, and to Bring Peace to the World.]

Mother of Aeneas and his race, delight of men and gods, life-giving Venus, it is your doing that under the wheeling constellations of the sky all nature teems with life, both the sea that buoys up our ships and the earth that yields our food. Through you all living creatures are conceived and come forth to look upon the sunlight. Before you the winds flee, and at your coming the clouds forsake the sky. For you the inventive earth flings up sweet flowers. For you the ocean levels laugh, the sky is calmed and glows with diffused radiance. When first the day puts on the aspect of spring, when in all its force the fertilizing breath of Zephyr is unleashed, then, great goddess, the birds of air give the first intimation of your entry; for yours is the power that has pierced them to the heart. Next the cattle run wild, frisk through the lush pastures and swim the swift-flowing streams. Spell-bound by your charm, they follow your lead with fierce desire. So throughout seas and uplands, rushing torrents, verdurous meadows and the leafy shelters of the birds, into the breasts of one and all you instil alluring love, so that with passionate longing they reproduce their several breeds.

Since you alone are the guiding power of the universe and without you nothing emerges into the shining sunlit world to grow in joy and loveliness, yours is the partnership I seek in striving to compose these lines *On the Nature of the Universe* for my noble Memmius. For him, great goddess, you have willed outstanding excellence in every field and everlasting fame. For his sake, therefore, endow my verse with everlasting charm.

Meanwhile, grant that this brutal business of war by sea and land may everywhere be lulled to rest. For you alone have power to bestow on mortals the blessing of quiet peace. In your bosom Mars himself, supreme commander in this brutal business, flings himself down at times, laid low by the irremediable wound of love. Gazing upward, his neck a prostrate column, he fixes hungry eyes on you, great goddess, and gluts them with love. As he lies outstretched, his breath hangs upon your lips. Stoop, then, goddess most glorious, and enfold him at rest in your hallowed bosom and whisper with those lips sweet words of prayer, beseeching for the people of Rome untroubled peace. In this evil hour of my country's history, I cannot pursue my task with a mind at ease, as an illustrious scion of the house of Memmius cannot at such a crisis withhold his service from the common well.

Translated by Robert Latham. Penguin Books, 1951. Reprinted by permission of Penguin Books, Ltd., Harmondsworth, Middlesex.

2. [Exhortation to Memmius to Listen to an Exhortation of "True Reason."]

For what is to follow, my Memmius, lay aside your cares and lend undistracted ears and an attentive mind to true reason. Do not scornfully reject, before you have understood them, the gifts I have marshalled for you with zealous devotion. I will set out to discourse to you on the ultimate realities of heaven and the gods. I will reveal those *atoms* from which nature creates all things and increases and feeds them and into which, when they perish, nature again resolves them. To these in my discourse I commonly give such names as the 'raw material', or 'generative bodies' or 'seeds' of things. Or I may call them 'primary particles', because they come first and everything else is composed of them.

3. [Praise of Epicurus for Delivering Mankind from Superstition.]

When human life lay groveling in all men's sight, crushed to the earth under the dead weight of superstition whose grim features loured menacingly upon mortals from the four quarters of the sky, a man of Greece was first to raise mortal eyes in defiance, first to stand erect and brave the challenge. Fables of the gods did not crush him, nor the lightning flash and the growling menace of the sky. Rather, they quickened his manhood, so that he, first of all men, longed to smash the constraining locks of nature's doors. The vital vigour of his mind prevailed. He ventured far out beyond the flaming ramparts of the world and voyaged in mind throughout infinity. Returning victor-

ious, he proclaimed to us what can be and what cannot: how a limit is fixed to the power of everything and an immovable frontier post. Therefore superstition in its turn lies crushed beneath his feet, and we by his triumph are lifted level with the skies.

4. [Superstition, Its Cause and Cure.]

One thing that worries me is the fear that you may fancy yourself embarking on an impious course, setting your feet on the path of sin. Far from it. More often it is this very superstition that is the mother of sinful and impious deeds. Remember how at Aulis the altar of the Virgin Goddess was foully stained with the blood of Iphigeneia by the leaders of the Greeks, the patterns of chivalry. The headband was bound about her virgin tresses and hung down evenly over both her cheeks. Suddenly she caught sight of her father standing sadly in front of the altar, the attendants beside him hiding the knife and her people bursting into tears when they saw her. Struck dumb with terror, she sank on her knees to the ground. Poor girl, at such a moment it did not help her that she had been first to give the name of father to a king. Raised by the hands of men, she was led trembling to the altar. Not for her the sacrament of marriage and the loud chant of Hymen. It was her fate in the very hour of marriage to fall a sinless victim to a sinful rite, slaughtered to her greater grief by a father's hand, so that a fleet might sail under happy auspices. Such are the heights of wickedness to which men are driven by superstition.

You yourself, if you surrender your

judgement at any time to the blood-curdling declamations of the prophets, will want to desert our ranks. Only think what phantoms they can conjure up to overturn the tenor of your life and wreck your happiness with fear. And not without cause. For, if men saw that a term was set to their troubles, they would find strength in some way to withstand the hocus-pocus and intimidations of the prophets. As it is, they have no power of resistance, because they are haunted by the fear of eternal punishment after death. They know nothing of the nature of the spirit. Is it born, or is it implanted in us at birth? Does it perish with us, dissolved by death, or does it visit the murky depths and dreary sloughs of Hades? Or is it transplanted by divine power into other creatures, as described in the poems of our own Ennius, who first gathered on the delectable slopes of Helicon an evergreen garland destined to win renown among the nations of Italy? Ennius indeed in his immortal verses proclaims that there is also a Hell, which is peopled not by our actual spirits or bodies but only by shadowy images, ghastly pale. It is from this realm that he pictures the ghost of Homer, of unfading memory, as appearing to him, shedding salt tears and revealing the nature of the universe.

I must therefore give an account of celestial phenomena, explaining the movements of sun and moon and also the forces that determine events on earth. Next, and no less important, we must look with keen insight into the make-up of spirit and mind: we must consider those alarming phantasms that strike upon our minds when they are awake but disordered by sickness, or when they are buried in slumber, so that we seem to see and hear before us men whose dead bones lie in the embraces of earth.

I am well aware that it is not easy to elucidate in Latin verse the obscure discoveries of the Greeks. The poverty of our language and the novelty of the theme compel me often to coin new words for the purpose. But your merit and the joy I hope to derive from our delightful friendship encourage me to face any task however hard. This it is that leads me to stay awake through the quiet of the night, studying how by choice of words and the poet's art I can display before your mind a clear light by which you can gaze into the heart of hidden things.

5. [Nothing Is Ever Created Out of Nothing.]

This dread and darkness of the mind cannot be dispelled by the sunbeams, the shining shafts of day, but only by an understanding of the outward form and inner workings of nature. In tackling this theme, our starting-point will be this principle: *Nothing can ever be created by divine power out of nothing.* The reason why all mortals are so gripped by fear is that they see all sorts of things happening on the earth and in the sky with no discernible cause, and these they attribute to the will of a god. Accordingly, when we have seen that nothing can be created out of nothing, we shall then have a clearer picture of the path ahead, the problem of how things are created and occasioned without the aid of the gods.

First then, if things were made out of nothing, any species could spring from any source and nothing would require seed. Men could arise from the sea and scaly fish from the earth, and birds could be hatched out of the sky. Cattle and other domestic animals and every kind of wild beast, multiplying indiscriminately, would occupy cultivated and waste lands alike. The same fruits would not grow constantly on the same trees, but they would keep changing: any tree might bear any fruit. If each species were not composed of its own generative bodies, why should each be born always of the same kind of mother? Actually, since each is formed out of specific seeds, it is born and emerges into the sunlit world only from a place where there exists the right material, the right kind of atoms. This is why everything cannot be born of everything, but a specific power of generation inheres in specific objects.

Again, why do we see roses appear in spring, grain in summer's heat, grapes under the spell of autumn? Surely, because it is only after specific seeds have drifted together at their own proper time that every created thing stands revealed, when the season is favourable and the life-giving earth can safely deliver delicate growths into the sunlit world. If they were made out of nothing, they would spring up suddenly after varying lapses of time and at abnormal seasons, since there would of course be no primary bodies which could be prevented by the harshness of the season from entering into generative unions. Similarly, in order that things might grow, there would be no need of any lapse of time for the accumulation of seed. Tiny tots would turn suddenly into grown men, and trees would shoot up spontaneously out of the earth. But it is obvious that none of these things happens, since everything grows gradually, as is natural, from a specific seed and retains its specific character. It is a fair inference that each is increased and nourished by its own raw material.

Here is a further point. Without seasonable showers the earth cannot send up gladdening growths. Lacking food, animals cannot reproduce their kind or sustain life. This points to the conclusion that many elements are common to many things, as letters are to words, rather than to the theory that anything can come into existence without atoms.

Or again, why has not nature been able to produce men on such a scale that they could ford the ocean on foot or demolish high mountains with their hands or prolong their lives over many generations? Surely, because each thing requires for its birth a particular material which determines what can be produced. It must therefore be admitted that nothing can be made out of nothing, because everything must be generated from a seed before it can emerge into the unresisting air.

Lastly, we see that tilled plots are superior to untilled, and their fruits are improved by cultivation. This is because the earth contains certain atoms which we rouse to productivity by turning the fruitful clods with the ploughshare and stirring up the soil. But for these, you would see great improvements arising spontaneously without any aid from our labours.

6. [Nothing Is Ever Annihilated.]

The second great principle is this: *nature resolves everything into its component atoms and never reduces anything to nothing.* If anything were perishable in all its parts, anything might perish all of a sudden and vanish from sight. There would be no need of any force to separate its parts and loosen their links. In actual fact, since everything is composed of indestructible seeds, nature obviously does not allow anything to perish till it has encountered a force that shatters it with a blow or creeps into chinks and unknits it.

If the things that are banished from the scene by age are annihilated through the exhaustion of their material, from what source does Venus bring back the several races of animals into the light of life? And, when they are brought back, where does the inventive earth find for each the special food required for its sustenance and growth? From what fount is the sea replenished by its native springs and the streams that flow into it from afar? Whence does the ether draw nutriment for the stars? For everything consisting of a mortal body must have been exhausted by the long day of time, the illimitable past. If throughout this bygone eternity there have persisted bodies from which the universe has been perpetually renewed, they must certainly be possessed of immortality. Therefore things cannot be reduced to nothing.

Again, all objects would regularly be destroyed by the same force and the same cause, were it not that they are sustained by imperishable matter more or less tightly fastened together. Why, a mere touch would be enough to bring about destruction supposing there were no imperishable bodies whose union could be dissolved only by the appropriate force. Actually, because the fastenings of the atoms are of various kinds while their matter is imperishable, compound objects remain intact until one of them encounters a force that proves strong enough to break up its particular constitution. Therefore nothing returns to nothing, but everything is resolved into its constituent bodies.

Lastly, showers perish when father ether has flung them down into the lap of mother earth. But the crops spring up fresh and gay; the branches on the trees burst into leaf; the trees themselves grow and are weighed down with fruit. Hence in turn man and brute draw nourishment. Hence we see flourishing cities blest with children and every leafy thicket loud with new broods of songsters. Hence in lush pastures cattle wearied by their bulk fling down their bodies, and the white milky juice oozes from their swollen udders. Hence a new generation frolic friskily on wobbly legs through the fresh grass, their young minds tipsy with undiluted milk. Visible objects therefore do not perish utterly, since nature repairs one thing from another and allows nothing to be born without the aid of another's death.

7. [Matter Exists in the Form of Invisible Particles (Atoms).]

Well, Memmius, I have taught you that things cannot be created out of nothing nor, once born be summoned back to nothing. Perhaps, however, you are becoming mistrustful of my words, because these atoms of mine are not visible to the eye. Consider, therefore, this further evidence of *bodies whose existence you must acknowledge though they cannot be seen.* First, wind, when its force is roused, whips up waves, founders tall ships and scatters cloud-rack. Sometimes scouring plains with hurricane force it strews them with huge trees and batters mountain peaks with blasts that hew down forests. Such is wind in its fury, when it whoops aloud with a mad menace in its shouting. Without question, therefore, there must be invisible particles of wind which sweep sea and land and the clouds in the sky, swooping upon them and whirling them along in a headlong hurricane. In the way they flow and the havoc they spread they are no different from a torrential flood of water when it rushes down in a sudden spate from the mountain heights, swollen by heavy rains, and heaps together wreckage from the forest and entire trees. Soft though it is by nature, the sudden shock of oncoming water is more than even stout bridges can withstand, so furious is the force with which the turbid, storm-flushed torrent surges against their piers. With a mighty roar it lays them low, rolling huge rocks under its waves and brushing aside every obstacle from its course. Such, therefore, must be the movement of blasts of wind also. When they have come surging along some course like a rushing river, they push obstacles before them and buffet them with repeated blows; and sometimes, eddying round and round, they snatch them up and carry them along in a swiftly circling vortex. Here then is proof upon proof that winds have invisible bodies, since in their actions and behaviour they are found to rival great rivers, whose bodies are plain to see.

Then again, we smell the various scents of things though we never see them approaching our nostrils. Similarly, heat and cold cannot be detected by our eyes, and we do not see sounds. Yet all these must be composed of bodies, since they are able to impinge upon our senses. For nothing can touch or be touched except body.

Again, clothes hung out on a surf-beaten shore grow moist. Spread in the sun they grow dry. But we do not see how the moisture has soaked into them, nor again how it has been dispelled by the heat. If follows that the moisture is split up into minute parts which the eye cannot possibly see.

Again, in the course of many annual revolutions of the sun a ring is worn thin next to the finger with continual rubbing. Dripping water hollows a stone. A curved ploughshare, iron though it is, dwindles imperceptibly in the furrow. We see the cobble-stones of the highway worn by the feet of many wayfarers. The bronze statues by the city gates show their right hands worn thin by the touch of travellers who have greeted them in passing. We see that all these are being diminished, since they are worn away. But to perceive what particles drop off at any particular time is a power grudged to us by our ungenerous sense of sight.

To sum up, whatever is added to things gradually by nature and the passage of days, causing a cumulative increase, eludes the most attentive scrutiny of our eyes. Conversely, you cannot see what objects lose by the wastage of age — sheer sea-cliffs, for instance, exposed to prolonged erosion by the mordant brine — or at what time the loss occurs. It follows that nature works through the agency of invisible bodies.

8. [Besides Matter, the Universe Contains Empty Space (Vacuity).]

On the other hand, things are not hemmed in by the pressure of solid bodies in a tight mass. This is because *there is vacuity in things.* A grasp of this fact will be helpful to you in many respects and will save you from much bewildered doubting and questioning about the universe and from mistrust of my teaching. Well then, by vacuity I mean intangible and empty space. If it did not exist, things could not move at all. For the distinctive action of matter, which is counteraction and obstruction, would be in force always and everywhere. Nothing could proceed, because nothing would give it a startingpoint by receding. As it is, we see with our own eyes at sea and on land and high up in the sky that all sorts of things in all sorts of ways are on the move. If there were no empty space, these things would be denied the power of restless movement — or rather, they could not possibly have come into existence, embedded as they would have been in motionless matter.

Besides, there are clear indications that things that pass for solid are in fact porous. Even in rocks a trickle of water seeps through into caves, and copious drops ooze from every surface. Food percolates to every part of an animal's body. Trees grow and bring forth their fruit in season, because their food is distributed throughout their length from the tips of the roots through the trunk and along every branch. Noises pass through walls and fly into closed buildings. Freezing cold penetrates to the bones. If there were no vacancies through which the various bodies could make their way, none of these phenomena would be possible.

Again, why do we find some things outweigh others of equal volume? If there is as much matter in a ball of wool as in one of lead, it is natural that it should weigh as heavily, since it is the function of matter to press everything downwards, while it is the function of space on the other hand to remain weightless. Accordingly, when one thing is not less bulky than another but obviously lighter, it plainly declares that there is more vacuum in it, while the heavier object proclaims that there is more matter in it and much less empty space. We have therefore reached the goal of our diligent inquiry: there is in things an admixture of what we call vacuity.

In case you should be misled on this question by the idle imagining of certain theorists, I must anticipate their argument. They maintain that water yields and opens a penetrable path to scaly bodies of fish that push against it, because they leave spaces behind them into which the yielding water can flow together. In the same way, they suppose, other things can move by mutually changing places, although every place remains filled. This theory has been adopted utterly without warrant. For how can the fish advance till the water has given way? And how can the water retire when the fish cannot move? There are thus only two alternatives: either all bodies are devoid of movement, or you must admit that things contain an admixture of vacuity whereby each is enabled to make the first move.

Lastly, if two bodies suddenly spring apart from contact on a broad surface, all the intervening space must be void until it is occupied by air. However quickly the air rushes in all round, the entire space cannot be filled instantaneously. The air must occupy one spot after another until it has taken possession of the whole space. If anyone supposes that this consequence of such springing apart is made possible by the condensation of air, he is mistaken. For condensation implies that something that was full becomes empty, or *vice versâ*. And I contend that air could not condense so as to produce this effect; or at any rate, if there were no vacuum, it could not thus shrink into itself and draw its parts together.

However many pleas you may advance to prolong the argument, you must end by admitting that there is vacuity in things. There are many other proofs I could add to the pile in order to strengthen conviction; but for an acute intelligence these small clues should suffice to enable you to discover the rest for yourself. As hounds that range the hills often smell out the lairs of wild beasts screened in thickets, when once they have got on to the right trail, so in such questions one thing will lead on to another, till you can succeed by yourself in tracking down the truth to its lurking-places and dragging it forth.

If you grow weary and relax from the chase, there is one thing, Memmius, that I can safely promise you: my honeyed tongue will pour from the treasury of my breast such generous draughts, drawn from inexhaustible springs, that I am afraid slow-plodding age may creep through my limbs and unbolt the bars of my life before the full flood of my arguments on any single point has flowed in verse through your ears.

9. [The Universe Consists of Matter (With Its Properties and Accidents) and of Vacuity and Nothing Else.]

To pick up the thread of my discourse, all nature as it is in itself consists of two things — bodies and the vacant space in which the bodies are situated and through which they move in different directions. The existence of bodies is vouched for by the agreement of the senses. If a belief resting directly on this foundation is not valid, there will be no standard to which we can refer any doubt on obscure questions for rational confirmation. If there were no place and space, which we call vacuity, these bodies could not be situated anywhere or move in any direction whatever. This I have just demonstrated. It remains to show that *nothing exists that is distinct both from body and from vacuity* and could be ranked with the others as a third substance. For whatever *is* must also be something. If it offers resistance to touch, however light and slight, it will increase the mass of body by such amount, great or small, as it may amount to, and will rank with it. If, on the other hand, it is intangible, so that it offers no resistance whatever to anything passing through it, then it will be that empty space which we call vacuity. Besides, whatever it may be in itself, either it will act in some way, or react to other things acting upon it, or else it will be such that things can be and happen in it. But without body nothing can act or react; and nothing can afford a place except emptiness and vacancy. Therefore, besides matter and vacuity, we cannot include in the number of things any third substance that can either affect our senses at any time or be grasped by the reasoning of our minds.

You will find that anything that can be named is either a property or an accident of these two. A *property* is something that cannot be detached or separated from a thing without destroying it, as weight is a property of rocks, heat of fire, fluidity of water, tangibility of all bodies, intangibility of vacuum. On the other hand, servitude and liberty, poverty and riches, war and peace, and all other things whose advent or departure leaves the essence of a thing intact, all these it is our practice to call by their appropriate name, *accidents*.

Similarly, time by itself does not exist; but from things themselves there results a sense of what has already taken place, what is now going on and what is to ensue. It must not be claimed that anyone can sense time by itself apart from the movement of things or their restful immobility.

Again, when men say it *is* a fact that Helen was ravished or the Trojans were conquered, do not let anyone drive you to the admission that any such event *is* independently of any object, on the ground that the generations of men of whom these events were accidents have been swept away by the irrevocable lapse of time. For we could put it that whatever has taken place is an accident of a particular tract of earth or of the space it occupied. If there had been no matter and no space or place in which things could happen, no spark of love kindled by the beauty of Tyndareus' daughter would ever have stolen into the breast of Phrygian Paris to light that dazzling blaze of pitiless war; no Wooden Horse, unmarked by the sons of Troy, would have set the towers of Ilium aflame through the midnight issue of Greeks from its womb. So you may see that events cannot be said to *be* by themselves like matter or in the same sense as space. Rather, you should describe them as accidents of matter, or of the place in which things happen.

10. [The Atoms Are Indestructible.]

Material objects are of two kinds, atoms and compounds of atoms. The atoms themselves cannot be swamped by any force, for they are preserved indefinitely by their absolute solidity. Admittedly, it is hard to believe that anything can exist that is absolutely solid. The lightning stroke from the sky penetrates closed buildings, as do shouts and other noises. Iron glows molten in the fire, and hot rocks are cracked by untempered scorching. Hard gold is softened and melted by heat; and bronze, ice-like, is liquefied by flame. Both heat and piercing cold seep through silver, since we feel both alike when a cooling shower of water is poured into a goblet that we hold ceremonially in our hands. All these facts point to the conclusion that nothing is really solid. But sound reasoning and nature itself drive us to the opposite conclusion. Pay attention, therefore, while I demonstrate in a few lines that there exist certain bodies that are absolutely solid and indestructible, namely those atoms which according to our teaching are the seeds or prime units of things from which the whole universe is built up.

In the first place, we have found that nature is twofold, consisting of two totally different things, matter and the space in which things happen. Hence each of these must exist by itself without admixture of the other. For, where there is empty space (what we call vacuity), there matter is not; where matter exists, there cannot be a vacuum. Therefore the prime units of matter are solid and free from vacuity.

Again, since composite things contain some vacuum, the surrounding matter must be solid. For you cannot reasonably maintain that anything can hide vacuity and hold it within its body unless you allow that the container itself is solid. And what contains the vacuum in things can only be an accumulation of matter. Hence matter, which possesses absolute solidity, can be everlasting when other things are decomposed.

Again, if there were no empty space, everything would be one solid mass; if there were not material objects with the property of filling the space they occupy, all existing space would be utterly void. It is clear, then, that there is an alternation of matter and vacuity, mutually distinct, since the whole is neither completely full nor completely empty. There are therefore solid bodies, causing the distinction between empty space and full. And these, as I have just shown, can be neither decomposed by blows from without nor invaded and unknit from within nor destroyed by any other form of assault. For it seems that a thing without vacuum can be neither knocked to bits nor snapped nor chopped in two by cutting; nor can it let in moisture or seeping cold or piercing fire, the universal agents of destruction. The more vacuum a thing contains within it, the more readily it yields to these assailants. Hence, if the units of matter are solid and without vacuity, as I have shown, they must be everlasting.

Yet again, if the matter in things had not been everlasting, everything by now would have gone back to nothing, and the things we see would be the product of rebirth out of nothing. But, since I have already shown that nothing can be created out of nothing nor any existing thing be summoned back to nothing, the atoms must be made of imperishable stuff into which everything can be resolved in the end, so that there may be a stock of matter for building the world anew. The atoms, therefore, are absolutely solid and unalloyed. In no other way could they have survived throughout infinite time to keep the world in being.

Furthermore, if nature had set no limit to the breaking of things, the particles of matter in the course of ages would have been ground so small that nothing could be generated from them so as to attain in the fullness of time to the summit of its growth. For we see that anything can be more speedily dis-integrated than put together again. Hence, what the long day of time, the bygone eternity, has already shaken and loosened to fragments could never in the residue of time be reconstructed. As it is, there is evidently a limit set to breaking, since we see that everything is renewed and each according to its kind has a fixed period in which to grow to its prime.

Here is a further argument. Granted that the particles of matter are abso-lutely solid, we can still explain the composition and behaviour of soft things — air, water, earth, fire — by their intermixture with empty space. On the other hand, supposing the atoms to be soft, we cannot account for the origin of hard flint and iron. For there would be no foundation for na-ture to build on. Therefore there must be bodies strong in their unalloyed so-lidity by whose closer clustering things can be knit together and display un-yielding toughness.

If we suppose that there is no limit set to the breaking of matter, we must still admit that material objects consist of particles which throughout eternity have resisted the forces of destruction. To say that these are breakable does not square with the fact that they have sur-vived throughout eternity under a per-petual bombardment of innumerable blows.

Again, there is laid down for each thing a specific limit to its growth and its tenure of life, and the laws of nature ordain what each can do and what it cannot. No species is ever changed, but each remains so much itself that every kind of bird displays on its body its

own specific markings. This is a further proof that their bodies are composed of changeless matter. For, if the atoms could yield in any way to change, there would be no certainty as to what could arise and what could not, at what point the power of everything was limited by an immovable frontier-post; nor could successive generations so regularly re-peat the nature, behaviour, habits and movements of their parents.

To proceed with our argument, there is an ultimate point in visible ob-jects which represents the smallest thing that can be seen. So also there must be an ultimate point in objects that lie below the limit of perception by our senses. This point is without parts and is the smallest thing that can exist. It never has been and never will be able to exist by itself, but only as one pri-mary part of something else. It is with a mass of such parts, solidly jammed to-gether in order, that matter is filled up. Since they cannot exist by themselves, they must needs stick together in a mass from which they cannot by any means be pried loose. The atoms there-fore are absolutely solid and unalloyed, consisting of a mass of least parts tightly packed together. They are not compounds formed by the coalescence of their parts, but bodies of absolute and everlasting solidity. To these na-ture allows no loss or diminution, but guards them as seeds for things. If there are no such least parts, even the small-est bodies will consist of an infinite number of parts, since they can always be halved and their halves halved again without limit. On this showing, what difference will there be between the whole universe and the very least of things? None at all. For, however endlessly infinite the universe may be, yet the smallest things will equally consist of an infinite number of parts. Since true reason cries out against this and denies that the mind can believe it, you must needs give in and admit that there are least parts which themselves are partless. Granted that these parts exist, you must needs admit that the atoms they compose are also solid and everlasting. But, if all things were compelled by all-creating nature to be broken up into these least parts, nature would lack the power to rebuild anything out of them. For partless objects cannot have the essential properties of generative matter—those varieties of attachment, weight, impetus, impact and movement on which everything depends. . . .

11. [Occasionally They Swerve Slightly From the Vertical.]

. . . There is another fact that I want you to grasp. *When the atoms are travelling straight down through empty space by their own weight, at quite indeterminate times and places they swerve ever so little from their course,* just so much that you can call it a change of direction. If it were not for this swerve, everything would fall downwards like rain-drops through the abyss of space. No collision would take place and no impact of atom on atom would be created. Thus nature would never have created anything.

If anyone supposes that heavier atoms on a straight course through empty space could outstrip lighter ones and fall on them from above, thus causing impacts that might give rise to generative motions, he is going far astray from the path of truth. The reason why objects falling through water or thin air vary in speed according to their weight is simply that the matter composing water or air cannot obstruct all objects equally, but is forced to give way more speedily to heavier ones. But empty space can offer no resistance to any object in any quarter at any time, so as not to yield free passage as its own nature demands. Therefore, through undisturbed vacuum all bodies must travel at equal speed though impelled by unequal weights. The heavier will never be able to fall on the lighter from above or generate of themselves impacts leading to that variety of motions out of which nature can produce things. We are thus forced back to the conclusion that the atoms swerve a little—but only a very little, or we shall be caught imagining slantwise movements, and the facts will prove us wrong. For we see plainly and palpably that weights, when they come tumbling down, have no power of their own to move aslant, so far as meets the eye. But who can possibly perceive that they do not diverge in the very least from a vertical course?

Again, if all movement is always interconnected, the new arising from the old in a determinate order—if the atoms never swerve so as to originate some new movement that will snap the bonds of fate, the everlasting sequence of cause and effect—what is the source of the free will possessed by living things throughout the earth? What, I repeat, is the source of that will-power snatched from the fates, whereby we follow the path along which we are severally led by pleasure, swerving from our course at no set time or place but at the bidding of our own hearts? There is no doubt that on these occasions the will of the individual originates the movements that trickle through his limbs. Observe, when the starting barriers are flung back, how the racehorses in the eagerness of their strength cannot break away as suddenly as their hearts desire. For the whole supply of matter must first be mobilized throughout every member of the body: only then, when it is mustered in a continuous array, can it respond to the prompting of the heart. So you may see that the beginning of movement is generated by the heart; starting from the voluntary action of the mind, it is then transmitted throughout the body and the limbs. Quite different is our experience when we are shoved along by a blow inflicted with compulsive force by someone else. In that case it is obvious that all the matter of our body is set going and pushed along involuntarily, till a check is imposed through the limbs by the will. Do you see the difference? Although many men are driven by an external force and often constrained involuntarily to advance or to rush headlong, yet there is within the human breast something that can fight against this force and resist it. At its command the supply of matter is forced to take a new course through our limbs and joints or is checked in its course and brought once more to a halt. So also in the atoms you must recognize the same possibility: besides weight and impact there must be a third cause of movement, the source of this inborn

power of ours, since we see that nothing can come out of nothing. For the weight of an atom prevents its movements from being completely determined by the impact of other atoms. But the fact that the mind itself has no internal necessity to determine its every act and compel it to suffer in helpless passivity — this is due to the slight swerve of the atoms at no determinate time or place.

12. [The Atoms Themselves Are Devoid of Colour.]

Give ear now to arguments that I have searched out with an effort that was also a delight. Do not imagine that white objects derive the snowy aspect they present to your eyes from white atoms, or that black objects are composed of a black element. And in general do not believe that anything owes the colour it displays to the fact that its atoms are tinted correspondingly. *The primary particles of matter have no colour whatsoever*, neither the same colour as the objects they compose nor a different one. If you think the mind cannot lay hold of such bodies, you are quite wrong. Men who are blind from birth and have never looked on the sunlight have knowledge by touch of bodies that have never from the beginning been associated with any colour. It follows that on our minds also an image can impinge of bodies not marked by any tint. Indeed the things that we ourselves touch in pitch darkness are not felt by us as possessing any colour.

Having proved that colourless bodies are not unthinkable, I will proceed to demonstrate that the atoms must be such bodies.

First, then, any colour may change completely to any other. But the atoms cannot possibly change colour. For something must remain changeless — or everything would be absolutely annihilated. For, if ever anything is so transformed as to overstep its own limits, this means the immediate death of what was before. So do not stain the atoms with colour — or you will find everything slipping back into nothing.

Let us suppose, then, that the atoms are naturally colourless and that it is through the variety of their shapes that they produce the whole range of colours, a great deal depending on their combinations and positions and their reciprocal motions. You will now find it easy to explain without more ado why things that were dark-coloured a moment since can suddenly become as white as marble — as the sea, for instance, when its surface is ruffled by a fresh breeze, is turned into white wave-crests of marble lustre. You could say that something we often see as dark is promptly transformed through the churning up of its matter and a reshuffling of atoms, with some additions and subtractions, so that it is seen as bleached and white. If, on the other hand, the waters of the sea were composed of blue atoms, they could not possibly be whitened; for, however you may stir up blue matter, it can never change its colour to the pallor of marble.

It might be supposed that the uniform lustre of the sea is made up of particles of different colours, as for instance a single object of a square shape is often made up of other objects of various shapes. But in the square we discern the different shapes. So in the surface of the sea or in any other uniform lustre we ought, on this hypothesis, to discern a variety of widely different colours. Besides, differences in the shapes of the parts are no hindrance to the whole being square in outline. But differences in colour completely prevent it from displaying an unvariegated lustre.

The seductive argument that sometimes tempts us to attribute colours to the atoms is demolished by the fact that white objects are not created from white material nor black from black, but both from various colours. Obviously, white could much more readily spring from no colour at all than from black, or from any other colour that interferes and conflicts with it.

Again, since there can be no colours without light and the atoms do not emerge into the light, it can be inferred that they are not clothed in any colour. For what colour can there be in blank darkness? Indeed, colour is itself changed by a change of light, according as the beams strike it vertically or aslant. Observe the appearance in sunlight of the plumage that rings the neck of a dove and crowns its nape: sometimes it is tinted with the brilliant red of a ruby; at others it is seen from a certain point of view to mingle emerald greens with the blue of the sky. In the same way a peacock's tail, profusely illumined, changes colour as it is turned this way or that. These colours, then, are created by a particular incidence of light. Hence, no light, no colour.

When the pupil of the eye is said to perceive the colour white, it experiences in fact a particular kind of impact. When it perceives black, or some other colour, the impact is different. But, when you touch things, it makes no odds what colour they may be, but only what is their shape. The inference is that the atoms have no need of colour, but cause various sensations of touch according to their various shapes.

Since there is no natural connexion between particular colours and particular shapes, atoms (if they were not colourless) might equally well be of any colour irrespective of their form. Why then are not their compounds tinted with every shade of colour irrespective of their kind? We should expect on this hypothesis that ravens in flight would often emit a snowy sheen from snowy wings; and that some swans would be black, being composed of black atoms, or would display some other uniform or variegated colour.

Again, the more anything is divided into tiny parts, the more you can see its colour gradually dimming and fading out. When red cloth, for instance, is pulled to pieces thread by thread, its crimson or scarlet colour, than which there is none brighter, is all dissipated. From this you may gather that, before its particles are reduced right down to atoms, they would shed all their colour.

Finally, since you acknowledge that not all objects emit noise or smell, you accept that as a reason for not attributing sounds and scents to everything. On the same principle, since we cannot perceive everything by eye, we may infer that some things are colourless, just as some things are scentless and soundless, and that these can be apprehended by the percipient mind as read-ily as things that are lacking in some other quality.

13. [The Atoms Are Also Devoid of Heat, Sound, Taste, and Smell.]

Do not imagine that colour is the only quality that is denied to the atoms. *They are also wholly devoid of warmth and cold and scorching heat; they are barren of sound and starved of savour, and emit no inherent odour from their bodies.* When you are setting out to prepare a pleasant perfume of marjoram or myrrh or flower of spikenard, breathing nectar into our nostrils, your first task is to select so far as possible an oil that is naturally odourless and sends out no exhalation to our nostrils. This will be least liable to corrupt the scents blended and concocted with its substance by contamination with its own taint. For the same reason the atoms must not impart to things at their birth a scent or sound that is their own property, since they can send nothing out of themselves; nor must they contribute any flavour or cold or heat, whether scorching or mild, or anything else of the kind.

These qualities, again, are perishable things, made pliable by the softness of their substance, breakable by its crumbliness and penetrable by its looseness of texture. They must be kept far apart from the atoms, if we wish to provide the universe with imperishable foundations on which it may rest secure; or else you will find everything slipping back into nothing.

14. [And of Sentience.]

At this stage you must admit that *whatever is seen to be sentient is neverthe-*

less composed of atoms that are insentient. The phenomena open to our observation do not contradict this conclusion or conflict with it. Rather, they lead us by the hand and compel us to believe that the animate is born, as I maintain, of the insentient.

As a particular instance, we can point to living worms, emerging from foul dung when the earth is soaked and rotted by intemperate showers. Besides, we see every sort of substance transformed in the same way. Rivers, foliage and lush pastures are transformed into cattle; the substance of cattle is transformed into our bodies; and often enough our bodies go to build up the strength of predatory beasts or the bodies of the lords of the air. So nature transforms all foods into living bodies and generates from them all the senses of animate creatures, just as it makes dry wood blossom out in flame and transfigures it wholly into fire. So now do you see that it makes a great difference in what order the various atoms are arranged and with what others they are combined so as to impart and take over motions?

What is it, then, that jogs the mind itself and moves and compels it to express certain sentiments, so that you do not believe that the sentient is generated by the insentient? Obviously it is the fact that a mixture of water and wood and earth cannot of itself bring about vital sensibility. There is one relevant point you should bear in mind: I am not maintaining that sensations are generated automatically from all the elements out of which sentient things are created. Everything depends on the size and shape of the sense-producing atoms

and on their appropriate motions, arrangements and positions. None of these is found in wood or clods. And yet these substances, when they are fairly well rotted by showers, give birth to little worms, because the particles of matter are jolted out of their old arrangements by a new factor and combined in such a way that animate objects must result.

Again, those who would have it that sensation can be produced only be sensitive bodies, which originate in their turn from others similarly sentient — these theorists are making the foundations of our senses perishable, because they are making them soft. For sensitivity is always associated with flesh, sinews, veins — all things that we see to be soft and composed of perishable stuff.

Let us suppose, for argument's sake, that particles of these substances could endure everlastingly. The sensation with which they are credited must be either that of a part or else similar to that of an animate being as a whole. But it is impossible for parts by themselves to experience sensation: all the sensations felt in our limbs are felt by us as a whole; a hand or any other member severed from the whole body is quite powerless to retain sensation on its own. There remains the alternative that such particles have senses like those of an animate being as a whole. They must then feel precisely what we feel, so as to share in all our vital sensations. How then can they pass for elements and escape the path of death, since they are animate beings, and animate and mortal are one and the same thing? Even supposing they could escape death, yet they will make nothing by their combination and conjunction but a mob or horde of living things, just as men and cattle and wild beasts obviously could not combine so as to give birth to a single thing. If we suppose that they shed their own sentience from their bodies and acquire another one, what is the point of giving them the one that is taken away? Besides, as we saw before, from the fact that we perceive eggs turning into live fledgelings and worms swarming out when the earth has been rotted by intemperate showers, we may infer that sense can be generated from the insentient.

Suppose someone asserts that sense can indeed emerge from the insentient, but only by some transformation or some creative process comparable to birth. He will be adequately answered by a clear demonstration that birth and transformation occur only as the result of union or combination. Admittedly sensation cannot arise in any body until an animate creature has been born. This of course is because the requisite matter is dispersed through air and streams and earth and the products of earth: it has not come together in the appropriate manner, so as to set in mutual operation those vitalizing motions that kindle the all-watchful senses which keep watch over every animate creature.

When any animate creature is suddenly assailed by a more powerful blow than its nature can withstand, all the senses of body and mind are promptly thrown into confusion. For the juxtapositions of the atoms are unknit, and the vitalizing motions are inwardly obstructed, until the matter, jarred and jolted throughout every limb, loosens the vital knots of the spirit from the body and expels the spirit in scattered particles through every pore. What other effect can we attribute to the infliction of a blow than this of shaking and shattering everything to bits? Besides, it often happens, when the blow is less violently inflicted, that such vitalizing motions as survive emerge victorious; they assuage the immense upheavals resulting from the shock, recall every particle to its own proper courses, break up the lethal motion when it is all but master of the body and rekindle the well-nigh extinguished senses. How else could living creatures on the very threshold of death rally their consciousness and return to life rather than make good their departure by a route on which they have already travelled most of the way?

Again, pain occurs when particles of matter have been unsettled by some force within the living flesh of the limbs and stagger in their inmost stations. When they slip back into place, that is blissful pleasure. It follows that the atoms cannot be afflicted by any pain or experience any pleasure in themselves, since they are not composed of any primal particles, by some reversal of whose movements they might suffer anguish or reap some fruition of vitalizing bliss. They cannot therefore be endowed with any power of sensation.

Again, if we are to account for the power of sensation possessed by animate creatures in general by attributing sentience to their atoms, what of those atoms that specifically compose the human race? Presumably they are not merely sentient, but also shake their sides with uproarious guffaws and besprinkle their cheeks with dewy teardrops and even discourse profoundly and at length about the composition of the universe and proceed to ask of what elements they are themselves composed. If they are to be likened to entire mortals, they must certainly consist of other elemental particles, and these again of others. There is no point at which you may call a halt, but I will follow you there with your argument that whatever speaks or laughs or thinks is composed of particles that do the same. Let us acknowledge that this is stark madness and lunacy: one can laugh without being composed of laughing particles, can think and proffer learned arguments though sprung from seeds neither thoughtful nor eloquent. Why then cannot the things that we see gifted with sensation by compounded of seeds that are wholly senseless?

Lastly, we are all sprung from heavenly seed. All alike have the same father, from whom all-nourishing mother earth receives the showering drops of moisture. Thus fertilized, she gives birth to smiling crops and lusty trees, to mankind and all the breeds of beasts. She it is that yields the food on which they all feed their bodies, lead their joyous lives and renew their race. So she has well earned the name of mother. In like manner this matter returns: what came from earth goes back into the earth; what was sent down from the ethereal vault is readmitted to the precincts of heaven. Death does not put an end to things by annihilating the component particles but by breaking up their conjunction. Then it links them in new combinations, making everything change in shape and colour and give up in an instant its acquired gift of sensa-

tion. So you may realize what a difference it makes in what combinations and positions the same elements occur, and what motions they mutually pass on and take over. You will thus avoid the mistake of conceiving as permanent properties of the atoms the qualities that are seen floating on the surface of things, coming into being from time to time and as suddenly perishing. Obviously it makes a great difference in these verses of mine in what context and order the letters are arranged. If not all, at least the greater part is alike. But differences in their position distinguish word from word. Just so with actual objects: when there is a change in the combination, motion, order, position or shapes of the component matter, there must be a corresponding change in the object composed. . . .

15. [Mind and Spirit Were Born and Will Die.]

A tree cannot exist high in air, or clouds in the depths of the sea, as fish cannot live in the fields, or blood flow in wood or sap in stones. There is a determined and allotted place for the growth and presence of everything. So mind cannot arise alone without body or apart from sinews and blood. If it could do this, then surely it could much more readily function in head or shoulders or the tips of the heels and be born in any other part, so long as it was held in the same container, that is to say in the same man. Since, however, even in the human body we see a determined and allotted place set aside for the growth and presence of spirit and mind, we have even stronger grounds for denying that they could survive or come to birth outside the body altogether. You must admit, therefore, that when the body has perished there is an end also of the spirit diffused through it. It is surely crazy to couple a mortal object with an eternal and suppose that they can work in harmony and mutually interact. What can be imagined more incongruous, what more repugnant and discordant, than that a mortal object and one that is immortal and everlasting should unite to form a compound and jointly weather the storms that rage about them?

Again, there can be only three kinds of everlasting objects. The first, owing to the absolute solidity of their substance, can repel blows and let nothing penetrate them so as to unknit their close texture from within. Such are the atoms of matter, whose nature I have already demonstrated. The second kind can last for ever because it is immune from blows. Such is empty space, which remains untouched and unaffected by any impact. Last is that which has no available place surrounding it into which its matter can disperse and disintegrate. It is for this reason that the sum total of the universe is everlasting, having no space outside it into which the matter can escape and no matter that can enter and disintegrate it by the force of impact.

Equally vain is the suggestion that the spirit is immortal because it is shielded by life-preserving powers; or because it is unassailed by forces hostile to its survival; or because such forces, if they threaten, are somehow arrested before we are conscious of the threat. Apart from the spirit's participation in the ailments of the body, it has maladies enough of its own. The prospect of the future torments it with fear and wearies it with worry, and past misdeeds leave the sting of remorse. Lastly, it may fall a prey to the mind's own specific afflictions, madness and amnesia, and plunge into the black waters of oblivion.

From all this it follows that *death is nothing to us* and no concern of ours, since our tenure of the mind is mortal. In days of old, we felt no disquiet when the hosts of Carthage poured in to battle on every side — when the whole earth, dizzied by the convulsive shock of war, reeled sickeningly under the high ethereal vault, and between realm and realm the empire of mankind by land and sea trembled in the balance. So, when we shall be no more — when the union of body and spirit that engenders us has been disrupted — to us, who shall then be nothing, nothing by any hazard will happen any more at all. Nothing will have power to stir our senses, not though earth be fused with sea and sea with sky. . . .

16. [Happiness Lies in Cheerful Acceptance of the Universal Lot.]

Here is something that you might well say to yourself from time to time: 'Even good king Ancus looked his last on the daylight — a better man than you, my presumptuous friend, by a long reckoning. Death has come to many another monarch and potentate, who lorded it over mighty nations. Even that King of Kings who once built a highway across the deep — who gave his legions a path to tread among the waves and taught them to march on foot over the briny gulfs and with his charger trampled scornfully upon the ocean's roar — even he was robbed of the light and poured out the spirit from a dying frame. Scipio, that thunderbolt of war, the terror of Carthage, gave his bones to the earth as if he had been the meanest of serfs. Add to this company the discoverers of truth and beauty. Add the attendants of the Muses, among them Homer who in solitary glory bore the sceptre but has sunk into the same slumber as the rest. Democritus, when ripe age warned him that the mindful motions of his intellect were running down, made his unbowed head a willing sacrifice to death. And the Master himself, when his daylit race was run, Epicurus himself died, whose genius outshone the race of men and dimmed them all, as the stars are dimmed by the rising of the fiery sun. And will *you* kick and protest against your sentence? You, whose life is next-door to death while you are still alive and looking on the light. You, who waste the major part of your time in sleep and, when you are awake, are snoring still and dreaming. You, who bear a mind hag-ridden by baseless fear and cannot find the commonest cause of your distress, hounded as you are, poor creature, by a pack of troubles and drifting in a drunken stupor upon a wavering tide of fantasy.'

Men feel plainly enough within their minds, a heavy burden, whose weight depresses them. If only they perceived with equal clearness the causes of this depression, the origin of this lump of evil within their breasts, they would not lead such a life as we now see all to commonly — no one knowing what he really wants and everyone for ever trying to get away from where he is, as though mere locomotion could throw off the load. Often the owner of some stately mansion, bored stiff by staying at home, takes his departure, only to return as speedily when he feels himself no better off out of doors. Off he goes to his country seat, driving his carriage and pair hot-foot, as though in haste to save a house on fire. No sooner has he crossed its doorstep than he starts yawning or retires moodily to sleep and courts oblivion, or else rushes back to revisit the city. In so doing the individual is really running away from himself. Since he remains reluctantly wedded to the self whom he cannot of course escape, he grows to hate him, because he is a sick man ignorant of the cause of his malady. If he did but see this, he would cast other thoughts aside and devote himself first to studying the nature of the universe. It is not the fortune of an hour that is in question, but of all time — the lot in store for mortals throughout the eternity that awaits them after death.

What is this deplorable lust of life that holds us trembling in bondage to such uncertainties and dangers? A fixed term is set to the life of mortals, and there is no way of dodging death. In any case the setting of our lives remains the same throughout, and by going on living we do not mint any new coin of pleasure. So long as the object of our craving is unattained, it seems more precious than anything besides. Once it is ours, we crave for something else. So an unquenchable thirst for life keeps us always on the gasp. There is no telling what fortune the future may bring—what chance may throw in our way, or what upshot lies in waiting. By prolonging life, we cannot subtract or whittle away one jot from the duration of our death. The time after our taking off remains constant. However many generations you may add to your store by living, there waits for you none the less the same eternal death. The time of not-being will be no less for him who made an end of life with yesterday's daylight than for him who perished many a moon and many a year before.

COMMENT

Ancient and Modern Materialism

Although Lucretius wrote his poem over two thousand years ago, his vision of a materialistic universe remains as fresh and vivid as ever. This may seem strange to a reader familiar with the history of ideas. Have not science and the naturalistic philosophy based on it undergone an immense revolution since the time of Lucretius? Even the more modern materialism of Hobbes and La Mettrie appears quaint and archaic in the light of recent science and philosophy. We can no longer conceive of matter in the form of tiny indivisible particles, like the motes of dust that we see dancing about in a shaft of sunlight. The atomic theory has been transplanted from metaphysical speculation to experimental research, and the resulting discoveries have radically transformed it.

Few people would now question the existence of atoms, but the atoms are no longer conceived as inert, eternal, and indivisible particles moving in a featureless void. Instead of being inert, they are made up of electrical charges, which behave like waves. Instead of being eternal, they emit radiations and are subject to splittings and fusions. Instead of being indivisible, they can be analyzed into electrons, protons, neutrons, mesons, positrons, and so on. Instead of moving in a void, they are enmeshed in electromagnetic fields within curved space-time. These modern concepts of radiation, fission, quanta, waves, fields, and relativity are a far cry from Lucretius.

Yet the naturalistic temper of his philosophy as distinguished from the archane details of his science remains as up to date as ever. Nothing in modern physics contradicts his vision of all things arising from and returning to a material base. The view of the world that some philosophers prefer to call naturalism rather than materialism remains as plausible as ever. This is the view that the universe as revealed in the physical sciences is primary and fundamental in the nature of things.

Can Materialism Explain Perceptual Appearances?

Extreme materialism tries to explain every process in terms of matter and motion quantitatively described. "Primary qualities", which are abstract and measurable, are conceived to be more ultimate or objective, whereas "secondary qualities", which are concrete and unmeasurable, are regarded as more derivative or subjective. This distinction was first clearly stated by Democritus: "There are two kinds of knowledge: real knowledge and obscure knowledge. To obscure knowledge belong all things of sight, sound, odor, taste, and touch; real knowledge is distinct from this. . . . Sweet and bitter, heat and cold, and color, are only opinions; there is nothing true but atoms and the void."[1] For Democritus, the only objective properties of things are size, shape, weight, and motion. All other qualities, such as sound, color, odor, taste, and touch, are sensations in us caused by the motions and arrangements of the atoms.

This theory was revived by Galileo and was reformulated by Hobbes, Locke, Newton, and other influential modern thinkers. It has figured very prominently in modern theories of perception. Warmth, for example, is explained as the reaction of our sense organs and nervous systems to molecular motions; sound, as our reaction to air waves; color, as our reaction to electromagnetic vibrations. Thus the "secondary qualities"—colors, sound, odors, and so on—exist, as such, only for our minds. In the absence of our mental reactions, the universe is a pretty dull and abstract affair—a collection of soundless, colorless, and odorless particles, in various arrangements, drifting through space and time.

Lucretius, departing from the views of Democritus, had a different theory. He agreed that the atoms individually are without any of the secondary qualities but maintained that these qualities spring into existence when the atoms are combined in certain ways. "The first-bodies," he tells us, are not only "bereft . . . of color, they are also sundered altogether from warmth and cold, and fiery heat, and are carried along barren of sound and devoid of taste, nor do they give off any scent of their own from their body." But these qualities *are* properties of compounds, formed by combinations of atoms. The compounds, being new and different entities, have color, sound, odor, taste, and heat, none of which can belong to the atoms as individual particles. When we perceive these secondary qualities we are grasping real objective properties, for the complex body perceived by our senses is as real as the atoms.

Whatever interpretation is adopted, whether that of Democritus, Lucretius, or a modern materialist, is subject to all the difficulties discussed

[1] *The Way of Philosophy*, translated by Philip Wheelwright (New York: Odyssey Press, 1954), p. 162.

by Bertrand Russell in Chapter 4. The qualities of perception belong to appearances ("sense-data"), which depend at least in part on the reactions of the sentient organism. To profess to know what is behind the sensory appearances is to leap into conjecture. Russell indicates just how conjectural this leap is.

Even if we accept the conclusions drawn from modern physical science, the electrons, protons, neutrons, mesons, positrons, and other abstract entities, with their fields of force and curved space-time environment, are very unlike human perceptions. To what extent are the appearances verifiable? To what extent are the *inferences* from these appearances also verifiable? To what extent are the appearances merely reactions in us? To what extent are they like "things" in the real external world? These are questions that should not be answered without reviewing the difficulties pointed out by Russell.

Can Materialism Explain Life?

Can a materialist account for the difference between animate and inanimate things?

Extreme materialists will not admit any such fundamental cleavage. Plant and animal activity, they will maintain, is reducible simply to physical and chemical forces exactly like those found in inorganic bodies. Living things are composed exclusively of substances that may also be found in nonliving things, and there are no teleological or vitalistic forces that explain life. In opposition to this point of view, "vitalists" such as Henri Bergson maintain that life is distinct and fundamentally different from nonlife.

Vitalism is not as plausible as it was earlier in this century. We are now aware of intermediate forms such as viruses that cannot be easily classified as either organic or inorganic. There are chemical substances that grow and multiply — they behave in some ways as if they were alive and in other ways as if they were not. Even machines, as Turing points out, display marks of behavior that were hitherto regarded as characteristic of living things only. It has become increasingly difficult to differentiate between the behavior of living and lifeless things.

More plausible than a sharp and everlasting dualism of the inorganic and the organic is the doctrine of emergence. This is the theory that life and mind evolve out of the nonliving and the nonmental. Lucretius can be called a believer in emergence. He pointed out that men can speak and laugh and think, whereas it would be absurd to attribute these capacities to atoms. A human organism, made up of innumerable atoms, has vital characteristics, which the atoms taken singly do not possess. Just as the meaning of a sentence results from the combinations of meaningless letters, so life and mind result from the meetings and configurations of lifeless and mindless atoms. Applied to evolution, this theory means the recognition of diverse levels of complexity and organization, each with its emergent qualities, and the interpretation of these levels as successive stages in an evolutionary process. We associate this type of theory with such modern philosophers as Samuel Alexander (1859–1938), but it was maintained by Lucretius two thousand years ago.

Its implications are, in the wide sense of the word, "materialistic." Mind, it declares, arises out of matter and is a function of complex material bodies. "Out of dust man arises and to dust will he return." Vital processes, including thought, cannot survive the dissolution of the body any more than a football game can continue after the disbanding of the opposing teams.

The type of materialism called *epiphenomenalism* admits that there are mental processes but regards them as mere ineffectual byproducts of physical processes. The only causal relations are between physical events and other physical events, or between physical antecedents and mental consequents. Our thoughts and feelings are caused by molecular changes in the brain or other physical processes and have no causal efficacy of their own. The mind has as little to do with the movement of the body as the shadow cast by a locomotive has to do with the racing of the locomotive.

Lucretius is not consistent enough to be called an epiphenomenalist, but for the most part he clings to a materialistic interpretation of the *causes* of mental events. He maintains, for example, that all knowledge is derived from sensations caused by the impact on the mind-atoms of surface-films emanating from external physical objects. But he departs from epiphenomenalism with its extreme mechanistic implications in his theory of "swerving" atoms and concomitant free will.

Consideration of these alternative theories — vitalism, emergence, and epiphenomenalism — will provide ample ground for discussion.

Can Materialism Explain Mind?

Can a materialist account for mental characteristics?

The most extreme kind of materialism, exemplified by some radical mechanists and behaviorists, is the virtual denial that we have minds at all. Since we are all aware that there are mental processes, such as reasoning, willing, feeling, perceiving, remembering, and imagining, we need not argue the point.

More sensible than the denial that human beings experience mental processes is the contention that machines can, in a sense "think." Since World War II there has been an amazing development of "electronic brains" or "thinking machines." They can perform lightning computations of the most complex kind—they can play chess, prove theorems, translate from one language to another, and guide rockets through interplanetary space. These astounding performances have reinforced the contention that the human mind is just a very complicated mechanism. In his article "Computing Machines and Intelligence," A. M. Turing argues that technicians will eventually be able to create machines with artificial intelligence so sophisticated that it cannot, under certain conditions (for example, "the imitation game"), be distinguished from human intelligence. Turing contends that we should then concede that machines can think.

An opponent would object that we cannot determine whether a machine can think by the mere observation of outputs, however cleverly they might simulate human behavior. It is not simply *what* the machine does but *how* it does it that must be considered. If by thought one means *conscious* deliberations and initiatives, the machine does not think.

Every conscious human being is aware of his or her own mental life—the sensations, feelings of pleasure and pain, hopes and dreams and fancies, loves and hates, plans and purposes. No machine has such an "inner life" or any self-conscious awareness. As Wladyslaw Sluckin, who is both a psychologist and an engineer, has written,

> Machines do not form their purposes in the manner of human beings, the purposes of machines are decided for them by their inventors or operators. It would be absurd to praise or blame a machine for results of its operations other than in a metaphorical way. Machines have no ethical sentiments and no effective attitudes. In no situation are machines expected to pass moral judgment. The question as to whether machines could possibly exhibit purpose in this sense of the word is nonsensical because it does not appear in any way feasible to describe robot behavior in terms which ascribe to it morality.[2]

---

[2]*Minds and Machines*, rev. ed. (Baltimore: Penguin Books, 1960), p. 213.

9

Idealism

"It is evident that the things I perceive are my own ideas, and that no idea can exist unless it be in a mind."

George Berkeley

GEORGE BERKELEY (1685–1753)

Berkeley was born in Kilkenny County, Ireland. His parents, having a comfortable income, gave him a good education at Kilkenny School and Trinity College, Dublin. While scarcely more than a boy, he began to fill notebooks with original philosophical reflections. His first major publication, *An Essay Toward a New Theory of Vision*, appeared when he was twenty-four, and *Principles of Human Knowledge*, which set forth his whole idealistic philosophy, was published only a year later. Finding that his ideas were ridiculed, if not neglected, he reformulated his argument in *Three Dialogues Between Hylas and Philonous*, which appeared in 1713. Thus, by the time he was twenty-eight, he had published his three major works, remarkable both for the felicity of their style and for the daring and profundity of their thought.

During this period of his greatest literary activity, Berkeley was a fellow and tutor at Trinity College, but he spent the next years after publishing his *Dialogues* in London, France, and Italy. In London he became the friend of Pope, Steele, Addison, and Swift. Subsequently he traveled in Europe as secretary and chaplain to an earl and tutor to a bishop's son. While in Sicily, he lost the manuscript of the second part of *The Principles of Human Knowledge* and never had the heart to rewrite it.

299

Returning to Ireland, he was appointed lecturer in Greek and theology at Trinity College and eventually an ecclesiastical dean (1724). Shortly thereafter, to his immense surprise, he inherited three thousand pounds from Hester Van Homrigh (Swift's former friend "Vanessa"), a lady whom he had met once and then only casually.

At about the same time, he conceived the project of founding a college in the Bermudas for training missionaries to the Indians and clergy for the American colonists. By his eloquence and personal charm, he was able to obtain a considerable sum to finance his project from private donors and the promise of twenty thousand pounds from the House of Commons. With a new wife, he set sail for America in 1728. But Walpole, the prime minister, refused to fulfill the promise of Parliament, and Berkeley remained for three years at Newport, Rhode Island, his hopes gradually diminishing. Finally, in 1731, despairing of further aid and saddened by the death of an infant daughter, he sailed with his wife and tiny son back to England.

His later life was spent as bishop of Cloyne and head of a growing family. He divided his time between ecclesiastical duties, philosophical studies, agitation for social reform, and family affairs. His main publication in these years was *Siris* (1744), a rather odd work in which he extolled the medicinal virtues of tar-water and expounded an idealistic interpretation of the universe. In the final year of his life, Berkeley and his family moved to Oxford, where, "suddenly and without the least previous notice or pain," he died in 1753.

Mind and Its Objects

THE FIRST DIALOGUE

PHILONOUS. Good morning, *Hylas*: I did not expect to find you abroad so early.

HYL. It is indeed something unusual; but my thoughts were so taken up with a subject I was discoursing of

last night, that finding I could not sleep, I resolved to rise and take a turn in the garden.

PHIL. It happened well, to let you see what innocent and agreeable pleasures you lose every morning. Can there be a pleasanter time of the day, or a more delightful season of the year? That purple sky, those wild but sweet notes of birds, the fragrant bloom upon the trees and flowers, the gentle influence of the rising sun, these and a thousand nameless

London, 1713. Second unchanged edition, 1725. Third edition, 1734. The present text is that of A. Campbell Fraser, *The Works of George Berkeley* (Oxford: Clarendon Press, 1871). (With omissions.)

beauties of nature inspire the soul with secret transports; its faculties too being at this time fresh and lively, are fit for these meditations, which the solitude of a garden and tranquillity of the morning naturally dispose us to. But I am afraid I interrupt your thoughts: for you seemed very intent on something.

HYL.   It is true, I was, and shall be obliged to you if you will permit me to go in the same vein; not that I would by any means deprive myself of your company, for my thoughts always flow more easily in conversation with a friend, than when I am alone: but my request is, that you would suffer me to impart my reflections to you.

PHIL.   With all my heart, it is what I should have requested myself if you had not prevented me.

HYL.   I was considering the odd fate of those men who have in all ages, through an affectation of being distinguished from the vulgar, or some unaccountable turn of thought, pretended either to believe nothing at all, or to believe the most extravagant things in the world. This however might be borne, if their paradoxes and scepticism did not draw after them some consequences of general disadvantage to mankind. But the mischief lieth here; that when men of less leisure see them who are supposed to have spent their whole time in the pursuits of knowledge professing an entire ignorance of all things, or advancing such notions as are repugnant to plain and commonly received principles, they will be tempted to entertain suspicions concerning the most important truths, which they had hitherto held sacred and unquestionable.

PHIL.   I entirely agree with you, as to the ill tendency of the affected doubts of some philosophers, and fantastical conceits of others. . . .

HYL.   I am glad to find there was nothing in the accounts I heard of you.

PHIL.   Pray, what were those?

HYL.   You were represented in last night's conversation, as one who maintained the most extravagant opinion that ever entered into the mind of man, to wit, that there is no such thing as *material substance* in the world.

PHIL.   That there is no such thing as what Philosophers call *material substance*, I am seriously persuaded: but, if I were made to see anything absurd or sceptical in this, I should then have the same reason to renounce this that I imagine I have now to reject the contrary opinion.

HYL.   What! can anything be more fantastical, more repugnant to common sense, or a more manifest piece of Scepticism, than to believe there is no such thing as *matter*?

PHIL.   Softly, good *Hylas*. What if it should prove, that you, who hold there is, are, by virtue of that opinion, a greater sceptic, and maintain more paradoxes and repugnances to common sense, than I who believe no such thing?

HYL.   You may as soon persuade me,

the part is greater than the whole, as that, in order to avoid absurdity and Scepticism, I should ever be obliged to give up my opinion in this point.

PHIL. Well then, are you content to admit that opinion for true, which, upon examination, shall appear most agreeable to common sense, and remote from Scepticism?

HYL. With all my heart. Since you are for raising disputes about the plainest things in nature, I am content for once to hear what you have to say. . . .

PHIL. Shall we therefore examine which of us it is that denies the reality of sensible things, or professes the greatest ignorance of them; since, if I take you rightly, he is to be esteemed the greatest *sceptic*?

HYL. That is what I desire.

PHIL. What mean you by Sensible Things?

HYL. Those things which are perceived by the senses. Can you imagine that I mean anything else?

PHIL. Pardon me, *Hylas*, if I am desirous clearly to apprehend your notions, since this may much shorten our inquiry. Suffer me then to ask you this further question. Are those things only perceived by the senses which are perceived immediately? Or, may those things properly be said to be *sensible* which are perceived mediately, or not without the intervention of others?

HYL. I do not sufficiently understand you.

PHIL. In reading a book, what I immediately perceive are the letters, but mediately, or by means of these, are suggested to my mind the notions of God, virtue, truth, &c. Now, that the letters are truly sensible things, or perceived by sense, there is no doubt: but I would know whether you take the things suggested by them to be so too.

HYL. No, certainly; it were absurd to think *God* or *virtue* sensible things, though they may be signified and suggested to the mind by sensible marks, with which they have an arbitrary connection.

PHIL. It seems then, that by *sensible things* you mean those only which can be perceived *immediately* by sense?

HYL. Right.

PHIL. Doth it not follow from this, that though I see one part of the sky red, and another blue, and that my reason doth thence evidently conclude there must be some cause of that diversity of colors, yet that cause cannot be said to be a sensible thing, or perceived by the sense of seeing?

HYL. It doth.

PHIL. In like manner, though I hear variety of sounds, yet I cannot be said to hear the causes of those sounds?

HYL. You cannot.

PHIL. And when by my touch I perceive a thing to be hot and heavy, I cannot say, with any truth or propriety, that I feel the cause of its heat or weight?

HYL. To prevent any more questions of this kind, I tell you once for all, that by *sensible things* I mean those only which are perceived by sense, and that in truth the senses perceive nothing which they do not perceive immediately: for they make no inferences. The deducing therefore of causes or occasions from effects and appearances, which alone are perceived by sense, entirely relates to reason.

PHIL. This point then is agreed between us — that *sensible things are those only which are immediately perceived by sense.* You will further inform me, whether we immediately perceive by sight anything beside light, and colors, and figures; or by hearing, anything but sounds; by the palate, anything beside tastes; by the smell, beside odors; or by the touch, more than tangible qualities.

HYL. We do not.

PHIL. It seems, therefore, that if you take away all sensible qualities, there remains nothing sensible?

HYL. I grant it.

PHIL. Sensible things therefore are nothing else but so many sensible qualities, or combinations of sensible qualities?

HYL. Nothing else.

PHIL. *Heat* is then a sensible thing?

HYL. Certainly.

PHIL. Doth the reality of sensible things consist in being perceived? or, is it something distinct from their being perceived, and that bears no relation to the mind?

HYL. To *exist* is one thing, and to be *perceived* is another.

PHIL. I speak with regard to sensible things only: and of these I ask, whether by their real existence you mean a subsistence exterior to the mind, and distinct from their being perceived?

HYL. I mean a real absolute being, distinct from, and without any relation to their being perceived.

PHIL. Heat therefore, if it be allowed a real being, must exist without the mind?

HYL. It must.

PHIL. Tell me, *Hylas*, is this real existence equally compatible to all degrees of heat, which we perceive; or is there any reason why we should attribute it to some, and deny it to others? and if there be, pray let me know that reason.

HYL. Whatever degree of heat we perceive by sense, we may be sure the same exists in the object that occasions it.

PHIL. What! the greatest as well as the least?

HYL. I tell you, the reason is plainly the same in respect of both: they are both perceived by sense; nay, the greater degree of heat is more sensibly perceived; and consequently, if there is any difference, we are more certain of its real existence than we can be of the reality of a lesser degree.

PHIL. But is not the most vehement and intense degree of heat a very great pain?

HYL. No one can deny it.

PHIL. And is any unperceiving thing capable of pain or pleasure?

HYL. No certainly.

PHIL. Is your material substance a senseless being, or a being endowed with sense and perception?

HYL. It is senseless without doubt.

PHIL. It cannot therefore be the subject of pain?

HYL. By no means.

PHIL. Nor consequently of the greatest heat perceived by sense, since you acknowledge this to be no small pain?

HYL. I grant it.

PHIL. What shall we say then of your external object; is it a material Substance, or no?

HYL. It is a material substance with the sensible qualities inhering in it.

PHIL. How then can a great heat exist in it, since you own it cannot in a material substance? I desire you would clear this point.

HYL. Hold, *Philonous*, I fear I was out in yielding intense heat to be a pain. It should seem rather, that pain is something distinct from heat, and the consequence or effect of it.

PHIL. Upon putting your hand near the fire, do you perceive one simple uniform sensation, or two distinct sensations?

HYL. But one simple sensation.

PHIL. Is not the heat immediately perceived?

HYL. It is.

PHIL. And the pain?

HYL. True.

PHIL. Seeing therefore they are both immediately perceived at the same time, and the fire affects you only with one simple, or uncompounded idea, it follows that this simple idea is both the intense heat immediately perceived, and the pain; and, consequently, that the intense heat immediately perceived, is nothing distinct from a particular sort of pain.

HYL. It seems so.

PHIL. Again, try in your thoughts, *Hylas*, if you can conceive a vehement sensation to be without pain or pleasure.

HYL. I cannot.

PHIL. Or can you frame to yourself an idea of sensible pain or pleasure, in general, abstracted from every particular idea of heat, cold, tastes, smells? &c.

HYL. I do not find that I can.

PHIL. Doth it not therefore follow, that sensible pain is nothing distinct from those sensations or ideas — in an intense degree?

HYL. It is undeniable; and, to speak the truth, I begin to suspect a very great heat cannot exist but in a mind perceiving it.

PHIL. What! are you then in that *sceptical* state of suspense, between affirming and denying?

HYL. I think I may be positive in the point. A very violent and painful heat cannot exist without the mind.

PHIL. It hath not therefore, according to you, any real being?

HYL. I own it.

PHIL. Is it therefore certain, that there is no body in nature really hot?

HYL. I have not denied there is any real heat in bodies. I only say, there is no such thing as an intense real heat.

PHIL. But, did you not say before that all degrees of heat were equally real; or, if there was any difference, that the greater were more undoubtedly real than the lesser?

HYL. True: but it was because I did not then consider the ground there is for distinguishing between them, which I now plainly see. And it is this: — because intense heat is nothing else but a particular kind of painful sensation; and pain cannot exist but in a perceiving being; it follows that no intense heat can really exist in an unperceiving corporeal substance. But this is no reason why we should deny heat in an inferior degree to exist in such a substance.

PHIL. But how shall we be able to discern those degrees of heat which exist only in the mind from those which exist without it?

HYL. That is no difficult matter. You know the least pain cannot exist unperceived; whatever, therefore, degree of heat is a pain exists only in the mind. But, as for all other degrees of heat, nothing obliges us to think the same of them.

PHIL. I think you granted before that no unperceiving being was capable of pleasure, any more than of pain.

HYL. I did.

PHIL. And is not warmth, or a more gentle degree of heat than what causes uneasiness, a pleasure?

HYL. What then?

PHIL. Consequently, it cannot exist without the mind in an unperceiving substance, or body.

HYL. So it seems.

PHIL. Since, therefore, as well those degrees of heat that are not painful, as those that are, can exist only in a thinking substance; may we not conclude that external bodies are absolutely incapable of any degree of heat whatsoever?

HYL. On second thoughts, I do not think it so evident that warmth is a pleasure, as that a great degree of heat is a pain.

PHIL. I do not pretend that warmth is as great a pleasure as heat is a pain. But, if you grant it to be even a small pleasure, it serves to make good my conclusion.

HYL. I could rather call it an *indolence*. It seems to be nothing more than a privation of both pain and pleasure. And that such a quality or state as this may agree to an unthinking substance, I hope you will not deny.

PHIL. If you are resolved to maintain that warmth, or a gentle degree of heat, is no pleasure, I know not how to convince you otherwise, than by appealing to your own sense. But what think you of cold?

HYL. The same that I do of heat. An intense degree of cold is a pain; for to feel a very great cold, is to perceive a great uneasiness: it cannot therefore exist without the mind; but a lesser degree of cold may, as well as a lesser degree of heat.

PHIL. Those bodies, therefore, upon whose application to our own, we perceive a moderate degree of heat, must be concluded to have a moderate degree of heat or warmth in them; and those, upon whose application we feel a like degree of cold, must be thought to have cold in them.

HYL. They must.

PHIL. Can any doctrine be true that necessarily leads a man into an absurdity?

HYL. Without doubt it cannot.

PHIL. Is it not an absurdity to think that the same thing should be at the same time both cold and warm?

HYL. It is.

PHIL. Suppose now one of your hands hot, and the other cold, and that they are both at once put into the same vessel of water, in an intermediate state; will not the water seem cold to one hand, and warm to the other?

HYL. It will.

PHIL. Ought we not therefore, by our principles, to conclude it is really both cold and warm at the same time, that is, according to your own concession, to believe an absurdity?

HYL. I confess it seems so.

PHIL. Consequently, the principles themselves are false, since you have granted that no true principle leads to an absurdity.

HYL. But, after all, can anything be more absurd than to say, *there is no heat in the fire*?

PHIL. To make the point still clearer; tell me whether, in two cases exactly alike, we ought not to make the same judgment?

HYL. We ought.

PHIL. When a pin pricks your finger, doth it not rend and divide the fibers of your flesh?

HYL. It doth.

PHIL. And when a coal burns your finger, doth it any more?

HYL. It doth not.

PHIL. Since, therefore, you neither judge the sensation itself occasioned by the pin, nor anything like it to be in the pin; you should not, conformably to what you have now granted, judge the sensation occasioned by the fire, or anything like it, to be in the fire.

HYL. Well, since it must be so, I am content to yield this point, and acknowledge that heat and cold are only sensations existing in our minds. But there still remain qualities enough to secure the reality of external things.

PHIL. But what will you say, *Hylas*, if it shall appear that the case is the same with regard to all other sensible qualities, and that they can no more be supposed to exist without the mind, than heat and cold?

HYL. Then indeed you will have done something to the purpose; but that is what I despair of seeing proved.

PHIL. Let us examine them in order. What think you of *tastes*—do they exist without the mind, or no?

HYL. Can any man in his senses doubt whether sugar is sweet, or wormwood bitter?

PHIL. Inform me, *Hylas*. Is a sweet taste a particular kind of pleasure or pleasant sensation, or is it not?

HYL. It is.

PHIL. And is not bitterness some kind of uneasiness or pain?

HYL. I grant it.

PHIL. If therefore sugar and wormwood are unthinking corporeal substances existing without the mind, how can sweetness and bitterness, that is, pleasure and pain, agree to them?

HYL. Hold, *Philonous*, I now see what

it was deluded me all this time. You asked whether heat and cold, sweetness and bitterness, were not particular sorts of pleasure and pain; to which I answered simply, that they were. Whereas I should have thus distinguished:—those qualities, as perceived by us, are pleasures or pains; but not as existing in the external objects. We must not therefore conclude absolutely, that there is no heat in the fire, or sweetness in the sugar, but only that heat or sweetness, as perceived by us, are not in the fire or sugar. What say you to this?

PHIL. I say it is nothing to the purpose. Our discourse proceeded altogether concerning sensible things, which you define to be, *the things we immediately perceive by our senses*. Whatever other qualities, therefore, you speak of, as distinct from these, I know nothing of them, neither do they at all belong to the point in dispute. You may, indeed, pretend to have discovered certain qualities which you do not perceive, and assert those insensible qualities exist in fire and sugar. But what use can be made of this to your present purpose, I am at a loss to conceive. Tell me then once more, do you acknowledge that heat and cold, sweetness and bitterness (meaning those qualities which are perceived by the senses), do not exist without the mind?

HYL. I see it is to no purpose to hold out, so I give up the cause as to those mentioned qualities. Though I profess it sounds oddly, to say that sugar is not sweet.

PHIL. But, for your further satisfaction, take this along with you: that which at other times seems sweet, shall, to a distempered palate, appear bitter. And, nothing can be plainer than that divers persons perceive different tastes in the same food; since that which one man delights in, another abhors. And how could this be, if the taste was something really inherent in the food?

HYL. I acknowledge I know not how.

PHIL. In the next place, *odors* are to be considered. And, with regard to these, I would fain know whether what has been said of tastes doth not exactly agree to them? Are they not so many pleasing or displeasing sensations?

HYL. They are.

PHIL. Can you then conceive it possible that they should exist in an unperceiving thing?

HYL. I cannot.

PHIL. Or, can you imagine that filth and ordure affect those brute animals that feed on them out of choice, with the same smells which we perceive in them?

HYL. By no means.

PHIL. May we not therefore conclude of smells, as of the other forementioned qualities, that they cannot exist in any but a perceiving substance or mind.

HYL. I think so.

PHIL. Then as to *sounds*, what must we think of them: are they accidents really inherent in external bodies, or not?

HYL. That they inhere not in the sonorous bodies is plain from hence; because a bell struck in the exhausted receiver of an air-pump sends forth no sound. The air, therefore, must be thought the subject of sound.

PHIL. What reason is there for that, *Hylas*?

HYL. Because, when any motion is raised in the air, we perceive a sound greater or lesser, according to the air's motion; but without some motion in the air, we never hear any sound at all.

PHIL. And granting that we never hear a sound but when some motion is produced in the air, yet I do not see how you can infer from thence, that the sound itself is in the air.

HYL. It is this very motion in the external air that produces in the mind the sensation of *sound*. For, striking on the drum of the ear, it causeth a vibration, which by the auditory nerves being communicated to the brain, the soul is thereupon affected with the sensation called *sound*.

PHIL. What!
Is sound then a sensation?

HYL. I tell you, as perceived by us, it is a particular sensation in the mind.

PHIL. And can any sensation exist without the mind?

HYL. No, certainly.

PHIL. How then can sound, being a sensation, exist in the air, if by the *air* you mean a senseless substance existing without the mind?

HYL. You must distinguish, *Philonous*, between sound as it is perceived by us, and as it is in itself; or (which is the same thing) between the sound we immediately perceive, and that which exists without us. The former, indeed, is a particular kind of sensation, but the latter is merely a vibrative or undulatory motion in the air.

PHIL. I thought I had already obviated that distinction, by the answer I gave when you were applying it in a like case before. But, to say no more of that, are you sure then that sound is really nothing but motion?

HYL. I am.

PHIL. Whatever therefore agrees to real sound, may with truth be attributed to motion?

HYL. It may.

PHIL. It is then good sense to speak of *motion* as of a thing that is *loud, sweet, acute, or grave.*

HYL. I see you are resolved not to understand me. It is not evident those accidents or modes belong only to sensible sound, or *sound* in the common acceptation of the word, but not to *sound* in the real and philosophic sense; which, as I just now told you, is nothing but a certain motion of the air?

PHIL. It seems then there are two sorts of sound—the one vulgar, or that which is heard, the other philosophical and real?

HYL. Even so.

PHIL. And the latter consists in motion?

HYL. I told you so before.

PHIL. Tell me, *Hylas*, to which of the senses, think you, the idea of motion belongs? to the hearing?

HYL. No, certainly; but to the sight and touch.

PHIL. It should follow then, that, according to you, real sounds may possibly be *seen* or *felt*, but never *heard*.

HYL. Look you, *Philonous*, you may, if you please, make a jest of my opinion, but that will not alter the truth of things. I own, indeed, the inferences you draw me into, sound something oddly; but common language, you know, is framed by, and for the use of the vulgar: we must not therefore wonder, if expressions adapted to exact philosophic notions seem uncouth and out of the way.

PHIL. Is it come to that? I assure you, I imagine myself to have gained no small point, since you make so light of departing from common phrases and opinions; it is being a main part of our inquiry, to examine whose notions are widest of the common road, and most repugnant to the general sense of the world. But, can you think it no more than a philosophical paradox, to say that *real sounds are never heard*, and that the idea of them is obtained by some other sense? And is there nothing in this contrary to nature and the truth of things?

HYL. To deal ingenuously, I do not like it. And, after the concessions already made, I had as well grant that sounds too have no real being without the mind.

PHIL. And I hope you will make no difficulty to acknowledge the same of *colors*.

HYL. Pardon me: the case of colors is very different. Can anything be plainer than that we see them on the objects?

PHIL. The objects you speak of are, I suppose, corporeal Substances existing without the mind.

HYL. They are.

PHIL. And have true and real colors inhering in them?

HYL. Each visible object hath that color which we see in it.

PHIL. How! is there anything visible but what we perceive by sight?

HYL. There is not.

PHIL. And, do we perceive anything by sense which we do not perceive immediately?

HYL. How often must I be obliged to repeat the same thing? I tell you, we do not.

PHIL. Have patience, good *Hylas*; and tell me once more, whether there is anything immediately perceived by the senses, except sensible qualities. I know you asserted there was not; but I would now be informed, whether you still persist in the same opinion.

HYL. I do.

PHIL. Pray, is your corporeal substance either a sensible quality, or made up of sensible qualities?

HYL. What a question that is! who ever thought it was?

PHIL. My reason for asking was, because in saying, *each visible object hath that color which we see in it*, you make visible objects to be corporeal substances; which implies either that corporeal substances are sensible qualities, or else that there is something beside sensible qualities perceived by sight: but, as this point was formerly agreed between us, and is still maintained by you, it is a clear consequence, that your corporeal substance is nothing distinct from sensible qualities.

HYL. You may draw as many absurd consequences as you please, and endeavor to perplex the plainest things; but you shall never persuade me out of my senses. I clearly understand my own meaning.

PHIL. I wish you would make me understand it too. But, since you are unwilling to have your notion of corporeal substance examined, I shall urge that point no further. Only be pleased to let me know, whether the same colors which we see exist in external bodies, or some other.

HYL. The very same.

PHIL. What! are then the beautiful red and purple we see on yonder clouds really in them? Or do you imagine they have in themselves any other form than that of a dark mist or vapor?

HYL. I must own, *Philonous*, those colors are not really in the clouds as they seem to be at this distance. They are only apparent colors.

PHIL. *Apparent* call you them? how shall we distinguish these apparent colors from real?

HYL. Very easily. Those are to be thought apparent which, appearing only at a distance, vanish upon a nearer approach.

PHIL. And those, I suppose, are to be thought real which are discovered by the most near and exact survey.

HYL. Right.

PHIL. Is the nearest and exactest survey made by the help of a microscope, or by the naked eye?

HYL. By a microscope, doubtless.

PHIL. But a microscope often discovers colors in an object different from those perceived by the unassisted sight. And, in case we had microscopes magnifying to any assigned degree, it is certain that no object whatsoever, viewed through them, would appear in the same color which it exhibits to the naked eye.

HYL. And what will you conclude from all this? You cannot argue that there are really and naturally no colors on objects: because by artificial managements they may be altered, or made to vanish.

PHIL. I think it may evidently be concluded from your own concessions, that all the colors we see with our naked eyes are only apparent as those on the clouds, since they vanish upon a more close and accurate inspection which is afforded us by a microspace. Then, as to what you say by way of prevention: I ask you whether the real and natural state of an object is better discovered by a very sharp and piercing sight, or by one which is less sharp?

HYL. By the former without doubt.

PHIL. Is it not plain from *Dioptrics* that microscopes make the sight more penetrating, and represent objects as they would appear to the eye in case it were naturally endowed with a most exquisite sharpness?

HYL. It is.

PHIL. Consequently the microscopical representation is to be thought that which best sets forth the real nature of the thing, or what it is in itself. The colors, therefore, by it perceived are more genuine and real than those perceived otherwise.

HYL. I confess there is something in what you say.

PHIL. Besides, it is not only possible but manifest, that there actually are animals whose eyes are by nature framed to perceive those things which by reason of their minuteness escape our sight. What think you of those inconceivably small animals perceived by glasses? must we suppose they are all stark blind? Or, in case they see, can it be imagined their sight hath not the same use in preserving their bodies from injuries, which appears in that of all other animals? And if it hath, is it not evident they must see particles less than their own bodies, which will present them with a far different view in each object from that which strikes our senses? Even our own eyes do not always represent objects to us after the same manner. In the *jaundice* every one knows that all things seem yellow. Is it not therefore highly probable those animals in whose eyes we discern a very different texture from that of ours, and whose bodies abound with different humors, do not see the same colors in every object that we do? From all which, should it not seem to follow that all colors are equally apparent, and that none of those which we perceive are really inherent in any outward object?

HYL. It should.

PHIL. The point will be past all doubt, if you consider that, in case colors were real properties or affections inherent in external bodies, they could admit of no alteration without some change wrought in the very bodies themselves; but, is it not evident from what hath been said that, upon the use of microscopes, upon a change happening in the humors of the eye, or a variation of distance, without any manner of real alteration in the thing itself, the colors of any object are either changed, or totally disappear? Nay, all other circumstances remaining the same,

change but the situation of some objects, and they shall present different colors to the eye. The same thing happens upon viewing an object in various degrees of light. And what is more known than that the same bodies appear differently colored by candlelight from what they do in the open day? Add to these the experiment of a prism which, separating the heterogeneous rays of light, alters the color of any object, and will cause the whitest to appear of a deep blue or red to the naked eye. And now tell me whether you are still of opinion that every body hath its true real color inhering in it; and, if you think it hath, I would fain know farther from you, what certain distance and position of the object, what peculiar texture and formation of the eye, what degree or kind of light is necessary for ascertaining that true color, and distinguishing it from apparent ones.

HYL. I own myself entirely satisfied, that they are all equally apparent, and that there is no such thing as color really inhering in external bodies, but that it is altogether in the light. And what confirms me in this opinion is that in proportion to the light, colors are still more or less vivid; and if there be no light, then are there no colors perceived. Besides, allowing there are colors on external objects, yet, how is it possible for us to perceive them? For no external body affects the mind, unless it acts first on our organs of sense. But the only action of bodies is motion; and motion cannot be communicated otherwise than by impulse. A distant object therefore cannot act on the eye, nor consequently make itself or its properties perceivable to the soul. Whence it plainly follows that it is immediately some contiguous substance, which, operating on the eye, occasions a perception of colors: and such is light.

PHIL.   How! is light then a substance?

HYL.   I tell you, *Philonous*, external light is nothing but a thin fluid substance, whose minute particles being agitated with a brisk motion, and in various manners reflected from the different surfaces of outward objects to the eyes, communicate different motions to the optic nerves; which, being propagated to the brain, cause therein various impressions; and these are attended with the sensations of red, blue, yellow, &c.

PHIL.   It seems then the light doth no more than shake the optic nerves.

HYL.   Nothing else.

PHIL.   And, consequent to each particular motion of the nerves, the mind is affected with a sensation, which is some particular color.

HYL.   Right.

PHIL.   And these sensations have no existence without the mind.

HYL.   They have not.

PHIL.   How then do you affirm that colors are in the light; since by *light* you understand a corporeal substance external to the mind?

HYL.   Light and colors, as immediately perceived by us, I grant cannot exist without the mind. But, in themselves they are only the motions and configurations of certain insensible particles of matter.

PHIL.   Colors, then, in the vulgar sense, or taken for the immediate objects of sight, cannot agree to any but a perceiving substance.

HYL.   That is what I say.

PHIL.   Well then, since you give up the point as to those sensible qualities which are alone thought colors by all mankind beside, you may hold what you please with regard to those invisible ones of the philosophers. It is not my business to dispute about them; only I would advise you to bethink yourself, whether, considering the inquiry we are upon, it be prudent for you to affirm—*the red and blue which we see are not real colors, but certain unknown motions and figures, which no man ever did or can see, are truly so.* Are not these shocking notions, and are not they subject to as many ridiculous inferences, as those you were obliged to renounce before in the case of sounds?

HYL.   I frankly own, *Philonous*, that it is in vain to stand out any longer. Colors, sounds, tastes, in a word all those termed *secondary qualities*, have certainly no existence without the mind. But, by this acknowledgment I must not be supposed to derogate anything from the reality of Matter or external objects; seeing it is no more than several philosophers maintain, who nevertheless are the farthest imaginable from denying Matter. For the clearer understanding of this, you must know sensible qualities are by philosophers divided into *primary* and *secondary.* The former are Extension, Figure, Solidity, Gravity, Motion, and Rest. And these they hold exist really in bodies. The latter are those above enumerated; or, briefly, all sensible qualities beside the Primary, which they assert are only so many sensations or ideas existing nowhere but in the mind. But all this, I doubt not, you are apprised of. For my part, I have been a long time sensible there was such an opinion current among philosophers, but was never thoroughly convinced of its truth until now.

PHIL. You are still then of opinion that *extension* and *figures* are inherent in external unthinking substances?

HYL. I am.

PHIL. But what if the same arguments which are brought against Secondary Qualities will hold good against these also?

HYL. Why then I shall be obliged to think, they too exist only in the mind.

PHIL. Is it your opinion the very figure and extension which you perceive by sense exist in the outward object or material substance?

HYL. It is.

PHIL. Have all other animals as good grounds to think the same of the figure and extension which they see and feel?

HYL. Without doubt, if they have any thought at all.

PHIL. Answer me, *Hylas.* Think you the senses were bestowed upon all animals for their preservation and well-being in life? or were they given to men alone for this end?

HYL. I make no question but they have the same use in all other animals.

PHIL. If so, it is not necessary they should be enabled by them to perceive their own limbs, and those bodies which are capable of harming them?

HYL. Certainly.

PHIL. A mite therefore must be supposed to see his own foot, and things equal or even less than it, as bodies of some considerable dimension; though at the same time they appear to you scarce discernible, or at best as so many visible points?

HYL. I cannot deny it.

PHIL. And to creatures less than the mite they will seem yet larger?

HYL. They will.

PHIL. Insomuch that what you can hardly discern will to another extremely minute animal appear as some huge mountain?

HYL. All this I grant.

PHIL. Can one and the same thing be at the same time in itself of different dimensions?

HYL. That were absurd to imagine.

PHIL. But, from what you have laid down it follows that both the extension by you perceived, and that perceived by the mite itself, as likewise all those perceived by lesser animals, are each of them the true extension of the mite's foot; that is to say, by your own principles you are led into an absurdity.

HYL. There seems to be some difficulty in the point.

PHIL. Again, have you not acknowledged that no real inherent property of any object can be changed without some change in the thing itself?

HYL. I have.

PHIL. But, as we approach to or recede from an object, the visible extension varies, being at one distance ten or a hundred times greater than at another. Doth it not therefore follow from hence likewise that it is not really inherent in the object?

HYL. I own I am at a loss what to think.

PHIL. Your judgment will soon be determined, if you will venture to think as freely concerning this quality as you have done concerning the rest. Was it not admitted as a good argument, that neither heat nor cold was in the water, because it seemed warm to one hand and cold to the other?

HYL. It was.

PHIL. Is it not the very same reasoning to conclude there is no extension or figure in an object, because to one eye it shall seem little, smooth, and round, when at the same time it appears to the other, great, uneven, and angular?

HYL. The very same. But does this latter fact ever happen?

PHIL. You may at any time make the experiment, by looking with one eye bare, and with the other through a microscope.

HYL. I know not how to maintain it, and yet I am loath to give up *extension*, I see so many odd consequences following upon such a concession.

PHIL. Odd, say you? After the concessions already made, I hope you will stick at nothing for its oddness. But, on the other hand, should it not seem very odd, if the general reasoning which includes all other sensible qualities did not also include extension? If it be allowed that no idea nor anything like an idea can exist in an unperceiving substance, then surely it follows that no figure or mode of extension, which we can either perceive or imagine, or have any idea of, can be really inherent in Matter; not to mention the peculiar difficulty there must be in conceiving a material substance, prior to and distinct from extension, to be the *substratum* of extension. Be the sensible quality what it will—figure, or sound, or color; it seems alike impossible it should subsist in that which doth not perceive it.

HYL. I give up the point for the

present, reserving still a right to retract my opinion, in case I shall hereafter discover any false step in my progress to it.

PHIL. That is a right you cannot be denied. Figures and extensions being dispatched, we proceed next to *motion. Can* a real motion in any external body be at the same time both very swift and very slow?

HYL. It cannot.

PHIL. Is not the motion of a body swift in a reciprocal proportion to the time it takes up in describing any given space? Thus a body that describes a mile in an hour moves three times faster than it would in case it described only a mile in three hours.

HYL. I agree with you.

PHIL. And is not time measured by the succession of ideas in our minds?

HYL. It is.

PHIL. And is it not possible ideas should succeed one another twice as fast in your mind as they do in mine, or in that of some spirit of another kind?

HYL. I own it.

PHIL. Consequently, the same body may to another seem to perform its motion over any space in half the time that it doth to you. And the same reasoning will hold as to any other proportion: that is to say, according to your principles (since the motions perceived are both really in the object) it is possible one and the same body shall be really moved the same way at once, both very swift and very slow. How is this consistent either with common sense, or with what you just now granted?

HYL. I have nothing to say to it.

PHIL. Then as for *solidity;* either you do not mean any sensible quality by that word, and so it is beside our inquiry: or if you do, it must be either hardness or resistance. But both the one and the other are plainly relative to our senses: it being evident that what seems hard to one animal may appear soft to another, who hath greater force and firmness of limbs. Nor is it less plain that the resistance I feel is not in the body.

HYL. I own the very sensation of resistance, which is all you immediately perceive, is not in the *body,* but the cause of that sensation is.

PHIL. But the causes of our sensations are not things immediately perceived, and therefore not sensible. This point I thought had been already determined.

HYL. I own it was; but you will pardon me if I seem a little embarrassed: I know not how to quit my old notions.

PHIL. To help you out, do but consider that if *extension* be once acknowledged to have no existence without the mind, the same must necessarily be granted of motion, solidity, and gravity—since they all evidently suppose extension. It is therefore superfluous to inquire particularly concerning each of them. In denying extension, you have denied them all to have any real existence. . . .

HYL. It is just come into my head, *Philonous*, that I have somewhere heard of a distinction between absolute and sensible extension. Now, though it be acknowledged that *great* and *small*, consisting merely in the relation which other extended beings have to the parts of our own bodies, do not really inhere in the Substances themselves; yet nothing obliges us to hold the same with regard to *absolute extension*, which is something abstracted from *great* and *small*, from this or that particular magnitude or figure. So likewise as to motion; *swift* and *slow* are altogether relative to the succession of ideas in our own minds. But, it doth not follow, because those modifications of motion exist not without the mind, that therefore absolute motion abstracted from them doth not.

PHIL. Pray what is it that distinguishes one motion, or one part of extension, from another? Is it not something sensible, as some degree of swiftness or slowness, some certain magnitude or figure peculiar to each?

HYL. I think so.

PHIL. These qualities, therefore, stripped of all sensible properties, are without all specific and numerical differences, as the schools call them.

HYL. They are.

PHIL. That is to say, they are extension in general, and motion in general.

HYL. Let it be so.

PHIL. But it is a universally received maxim that *Everything which exists is particular*. How then can motion in general, or extension in general, exist in any corporeal Substance?

HYL. I will take time to solve your difficulty.

PHIL. But I think the point may be speedily decided. Without doubt you can tell whether you are able to frame this or that idea. Now I am content to put our dispute on this issue. If you can frame in your thoughts a distinct abstract idea of motion or extension; divested of all those sensible modes, as swift and slow, great and small, round and square, and the like, which are acknowledged to exist only in the mind, I will then yield the point you contend for. But, if you cannot, it will be unreasonable on your side to insist any longer upon what you have no notion of.

HYL. To confess ingenuously, I cannot.

PHIL. Can you even separate the ideas of extension and motion from the ideas of all those qualities which they who make the distinction term *secondary*?

HYL. What! is it not an easy matter to consider extension and motion by themselves, abstracted from all other sensible qualities? Pray how do the mathematicians treat of them?

PHIL. I acknowledge, *Hylas*, it is not difficult to form general propositions and reasonings about those qualities, without mentioning any other; and, in this sense, to consider or treat of them abstractedly. But, how doth it follow that, because I can pronounce the word *motion* by itself, I can form the idea of it in my mind exclusive of body? Or, because theorems may be made of extension and figures, without any mention of *great* or *small*, or any other sensible mode or quality, that therefore it is possible such an abstract idea of extension, without any particular size or figure, or sensible quality, should be distinctly formed, and apprehended by the mind? Mathematicians treat of quantity, without regarding what other sensible qualities it is attended with, as being altogether indifferent to their demonstrations. But when laying aside the words, they contemplate the bare ideas, I believe you will find, they are not the pure abstracted ideas of extension.

HYL.   But what say you to *pure intellect*? May not abstracted ideas be framed by that faculty?

PHIL.   Since I cannot frame abstract ideas at all, it is plain I cannot frame them by the help of *pure intellect*; whatsoever faculty you understand by those words. Besides, not to inquire into the nature of pure intellect and its spiritual objects, as *virtue, reason, God*, or the like, thus much seems manifest, that sensible things are only to be perceived by sense, or represented by the imagination. Figures, therefore, and extension, being originally perceived by sense, do not belong to pure intel-

lect: but, for your further satisfaction, try if you can frame the idea of any figure, abstracted from all particularities of size, or even from other sensible qualities.

HYL.   Let me think a little. . . . I do not find that I can.

PHIL.   And can you think it possible that should really exist in nature which implies a repugnancy in its conception?

HYL.   By no means.

PHIL.   Since therefore it is impossible even for the mind to disunite the ideas of extension and motion from all other sensible qualities, doth it not follow, that where the one exist there necessarily the other exist likewise?

HYL.   It should seem so.

PHIL.   Consequently, the very same arguments which you admitted as conclusive against the Secondary Qualities are, without any further application of force, against the Primary too. Besides, if you will trust your senses, is it not plain all sensible qualities coexist, or to them appear as being in the same place? Do they ever represent a motion, or figure, as being divested of all other visible and tangible qualities?

HYL.   You need say no more on this head. I am free to own, if there be no secret error to oversight in our proceedings hitherto, that all sensible qualities are alike to be denied existence without the mind. But, my fear is that I have been too liberal in my former concessions, or overlooked some fallacy or other. In short, I did not take time to think.

PHIL. For that matter, *Hylas*, you may take what time you please in reviewing the progress of our inquiry. You are at liberty to recover any slips you might have made, or offer whatever you have omitted which makes for your first opinion.

HYL. One great oversight I take to be this — that I did not sufficiently distinguish the *object* from the *sensation*. Now, though this latter may not exist without the mind, yet it will not thence follow that the former cannot.

PHIL. What object do you mean? The object of the senses?

HYL. The same.

PHIL. It is then immediately perceived?

HYL. Right.

PHIL. Make me to understand the difference between what is immediately perceived, and a sensation.

HYL. The sensation I take to be an act of the mind perceiving; besides which, there is something perceived; and this I call the *object*. For example, there is red and yellow on that tulip. But then the act of perceiving those colors, is in me only, and not in the tulip.

PHIL. What tulip do you speak of? Is it that which you see?

HYL. The same.

PHIL. And what do you see beside color, figure, and extension?

HYL. Nothing.

PHIL. What you would say then is that the red and yellow are coexistent with the extension, is it not?

HYL. That is not all; I would say they have a real existence without the mind, in some unthinking substance.

PHIL. That the colors are really in the tulip which I see is manifest. Neither can it be denied that this tulip may exist independent of your mind or mine; but, that any immediate object of the senses — that is, any idea, or combination of ideas — should exist in an unthinking substance, or exterior to all minds, is in itself an evident contradiction. Nor can I imagine how this follows from what you said just now, to wit, that the red and yellow were on the tulip *you saw*, since you do not pretend to *see* that unthinking substance. . . .

HYL. Pray what think you of this? It is just come into my head that the ground of all our mistake lies in your treating of each quality by itself. Now, I grant that each quality cannot singly subsist without the mind. Color cannot without extension, neither can figure without some other sensible quality. But, as the several qualities united or blended together form entire sensible things, nothing hinders why such things may not be supposed to exist without the mind.

PHIL. Either, *Hylas*, you are jesting, or have a very bad memory. Though indeed we went through all the qualities by name one after another, yet my arguments, or rather your concessions, nowhere tended to prove that the Secondary Qualities did not subsist each alone by itself; but, that they were not *at all* without the mind. Indeed, in treating of figure and motion we concluded they could not exist without the mind, because it was impossible even in thought to separate them from all secondary qualities, so as to conceive them existing by themselves. But then this was not the only argument made use of upon that occasion. But (to pass by all that hath been hitherto said, and reckon it for nothing, if you will have it so) I am content to put the whole upon this issue. If you can conceive it possible for any mixture or combination of qualities, or any sensible object whatever, to exist without the mind, then I will grant it actually to be so.

HYL.   If it comes to that the point will soon be decided. What more easy than to conceive a tree or house existing by itself, independent of, and unperceived by, any mind whatsoever? I do at this present time conceive them existing after that manner.

PHIL.   How say you, *Hylas*, can you see a thing which is at the same time unseen?

HYL.   No, that were a contradiction.

PHIL.   Is it not as great a contradiction to talk of *conceiving* a thing which is *unconceived*?

HYL.   It is.

PHIL.   The tree or house therefore which you think of is conceived by you?

HYL.   How should it be otherwise?

PHIL.   And what is conceived is surely in the mind?

HYL.   Without question, that which is conceived is in the mind.

PHIL.   How then came you to say, you conceived a house or tree existing independent and out of all minds whatsoever?

HYL.   That was I own an oversight; but stay, let me consider what led me into it. — It is a pleasant mistake enough. As I was thinking of a tree in a solitary place where no one was present to see it, methought that was to conceive a tree as existing unperceived or unthought of — not considering that I myself conceived it all the while. But now I plainly see that all I can do is to frame ideas in my own mind. I may indeed conceive in my own thoughts the idea of a tree, or a house, or a mountain, but that is all. And his is far from proving that I can conceive them *existing out of the minds of all Spirits*.

PHIL.   You acknowledge then that you cannot possibly conceive how any one corporeal sensible thing should exist otherwise than in a mind? . . .

HYL.   To speak the truth, *Philonous*, I think there are two kinds of objects: —the one perceived immediately, which are likewise called *ideas*; the other are real things of external objects, perceived by the mediation of ideas, which are their images and representations. Now, I own ideas do not exist without the mind; but the latter sort of objects do. I am sorry I did not think of this distinction sooner; it would probably have cut short your discourse.

PHIL. Are those external objects perceived by sense, or by some other faculty?

HYL. They are perceived by sense.

PHIL. How! is there anything perceived by sense which is not immediately perceived?

HYL. Yes, *Philonous*, in some sort there is. For example, when I look on a picture or statue of Julius Caesar, I may be said after a manner to perceive him (though not immediately) by my senses.

PHIL. It seems then you will have our ideas, which alone are immediately perceived, to be pictures of external things: and that these also are perceived by sense, inasmuch as they have a conformity or resemblance to our ideas?

HYL. That is my meaning.

PHIL. And, in the same way that Julius Caesar, in himself invisible, is nevertheless perceived by sight; real things, in themselves imperceptible, are perceived by sense.

HYL. In the very same.

PHIL. Tell me, *Hylas*, when you behold the picture of Julius Caesar, do you see with your eyes any more than some colors and figures, with a certain symmetry and composition of the whole?

HYL. Nothing else.

PHIL. And would not a man who had never known anything of Julius Caesar see as much?

HYL. He would.

PHIL. Consequently he hath his sight, and the use of it, in as perfect a degree as you?

HYL. I agree with you.

PHIL. Whence comes it then that your thoughts are directed to the Roman emperor, and his are not? This cannot proceed from the sensations or ideas of sense by you then perceived; since you acknowledge you have no advantage over him in that respect. It should seem therefore to proceed from reason and memory: should it not?

HYL. It should.

PHIL. Consequently, it will not follow from that instance that anything is perceived by sense which is not immediately perceived. Though I grant we may, in one acceptation, be said to perceive sensible things mediately by sense — that is, when, from a frequently perceived connection, the immediate perception of ideas by one sense suggest to the mind others, perhaps belonging to another sense, which are wont to be connected with them. For instance, when I hear a coach drive along the streets, immediately I perceive only the sound; but, from the experience I have had that such a sound is connected with a coach, I am said to hear the coach. It is nevertheless evident that, in truth and strictness, nothing can be *heard* but *sound*; and the coach is not then properly perceived by sense, but suggested from experience. So likewise when we are said to see a red-hot bar of iron; the solidity and heat of the iron are not the objects of sight, but suggested to the imagination by the color and figure which are properly perceived by that sense. In short, those things alone are actually and strictly perceived by any sense, which would have been perceived in case that same sense had then been first conferred on use. As for other things, it is plain they are only suggested to the mind by experience, grounded on former perceptions. But, to return to your comparison of Caesar's picture, it is plain, if you keep to that, you must hold the real things or archetypes of our ideas are not perceived by sense, but by some internal faculty of the soul, as reason or memory. I would therefore fain know what arguments you can draw from reason for the existence of what you call *real things* or *material objects*. Or, whether you remember to have seen them formerly as they are in themselves; or, if you have heard or read of any one that did.

HYL.   I see, *Philonous*, you are disposed to raillery; but that will never convince me.

PHIL.   My aim is only to learn from you the way to come at the knowledge of *material beings*. Whatever we perceive is perceived immediately or mediately: by sense; or by reason and reflection. But, as you have excluded sense, pray show me

what reason you have to believe their existence; or what *medium* you can possibly make use of to prove it, either to mine or your own understanding.

HYL.   To deal ingenuously, *Philonous*, now I consider the point, I do not find I can give you any good reason for it. But, thus much seems pretty plain, that it is at least possible such things may really exist. And, as long as there is no absurdity in supposing them, I am resolved to believe as I did, till you bring good reasons to the contrary.

PHIL.   What! is it come to this, that you only believe the existence of material objects, and that your belief is founded barely on the possibility of its being true? Then you will have me bring reasons against it: though another would think it reasonable the proof should lie on him who holds the affirmative. And, after all, this very point which you are now resolved to maintain, without any reason, is in effect what you have more than once during this discourse seen good reason to give up. But, to pass over all this; if I understand you rightly, you say our ideas do not exist without the mind; but that they are copies, images, or representations, of certain originals that do?

HYL.   You take me right.

PHIL.   They are then like external things?

HYL.   They are.

PHIL.   Have those things a stable and

permanent nature, independent of our senses; or are they in a perpetual change, upon our producing any motions in our bodies, suspending, exerting, or altering, our faculties or organs of sense?

HYL. Real things, it is plain, have a fixed and real nature, which remains the same notwithstanding any change in our senses, or in the posture and motion of our bodies; which indeed may affect the ideas in our minds, but it were absurd to think they had the same effect on things existing without the mind.

PHIL. How then is it possible that things perpetually fleeting and variable as our ideas should be copies or images of anything fixed and constant? Or, in other words, since all sensible qualities, as size, figure, colour, &c., that is, our ideas, are continually changing upon every alteration in the distance, medium, or instruments of sensation; how can any determinate material objects be properly represented or painted forth by several distinct things, each of which is so different from and unlike the rest? Or, if you say it resembles some one only of our ideas, how shall we be able to distinguish the true copy from all the false ones?

HYL. I profess, *Philonous*, I am at a loss. I know not what to say to this.

PHIL. But neither is this all. Which are material objects in themselves — perceptible or imperceptible.

HYL. Properly and immediately nothing can be perceived but ideas. All material things, therefore, are in themselves insensible, and to be perceived only by our ideas.

PHIL. Ideas then are sensible, and their archetypes or originals insensible?

HYL. Right.

PHIL. But how can that which is sensible be like that which is insensible? Can a real thing, in itself *invisible*, be like a *colour*; or a real thing, which is not *audible*, be like a *sound*? In a word, can anything be like a sensation or idea, but another sensation or idea?

HYL. I must own, I think not.

PHIL. Is it possible there should be any doubt on the point? Do you not perfectly know your own ideas?

HYL. I know them perfectly; since what I do not perceive or know can be no part of my idea.

PHIL. Consider, therefore, and examine them, and then tell me if there be anything in them which can exist without the mind? or if you can conceive anything like them existing without the mind?

HYL. Upon inquiry, I find it is impossible for me to conceive or understand how anything but an idea can be like an idea. And it is most evident that *no idea can exist without the mind.*

PHIL. You are therefore, by our principles, forced to deny the reality of sensible things; since you made it to consist in an absolute existence exterior to the mind. That is to say, you are a downright sceptic. So I have gained my point, which was to show your principles led to Scepticism.

HYL. For the present I am, if not entirely convinced, at least silenced. . . .

THE SECOND DIALOGUE

HYLAS. I beg your pardon, *Philonous*, for not meeting you sooner. All this morning my head was so filled with our late conversation that I had not leisure to think of the time of the day, or indeed of anything else.

PHILONOUS. I am glad you were so intent upon it, in hopes if there were any mistakes in your concessions, or fallacies in my reasonings from them, you will now discover them to me. . . .

HYL. I own there is a great deal in what you say. Nor can any one be more entirely satisfied of the truth of those odd consequences, so long as I have in view the reasonings that lead to them. But, when these are out of my thoughts, there seems, on the other hand, something so satisfactory, so natural and intelligible, in the modern way of explaining things that, I profess, I know not how to reject it.

PHIL. I know not what way you mean.

HYL. I mean the way of accounting for our sensations or ideas.

PHIL. How is that?

HYL. It is supposed the soul makes her residence in some part of the brain, from which the nerves take their rise, and are thence extended to all parts of the body; and that outward objects, by the different impressions they make on the organs of sense, communicate certain vibrative motions to the nerves; and these being filled with spirits propagate them to the brain or seat of the soul, which, according to the various impressions or traces thereby made in the brain, is variously affected with ideas.

PHIL. And call you this an explication of the manner whereby we are effected with ideas?

HYL. Why not, *Philonous*; have you anything to object against it?

PHIL. I would first know whether I rightly understand your hypothesis. You make certain traces in the brain to be the causes or occasions of our ideas. Pray tell me whether by the *brain* you mean any sensible thing.

HYL. What else think you I could mean?

PHIL. Sensible things are all immediately perceivable; and those things which are immediately perceivable are ideas; and these exist only in the mind. Thus much you have, if I mistake not, long since agreed to.

HYL. I do not deny it.

PHIL. The brain therefore you speak of, being a sensible thing, exists only in the mind. Now, I would fain know whether you think it reasonable to suppose that one idea or thing existing in the mind occasions all other ideas. And, if you think so, pray how do you account for the origin of that primary idea or brain itself?

HYL.   I do not explain the origin of our ideas by that brain which is perceivable to sense, this being itself only a combination of sensible ideas, but by another which I imagine.

PHIL.   But are not things imagined as truly *in the mind* as things perceived?

HYL.   I must confess they are.

PHIL.   It comes, therefore, to the same thing; and you have been all this while accounting for ideas by certain motions or impressions of the brain, that is, by some alterations in an idea, whether sensible or imaginable it matters not.

HYL.   I begin to suspect my hypothesis.

PHIL.   Besides spirits, all that we know or conceive are our own ideas. When, therefore, you say all ideas are occasioned by impressions in the brain, do you conceive this brain or no? If you do, then you talk of ideas imprinted in an idea causing that same idea, which is absurd. If you do not conceive it, you talk unintelligibly, instead of forming a reasonable hypothesis.

HYL.   I now clearly see it was a mere dream. There is nothing in it.

PHIL.   You need not be much concerned at it; for after all, this way of explaining things, as you called it, could never have satisfied any reasonable man. What connection is there between a motion in the nerves, and the sensations of sound or colour in the mind? Or how is it possible these should be the effect of that?

HYL.   But I could never think it had so little in it as now it seems to have.

PHIL.   Well then, are you at length satisfied that no sensible things have a real existence; and that you are in truth an arrant *sceptic*?

HYL.   It is too plain to be denied.

PHIL.   Look! are not the fields covered with a delightful verdure? Is there not something in the woods and groves, in the rivers and clear springs, that soothes, that delights, that transports the soul? At the prospect of the wide and deep ocean, or some huge mountain whose top is lost in the clouds, or of an old gloomy forest, are not our minds filled with a pleasing horror? Even in rocks and deserts is there not an agreeable wildness? How sincere a pleasure is it to behold the natural beauties of the earth! To preserve and renew our relish for them, is not the veil of night alternately drawn over her face, and doth she not change her dress with the seasons? How aptly are the elements disposed! What variety and use in the meanest productions of nature! What delicacy, what beauty, what contrivance, in animal and vegetable bodies! How exquisitely are all things suited, as well to their particular ends, as to constitute opposite parts of the whole! And, while they mutually aid and support, do they not also set off and illustrate each other? Raise now your thoughts from this ball of earth to all those glorious luminaries that adorn the high arch of heaven. The motion and situation of the planets, are they not admirable for use and order? Were those (miscalled *erratic*) globes ever known to stray, in their repeated journeys through the pathless void? Do they not measure areas round the sun ever proportioned to the times? So fixed, so immutable are the laws by which the unseen Author of nature actuates the universe. How vivid and radiant is the luster of the fixed stars! How magnificent and rich that negligent profusion with which they appear to be scattered throughout the whole azure vault! Yet, if you take the telescope, it brings into your sight a new host of stars that escape the naked eye. Here they seem contiguous and minute, but to a nearer view immense orbs of light at various distances, far sunk in the abyss of space. Now you must call imagination to your aid. The feeble narrow sense cannot descry innumerable worlds revolving round the central fires; and in those worlds the energy of an all-perfect Mind displayed in endless forms. But, neither sense nor imagination are big enough to comprehend the boundless extent, with all its glittering furniture. Though the laboring mind exert and strain each power to its utmost reach, there still stands out ungrasped a surplusage immeasurable. Yet all the vast bodies that compose this mighty frame, how distant and remote soever, are by

some secret mechanism, some divine art and force, linked in a mutual dependence and intercourse with each other, even with this earth, which was almost slipped from my thoughts and lost in the crowd of worlds. Is not the whole system immense, beautiful, glorious beyond expression and beyond thought! What treatment, then, do those philosophers deserve, who would deprive these noble and delightful scenes of all reality? How should those Principles be entertained that lead us to think all the visible beauty of the creation a false imaginary glare? To be plain, can you expect this Scepticism of yours will not be thought extravagantly absurd by all men of sense?

HYL. Other men may think as they please; but for your part you have nothing to reproach me with. My comfort is, you are as much a sceptic as I am.

PHIL. There, *Hylas*, I must beg leave to differ from you.

HYL. What have you all along agreed to the premises, and do you now deny the conclusion, and leave me to maintain those paradoxes by myself which you led me into? This surely is not fair.

PHIL. I deny that I agreed with you in those notions that led to Scepticism. You indeed said the *reality* of sensible things consisted in an *absolute existence* out of the minds of spirits, or distinct from their being perceived. And, pursuant to this notion of reality, you are obliged to deny sensible things any real existence: that is, according to your own definition, you profess yourself a sceptic. But I neither said nor thought the reality of sensible things was to be defined after that manner. To me it is evident, for the reasons you allow of, that sensible things cannot exist otherwise than in a mind or spirit. Whence I conclude, not that they have no real existence, but that, seeing they depend not on my thought, and have an existence distinct from being perceived by me, *there must be some other mind wherein they exist.* As sure, therefore, as the sensible world really exists, so sure is there an infinite omnipresent Spirit, who contains and supports it.

HYL. What! this is no more than I and all Christians hold, nay and all others too who believe there is a God, and that He knows and comprehends all things.

PHIL. Aye, but here lies the difference. Men commonly believe that all things are known or perceived by God, because they believe the being of a God; whereas I, on the other side, immediately and necessarily conclude the being of a God, because all sensible things must be perceived by him. . . . It is evident that the things I perceive are my own ideas, and that no idea can exist unless it be in a mind. Nor is it less plain that these ideas or things by me perceived, either themselves or their archetypes, exist independently of my mind; since I know myself not to be

their author, it being out of my power to determine at pleasure what particular ideas I shall be affected with upon opening my eyes or ears. They must therefore exist in some other mind, whose will it is they should be exhibited to me. The things, I say, immediately perceived are ideas or sensations, call them which you will. But how can any idea or sensation exist in, or be produced by, anything but a mind or spirit? This indeed is inconceivable; and to assert that which is inconceivable is to talk nonsense: is it not?

HYL. Without doubt.

PHIL. But, on the other hand, it is very conceivable that they should exist in and be produced by a Spirit; since this is no more than I daily experience in myself, inasmuch as I perceive numberless ideas; and, by an act of my will, can form a great variety of them, and raise them up in my imagination: though, it must be confessed, these creatures of the fancy are not altogether so distinct, so strong, vivid, and permanent, as those perceived by my senses, which latter are called *real things.* From all which I conclude, *there is a Mind which affects me every moment with all the sensible impressions I perceive.* And, from the variety, order, and manner of these, I conclude the Author of them to be *wise, powerful, and good, and beyond comprehension.* . . .

[*The Third Dialogue is omitted.*]

COMMENT

The speakers in Berkeley's *Dialogues* are Hylas, a "materialist," and Philonous, who represents the point of view of the author. Physical objects, according to Philonous, have no existence independent of thought. The whole universe is made up of minds and the immaterial objects of minds, and nothing more. This doctrine, which is called *idealism* (*idea-ism*, with the *l* inserted for the sake of euphony), may strike beginning students as exceedingly odd; but it is quite possible that the universe *is* very odd, and the arguments for idealism are strong. Since Berkeley's presentation of these arguments is lucid, I shall not summarize them.

Some of Berkeley's arguments are similar to the arguments of Russell in discussing the nature and existence of matter (see pages 161–165). Other arguments are unique to Berkeley. Altogether they constitute a powerful case for idealism. But certain critical questions are worth reviewing:

1. IS THE ESSENCE OF AN OBJECT TO BE PERCEIVED? Over and over again, Berkeley insisted that "things" are mere collections of "ideas" and that ideas cannot exist unless they are perceived. The plausibility of his contention depends on his constant use of the word *idea*. We think of "idea" as something in the mind and therefore as incapable of existing apart from the mind. Hence, if we are told that an apple consists entirely of "ideas", it is natural for us to suppose that the apple can exist only in some mind. But *idea*, as Berkeley used it, really means "immediate object of thought or experience" (including both imaginative and perceptual experience). If we understand idea in this sense, there is a possibility — not lightly to be dismissed — that an object known as a set of ideas may continue to exist when the thought of it ceases.

The point can be illustrated by an amusing passage from Lewis Carroll's *Through the Looking Glass*. Alice is warned by Tweedledum and Tweedledee not to awaken the Red King:

> "He's dreaming now," said Tweedledee: "and what do you think he's dreaming about?"
>
> Alice said, "Nobody can guess that."
>
> "What about *you!*" Tweedledee exclaimed, clapping his hands triumphantly. "And if he left off dreaming about you, where do you suppose you'd be?"
>
> Where I am now, of course," said Alice.
>
> "Not you!" Tweedledee retorted contemptuously. "You'd be nowhere. Why, you're only a sort of thing in his dream!"
>
> "If that there King was to wake," added Tweedledum, "you'd go out — bang! — just like a candle!"

The delicious absurdity of this passage depends upon the supposition of Tweedledum and Tweedledee that to *exist* is to be *borne in mind*, and that when Alice is not borne in mind by the Red King she cannot exist. But no real person is merely a thought or idea in anybody's mind.

This point would be admitted by Berkeley. His formula for summing up the nature of reality is *"esse est percipi aut percipere"* [essence is to be perceived or to perceive], not just *"esse est percipi."* But if people can exist independently of someone's idea of them, why cannot a *thing* exist independently? To argue that an apple must be in our minds because we are thinking of it is like arguing that a person must be in our minds because we are thinking of him or her. If we distinguish clearly between the act of thinking and the object of thought, the act of perceiving and the object perceived, there is no absurdity in supposing that things may exist even when they are unperceived or unthought.

2. IS THE "EGOCENTRIC PREDICAMENT" A REASON FOR BELIEVING IN IDEALISM? Berkeley pointed out that everyone's knowledge is incurably egocentric. Even when I think of the unobserved interior of the earth, I am *thinking* about it, and, in that sense, it is an object before my mind. Every object we ever perceive or think about in any way stands ipso facto in relation to our minds. Does this "egocentric predicament"[1] provide a valid argument for idealism?

Ralph Barton Perry answers in the negative. The fact that we can not eliminate ourselves as the subject of our own experiences proves nothing at all about the nature of the external world. We may have good reason to suppose that there are unknown stars, unexperienced atoms, unsighted grains of sand in the Sahara Desert, and unobserved physical processes beneath the earth's crust. Our reasons for believing in them should be judged on the basis of logic and evidence and should not be rejected merely because no one can think about these matters without using one's mind.

3. DOES THE RELATIVITY OF PERCEPTION PROVE IDEALISM? The fact that sense data are relative to the perceiver can scarcely be denied; but does it prove idealism? So long as we can explain *why* things appear differently to different observers, we can still maintain that there are real objective qualities.

Let us consider one of Berkeley's own examples. He pointed out that if one hand has been chilled and the other warmed, and both hands are put simultaneously into the same pan of water, the water will seem warm to one hand and cool to the other. But this is just what we should expect if

---

[1] See also Ralph Barton Perry, *Present Philosophical Tendencies* (New York: Longmans, Green, 1929), pp. 129–132.

the water is *really tepid*. What the person who puts his hands in the water feels is not the temperature of the water but the temperature in his or her hands — and the preheated hand naturally has a different temperature than the prechilled hand. If the two hands remain in the water long enough, the temperature of the water will finally pervade them, and then the water will feel tepid to *both* hands. Similarly, if light and color are truly objective, an object will naturally appear to have a different color in a different light. Or if a microscope enables us to see features of an object that were before invisible, it is not surprising that we see colors and shapes that we did not see before. However variously things may *appear*, we can often distinguish between "appearances" and "realities." Whether we can do so in a sufficient number of cases to invalidate Berkeley's argument is a question worth debating.

4.   DOES THE INSEPARABILITY OF PRIMARY AND SECONDARY QUALITIES COMMIT US TO IDEALISM? Suppose we grant Berkeley's contention that primary and secondary qualities are inseparable. We might therefore conclude that both are objective (*not* mind-dependent) rather than that both are subjective (mind-dependent). Some critics maintain that Berkeley's arguments fail to show that even secondary qualities are "in the mind." They believe that colors, sounds, odors, and textures (though perhaps not tastes) are no less objective than the primary qualities.

Another alternative would be the agnostic position that things-in-themselves are unknowable, and that consequently we can no more assert idealism than we can assert materialism. This is the position favored by Kant, Hume, and the positivists — all of whom admit the inseparability of primary and secondary qualities.

But it is also possible to reject Berkeley's thesis that primary and secondary qualities are inseparable. Actually, there is a very significant difference between the two sets of qualities. The secondary qualities are *sensory* properties, whereas the primary qualities are *formal* characteristics — the structures, relations, and quantities of things. This difference may justify the supposition that the primary qualities have a different epistemological status than the secondary qualities.

According to modern scientific theories of perception, the secondary qualities seem to depend on physiological and mental factors and thus appear to be qualitative events in the perceiving organisms. Sounds seem to depend on organic reactions to airwaves; colors, on organic reactions to electromagnetic vibrations; and so on. Our *impressions* of primary qualities are similarly dependent on our minds, but there is a significant difference: The laws of physics are framed in terms of abstract orders and quantitative relations — primary qualities — rather than in terms of concrete secondary qualities. We therefore have scientific warrant for believing that our impressions of primary but not of secondary qualities have objective counterparts — *if* science is dealing with a real objective world.

Relational properties cannot exist all by themselves; they must attach to the things related. On this point Berkeley is perfectly right. Yet it is conceivable that physical science reveals the relational structure of the real world without revealing its content. Atoms may exist and conform to Einstein's equations even though their ultimate qualitative nature remains a mystery.

5. CAN WE TEST THE CORRESPONDENCE BETWEEN IDEAS AND THINGS? Once we distinguish between objects as we apprehend them and objects as they really are, how can we ever know that the former agree with the latter? Not only Berkeley, but Kant and Hegel as well, maintain that the correspondence test of truth is unworkable.

The impossibility of directly comparing ideas (or sense data) with things outside experience must be admitted. But we can *infer* things that we do not experience. No one, for example, *directly* observes another person's toothache, but one can be reasonably certain that the other person *is* suffering from a toothache. Such indirect knowledge involves the interpretation of signs, and we can often infer from signs what we cannot observe.

It is a striking fact that the signs of minds differ very markedly from the signs of eternal things. When we hear people talk, see them gesture, or read what they have written, we are interpreting signs of a very different sort than when we are looking at a rock. The first set of signs are clearly indicative of thinking people and their thoughts, whereas the second set of signs, to all appearances, indicates something nonconscious and nonintelligent. It seems a bit fantastic and gratuitous to attribute a *mind* to the rock, or even to the system of nature of which the rock is a minute part. The sensible aspects of human behavior from which we infer a human mind have little resemblance to the sensible characteristics of nature from which Berkeley would have us infer God. Perhaps Kant and the positivists are right — perhaps we can never know the rock as a thing-in-itself — but such clues as we have for judging the nature of inorganic things are quite different from the clues whereby we infer the minds of our friends and acquaintances. Reality *appears* to be dualistic, made up of both mental and physical qualities, and it involves a sharp break with common sense to suppose that this appearance is quite illusory.

10

Pantheism

"I have shown that God necessarily exists; that He is one God; that from the necessity alone of His nature He is and acts; that He is . . . the free cause of all things; that all things are in Him, and so depend upon him, that without Him they can neither be nor be conceived; and, finally, that all things have been predetermined by Him."

Baruch Spinoza

BARUCH SPINOZA (1632–1677)

Born into the Jewish community of Amsterdam, Spinoza was educated in the rabbinical tradition but studied such non-Jewish philosophers as Bruno and Descartes. By the time he was twenty-three he rebelled against orthodox Judaism, even refusing a bribe to conceal his views. In consequence, he was cursed in the name of God and His Holy Angels by the Jewish authorities and excommunicated from the synagogue. Changing his Jewish name, Baruch, to its Latin equivalent, Benedictus, he dwelt for many years in a nearby village earning a modest living by polishing optical lenses. Later he moved to The Hague. As an excommunicated Jew, he had few ties with either his Dutch or his Jewish neighbors, but he was loved and respected by the few who knew him.

He devoted much of his time to studying philosophy and corresponding with the great scientists, mathematicians, and philosophers of the period. In 1663 he published an expository account of Descartes's philosophy and in 1670 published his *Tractatus Theologico-Politicus.* The latter, a work of biblical criticism and political theory, although prohibited by both

Catholics and Protestants, achieved fame in learned and emancipated circles. As result, Spinoza was offered a professorship at the University of Heidelberg if he would promise not to disturb the established religion. He refused the offer because the proviso would restrict his freedom of speech and the academic duties would cut into his studies.

The grinding of lenses may have brought on or aggravated the tuberculosis of which he died at the age of forty-three. At the time of his death, he left behind a few personal belongings and some unpublished manuscripts, including the *Ethics*. It was one of the richest estates ever left by any man.

Monism

I have now explained the nature of God and its properties. I have shown that He necessarily exists; that He is one God; that from the necessity alone of His own nature He is and acts; that He is, and in what way He is, the free cause of all things; that all things are in Him, and so depend upon Him that without Him they can neither be nor can be conceived; and, finally, that all things have been predetermined by Him, not indeed from freedom of will or from absolute good pleasure, but from His absolute nature or infinite power.

Moreover, wherever an opportunity was afforded, I have endeavoured to remove prejudices which might hinder the perception of the truth of what I have demonstrated; but because not a few still remain which have been and are now sufficient to prove a very great hindrance to the comprehension of the connection of things in the manner in which I have explained it, I have thought it worth while to call them up to be examined by reason. But all these prejudices which I here undertake to point out depend upon this solely: that it is commonly supposed that all things in nature, like men, work to some end; and indeed it is thought to be certain that God himself directs all things to some sure end, for it is said that God has made all things for man, and man that he may worship God. This, therefore, I will first investigate by inquiring, firstly, why so many rest in this prejudice, and why all are so naturally inclined to embrace it? I shall then show its falsity, and, finally, the manner in which there have arisen from it prejudices concerning *good* and *evil*, *merit* and *sin*, *praise* and *blame*, *order* and *disorder*, *beauty* and *deformity*, and so forth. This, however, is not the place to deduce these things from the nature of the human mind. It will be sufficient if I here take as an axiom that which no one ought to dispute, namely

From Benedict Spinoza, *Ethics*, Appendix to Part I, trans. from the Latin by William Hale White (London: Trübner and Company, 1883).

that man is born ignorant of the causes of things, and that he has a desire, of which he is conscious, to seek that which is profitable to him. From this it follows, firstly, that he thinks himself free because he is conscious of his wishes and appetites, whilst at the same time he is ignorant of the causes by which he is led to wish and desire, not dreaming what they are; and, secondly, it follows that man does everything for an end, namely, for that which is profitable to him, which is what he seeks. Hence it happens that he attempts to discover merely the final causes of that which has happened; and when he has heard them he is satisfied, because there is no longer any cause for further uncertainty. But if he cannot hear from another what these final causes are, nothing remains but to turn to himself and reflect upon the ends which usually determine him to the like actions, and thus by his own mind he necessarily judges that of another. Moreover, since he discovers, both within and without himself, a multitude of means which contribute not a little to the attainment of what is profitable to himself — for example, the eyes, which are useful for seeing, the teeth for mastication, plants and animals for nourishment, the sun for giving light, the sea for feeding fish, &c. — it comes to pass that all natural objects are considered as means for obtaining what is profitable. These too being evidently discovered and not created by man, hence he has a cause for believing that some other person exists, who has prepared them for man's use. For having considered them as means it was impossible to believe that they had created themselves, and so he was obliged to infer from the means which he was in the habit of providing for himself that some ruler or rulers of nature exist, endowed with human liberty, who have taken care of all things for him, and have made all things for his use. Since he never heard anything about the mind of these rulers, he was compelled to judge of it from his own, and hence he affirmed that the gods direct everything for his advantage, in order that he may be bound to them and hold them in the highest honour. This is the reason why each man has devised for himself, out of his own brain, a different mode of worshipping God, so that God might love him above others, and direct all nature to the service of his blind cupidity and insatiable avarice.

Thus has this prejudice been turned into a superstition and has driven deep roots into the mind — a prejudice which was the reason why every one has so eagerly tried to discover and explain the final causes of things. The attempt, however, to show that nature does nothing in vain (that is to say, nothing which is not profitable to man), seems to end in showing that nature, the gods, and man are alike mad.

Do but see, I pray, to what all this has led. Amidst so much in nature that is beneficial, not a few things must have been observed which are injurious, such as storms, earthquakes, diseases, and it was affirmed that these things happened either because the gods were angry because of wrongs which had been inflicted on them by man, or because of sins committed in the method of worshipping them; and although experience daily contradicted this, and showed by an infinity of examples that both the beneficial and the injurious were indiscriminately bestowed on the pious and the impious, the inveterate prejudices on this point have not therefore been abandoned. For it was much easier for a man to place these things aside with others of the use of which he was ignorant, and thus retain his present and inborn state of ignorance, than to destroy the whole superstructure and think out a new one. Hence it was looked upon as indisputable that the judgments of the gods far surpass our comprehension; and this opinion alone would have been sufficient to keep the human race in darkness to all eternity, if mathematics, which does not deal with ends, but with the essences and properties of forms, had not placed before us another rule of truth. In addition to mathematics, other causes also might be assigned, which it is superfluous here to enumerate, tending to make men reflect upon these universal prejudices, and leading them to a true knowledge of things.

I have thus sufficiently explained what I promised in the first place to explain. There will now be no need of many words to show that nature has set no end before herself, and that all final causes are nothing but human fictions. For I believe that this is sufficiently evident both from the foundations and causes of this prejudice, and from Prop. 16 and Corol. Prop. 32, as well as from all those propositions in which I have shown that all things are begotten by a certain eternal necessity of nature and in absolute perfection. Thus much, nevertheless, I will add, that this doctrine concerning an end altogether overturns nature. For that which is in truth the cause it considers as the effect, and *vice versa*. Again, that which is first in nature it puts last; and, finally, that which is supreme and most perfect it makes the most imperfect. For (passing by the first two assertions as self-evident) it is plain from Props. 21, 22, and 23, that the effect is the most perfect which is immediately produced by God, and in proportion as intermediate causes are necessary for the production of a thing is it imperfect. But if things which are immediately produced by God were made in order that He might obtain the end He had in view, then the last things for the sake of which the first exist, must be the most perfect of all. Again, this doctrine does away with God's perfection. For if God works to obtain an end, He necessarily seeks something of which he stands in need. And although theologians and metaphysicians distinguish between the end of want and the end of assimilation (*finem indegentiae et finem assimilationis*), they confess that God has done all things for His own sake, and not for the sake of the things to be created, because before the creation they can assign nothing excepting God for the sake of which God could do anything; and therefore they are necessarily compelled to admit that God stood in need of and desired those things for which He determined to prepare means. This is self-evident. Nor is it here to be overlooked that the adherents of this doctrine, who have found a pleasure in displaying their ingenuity in assigning the ends of things, have introduced a new species of argument, not the *reductio ad impossible*, but the *reductio ad ignorantiam*, to prove their position, which shows that it had no other method of defence left. For, by way of example, if a stone has fallen from some roof on somebody's head and killed him, they will demonstrate in this manner that the stone has fallen in order to kill the man. For if it did not fall for that purpose by the will of God, how could so many circumstances concur through chance (and a number often simultaneously do concur)? You will answer, perhaps, that the event happened because the wind blew and the man was passing that way. But, they will urge, why did the wind blow at that time, and why did the man pass that way precisely at the same moment? If you again reply that the wind rose then because the sea on the preceding day began to be stormy, the weather hitherto having been calm, and that the man had been invited by a friend, they will urge again—because there is no end of questioning—But why was the sea agitated? why was the man invited at that time? And so they will not cease from asking the causes of causes, until at last you fly to the will of God, the refuge for ignorance.

So, also, when they behold the structure of the human body, they are amazed; and because they are ignorant of the causes of such art, they conclude that the body was made not by mechanical but by a supernatural or divine art, and has been formed in such a way so that the one part may not injure the other. Hence it happens that the man who endeavours to find out the true causes of miracles, and who desires as a wise man to understand nature, and not to gape at it like a fool, is generally considered and proclaimed to be a heretic and impious by those whom the vulgar worship as the interpreters both of nature and the gods. For these know that if ignorance be removed, amazed stupidity, the sole ground on which they rely in arguing or in defending their authority, is taken away also. But these things I leave and pass on to that which I determined to do in the third place.

After man has persuaded himself that all things which exist are made for him, he must in everything adjudge that to be of the greatest importance which is most useful to him, and he must esteem that to be of surpassing worth by which he is most beneficially affected. In this way he is compelled to form those notions by which he explains nature; such, for instance, as *good*, *evil*, *order*, *confusion*, *heat*, *cold*, *beauty*, and *deformity*, &c.; and because he supposes himself to be free, notions like those of *praise* and *blame*, *sin* and *merit*, have arisen. These latter I shall hereafter explain when I have treated of human nature; the former I will here briefly unfold.

It is to be observed that man has given the name *good* to every thing which leads to health and the worship of God; on the contrary, everything which does not lead thereto he calls *evil*. But because those who do not understand nature affirm nothing about things themselves, but only imagine them, and take the imagination to be understanding, they therefore, ignorant of things and their nature, firmly believe an *order* to be in things; for when things are so placed that, if they are represented to us through the senses, we can easily imagine them, and consequently easily remember them, we call them well arranged; but if they are not placed so that we can imagine and remember them, we call them badly arranged or *confused*. Moreover, since those things are more especially pleasing to us which we can easily imagine, men therefore prefer order to confusion, as if order were something in nature apart from our own imagination; and they say that God has created everything in order, and in this manner they ignorantly attribute imagination to God, unless they mean perhaps that God, out of consideration for the human imagination, has disposed things in the manner in which they can most easily be imagined. No hesitation either seems to be caused by the fact that an infinite number of things are discovered which far surpass our imagination, and very many which confound it through its weakness. But enough of this. The other notions which I have mentioned are nothing but modes in which the imagination is affected in different ways, and nevertheless they are regarded by the ignorant as being specially attributes of things, because, as we have remarked, men consider all things as made for themselves, and call the nature of a thing good, evil, sound, putrid, or corrupt, just as they are affected by it. For example if the motion by which the nerves are affected by means of objects represented to the eye conduces to well-being, the objects by which it is caused are called *beautiful*; while those exciting a contrary motion are called *deformed*. Those things, too, which stimulate the senses through the nostrils are called

sweet-smelling or stinking; those which act through the taste are called sweet or bitter, full-flavoured or insipid; those which act through the touch, hard or soft, heavy or light; those, lastly, which act through the ears are said to make a noise, sound, or harmony, the last having caused men to lose their senses to such a degree that they have believed that God even is delighted with it. Indeed, philosophers may be found who have persuaded themselves that the celestial motions beget a harmony. All these things sufficiently show that every one judges things by the constitution of his brain, or rather accepts the affections of his imagination in the place of things. It is not, therefore, to be wondered at, as we may observe in passing, that all those controversies which we see have arisen amongst men, so that at last scepticism has been the result. For although human bodies agree in many things, they differ in more, and therefore that which to one person is good will appear to another evil, that which to one is well arranged to another is confused, that which pleases one will displease another, and so on in other cases which I pass by both because we cannot notice them at length here, and because they are within the experience of every one. For every one has heard the expressions: So many heads, so many ways of thinking; Every one is satisfied with his own way of thinking; Differences of brains are not less common than differences of taste;—all which maxims show that men decide upon matters according to the constitution of their brains, and imagine rather than understand things. If men understood things, they would, as mathematics prove, at least be all alike convinced if they were not all alike attracted. We see, therefore, that all those methods by which the common people are in the habit of explaining nature are only different sorts of imaginations, and do not reveal the nature of anything in itself, but only the constitution of the imagination; and because they have names as if they were entities existing apart from the imagination, I call them entities not of the reason but of the imagination. All argument, therefore, urged against us based upon such notions can be easily refuted. Many people, for instance, are accustomed to argue thus: — If all things have followed from the necessity of the most perfect nature of God, how is it that so many imperfections have arisen in nature — corruption, for instance, of things till they stink; deformity, exciting disgust; confusion, evil, crime, &c.? But, as I have just observed, all this is easily answered. For the perfection of things is to be judged by their nature and power alone; nor are they more or less perfect because they delight or offend the human senses, or because they are beneficial or prejudicial to human nature. But to those who ask why God has not created all men in such a manner that they might be controlled by the dictates of reason alone, I give but this answer: Because to Him material was not wanting for the creation of everything, from the highest down to the very lowest grade of perfection; or, to speak more properly, because the laws of His nature were so ample that they suffered for the production of everything which can be conceived by an infinite intellect, as I have demonstrated in Prop. 16.

These are the prejudices which I undertook to notice here. If any others of a similar character remain, they can easily be rectified with a little thought by any one.

Correspondence

LETTER XXXII

To the Very Noble and Learned Mr. HENRY OLDENBURG.

Most noble Sir,

I thank you and the very Noble Mr. Boyle very much for kindly encouraging me to go on with my Philosophy. I do indeed proceed with it, as far as my slender powers allow, not doubting meanwhile of your help and goodwill.

When you ask me what I think about the question which turns on *the Knowledge how each part of Nature accords with the whole of it, and in what way it is connected with the other parts*, I think you mean to ask for the reasons on the strength of which we believe that each part of Nature accords with the whole of it, and is connected with

From *The Correspondence of Spinoza*, trans. and ed. Abraham Wolf, 1928, new impression, 1966. By permission of George Allen & Unwin, London, and Russell & Russell, New York.

the other parts. For I said in my preceding letter that I do not know how the parts are really interconnected, and how each part accords with the whole; for to know this it would be necessary to know the whole of Nature and all its Parts.

I shall therefore try to show the reason which compels me to make this assertion; but I should like first to warn you that I do not attribute to Nature beauty or ugliness, order or confusion. For things cannot, except with respect to our imagination, be called beautiful, or ugly, ordered or confused.

By connection of the parts, then, I mean nothing else than that the laws, or nature, of one part adapt themselves to the laws, or nature, of another part in such a way as to produce the least possible opposition. With regard to whole and parts, I consider things as parts of some whole, in so far as their natures are mutually adapted so that they are in accord among themselves, as far as possible; but in so far as things differ among themselves, each produces an idea in our mind, which is distinct from the others, and is therefore considered to be a whole, not a part. For instance, since the motions of the particles of lymph, chyle, etc., are so mutually adapted in respect of magnitude and figure that they clearly agree among themselves, and all together constitute one fluid, to that extent only, chyle, lymph, etc., are considered to be parts of the blood: but in so far as we conceive the lymph particles as differing in respect of figure and motion from the particles of chyle, to that extent we consider them to be a whole, not a part.

Let us now, if you please, imagine that a small worm lives in the blood, whose sight is keen enough to distinguish the particles of blood, lymph, etc., and his reason to observe how each part on collision with another either rebounds, or communicates a part of its own motion, etc. That worm would live in this blood as we live in this part of the universe, and he would consider each particle of blood to be a whole, and not a part. And he could not know how all the parts are controlled by the universal nature of blood, and are forced, as the universal nature of blood demands, to adapt themselves to one another, so as to harmonize with one another in a certain way. For if we imagine that there are no causes outside the blood to communicate new motions to the blood, and that outside the blood there is no space, and no other bodies, to which the particles of blood could transfer their motion, it is certain that the blood would remain always in its state, and its particles would suffer no changes other than those which can be conceived from the given relation of the motion of the blood to the lymph and chyle, etc., and so blood would have to be considered always to be a whole and not a part. But, since there are very many other causes which in a certain way control the laws of the nature of blood, and are in turn controlled by the blood, hence it comes about that other motions and other changes take place in the blood, which result not only from the mere relation of the motion of its parts to one another, but from the relation of the motion of the blood and also the external causes to one another: in this way the blood has the character of a part and not of a whole. I have only spoken of whole and part.

Now, all the bodies of nature can and should be conceived in the same way as we have here conceived the blood: for all bodies are surrounded by others, and are mutually determined to exist and to act in a definite and determined manner, while there is preserved in all together, that is, in the whole universe, the same proportion of motion and rest. Hence it follows that every body, in so far as it exists modified in a certain way, must be considered to be a part of the whole universe, to be in accord with the whole of it, and to be connected with the other parts. And since the nature of the universe is not limited, like the nature of the blood, but absolutely infinite, its parts are controlled by the nature of this infinite power in infinite ways, and are compelled to suffer infinite changes. But I conceive that with regard to substance each part has a closer union with its whole. For as I endeavoured to show in my first letter, which I wrote to you when I was still living at Rhynsburg, since it is of the nature of substance to be infinite, it follows that each part belongs to the nature of corporeal substance, and can neither exist nor be conceived without it.

You see, then, in what way and why I think that the human Body is a part of Nature. As regards the human Mind I think it too is a part of Nature: since I state that there exists in Nature an infinite power of thought, which in so far as it is infinite, contains in itself subjectively the whole of Nature, and its thoughts proceed in the same way as Nature, which, to be sure, is its ideatum.

Then I declare that the human mind is this same power, not in so far as it is infinite, and perceives the whole of Nature, but in so far as it is finite and perceives only the human Body, and in this way I declare that the human Mind is a part of a certain infinite intellect. . . .

In all affection yours

B. de SPINOZA

[Voorburg, 20 November 1665]

LETTER LVI

To the Very Honourable and Prudent Mr. HUGO BOXEL.

Most honourable Sir,

I hasten to answer your letter, which I received yesterday, because if I go on delaying longer I shall be compelled to postpone my reply longer than I should wish. Your health would cause me anxiety if I had not heard that you are better, and I hope you are now entirely recovered.

How difficult it is for two persons who follow different principles to meet one another and agree on a subject which depends on many others, would be clear from this question alone, even if no argument demonstrated it. Tell me, I pray, whether you have seen or read any Philosophers who hold the opinion that the world was made by chance, that is, in the sense in which you understand it, namely, that God, when creating the world had set Himself a definite aim, and yet transgressed His own decree. I do not know that such a thing even occurred to any man's thought. Similarly, I am in the dark about the arguments by which you endeavour to persuade me to believe that *Fortuitious* and *Necessary* are not contraries. As soon as I realize that the three angles of a triangle are necessarily equal to two right angles, I also deny that this is the result of chance. Similarly as soon as I realize that heat is the necessary effect of fire, I also deny that it occurs by chance. It seems no less absurd and opposed to reason to suppose that *Necessary* and *Free* are contraries. For no one can deny that God knows Himself and everything else freely, and yet all are agreed in admitting that God knows Himself necessarily. Thus you seem to me to make no distinction between coercion or force, and Necessity. That man desires to live, to love, etc., is not a compulsory activity, but it is none the less necessary, and much more so is God's will to be, and to know, and to act. If, apart from these remarks, you turn over in your mind the fact that indifference is nothing but ignorance or doubt, and that a will ever constant and determined in all things is a virtue, and a necessary property of the intellect, then you will see that my words are thoroughly in accord with the truth. If we assert that God had it in His power not to will a thing, and did not have it in His power not to understand it, then we attribute to God two different kinds of freedom, one being that of necessity, the other that of indifference, and consequently we shall conceive the will of God as differing from His essence and His intellect, and in that case we shall fall into one absurdity after another. . . .

Further, when you say that if I deny to God the acts of seeing, of hearing, of attending and of willing, etc., and their occurrence in Him in an eminent degree, then you do not know what kind of God I have, I suspect therefrom that you believe that there is no perfection greater than that which is unfolded in the said attributes. I do not wonder at this, since I believe that a triangle, if only it had the power of speech, would say in like manner that God is eminently triangular, and a circle would say that the Divine Nature is eminently circular, and in this way each thing would ascribe its own attributes to God, and make itself like unto God, while all else would appear to it deformed.

The small compass of a letter, and limitation of time, do not permit me to explain in detail my opinion about the Divine Nature, or the other Questions which you put forward, to say nothing of the fact that to raise difficulties is not the same as to advance reasons. It is true that in the world we often act on conjecture; but it is false that our reflections are based on conjecture. In ordinary life we must follow what is most probable, but in philosophical speculations, the truth. Man would perish of thirst and hunger if he would not eat or drink until he had obtained a perfect proof that food and drink would do him good. But in contemplation this has no place. On the contrary, we must be cautious not to admit as true something which is merely probable. For when we admit one falsity, countless others follow.

Further, from the fact that divine and human sciences are full of disputes and controversies it cannot be inferred that all the things which are treated therein are uncertain: for there have been very many people who were so possessed by the love of contradiction that they laughed even at Geometrical proofs. Sextus Empiricus and other Sceptics whom you cite say that it is not true that the whole is greater than its part, and they have the same view of the other axioms.

But, putting aside and admitting the fact that in default of proofs we must be satisfied with probabilities, I say that a probable Proof ought to be such that, although we can doubt it, yet we cannot contradict it; because that which can be contradicted is not likely to be true, but likely to be false. If, for instance, I say that Peter is alive, because I saw him in good health yesterday, this is indeed likely to be true so long as no one can contradict me; but if someone else says that yesterday he saw Peter suffering from loss of consciousness, and that he believes that Peter died from it, he makes my words seem false. That your conjecture about spectres and ghosts seems false and not even probable, I have so clearly shown that I find nothing worthy of consideration in your answer.

To your question whether I have as clear an idea of God as I have of a triangle, I answer in the affirmative. But if you ask me whether I have as clear a mental image of God as I have of a triangle, I shall answer No. For we cannot imagine God, but we can, indeed, conceive Him. Here also it should be noted that I do not say that I know God entirely, but only that I understand some of His attributes, though not all, nor

even the greater part of them, and it is certain that our ignorance of the majority of them does not hinder our having a knowledge of some of them. When I learnt Euclid's elements I first understood that the three angles of a triangle are equal to two right angles, and I clearly perceived this property of a triangle although I was ignorant of many others.

As regards spectres, or ghosts, I have never yet heard of an intelligible property of theirs, but only of Phantasies which no-one can grasp. When you say that spectres, or ghosts, here in this lower region (I follow your form of expression, although I do not know that the matter here in this lower region is less valuable than that above) consist of the finest, thinnest, and most subtle substance, you seem to be speaking of spiders' webs, of air, or of vapours. To say that they are invisible means for me as much as if you said what they are not, but not what they are; unless perhaps you want to indicate that, according as they please, they make themselves now visible, now invisible, and that in these as in other impossibilities, the imagination will find no difficulty.

The authority of Plato, Aristotle, and Socrates has not much weight with me. I should have been surprised had you mentioned Epicurus, Democritus, Lucretius or any one of the Atomists, or defenders of the atoms. It is not surprising that those who invented occult Qualities, intentional Species, substantial Forms, and a thousand other trifles, should have devised spectres and ghosts, and put their faith in old women, in order to weaken the authority of Democritus, of whose good repute they were so envious that they burnt all his books, which he had published amidst so much praise. If you have a mind to put faith in them, what reasons have you for denying the miracles of the Holy Virgin, and of all the Saints, which have been described by so many very famous Philosophers, Theologians, and Historians that I can produce an hundred of them to scarcely one of the others?

Lastly, most honoured Sir, I have gone further than I intended. I do not wish to annoy you further with things which (I know) you will not admit, since you follow other principles which differ widely from my own, etc.

[The Hague, October 1674]

LETTER LVIII

To the Very Learned and Expert Mr. G. H. SCHULLER.

Most Expert Sir,

. . . I say that that thing is free which exists and acts solely from the necessity of its own nature; but that that thing is under compulsion which is determined by something else to exist, and to act in a definite and determined manner. For example, God, although He exists necessarily, nevertheless exists freely, since He exists solely from the necessity of His own nature. So also God freely understands Himself and absolutely all things, since it follows solely from the necessity of His own nature that He should understand everything. You see, therefore, that I do not place Freedom in free decision, but in free necessity.

Let us, however, descend to created things, which are all determined by external causes to exist, and to act in a definite and determined manner. In order that this may be clearly understood, let us think of a very simple thing. For instance, a stone receives from an external cause, which impels it, a certain quantity of motion, with which it will afterwards necessarily continue to move when the impact of the external cause has ceased. This continuance of the stone in its motion is compelled, not because it is necessary, but because it must be defined by the impact of an external cause. What is here said of the stone must be understood of each individual thing, however composite and however adapted to various ends it may be thought to be: that is, that each thing is necessarily determined by an external cause to exist and to act in a definite and determinate manner.

Next, conceive, if you please, that the stone while it continues in motion thinks, and knows that it is striving as much as possible to continue in motion. Surely this stone, inasmuch as it is conscious only of its own effort, and is far from indifferent, will believe that it is completely free, and that it continues in motion for no other reason than because it wants to. And such is the human freedom which all men boast that they possess, and which consists solely in this, that men are conscious of their desire, and ignorant of the causes by which they are determined. So the infant believes that it freely wants milk; the boy when he is angry that he freely wants revenge; the timid that he wants to escape. Then too the drunkard believes that, by the free decision of his mind, he says those things which afterwards when sober he would prefer to have left unsaid. So the delirious, the garrulous and many others of the same sort, believe that they are acting in accordance with the free decision of their mind, and not that they are carried away by impulse. Since this preconception is innate in all men, they are not so easily freed from it. For, although experience teaches sufficiently and more than sufficiently that the last thing that men can do is to moderate their appetites, and that often, when they are tormented by conflicting feelings, they see the better and follow the worse, yet they believe themselves to be free, because they desire some things slightly, and their appetites for these can easily be repressed by the memory of some other thing, which we frequently call to mind.

With these remarks, unless I am mistaken, I have sufficiently explained what my view is about free and compelled necessity, and about imaginary human freedom: and from this it will be easy to answer the objections of your friend. For, when he says with Descartes, that he is free who is compelled by no external cause, if by a man who is compelled he means one who acts against his will, I admit that in certain matters we are in no way compelled, and that in this respect we have a free will. But if by compelled he means one who, although he does not act against his will, yet acts necessarily (as I explained above), then I deny that we are free in anything.

Your friend, on the contrary, asserts that *we can exercise our reason with complete freedom, that is, absolutely.* He persists in this opinion with sufficient, not to say too much, confidence. *For who*, he says, *without contradicting his own consciousness, would deny that in my thoughts I can think that I want to write, and that I do not want to do so.* I should very much like to know of what consciousness he speaks, other than that which I explained above in my example of the stone. Indeed, in order not to contradict my consciousness, that is, my reason and experience, and in order not to foster preconceived ideas and ignorance, I deny that I can, by any absolute power of thought, think that I want, and that I do not want to write. But I appeal to his own consciousness, for he has doubtless experienced the fact that in dreams he has not the power of thinking that he wants, and does not want to write; and that when he dreams that he wants to write he has not the power of not dreaming that he wants to write. I believe he has had no less experience of the fact that the mind is not always equally capable of thinking about the same subject; but that according as the body is more fit for the excitation of the image of this or that object, so the mind is more capable of contemplating this or that object.

When he adds, further, that the causes of his applying himself to writing have stimulated him to write, but have not compelled him, he means nothing else (if you will examine the matter fully) than that his mind was at that time so constituted that the causes which on other occasions, that is, when they were in conflict with some powerful feeling, could not influence him, could now influence him easily, that is, that causes which on other occasions could not compel him, have now compelled him, not to write against his will, but necessarily to desire to write.

Again, as to his statement that *if we were compelled by external causes then no one would be able to acquire the habit of virtue*, I do not know who has told him that we cannot be of a firm and constant disposition as a result of fatalistic necessity, but only from the free decision of the Mind.

As to his last addition, that *if this were granted all wickedness would be excusable*; what then? For wicked men are no less to be feared, and no less pernicious, when they are necessarily wicked. But on these things, look up, if you please, Part II, Chapter VIII, of my *Appendix to Descartes' Principles, Books I and II, geometrically demonstrated.*

Lastly, I should like your friend, who makes these objections to my theory, to tell me how he conceives human virtue, which he says arises from the free decision of the mind, together with the preordination of God. For if, with Descartes, he admits that he does not know how to reconcile them, then he is endeavouring to hurl against me the weapon by which he has already been pierced. But in vain. For if you will attentively examine my view, you will see that it is entirely consistent, etc.

[The Hague, October 1674]

COMMENT

Spinoza's Monism

Monism is the name commonly given to theories that stress the oneness of reality. *Dualism* is the doctrine that there are at least two distinct kinds of things — mind and matter. *Pluralism* is the doctrine that there is not one (monism), not two (dualism), but a larger number of ultimate kinds or things.

How many things are there in the world? Quantitative monism is the doctrine that there is only one thing. Spinoza is a quantitative monist. How many *kinds* are there in the world? Qualitative monism answers "Only one kind." Spinoza distinguishes between mind and matter as qualitatively different aspects ("attributes") of the one cosmic being. Hence he is not a qualitative monist in the sense of maintaining that all reality is mental (idealism) or that all reality is material (materialism). But in another sense he is a monist. He believes that mind and matter pervade the entire universe and are attributes of the same ultimate substance. In the human being, as well as in the universe at large, mind is not reducible to matter nor matter to mind, but both are aspects of a single reality. This view is sometimes called "the double-aspect theory." Finally Spinoza believes that the one cosmic being is infinite in an infinite number of other ways, each of which is as ultimate and unique as mind and matter. In addition to the one substance and its infinite attributes, there are so-called individual things — a rock, a horse, a man, a planet — which Spinoza calls "modes." To call them modes is to emphasize their adjectival nature — they are merely modifications of the single substance.

Spinoza seizes on the Cartesian notion (derived from Aristotle) that substance is an enduring thing independent of other things, but he rejects utterly the notion of a finite substance or a plurality of substances. "By substance," he says, "I understand that which is in itself and is conceived through itself; in other words, that the conception of which does not need the conception of another thing from which it must be formed."[1] Substance is thus, by definition absolutely independent and self-sustaining. Spinoza then proceeds to prove that there can be only one substance, and that this substance is infinite and all-inclusive. Finally he "proves" that this single substance, which he calls God or Nature, must exist. The argument, which we shall not trace, is modeled after geometry, being based on definitions and axioms from which various propositions are deduced.

In the Appendix, Spinoza sums up his argument briefly and combats misconceptions of Nature or God. These all arise from the idea that the God-Universe works toward some goal, or "final cause". Human beings interpret themselves as goal seeking and God as like themselves. They think that God has created every natural object and guided every event for an end or purpose. According to Spinoza, this whole approach is false because God, who is absolutely infinite and self-complete, is made to appear in need of, and dependent on, an end not yet attained. Those who accept this anthropomorphic belief make the will of God a "refuge of ignorance" by referring every event of which they do not know the cause to God.

Pitted against these "superstitions" is Spinoza's own interpretation of the nature of things. God's causality, far from being teleological, must be conceived on the analogy of logical ground and consequent. ". . . From the supreme power of God, or from God's infinite nature, infinite things in infinite ways, that is to say, all things, have necessarily flowed, or continually follow by the same necessity, in the same way as it follows from the nature of a triangle, from eternity to eternity, that its three angles are equal to two right angles."[2] This kind of causality precludes all chance anywhere and anytime. "Necessary" alone expresses what is, and "impossible" what is not. Hence there is no divine purpose and no inde-

[1] *Ethics*, First Part, Def. III.
[2] *Ethics*, Prop. XVII, Scholium.

terminism. People, in distinction from God, think they act freely and purposively, but ultimately their action is determined by forces over which they have no exclusive control since the only completely adequate ground, and the only real and ultimate agent, is God, from whom everything follows by logical necessity.

According to Spinoza, happiness depends on the quality of the object of one's love, and love toward the greatest of objects, God or Nature, feeds the mind with a profound joy. This joy, accompanied with a clear understanding of its cause, is called by Spinoza "intellectual love". They who have comprehensive knowledge of themselves and the natural world love God: Their intellectual love, in effect, is that very love of God whereby God loves God's self. The finite human being is then virtually at one with the eternal nature of things. Our life is a communion with that sublime and marvelous order of nature in which God is manifest. Whoever loves God in this "intellectual" way is free; he is caught up into the impersonal infinitude of being and knows the deepest happiness of which a human being is capable. Because his account of the nature of things culminates in this ecstatic vision, Spinoza regarded metaphysics as a prelude to ethics and gave to his great metaphysical treatise the name *Ethics*.

Even highly trained philosophers find the *Ethics* a very difficult book to understand. But in the Appendix and the Correspondence that we have quoted the doctrine is easier to grasp.

No one today would altogether accept Spinoza's rationalism and extreme monism. To set up cosmic monism and determinism as necessary truths, and to demonstrate them in the style of Euclid's geometry, with definitions, axioms, and theorems, is no longer plausible. Nevertheless, his vision of an integrated, deterministic, and nonpurposive universe retains a kind of impersonal grandeur, and his conception of freedom as the understanding of necessity has a deep and enduring appeal.

Dualism

RENÉ DESCARTES (1596–1650)

For a biographical note, see page 60–61.

Meditation I

Of the Things Which May Be Brought Within the Sphere of the Doubtful.

It is now some years since I detected how many were the false beliefs that I had from my earliest youth admitted as true, and how doubtful was everything I had since constructed on this basis; and from that time I was convinced that I must once for all seriously undertake to rid myself of all the opinions which I had formerly accepted, and commence to build anew from the foundation, if I wanted to establish any firm and permanent structure in the sciences. But as this enterprise appeared to be a very great one, I waited until I had attained an age so mature

The following excerpts from the *Meditations* are from *The Philosophical Works of Descartes*, trans. from the Latin by Elizabeth S. Haldane and G. R. T. Ross, and published by Cambridge University Press, 1931. Where it seems desirable, an alternative reading from the French is given in brackets. Reprinted by permission.

348

that I could not hope that at any later date I should be better fitted to execute my design. This reason caused me to delay so long that I should feel that I was doing wrong were I to occupy in deliberation the time that yet remains to me for action. Today, then, since very opportunely for the plan I have in view I have delivered my mind from every care [and am happily agitated by no passions] and since I have procured for myself an assured leisure in a peaceable retirement, I shall at last seriously and freely address myself to the general upheaval of all my former opinions.

Now for this object it is not necessary that I should show that all of these are false—I shall perhaps never arrive at this end. But inasmuch as reason already persuades me that I ought no less carefully to withhold my assent from matters which are not entirely certain and indubitable than from those which appear to me manifestly to be false, if I am able to find in each one some reason to doubt, this will suffice to justify my rejecting the whole. And for that end it will not be requisite that I should examine each in particular, which would be an endless undertaking; for owing to the fact that the destruction of the foundations of necessity brings with it the downfall of the rest of the edifice, I shall only in the first place attack those principles upon which all my former opinions rested.

All that up to the present time I have accepted as most true and certain I have learned either from the senses or through the senses; but it is sometimes proved to me that these senses are deceptive, and it is wiser not to trust entirely to any thing by which we have once been deceived.

But it may be that although the senses sometimes deceive us concerning things which are hardly perceptible, or very far away, there are yet many others to be met with as to which we cannot reasonably have any doubt, although we recognize them by their means. For example, there is the fact that I am here, seated by the fire, attired in a dressing gown, having this paper in my hands and other similar matters. And how could I deny that these hands and this body are mine, were it not perhaps that I compare myself to certain persons, devoid of sense, whose cerebella are so troubled and clouded by the violent vapors of black bile, that they constantly assure us that they think they are kings when they are really quite poor, or that they are clothed in purple when they are really without covering, or who imagine that they have an earthenware head or are nothing but pumpkins or are made of glass. But they are mad, and I should not be any the less insane were I to follow examples so extravagant.

At the same time I must remember that I am a man, and that consequently I am in the habit of sleeping, and in my dreams representing to myself the same things or sometimes even less probable things, than do those who are insane in their waking moments. How often has it happened to me that in the night I dreamt that I found myself in this particular place, that I was dressed and seated near the fire, whilst in reality I was lying undressed in bed! At this moment it does indeed seem to me that it is with eyes awake that I am looking at this paper; that this head which I move is not asleep, that it is deliberately and of set purpose that I extend my hand

and perceive it; what happens in sleep does not appear so clear nor so distinct as does all this. But in thinking over this I remind myself that on many occasions I have in sleep been deceived by similar illusions, and in dwelling carefully on this reflection I see so manifestly that there are no certain indications by which we may clearly distinguish wakefulness from sleep that I am lost in astonishment. And my astonishment is such that it is almost incapable of persuading me that I now dream.

Now let us assume that we are asleep and that all these particulars, e.g., that we open our eyes, shake our head, extend our hands, and so on, are but false delusions; and let us reflect that possibly neither our hands nor our whole body are such as they appear to us to be. At the same time we must at least confess that the things which are represented to us in sleep are like painted representations which can only have been formed as the counterparts of something real and true, and that in this way those general things at least, i.e. eyes, a head, hands, and a whole body, are not imaginary things, but things really existent. For, as a matter of fact, painters, even when they study with the greatest skill to represent sirens and satyrs by forms the most strange and extraordinary, cannot give them natures which are entirely new, but merely make a certain medley of the members of different animals; or if their imagination is extravagant enough to invent something so novel that nothing similar has ever before been seen, and that then their work represents a thing purely fictitious and absolutely false, it is certain all the same

that the colors of which this is composed are necessarily real. And for the same reason, although these general things, to wit, [a body], eyes, a head, and such like, may be imaginary, we are bound at the same time to confess that there are at least some other objects yet more simple and more universal, which are real and true; and of these just in the same way as with certain real colors, all these images of things which dwell in our thoughts, whether true and real or false and fantastic, are formed.

To such a class of things pertains corporeal nature in general, and its extension, the figure of extended things, their quantity or magnitude and number, as also the place in which they are, the time which measures their duration, and so on.

That is possibly why our reasoning is not unjust when we conclude from this that Physics, Astronomy, Medicine and all other sciences which have as their end the consideration of composite things, are very dubious and uncertain; but that Arithmetic, Geometry and other sciences of that kind which only treat of things that are very simple and very general, without taking great trouble to ascertain whether they are actually existent or not, contain some measure of certainty and an element of the indubitable. For whether I am awake or asleep, two and three together always form five, and the square can never have more than four sides, and it does not seem possible that truths so clear and apparent can be suspected of any falsity [or uncertainty].

Nevertheless I have long had fixed in my mind the belief that an all-powerful God existed by whom I have been created such as I am. But how do I know that He has not brought it to pass that there is no earth, no heaven, no extended body, no magnitude, no place, and that nevertheless [I possess the perceptions of all these things and that] they seem to me to exist just exactly as I now see them? And, besides, as I sometimes imagine that others deceive themselves in the things which they think they know best, how do I know that I am not deceived every time that I add two and three, or count the sides of a square, or judge of things yet simpler, if anything simpler can be imagined? But possibly God has not desired that I should be thus deceived, for He is said to be supremely good. If, however, it is contrary to His goodness to have made me such that I constantly deceive myself, it would also appear to be contrary to His goodness to permit me to be sometimes deceived, and nevertheless I cannot doubt that He does permit this.

There may indeed be those who would prefer to deny the existence of a God so powerful, rather than believe that all other things are uncertain. But let us not oppose them for the present, and grant that all that is said of a God is a fable; nevertheless in whatever way they suppose that I have arrived at the state of being that I have reached — whether they attribute it to fate or to accident, or make out that it is by a continual succession of antecedents, or by some other method — since to err and deceive oneself is a defect, it is clear that the greater will be the probability of my being so imperfect as to deceive myself ever, as is the Author to whom they assign my origin the less powerful. To these reasons I have cer-

tainly nothing to reply, but at the end I feel constrained to confess that there is nothing in all that I formerly believed to be true, of which I cannot in some measure doubt, and that not merely through want of thought or through levity, but for reasons which are very powerful and maturely considered; so that henceforth I ought not the less carefully to refrain from giving credence to these opinions than to that which is manifestly false, if I desire to arrive at any certainty [in the sciences].

But it is not sufficient to have made these remarks, we must also be careful to keep them in mind. For these ancient and commonly held opinions still revert frequently to my mind, long and familiar custom having given them the right to occupy my mind against my inclination and rendered them almost masters of my belief; nor will I ever lose the habit of deferring to them or of placing my confidence in them, so long as I consider them as they really are, *i.e.* opinions in some measure doubtful, as I have just shown, and at the same time highly probable, so that there is much more reason to believe than to deny them. That is why I consider that I shall not be acting amiss, if, taking of set purpose a contrary belief, I allow myself to be deceived, and for a certain time pretend that all these opinions are entirely false and imaginary, until at last, having thus balanced my former prejudices with my latter [so that they cannot divert my opinions more to one side than to the other], my judgment will no longer be dominated by bad usage or turned away from the right knowledge of the truth. For I am assured that there can be neither peril nor error in this course, and that I cannot at present yield too much to distrust, since I am not considering the question of action, but only of knowledge.

I shall then suppose, not that God who is supremely good and the fountain of truth, but some evil genius not less powerful than deceitful, has employed his whole energies in deceiving me; I shall consider that the heavens, the earth, colors, figures, sound, and all other external things are nought but the illusions and dreams of which this genius has availed himself in order to lay traps for my credulity; I shall consider myself as having no hands, no eyes, no flesh, no blood, nor any senses, yet falsely believing myself to possess all these things; I shall remain obstinately attached to this idea, and if by this means it is not in my power to arrive at the knowledge of any truth, I

may at least do what is in my power [i.e. suspend my judgment], and with firm purpose avoid giving credence to any false thing, or being imposed upon by this arch deceiver, however powerful and deceptive he may be. But this task is a laborious one, and insensibly a certain lassitude leads me into the course of my ordinary life. And just as a captive who in sleep enjoys imaginary liberty, when he begins to suspect that his liberty is but a dream, fears to awaken, and conspires with these agreeable illusions that the deception may be prolonged, so insensibly of my own accord I fall back into my former opinions, and I dread awakening from this slumber, lest the laborious wakefulness which would follow the tranquillity of this repose should have to be spent not in daylight, but in the excessive darkness of the difficulties which have just been discussed.

Meditation II

Of the Nature of the Human Mind; and That It Is More Easily Known Than the Body.

The Meditation of yesterday filled my mind with so many doubts that it is no longer in my power to forget them. And yet I do not see in what manner I can resolve them; and, just as if I had all of a sudden fallen into very deep water, I am so disconcerted that I can neither make certain of setting my feet on the bottom, nor can I swim and so support myself on the surface. I shall neverthe-

less make an effort and follow anew the same path as that on which I yesterday entered, i.e. I shall proceed by setting aside all that in which the least doubt could be supposed to exist, just as if I had discovered that it was absolutely false; and I shall ever follow in this road until I have met with something which is certain, or at least, if I can do nothing else, until I have learned for certain that there is nothing in the world that is certain. Archimedes, in order that he might draw the terrestrial globe out of its place, and transport it elsewhere, demanded only that one point should be fixed and immovable; in the same way I shall have the right to conceive high hopes if I am happy enough to discover one thing only which is certain and indubitable.

I suppose, then, that all the things that I see are false; I persuade myself that nothing has ever existed of all that my fallacious memory represents to me. I consider that I possess no senses; I imagine that body, figure, extension, movement and place are but the fictions of my mind. What, then, can be esteemed as true? Perhaps nothing at all, unless that there is nothing in the world that is certain.

But how can I know there is not something different from those things that I have just considered, of which one cannot have the slightest doubt? Is there not some God, or some other being by whatever name we call it, who puts these reflections into my mind? That is not necessary, for is it not possible that I am capable of producing them myself? I myself, am I not at least something? But I have already denied that I had senses and body. Yet I hesitate, for what follows from that? Am I so dependent on body and senses that I cannot exist without these? But I was persuaded that there was nothing in all the world, that there was no heaven, no earth, that there were no minds, nor any bodies: was I not then likewise persuaded that I did not exist? Not at all; of a surety I myself did exist since I persuaded myself of something [or merely because I thought of something]. But there is some deceiver or other, very powerful and very cunning, who ever employs his ingenuity in de-

ceiving me. Then without doubt I exist also if he deceives me, and let him deceive me as much as he will, he can never cause me to be nothing so long as I think that I am something. So that after having reflected well and carefully examined all things, we must come to the definite conclusion that this proposition: I am, I exist, is necessarily true each time that I pronounce it, or that I mentally conceive it.

But I do not yet know clearly enough what I am, I who am certain that I am; and hence I must be careful to see that I do not imprudently take some other object in place of myself, and thus that I do not go astray in respect of this knowledge that I hold to be the most certain and most evident of all that I have formerly learned. That is why I shall now consider anew what I believed myself to be before I embarked upon these last reflections; and of my former opinions I shall withdraw all that might even in a small degree be invalidated by the reasons which I have just brought forward, in order that there may be nothing at all left beyond what is absolutely certain and indubitable.

What then did I formerly believe myself to be? Undoubtedly I believed myself to be a man. But what is a man? Shall I say a reasonable animal? Certainly not; for then I should have to inquire what an animal is, and what is reasonable; and thus from a single question I should insensibly fall into an infinitude of others more difficult; and I should not wish to waste the little time and leisure remaining to me in trying to unravel subtleties like these. But I shall rather stop here to consider the thoughts which of themselves spring up in my mind, and which were not inspired by anything beyond my own nature alone when I applied myself to the consideration of my being. In the first place, then, I considered myself as having a face, hands, arms, and all that system of members composed of bones and flesh as seen in a corpse which I designated by the name of body. In addition to this I considered that I was nourished, that I walked, that I felt, and that I thought, and I referred all these actions to the soul: but I did not stop to consider what the soul was, or if I did stop, I imagined that it was something extremely rare and subtle like a wind, a flame, or an ether, which was spread throughout my grosser parts. As to body I had no manner of doubt about its nature, but thought I had a very clear knowledge of it; and if I had desired to explain it according to the notions that I had then formed of it, I should have described it thus: By the body I understand all that which can be defined by a certain figure: something which can be confined in a certain place, and which can fill a given space in such a way that every other body will be excluded from it; which can be perceived either by touch, or by sight, or by hearing, or by taste, or by smell: which can be moved in many ways not, in truth, by itself, but by something which is foreign to it, by which it is touched [and from which it receives impressions]: for to have the power of self-movement, as also of feeling or of thinking, I did not consider to appertain to the nature of body: on the contrary, I was rather astonished to find that faculties similar to them existed in some bodies.

But what am I, now that I suppose that there is a certain genius which is extremely powerful, and, if I may say so, malicious, who employs all his powers in deceiving me? Can I affirm that I possess the least of all those things which I have just said pertain to the nature of body? I pause to consider, I resolve all these things in my mind, and find none of which I can say that it pertains to me. It would be tedious to stop to enumerate them. Let us pass to the attributes of soul and see if there is any one which is in me? What of nutrition or walking [the first mentioned]? But if it is so that I have no body, it is also true that I can neither walk nor take nourishment. Another attribute is sensation. But one cannot feel without body, and besides I have thought I perceived many things during sleep that I recognized in my waking moments as not having been experienced at all. What of thinking? I find here that thought is an attribute that belongs to me; it alone cannot be separated from me. I am, I exist, that is certain. But how often? Just when I think; for it might possibly be the case if I ceased entirely to think, that I should likewise cease altogether to exist. I do not now admit anything which is not necessarily true: to speak accurately I am not more than a thing which thinks, that is to say a mind or a soul, or an understanding, or a reason, which are terms whose significance was formerly unknown to me. I am, however, a real thing and really exist; but what thing? I have answered: a thing which thinks.

And what more? I shall exercise my imagination [in order to see if I am not something more]. I am not a collection of members which we call the human body: I am not a subtle air distributed through these members, I am not a wind, a fire, a vapor, a breath, nor anything at all which I can imagine or conceive; because I have assumed that all these were nothing. Without changing that supposition I find that I only leave myself certain of the fact that I am somewhat. But perhaps it is true that these same things which I supposed were non-existent because they are unknown to me, are really not different from the self which I know. I am not sure about this, I shall not dispute about it now; I can only give judgment on things that are known to me. I know that I exist, and I inquire what I am, I whom I know to exist. But it is very certain that the knowledge of my existence taken in its precise significance does not depend on things whose existence is not yet known to me; consequently it does not depend on those which I can feign in imagination. And indeed the very term *feign* in imagination proves to me my error, for I really do this if I image myself a something, since to imagine is nothing else than to contemplate the figure or image of a corporeal thing. But I already know for certain that I am, and that it may be that all these images, and, speaking generally, all things that relate to the nature of body are nothing but dreams [and chimeras]. For this reason I see clearly that I have as little reason to say, "I shall stimulate my imagination in order to know more distinctly what I am," than if I were to say, "I am now awake," and I perceive somewhat that is real and true: but because I do not yet perceive it distinctly enough, I shall go to sleep of express purpose, so that my dreams may represent the perception

with greatest truth and evidence." And, thus, I know for certain that nothing of all that I can understand by means of my imagination belongs to this knowledge which I have of myself, and that it is necessary to recall the mind from this mode of thought with the utmost diligence in order that it may be able to know its own nature with perfect distinctness.

But what then am I? A thing which thinks. What is a thing which thinks? It is a thing which doubts, understands, [conceives], affirms, denies, wills, refuses, which also imagines and feels.

Certainly it is no small matter if all these things pertain to my nature. But why should they not so pertain? Am I not that being who now doubts nearly everything, who nevertheless understands certain things, who affirms that one only is true, who denies all the others, who desires to know more, is averse from being deceived, who imagines many things, sometimes indeed despite his will, and who perceives many likewise, as by the intervention of the bodily organs? Is there nothing in all this which is as true as it is certain that I exist, even though I should always sleep and though he who has given me being employed all his ingenuity in deceiving me? Is there likewise any one of these attributes which can be distinguished from my thought, or which might be said to be separated from myself? For it is so evident of itself that it is I who doubts, who understands, and who desires, that there is no reason here to add anything to explain it. And I have certainly the power of imagining likewise; for although it may happen (as I formerly supposed) that none of the things which I imagine are true, nevertheless this power of imagining does not cease to be really in use, and it forms part of my thought. Finally, I am the same who feels, that is to say, who perceives certain things, as by the organs of sense, since in truth I see light, I hear noise, I feel heat. But it will be said that these phenomena are false and that I am dreaming. Let it be so; still it is at least quite certain that it seems to me that I see light, than I hear noise and that I feel heat. That cannot be false; properly speaking it is what is in me called feeling; and used in this precise sense that is no other thing than thinking.

From this time I begin to know what I am with a little more clearness and distinction than before; but nevertheless it still seems to me, and I cannot prevent myself from thinking, that corporeal things, whose images are framed by thought, which are tested by the senses, are much more distinctly known than that obscure part of me which does not come under the imagination. Although really it is very strange to say that I know and understand more distinctly these things whose existence seems to me dubious, which are unknown to me, and which do not belong to me, than others of the truth of which I am convinced, which are known to me and which pertain to my real nature, in a word, than myself. But I see clearly how the case stands: my mind loves to wander, and cannot yet suffer itself to be retained within the just limits of truth. Very good, let us once more give it the freest rein, so that, when afterwards we seize the proper occasion for pulling up, it may the more easily be regulated and controlled.

Let us begin by considering the commonest matters, those which we believe to be the most distinctly comprehended, to wit, the bodies which we touch and see; not indeed bodies in general, for these general ideas are usually a little more confused, but let us consider one body in particular. Let us take for example, this piece of wax: it has been taken quite freshly from the hive, and it has not yet lost the sweetness of the honey which it contains; it still retains somewhat of the odor of the flowers from which it has been culled; its color, its figure, its size are apparent; it is hard, cold, easily handled, and if you strike it with the finger, it will emit a sound. Finally all the things which are requisite to cause us distinctly to recognize a body, are met within it. But notice that while I speak and approach the fire what remained of the taste is exhaled, the smell evaporates, the color alters, the figure is destroyed, the size increases, it becomes liquid, it heats, scarcely can one handle it, and when one strikes it, no sound is emitted. Does the same wax remain after this change? We must confess that it remains; none would judge otherwise. What then did I know so distinctly in this piece of wax? It could certainly be nothing of all that the senses brought to my notice, since all these things which fall under taste, smell, sight, touch, and hearing, are found to be changed, and yet the same wax remains.

Perhaps it was what I now think, viz. that this wax was not that sweetness of honey, nor that agreeable scent of flowers, nor that particular whiteness, nor that figure, nor that sound, but simply a body which a little before appeared to me as perceptible under these forms, and which is now perceptible under others. But what, precisely, is that I imagine when I form such conceptions? Let us attentively consider this, and, abstracting from all that does not belong to the wax, let us see what remains. Certainly nothing remains excepting a certain extended thing which is flexible and movable. But what is the meaning of flexible and movable? Is it not that I imagine that this piece of wax being round is capable of becoming square and of passing from a square to a triangular figure? No, certainly it is not that, since I imagine it admits of an infinitude of similar changes, and I nevertheless do not know how to compass the infinitude by my imagination, and consequently this conception which I have of the wax is not brought about by the faculty of imagination. What now is this extension? Is it not also unknown? For it becomes greater when the wax is melted, greater when it is boiled, and greater still when the heat increases; and I should not conceive [clearly] according to truth what wax is, if I did not think that even this piece that we are considering is capable of receiving more variations in extension than I have ever imagined. We must then grant that I could not even understand through the imagination what this piece of wax is, and that it is my mind alone which perceives it. I say this piece of wax in particular, for as to wax in general it is yet clearer. But what is this piece of wax which cannot be understood excepting by the [understanding or] mind? It is certainly the same that I see, touch, imagine, and finally it is the same which I have always believed it to be from the beginning.

But what must particularly be observed is that its perception is neither an act of vision, nor of touch, nor of imagination, and has never been such although it may have appeared formerly to be so, but only an intuition of the mind, which may be imperfect and confused as it was formerly, or clear and distinct as it is at present, according as my attention is more or less directed to the elements which are found in it, and of which it is composed.

Yet in the meantime I am greatly astonished when I consider [the great feebleness of mind] and its proneness to fall [insensibly] into error; for although without giving expression to my thoughts I consider all this in my own mind, words often impede me and I am almost deceived by the terms of ordinary language. For we say that we see the same wax, if it is present, and not that we simply judge that it is the same from its having the same color and figure. From this I should conclude that I knew the wax by means of vision and not simply by the intuition of the mind; unless by chance I remember that, when looking from a window and saying I see men who pass in the street, I really do not see them, but infer that what I see is men, just as I say that I see wax. And yet what do I see from the window but hats and coats which may cover automatic machines? Yet I judge these to be men. And similarly solely by the faculty of judgment which rests in my mind, I comprehend that which I believed I saw with my eyes.

A man who makes it his aim to raise his knowledge above the common should be ashamed to derive the occasion for doubting from the forms of speech invented by the vulgar; I prefer to pass on and consider whether I had a more evident and perfect conception of what the wax was when I first perceived it, and when I believed I knew it by means of the external senses or at least by the common sense as it is called, that is to say by the imaginative faculty, or whether my present conception is clearer now that I have most carefully examined what it is, and in what way it can be known. It would certainly be absurd to doubt as to this. For what was there in this first perception which was distinct? What was there which might not as well have been perceived by any of the animals? But when I distinguish the wax from its external forms, and when, just as if I had taken from it its vestments, I consider it quite naked, it is certain that although some error may still be found in my judgment, I can nevertheless not perceive it thus without a human mind.

But finally what shall I say of this mind, that is, of myself, for up to this point I do not admit in myself anything but mind? What then, I who seem to perceive this piece of wax distinctly, do I not know myself, not only with much more truth and certainty, but also with much more distinctness and clearness? For if I judge that the wax is or exists from the fact that I see it, it certainly follows much more clearly that I am or that I exist myself from the fact that I see it. For it may be that what I see is not really wax, it may also be that I do not possess eyes with which to see anything; but it cannot be that when I see, or (for I no longer take account of the distinction) when I think I see, that I myself who think am nought. So if I judge that the wax exists from the fact that I touch it, the same thing will follow, to wit, that I am; and if I judge that my imagination, or some other cause, whatever it is, persuades me that the wax exists, I shall still conclude the same. And what I have here remarked of wax may be applied to all other things which are external to me [and which are met with outside of me]. And further, if the [notion or] perception of wax has seemed to me clearer and more distinct, not only after the sight or the touch, but also after many other causes have rendered it quite manifest to me, with how much more [evidence] and distinctness must it be said that I now know myself, since all the reasons which contribute to the knowledge of wax, or any other body whatever, are yet better proofs of the nature of my mind! And there are so many other things in the mind itself which may contribute to the elucidation of its nature, that those which depend on body such as these just mentioned, hardly merit being taken into account.

But finally here I am, having insensibly reverted to the point I desired, for, since it is now manifest to me that even bodies are not properly speaking known by the senses or by the faculty of imagination, but by the understanding only, and since they are not known from the fact that they are seen or touched, but only because they are understood, I see clearly that there is nothing which is easier for me to know than my mind. But because it is difficult to rid oneself so promptly of an opinion to which one was accustomed for so long, it will be well that I should halt a little at this point, so that by the length of my meditation I may more deeply imprint on my memory this new knowledge.

Meditation III

Of God: That He Exists.

I shall now close my eyes, I shall stop my ears, I shall call away all my senses, I shall efface even from my thoughts all the images of corporeal things, or at least (for that is hardly possible) I shall esteem them as vain and false; and thus holding converse only with myself and considering my own nature, I shall try little by little to reach a better knowledge of and a more familiar acquaintanceship with myself. I am a thing that thinks, that is to say, that doubts, affirms, denies, that knows a few things, that is ignorant of many, [that loves, that hates], that wills, that desires, that also imagines and perceives; for as I remarked before, although the things which I perceive and imagine are perhaps nothing at all apart from me and in themselves, I am nevertheless assured that these modes of thought that I call perceptions and imaginations, inasmuch only as they are modes of thought, certainly reside [and are met with] in me.

And in the little that I have just said, I think I have summed up all that I really know, or at least all that hitherto I was aware that I knew. In order to try to extend my knowledge further, I shall now look around more carefully and see whether I cannot still discover in myself some other things which I have not hitherto perceived. I am certain that I am a thing which thinks; but do I not then likewise know what is requisite to render me certain of a truth? Certainly in this first knowledge there is nothing that assures me of its truth, excepting the clear and distinct perception of that which I state, which would not indeed suffice to assure me that what I say is true, if it could ever happen that a thing which I conceived so clearly and distinctly could be false; and accordingly it seems to me that already I can establish as a general rule that all things which I perceive very clearly and very distinctly are true.

At the same time I have before received and admitted many things to be very certain and manifest, which yet I afterwards recognized as being dubious. What then were these things? They were the earth, sky, stars and all other objects which I apprehended by means of the senses. But what did I clearly [and distinctly] perceive in them? Nothing more than that the ideas or thoughts of these things were presented to my mind. And not even now do I deny that these ideas are met with in me. But there was yet another thing which I affirmed, and which, owing to the habit which I had formed of believing it, I thought I perceived very clearly, although in truth I did not perceive it at all, to wit, that there were objects outside of me from which these ideas proceeded, and to which they were entirely similar. And it was in this that I erred, or, if perchance my judgment was correct, this was not due to any knowledge arising from my perception.

But when I took anything very simple and easy in the sphere of arithmetic or geometry into consideration, *e.g.*

that two and three together made five, and other things of the sort, were not these present to my mind so clearly as to enable me to affirm that they were true? Certainly if I judged that since such matters could be doubted, this would not have been so for any other reason than that it came into my mind that perhaps a God might have endowed me with such a nature that I may have been deceived even concerning things which seemed to me most manifest. But every time that this preconceived opinion of the sovereign power of a God presents itself to my thought, I am constrained to confess that it is easy to Him, if He wishes it, to cause me to err, even in matters in which I believe myself to have the best evidence. And, on the other hand, always when I direct my attention to things which I believe myself to perceive very clearly, I am so persuaded of their truth that I let myself break out into words such as these: Let who will deceive me, He can never cause me to be nothing while I think that I am, or some day cause it to be true to say that I have never been, it being true now to say that I am, or that two and three make more or less than five, or any such thing in which I see a manifest contradiction. And certainly, since I have no reason to believe that there is a God who is a deceiver, and as I have not yet satisfied myself that there is a God at all, the reason for doubt which depends on this opinion alone is very slight, and so to speak metaphysical. But in order to be able altogether to remove it, I must inquire whether there is a God as soon as the occasion presents itself; and if I find that there is

a God, I must also inquire whether He may be a deceiver; for without a knowledge of these two truths I do not see that I can ever be certain of anything.

[*To answer this lingering doubt, Descartes "proves" that there is a God who, as perfect, would not deceive me. Since arguments for the existence of God have been considered in detail in Chapter 7, a brief summary of Descartes' arguments will here be sufficient.*

His first argument for the existence of God consists of four steps: (1) I have an idea of God. (2) Everything, including my idea, has a cause. (3) Since the greater cannot proceed from the less, nothing less than God is adequate to explain my idea of God. This step involves the notion that the idea of a Perfect Being is, in conception, perfect; that no imperfect being is capable of producing such an idea; and that hence it requires a perfect Cause to produce it. (4) Therefore God exists.

Descartes advances a second argument for God, once again starting with "I think, therefore I am." He argues (still using the first person pronoun) that God is the cause, not only of my idea of God, but of me. This is an argument by elimination: (1) I am not the cause of myself, for if I were, I would not be the highly imperfect and fallible being that I know myself to be. (2) No other finite being could be the sufficient cause of my existence, for if such a being existed, it in turn would have to be explained, as would any prior finite cause as well. I would thus have to trace the causal process back from stage to stage to the ultimate *cause*, an eternal and necessary being who requires no explanation beyond itself. Only such an infinite cause could be conceived as existing, not merely through my life, but through all the lives involved in the total succession of finite beings—and only such a cause would be adequate to maintain as well as to originate the entire succession. (3) The ultimate cause could not be multiple, because I conceive of God as absolutely one, and the cause of this idea must be no less perfect than its effect, not falling short of the idea in its unity or in any other respect. (4) The only possibility that remains is that an infinite and monotheistic God is the cause. Therefore God exists.

In *Meditation V* which has been omitted in the present book, Descartes presents a third argument for God's existence—a restatement of the so-called Ontological Argument of Saint Anselm, an early medieval philosopher. Since this argument is dealt with in Chapter 7, we shall not consider it here.

The importance of God in Descartes' system is that God is used to guarantee not a system of dogma but science and philosophy. Science and philosophy are based upon reason and memory, and God is needed to guarantee their reliability. God, being perfect, would not deceive me—God would not, like a malignant demon, so mislead me as to invalidate my most vivid memory and careful reasoning. Descartes' constructive argument starts with "I think, therefore I am." But, almost surreptitiously, he admits three other "self-evident truths":

1. Whatever is clearly and distinctly perceived is true.
2. Nothing can be without a cause.
3. The cause must be at least as great as the effect.

From these premises he deduces two additional "truths":

4. God exists.
5. God, being perfect, cannot deceive me.

The rest of his argument follows rather quickly. He argues for the existence of other minds and material objects alike on the grounds of God's veracity. This means not that all my ideas are true but simply that the faculties God has given me are reliable when used correctly—without prejudice, hastiness, or naïveté. I can trust only "firm conceptions born in a sound and attentive mind from the light of reason alone" and rigorous deductions from these conceptions.

The remainder of Meditation III and Meditations IV and V are omitted.]

Meditation VI

Of the Existence of Material Things, and of the Real Distinction Between the Soul and Body of Man.

. . . First of all I shall recall to my memory those matters which I hitherto held to be true, as having perceived them through the senses, and the foundations on which my belief has rested; in the next place I shall examine the reasons which have since obliged me to place them in doubt; in the last place I shall consider which of them I must now believe.

First of all, then, I perceived that I had a head, hands, feet, and all other members of which this body — which I considered as a part, or possibly even as the whole, of myself — is composed. Further I was sensible that this body was placed amidst many others, from which it was capable of being affected in many different ways, beneficial and hurtful, and I remarked that a certain feeling of pleasure accompanied those that were beneficial, and pain those which were harmful. And in addition to this pleasure and pain, I also experienced hunger, thirst, and other similar appetites, as also certain corporeal inclinations towards joy, sadness, anger, and other similar passions. And outside myself, in addition to extension, figure, and motions of bodies, I remarked in them hardness, heat, and all other tactile qualities, and, further, light and color, and scents and sounds, the variety of which gave me the means of distinguishing the sky, the earth, the sea, and generally all the other bodies, one from the other. And certainly, considering the ideas of all these qualities which presented themselves to my mind, and which alone I perceived properly or immediately, it was not without reason that I believed myself to perceive objects quite different from my thought, to wit, bodies from which those ideas proceeded; for I found by experience that these ideas presented themselves to me without my consent being requisite, so that I could not perceive any object, however desirous I might be, unless it were present to the organs of sense; and it was not in my power not to perceive it, when it was present. And because the ideas which I perceived through the senses were much more lively, more clear, and even, in their own way, more distinct than any of those which I could of myself frame in meditation, or than those I found impressed on my memory, it appeared as though they could not have proceeded from my mind, so that they must necessarily have been produced in me by some other things. And having no knowledge of those objects excepting the knowledge which the ideas themselves gave me, nothing was more likely to occur to my mind than that the objects were similar to the ideas which were caused. And because I likewise remembered that I had formerly made use of my senses rather than my reason, and recognized that the ideas which I formed of myself were not so distinct as those which I perceived through the senses, and that they were most frequently even composed of portions of these last, I persuaded myself easily that I had no idea in my mind which had not formerly come to me through the senses. Nor was it without some reason that I believed that this body (which by a certain special right I call my own) belonged to me more properly and more strictly than any other; for in fact I could never be separated from it as from other bodies; I experienced in it and on account of it all my appetites and affections, and finally I was touched by the feeling of pain and the titillation of pleasure in its parts, and not in the parts of other bodies which were separated from it. But when I inquired, why, from some, I know not what, painful sensation, there follows sadness of mind, and from the pleasurable sensation there arises joy, or why this mysterious emotion of the stomach which I call hunger causes me to desire to eat, and dryness of throat causes a desire to drink, and so on, I could give no reason excepting that nature taught me so; for there is certainly no affinity (that I at least can understand) between the craving of the stomach and the desire to eat, any more than between the perception of whatever causes pain and the thought of sadness which arises from this perception. And in the same way it appeared to me that I had learned from nature all the other judgments which I formed regarding the objects of my senses, since I remarked that these judgments were formed in me before I had the leisure to weigh and consider any reasons which might oblige me to make them.

But afterwards many experiences little by little destroyed all the faith which I had rested in my senses; for I from time to time observed that those towers which from afar appeared to me to be round, more closely observed seemed square, and that colossal statues raised on the summit of these towers, appeared as quite tiny statues when viewed from the bottom; and so in an infinitude of other cases I found error in judgments founded on the external senses. And not only in those founded on the external senses, but even in those founded on the internal as well; for is there anything more intimate or more internal than pain? And yet I have learned from some persons whose arms or legs have been cut off, that they sometimes seemed to feel pain in the part which had been amputated, which made me think that I could not be quite certain that it was a certain member which pained me, even although I felt pain in it. And to those grounds of doubt I have lately added two others, which are very general; the first is that I never have believed myself to feel anything in waking moments which I cannot also sometimes believe myself to feel when I sleep, and as I do not think that these things which I seem to find in sleep, proceed from objects outside of me, I do not see any reason why I should have this belief regarding objects which I seem to perceive while awake. The other was that being still ignorant, or rather supposing myself to be ignorant, of the author of my being, I saw nothing to prevent me from having been so constituted by nature that I might be deceived even in matters which seemed to me to be most certain. And as to the grounds on which I was formerly persuaded of the truth of sensible objects, I had not much trouble in replying to them. For since nature seemed to cause me to lean towards many things from which reason repelled me, I did not believe that I should trust much to the teachings of nature. And although the ideas which I receive by the senses do not depend on my will, I did not think that one should for that reason conclude that they proceeded from things different from myself, since possibly some faculty might be discovered in me—though hitherto unknown to me—which produced them.

But now that I begin to know myself better, and to discover more clearly the author of my being, I do not in truth think that I should rashly admit all the matters which the senses seem to teach us, but, on the other hand, I do not think that I should doubt them all universally.

And first of all, because I know that all things which I apprehend clearly and distinctly can be created by God as I apprehend them, it suffices that I am able to apprehend one thing apart from another clearly and distinctly in order to be certain that the one is different from the other, since they may be made to exist in separation at least by the omnipotence of God; and it does not signify by what power this separation is made in order to compel me to judge them to be different: and, therefore, just because I know certainly that I exist, and that meanwhile I do not remark that any other thing necessarily pertains to my nature or essence, excepting that I am a thinking thing, I

rightly conclude that my essence consists solely in the fact that I am a thinking thing [or a substance whose whole essence or nature is to think]. And although possibly (or rather certainly, as I shall say in a moment) I posses a body with which I am very intimately conjoined, yet because, on the one side, I have a clear and distinct idea of myself inasmuch as I am only a thinking and unextended thing, and as, on the other, I possess a distinct idea of body, inasmuch as it is only an extended and unthinking thing, it is certain that this I [that is to say, my soul by which I am what I am], is entirely and absolutely distinct from my body, and can exist without it. . . .

. . . There is a great difference between mind and body, inasmuch as body is by nature always divisible, and the mind is entirely indivisible. For, as a matter of fact, when I consider the mind, that is to say, myself inasmuch as I am only a thinking thing, I cannot distinguish in myself any parts, but apprehend myself to be clearly one and entire; and although the whole mind seems to be united to the whole body, yet if a foot, or an arm, or some other part, is separated from my body, I am aware that nothing has been taken away from my mind. And the faculties of willing, feeling, conceiving, etc., cannot be properly speaking said to be its parts, for it is one and the same mind which employs itself in willing and in feeling and understanding. But it is quite otherwise with corporeal or extended objects, for there is not one of these imaginable by me which my mind cannot easily divide into parts, and which consequently I do not recognize

as being divisible; this would be sufficient to teach me that the mind or soul
of man is entirely different from the
body, if I have not already learned it
from other sources. . . .

From this it is quite clear that, notwithstanding the supreme goodness of
God, the nature of man, inasmuch as it
is composed of mind and body, cannot
be otherwise than sometimes a source
of deception. For if there is any cause
which excites, not in the foot but in
some parts of the nerves which are extended between the foot and the brain,
or even the brain itself, the same movement which usually is produced when
the foot is detrimentally affected, pain
will be experienced as though it were in
the foot, and the sense will thus naturally be deceived; for since the same
movement in the brain is capable of
causing but one sensation in the mind,
and this sensation is much more frequently excited by a cause which hurts
the foot than by another existing in
some other quarter, it is reasonable that
it should convey to the mind pain in the
foot rather than in any other part of the
body. And although the parchedness of
the throat does not always proceed, as
it usually does, from the fact that
drinking is essential for the health of
the body, but sometimes comes from
quite a different cause, as is the case
with dropsical patients, it is yet much
better that it should mislead on this occasion than if, on the other hand, it
were always to deceive us when the
body is in good health; and so on in
similar cases.

And certainly this consideration is
of great service to me, not only in enabling me to recognize all the errors to
which my nature is subject, but also in
enabling me to avoid them or to correct
them more easily. For knowing that all
my senses more frequently indicate to
me truth than falsehood respecting the
things which concern that which is
beneficial to the body, and being able
almost always to avail myself of many
of them in order to examine one particular thing, and, besides that, being able
to make use of my memory in order to
connect the present with the past, and
of my understanding which already has
discovered all the causes of my errors, I
ought no longer to fear that falsity may
be found in matters every day presented to me by my senses. And I ought
to set aside all the doubts of these past
days as hyperbolical and ridiculous,
particularly that very common uncertainty respecting sleep, which I could
not distinguish from the waking state;
for at present I find a very notable difference between the two, inasmuch as
our memory can never connect our
dreams one with the other, or with the
whole course of our lives, as it unites
events which happen to us while we are
awake. And, as a matter of fact, if
someone, while I was awake, quite suddenly appeared to me and disappeared
as fast as do the images which I see in
sleep, so that I could not know from
whence the form came nor whither it
went, it would not be without reason
that I should deem it a specter or a
phantom formed by my brain [and similar to those which I form in sleep],
rather than a real man. But when I perceive things as to which I know distinctly both the place from which they
proceed, and that in which they are,
and the time at which they appeared to

me; and when, without any interruption, I can connect the perceptions which I have of them with the whole course of my life, I am perfectly assured that these perceptions occur while I am waking and not during sleep. And I ought in no wise to doubt the truth of such matters, if, after having called up all my senses, my memory, and my understanding, to examine them, nothing is brought to evidence by any one of them which is repugnant to what is set forth by the others. For because God is in no wise a deceiver, it follows that I am not deceived in this. But because the exigencies of action often oblige us to make up our minds before having leisure to examine matters carefully, we must confess that the life of man is very frequently subject to error in respect to individual objects, and we must in the end acknowledge the infirmity of our nature.

COMMENT

Dualism Attacked

The distinction between mind and body is closely related to the method of doubt. Descartes notes that he can be certain that he exists as a thinking being even when he is still in doubt whether he has a body, hence he concludes that the mind and body must be distinct and that his real essence is to think.

Descartes recognized two distinct realms of being. One is the world described by physics, a world that does not depend on our thoughts. It would continue to exist and operate if there were no human beings at all. Its essence is to be extended. The other is the world whose essence is thought — perception, willing, feeling, reasoning, imagining, and the corresponding ideas or mental representations.

A human being, as a compound of mind and body, belongs to both realms. How a person can thus be both two and one poses a difficult problem. Despite the apparent paradox, Descartes believed that mind and body, although radically different, are harmoniously combined in the human organism and that the unextended mind somehow interacts with the extended body.

This dualism is attacked in Gilbert Ryle's famous polemic against "the ghost in the machine." He characterizes the "official theory" of mind and body that stems from Descartes as based on a "category mistake." A mistake of this sort occurs when something is taken to belong to a different type or class than its true one. For example, it would be a category mistake if a spectator at a baseball game wanted to know which player did the pitching, which the catching, and which the exercising of "team spirit." The mistake, in this instance, would be to suppose that exercising team spirit is the same sort of thing as catching and pitching.

The category mistake involved in dualism is to regard both minds and bodies as things of the same logical type, or to use Descartes' terms, as "substances." This leads, declares Ryle, to the false supposition that the mind is an invisible thing somehow having dealings with another thing, the visible body. Each thing is described as having unique and independent properties, bodies being in space and subject to mechanical laws, minds being spaceless and characterized by spiritual capacities. The mental ghost thinks and the bodily machine moves: Somehow each influences the other, although it is strange and mysterious how this interaction takes place.

Ryle objects to the tendency to partition off the mental from the physical. For example, he says,

> When we read novels, biographies, and reminiscences, we do not find the chapters partitioned into section "A," covering the hero's "bodily" doings, and section "B," covering his "mental" doings. We find unpartitioned accounts of what he did and thought and felt, of what he said to others and to himself, of the mountains he tried to climb and the problems he tried to solve.[1]

Reacting against introspectionism, Ryle tries to explain mental life in terms of witnessable activities. "Overt intelligent performances," he declares, "are not clues to the workings of minds; they *are* those workings. Boswell described Johnson's mind when he described how he wrote, talked, ate, fidgeted and fumed."[2]

Whether Ryle succeeds in refuting dualism is debatable. Some critics contend that he is too behavioristic and skips over the more private aspects of mental life. A dream, for example, is directly knowable only by the dreamer. It is different from a table, which you and I and others can inspect. But Ryle does not deny states of consciousness even though he distrusts introspection. He is quite aware that human beings are more than complicated mechanisms. "Man need not be degraded to a machine by being denied to be a ghost in a machine . . ." he writes. "There has yet to be ventured the hazardous leap to the hypothesis that perhaps he is a man."[3]

[1]Professor Le Gros Clark, Ed., *The Physical Basis of Mind* (Oxford: Basil Blackwell, 1952), p. 77.
[2]*The Concept of Mind*, p. 58. Barnes and Noble, NY 1949.
[3]Ibid., p. 328.

12

Relationalism

"For Whitehead the fundamental 'units' of reality are actually 'events', not 'things'. He termed these free-flowing interchanging happenings 'occasions' or 'actual entities', and he saw them as the intersections of the world's continuously evolving energy."

J. H. Gill

ALFRED NORTH WHITEHEAD (1861–1947)

The son of a vicar in the Anglican Church, Whitehead was born at Ramsgate, a village near Canterbury Cathedral. He was educated at Sherborne, one of England's oldest boarding schools, and at Trinity College, Cambridge. He remained in the college for a quarter of a century as a teacher of mathematics and then taught for an additional thirteen years at the University of London.

Meanwhile he had married Evelyn Wade, who bore him a daughter and two sons. "Her vivid life," he wrote in an autobiographical sketch, "has taught me that beauty, moral and esthetic, is the aim of existence; and that kindness, and love, and artistic satisfaction are among its modes of attainment."[1]

In 1924, at the age of sixty-three, he joined the Philosophy Department at Harvard, where he taught until his retirement in 1937. Although he had collaborated with Bertrand Russell in writing the great *Principia Mathematica* (1910–1913), it was not until his later life that he turned to speculative philosophy, writing a brilliant series of books, including *The*

---

[1] Paul Arthur Schilpp, *The Philosophy of Alfred North Whitehead* (Evanston, IL: Northwestern University, 1941), p. 8.

Concept of Nature (1920), *Science and the Modern World* (1925), *Process and Reality* (1929), and *Adventures of Ideas* (1933). These works established his reputation as one of the towering figures in modern thought. He died in his eighty-seventh year in his small apartment near Harvard Yard.

Objects and Subjects

. . . Τὸ παοὸν ἑχάστῳ πάθος, ἐξ ὧν αἱ αἰσθήσεις χαὶ αἱ χατὰ χαύτας δόξαι γίγνονται, . . . *Theaetetus*, 179 C.

§1. *Prefatory.* — When Descartes, Locke, and Hume undertake the analysis of experience, they utilize those elements in their own experience which lie clear and distinct, fit for the exactitude of intellectual discourse. It is tacitly assumed, except by Plato, that the more fundamental factors will ever lend themselves for discrimination with peculiar clarity. This assumption is here directly challenged.

§2. *Structure of Experience.* — No topic has suffered more from this tendency of philosophers than their account of the object-subject structure of experience. In the first place, this structure has been identified with the bare relation of knower to known. The subject is the knower, the object is the known. Thus, with this interpretation, the object-subject relation is the known-knower relation. It then follows that the more clearly any instance of

this relation stands out for discrimination, the more safely we can utilize it for the interpretation of the status of experience in the universe of things. Hence Descartes' appeal to clarity and distinctness.

This deduction presupposes that the subject-object relation is the fundamental structural pattern of experience. I agree with this presupposition, but not in the sense in which subject-object is identified with knower-known. I contend that the notion of mere knowledge is a high abstraction, and that conscious discrimination itself is a variable factor only present in the more elaborate examples of occasions of experience. The basis of experience is emotional. Stated more generally, the basic fact is the rise of an affective tone originating from things whose relevance is given.

§3. *Phraseology.* — Thus the Quaker word 'concern', divested of any suggestion of knowledge, is more fitted to express this fundamental structure. The occasion as subject has a 'concern' for the object. And the 'concern' at once places the object as a component in the experience of the subject, with an affective tone drawn from this object and directed towards it. With this interpretation the subject-object relation is the fundamental structure of experience.

Quaker usages of language are not

widely spread. Also each phraseology leads to a crop of misunderstandings. The subject-object relation can be conceived as Recipient and Provoker, where the fact provoked is an affective tone about the status of the provoker in the provoked experience. Also the total provoked occasion is a totality involving many such examples of provocation. Again this phraseology is unfortunate; for the word 'recipient' suggests a passivity which is erroneous.

§4. *Prehensions.* — A more formal explanation is as follows. An occasion of experience is an activity, analysable into modes of functioning which jointly constitute its process of becoming. Each mode is analysable into the total experience as active subject, and into the thing or object with which the special activity is concerned. This thing is a datum, that is to say, is describable without reference to its entertainment in that occasion. An object is anything performing this function of a datum provoking some special activity of the occasion in question. Thus subject and object are relative terms. An occasion is a subject in respect to its special activity concerning an object; and anything is an object in respect to its provocation of some special activity within a subject. Such a mode of activity is termed a 'prehension'. Thus a prehension involves three factors. There is the occasion of experience within which the prehension is a detail of activity; there is the datum whose relevance provokes the origination of this prehension; this datum is the prehended object; there is the subjective form, which is the affective tone determining the effectiveness of that prehension in that occasion of experience. How the experience consti-

tutes itself depends on its complex of subjective forms.

§5. *Individuality.* — The individual immediacy of an occasion is the final unity of subjective form, which is the occasion as an absolute reality. This immediacy is its moment of sheer individuality, bounded on either side by essential relativity. The occasion arises from relevant objects, and perishes into the status of an object for other occasions. But it enjoys its decisive moment of absolute self-attainment as emotional unity. As used here the words 'individual' and 'atom' have the same meaning, that they apply to composite things with an absolute reality which their components lack. These words properly apply to an actual entity in its immediacy of self-attainment when it stands out as for itself alone, with its own affective self-enjoyment. The term 'monad' also expresses this essential unity at the decisive moment, which stands between its birth and its perishing. The creativity of the world is the throbbing emotion of the past hurling itself into a new transcendent fact. It is the flying dart, of which Lucretius speaks, hurled beyond the bounds of the world.

§6. *Knowledge.* — All knowledge is conscious discrimination of objects experienced. But this conscious discrimination, which is knowledge, is nothing more than an additional factor in the subjective form of the interplay of subject with object. This interplay is the stuff constituting those individual things which make up the sole reality of the Universe. These individual things are the individual occasions of experience, the actual entities.

But we do not so easily get rid of

knowledge. After all, it is knowledge that philosophers seek. And all knowledge is derived from, and verified by, direct intuitive observation. I accept this axiom of empiricism as stated in this general form. The question then arises how the structure of experience outlined above is directly observed. In answering this challenge I remind myself of the old advice that the doctrines which best repay critical examination are those which for the longest period have remained unquestioned.

§7. *Sense-perception.* — The particular agelong group of doctrines which I have in mind is: (1) that all perception is by the mediation of our bodily sense-organs, such as eyes, palates, noses, ears, and the diffused bodily organization furnishing touches, aches, and other bodily sensations; (2) that all percepta are bare sensa, in patterned connections, given in the immediate present; (3) that our experience of a social world is an interpretative reaction wholly derivative from this perception; (4) that our emotional and purposive experience is a reflective reaction derived from the original perception, and intertwined with the interpretative reaction and partly shaping it. Thus the two reactions are different aspects of one process, involving interpretative, emotional, and purposive factors. Of course, we are all aware that there are powerful schools of philosophy which explicitly reject this doctrine. Yet I cannot persuade myself that this rejection has been taken seriously by writers belonging to the schools in question. When the direct question as to things perceived arises, it seems to me that the answer is always returned in terms of sensa perceived.

§8. *Perceptive Functions.* — In the examination of the sensationalist doctrine, the first question to be asked concerns the general definition of what we mean by those functions of experience which we term 'perceptions'. If we define them as those experiential functions which arise directly from the stimulation of the various bodily sense-organs, then argument ceases. The traditional doctrine then becomes a mere matter of definition of the use of the word 'perception'. Indeed, having regard to long-standing usage, I am inclined to agree that it may be advisable for philosophers to confine the word 'perception' to this limited meaning. But the point on which I am insisting is that this meaning *is* limited, and that there is a wider meaning with which this limited use of the term 'perception' has been tacitly identified.

§9. *Objects.* — The process of experiencing is constituted by the reception of entities, whose being is antecedent to that process, into the complex fact which is that process itself. These antecedent entities, thus received as factors into the process of experiencing, are termed 'objects' for that experiential occasion. Thus primarily the term 'object' expresses the relation of the entity, thus denoted, to one or more occasions of experiencing. Two conditions must be fulfilled in order that an entity may function as an object in a process of experiencing: (1) the entity must be *antecedent*, and (2) the entity must be experienced in virtue of its antecedence; it must be *given*. Thus an object must be a thing received, and must not be either a *mode* of reception or a thing *generated* in that occasion. Thus the process of experiencing is constituted by the reception of objects into the unity of that complex occasion which is the process itself. The process creates itself, but it does not create the objects which it receives as factors in its own nature.

'Objects' for an occasion can also be termed the 'data' for that occasion. The choice of terms entirely depends on the metaphor which you prefer. One word carries the literal meaning of 'lying in the way of', and the other word carries the literal meaning of 'being given to'. But both words suffer from the defect of suggesting that an occasion of experiencing arises out of a passive situation which is a mere welter of many data.

§10. *Creativity.* — The exact contrary is the case. The initial situation includes a factor of activity which is the reason for the origin of that occasion of experience. This factor of activity is what I have called 'Creativity'. The initial situation with its creativity can be termed the initial phase of the new occasion. It can equally well be termed the 'actual world' relative to that occasion. It has a certain unity of its own, expressive of its capacity for providing the objects requisite for a new occasion, and also expressive of its conjoint activity whereby it is essentially the primary phase of a new occasion. It can thus be termed a 'real potentiality'. The 'potentiality' refers to the passive capacity, the term 'real' refers to the creative activity, where the Platonic definition of 'real' in the *Sophist* is referred to. This basic situation, this actual world, this primary phase, this real potentiality — however you characterize it — as a whole is active with its inherent crea-

tivity, but in its details it provides the passive objects which derive their activity from the creativity of the whole. The creativity is the actualization of potentiality, and the process of actualization is an occasion of experiencing. Thus viewed in abstraction objects are passive, but viewed in conjunction they carry the creativity which drives the world. The process of creation is the form of unity of the Universe.

§11. *Perception.* — In the preceding sections, the discovery of objects as factors in experience was explained. The discussion was phrased in terms of an ontology which goes beyond the immediate purpose, although the status of objects cannot be understood in the absence of some such ontology explaining their function in experience, that is to say, explaining why an occasion of experience by reason of its nature requires objects.

The objects are the factors in experience which function so as to express that that occasion originates by including a transcendent universe of other things. Thus it belongs to the essence of each occasion of experience that it is concerned with an otherness transcending itself. The occasion is one among others, and including the others which it is among. Consciousness is an emphasis upon a selection of these objects. Thus perception is consciousness analysed in respect to those objects selected for this emphasis. Consciousness is the acme of emphasis.

It is evident that this definition of perception is wider than the narrow definition based upon sense-perception, sensa, and the bodily sense-organs.

§12. *Non-Sensuous Perception.* — This wider definition of perception can be of no importance unless we can detect occasions of experience exhibiting modes of functioning which fall within its wider scope. If we discover such instances of non-sensuous perception, then the tacit identification of perception with sense-perception must be a fatal error barring the advance of systematic metaphysics.

Our first step must involve the clear recognition of the limitations inherent in the scope of sense-perception. This special mode of functioning essentially exhibits percepta as *here, now, immediate*, and *discrete.* Every impression of sensation is a distinct existence, declares Hume; and there can be no reasonable doubt of this doctrine. But even Hume clothes each impression with force and liveliness. It must be distinctly understood that no prehension, even of bare sensa, can be divested of its affective tone, that is to say, of its character of a 'concern' in the Quaker sense. Concernedness is of the essence of perception.

Gaze at a patch of red. In itself as an object, and apart from other factors of concern, this patch of red, as the mere object of that present act of perception, is silent as to the past or the future. How it originates, how it will vanish, whether indeed there was a past, and whether there will be a future, are not disclosed by its own nature. No material for the interpretation of sensa is provided by the sensa themselves, as they stand starkly, barely, present and immediate. We *do* interpret them; but no thanks for the feat is due to them. The epistemologies of the last two hundred years are employed in the tacit introduction of alien considerations by the uncritical use of current forms of speech. A copious use of simple literary forms can thus provide a philosophy delightful to read, easy to understand, and entirely fallacious. Yet the usages of language do prove that our habitual interpretations of these barren sensa are in the main satisfying to common sense, though in particular instances liable to error. But the evidence on which these interpretations are based is entirely drawn from the vast background and foreground of non-sensuous perception with which sense-perception is fused, and without which it can never be. We can discern no clean-cut sense-perception wholly concerned with present fact.

In human experience, the most compelling example of non-sensuous perception is our knowledge of our own immediate past. I am not referring to our memories of a day past, or of an hour past, or of a minute past. Such memories are blurred and confused by the intervening occasions of our personal existence. But our immediate past is constituted by that occasion, or by that group of fused occasions, which enters into experience devoid of any perceptible medium intervening between it and the present immediate fact. Roughly speaking, it is that portion of our past lying between a tenth of a second and half a second ago. It is gone, and yet it is here. It is our indubitable self, the foundation of our present existence. Yet the present occasion while claiming self-identity, while sharing the very nature of the byegone occasion in all its living activities, nevertheless is engaged in modifying it, in adjusting it to *other* influences, in completing it with *other* values, in deflecting it to *other* purposes. The present moment is constituted by the influx of *the other* into that self-identity which is the continued life of the immediate past within the immediacy of the present.

§13. *Illustration.* — Consider a reasonably rapid speaker enunciating the proper name 'United States'. There are four syllables here. When the third syllable is reached, probably the first is in the immediate past; and certainly during the word 'States' the first syllable of the phrase lies beyond the immediacy of the present. Consider the speaker's own occasions of existence. Each occasion achieves for him the immediate sense-presentation of sounds, the earlier syllables in the earlier occasions, the word 'States' in the final occasion. As mere sensuous perception, Hume is right in saying that the sound 'United' as a mere sensum has nothing in its nature referent to the sound 'States', yet the speaker is carried from 'United' to 'States', and the two conjointly live in the present, by the energizing of the past occasion as it claims its self-identical existence as a living issue in the present. The immediate past as surviving to be again lived through in the present is the palmary instance of non-sensuous perception.

The Humian explanation, involving the 'association of ideas', has its importance for this topic. But it is not to the point for this example. The speaker, a citizen of the United States and therefore dominated by an immense familiarity with that phrase, may in fact have been enunciating the phrase 'United Fruit Company' — a corporation which, for all its importance, he may not have heard of till half a minute earlier. In his experience the relation of the later to the earlier parts of this phrase is entirely the same as that described above for the phrase 'United States'. In this latter example it is to be noted that while association would have led him to 'States', the fact of the energizing of the immediate past compelled him to conjoin 'Fruit' in the immediacy of the present. He uttered the word 'United' with the non-sensuous anticipation of an immediate future with the sensum 'Fruit', and he then uttered the word 'Fruit' with the non-sensuous perception of the immediate past with the sensum 'United'. But, unfamiliar as he was with the United Fruit Company, he had no association connecting the various words in the phrase 'United Fruit Company'; while, patriot as he was, the orator had the strongest association connecting the words 'United' and 'States'. Perhaps, indeed, he was the founder of the Company, and also invented the name. He then uttered the mere sounds 'United Fruit Company' for the first time in the history of the English language. There could not have been the vestige of an association to help him along. The final occasion of his experience which drove his body to the utterance of the sound 'Company' is only explicable by his concern with the earlier occasions with their subjective forms of intention to procure the utterance of the complete phrase. Also, in so far as there was consciousness, there was direct observation of the past with its intention finding its completion in the present fact. This is an instance of direct intuitive observation which is incapable of reduction to the sensationalist formula. Such observations have not the clear sharp-cut precision of sense-perception. But surely there can be no doubt about them. For instance, if the speaker had been interrupted after the words 'United Fruit', he might have resumed his speech with the words 'I meant to add the word Company'. Thus during the interruption, the past was energizing in his experience as carrying in itself an unfulfilled intention.

§14. *Conformation of Feeling.* — Another point emerges in this explanation, namely, the doctrine of the continuity of nature. This doctrine balances and limits the doctrine of the absolute individuality of each occasion of experience. There is a continuity between the subjective form of the immediate past occasion and the subjective form of its primary prehension in the origination of the new occasion. In the process of synthesis of the many basic prehensions modifications enter. But the subjective forms of the immediate past are continuous with those of the present. I will term this doctrine of continuity, the Doctrine of Conformation of Feeling.

Suppose that for some period of time some circumstance of his life has aroused anger in a man. How does he now know that a quarter of a second ago he was angry? Of course, he remembers it; we all know that. But I am enquiring about this very curious fact of memory, and have chosen an overwhelmingly vivid instance. The mere word 'memory' explains nothing. The first phase in the immediacy of the new occasion is that of the conformation of feelings. The feeling as enjoyed by the past occasion is present in the new occasion as datum felt, with a subjective form conformal to that of the datum. Thus if A be the past occasion, D the datum felt by A with subjective form describable as A angry, then this feeling—namely, A feeling D with subjective form of anger—is initially felt by the new occasion B with the same subjective form of anger. The anger is continuous throughout the successive occasions of experience. This continuity of subjective form is the initial sympathy of B for A. It is the primary ground for the continuity of nature.

Let us elaborate the consideration of the angry man. His anger is the subjective form of his feeling some datum D. A quarter of a second later he is, consciously, or unconsciously, embodying his past as a datum in the present, and maintaining in the present the anger which is a datum from the past. In so far as that feeling has fallen within the illumination of consciousness, he enjoys a non-sensuous perception of the past emotion. He enjoys this emotion both objectively, as belonging to the past, and also formally as continued in the present. This continuation is the continuity of nature. I have labored this point, because traditional doctrines involve its denial.

Thus non-sensuous perception is one aspect of the continuity of nature. . . .

§17. *Mind and Nature Compared.* — The doctrine of human experience which I have outlined above, also for its own purposes preserves a doctrine of distinguishable individualities which are the separate occasions of experience, and a doctrine of continuity expressed by the identity of subjective form inherited conformally from one occasion to the other. The physical flux corresponds to the conformal inheritance at the base of each occasion of experience. This inheritance, in spite of its continuity of subjective form, is nevertheless an inheritance from definite individual occasions. Thus, if the analogy is to hold, in the account of the general system of relations binding the past to the present, we should expect a doctrine of quanta, where the individualities of the occasions are relevant, and a doctrine of continuity where the conformal transference of subjective form is the dominating fact.

The notion of physical energy, which is at the base of physics, must then be conceived as an abstraction from the complex energy, emotional and purposeful, inherent in the subjective form of the final synthesis in which each occasion completes itself. It is the total vigor of each activity of experience. The mere phrase that 'physical science is an abstraction', is a confession of philosophic failure. It is the business of rational thought to describe the more concrete fact from which that abstraction is derivable.

§18. *Personality.* — In our account of human experience we have attenuated human personality into a genetic relation between occasions of human experience. Yet personal unity is an inescapable fact. The Platonic and Christian doctrines of the Soul, the Epicurean doctrine of a Concilium of subtle atoms, the Cartesian doctrine of Thinking Substance, the Humanitarian doctrine of the Rights of Man, the general Common Sense of civilized mankind, —these doctrines between them dominate the whole span of Western thought. Evidently there is a fact to be accounted for. Any philosophy must provide some doctrine of personal identity. In some sense there is a unity in the life of each man, from birth to death. The two modern philosophers who most consistently reject the notion of a self-identical Soul-Substance are Hume and William James. But the problem remains for them, as it does for the philosophy of organism, to provide an adequate account of this undoubted personal unity, maintaining itself amidst the welter of circumstance. . . .

§20. *Immanence.* — This is at once the doctrine of the unity of nature, and of the unity of each human life. The conclusion follows that our consciousness of the self-identity pervading our life-thread of occasions, is nothing other than knowledge of a special strand of unity within the general unity of nature. It is a locus within the whole, marked out by its own peculiarities, but otherwise exhibiting the general principle which guides the constitution of the whole. This general principle is the object-to-subject structure of experience. It can be otherwise stated as the vector-structure of nature. Or otherwise, it can be conceived as the doctrine of the immanence of the past energizing in the present.

This doctrine of immanence is practically that doctrine adumbrated by the Hellenistic Christian theologians of Egypt. But they applied the doctrine only to the relation of God to the World, and not to all actualities. . . .

COMMENT

Whitehead's Philosophy of Organism

Certain philosophers are especially difficult to understand because in addition to dealing with profound issues and engaging in complex analysis, they invent their own vocabulary. Whitehead is one such philosopher. However, in the twentieth century, few thinkers have accomplished as much or become as influential as Whitehead, even though his writings are notoriously difficult to understand. Generally his theory of the nature of reality is termed *process philosophy*. Its chief characteristic is its insistence on the *interrelatedness* of all aspects of reality, from the most complex to the simplest. Whitehead saw the world as a vast, organic, weblike reality evolving through time and space by means of continuous connections, disconnections, and reconnections.

Whitehead begins by rejecting traditional approaches to metaphysics and epistemology, which assume that the world and our knowledge of it are based on and can be broken down into individual units known as subjects and objects. Adherents of such "atomism" are guilty of what he called "the fallacy of misplaced concreteness". For Whitehead the fundamental "units" of reality are actually "events", not "things". He termed these free-flowing interchanging happenings *occasions* or *actual entities*, and he saw them as the intersections of the world's continuously evolving energy.

When these events or interactions occur, they are drawn together or coalesce out of what Whitehead calls a mutual "concern"; a relevance arises in which that which functions as the subject and that serving as the object are conjoined. This relationship is always a *relative* one in the sense that the subject can serve as the object for yet another subject, or even for its own object at another time and place, or even simultaneously. The unity formed by this reciprocal interaction is termed by Whitehead a *prehension*. Thus the fundamental nature of reality is relational and processional. Actual entities really are events occurring within the flux of the ongoing process of energy constituting the totality of all that is.

Perhaps a simple, though necessarily limited, illustration will be of help at this juncture. Consider the philosophy class you are presently enrolled in. Rather than thinking of the students in it as the individual units that make it real, try thinking of the interrelatedness of the class itself as that which contributes to the reality of the individual students. This class, as an "actual entity," has come into being and serves to define the students as members of itself. Although each student did exist prior to the class, the class makes a definitive contribution to each individual's identity and character from this point on. Moreover, the whole of reality, consisting of the sum total of all current and previous relationships, not only existed prior to the students but also has functioned as the determining and constitutive factor in their becoming who they are. In short, we are all a function of the relationships in which we find ourselves.

This way of looking at reality is, admittedly, somewhat mind-bending because it asks us to reverse the usual way we think of things. We generally think of relationships as being the result of the individuals that constitute them rather than the other way around. It is a bit like altering our way of locating addresses, according to street names and numbers, to that of the Japanese, who locate places by naming and numbering intersections rather than streets. It takes some getting used to, but Whitehead insists that relational reality is more fundamental than individual reality, that the whole is more than and logically prior to the parts.

The so-called "knowledge" that arises within the prehension that comprises an "occasion" is said by Whitehead to be the result of the creative energy or process that drives the natural order. Both perceptual and non-sensuous knowledge are, for Whitehead, relational realities. In other words, there is no such thing as mere "objective" knowledge; all cognition is based on "concern", or our interactive awareness. This is the point of his example of our knowledge of our immediate past. Knowing is what defines the knower and the known, not vice versa.

Finally, there is, according to Whitehead's view, a basic continuity that runs through all of reality, a kind of networking that ties it all together and provides a sense of "closure" on both the metaphysical and personal levels. There is a dynamic process or energy that animates all reality, from rocks to minds, and that provides a general organic unity to the whole. Individual or personal identity is only "a strand of unity within the general unity of nature." Each occasion is knitted to the next, and together they form what Whitehead calls a nexus. Should a nexus take on increased relevance and prehension, thereby achieving a measurable place in time and space, such as is the case with individual persons, it can be said to exist as a "society."

There are, to be sure, those philosophers who find all this talk of organisms, occasions, and process quite confusing and even misleading. It is one thing, they might say, to invent a fancy vocabulary, quite another to establish its application to reality. There seems to be a stubborn "rightness" about our way of talking about things and qualities as the fundamental building blocks of reality. Moreover, Whitehead's philosophy of relationality does not actually explain how truth can be distinguished from error, even and especially in reference to this own theories. Nonetheless, Whitehead's approach does have the advantage of seeming to be in harmony with the Einsteinian relativity and quantum physics of the twentieth century. At the very least it must be admitted that it is a highly creative and influential approach to metaphysics.

THE BASIS
OF MORALITY

There are few words more common in the English language than *good*, *better*, *worse*, *right*, *wrong*, and *ought*. We use these words, or their synonyms, every day: "What a good piece of pie!"; "You had better see that movie"; "You ought to obey that traffic signal!"; "That is the wrong way to study for exams"; and so on. Each of these utterances expresses a judgment, favorable or unfavorable. Although there are factual implications in each instance, the primary intention is to *evaluate* something rather than merely to state a fact. Purely descriptive sentences, such as "That man is six feet tall," stand in obvious contrast.

Corresponding to these two types of sentences, the evaluative and the descriptive, are two distinct fields of philosophy: *axiology*, or the theory of values, and *metaphysics*, or the theory of reality. In Part Two we have been concerned with metaphysics; in Part Three we shall turn to axiology. In its total scope, axiology is the theory of all types of value — not only the moral good or right, but the holy, the beautiful, the useful, or anything else that is prizeworthy. However, we shall confine ourselves to moral values, which are the subject matter of ethics.

The function of ethics is not to tell you what human beings do but to tell you what they *ought*, in a moral sense, to do. Its fundamental concepts are *good* and *bad* and *right* and *wrong*. How can we tell a good life from a bad one? How can we distinguish between right and wrong acts? These are the questions that ethics seeks to answer. Although such words as *good* and *right* can be used in a nonmoral sense, we shall be concerned with their moral usage.

The readers of this book have already been introduced to ethics in Part One. Socrates, in the *Apology*, was criticizing the ethics of custom and expediency and defending the ideal of wisdom. In Part Four, we shall again meet Socrates, this time as a character in Plato's *Republic.* In this dialogue, Socrates maintains that goodness is the harmonious development of all parts of the personality under the control of reason. Similarly, he defines the good of the state as the harmonious development of all classes under the control of wise men. Some readers of this book will prefer to consider the selections from the *Republic* in connection with the ethical problems of Part Three rather than the social problems of Part Four.

In an introductory book, it is impossible to survey the many types of ethics. We have confined our discussion to the following:

1. *Aristotle's theory of rational development.* The good is the active exercise of those faculties distinctive of human beings, especially reason.

2. *Epicurus' theory of harmonious pleasure.* Pleasure is defined as the absence of pain, especially the pain caused by the fear of death. Epicurus advocated withdrawal from the chaos of worldly concerns to the peaceful environment of contemplation.

3. *Theory of natural law.* The good is the life according to nature — both the nature of humans and the nature of their environment.

4. *Kant's theory of duty for duty's sake.* The only unqualified good is good will, which is based on respect for duty. Our duty is to obey universal moral laws, regardless of the particular consequences.

5. *Mill's theory of happiness.* The good life excels in both quantity and quality of pleasure. Right acts are the most useful in achieving this goal.

6. *Nietzsche's theory of will to power.* Human well-being is defined in terms of maximizing the potential for volitional growth. Moral worth is determined by an individual's integrity as opposed to conformity to cultural conventions.

7. *Dewey's theory of moral experiment.* The good life is experimental and has no final end or goal except growth.

13

The Way of Reason

"We shall conclude that the life of the intellect is best and pleasantest for man, because the intellect more than anything else is man. Thus it will be the happiest life as well."

Aristotle

ARISTOTLE (384 B.C. – 322 B.C.)

Aristotle was born in Stagira, a town in Macedonia colonized by Greeks. At the time of his birth, Socrates had been dead for fifteen years and Plato was thirty-three. Aristotle's father, Nichomachus, having achieved some renown, became court physician to King Amyntas II of Macedonia. Refusing to follow his father's profession, Aristotle at the age of eighteen migrated to Athens, where he lived for twenty years as a member of Plato's school, the Academy. When the master died, Aristotle left Athens to spend four years on the coast of Asia Minor, engaged mainly in biological research. During this period he married, and his wife eventually bore him a daughter. Subsequently he married a second time and had two sons, one of them adopted.

Meanwhile Philip, the son of Amyntas, having become king of Macedonia, invited Aristotle to take charge of the education of his son Alexander, then thirteen years old. In consequence of accepting this invitation, Aristotle must have acquired intimate knowledge of court affairs, but he makes no mention of the great Macedonian empire built up by Philip and Alexander the Great. Perhaps he was too close to kings to be greatly impressed by courtly glitter.

He stayed with Philip for seven years, until the monarch's death, and lingered at the court for about a year after Alexander's accession to the throne. Then he returned to Athens to resume his philosophical career. At this time the Academy was being reorganized, and Xenocrates, a second-rate philosopher, was made head. Evidently disappointed at the choice, Aristotle withdrew and founded a school of his own, the Lyceum, which he directed for twelve years. It was during this period that he was his most productive.

Aristotle's reputation and the prosperity of his school suffered from the anti-Macedonian reaction that occurred after Alexander's death in 323 B.C. Accused of impiety, Aristotle, unlike Socrates, fled to the island of Euboea, vowing that he would not "give the Athenians a second chance of sinning against philosophy." A year later, in 322 B.C., he died of a stomach disease, at the age of sixty-three.

His writings, as they have come down to us, lack the beauty of Plato's dialogues and are without wit, personal charm, or poetry. He also wrote popular works, including dialogues, which were praised by Cicero for "the incredible flow and sweetness of their diction"; but like many other ancient compositions, these dialogues have been lost. The works that remain touch on almost every phase of human knowledge, and they establish Aristotle's reputation not only as an extremely versatile philosopher but also as an accomplished biologist.

Happiness and Virtue

1 [The Nature of Happiness]

[*Aristotle begins, in a way characteristic of his method, with a generalization which, if accepted, will lead to a more exact account of his subject. It is a generalization which is fundamental to his philosophy and in his own mind there is no doubt about the truth of it. Yet he is not at this point asserting its truth.*

The Ethics of Aristotle, trans. J. A. K. Thomson, George Allen and Unwin, London, and Barnes and Noble, New York, 1953. Reprinted by permission. The sentences in italics are explanatory comments by the translator except where initialed *M.R.*

He is content to state a position which he has found reason to hold. It may be defined in some such words as these: The good is that at which all things aim. If we are to understand this, we must form to ourselves a clear notion of what is meant by an aim or, in more technical language, an "end." The first chapter of the Ethics *is concerned with making the notion clear.*]

It is thought that every activity, artistic or scientific, in fact every deliberate action or pursuit, has for its object the attainment of some good. We may therefore assent to the view which has been expressed that "the good" is "that at which all things aim." . . . Since modes of action involving the practiced hand and the instructed brain are numerous, the number of their ends is proportionately large. For instance, the end of medical science is health; of military science, victory; of economic science, wealth. All skills of that kind which come under a single "faculty"—a skill in making bridles or any other part of a horse's gear comes under the faculty or art of horsemanship, while horsemanship itself and every branch of military practice comes under the art of war, and in like manner other arts and techniques are subordinate to yet others—in all these the ends of the master arts are to be preferred to those of the subordinate skills, for it is the former that provide the motive for pursuing the latter. . . .

Now if there is an end which as moral agents we seek for its own sake, and which is the cause of our seeking all the other ends—if we are not to go on choosing one act for the sake of another, thus landing ourselves in an infinite progression with the result that desire will be frustrated and ineffectual—it is clear that this must be the good, that is the absolutely good. May we not then argue from this that a knowledge of the good is a great advantage to us in the conduct of our lives? Are we not more likely to hit the mark if we have a target? If this be true, we must do our best to get at least a rough idea of what the good really is, and which of the sciences, pure or applied, is concerned with the business of achieving it.

[*Ethics is a branch of politics. That is to say, it is the duty of the statesman to create for the citizen the best possible opportunity of living the good life. It will be seen that the effect of this injunction is not to degrade morality but to moralize politics. The modern view that "you cannot make men better by act of parliament" would have been repudiated by Aristotle as certainly as by Plato and indeed by ancient philosophers in general.*]

Now most people would regard the good as the end pursued by that study which has most authority and control over the rest. Need I say that this is the science of politics? Is it political science that prescribes what subjects are to be taught in states, which of these the different sections of the population are to learn, and up to what point. We see also that the faculties which obtain most regard come under this science: for example, the art of war, the management of property, the ability to state a case. Since, therefore, politics makes use of the other practical sciences, and lays it down besides what we must do and what we must not do, its end must include theirs. And that end, in politics as well as in ethics, can only be the good for man. For even if the good of the community coincides with that of the individual, the good of the community is clearly a greater and more perfect good both to get and to keep. This is not to deny that the good of the individual is worth while. But what is good for a nation or a city has a higher, a diviner, quality.

Such being the matters we seek to investigate, the investigation may fairly be represented as the study of politics. . . .

[. . . *Let us consider what is the end*

*of political science. For want of a better
word we call it "Happiness." People are
agreed on the word but not on its
meaning.]*

. . . Since every activity involving
some acquired skill or some moral decision aims at some good, what do we
take to be the end of politics — what is
the supreme good attainable in our actions? Well, so far as the name goes
there is pretty general agreement. "It is
happiness," say both intellectuals and
the unsophisticated, meaning by "happiness" living well or faring well. But
when it comes to saying in what happiness consists, opinions differ and the
account given by the generality of mankind is not at all like that given by the
philosophers. The masses take it to be
something plain and tangible, like pleasure or money or social standing. Some
maintain that it is one of these, some
that it is another, and the same man
will change his opinion about it more
than once. When he has caught an illness he will say that it is health, and
when he is hard up he will say that it is
money. Conscious that they are out of
their depths in such discussions, most
people are impressed by anyone who
pontificates and says something that is
over their heads. Now it would no
doubt be a waste of time to examine all
these opinions; enough if we consider
those which are most in evidence or
have something to be said for them.
Among these we shall have to discuss
the view held by some that, over and
above particular goods like those I have
just mentioned, there is another which
is good in itself and the cause of whatever goodness there is in all these
others. . . .

*[A man's way of life may afford a
clue to his genuine views upon the nature of happiness. It is therefore worth
our while to glance at the different
types of life.]*

. . . There is a general assumption
that the manner of a man's life is a clue
to what he on reflection regards as the
good — in other words happiness. Persons of low tastes (always in the majority) hold that it is pleasure. Accordingly
they ask for nothing better than the
sort of life which consists in having a
good time. (I have in mind the three
well-known types of life — that just
mentioned, that of the man of affairs,
that of the philosophic student.) The
utter vulgarity of the herd of men
comes out in their preference for the
sort of existence a cow leads. Their
view would hardly get a respectful
hearing, were it not that those who occupy great positions sympathize with a
monster of sensuality like Sardana-
palus. The gentleman, however, and
the man of affairs identify the good
with honor, which may fairly be described as the end which men pursue in
political or public life. Yet honor is
surely too superficial a thing to be the
good we are seeking. Honor depends
more on those who confer than on him
who receives it, and we cannot but feel
that the good is something personal and
almost inseparable from its possessor.
Again, why do men seek honor? Surely
in order to confirm the favorable opinion they have formed of themselves. It
is at all events by intelligent men who
know them personally that they seek to
be honored. And for what? For their
moral qualities. The inference is clear;
public men prefer virtue to honor. It

might therefore seem reasonable to suppose that virtue rather than honor is the end pursued in the life of the public servant. But clearly even virtue cannot be quite the end. It is possible, most people think, to possess virtue while you are asleep, to possess it without acting under its influence during any portion of one's life. Besides, the virtuous man may meet with the most atrocious luck or ill-treatment; and nobody, who was not arguing for argument's sake, would maintain that a man with an existence of that sort was "happy." . . . The third type of life is the "contemplative," and this we shall discuss later.

As for the life of the business man, it does not give him much freedom of action. Besides, wealth obviously is not the good we seek, for the sole purpose it serves is to provide the means of getting something else. So far as that goes, the ends we have already mentioned would have a better title to be considered the good, for they are desired on their own account. But in fact even their claim must be disallowed. We may say that they have furnished the ground for many arguments, and leave the matter at that. . . .

[*What then is the good? If it is what all men in the last resort aim at, it must be happiness. And that for two reasons: (1) happiness is everything it needs to be, (2) it has everything it needs to have.*]

. . . [The good] is one thing in medicine and another in strategy, and so in the other branches of human skill. We must inquire, then, what is the good which is the end common to all of them. Shall we say it is that for the sake of which everything else is done? In medicine this is health, in military science victory, in architecture a building, and so on — different ends in different arts; every consciously directed activity has an end for the sake of which everything that it does is done. This end may be described as its good. Consequently, if there be some one thing which is the end of all things consciously done, this will be the double good; or, if there be more than one end, then it will be all of these. . . .

In our actions we aim at more ends than one — that seems to be certain — but, since we choose some (wealth, for example, or flutes and tools or instruments generally) as means to something else, it is clear that not all of them are ends in the full sense of the word, whereas the good, that is the supreme good, is surely such an end. Assuming then that there is some one thing which alone is an end beyond which there are no further ends, we may call *that* the good of which we are in search. If there be more than one such final end, the good will be that end which has the highest degree of finality. An object pursued for its own sake possesses a higher degree of finality than one pursued with an eye to something else. A corollary to that is that a thing which is never chosen as a means to some remoter object has a higher degree of finality than things which are chosen both as ends in themselves and as means to such ends. We may conclude, then, that something which is always chosen for its own sake and never for the sake of something else is without qualification a final end.

Now happiness more than anything

else appears to be just such an end, for we always choose it for its own sake and never for the sake of some other thing. It is different with honor, pleasure, intelligence and good qualities generally. We choose them indeed for their own sake in the sense that we should be glad to have them irrespective of any advantage which might accrue from them. But we also choose them for the sake of our happiness in the belief that they will be instrumental in promoting that. On the other hand nobody chooses happiness as a means of achieving them or anything else whatsoever than just happiness.

The same conclusion would seem to follow from another consideration. It is a generally accepted view that the final good is self-sufficient. By "self-sufficient" is meant not what is sufficient for oneself living the life of a solitary but includes parents, wife and children, friends and fellow-citizens in general. For man is a social animal. . . . A self-sufficient thing, then, we take to be one which on its own footing tends to make life desirable and lacking in nothing. And we regard happiness as such a thing. . . .

[*But we desire a clearer definition of happiness. The way to this may be prepared by a discussion of what is meant by the "function" of a man.*]

But no doubt people will say, "To call happiness the highest good is a truism. We want a more distinct account of what it is." We might arrive at this if we could grasp what is meant by the "function" of a human being. If we take a flutist or a sculptor or any craftsman—in fact any class of men at all who have some special job or profession—we find that his special talent and excellence comes out in that job, and this is his function. The same thing will be true of man simply as man—that is of course if "man" does have a function. But is it likely that joiners and shoemakers have certain functions or specialized activities, while man as such has none but has been left by Nature a functionless being? Seeing that eye and hand and foot and every one of our members has some obvious function, must we not believe that in like manner a human being has a function over and above these particular functions? Then what exactly is it? The mere act of living is not peculiar to man—we find it even in the vegetable kingdom—and what we are looking for is something peculiar to him. We must therefore exclude from our definition the life that manifests itself in mere nurture and growth. A step higher should come the life that is confined to experiencing sensations. But that we see is shared by horses, cows and the brute creation as a whole. We are left, then, with a life concerning which we can make two statements. First, it belongs to the rational part of man. Secondly, it finds expression in actions. The rational part may be either active or passive: passive in so far as it follows the dictates of reasoning. A similar distinction can be drawn within the rational life; that is to say, the reasonable element in it may be active or passive. Let us take it that what we are concerned with here is the reasoning power in action, for it will be generally allowed that when we speak of "reasoning" we really mean *exercising* our reasoning faculties. (This seems the more correct use of the word.)

Now let us assume for the moment the truth of the following propositions. (*a*) The function of a man is the exercise of his non-corporeal faculties or "soul" in accordance with, or at least not divorced from, a rational principle. (*b*) The function of an individual and of a *good* individual in the same class —a harp player, for example, and a good harp player, and so through the classes — is generically the same, except that we must add superiority in accomplishment to the function, the function of the harp player being merely to play on the harp, while the function of the good harp player is to play on it well. (*c*) The function of man is a certain form of life, namely an activity of the soul exercised in combination with a rational principle or reasonable ground of action. (*d*) The function of a good man is to exert such activity well. (*e*) A function is performed well when performed in accordance with the excellence proper to it. — If these assumptions are granted, we conclude that the good for man is "an activity of soul in accordance with goodness" or (on the supposition that there may be more than one form of goodness) "in accordance with the best and most complete form of goodness."

[*Happiness is more than momentary bliss.*]

There is another condition of happiness; it cannot be achieved in less than a complete lifetime. One swallow does not make a summer; neither does one fine day. And one day, or indeed any brief period of felicity, does not make a man entirely and perfectly happy. . . .

[. . . *Our first principle — our definition of happiness — should be tested not only by the rules of logic but also by the application to it of current opinions on the subject.*]

So we must examine our first principle not only logically, that is as a conclusion from premises, but also in the light of what is currently said about it. For if a thing be true, the evidence will be found in harmony with it; and, if it be false, the evidence is quickly shown to be discordant with it.

But first a note about "goods." They have been classified as (*a*) external, (*b*) of the soul, (*c*) of the body. Of these we may express our belief that goods of the soul are the best and are most properly designated as "good." Now according to our definition happiness is an expression of the soul in considered actions, and that definition seems to be confirmed by this belief, which is not only an old popular notion but is accepted by philosophers. We are justified, too, in saying that the end consists in certain acts or activities, for this enables us to count it among goods of the soul and not among external goods. We may also claim that our description of the happy man as the man who lives or fares well chimes in with our definition. For happiness has pretty much been stated to be a form of such living or faring well. Again, our definition seems to include the elements detected in the various analyses of happiness — virtue, practical wisdom, speculative wisdom, or a combination of these, or one of them in more or less intimate association with pleasure. All these definitions have their supporters, while still others are for adding material prosperity to the conditions of a happy life. Some of these views are popular convictions of long standing; others are set forth by a distinguished minority. It is reasonable to think that neither the mass of men nor the sages are mistaken altogether, but that on this point or that, or indeed on most points, there is justice in what they say.

Now our definition of happiness as an activity in accordance with virtue is so far in agreement with that of those who say that it *is* virtue, that such an activity *involves* virtue. But of course it makes a great difference whether we think of the highest good as consisting in the *possession* or in the *exercise* of virtue. It is possible for a disposition to goodness to exist in a man without anything coming of it; he might be asleep or in some other way have ceased to exercise his function of a man. But that is not possible with the activity in our definition. For in "doing well" the happy man will of necessity *do.* Just as at the Olympic Games it is not the best-looking or the strongest men present who are crowned with victory but competitors — the successful competitors, so in the arena of human life the honors and rewards fall to those who show their good qualities in action.

Observe, moreover, that the life of the actively good is inherently pleasant. Pleasure is a psychological experience, and every man finds that pleasant for which he has a liking — "fond of" so and so is the expression people use. For example, a horse is a source of pleasure to a man who is fond of horses, a show

to a man who is fond of sight-seeing. In the same way just actions are a source of pleasure to a man who likes to see justice done, and good actions in general to one who likes goodness. Now the mass of men do not follow any consistent plan in the pursuit of their pleasures, because their pleasures are not inherently pleasurable. But men of more elevated tastes and sentiments find pleasure in things which are in their own nature pleasant, for instance virtuous actions, which are pleasant in themselves and not merely to such men. So their life does not need to have pleasure fastened about it like a necklace, but possesses it as a part of itself. We may go further and assert that he is no good man who does not find pleasure in noble deeds. Nobody would admit that a man is just, unless he takes pleasure in just actions; or liberal, unless he takes pleasure in acts of liberality; and so with the other virtues. Grant this, and you must grant that virtuous actions are a source of pleasure in themselves. And surely they are also both good and noble, and that always in the highest degree, if we are to accept, as accept we must, the judgment of the good man about them, he judging in the way I have described. Thus, happiness is the best, the noblest, the most delightful thing in the world, and in it meet all those qualities which are separately enumerated in the inscription upon the temple at Delos:

Justice is loveliest, and health is
*   best,*
And sweetest to obtain is heart's
*   desire.*

All these good qualities inhere in the

activities of the virtuous soul, and it is these, or the best of them, which we say constitute happiness.

For all that those are clearly right who, as I remarked, maintain the necessity to a happy life of an addition in the form of material goods. It is difficult, if not impossible, to engage in noble enterprises without money to spend on them; many can only be performed through friends, or wealth, or political influence. There are also certain advantages, such as the possession of honored ancestors or children, or personal beauty, the absence of which takes the bloom from our felicity. For you cannot quite regard a man as happy if he be very ugly to look at, or of humble origin, or alone in the world and childless, or — what is probably worse — with children or friends who have not a single good quality. . . .

[*Our definition of happiness compels us to consider the nature of virtue. But before we can do this we must have some conception of how the human soul is constituted. It will serve our purpose to take over (for what it is worth) the current psychology which divides the soul into "parts."*]

Happiness, then, being an activity of the soul in conformity with perfect goodness, it follows that we must examine the nature of goodness. . . . The goodness we have to consider is human goodness. This — I mean human goodness or (if you prefer to put it that way) human happiness — was what we set out to find. By human goodness is meant not fineness of physique but a right condition of the soul, and by happiness a condition of the soul. That being so, it is evident that the states-

man ought to have some inkling of psychology, just as the doctor who is to specialize in diseases of the eye must have a general knowledge of physiology. Indeed, such a general background is even more necessary for the statesman in view of the fact that his science is of a higher order than the doctor's. Now the best kind of doctor takes a good deal of trouble to acquire a knowledge of the human body as a whole. Therefore the statesman should also be a psychologist and study the soul with an eye to his profession. Yet he will do so only as far as his own problems make it necessary; to go into greater detail on the subject would hardly be worth the labor spent on it.

Psychology has been studied elsewhere and some of the doctrines stated there may be accepted as adequate for our present purpose and used by us here. The soul is represented as consisting of two parts, a rational and an irrational. . . . As regards the irrational part there is one subdivision of it which appears to be common to all living things, and this we may designate as having a "vegetative" nature, by which I mean that it is the cause of nutrition and growth, since one must assume the existence of some vital force in all things that assimilate food. . . . Now the excellence peculiar to this power is evidently common to the whole of animated nature and not confined to man. This view is supported by the admitted fact that the vegetative part of us is particularly active in sleep, when the good and the bad are hardest to distinguish. . . . Such a phenomenon would be only natural, for sleep is a cessation of that function on the operation of which depends the goodness or badness of the soul. . . . But enough of this, let us say no more about the nutritive part of the soul, since it forms no portion of goodness in the specifically *human* character.

But there would seem to be another constituent of the soul which, while irrational, contains an element of rationality. It may be observed in the types of men we call "continent" and "incontinent." They have a principle—a rational element in their souls—which we commend, because it encourages them to perform the best actions in the right way. But such natures appear at the same time to contain an irrational element in active opposition to the rational. In paralytic cases it often happens that when the patient wills to move his limbs to the right they swing instead to the left. Exactly the same thing may happen to the soul; the impulses of the incontinent man carry him in the opposite direction from that towards which he was aiming. The only difference is that, where the body is concerned, we see the uncontrolled limb, while the erratic impulse we do not see. Yet this should not prevent us from believing that besides the rational an irrational principle exists running opposite and counter to the other. . . . Yet, as I said, it is not altogether irrational; at all events it submits to direction in the continent man, and may be assumed to be still more amenable to reason in the "temperate" and in the brave man, in whose moral make-up there is nothing which is at variance with reason.

We have, then, this clear result. The irrational part of the soul, like the soul itself, consists of two parts. The first of these is the vegetative, which has nothing rational about it at all. The second is that from which spring the appetites and desire in general; and this does in a way participate in reason, seeing that it is submissive and obedient to it. . . . That the irrational element in us need not be heedless of the rational is proved by the fact that we find admonition, indeed every form of censure and exhortation, not ineffective. It may be, however, that we ought to speak of the appetitive part of the soul as rational, too. In that event it will rather be the rational part that is divided in two, one division rational in the proper sense of the word and in its nature, the other in the derivative sense in which we speak of a child as "listening to reason" in the person of its father.

These distinctions within the soul supply us with a classification of the virtues. Some are called "intellectual," as wisdom, intelligence, prudence. Others are "moral," as liberality and temperance. When we are speaking of a man's *character* we do not describe him as wise or intelligent but as gentle or temperate. Yet we praise a wise man, too, on the ground of his "disposition" or settled habit of acting wisely. The dispositions so praised are what we mean by "virtues."

2. [Moral Goodness]

[. . . *We have to ask what moral virtue or goodness is. It is a confirmed disposition to act rightly, the disposition being itself formed by a continuous series of right actions.*]

Virtue, then, is of two kinds, intel-

lectual and moral. Of these the intellectual is in the main indebted to teaching
for its production and growth, and this
calls for time and experience. Moral
goodness, on the other hand, is the
child of habit, from which it has got its
very name, ethics being derived from
ethos, "habit." . . . This is an indication that none of the moral virtues is
implanted in us by nature, since nothing that nature creates can be taught by
habit to change the direction of its development. For instance a stone, the
natural tendency of which is to fall
down, could never, however often you
threw it up in the air, be trained to go in
that direction. No more can you train
fire to burn downwards. Nothing in
fact, if the law of its being is to behave
in one way, can be habituated to behave
in another. The moral virtues, then, are
produced in us neither *by* Nature nor
against Nature. Nature, indeed, prepares in us the ground for their reception, but their complete formation is
the product of habit.

Consider again these powers or faculties with which Nature endows us.
We acquire the ability to use them before we do use them. The senses provide us with a good illustration of this
truth. We have not acquired the sense
of sight from repeated acts of seeing, or
the sense of hearing from repeated acts
of hearing. It is the other way round.
We had these senses before we used
them, we did not acquire them as a result of using them. But the moral virtues we do acquire by first exercising
them. The same is true of the arts and
crafts in general. The craftsman has to
learn how to make things, but he learns
in the process of making them. So men

become builders by building, harp
players by playing the harp. By a similar
process we become just by performing
just actions, temperate by performing
temperate actions, brave by performing brave actions. Look at what happens in political societies — it confirms
our view. We find legislators seeking to
make good men of their fellows by
making good behavior habitual with
them. . . .

We may sum it all up in the generalization, "Like activities produce like
dispositions." This makes it our duty
to see that our activities have the right
character, since the differences of quality in them are repeated in the dispositions that follow in their train. So it is a
matter of real importance whether our
early education confirms us in one set
of habits or another. It would be nearer
the truth to say that it makes a very
great difference indeed, in fact all the
difference in the world. . . .

[*There is one way of discovering
whether we are in full possession of a
virtue or not. We possess it if we feel
pleasure in its exercise; indeed, it is
just with pleasures and pains that virtue is concerned.*]

We may use the pleasure (or pain)
that accompanies the exercise of our
dispositions as an index of how far they
have established themselves. A man is
temperate who abstaining from bodily
pleasures finds this abstinence pleasant; if he finds it irksome, he is intemperate. Again, it is the man who encounters danger gladly, or at least
without painful sensations, who is
brave; the man who has these sensations is a coward. In a word, moral virtue has to do with pains and pleasures.

There are a number of reasons for believing this. (1) Pleasure has a way of making us do what is disgraceful; pain deters us from doing what is right and fine. Hence the importance—I quote Plato—of having been brought up to find pleasure and pain in the right things. True education is just such a training. (2) The virtues operate with actions and emotions, each of which is accompanied by pleasure or pain. This is only another way of saying that virtue has to do with pleasures and pains. (3) Pain is used as an instrument of punishment. For in her remedies Nature works by opposites, and pain can be remedial. (4) When any disposition finds its complete expression it is, as we noted, in dealing with just those things by which it is its nature to be made better or worse, and which constitute the sphere of its operations. Now when men become bad it is under the influence of pleasures and pains when they seek the wrong ones among them, or seek them at the wrong time, or in the wrong manner, or in any of the wrong forms which such offenses may take; and in seeking the wrong pleasures and pains they shun the right. . . .

So far, then, we have got this result. Moral goodness is a quality disposing us to act in the best way when we are dealing with pleasures and pains, while vice is one which leads us to act in the worst way when we deal with them. . . .

[We have now to state the "differentia" of virtue. Virtue is a disposition; but how are we to distinguish it from other dispositions? We may say that it is such a disposition as enables the good man to perform his function well. And he performs it well when he avoids the extremes and chooses the mean in actions and feelings.]

. . . Excellence of whatever kind affects that of which it is the excellence in two ways. (1) It produces a good state in it. (2) It enables it to perform its function well. Take eyesight. The goodness of your eye is not only that which makes your eye good, it is also that which makes it function well. Or take the case of a horse. The goodness of a horse makes him a good horse, but it also makes him good at running, carrying a rider and facing the enemy. Our proposition, then, seems to be true, and it enables us to say that virtue in a man will be the disposition which (a) makes him a good man, (b) enables him to perform his function well. . . .

Every form . . . of applied knowledge, when it performs its function well, looks to the mean and works to the standard set by that. It is because people feel this that they apply the cliché, "You couldn't add anything to it or take anything from it" to an artistic masterpiece, the implication being that too much and too little alike destroy perfection, while the mean preserves it. Now if this be so, and if it be true, as we say, that good craftsmen work to the standard of the mean, then, since goodness like nature is more exact and of a higher character than any art, it follows that goodness is the quality that hits the mean. By "goodness" I mean goodness of moral character, since it is moral goodness that deals with feelings and actions, and it is in them that we find excess, deficiency and a mean. It is possible, for example, to experience fear, boldness, desire, anger, pity, and pleasures and pains generally, too much or too little or to the right amount. If we feel them too much or too little, we are wrong. But to have these feelings at the right times on the right occasions towards the right people for the right motive and in the right way is to have them in the right measure, that is somewhere between the extremes; and this is what characterizes goodness. The same may be said of the mean and extremes in actions. Now it is in the field of actions and feelings that goodness operates; in them we find excess, deficiency and, between them, the mean, the first two being wrong, the mean right and praised as such. . . . Goodness, then, is a mean condition in the sense that it aims at and hits the mean. Consider, too, that it is possible to go wrong in more ways than one. (In Pythagorean terminology evil is a form of the Unlimited, good of the Limited.) But there is only one way of being right. That is why going wrong is easy, and going right difficult; it is easy to miss the bull's eye and difficult to hit it. Here, then, is another explanation of why the too much and the too little are connected with evil and the mean with good. As the poet says,

Goodness is one, evil is multiform.

[*We are now in a position to state our definition of virtue with more precision. Observe that the kind of virtue meant here is moral, not intellectual, and that Aristotle must not be taken as saying that the kind of virtue which he regards as the highest and truest is any sort of mean.*]

We may now define virtue as a disposition of the soul in which, when it has to choose among actions and feelings, it observes the mean relative to us, this being determined by such a rule or principle as would take shape in the mind of a man of sense or practical wisdom. We call it a mean condition as lying between two forms of badness, one being excess and the other deficiency; and also for this reason, that, whereas badness either falls short of or exceeds the right measure in feelings and actions, virtue discovers the mean and deliberately chooses it. Thus, looked at from the point of view of its essence as embodied in its definition, virtue no doubt is a mean; judged by the standard of what is right and best, it is an extreme.

[*Aristotle enters a caution. Though we have said that virtue observes the mean in actions and passions, we do not say this of all acts and all feelings. Some are essentially evil and, when these are involved, our rule of applying the mean cannot be brought into operation.*]

But choice of a mean is not possible in every action or every feeling. The very names of some have an immediate connotation of evil. Such are malice, shamelessness, envy among feelings, and among actions adultery, theft, murder. All these and more like them have a bad name as being evil in themselves; it is not merely the excess or deficiency of them that we censure. In their case, then, it is impossible to act rightly; whatever we do is wrong. . . .

[*Aristotle now suggests some rules for our guidance.*]

. . . We shall find it useful when

aiming at the mean to observe these rules. (1) *Keep away from that extreme which is the more opposed to the mean.* It is Calpyso's advice:

> *Swing round the ship; clear of this surf and surge.*

For one of the extremes is always a more dangerous error than the other; and — since it is hard to hit the bull's-eye — we must take the next best course and choose the least of the evils. And it will be easiest for us to do this if we follow the rule I have suggested. (2) *Note the errors into which we personally are most liable to fall.* (Each of us has his natural bias in one direction or another.) We shall find out what ours are by noting what gives us pleasure and pain. After that we must drag ourselves in the opposite direction. For our best way of reaching the middle is by giving a wide berth to our darling sin. It is the method used by a carpenter when he is straightening a warped board. (3) *Always be particularly on your guard against pleasure and pleasant things.* When Pleasure is at the bar the jury is not impartial. So it will be best for us if we feel towards her as the Trojan elders felt towards Helen, and regularly apply their words to her. If we are for packing her off, as they were with Helen, we shall be the less likely to go wrong.

3. [Particular Virtues]

[*Aristotle now embarks upon a long analysis of the virtues and vices. These do not include the characteristically Christian virtues of piety, chastity and humility, which are not regarded by him as independent virtues at all. Yet however he may classify and name the moral feelings and habits which form the material for his analysis, that material is substantially the same for him as for us. The picture of the good man which emerges is perfectly recognizable and even familiar to us.*]

Let us begin with courage.

We have seen that it is a disposition which aims at the mean in situations inspiring fear and confidence. What we fear are of course things of a nature to inspire fear. Now these are, speaking generally, evil things, so that we get the definition of fear as 'an anticipation of evil.' Well, we do fear all evil things — ill-repute, poverty, sickness, friendlessness, death and so on — but in the opinion of most people courage is to be distinguished from the simple fear of all these. There are some evils which it is proper and honourable to fear and discreditable not to fear — disgrace, for example. The man who fears disgrace has a sense of what is due to himself as a man of character and to other people; the man who does not fear it has a forehead of brass. Such a man indeed is occasionally styled a brave fellow, but only by a transference of epithet made possible by the fact that there is one point of similarity between him and the truly brave man, namely their freedom from timidity. Then one ought not, of course, to fear poverty or illness or, indeed, anything at all that is not a consequence of vice or of one's own misconduct; still we do not call a man who is fearless in facing these things 'brave' except once more by analogy. For we find individuals who are cowardly on the field of battle and yet spend money lavishly and meet the loss of it with equanimity. And surely a man is not to be dubbed a coward because he dreads brutality to his wife and children, or the effects of envy towards himself, or anything of that nature. Nor is a man described as brave if he does not turn a hair at the prospect of a whipping.

What, then, are the objects of fear confronting which the brave man comes out in his true colours? Surely one would say the greatest, for it is just in facing fearful issues that the brave man excels. Now the most fearful thing is death; for death is an end, and to the dead man nothing seems good or evil any more for ever. Yet even death may be attended by circumstances which make it seem inappropriate to describe the man confronted by it as 'brave.' For instance, he might be drowned at sea or pass away in his bed. In what dangers, then, is courage most clearly displayed? Shall we not say, in the noblest? Well, the noblest death is the soldier's, for he meets it in the midst of the greatest and most glorious dangers. This is recognized in the honours conferred on the fallen by republics and monarchs alike. So in the strict meaning of the word the brave man will be one who fearlessly meets an honourable death or some instant threat to life; and it is war which presents most opportunities of that sort. Not but what the brave man will be fearless in plague, or in peril by sea, although it will be a different kind of fearlessness from that of the old salt. For in a shipwreck the brave man does not expect to be rescued, and he hates the thought of the inglorious end which threatens him, whereas the seaman who has weathered many a storm never gives up hope. Courage, too, may be shown on occasions when a man can put up a fight or meet a glorious death. But there is no opportunity for either when you are going down in a ship.

All men have not the same views about what is to be feared, although there are some terrors which are admitted to be more than human nature can face. Terrors of that order are experienced of course by every sane person. But there are great diversities in the extent and degree of the dangers that are humanly tolerable; and there is the same variety in the objects which instil courage. What characterizes the brave man is his unshaken courage wherever courage is humanly possible. No doubt even then he will not always be exempt from fear; but when he fears it will be in the right way, and he will meet the danger according to the rule or principle he has taken to guide his conduct, his object being to achieve moral dignity or beauty in what he does, for that is the end of virtue. Yet it is possible to feel such dangers too much, and possible to fear them too little, and possible also to fear things that are not fearful as much as if they were. One may fear what one ought not to fear, and that is one kind of error; one may fear it in the wrong way, and that is another. A third error is committed when one fears at the wrong time. And so on. We have the same possibilities of error when we deal with things that give us confidence. The brave man is the man who faces or fears the right thing for the right purpose in the right manner at the right moment, or who shows courage in the corresponding ways. . . .

The man who goes to the extreme in fear is a coward—one who fears the wrong things in the wrong way and all the rest of it. He also exhibits a deficiency in boldness. But what one particularly notices is the extremity of his fear in the face of pain. We may therefore describe the coward as a poor-spirited person scared of everything. This is the very opposite of the brave man, for a bold heart indicates a confident temper.

We may say, then, that the coward, the rash man, and the brave man work as it were with the same materials, but their attitudes to them are different. The coward has too much fear and too little courage, the rash man too much courage and too little fear. It is the brave man who has the right attitude, for he has the right disposition, enabling him to observe the mean. We may add that the rash man is foolhardy, ready for anything before the danger arrives; but, when it does, sheering off. On the other hand the brave man is gallant in action but undemonstrative beforehand.

Summing up, let us say that courage is the disposition which aims at the mean in conditions which inspire confidence or fear in the circumstances I have described; it feels confidence and faces danger because it is the fine thing to do so and because it is base to shrink from doing it. Yet to kill oneself as a means of escape from poverty or disappointed love or bodily or mental anguish is the deed of a coward rather than a brave man. To run away from trouble is a form of cowardice and, while it is true that the suicide braves death, he does it not for some noble object but to escape some ill.

[*The virtue of which Aristotle now gives an account is* Sophrosyne, *a word which cannot be rendered by any modern English equivalent. It is, however, what our moralists until quite recently called 'temperance,' and this, with its opposite 'intemperance,' will be used here. What Aristotle means by* Sophrosyne *will gradually appear.*]

Let us next say something about temperance, which like courage is considered to be one of the virtues developed in the irrational parts of the soul.

We have already described it as aiming at the mean in pleasurable experiences. Intemperance is shown in the same field. So we must now say something definite about the quality of the pleasures which are the material on which temperance and its opposite work. Let us begin by drawing a distinction between (a) pleasures of the soul and (b) pleasures of the body.

(a) As an instance of pleasures of the soul consider the love of distinction in public life or in some branch of learning. The devotee in either case takes pleasure in what he loves without any physical sensations. What he feels is a spiritual or intellectual pleasure, and we do not speak of men who seek that kind of pleasure as 'temperate' or 'intemperate.' Nor do we apply these terms to any class of persons whose pleasures are not those of the flesh. For example, the kind of person who likes to swap stories and anecdotes, and wastes his time discussing trivialities, we call a 'gossip' or a 'chatterbox,' but not 'intemperate.' Neither should we so describe a man who makes a tragedy out of some loss he has met with of money or of friends.

(b) It is then the pleasures of sense

that are the concern of temperance, though not all of these. The people who find pleasure in looking at things like colours and forms and pictures are not called temperate or intemperate. At the same time we must suppose that pleasure in these things can be felt too much or too little or in due measure. It is so with the pleasures of listening. A man may take inordinate delight in music or acting. But nobody is prepared to call him intemperate on that account; nor, if he takes neither too much nor too little, do we think of describing him as temperate. It is the same with the pleasures of smell, except when some association comes in. A man is not called intemperate if he happens to like the smell of apples or roses or incense. Yet he may be, if he inhales essences or the emanations of the cuisine, for these are odours which appeal to the voluptuary, because they remind him of the things that arouse his desires. And not only the voluptuary; everybody likes the smell of things to eat when he is hungry. Still the delight in such things is specially characteristic of the voluptuary or intemperate man, because it is on these that his heart is set. And if we extend our observation to the lower animals, we note that they, too, find nothing intrinsically pleasant in these sensations. A hunting-dog gets no pleasure from the scent of a hare. The pleasure is in eating it; all the scent did was to tell him the hare was there. It is not the lowing of an ox that gratifies a lion but the eating it, though the lowing tells him the ox is somewhere about, and that evidently gives him pleasure. Nor does he, as Homer thinks, rejoice when he has caught sight of 'stag or goat of the wild,' but because he is promising himself a meal.

Such are the pleasures with which temperance and intemperance deal, and they are pleasures in which the lower animals also share. On that account they have the name of being illiberal and brutish, confined as they are to touch and taste. And even taste seems to count for little or nothing in the practice of temperance. It is the function of taste to discriminate between flavours, as connoisseurs do when they sample wines, and chefs when they prepare entrées; although it is not exactly the flavours that please (except, perhaps, with the intemperate), it is the enjoyment of the flavorous article, and that is wholly a tactile experience, whether in eating, drinking or what are called the pleasures of sex. This explains the anecdote of the epicure who prayed that his throat might be made longer than a crane's — the longer the contact, he thought, the more protracted the pleasure. So the sense in respect of which we give an intemperate man that name is the sense that comes nearest to being universal. This may seem to justify its ill-repute, for it belongs to us not as men but as animals. Therefore to delight in such sensations, and to prefer them to any other pleasure, is brutish.

[*Aristotle discusses other virtues, such as liberality, the golden mean between stinginess and prodigality; dignified self-respect, between humility and vanity; and friendliness, between quarrelsomeness and obsequiousness. He points out that acts like theft, adultery, and murder, and emotions like shamelessness, envy, and spite, are already excesses or defects and therefore can-*

not exist in proper moderation. The virtue of justice, as a kind of fairness or impartiality, consists in treating equals equally and unequals unequally in proportion to their deserts. It is a mean, not as the other virtues are, but only in the sense that it produces a state of affairs intermediate between giving too much or too little to one person compared with another.—M.R.]

4. [Self-love and Friendship]

[How far, and with what justification, may a man love himself?]

Another problem is whether one ought to love oneself or another most. The world blames those whose first thoughts are always for themselves and stigmatizes them as self-centred. It is also generally believed that a bad man does everything from a selfish motive, and does this the more, the worse he is.[1] On the other hand the good man is supposed never to act except on some lofty principle—the loftier the principle, the better the man—and to neglect his own interest in order to promote that of his friend. It is a view which is not borne out by the facts. Nor need this surprise us. It is common ground that a man should love his best friend most. But my best friend is the man who in wishing me well wishes it for my sake, whether this shall come to be known or not. Well, there is no one who fulfills this condition as well as I do in my behaviour towards myself; indeed it may be said of every quality which enters into the definition of a

friend—I have it in a higher degree than any of my friends. For, as I have already observed, all the affectionate feelings of a man for others are an extension of his feelings for himself. You will find, too, that all the popular bywords agree on this point. ('Two bodies and one soul,' 'Amity is parity,' 'The knee is nearer than the shin.') All the proverbs show how close are the ties of friendship, and they all apply best to oneself. For a man is his own best friend. From this it follows that he ought to love himself best.— Which then of these two opinions ought we to accept in practice? It is a reasonable question, since there is a degree of plausibility in both.

No doubt the proper method of dealing with divergent opinions of this sort is to distinguish between them, and so reach a definite conclusion on the point of how far and in what way each of them is true. So the present difficulty may be cleared up if we can discover what meaning each side attaches to the word 'self-love.' Those who make it a term of reproach give the epithet of 'self-loving' to those who assign to themselves more than they are entitled to in money, public distinctions and bodily pleasures, these being what most men crave for and earnestly pursue as the greatest blessings, so that they contend fiercely for the possession of them. Well, the man who grasps at more than his fair share of these things is given to the gratification of his desires and his passions generally and the irrational part of his soul. Now most men are like that, and we see from this that the censorious use of the epithet 'self-loving' results from the fact that

[1] A bad man is often accused of 'doing nothing until he has to.'

the self-love of most men is a bad thing. Applied to them, the censorious epithet is therefore justified. And unquestionably it is people who arrogate too much of such things to themselves who are called 'self-loving' by the ordinary man. For if anybody were to make it his constant business to take the lead himself over everyone else in the performance of just or temperate or any other kind whatever of virtuous actions, generally claiming the honourable rôle for himself, nobody would stigmatize *him* as a 'self-lover.' Yet the view might be taken that such a man was exceptionally self-loving. At any rate he arrogates to himself the things of greatest moral beauty and excellence, and what he gratifies and obeys throughout is the magistral part of himself, his higher intelligence. Now just as in a state or any other composite body it is the magistral or dominant part of it that is considered more particularly to *be* the state or body, so with a man; his intelligence, the governing part of him, *is* the man. Therefore he who loves and indulges this part is to the fullest extent a lover of himself. Further, we may note that the terms 'continent' and 'incontinent' imply that the intellect is or is not in control, which involves the assumption that the intellect is the man. Again, it is our reasoned acts that are held to be more especially those which we have performed ourselves and by our own volition. All which goes to show that a man is, or is chiefly the ruling part of himself, and that a good man loves it beyond any other part of his nature. It follows that such a man will be self-loving in a different sense from that attached to the word when it is used as a term of reproach. From the vulgar self-lover he differs as far as the life of reason from the life of passion, and as far as a noble purpose differs from mere grasping at whatever presents itself as an expedient. Hence those who are exceptionally devoted to the performance of fine and noble actions receive the approval and commendation of all. And if everyone sought to outdo his neighbour in elevation of character, and laboured strenuously to perform the noblest actions, the common weal would find its complete actualization and the private citizen would realize for himself the greatest of goods, which is virtue.

Therefore it is right for the *good* man to be self-loving, because he will thereby himself be benefited by performing fine actions; and by the same process he will be helpful to others. The bad man on the other hand should not be a self-lover, because he will only be injuring himself and his neighbours by his subservience to base passions. As a result of this subservience what he does is in conflict with what he ought to do, whereas the good man does what he ought to do. For intelligence never fails to choose the course that is best for itself, and the good man obeys his intelligence.

But there is something else which we can truly say about the good man. Many of his actions are performed to serve his friends or his country, even if this should involve dying for them. For he is ready to sacrifice wealth, honours, all the prizes of life in his eagerness to play a noble part. He would prefer one crowded hour of glorious life to a protracted period of quiet existence and mild enjoyment spent as an ordinary man would spend it — one great and dazzling achievement to many small successes. And surely this may be said of those who lay down their lives for others; they choose for themselves a crown of glory. It is also a characteristic trait of the good man that he is prepared to lose money on condition that his friends get more. The friend gets the cash, and he gets the credit, so that he is assigning the greater good to himself. His conduct is not different when it comes to public honours and offices. All these he will freely give up to his friend, because that is the fine and praiseworthy thing for him to do. It is natural then that people should think him virtuous, when he prefers honour to everything else. He may even create opportunities for his friend to do a fine action which he might have done himself, and this may be the nobler course for him to take. Thus in the whole field of admirable conduct we see the good man taking the larger share of moral dignity. In this sense then it is, as I said before, right that he should be self-loving. But in the vulgar sense no one should be so.

[*It has been questioned whether the possession of friends is necessary to happiness. Aristotle has no doubt that it is so, and gives his reasons.*]

Another debatable point concerning the happy man is this. Will friends be necessary to his happiness or not? It is commonly said that the happy, being sufficient to themselves, have no need of friends. All the blessings of life are theirs already; so, having all resources within themselves, they are not in need of anything else, whereas a friend, being an *alter ego*, is only there to supply what one cannot supply for oneself. Hence that line in the *Orestes* of Euripides:

When Fortune smiles on us, what need of friends?

Yet it seems a strange thing that in the process of attributing every blessing to the happy man we should not assign him friends, who are thought to be the greatest of all external advantages. Besides, if it is more like a friend to confer than to receive benefits, and doing good to others is an activity which especially belongs to virtue and the virtuous man, and if it is better to do a kindness to a friend than to a stranger, the good man will have need of friends as objects of his active benevolence. Hence a second question. Does one need friends more in prosperity than in adversity? There is a case for either of these alternatives. The unfortunate need people who will be kind to them; the prosperous need people to be kind to.

Surely also there is something strange in representing the man of perfect blessedness as a solitary or a recluse. Nobody would deliberately choose to have all the good things in the world, if there was a condition that he was to have them all by himself. Man is a social animal, and the need for company is in his blood. Therefore the happy man must have company, for he has everything that is naturally good, and it will not be denied that it is better to associate with friends than with strangers, with men of virtue than with the ordinary run of persons. We conclude then that the happy man needs friends. . . .

[*A little chapter on the value and influence of Friendship.*]

Well then, are we to say that, just as lovers find their chief delight in gazing upon the beloved and prefer sight to all the other senses — for this is the seat and source of love — so friends find the society of one another that which they prefer to all things else? For in the first place friendship is a communion or partnership. Secondly, a man stands in the same relation to his friend as to himself. Now the consciousness which he has of his own existence is something that would be chosen as a good. So the consciousness of his friend's existence must be a good. This consciousness becomes active in the intercourse of the friends, which accordingly they instinctively desire. Thirdly, every man wishes to share with his friends that occupation, whatever it may be, which forms for him the essence and aim of his existence. So we find friends who drink together, and others who dice together, while yet others go in together for physical training, hunting or philosophy. Each set spend their time in one another's company following the pursuit which makes the great pleasure of their lives. As their wish is to be always with their friends, they do what these do and take part with them in these pursuits to the best of their ability. But this means that the friendship of the unworthy is evil, for they associate in unworthy pursuits; and so becoming more and more like each other they turn out badly. But the friendship of the good is good and increases in goodness in consequence of their associa-

tion. They seem to become positively better men by putting their friendship into operation and correcting each other's faults. For each seeks to transfer to himself the traits he admires in the other. Hence the famous saying:

From noble men you may learn noble deeds . . .

5. [Intellectual Goodness]

[. . . *Aristotle gives reasons for thinking that happiness in its highest and best manifestation is found in cultivating the "contemplative" life.*]

. . . If happiness is an activity in accordance with virtue, it is reasonable to assume that it will be in accordance with the highest virtue; and this can only be the virtue of the best part of us. Whether this be the intellect or something else — whatever it is that is held to have a natural right to govern and guide us, and to have an insight into what is noble and divine, either as being itself also divine or more divine than any other part of us — it is the activity of this part in accordance with the virtue proper to it that will be perfect happiness. Now we have seen already that this activity has a speculative or contemplative character. This is a conclusion which may be accepted as in harmony with our earlier arguments and with the truth. For "contemplation" is the highest form of activity, since the intellect is the highest thing in us and the objects which come within its range are the highest that can be known. But it is also the most continuous activity, for we can think about intellectual problems more continuously than we can keep up any sort of physical action. Again, we feel sure that a modicum of pleasure must be one of the ingredients of happiness. Now it is admitted that activity along the lines of "wisdom" is the pleasantest of all the good activities. At all events it is thought that philosophy ("the pursuit of wisdom") has pleasures marvelous in purity and duration, and it stands to reason that those who have knowledge pass their time more pleasantly than those who are engaged in its pursuit. Again, self-sufficiency will be found to belong in an exceptional degree to the exercise of the speculative intellect. The wise man, as much as the just man and everyone else, must have the necessaries of life. But, given an adequate supply of these, the just man also needs people with and towards whom he can put his justice into operation; and we can use similar language about the temperate man, the brave man, and so on. But the wise man can do more. He can speculate all by himself, and the wiser he is the better he can do it. Doubtless it helps to have fellow workers, but for all that he is the most self-sufficing of men. Finally it may well be thought that the activity of contemplation is the only one that is praised on its own account, because nothing comes of it beyond the act of contemplation, whereas from practical activities we count on gaining something more or less over and above the mere action. Again, it is commonly believed that, to have happiness, one must have leisure; we occupy ourselves in order that we may have leisure, just as we make war for the sake of peace. Now the practical virtues find opportunity for their exercise in politics and in war, but there are occupations which are supposed to leave no room for leisure. Certainly it is true of the trade of war, for no one deliberately chooses to make war for the sake of making it or tries to bring about a war. A man would be regarded as a bloodthirsty monster if he were to make war on a friendly state just to produce battles and slaughter. The business of the politician also makes leisure impossible. Besides the activity itself, politics aims at securing positions of power and honor or the happiness of the politician himself or his fellow citizens—a happiness obviously distinct from that which we are seeking.

We are now in a position to suggest the truth of the following statements. (a) Political and military activities, while preeminent among good activities in beauty and grandeur, are incompatible with leisure, and are not chosen for their own sake but with a view to some remoter end, whereas the activity of the intellect is felt to excel in the serious use of leisure, taking as it does the form of contemplation, and not to aim at any end beyond itself, and to own a pleasure peculiar to itself, thereby enhancing its activity. (b) In this activity we easily recognize self-sufficiency, the possibility of leisure and such freedom from fatigue as is humanly possible, together with all the other blessings of pure happiness. Now if these statements are received as true, it will follow that it is this intellectual activity which forms perfect happiness for a man—provided of course that it ensures a complete span of life, for nothing incomplete can be an element in happiness.

Yes, but such a life will be too high

for *human* attainment. It will not be lived by us in our merely human capacity but in virtue of something divine within us, and so far as this divine particle is superior to man's composite nature, to that extent will its activity be superior to that of the other forms of excellence. If the intellect is divine compared with man, the life of the intellect must be divine compared with the life of a human creature. And we ought not to listen to those who counsel us *O man, think as man should* and *O mortal, remember your mortality.* Rather ought we, so far as in us lies, to put on immortality and to leave nothing unattempted in the effort to live in conformity with the highest thing within us. Small in bulk it may be, yet in power and preciousness it transcends all the rest. We may in fact believe that this is the true self of the individual, being the sovereign and better part of him. It would be strange, then, if a man should choose to live not his own life but another's. Moreover the rule, as I stated it a little before, will apply here —the rule that what is best and pleasantest for each creature is that which intimately belongs to it. Applying it, we shall conclude that the life of the intellect is the best and pleasantest for man, because the intellect more than anything else *is* the man. Thus it will be the happiest life as well.

COMMENT

In considering the merits of Aristotle's theory, we should keep certain key questions in mind:

1. *Can we deduce good from the nature of things?* The presupposition of Aristotle's ethics is that each kind of thing has certain characteristic tendencies and that the good is the fulfillment of these tendencies. Man's good, accordingly, can be deduced from human nature. It may be objected that this implies an optimistic and undemonstrated premise (that developed reality is fully good) and allows the tendencies of the actual world to dictate our standards of value. Some philosophers, such as Kant, deny that the *ought* (good and right) can be derived from the *is* (matters of fact), and thus take fundamental issue with the basis of Aristotle's ethics.

2. *Is the wider definition of good correct?* We can distinguish, in Aristotle's theory, between a "wide" and a "narrow" definition of ultimate good. In its wide meaning, good is the actualization of potentialities. In its narrow meaning, it is the actualization of *human* potentialities, which are taken to be essentially rational.

Let us first consider the wider definition. It is very wide indeed, for it applies to animals, plants, and even inanimate things. Whether Aristotle would interpret it so broadly is not altogether clear. In his teleological metaphysics, he speaks of "end" or "final cause" in this very inclusive way, but he does not state explicitly that every end is good. If, however, the actualization of potentialities is taken to be the essence of good, there is no logical reason to stop short with conscious or even unconscious organisms.

This very wide definition, a critic might say, confuses an "end" in a temporal sense (the *finis* of a process) with an "end" in an ethical sense (good as an end rather than as a means). Another type of confusion may also be involved. We often say that something is a *good* example of its kind, and good in this sense, a biologist might claim, applies only to a fully developed animal, which clearly exhibits the powers and abilities of its species. But "good" in this sense does not imply positive value; a cancer specialist might speak of a perfectly good case of cancer, meaning a case so far developed that it clearly exhibits the generic characteristics of the malignancy. Has Aristotle confused good in this sense with good in its value import?

The attempt to extend the meaning of intrinsic goodness to include nonconscious things has often been challenged. If there were no feelings, no desires, no thoughts whatsoever — if all things in the universe were as unconscious as sticks and stones — would there be any value? Some philosophers maintain that a world without consciousness would be without value; if this were so, we should have to reject Aristotle's wider interpretation of good.

3.   *Is the narrower definition of good correct?* Aristotle's interpretation of human goodness rests upon two premises: (a) The good is to be found in the life and work peculiar to people, and (b) rationality is the distinctive mark of the human creature. Both premises can be challenged.

(a) Why should we suppose that the human good is to be found in what is distinctive to people? That a certain factor is peculiar to a species does not necessarily imply any ethical superiority in that factor. If all human beings were just like other animals except that they alone had bowlegs, this would not prove that human good is bowleggedness. Perhaps Aristotle is taking it for granted that people *are* superior to other animals and that this superiority must lie in that which people alone possess. But some philosophers would question this view. Hedonists, for example, would say that good is pleasure, and the fact that a dog can feel pleasure does not detract from human good. We may or may not believe that this view is mistaken and Aristotle's theory correct — but is there any way of supporting our conviction?

(b. Is reason the differentia of humankind? Certain psychologists, such as Wolfgang Köhler, have demonstrated that chimpanzees also have the capacity to reason. These clever animals can figure out ways of piling up and mounting boxes, for example, to reach a bunch of bananas hanging high from the top of their cage. Aristotle would no doubt reply that this is only *practical*, not *theoretical*, reason, but it may be that chimpanzees also have curiosity and enjoy satisfying it. At least it is not at all obvious that reason is *the* distinctive mark of human beings or that any faculty is exclusively human. What fundamentally distinguishes people, it can be argued, is the whole development of their culture, including art and religion and social institutions in addition to philosophy and science. Does Aristotle's rather exclusive emphasis on reason betray the natural bias of a philosopher?

4. *Does Aristotle, in stressing the generic nature of humans, neglect the importance of individuality?* His emphasis is on the reason that all humans share, and only in rare passages does he speak of self-realization in individualistic terms. He would probably have admitted, for example, that a person with very great musical talent should develop that special gift. But an existentialist such as Kierkegaard would charge that Aristotle shows too little respect for the matchless individuality that is the core of every human life. Who is right?

5. *Is moral virtue to be found in adherence to a mean between the extremes of excess and deficiency?* How adequate is Aristotle's theory of the golden mean? "Be cautious; avoid extremes; follow the mean," it can be argued, is a counsel of prudence and not necessarily of morality — even the wicked and crafty can find it useful. From the standpoint of attaining happiness, does it need to be counterbalanced by a relish for adventure and the careless rapture of intense moments of experience?

Still other questions can be posed. Is pleasure merely contributory to the happy life, as Aristotle supposed, or is it the very essence of happiness, as the hedonists contend? Is the ideal of intellectual contemplation unrealizable by all but the aristocratic few, and if so, should we favor the development of an intellectual elite rather than the cultivation of the masses? Are ethics and politics inseparable in the way in which Aristotle supposed? Do you agree with his characterization of the nature and value of self-love? Of friendship? Other questions will probably occur to the reader.

14

The Way of Pleasure

"When we say, then, that pleasure is the end and aim, we do not mean the pleasures of the prodigal or the pleasures of sensuality . . . By pleasure we mean the absence of pain in the body and of trouble in the soul."

Epicurus

EPICURUS (341–270 B.C.)

Epicurus was born on the island of Samos, although his parents originally were from Athens. After encountering students of both Plato and Democritus, he began to teach on the island of Lesbos in the year 311. Soon he moved to Athens and founded a community and school, which he called the Garden. Here Epicurus and his followers followed a life of quiet seclusion in order to maximize peaceful and harmonious pleasure and minimize pain and fear. The Garden was open to both men and women, slaves and free persons, from all walks of life.

In addition to three letters preserved in Diogenes Laertius' *Life of Epicurus*, there is also extant a collection of chief beliefs and rules by which those in the Garden lived. All but a few fragments of Epicurus' many other writings have been lost. The main doctrines of his philosophy include a belief in the simple material basis of reality, even mental activity; the superiority of the pleasures of the mind over those of the body; and a commitment to the cultivation of friendship.

The Absence of Pain

LETTER TO MENOECEUS

Epicurus to Menoeceus, greeting.

Let no one be slow to seek wisdom when he is young nor weary in the search thereof when he is grown old. For no age is too early or too late for the health of the soul. And to say that the season for studying philosophy has not yet come, or that it is past and gone, is like saying that the season for happiness is not yet or that it is now no more. Therefore, both old and young ought to seek wisdom, the former in order that, as age comes over him, he may be young in good things because of the grace of what has been, and the latter in order that, while he is young, he may at the same time be old, because he has no fear of the things which are to come. So we must exercise ourselves in the things which bring happiness, since, if that be present, we have everything, and, if that be absent, all our actions are directed toward attaining it.

Those things which without ceasing I have declared unto thee, those do, and exercise thyself therein, holding them to be the elements of right life. First believe that god is a living being immortal and blessed, according to the notion of a god indicated by the common sense of mankind; and so believing, thou shalt not affirm of him ought that is foreign to his immortality or that agrees not with blessedness, but shalt believe about him whatever may uphold both his blessedness and his immortality. For verily there are gods, and the knowledge of them is manifest; but they are not such as the multitude believe, seeing that men do not steadfastly maintain the notions they form respecting them. Not the man who denies the gods worshipped by the multitude, but he who affirms of the gods what the multitude believes about them is truly impious. For the utterances of the multitude about the gods are not true preconceptions but false assumptions; hence it is that the greatest evils happen to the wicked and the greatest blessings happen to the good from the hand of the gods, seeing that they are always favourable to their own good qualities and take pleasure in men like unto themselves, but reject as alien whatever is not of their kind.

Accustom thyself to believe that death is nothing to us, for good and evil imply sentience, and death is the privation of all sentience; therefore a right understanding that death is nothing to us makes the mortality of life enjoyable, not by adding to life an illimitable time, but by taking away the yearning after immortality. For life has no terrors for him who has thoroughly apprehended that there are no terrors for him in ceasing to live. Foolish, therefore, is the man who says that he fears death, not because it will pain when it comes, but because it pains in the prospect. Whatsoever causes no annoyance when it is present, causes only a groundless pain in the expectation. Death, therefore, the most awful of evils, is nothing to us, seeing that, when we are, death is not come, and, when death is come, we are not. It is nothing, then, either to the living or to the dead, for with the living it is not and the dead exist no longer. But in the world, at one time men shun death as the greatest of all evils, and at another time choose it as a respite from the evils in life. The wise man does not deprecate life nor does he fear the cessation of life. The thought of life is no offense to him, nor is the cessation of life regarded as an evil. And even as men choose of food not merely and simply the larger portion, but the more pleasant, so the wise seek to enjoy the time which is most pleasant and not merely that which is longest. And he who admonishes the young to live well and the old to make a good end speaks foolishly, not merely because of the desirableness of life, but because the same exercise at once teaches to live well and die well. Much worse is he who says that it were good not to be born, but when once one is born to pass with all speed through the gates of Hades. For if he truly believes this, why does he not depart from life? If were easy for him to do so, if once he were firmly convinced. If he speaks only in mockery, his words are foolishness, for those who hear believe him not.

We must remember that the future is neither wholly ours nor wholly not ours, so that neither must we count upon it as quite certain to come nor despair of it as quite certain not to come.

We must also reflect that of desires some are natural, others are groundless; and that of the natural some are necessary as well as natural, and some natural only. And of the necessary desires some are necessary if we are to be happy, some if the body is to be rid of uneasiness, some if we are even to live. He who has a clear and certain understanding of these things will direct every preference and aversion toward securing health of body and tranquillity of mind, seeing that this is the sum and end of a blessed life. For the end of all our actions is to be free from pain and fear, and, when once we have attained all this, the tempest of the soul is laid; seeing that the living creature has no need to go in search of something that is lacking, nor to look for anything else by which the good of the soul and of the body will be fulfilled. When we are pained because of the absence of pleasure, then, and then only, do we feel the need of pleasure. Wherefore we call pleasure the alpha and omega of a blessed life. Pleasure is our first and kindred good. It is the starting point of every choice and of every aversion, and to it we come back, inasmuch as we make feeling the rule by which to judge of every good thing. And since pleasure is our first and native good, for that reason we do not choose every pleasure whatsoever, but ofttimes pass over many pleasures when a greater annoyance ensues from them. And ofttimes we consider pains superior to pleasures when submission to the pains for a long time brings us as a consequence a greater pleasure. While therefore all pleasure because it is naturally akin to us is good, not all pleasure is choiceworthy, just as all pain is an evil and yet not all pain is to be shunned. It is, however, by measuring one against another, and by looking at the conveniences and inconveniences, that all these matters must be judged. Sometimes we treat the good as an evil, and the evil, on the contrary, as a good. Again, we regard independence of outward things as a great good, not so as in all cases to use little, but so as to be contented with little if we have not much, being honestly persuaded that they have the sweetest enjoyment of luxury who stand least in need of it, and that whatever is natural is easily procured and only the vain and worthless hard to win. Plain fare gives as much pleasure as a costly diet, when once the pain of want has been removed, while bread and water confer the highest possible pleasure when they are brought to hungry lips. To habituate one's self, therefore, to simple and inexpensive diet supplies all that is needful for health, and enables a man to meet the necessary requirements of life without shrinking, and it places us in a better condition when we approach at intervals a costly fare and renders us fearless of fortune.

When we say, then, that pleasure is the end and aim, we do not mean the pleasures of the prodigal or the pleasures of sensuality, as we are understood to do by some through ignorance, prejudice, or wilful misrepresentation. By pleasure we mean the absence of pain in the body and of trouble in the soul. It is not an unbroken succession of drinking bouts and of revelry, not sexual love, not the enjoyment of the fish and other delicacies of a luxurious table, which produce a pleasant life; it is sober reasoning, searching out the grounds of every choice and avoidance, and banishing those beliefs through which the greatest tumults take possession of the soul. Of all this the beginning and the greatest good is prudence. Wherefore prudence is a more precious thing even than philosophy; from it spring all the other virtues, for it teaches that we cannot lead a life of pleasure which is not also a life of prudence, honor, and justice; nor lead a life of prudence, honor, and justice, which is not also a life of pleasure. For the virtues have grown into one with a pleasant life, and a pleasant life is inseparable from them.

Who, then, is superior in thy judgement to such a man? He holds a holy belief concerning the gods, and is altogether free from the fear of death. He has diligently considered the end fixed by nature, and understands how easily the limit of good things can be reached and attained, and how either the duration or the intensity of evils is but slight. Destiny, which some introduce as sovereign over all things, he laughs to scorn, affirming rather that some things happen of necessity, others by chance, others through our own agency. For he sees that necessity destroys responsibility and that chance or fortune is inconstant; whereas our own actions are free, and it is to them that praise and blame naturally attach. It were better, indeed, to accept the legends of the gods than to bow beneath that yoke of destiny which the natural philosophers have imposed. The one holds out some faint hope that we may escape if we honor the gods, while the necessity of the naturalists is deaf to all entreaties. Nor does he hold chance to be a god, as the world in general does, for in the acts of a god there is no disorder; nor to be a cause, though an uncertain one, for he believes that no good or evil is dispensed by chance to men so as to make life blessed, though it supplies the starting-point of great good and great evil. He believes that the misfortune of the wise is better than the prosperity of the fool. It is better, in short, that what is well judged in action should not owe its successful issue to the aid of chance.

Exercise thyself in these and kindred precepts day and night, both by thyself and with him who is like unto thee; then never, either in waking or in dream, wilt thou be disturbed; but wilt live as a god among men. For man loses all semblance of mortality by living in the midst of immortal blessings.

Principal Doctrines

1.   A blessed and eternal being has no trouble himself and brings no trouble upon any other being; hence he is exempt from movements of anger and partiality, for every such movement implies weakness.

2.   Death is nothing to us; for the body, when it has been resolved into its elements, has no feeling, and that which has no feeling is nothing to us.

3.   The magnitude of pleasure reaches its limit in the removal of all pain. When pleasure is present, so long as it is uninterrupted, there is no pain either of body or of mind or of both together.

4.   Continuous pain does not last long in the flesh; on the contrary, pain, if extreme, is present a very short time, and even that degree of pain which barely outweighs pleasure in the flesh does not last for many days together. Illnesses of long duration even permit of an excess of pleasure over pain in the flesh.

5.   It is impossible to live a pleasant life without living wisely and well and justly, and it is impossible to live wisely and well and justly without living pleasantly. Whenever any one of these is lacking, when, for instance, the man is not able to live wisely, though he lives well and justly, it is impossible for him to live a pleasant life.

6.   In order to obtain security from other men any means whatsoever of procuring this was a natural good.

7.   Some men have sought to become famous and renowned, thinking that thus they would make themselves secure against their fellow-men. If, then, the life of such persons really was secure, they attained natural good; if, however, it was insecure, they have not attained the end which by nature's own prompting they originally sought.

8.   No pleasure is in itself evil, but the things which produce certain pleasures entail annoyances many times greater than the pleasures themselves.

9. If all pleasures had been capable of accumulation, — if this had gone on not only by recurrence in time, but all over the frame or, at any rate, over the principal parts of man's nature, there would never have been any difference between one pleasure and another, as in fact there is.

10. If the objects which are productive of pleasures to profligate persons really freed them from fears of the mind, — the fears, I mean, inspired by celestial and atmospheric phenomena, the fear of death, the fear of pain; if, further, they taught them to limit their desires, we should never have any fault to find with such persons, for they would then be filled with pleasures to overflowing on all sides and would be exempt from all pain, whether of body or mind, that is, from all evil.

11. If we had never been molested by alarms at celestial and atmospheric phenomena, nor by the misgiving that death somehow affects us, nor by neglect of the proper limits of pains and desires, we should have had no need to study natural science.

12. It would be impossible to banish fear on matters of the highest importance, if a man did not know the nature of the whole universe, but lived in dread of what the legend tells us. Hence without the study of nature there was no enjoyment of unmixed pleasures.

13. There would be no advantage in providing security against our fellow-men, so long as we were alarmed by occurrences over our heads or beneath the earth or in general by whatever happens in the boundless universe.

14. When tolerable security against our fellow-men is attained, then on a basis of power sufficient to afford support and of material prosperity arises in most genuine form the security of a quiet private life withdrawn from the multitude.

15. Nature's wealth at once has its bounds and is easy to procure; but the wealth of vain fancies recedes to an infinite distance.

16. Fortune but seldom interferes with the wise man; his greatest and highest interests have been, are, and will be, directed by reason throughout the course of his life.

17. The just man enjoys the greatest peace of mind, while the unjust is full of the utmost disquietude.

18. Pleasure in the flesh admits no increase when once the pain of want has been removed; after that it only admits of variation. The limit of pleasure in the mind, however, is reached when we reflect on the things themselves and their congeners which cause the mind the greatest alarms.

19. Unlimited time and limited time afford an equal amount of pleasure, if we measure the limits of that pleasure by reason.

20. The flesh receives as unlimited the limits of pleasure; and to provide it requires unlimited time. But the mind, grasping in thought what the end and limit of the flesh is, and banishing the terrors of futurity, procures a complete and perfect life, and has no longer any need of unlimited time. Nevertheless it does not shun pleasure, and even in the hour of death, when ushered out of existence by circumstances, the mind does not lack enjoyment of the best life.

21. He who understands the limits

of life knows how easy it is to procure enough to remove the pain of want and make the whole of life complete and perfect. Hence he has no longer any need of things which are not to be won save by labor and conflict.

22. We must take into account as the end all that really exists and all clear evidence of sense to which we refer our opinions; for otherwise everything will be full of uncertainty and confusion.

23. If you fight against all your sensations, you will have no standard to which to refer, and thus no means of judging even those judgments which you pronounce false.

24. If you reject absolutely any single sensation without stopping to discriminate with respect to that which awaits confirmation between matter of opinion and that which is already present, whether in sensation or in feelings or in any presentative perception of the mind, you will throw into confusion even the rest of your sensations by your groundless belief and so you will be rejecting the standard of truth altogether. If in your ideas based upon opinion you hastily affirm as true all that awaits confirmation as well as that which does not, you will not escape error, as you will be maintaining complete ambiguity whenever it is a case of judging between right and wrong opinion.

25. If you do not on every separate occasion refer each of your actions to the end prescribed by nature, but instead of this in the act of choice or avoidance swerve aside to some other end, your acts will not be consistent with your theories.

26. All such desires as lead to no pain when they remain ungratified are unnecessary, and the longing is easily got rid of, when the thing desired is difficult to procure or when the desires seem likely to produce harm.

27. Of all the means which are procured by wisdom to ensure happiness throughout the whole of life, by far the most important is the acquisition of friends.

28. The same conviction which inspires confidence that nothing we have to fear is eternal or even of long duration, also enables us to see that even in our limited conditions of life nothing enhances our security so much as friendship.

29. Of our desires some are natural and necessary; others are natural, but not necessary; others, again, are neither natural nor necessary, but are due to illusory opinion. [Epicurus regards as natural and necessary desires which bring relief from pain, as *e.g.* drink when we are thirsty; while by natural and not necessary he means those which merely diversify the pleasure without removing the pain, as *e.g.* costly viands; by the neither natural nor necessary he means desires for crowns and the erection of statues in one's honor.][1]

30. Those natural desires which entail no pain when not gratified, though their objects are vehemently pursued, are also due to illusory opinion; and when they are not got rid of, it is not because of their own nature, but because of the man's illusory opinion.

31. Natural justice is a symbol or

[1]The bracketed remarks are by an ancient commentator.

expression of expediency, to prevent one man from harming or being harmed by another.

32. Those animals which are incapable of making covenants with one another, to the end that they may neither inflict nor suffer harm, are without either justice or injustice. And those tribes which either could not or would not form mutual covenants to the same end are in like case.

33. There never was an absolute justice, but only an agreement made in reciprocal intercourse in whatever localities now and again from time to time, providing against the infliction or suffering of harm.

34. Injustice is not in itself an evil, but only in its consequence, viz. the terror which is excited by apprehension that those appointed to punish such offences will discover the injustice.

35. It is impossible for the man who secretly violates any article of the social compact to feel confident that he will remain undiscovered, even if he has already escaped ten thousand times; for right on to the end of his life he is never sure he will not be detected.

36. Taken generally, justice is the same for all, to wit, something found expedient in mutual intercourse; but in its application to particular cases of locality or conditions of whatever kind, it varies under different circumstances.

37. Among the things accounted just by conventional law, whatever in the needs of mutual intercourse is attested to be expedient, is thereby stamped as just, whether or not it be the same for all; and in case any law is made and does not prove suitable to the expediencies of mutual intercourse, then this is no longer just. And should the expediency which is expressed by the law vary and only for a time correspond with the prior conception, nevertheless for the time being it was just, so long as we do not trouble ourselves about empty words, but look simply at the facts.

38. Where without any change in circumstances the conventional laws, when judged by their consequences, were seen not to correspond with the notion of justice, such laws were not really just; but wherever the laws have ceased to be expedient in consequence of a change in circumstances, in that case the laws were for the time being just when they were expedient for the mutual intercourse of the citizens, and subsequently ceased to be just when they ceased to be expedient.

39. He who best knew how to meet fear of external foes made into one family all the creatures he could; and those he could not, he at any rate did not treat as aliens; and where he found even this impossible, he avoided all intercourse, and, so far as was expedient, kept them at a distance.

40. Those who were best able to provide themselves with the means of security against their neighbors, being thus in possession of the surest guarantee, passed the most agreeable life in each other's society; and their enjoyment of the fullest intimacy was such that, if one of them died before his time, the survivors did not lament his death as if it called for commiseration.

COMMENT

Epicurean Metaphysics

Although he acknowledges the possible existence of the gods, Epicurus shows no inclination to suppose that they involve themselves in the lives of human beings or that there is any final judgment or afterlife. Nevertheless, he admits that it cannot hurt to pattern one's life according to what one thinks would please the gods. The real basis for the "ethics of pleasure" is the materialist doctrine, borrowed from Lucretius and Democritus, that all that exists are individual, indestructible "atoms" continually rearranging themselves in relation to one another in empty space, referred to as "the void."

Such a metaphysic is extremely comforting, according to Epicurus, for several reasons. First, it means that death is not to be feared, because when we die, the atoms of which we are composed rearrange themselves, causing us to cease to exist. Thus we shall not be present to "experience" our own death. Moreover, if we no longer exist, there is nothing that can cause us pain after we are dead. Only pain itself is to be feared, and only those who are alive can experience pain.

Second, since the various permutations of atomic and molecular structuring are beyond our full knowledge, we cannot hope to control them completely. However, the more we adjust our wants to our needs and the less we seek to alter the natural course of events, the less pain we shall encounter. In other words, if we learn to distinguish between natural and unnatural desires, we shall be able to maximize our satisfaction by minimizing our frustrations. Epicurus and those who lived in his Garden sought to effect an *external* withdrawal from life and its vicissitudes rather than the *internal* withdrawal advocated by their Hellenistic counterparts, the Stoics, who will be presented in the next chapter.

Thus the goal of Epicureanism is a life of peaceful contemplation based on a materialist conception of reality. Pleasure is defined as the absence of pain. The method devised for achieving this pleasurable state is the adoption of a simple life in which one's wants are few and the long-term pleasures of the mind are preferred over the short-term pleasures of the body. In addition, the contemplation of the finer things in life and commitment to the cultivation of friendship are pleasure-producing activities.

The crucial ingredient for such a life is, of course, a strong dose of *rationality.* Only by studying the processes and patterns of nature can we hope to anticipate and avoid those events and situations that will bring us pain. By developing our reasoning powers, Epicurus maintained, we can fit our expectations to our limits and ensure our own harmony of being and peace of mind. Thus there is a certain intellectual stringency, as well as integrity of character, to the life advocated by the Epicureans.

Epicurus' concluding remarks in the selection reprinted here focus on the concept of justice. Here, too, everything becomes a means to the end of producing pleasure and avoiding pain. Justice is to be valued because it is expedient in bringing about a happy life; to live unjustly renders one susceptible to the constant fear of being found out and perhaps even punished. For Epicurus there are no forms of behavior that are evil in and of themselves; all actions are good or bad to the degree that they promote pleasure and negate pain. Only the *results* of lying, for instance, are bad because it is painful to be caught.

Some Problems

There does seem to be an inconsistency in what Epicurus says about the gods on the one hand and what he says about death on the other. If there is no afterlife, why bother to please the gods, especially since they do not seem to interfere in human affairs while we are alive? Perhaps Epicurus was only trying to avoid public disapproval by including a belief in the gods among his principle doctrines. Also, since many materialists believed that the mind is actually a specific kind of atom, it would seem that a consciousness after death is not ruled out by the rearrangement of the atoms from which we are made. Perhaps the gods are also mind-atoms who judge us according to our thoughts, both before and after death.

Many philosophers also object to the Epicurean definition of pleasure in terms of the absence of pain. Surely there is a gray middle ground between pleasure and pain that is neither. Just because we are not in pain is no reason to believe that we are experiencing pleasure. Moreover, by the time Epicurus is finished defining pleasure, he may have eliminated everything that most people generally regard as the basic pleasures of life. By withdrawing into his Garden, perhaps Epicurus has shut himself off not only from the realities of life but also from its paradoxical yet most meaningful pleasures, such as the thrill of achievement or the satisfaction of having overcome great difficulty. In short, a life of no risks may turn out, in the long run, to be quite meaningless indeed.

Finally, there seems to be a basic tension between Epicurus' commitment to the cultivation of friendship and his emphasis on the ethics of expediency. If "honesty is the best policy" simply because its opposite causes the fear of getting caught, what happens to friendship and all of its inherent virtues? Surely we all find friendship mutually pleasurable, but if our behavior toward our friends never transcends mere expediency, we have lost the meaning of friendship. Likewise, virtues such as justice may well be, as Plato taught, their own reward, even though practicing them may in given circumstances cause us great pain.

15

The Way of Nature

"By remembering, then, that I am a part of such a whole, I shall be content with everything that happens . . . and I shall turn all my efforts to the common interest."

Marcus Aurelius

MARCUS AURELIUS (A.D. 121–180)

Marcus Aurelius was the adopted son of his uncle, the Emperor Antoninus Pius. In early boyhood he was introduced to the doctrines of Stoicism, and he assumed the simple dress and practiced the austere way of life of the Stoics. After his marriage to the emperor's daughter Faustina, who bore him thirteen children, he was occupied with family affairs and learning the arts of government. At the death of Antoninus in 161 he became the ruler of the vast Roman Empire.

The remaining nineteen years of his life called for all the Stoic fortitude he could muster, for his reign was beset with calamities — floods, fires, earthquakes, pestilences, insurrections, wars, and barbarian invasions. He instituted many reforms and founded charitable institutions, but he violently persecuted the Christians, whom he regarded as subversive. His *Meditations*, which apparently were private soliloquies intended for no eyes but his own, were written during military campaigns, the hardships of which eventually caused his death at his headquarters near present-day Vienna.

Harmony with Nature

BOOK II

Begin the morning by saying to thyself, I shall meet with the busybody, the ungrateful, arrogant, deceitful, envious, unsocial. All these things happen to them by reason of their ignorance of what is good and evil. But I who have seen the nature of the good that it is beautiful, and of the bad that it is ugly, and the nature of him who does wrong, that it is akin to me, not only of the same blood or seed, but that it participates in the same intelligence and the same portion of the divinity, I can neither be injured by any of them, for no one can fix on me what is ugly, nor can I be angry with my kinsman, nor hate him. For we are made for co-operation, like feet, like hands, like eyelids, like the rows of the upper and lower teeth. To act against one another then is contrary to nature; and it is acting against one another to be vexed and to turn away.

9. This thou must always bear in mind, what is the nature of the whole, and what is my nature, and how this is related to that, and what kind of a part it is of what kind of a whole; and that there is no one who hinders thee from always doing and saying the things which are according to the nature of which thou are a part.

From *The Meditations of Marcus Aurelius Antoninus*, translated by George Long (1862).

16. The soul of man does violence to itself, first of all, when it becomes an abscess and, as it were, a tumour on the universe, so far as it can. For to be vexed at anything which happens is a separation of ourselves from nature, in some part of which the natures of all other things are contained. In the next place, the soul does violence to itself when it turns away from any man, or even moves towards him with the intention of injuring, such as are the souls of those who are angry. In the third place, the soul does violence to itself when it is overpowered by pleasure or by pain. Fourthly, when it plays a part, and does or says anything insincerely and untruly. Fifthly, when it allows any act of its own and any movement to be without an aim, and does anything thoughtlessly and without considering what it is, it being right that even the smallest things be done with reference to an end; and the end of rational animals is to follow the reason and the law of the most ancient city and polity.

17. Of human life the time is a point, and the substance is in a flux, and the perception dull, and the composition of the whole body subject to putrefaction, and the soul a whirl, and fortune hard to divine, and fame a thing devoid of judgement. And, to say all in a word, everything which belongs to the body is a stream, and what belongs to the soul is a dream and vapour, and life is a warfare and a stranger's sojourn, and after-fame is oblivion. What then is that which is able to conduct a man? One

thing and only one, philosophy. But this consists in keeping the daemon within a man free from violence and unharmed, superior to pains and pleasures, doing nothing without a purpose, nor yet falsely and with hypocrisy, not feeling the need of another man's doing or not doing anything; and besides, accepting all that happens, and all that it allotted, as coming from thence, wherever it is, from whence he himself came; and, finally, waiting for death with a cheerful mind, as being nothing else than a dissolution of the elements of which every living being is compounded. But if there is no harm to the elements themselves in each continually changing into another, why should a man have any apprehension about the change and dissolution of all the elements? For it is according to nature, and nothing is evil which is according to nature.

BOOK III

2. We ought to observe also that even the things which follow after the things which are produced according to nature contain something pleasing and attractive. For instance, when bread is baked some parts are split at the surface, and these parts which thus open, and have a certain fashion contrary to the purpose of the baker's art, are beautiful in a manner, and in a peculiar way excite a desire for eating. And again, figs, when they are quite ripe, gape open; and in the ripe olives the very circumstance of their being near to rottenness adds a peculiar beauty to the fruit. And the ears of corn bending down, and the lion's eyebrows, and the foam which flows from the mouth of wild boars, and many other things — though they are far from being beautiful, if a man should examine them severally — still, because they are consequent upon the things which are formed by nature, help to adorn them, and they please the mind; so that if a man should have a feeling and deeper insight with respect to the things which are produced in the universe, there is hardly one of those which follow by way of consequence which will not seem to him to be in a manner disposed so as to give pleasure. And so he will see even the real gaping jaws of wild beasts with no less pleasure than those which painters and sculptors show by imitation; and in an old woman and an old man he will be able to see a certain maturity and comeliness; and the attractive loveliness of young persons he will be able to look on with chaste eyes; and many such things will present themselves, not pleasing to every man, but to him only who has become truly familiar with nature and her works.

11. To the aids which have been mentioned let this one still be added: — Make for thyself a definition or description of the thing which is presented to thee, so as to see distinctly what kind of a thing it is in its substance, in its nudity, in its complete entirety, and tell thyself its proper name, and the names of the things of which it has been compounded, and into which it will be resolved. For nothing is so productive of elevation of mind as to be able to examine methodically and truly every object which is presented to thee in life, and always to look at things so as to see at the same time what kind of

universe this is, and what kind of use everything performs in it, and what value everything has with reference to the whole, and what with reference to man, who is a citizen of the highest city, of which all other cities are like families; what each thing is, and of what it is composed, and how long it is the nature of this thing to endure which now makes an impression on me, and what virtue I have need of with respect to it, such as gentleness, manliness, truth, fidelity, simplicity, contentment, and the rest. Wherefore, on every occasion a man should say: this comes from God; and this is according to the apportionment and spinning of the thread of destiny, and such-like coincidence and chance; and this is from one of the same stock, and a kinsman and partner, one who knows not however what is according to his nature. But I know; for this reason I behave towards him according to the natural law of fellowship with benevolence and justice. At the same time however in things indifferent I attempt to ascertain the value of each.

BOOK IV

4. If our intellectual part is common, the reason also, in respect of which we are rational beings, is common: if this is so, common also is the reason which commands us what to do, and what not to do; if this is so, there is a common law also; if this is so, we are fellow-citizens; if this is so, we are members of some political community; if this is so, the world is in a manner a state. For of what other common political community will any one say that the whole human race are members? And from thence, from this common political community comes also our very intellectual faculty and reasoning faculty and our capacity for law; or whence do they come? For as my earthly part is a portion given to me from certain earth, and that which is watery from another element, and that which is hot and fiery from some peculiar source (for nothing comes out of that which is nothing, as nothing also returns to non-existence), so also the intellectual part comes from some source.

23. Everything harmonizes with me, which is harmonious to thee, O Universe. Nothing for me is too early nor too late, which is in due time for thee. Everything is fruit to me which thy seasons bring, O Nature: from thee are all things; in thee are all things, to thee all things return. The poet says, Dear city of Cecrops; and wilt not thou say, Dear city of Zeus?

48. Think continually how many physicians are dead after often contracting their eyebrows over the sick; and how many astrologers after predicting with great pretensions the deaths of others; and how many philosophers after endless discourses on death or immortality; how many heroes after killing thousands; and how many tyrants who have used their power over men's lives with terrible insolence as if they were immortal; and how many cities are entirely dead, so to speak, Helice and Pompeii and Herculaneum, and others innumerable. Add to the reckoning all whom thou hast known, one after another. One man after burying another has been laid out dead, and another buries him: and all this in a

short time. To conclude, always observe how ephemeral and worthless human things are, and what was yesterday a little mucus tomorrow will be a mummy or ashes. Pass then through this little space of time conformably to nature, and end thy journey in content, just as an olive falls off when it is ripe, blessing nature who produced it, and thanking the tree on which it grew.

49. Be like the promontory against which the waves continually break, but it stands firm and tames the fury of the water around it.

Unhappy am I, because this has happened to me. — Not so, but happy am I, though this has happened to me, because I continue free from pain, neither crushed by the present nor fearing the future. For such a thing as this might have happened to every man; but every man would not have continued free from pain on such an occasion. Why then is that rather a misfortune than this a good fortune? And dost thou in all cases call that a man's misfortune, which is not a deviation from man's nature? And does a thing seem to thee to be a deviation from man's nature, when it is not contrary to the will of man's nature? Well, thou knowest the will of nature. Will then this which has happened prevent thee from being just, magnanimous, temperate, prudent, secure against inconsiderate opinions and falsehood; will it prevent thee from having modesty, freedom, and everything else, by the presence of which man's nature obtains all that is its own? Remember too on every occasion which leads thee to vexation to apply this principle: not that this is a mis-

fortune, but that to bear it nobly is good fortune.

BOOK V

In the morning when thou risest unwillingly, let this thought be present — I am rising to the work of a human being. Why then am I dissatisfied if I am going to do the things for which I exist and for which I was brought into the world? Or have I been made for this, to lie in the bed-clothes and keep myself warm? — But this is more pleasant. — Dost thou exist then to take thy pleasure, and not at all for action or exertion? Dost thou not see the little plants, the little birds, the ants, the spiders, the bees working together to put in order their several parts of the universe? And art thou willing to do the work of a human being, and dost thou not make haste to do that which is according to thy nature? — But it is necessary to take rest also. — It is necessary: however nature has fixed bounds to this too: she has fixed bounds both to eating and drinking, and yet thou goest beyond these bounds, beyond what is sufficient; yet in thy acts it is not so, but thou stoppest short of what thou canst do. So thou lovest not thyself, for it thou didst, thou wouldst love thy nature and her will. But those who love their several arts exhaust themselves in working at them unwashed and without food; but thou valuest thy own nature less than the turner values the turning art, or the dancer the dancing art, or the lover of money values his money, or the vainglorious man his little glory. And such men, when they have a violent affection to a thing, choose neither to eat nor to sleep rather than to perfect the things which they care for. But are the acts which concern society more vile in thy eyes and less worthy of thy labour?

2. How easy it is to repel and to wipe away every impression which is troublesome or unsuitable, and immediately to be in all tranquillity.

3. Judge every word and deed which are according to nature to be fit for thee; and be not diverted by the blame which follows from any people nor by their words, but if a thing is good to be done or said, do not consider it unworthy of thee. For those persons have their peculiar leading principle and follow their peculiar movement; which things do not thou regard, but go straight on, following thy own nature and the common nature; and the way of both is one.

16. Such as are thy habitual thoughts, such also will be the character of thy mind; for the soul is dyed by the thoughts. Dye it then with a continuous series of such thoughts as these: for instance, that where a man can live, there he can also live well. But he must live in a place; — well then, he can also live well in a palace. And again, consider that for whatever purpose each thing has been constituted, for this it has been constituted, and towards this it is carried; and its end is in that towards which it is carried; and where the end is, there also is the advantage and the good of each thing. Now the good for the reasonable animal is society; for that we are made for society has been shown above. Is it not plain that the inferior exist for the sake of the superior? But the things which have life are superior to those which have not life, and of those which have life the superior are those which have reason.

BOOK VI

15. Some things are hurrying into existence, and others are hurrying out of it; and of that which is coming into existence part is already extinguished. Motions and changes are continually renewing the world, just as the uninterrupted course of time is always renewing the infinite duration of ages. In this flowing stream then, on which there is no abiding, what is there of the things which hurry by on which a man would set a high price? It would be just as if a man should fall in love with one of the sparrows which fly by, but it has already passed out of sight. Something of this kind is the very life of every man, like the exhalation of the blood and the respiration of the air. For such as it is to have once drawn in the air and to have given it back, which we do every moment, just the same is it with the whole respiratory power, which thou didst receive at thy birth yesterday and the day before, to give it back to the element from which thou didst first draw it.

16. Neither is transpiration, as in plants, a thing to be valued, nor respiration, as in domesticated animals and wild beasts, nor the receiving of impressions by the appearances of things, nor being moved by desires as puppets by strings, nor assembling in herds, nor being nourished by food; for this is just like the act of separating and parting with the useless part of our food. What then is worth being valued? To be received with clapping of hands? No.

Neither must we value the clapping of tongues, for the praise which comes from the many is a clapping of tongues. Suppose then that thou hast given up this worthless thing called fame, what remains that is worth valuing? This is my opinion, to move thyself and to re-strain thyself in conformity to thy proper constitution, to which end both all employments and arts lead. For every art aims at this, that the thing which has been made should be adapted to the work for which it has been made; and both the vine-planter who looks after the vine, and the horse-breaker, and he who trains the dog, seek this end. But the education and the teaching of youth aim at something. In this then is the value of the education and the teaching. And if this is well, thou wilt not seek anything else. Wilt thou not cease to value many other things too? Then thou wilt be neither free, nor suf-ficient for thy own happiness, nor without passion. For of necessity thou must be envious, jealous, and suspi-cious of those who can take away those things, and plot against those who have that which is valued by thee. Of neces-sity a man must be altogether in a state of perturbation who wants any of these things; and besides, he must often find fault with the gods. But to reverence and honour thy own mind will make thee content with thyself, and in har-mony with society, and in agreement with the gods, that is, praising all that they give and have ordered.

BOOK VII

9. All things are implicated with one another, and the bond is holy; and there is hardly anything unconnected with any other thing. For things have been co-ordinated, and they combine to form the same universe (order). For there is one universe made up of all things, and one God who pervades all things, and one substance, and one law, one common reason in all intelligent animals, and one truth; if indeed there is also one perfection for all animals which are of the same stock and partici-pate in the same reason.

55. Do not look around thee to dis-cover other men's ruling principles, but look straight to this, to what na-ture leads thee, both the universal nature through the things which hap-pen to thee, and thy own nature through the acts which must be done by thee. But every being ought to do that which is according to its constitution; and all other things have been consti-tuted for the sake of rational beings, just as among irrational things the in-ferior for the sake of the superior, but the rational for the sake of one an-other.

The prime principle then in man's constitution is the social. And the sec-ond is not to yield to the persuasions of the body, for it is the peculiar office of the rational and intelligent motion to circumscribe itself, and never to be overpowered either by the motion of the senses or of the appetites, for both are animal; but the intelligent motion claims superiority and does not permit itself to be overpowered by the others. And with good reason, for it is formed by nature to use all of them. The third thing in the rational constitution is freedom from error and from decep-tion. Let then the ruling principle holding fast to these things go straight on, and it has what is its own.

BOOK VIII

7. Every nature is contented with itself when it goes on its way well; and a rational nature goes on its way well, when in its thoughts it assents to nothing false or uncertain, and when it directs its movements to social acts only, and when it confines its desires and aversions to the things which are in its power, and when it is satisfied with everything that is assigned to it by the common nature. For of this common nature every particular nature is a part, as the nature of the leaf is a part of the nature of the plant; except that in the plant the nature of the leaf is part of a nature which has not perception or reason, and is subject to be impeded; but the nature of man is part of a nature which is not subject to impediments, and is intelligent and just, since it gives to everything in equal portions and according to its worth, times, substance, cause (form), activity, and incident. But examine, not to discover that any one thing compared with any other single thing is equal in all respects, but by taking all the parts together of one thing comparing them with all the parts together of another.

34. If thou didst ever see a hand cut off, or a foot, or a head, lying anywhere apart from the rest of the body, such does a man make himself, as far as he can, who is not content with what happens, and separates himself from others, or does anything unsocial. Suppose that thou hast detached thyself from the natural unity—for thou wast made by nature a part, but now thou hast cut thyself off—yet here there is this beautiful provision, that it is in thy power again to unite thyself. God has allowed this to no other part, after it has been separated and cut asunder, to come together again. But consider the kindness by which he has distinguished man, for he has put it in his power not to be separated at all from the universal; and when he has been separated, he has allowed him to return and to be united and to resume his place as a part.

47. If thou art pained by any external thing, it is not this thing that disturbs thee, but thy own judgement about it. And it is in thy power to wipe out this judgement now. But if anything in thy own disposition gives thee pain, who hinders thee from correcting thy opinion? And even if thou are pained because thou art not doing some particular thing which seems to thee to be right, why dost thou not rather act than complain?—But some insuperable obstacle is in the way?—Do not be grieved then, for the cause of its not being done depends not on thee.—But it is not worth while to live, if this cannot be done.—Take thy departure then from life contentedly, just as he dies who is in full activity, and well pleased too with things which are obstacles.

BOOK IX

3. Do not despise death, but be well content with it, since this too is one of those things which nature wills. For such as it is to be young and to grow old, and to increase and to reach maturity, and to have teeth and beard and grey hairs, and to beget, and to be preg-

nant and to bring forth, and all the other natural operations which the seasons of thy life bring, such also is dissolution. This, then, is consistent with the character of a reflecting man, to be neither careless nor impatient nor contemptuous with respect to death, but to wait for it as one of the operations of nature. As thou now waitest for the time when the child shall come out of thy wife's womb, so be ready for the time when thy soul shall fall out of this envelope. But if thou requirest also a vulgar kind of comfort which shall reach thy heart, thou wilt be made best reconciled to death by observing the objects from which thou art going to be removed, and the morals of those with whom thy soul will no longer be mingled. For it is no way right to be offended with men, but it is thy duty to care for them and to bear with them gently; and yet to remember that thy departure will be not from men who have the same principles as thyself. For this is the only thing, if there be any, which could draw us the contrary way and attach us to life, to be permitted to live with those who have the same principles as ourselves. But now thou seest how great is the trouble arising from the discordance of those who live together, so that thou mayest say, Come quick, O death, lest perchance I, too, should forget myself.

9. All things which participate in anything which is common to them all move towards that which is of the same kind with themselves. Everything which is earthy turns towards the earth, everything which is liquid flows together, and everything which is of an aërial kind does the same, so that they require something to keep them asunder, and the application of force. Fire indeed moves upwards on account of the elemental fire, but it is so ready to be kindled together with all the fire which is here, that even every substance which is somewhat dry, is easily ignited, because there is less mingled with it of that which is a hindrance to ignition. Accordingly then everything also which participates in the common intelligent nature moves in like manner towards that which is of the same kind with itself, or moves even more. For so much as it is superior in comparison with all other things, in the same degree also is it more ready to mingle with and to be fused with that which is akin to it. Accordingly among animals devoid of reason we find swarms of bees, and herds of cattle, and the nurture of young birds, and in a manner, loves; for even in animals there are souls, and that power which brings them together is seen to exert itself in the superior degree, and in such a way as never has been observed in plants nor in stones nor in trees. But in rational animals there are political communities and friendships, and families and meetings of people; and in wars, treaties and armistices. But in the things which are still superior, even though they are separated from one another, unity in a manner exists, as in the stars. Thus the ascent to the higher degree is able to produce a sympathy even in things which are separated. See, then, what now takes place. For only intelligent animals have now forgotten this mutual desire and inclination, and in them alone the property of flowing together is not seen. But still though men

strive to avoid this union, they are caught and held by it, for their nature is too strong for them; and thou wilt see what I say, if thou only observest. Sooner, then, will one find anything earthy which comes in contact with no earthy thing than a man altogether separated from other men.

42. When thou art offended with any man's shameless conduct, immediately ask thyself, Is it possible, then, that shameless men should not be in the world? It is not possible. Do not, then, require what is impossible. For this man also is one of those shameless men who must of necessity be in the world. Let the same considerations be present to thy mind in the case of the knave, and the faithless man, and of every man who does wrong in any way. For at the same time that thou dost remind thyself that it is impossible that such kind of men should not exist, thou wilt become more kindly disposed towards every one individually. It is useful to perceive this, too, immediately when the occasion arises, what virtue nature has given to man to oppose to every wrongful act. For she has given to man, as an antidote against the stupid man, mildness, and against another kind of man some other power. And in all cases it is possible for thee to correct by teaching the man who is gone astray; for every man who errs misses his object and is gone astray. Besides wherein hast thou been injured? For thou wilt find that no one among those against whom thou art irritated has done anything by which thy mind could be made worse; but that which is evil to thee and harmful has its foundation only in the mind. And what harm is done or what

is there strange, if the man who has not been instructed does the acts of an uninstructed man? Consider whether thou shouldst not rather blame thyself, because thou didst not expect such a man to err in such a way. For thou hadst means given thee by the reason to suppose that it was likely that he would commit this error, and yet thou hast forgotten and art amazed that he has erred. But most of all when thou blamest a man as faithless or ungrateful, turn to thyself. For the fault is manifestly thy own, whether thou didst trust that a man who had such a disposition would keep his promise, or when conferring thy kindness thou didst not confer it absolutely, nor yet in such way as to have received from thy very act all the profit. For what more dost thou want when thou hast done a man a service? Are thou not content that thou hast done something comformable to thy nature, and dost thou seek to be paid for it? Just as if the eye demanded a recompense for seeing, or the feet for walking. For as these members are formed for a particular purpose, and by working according to their several constitutions obtain what is their own; so also as man is formed by nature to acts of benevolence, when he has done anything benevolent or in any other way conducive to the common interest, he has acted conformably to his constitution, and he gets what is his own.

BOOK X

2. Observe what thy nature requires, so far as thou art governed by nature only: then do it and accept it, if thy nature, so far as thou art a living being, shall not

be made worse by it. And next thou must observe what thy nature requires so far as thou art a living being. And all this thou mayest allow thyself, if thy nature, so far as thou art a rational animal, shall not be made worse by it. But the rational animal is consequently also a political (social) animal. Use these rules, then, and trouble thyself about nothing else.

6. Whether the universe is a concourse of atoms, or nature is a system, let this first be established, that I am a part of the whole which is governed by nature; next, I am in a manner intimately related to the parts which are of the same kind with myself. For remembering this, inasmuch as I am a part, I shall be discontented with none of the things which are assigned to me out of the whole; for nothing is injurious to the part, if it is for the advantage of the whole. For the whole contains nothing which is not for its advantage; and all natures indeed have this common principle, but the nature of the universe has this principle besides, that it cannot be compelled even by any external cause to generate anything harmful to itself. By remembering, then, that I am a part of such a whole, I shall be content with everything that happens. And inasmuch as I am in a manner intimately related to the parts which are of the same kind with myself, I shall do nothing unsocial, but I shall rather direct myself to the things which are of the same kind with myself, and I shall turn all my efforts to the common interest, and divert them from the contrary. Now, if these things are done so, life must flow on happily, just as thou mayest observe that the life of a citizen is happy, who continues a course of action which is advantageous to his fellow-citizens, and is content with whatever the state may assign to him.

BOOK XI

19. There are four principal aberrations of the superior faculty against which thou shouldst be constantly on thy guard, and when thou hast detected them, thou shouldst wipe them out and say on each occasion thus: this thought is not necessary: this tends to destroy social union: this which thou art going to say comes not from the real thoughts; for thou shouldst consider it among the most absurd of things for a man not to speak from his real thoughts. But the fourth is when thou shalt reproach thyself for anything, for this is an evidence of the diviner part within thee being overpowered and yielding to the less honourable and to the perishable part, the body, and to its gross pleasures.

20. Thy aërial part and all the fiery parts which are mingled in thee, though by nature they have an upward tendency, still in obedience to the disposition of the universe they are overpowered here in the compound mass (the body). And also the whole of the earthy part in thee and the watery, though their tendency is downward, still are raised up and occupy a position which is not their natural one. In this manner then the elemental parts obey the universal, for when they have been fixed in any place perforce they remain there until again the universal shall sound the signal for dissolution. Is it not then strange that thy intelligent

part only should be disobedient and discontented with its own place? And yet no force is imposed on it, but only those things which are conformable to its nature: still it does not submit, but is carried in the opposite direction. For the movement towards injustice and intemperance and to anger and grief and fear is nothing else than the act of one who deviates from nature. And also when the ruling faculty is discontented with anything that happens, then too it deserts its post: for it is constituted for piety and reverence towards the gods no less than for justice. For these qualities also are comprehended under the generic term of contentment with the constitution of things, and indeed they are prior to acts of justice.

BOOK XII

26. When thou art troubled about anything, thou hast forgotten this, that all things happen according to the universal nature; and forgotten this, that a man's wrongful act is nothing to thee; and further thou hast forgotten this, that everything which happens, always happened so and will happen so, and now happens so everywhere; forgotten this too, how close is the kinship between a man and the whole human race, for it is a community, not of a little blood or seed, but of intelligence. And thou hast forgotten this too, that every man's intelligence is a god, and is an efflux of the deity; and forgotten this, that nothing is a man's own, but that his child and his body and his very soul came from the deity; forgotten this, that everything is opinion; and lastly thou hast forgotten that every man lives the present time only, and loses only this.

36. Man, thou has been a citizen in this great state (the world): what difference does it make to thee whether for five years (or three)? For that which is conformable to the laws is just for all. Where is the hardship then, if no tyrant nor yet an unjust judge sends thee away from the state, but nature who brought thee into it? The same as if a praetor who has employed an actor dismisses him from the stage. — 'But I have not finished the five acts, but only three of them.' — Thou sayest well, but in life the three acts are the whole drama; for what shall be a complete drama is determined by him who was once the cause of its composition, and now of its dissolution: but thou art the cause of neither. Depart then satisfied, for he also who releases thee is satisfied.

COMMENT

Human Harmony with the Natural Environment

In the writings of Marcus Aurelius, there is a strong overtone of pantheism in the doctrine that people should live in harmony with nature. Just as a soul or life force animates the human body, he maintained, so a spiritual force rolls through all things. This soul or life force can be called

God, Nature, Reason — synonyms for the inner essence and animating principle of the universe. It is the productive, formative power, the force that makes for movement and growth. It is divine reason, all-pervasive and all-powerful. Hence Marcus Aurelius maintained that there is no sheer evil in the world, and nothing is left to chance. From this standpoint the force is also fate — not a blind mechanical necessity but a purposive, providential force, the living activity of the whole expressing itself through every natural event.

The divine essence is in every person: Reason is our governing principle, the core and center of our being. What corresponds to this reason and expresses our nature also corresponds to the world soul and expresses the universal nature. To "live according to nature" is to express our rational nature and to be in harmony with the rational order of the world. The essence of morality is to make the "things in our power" — our inner attitudes — harmonize with the "things not in our power" — the rational outward course of events.

The need to live in harmony with nature is not just an ancient doctrine. It has been echoed and reechoed during our modern ecological crisis. We may choose to express this need more in scientific than in religious terms, but we too must recognize the necessity to live in symbiotic harmony with nature. Willy-nilly, we have to dwell on this earth if we are to live at all. If the future is to be tolerable, we must bring human breeding under sensible control, we must conserve our dwindling natural resources, and we must bring to a halt the air and water pollution and the bulldozed devastation of the landscape.

Some Major Questions

The great question that is posed by the readings in this chapter is the relation between "facts" and "ideals", between "what is" and "what ought to be." This is a question to which the philosophers represented here in Part Three will return again and again, and it is one of the most important and difficult questions in ethics. The serious student of philosophy will need to ponder its meaning and implications and to decide as best as possible what is a reasonable answer.

It seems clear that *good*, in the sense of *what ought to be*, and *right*, in the sense of *what ought to be done*, are not natural characteristics, as are rectangularity or absent-mindedness. Many philosophers have concluded that these concepts have a distinctly *ethical* meaning — a meaning that must be grasped by intuition or a priori reason or a peculiar moral sense rather than by empirical science or a descriptive metaphysics. If so, does this invalidate the doctrine discussed in this chapter that morality is based on nature? Here is a question that the reader might ponder.

Another very fundamental question is whether the antirelativistic implications of the theory of natural law are valid. Can we define our legitimate aim as the unfolding of our basic powers according to the laws of our nature and in harmony with our natural environment? Or should we conclude that people are so variously molded by patterns of culture that "human nature" is largely an empty phrase? Or that the natural environment counts less and less in comparison with the artificialities of urban civilization? If so, is this a disaster?

Other questions concern the relation between natural rights and democratic theory. The concept of natural rights has often been linked with the "social contract." This is the idea of an original covenant by which individuals, who possessed natural rights in an original, nonpolitical "state of nature," joined together and through mutual consent formed a state and placed a fiduciary trust in the supreme power of government. The purpose of the covenant is to make these rights more secure, and if the government fails to do so, it forfeits the right to rule. Thus phrased the theory of the state of nature, natural rights, and the social contract formed the basis of democratic, sometimes revolutionary, tendencies. In Rousseau's formulation and even more clearly in Kant's, the state of nature and the social contract were treated as useful fictions, meant to serve as a criterion for judging the legitimacy of acts of the state. This constellation of ideas has been elaborated by John Rawl's much discussed book, *The Theory of Justice* (Harvard University Press, 1971). The reader may wish to consider whether the tradition of natural law and natural rights is a satisfactory basis for a theory of democratic sovereignty and social justice. Is it an effective way to delineate the meaning of human rights? Or is it too abstract and nonhistorical? Must we seek some other basis for democratic theory, for example, the instrumentalist approach of John Dewey or the socialist approach of Karl Marx? Or should we reject democracy altogether, as Plato and Nietzsche would have us do?

There is also the question of whether Marcus Aurelius' interpretation of nature is coherent. Is he being inconsistent in clinging to the doctrines of both fate and free will, cosmopolitanism and self-sufficiency, tacit admission that certain things are preferable and yet explicit teaching that all happens for the best? If he *is* inconsistent, can we somehow reconcile these clashing doctrines, or must we choose some and abandon others? If so, how much can we salvage? Can we still admire the main tenets of his Stoicism: the courage, the tranquility, the cosmopolitanism, the sense of universal fellowship, the attempt to see the rational connections and necessity of things, the poise and magnanimity of outlook that result from identifying oneself with the whole frame of nature?

Finally there is the question of ecological adjustment. As I have already intimated, this is a crucial issue for the whole of humanity. Our present technology is suicidal — so much of it is devoted to the instruments of death rather than to the means of life, and so much is based on the extraction of exhaustible ores and fossil fuels. These diminishing resources are combined with mounting overpopulation. Control is an unsolved problem even in the developed countries, and starvation is the only sure-fire method of controlling population in the undeveloped countries. The present rate of population growth cannot continue indefinitely, for it would rapidly exhaust the physical resources and limit of our world. Can we cope with these threats without a fairly radical interference with cherished freedoms and traditional institutions? Can we limit growth without precipitating a new depression? What far-reaching changes in human values will be required?

16

The Way of Duty

"In all cases I must act in such a way that I can at the same time will that my maxim should become a universal law . . . and this is the principal which serves, and must serve, to determine the will, if the idea of duty is not to be regarded as empty."

Immanuel Kant

IMMANUEL KANT (1724–1804)

For a biographical note, see pages 99–100.

The Categorical Imperative

SECTION I

Transition from Ordinary Moral Conceptions to the Philosophical Conception of Morality

Nothing in the whole world, or even outside of the world, can possibly be regarded as good without limitation except a *good will*. No doubt it is a good and desirable thing to have intelligence, sagacity, judgment, and other intellectual gifts, by whatever name they may be called; it is also good and desirable in many respects to possess by nature such qualities as courage, resolution, and perseverance; but all these gifts of nature may be in the highest degree pernicious and hurtful, if the will which directs them, or what is called the *character*, is not itself good. The same thing applies to *gifts of fortune*. Power, wealth, honor, even good health, and that general well-being and contentment with one's lot which we call *happiness*, give rise to pride and not infrequently to insolence, if a man's will is not good; nor can a reflective and impartial spectator ever look with satisfaction upon the unbroken prosperity of a man who is destitute of

The *Philosophy of Kant as Contained in Extracts from His Own Writings*, selected and translated by John Watson. (Glasgow: Jackson, Wylie and Company, 1888; second edition, 1891). In this version, the original in *The Foundations of the Metaphysic of Morals* is somewhat condensed.

the ornament of a pure and good will. A good will would therefore seem to be the indispensable condition without which no one is even worthy to be happy.

A man's will is good, not because the consequences which flow from it are good, nor because it is capable of attaining the end which it seeks, but it is good in itself, or because it wills the good. By a good will is not meant mere well-wishing; it consists in a resolute employment of all the means within one's reach, and its intrinsic value is in no way increased by success or lessened by failure.

This idea of the absolute value of mere will seems so extraordinary that, although it is endorsed even by the popular judgment, we must subject it to careful scrutiny.

If nature had meant to provide simply for the maintenance, the well-being, in a word the happiness, of beings which have reason and will, it must be confessed that, in making use of their reason, it has hit upon a very poor way of attaining its end. As a matter of fact the very worst way a man of refinement and culture can take to secure enjoyment and happiness is to make use of his reason for that purpose. Hence there is apt to arise in his mind a certain degree of *misology*, or hatred of reason. Finding that the arts which minister to luxury, and even the sciences, instead of bringing him happiness, only lay a heavier yoke on his neck, he at length comes to envy, rather than to despise, men of less refinement, who follow more closely the promptings of their natural impulses, and pay little heed to what reason tells them to do or to leave undone. It must at least be admitted, that one may deny reason to have much or indeed any value in the production of happiness and contentment, without taking a morose or ungrateful view of the goodness with which the world is governed. Such a judgment really means that life has another and a much nobler end than happiness, and that the true vocation of reason is to secure that end.

The true object of reason then, in so far as it is practical, or capable of influencing the will, must be to produce a will which is *good in itself*, and not merely good *as a means* to something else. This will is not the only or the whole good, but it is the highest good, and the condition of all other good, even of the desire for happiness itself. It is therefore not inconsistent with the wisdom of nature that the cultivation of reason which is essential to the furtherance of its first and unconditioned object, the production of a good will, should, in this life at least, in many ways limit, or even make impossible, the attainment of happiness, which is its second and conditioned object.

To bring to clear consciousness the conception of a will which is good in itself, a conception already familiar to the popular mind, let us examine the conception of *duty*, which involves the idea of a good will as manifested under certain subjective limitations and hindrances.

I pass over actions which are admittedly violations of duty, for these, however useful they may be in the attainment of this or that end, manifestly do not proceed *from* duty. I set aside also those actions which are not actually inconsistent with duty, but which yet are done under the impulse of some natural inclination, although *not a direct inclination* to do these particular actions; for in these it is easy to determine whether the action that is consistent with duty, is done *from duty* or with some selfish object in view. It is more difficult to make a clear distinction of motives when there is a *direct* inclination to do a certain action, which is itself in conformity with duty. The preservation of one's own life, for instance, is a duty; but, as everyone has a natural inclination to preserve his life, the anxious care which most men usually devote to this object, has no intrinsic value, nor the maxim from which they act any moral import. They preserve their life *in accordance with* duty, but not *because of* duty. But, suppose adversity and hopeless sorrow to have taken away all desire for life; suppose that the wretched man would welcome death as a release, and yet takes means to prolong his life simply from a sense of duty: then his maxim has a genuine moral import.

But, secondly, an action that is done from duty gets its moral value, *not from the object* which it is intended to secure, but from the maxim by which it is determined. Accordingly, the action has the same moral value whether the object is attained or not, if only the *principle* by which the will is determined to act is independent of every object of sensuous desire. What was said above makes it clear, that it is not the object aimed at, or, in other words, the consequences which flow from an action when these are made the end and motive of the will, that can give to the action an unconditioned and moral value. In what, then, can the moral value of an action consist, if it does not lie in the will itself, as directed to the attainment of a certain object? It can lie only in the principle of the will, no matter whether the object sought can be attained by the action or not. For the will stands as it were at the parting of the ways, between its *a priori* principle, which is formal, and its *posteriori* material motive. As so standing it must be determined by something, and, as no action which is done from duty can be determined by a material principle, it can be determined only by the formal principle of all volition.

From the two propositions just set forth a third directly follows, which may be thus stated. *Duty is the obligation to act from reverence for law.* Now, I may have a natural *inclination* for the object that I expect to follow from my action, but I can never have *reverence* for that which is not a spontaneous activity of my will, but merely an effect of it; neither can I have reverence for any natural inclination, whether it is my own or another's. If it is my own, I can at most only approve of it; if it is manifested by another, I may regard it as conducive to my own interest, and hence I may in certain cases even be said to have a love for it. But the only thing which I can reverence or which can lay me under an obligation to act, is the law which is connected with my will, not as a consequence, but as a principle; a prin-

ciple which is not dependent upon natural inclination, but overmasters it, or at least allows it to have no influence whatever in determining my course of action. Now if an action which is done out of regard for duty sets entirely aside the influence of natural inclination and along with it every object of the will, nothing else is left by which the will can be determined but objectively the *law* itself, and subjectively *pure reverence* for the law as a principle of action. Thus there arises the maxim, to obey the moral law even at the sacrifice of all my natural inclinations.

The supreme good which we call moral can therefore be nothing but the *idea of the law* in itself, in so far as it is this idea which determines the will, and not any consequences that are expected to follow. Only a *rational* being can have such an idea, and hence a man who acts from the idea of the law is already morally good, no matter whether the consequences which he expects from his action follow or not.

Now what must be the nature of a law, the idea of which is to determine the will, even apart from the effects expected to follow, and which is therefore itself entitled to be called good absolutely and without qualification? As the will must not be moved to act from any desire for the results expected to follow from obedience to a certain law, the only principle of the will which remains is that of the conformity of actions to universal law. In all cases I must act in such a way *that I can at the same time will that my maxim should become a universal law.* This is what is meant by conformity to law pure and simple; and this is the principle which serves, and must serve, to determine the will, if the idea of duty is not to be regarded as empty and chimerical. As a matter of fact the judgments which we are wont to pass upon conduct perfectly agree with this principle, and in making them we always have it before our eyes.

May I, for instance, under the pressure of circumstances, make a promise which I have no intention of keeping? The question is not, whether it is prudent to make a false promise, but whether it is morally right. To enable me to answer this question shortly and conclusively, the best way is for me to ask myself whether it would satisfy me that the maxim to extricate myself from embarrassment by giving a false promise should have the force of a universal law, applying to others as well as to myself. And I see at once, that, while I can certainly will the lie, I cannot will that lying should be a universal law. If lying were universal, there would, properly speaking, be no promises whatever. I might say that I intended to do a certain thing at some future time, but nobody would believe me, or if he did at the moment trust to my promise, he would afterwards pay me back in my own coin. My maxim thus proves itself to be self-destructive, so soon as it is taken as a universal law.

Duty, then, consists in the obligation to act from *pure* reverence for the moral law. To this motive all others must give way, for it is the condition of a will which is good *in itself*, and which has a value with which nothing else is comparable.

There is, however, in man a strong feeling of antagonism to the commands of duty, although his reason tells him that those commands are worthy of the highest reverence. For man not only possesses reason, but he has certain natural wants and inclinations, the complete satisfaction of which he calls happiness. These natural inclinations clamorously demand to have their seemingly reasonable claims respected; but reason issues its commands inflexibly, refusing to promise anything to the natural desires, and treating their claims with a sort of neglect and contempt. From this there arises a *natural dialectic*, that is, a disposition to explain away the strict laws of duty, to cast doubt upon their validity, or at least, upon their purity and stringency, and in this way to make them yield to the demands of the natural inclinations.

Thus men are forced to go beyond the narrow circle of ideas within which their reason ordinarily moves, and to take a step into the field of *moral philosophy*, not indeed from any perception of speculative difficulties, but simply on practical grounds. The practical reason of men cannot be long exercised any more than the theoretical, without falling insensibly into a dialectic, which compels it to call in the aid of philosophy; and in the one case as in the other, rest can be found only in a thorough criticism of human reason.

SECTION II

Transition from Popular Moral Philosophy to the Metaphysic of Morality

So far, we have drawn our conception of duty from the manner in which men employ it in the ordinary exercise of their practical reason. The conception of duty, however, we must not suppose to be therefore derived from experience. On the contrary, we hear frequent complaints, the justice of which we cannot but admit, that no one can point to a single instance in which an action has undoubtedly been done purely from a regard for duty; that there are certainly many actions which are not *opposed* to duty, but none which are indisputably done *from* duty and therefore have a moral value. Nothing indeed can secure us against the complete loss of our ideas of duty, and maintain in the soul a well-grounded respect for the moral law, but the clear conviction, that reason issues its commands on its own authority, without caring in the least whether the actions of men have, as a matter of fact, been done purely from ideas of duty. For reason commands inflexibly that certain actions should be done, which perhaps never have been done; actions, the very possibility of which may seem doubtful to one who bases everything upon experience. Perfect disinterestedness in friendship, for instance, is demanded of every man, although there may never have been a sincere friend; for pure friendship is bound up with the idea of duty as duty, and belongs to the very idea of a reason which determines the will on *a priori* grounds, prior to all experience.

It is, moreover, beyond dispute, that unless we are to deny to morality all truth and all reference to a possible object, the moral law has so wide an application that it is binding, not merely upon man, but upon all *rational beings*, and no merely under certain contingent conditions, and with certain limitations, but absolutely and necessarily. . . .

Only a rational being has the faculty of acting in conformity with the *idea* of law, or from principles; only a rational being, in other words, has a will. And as without reason actions cannot proceed from laws, will is simply practical reason. If the will is infallibly determined by reason, the actions of a rational being are subjectively as well as objectively necessary; that is, will must be regarded as a faculty of choosing *that only* which reason, independently of natural inclination, declares to be practically necessary or good. On the other hand, if the will is not invariably determined by reason alone, but is subject to certain subjective conditions or motives, which are not always in harmony with the objective conditions; if the will, as actually is the case with man, is not in perfect conformity with reason; actions which are recognized to be objectively necessary, are subjectively contingent. The determination of such a will according to objective laws is therefore called *obligation*. That is to say, if the will of a rational being is not absolutely good, we conceive of it as capable of being determined by objective laws of reason, but not as by its very nature necessarily obeying them.

The idea that a certain principle is objective, and binding upon the will, is a command of reason, and the statement of the command in a formula is an *imperative*.

All imperatives are expressed by the word *ought*, to indicate that the will upon which they are binding is not by its subjective constitution necessarily determined in conformity with the objective law of reason. An imperative says, that the doing, or leaving undone of a certain thing would be good, but it addresses a will which does not always do a thing simply because it is good. Now, that is practically *good* which determines the will by ideas of reason, in other words, that which determines it, not by subjective influences, but by principles which are objective, or apply to all rational beings as such. *Good* and *pleasure* are quite distinct. Pleasure results from the influence of purely subjective causes upon the will of the subject, and these vary with the susceptibility of this or that individual, while a principle of reason is valid for all.

A perfectly good will would, like the will of man, stand under objective laws, laws of the good, but it could not be said to be under an *obligation* to act in conformity with those laws. Such a will by its subjective constitution could be determined only by the idea of the good. In reference to the Divine will, or any other holy will, imperatives have no meaning; for here the will is by its very nature necessarily in harmony with the law, and therefore *ought* has no application to it. Imperatives are formulae, which express merely the relation of objective laws of volition in general to the imperfect will of this or that rational being, as for instance, the will of man.

Now, all imperatives command either *hypothetically* or *categorically*. A hypothetical imperative states that a certain thing must be done, if something else which is willed, or at least might be willed, is to be attained. The categorical imperative declares that an act is in itself or objectively necessary, without any reference to another end.

Every practical law represents a possibly action as good, and therefore as obligatory for a subject that is capable of being determined to act by reason. Hence all imperatives are formulae for the determination of an action which is obligatory according to the principle of a will that is in some sense good. If the action is good only because it is a means to *something else*, the imperative is *hypothetical*; if the action is conceived to be good *in itself*, the imperative, as the necessary principle of a will than in itself conforms to reason, is *categorical*.

An imperative, then, states what possible action of mine would be good. It supplies the practical rule for a will which does not at once do an act simply because it is good, either because the subject does not know it to be good, or because, knowing it to be good, he is influenced by maxims which are opposed to the objective principles of a practical reason.

The hypothetical imperative says only that an action is good relatively to a certain *possible* end or to a certain *actual* end. In the former case it is *problematic*, in the latter case *assertoric*. The categorical imperative, which affirms that an action is in itself or objectively necessary without regard to an end, that is, without regard to any other end than itself, is an *apodictic* practical principle.

Whatever is within the power of a rational being may be conceived to be capable of being willed by some rational being, and hence the principles which determine what actions are necessary in the attainment of certain possible ends, are infinite in number.

Yet there is one thing which we may assume that all finite rational beings actually make their end, and there is therefore one object which may safely be regarded, not simply as something that they *may* seek, but as something that by a necessity of their nature they actually *do* seek. This object is *happiness*. The hypothetical imperative, which affirms the practical necessity of an action as the means of attaining happiness, is *assertoric*. We must not think of happiness as simply a possible and problematic end, but as an end that we may with confidence presuppose *a priori* to be sought by everyone, belonging as it does to the very nature of man. Now skill in the choice of means to his own greatest well-being may be called *prudence*, taking the word in its more restricted sense. An imperative, therefore, which relates merely to the choice of means to one's own happiness, that is, a maxim of prudence, must be hypothetical; it commands an action, not absolutely, but only as a means to another end.

Lastly, there is an imperative which directly commands an action, without presupposing as its condition that some other end is to be attained by means of that action. This imperative is *categorical*. It has to do, not with the matter of an action and the result expected to follow from it, but simply with the form and principle from which the action itself proceeds. The action is essentially good if the motive of the agent is good, let the consequences be what they may.

This imperative may be called the imperative of *morality*.

How are all these imperatives possible? The question is not, How is an action which an imperative commands actually realized? but, How can we think of the will as placed under obligation by each of those imperatives? Very little need be said to show how an imperative of skill is possible. He who wills the end, wills also the means in his power which are indispensable to the attainment of the end. Looking simply at the act of will, we must say that this proposition is analytic. If a certain object is to follow as an effect from my volition, my causality must be conceived as active in the production of the effect, or as employing the means by which the effect will take place. The imperative, therefore, simply states that in the conception of the willing of this end there is directly implied the conception of actions necessary to this end. No doubt certain synthetic propositions are required to determine the particular means by which a given end may be attained, but these have nothing to do with the principle or act of the will, but merely state how the object may actually be realized.

Were it as easy to give a definite conception of happiness as of a particular end, the imperatives of prudence would be of exactly the same nature as the imperatives of skill, and would therefore be analytic. For, we should be able to say, that he who wills the end wills also the only means in his power for the attainment of the end. But, unfortunately, the conception of happiness is so indefinite, that, although every man desires to obtain it, he is unable to give a definite and self-consistent statement of what he actually desires and wills. The truth is, that, strictly speaking, the imperatives of prudence are not commands at all. They do not say that actions are objective or *necessary*, and hence they must be regarded as counsels, not as commands of reason. Still, the imperative of prudence would be an analytic proposition, if the means to happiness could only be known with certainty. For the only difference in the two cases is that in the imperative of skill the end is merely possible, in the imperative of prudence it is actually given; and as in both all that is commanded is the means to an end which is assumed to be willed, the imperative which commands that he who wills the end should also will the means, is in both cases analytic. There is therefore no real difficulty in seeing how an imperative of prudence is possible.

The only question which is difficult of solution, is, how the imperative of morality is possible. Here the imperative is not hypothetical, and hence we cannot derive its objective necessity from any presupposition. Nor must it for a moment be forgotten, that an imperative of this sort cannot be established by instances taken from experience. We must therefore find out by careful investigation, whether imperatives which seem to be categorical may not be simply hypothetical imperatives in disguise.

One thing is plain at the very outset, namely, that only a categorical imperative can have the dignity of a practical *law*, and that the other imperatives, while they may no doubt be called *principles* of the will, cannot be called laws. An action which is necessary merely as a means to an arbitrary end, may be regarded as itself contingent, and if the end is abandoned, the maxim which prescribes the action has no longer any force. An unconditioned command, on the other hand, does not permit the will to choose the opposite, and therefore it carries with it the necessity which is essential to a law.

It is, however, very hard to see how there can be a categorical imperative or law of morality at all. Such a law is an *a priori* synthetic proposition, and we cannot expect that there will be less difficulty in showing how a proposition of that sort is possible in the sphere of morality than we have found it to be in the sphere of knowledge.

In attempting to solve this problem, we shall first of all inquire, whether the mere conception of a categorical imperative may not perhaps supply us with a formula, which contains the only proposition that can possibly be a categorical imperative. . . .

If I take the mere conception of a hypothetical imperative, I cannot tell what it may contain until the condition under which it applies is presented to me. But I can tell at once from the very conception of a categorical imperative what it must contain. Viewed apart from the law, the imperative simply affirms that the maxim, or subjective principle of action, must conform to the objective principle or law. Now the law contains no condition to which it is restricted, and hence nothing remains but the statement, that the maxim ought to conform to the universality of the law as such. It is only this conformity to law that the imperative can be said to represent as necessary.

There is therefore but one categorical imperative, which may be thus stated: *Act in conformity with that maxim, and that maxim only, which you can at the same time will to be a universal. . . .*

The universality of the law which governs the succession of events, is what we mean by *nature*, in the most general sense, that is, the existence of things, in so far as their existence is determined in conformity with universal laws. The universal imperative of duty might therefore be put in this way: *Act as if the maxim from which you act were to become through your will a universal law of nature.*

If we attend to what goes on in ourselves in every transgression of a duty, we find, that we do not will that our maxim should become a universal law. We find it in fact impossible to do so, and we really will that the opposite of our maxim should remain a universal law, at the same time that we assume the liberty of making an exception in favor of natural inclination in our own case, or perhaps only for this particular occasion. Hence, if we looked at all cases from the same point of view, that is, from the point of view of reason, we should see that there was here a contradiction in our will. The contradiction is, that a certain principle is admitted to be necessary objectively or as a universal law, and yet is held not to be universal subjectively, but to admit of exceptions. What we do is, to consider our action at one time from the point of view of a will that is in perfect conformity with reason, and at another

time from the point of view of a will that is under the influence of natural inclination. There is, therefore, here no real contradiction, but merely an antagonism of inclination to the command of reason. The universality of the principle is changed into a mere generality, in order that the practical principle of reason may meet the maxim half way. Not only is this limitation condemned by our own impartial judgment, but it proves that we actually recognize the validity of the categorical imperative, and merely allow ourselves to make a few exceptions in our own favor which we try to consider as of no importance, or as a necessary concession to circumstances.

This much at least we have learned, that if the idea of duty is to have any meaning and to lay down the laws of our actions, it must be expressed in categorical and not in hypothetical imperatives. We have also obtained a clear and distinct conception (a very important thing), of what is implied in a categorical imperative which contains the principle of duty for all cases, granting such an imperative to be possible at all. But we have not yet been able to prove *a priori*, that there actually is such an imperative; that there is a practical law which commands absolutely on its own authority, and is independent of all sensuous impulses; and that duty consists in obedience to this law.

In seeking to reach this point, it is of the greatest importance to observe, that the reality of this principle cannot possibly be derived from the *peculiar constitution of human nature.* For by duty is meant the practically unconditioned necessity of an act, and hence we can show that duty is a law for the will of all human beings, only by showing that it is applicable to all rational beings, or rather to all rational beings to whom an imperative applies at all. . . .

Practical principles that abstract from all subjective ends are *formal*; those that presuppose subjective ends, and therefore natural inclinations, are *material*. The ends which a rational being arbitrarily sets before himself as material ends to be produced by his actions, are all merely relative; for that which gives to them their value is simply their relation to the peculiar susceptibility of the subject. They can therefore yield no universal and necessary principles, or practical laws, applicable to all rational beings, and binding upon every will. Upon such relative ends, therefore, only hypothetical imperatives can be based.

Suppose, however, that there is something the existence of which has in itself an absolute value, something which, *as an end in itself*, can be a ground of definite laws; then, there would lie in that, and only in that, the ground of a possible categorical imperative or practical law.

Now, I say, that man, and indeed every rational being as such, *exists* as an end in himself, *not merely as a means* to be made use of by this or that will, and therefore man in all his actions, whether these are directed towards himself or towards other rational beings, must always be regarded as an end. No object of natural desire has more than a conditioned value; for if the natural desires, and the wants to which they give rise, did not exist, the object to which they are directed would have no value at all. So far are the natural desires and wants from having an absolute value, so far are they from being sought simply for themselves, that every rational being must wish to be entirely free from their influence. The value of every object which human action is the means of obtaining, is, therefore, always conditioned. And even beings whose existence depends upon nature, not upon our will, if they are without reason, have only the relative value of means, and are therefore called *things*. Rational beings, on the other hand, are called *persons*, because their very nature shows them to be ends in themselves, that is, something which cannot be made use of simply as a means. A person being thus an object of respect, a certain limit is placed upon arbitrary will. Persons are not purely subjective ends, whose existence has a value *for us* as the effect of our actions, but they are *objective ends*, or beings whose existence is an end in itself, for which no other end can be substituted. If all value were conditioned, and therefore contingent, it would be impossible to show that there is any supreme practical principle whatever.

If, then, there is a supreme practical principle, a principle which in relation to the human will is a categorical imperative, it must be an *objective* principle of the will, and must be able to serve as a universal practical law. For, such a principle must be derived from the idea of that which is necessarily an end for every one because it is an *end in itself*. Its foundation is this, that *rational nature exists as an end in itself*. Man necessarily conceives of his own existence in this way, and so far this is a *subjective* principle of human action. But in this way also every other rational being conceives of his own existence, and for the very same reason; hence the principle is also *objective*, and from it, as the highest practical ground, all laws of the will must be capable of being derived. The practical imperative will therefore be this: *Act so as to use humanity, whether in your own person or in the person of another, always as an end, never as merely a means.*

The principle, that humanity and every rational nature is an end in itself, is not borrowed from experience. For, in the first place, because of its universality it applies to all rational beings, and no experience can apply so widely. In the second place, it does not regard humanity subjectively, as an end of man, that is, as an object which the subject of himself actually makes his end, but as an objective end, which ought to be regarded as a law that constitutes the supreme limiting condition of all subjective ends, and which must therefore have its source in pure reason. The objective ground of all practical laws consists in the *rule* and the form of universality, which makes them capable of serving as laws, but their *subjective* ground consists in the *end* to which they are directed. Now, by the second principle, every rational being, as an end in himself, is the subject of all ends. From this follows the third practical principle of the will, which is the supreme condition of its harmony with universal practical reason, namely, the idea of *the will of every rational being as a will which lays down universal laws of action.* . . .

At the point we have now reached, it does not seem surprising that all previous attempts to find out the principle of morality should have ended in failure. It was seen that man is bound under law by duty, but it did not strike anyone, that the *universal* system of laws to which he is subject are laws which he *imposes upon himself*, and that he is only under obligation to act in conformity with his own will, a will which by the purpose of nature prescribes universal laws. Now so long as man is thought to be merely subject to law, no matter what the law may be, he must be regarded as stimulated or constrained to obey the law from interest of some kind; for as the law does not proceed from *his own* will, there must be *something external* to his will which compels him to act in conformity with it. This perfectly necessary conclusion frustrated every attempt to find a supreme principle of duty. Duty was never established, but merely the necessity of acting from some form of interest, private or public. The imperative was therefore necessarily always conditioned, and could not possibly have the force of a moral command. The supreme principle of morality I shall therefore call the principle of the *autonomy* of the will, to distinguish it from all other principles, which I call principles of *heteronomy*.

The conception that every rational being in all the maxims of his will must regard himself as prescribing universal laws, by reference to which himself and all his actions are to be judged, leads to a cognate and very fruitful conception, that of a *kingdom of ends.*

By *kingdom*, I mean the systematic combination of different rational beings through the medium of common laws. Now, laws determine certain ends as universal, and hence, if abstraction is made from the individual differences of rational beings, and from all that is peculiar to their private ends, we get the idea of a complete totality of ends combined in a system; in other words, we are able to conceive of a kingdom of ends, which conforms to the principles formulated above.

All rational beings stand under the law, that each should treat himself and others, *never simply as means*, but always as *at the same time ends in themselves*. Thus there arises a systematic combination of rational beings through the medium of common objective laws. This may well be called a kingdom of ends, because the object of those laws is just to relate all rational beings to one another as ends and means. Of course this kingdom of ends is merely an ideal.

Morality, then, consists in the relation of all action to the system of laws which alone makes possible a kingdom of ends. These laws must belong to the nature of every rational being, and must proceed from his own will. The principle of the will, therefore, is, that no action should be done from any other maxim than one which is consistent with a universal law. This may be expressed in the formula: *Act so that the will may regard itself as in its maxims laying down universal laws.* Now, if the maxims of rational beings are not by their very nature in harmony with this objective principle, the principle of a universal system of laws, the necessity of acting in conformity with that principle is called practical obligation or *duty. . . . Autonomy* is thus the foundation of the moral value of man and of every other rational being.

The three ways in which the principle of morality has been formulated are at bottom simply different statements of the same law, and each implies the other two.

COMMENT

Some Main Issues Presented by Kant's Ethics

The ethics of Kant is the most famous example of a "deontological" type of ethics. The adjective *deontological* is derived from the Greek words *deon* ("duty") and *logos* ("science," or "theory"). A deontological ethics is one based on the theory of duty. As the term is commonly used, it means an ethics of duty for duty's sake, expressed in its most uncompromising form in the motto "Let me do right though the heavens fall." The opposite, or utilitarian, point of view is that an act would be wrong because disastrous *if* the heavens fell. As indicated by the next chapter, utilitarians such as Bentham and Mill judge the morality of actions in terms of their consequences for weal or woe. Quite different is Kant's view that the moral quality of acts depends on conformity to laws, rules, or principles of action rather than on goals or results.

Whatever our opinion of Kant's ethics — and there is much to admire as well as to criticize — we cannot deny that he presents issues of great importance. Some of these are as follows:

1. ARE ETHICAL PRINCIPLES EMPIRICAL OR A PRIORI? The motive of Kant's philosophy is the discovery and justification of a priori forms, concepts, and principles. In ethics, he draws a sharp distinction between *is* and *ought* and contends that the moral *ought* must be formulated in a priori principles. Is he correct?

If empirical science is a knowledge of *existence*, and if an "ideal" or "norm" is what ought to be but *is not*, the conception of a "normative empirical science" is contradictory. And if so, ethics is either merely subjective — as the advocates of the emotive theory contend — or it is a priori. Modern philosophers have been deeply disturbed by the problem thus posed.

The proponents of natural law, such as Cicero, try to solve the problem by denying the sharp antithesis between *what is* and *what ought to be* — and on this point they receive support from utilitarians such as Mill and pragmatists such as Dewey. What ought to be, it can be argued, is what satisfies genuine needs. A need arises when there is an uncompleted tendency in human nature — a frustrated, or at least unconsummated, impulse or desire. These needs can be determined scientifically, and plans to satisfy them can be elaborated with due regard to facts. The objective of securing the greatest possible fulfillment should determine which needs are to receive preferential treatment, and here, too, there are facts to guide us.

Kant would reply that such an empirical procedure is a mere begging of the question. It *assumes* that morality consists in the fulfillment of our needs — but this assumption he would sharply challenge. If *need* is interpreted in a nonmoral sense, it is not a moral concept and hence is irrelevant; but if it is interpreted in a moral sense, it must be connected with obligation — and obligation is not the sort of thing that empirical science can discover and justify. *Moral* objectivity is quite different from *scientific* objectivity, and an objective moral *ought* can never be determined scientifically. Rejecting the emotive view that morality is subjective, Kant concludes that moral objectivity must rest on a priori foundations.

2. IS GOOD WILL, AND GOOD WILL ALONE, UNCONDITIONALLY GOOD? Let us consider Kant's contention that pleasure is good if combined with a good will but evil if combined with a bad will. A hedonist would agree that pleasure gained from wanton torture is bad but would say that it is bad not *in* and *of itself* but in its evil consequences. Its bad effects greatly outweigh its intrinsic goodness — but *as pleasure*, it is intrinsically good. The hedonist would add that what makes good will

"intrinsically good" is simply the pleasure that it involves, rather than the accompanying sense of duty. A nonhedonist might admit that good will is intrinsically good but maintain that there are other intrinsic goods, such as truth and beauty, that are no less ultimate and unconditional.

We can ask the question whether there is *any* unconditional good — pleasure or love or respect for duty or anything else. Pleasure can be sadistic, respect for duty can be chill and puritanical, and anything else can be degraded by its context.

3. IS KANT'S DISTINCTION BETWEEN A HYPOTHETICAL AND A CATEGORICAL IMPERATIVE SOUND? If the criterion of right volition is neither inclination nor consequences, what is it? Kant answers that the rightness of the volition depends on two factors: *right incentive* and *right maxim*.

The right incentive is respect and reverence for moral law. A moral act must be done for duty's sake (although other motivations may be involved). This requirement has already been discussed under the name "good will."

The right maxim is the principle of "the categorical imperative." An imperative is an injunction or command; it says that a person ought to do so and so. A hypothetical imperative always takes a conditional form: "*If you want to achieve x, then you ought to do y.*" Rules of skill and counsels of prudence are hypothetical imperatives: They tell us what we ought to do — "ought" in the sense of what we would be well advised to do — if we desire certain ends. They may be legitimate but they are not moral. A categorical imperative, on the other hand, asserts unconditionally, "You ought to act so and so." There is no *if* in front of the *ought*. Obligation is not determined by inclination or expediency but by objective moral necessity, which can be stated in a universal rule.

The question is whether this distinction between a categorical and a hypothetical imperative is sound? Has Kant drawn the distinction too sharply? Is he, in pressing this distinction, too much the absolutist, not enough the relativist? Or is Kant right? Don't we believe that moral imperatives are, somehow or other, distinctive? And has he not correctly formulated the distinction? These are questions for the reader to ponder.

4. DOES KANT'S ETHICS PROVIDE A SOUND TEST OF RIGHT? An opponent might concede that there are categorical imperatives and still find Kant's formulas for determining them unsatisfactory.

His first formula is "Act only on that maxim which you can will as a universal law." One may object that this does not take account of individual differences, which may be ethically decisive. Consider Kant's dispute with the French philosopher Benjamin Constant. The moral duty to tell the truth, Constant argued, is not unconditional. It would be ethically right to lie to a would-be murderer in order to save the intended victim, for a person bent on murder has forfeited all right to a truth that would abet a plot. To this contention Kant replied, "The duty of truthfulness makes no distinction between persons to whom one has this duty and to whom one can exempt himself from this duty; rather, it is an unconditional duty which holds in all circumstances."[1] Hence, we are duty-bound to tell even a truth that would result in murder. This is an extreme position that very few thinkers, whether philosophers or laypeople, would endorse. In the case cited by Constant, there is a conflict between two duties: the duty to tell the truth and the duty to save a life. In such instances, how can we decide which duty is paramount without a consideration of consequences?

Kant would reply that there are "perfect duties," and that the duty to tell the truth is such a duty. We recognize a perfect obligation when we see that it is possible to universalize it and impossible to universalize its violation. For example, it is impossible to universalize lying (the violation of truth-telling) because if everybody lied, no one would believe you — lying is parasitic on truth-telling. Hence telling the truth, which can be universalized with perfect consistency, is an absolute duty, and lying is an absolute violation of this duty. The duty to protect a life that is threatened is only an "imperfect duty" — derived from the fact that no one could consistently will that one's own life be unprotected under such circumstances. The duties of perfect obligation, forbidding us to lie, break promises, steal, murder, and so forth, admit of no exceptions whatever in favor of duties of imperfect obligation.

Some writers have argued, in Kant's defense, that his universalization formula can be interpreted flexibly enough to meet commonsense objections. For example, we could universalize the principle that people should steal rather than starve to death. Or (to revert to the question that Constant raised) we could universalize the principle that one should lie in order to save an innocent person from the threat of murder. But can we reason in this way without a more empirical approach to ethics than Kant was prepared to admit? Can we do so without setting aside his concept of "perfect duties"?

A utilitarian could agree with Kant up to a certain point: Granted that an act is right for one person, it must be right *under the same conditions* for everybody. But when the conditions (physical or psychological or cultural) vary, philanthropic exception to the general rule may be warranted. If this is so, can morality be a priori and universal, as Kant supposed?

His second formula of the categorical imperative is "Act so as to treat humanity, whether in your own person or in that of another, always as an end and never as a means only." This formula expresses our sense of the intrinsic value of the human spirit, and it has a profound moral appeal. But is it possible to carry out the formula without a view to the effects of our actions? Must we not have some positive idea of the ends of humanity and how to achieve them? If so, is the second formula consistent with the first formula? The first formula, it could be argued, is a "right for right's sake" principle, and the second is a "right for good's sake" principle.

The third formula is "Act as a member of a kingdom of ends." Spelled out, this means that every person, as a rational agent, is ideally a member of a moral community, in which one is both sovereign (free) and subject (responsible), willing the universal laws of morality for oneself and others. The moral law, according to this formula, must be the person's own free voice and is not a whit less a universal law for being freely chosen. But is genuine freedom consistent with Kant's interpretation of universality? Freedom, it might be objected, does not consist merely in willing the dictates of universal abstract reason; it is warmer, more personal, and creative. In maintaining that morality is obedience to universal law, without regard to the individual and his or her peculiar circumstances, Kant dissolves the individual personality in an ocean of ethical abstraction, like an individual grain of sand dissolved in a vast sea. In so doing, he undermines his very demand for a moral community of free and responsible human beings. So at least might existentialists, with their strong emphasis on human individuality, argue.

In Kant's defense, it can be pointed out that *The Foundations of the Metaphysic of Morals*, from which our selection is taken, is the most abstract and formalistic of his ethical works. In the *Critique of Practical Reason*, Kant corrects the one-sidedness of the *Foundations* by discoursing at length on the concept of "good" as well as "duty," and in his *Lectures on Ethics* and *Metaphysics of Morals* (not to be confused with the *Foundations*), Kant discusses particular duties in a concrete way. The more teleological and less absolutistic elements in his theory emerge in these works.

17

The Way of Utility

"By the principle of utility is meant that principle which approves or disapproves of every action whatsoever, according to the tendency which it appears to have to augment or diminish the happiness of the party whose interest is in question."

Jeremy Bentham

JEREMY BENTHAM (1748–1832)

The son of a well-to-do London barrister, Bentham studied law but never practiced it. He set himself to work out a new system of jurisprudence and to reform both the penal and the civil law. In pursuit of this aim he wrote thousands of pages but was curiously indifferent about publishing them. Although his works were collected in eleven large volumes, the only major theoretical work that he published himself was the *Introduction to the Principles of Morals and Legislation* (1789), which contains an exposition of his hedonistic and utilitarian ethics.

Painfully shy, he could hardly endure the company of strangers, and yet he became a powerful political force. As a leader of the "Philosophical Radicals," he attracted such distinguished followers as James Mill and John Stuart Mill. He established the *Westminster Review*, at his own expense, as an organ of his movement, and he and his associates succeeded in founding University College, London. There his embalmed body, dressed in his customary clothes and topped with a wax model of his head, is still to be seen.

The Hedonistic Calculus

CHAPTER I

Of the Principle of Utility

I. Nature has placed mankind under the governance of two sovereign masters, *pain* and *pleasure*. It is for them alone to point out what we ought to do, as well as to determine what we shall do. On the one hand the standard of right and wrong, on the other the chain of causes and effects, are fastened to their throne. They govern us in all we do, in all we say, in all we think: every effort we can make to throw off our subjection, will serve but to demonstrate and confirm it. In words a man may pretend to abjure their empire: but in reality he will remain subject to it all the while. The *principle of utility*[1] recognizes this subjection, and assumes it for the foundation of that system, the object of which is to rear the fabric of felicity by the hands of reason and of law. Systems which attempt to question it, deal in sounds instead of sense, in caprice instead of reason, in darkness instead of light.

From *An Introduction to the Principles of Morals and Legislation*, new edition, Oxford, 1823. Some of Bentham's footnotes have been omitted. First published in 1789.

[1] Note by the Author, July 1822: To this denomination has of late been added, or substituted, the *greatest happiness or greatest felicity* principle: this for shortness, instead of saying at length *that principle* which states the greatest happiness of all those whose interest is in question, as being the

But enough of metaphor and declamation: it is not by such means that moral science is to be improved.

II. The principle of utility is the foundation of the present work: it will be proper therefore at the outset to give an explicit and determinate account of what is meant by it. By the principle of utility is meant that principle which approves or disapproves of every action whatsoever, according to the tendency which it appears to have to augment or diminish the happiness of the party whose interest is in question: or, what is the same thing in other words, to promote or to oppose that happiness. I say of every action whatsoever; and

right and proper, and only right and proper and universally desirable, end of human action: of human action in every situation, and in particular in that of a functionary or set of functionaries exercising the powers of Government. The word *utility* does not so clearly point to the ideas of *pleasure* and *pain* as the words *happiness* and *felicity* do: nor does it lead us to the consideration of the *number*, of the interests affected; to the *number*, as being the circumstance, which contributes, in the largest proportion, to the formation of the standard here in question; the *standard of right and wrong*, by which alone the propriety of human conduct, in every situation can with propriety be tried. This want of a sufficiently manifest connexion between the ideas of *happiness* and *pleasure* on the one hand, and the idea of *utility* on the other, I have every now and then found operating, and with but too much efficiency, as a bar to the acceptance, that might otherwise have been given, to this principle.

therefore not only of every action of a private individual, but of every measure of government.

III. By utility is meant that property in any object, whereby it tends to produce benefit, advantage, pleasure, good, or happiness, (all this in the present case comes to the same thing) to prevent the happening of mischief, pain, evil, or unhappiness to the party whose interest is considered: if that party be the community in general, then the happiness of the community: if a particular individual, then the happiness of that individual.

IV. The interest of the community is one of the most general expressions that can occur in the phraseology of morals: no wonder that the meaning of it is often lost. When it has a meaning, it is this. The community is a fictitious *body*, composed of the individual persons who are considered as constituting as it were its *members*. The interest of the community then is, what?—the sum of the interests of the several members who compose it.

V. It is in vain to talk of the interest of the community, without understanding what is the interest of the individual. A thing is said to promote the interest, or to be *for* the interest, of an individual, when it tends to add to the sum total of his pleasures: or, what comes to the same thing, to diminish the sum total of his pains.

VI. An action then may be said to be conformable to the principle of utility, or, for shortness sake, to utility, (meaning with respect to the community at large) when the tendency it has to augment the happiness of the community is greater than any it has to diminish it.

VII. A measure of government (which is but a particular kind of action, performed by a particular person or persons) may be said to be conformable to or dictated by the principle of utility, when in like manner the tendency which it has to augment the happiness of the community is greater than any which it has to diminish it.

VIII. When an action, or in particular a measure of government, is supposed by a man to be conformable to the principle of utility, it may be convenient, for the purposes of discourse, to imagine a kind of law or dictate, called a law or dictate of utility: and to speak of the action in question, as being conformable to such law or dictate.

IX. A man may be said to be a partizan of the principle of utility, when the approbation or disapprobation he annexes to any action, or to any measure, is determined by and proportioned to the tendency which he conceives it to have to augment or to diminish the happiness of the community: or in other words, to its conformity or unconformity to the laws or dictates of utility.

X. Of an action that is conformable to the principle of utility one may always say either that it is one that ought to be done, or at least that it is not one that ought not to be done. One may say also, that it is right it should be done; at least that it is not wrong it should be done: that it is a right action; at least that it is not a wrong action. When thus interpreted, the words *ought*, and *right* and *wrong*, and others of that stamp, have a meaning: when otherwise, they have none.

XI. Has the rectitude of this principle been ever formally contested? It should seem that it had, by those who have not known what they have been meaning. Is it susceptible of any direct proof? it should seem not: for that which is used to prove every thing else, cannot itself be proved: a chain of proofs must have their commencement somewhere. To give such proof is as impossible as it is needless.

XII. Not that there is or ever has been that human creature breathing, however stupid or perverse, who has not on many, perhaps on most occasions of his life, deferred to it. By the natural constitution of the human frame, on most occasions of their lives men in general embrace this principle, without thinking of it: if not for the ordering of their own actions, yet for the trying of their own actions, as well as those of other men. There have been, at the same time, not many, perhaps, even of the most intelligent, who have been disposed to embrace it purely and without reserve. There are even few who have not taken some occasion or other to quarrel with it, either on account of their not understanding always how to apply it, or on account of some prejudice or other which they were afraid to examine into, or could not bear to part with. For such is the stuff that man is made of: in principle and in practice, in a right track and in a wrong one, the rarest of all human qualities is consistency.

XIII. When a man attempts to combat the principle of utility, it is with reasons drawn, without his being aware of it, from that very principle itself. His arguments, if they prove any thing, prove not that the principle is *wrong*, but that, according to the applications he supposes to be made of it, it is *misapplied*. Is it possible for a man to move

the earth? Yes; but he must first find out another earth to stand upon.

XIV. To disprove the propriety of it by arguments is impossible; but, from the causes that have been mentioned, or from some confused or partial view of it, a man may happen to be disposed not to relish it. Where this is the case, if he thinks the settling of his opinions on such a subject worth the trouble, let him take the following steps, and at length, perhaps, he may come to reconcile himself to it.

1. Let him settle with himself, whether he would wish to discard this principle altogether; if so, let him consider what it is that all his reasonings (in matters of politics especially) can amount to?

2. If he would, let him settle with himself, whether he would judge and act without any principle, or whether there is any other he would judge and act by?

3. If there be, let him examine and satisfy himself whether the principle he thinks he has found is really any separate intelligible principle; or whether it be not a mere principle in words, a kind of phrase, which at bottom expresses neither more nor less than the mere averment of his own unfounded sentiments; that is, what in another person he might be apt to call caprice?

4. If he is inclined to think that his own approbation or disapprobation, annexed to the idea of an act, without any regard to its consequences, is a sufficient foundation for him to judge and act upon, let him ask himself whether his sentiment is to be a standard of right and wrong, with respect to every other man, or whether every man's sen-

timent has the same privilege of being a standard to itself?

5. In the first case, let him ask himself whether his principle is not despotical, and hostile to all the rest of the human race?

6. In the second case, whether it is not anarchical, and whether at this rate there are not as many different standards of right and wrong as there are men? and whether even to the same man, the same thing, which is right today, may not (without the least change in its nature) be wrong tomorrow? and whether the same thing is not right and wrong in the same place at the same time? and in either case, whether all argument is not at an end? and whether, when two men have said, 'I like this,' and 'I don't like it,' they can (upon such a principle) have any thing more to say?

7. If he should have said to himself, No: for that sentiment which he proposes as a standard must be grounded on reflection, let him say on what particulars the reflection is to turn? if on particulars having relation to the utility of the act, then let him say whether this is not deserting his own principle, and borrowing assistance from that very one in opposition to which he sets it up: or if not on those particulars, on what other particulars?

8. If he should be for compounding the matter, and adopting his own principle in part, and the principle of utility in part, let him say how far he will adopt it?

9. When he has settled with himself where he will stop, then let him ask himself how he justifies to himself the adopting it so far? and why he will not adopt it any farther?

10. Admitting any other principle than the principle of utility to be a right principle, a principle that it is right for a man to pursue; admitting (what is not true) that the word *right* can have a meaning without reference to utility, let him say whether there is any such thing as a *motive* that a man can have to pursue the dictates of it: if there is, let him say what that motive is, and how it is to be distinguished from those which enforce the dictates of utility: if not, then lastly let him say what it is this other principle can be good for? . . .

Value of a Lot of Pleasure or Pain, How To Be Measured

I. PLEASURES then, and the avoidance of pains, are the *ends* which the legislator has in view: it behoves him therefore to understand their *value*. Pleasures and pains are the *instruments* he has to work with: it behoves him therefore to understand their *force*, which is again, in other words, their value.

II. To a person considered *by himself*, the value of a pleasure or pain considered *by itself*, will be greater or less, according to the four following circumstances:[2]

[2] These circumstances have since been denominated *elements* or *dimensions* of *value* in a pleasure or a pain.

Not long after the publication of the first edition, the following memoriter verses were framed, in the view of lodging more effectually, in the memory, these points, on which the whole fabric of morals and legislation may be seen to rest.

Intense, long, certain, speedy, fruitful, pure —Such marks in *pleasures* and in *pains* endure. Such pleasures seek, if *private* be thy end:
If it be *public*, wide let them *extend*.
Such *pains* avoid, whichever be thy view:
If pains *must* come, let them *extend* to few.

1. Its *intensity*.
2. Its *duration*.
3. Its *certainty* or *uncertainty*.
4. Its *propinquity* or *remoteness*.

III. These are the circumstances which are to be considered in estimating a pleasure or a pain considered each of them by itself. But when the value of any pleasure or pain is considered for the purpose of estimating the tendency of any *act* by which it is produced, there are two other circumstances to be taken into the account; these are,

5. Its *fecundity*, or the chance it has of being followed by sensations of the *same* kind: that is, pleasures, if it be a pleasure: pains, if it be a pain.

6. Its *purity*, or the chance it has of *not* being followed by sensations of the *opposite* kind: that is, pains, if it be a pleasure: pleasures, if it be a pain.

These two last, however, are in strictness scarcely to be deemed properties of the pleasure or the pain itself; they are not, therefore, in strictness to be taken into the account of the value of that pleasure or that pain. They are in strictness to be deemed properties only of the act, or other event, by which such pleasure or pain has been produced; and accordingly are only to be taken into the account of the tendency of such act or such event.

IV. To a *number* of persons, with reference to each of whom the value of a pleasure or a pain is considered, it will be greater or less, according to seven circumstances: to wit, the six preceding ones; viz.

1. Its *intensity*.

2. Its *duration*.
3. Its *certainty* or *uncertainty*.
4. Its *propinquity* or *remoteness*.
5. Its *fecundity*.
6. Its *purity*.

And one other; to wit:

7. Its *extent*; that is, the number of persons to whom it *extends*; or (in other words) who are affected by it.

V. To take an exact account then of the general tendency of any act, by which the interests of a community are affected, proceed as follows. Begin with any one person of those whose interests seem most immediately to be affected by it: and take an account,

1. Of the value of each distinguishable *pleasure* which appears to be produced by it in the *first* instance.

2. Of the value of each *pain* which appears to be produced by it in the *first* instance.

3. Of the value of each pleasure which appears to be produced by it *after* the first. This constitutes the *fecundity* of the first *pleasure* and the *impurity* of the first *pain*.

4. Of the value of each *pain* which appears to be produced by it after the first. This constitutes the *fecundity* of the first *pain*, and the *impurity* of the first *pleasure*.

5. Sum up all the values of all the *pleasures* on the one side, and those of all the *pains* on the other. The balance, if it be on the side of pleasure, will give the *good* tendency of the act upon the whole, with respect to the interests of that *individual* person; if on the side of pain, the *bad* tendency of it upon the whole.

6. Take an account of the *number* of persons whose interests appear to be concerned; and repeat the above process with respect to each. *Sum up the* numbers expressive of the degrees of *good* tendency which the act has, with respect to each individual, in regard to whom the tendency of it is *good* upon the whole: . . . do this again with respect to each individual, in regard to whom the tendency of it is *bad* upon the whole. Take the *balance*; which, if on the side of *pleasure*, will give the general *good tendency* of the act, with respect to the total number or community of individuals concerned; if on the side of pain, the general *evil tendency*, with respect to the same community.

VI. It is not to be expected that this process should be strictly pursued previously to every moral judgment, or to every legislative or judicial operation. It may, however, be always kept in view: and as near as the process actually pursued on these occasions approaches to it, so near will such process approach to the character of an exact one.

VII. The same process is alike applicable to pleasure and pain, in whatever shape they appear: and by whatever denomination they are distinguished: to pleasure, whether it be called *good* (which is properly the cause or instrument of pleasure) or *profit* (which is distant pleasure, or the cause or instrument of distant pleasure,) or *convenience*, or *advantage*, *benefit*, *emolu-ment, happiness*, and so forth: to pain, whether it be called *evil*, (which corresponds to *good*) or *mischief*, or *inconvenience*, or *disadvantage*, or *loss*, or *unhappiness*, and so forth.

VIII. Nor is this a novel and unwarranted, any more than it is a useless theory. In all this there is nothing but what the practice of mankind, wheresoever they have a clear view of their own interest, is perfectly conformable to. An article of property, an estate in land, for instance, is valuable, on what account? On account of the pleasures of all kinds which it enables a man to produce, and what comes to the same thing the pains of all kinds which it enables him to avert. But the value of such an article of property is universally understood to rise or fall according to the length or shortness of the time which a man has in it: the certainty or uncertainty of its coming into possession: and the nearness or remoteness of the time at which, if at all, it is to come into possession. As to the *intensity* of the pleasures which a man may derive from it, this is never thought of, because it depends upon the use which each particular person may come to make of it; which cannot be estimated till the particular pleasures he may come to derive from it, or the particular pains he may come to exclude by means of it, are brought to view. For the same reason, neither does he think of the *fecundity* or *purity* of those pleasures.

JOHN STUART MILL (1806–1873)

Mill was reared in London and was educated privately by his father, James Mill, a famous political philosopher. No child ever received a more prodigious education. Mill was reading Plato and Thucydides in the original Greek at an age when most children are reading nursery stories in their native language. His father set him to learn Greek at the age of three; Latin, algebra, and geometry at the age of eight; logic at twelve; and political economy at thirteen. Jeremy Bentham was an intimate friend of the family, and young John was thoroughly indoctrinated in his philosophy.

When Mill reached the age of seventeen, he was appointed a clerk in the East India Company, in whose service he remained for thirty-five years, rising steadily to the highest post in his department, that of examiner of correspondence and dispatches to India. This position afforded him considerable leisure for his intense intellectual pursuits.

In his twenty-first year, he fell into a deep mental depression, evidently the result of his unnatural childhood and years of intellectual cramming. He gradually emerged from this illness, but with a new sense of the insufficiency of his father's doctrinaire philosophy and a keener appreciation of the value of poetry, especially Wordsworth's. Thereafter he sought to broaden his outlook and succeeded in becoming a much better-rounded (though less consistent) philosopher than either Bentham or his father. An important influence on Mill was Harriet Taylor, the beautiful and talented wife of a London merchant, who finally married him (in 1851) after her husband died. They lived happily together for seven years, until they were separated by her untimely death. It was through her, Mill said, that he came to be more of a democrat and socialist, and *On Liberty* was their joint work.

After his long service in the East India office, he retired on a pension at the age of fifty-two. The remaining fifteen years of his life, although marred by ill health, were packed with intellectual and political activity. In 1865 he consented to run for Parliament as a representative of the working people for the constituency of Westminster; and during his single term of office (1866–1868), he made a considerable impression by his vigorous championing of reform. In 1869 he retired with his stepdaughter, Helen Taylor, to a small white stone cottage near Avignon, in France, where he continued to write. In May 1873 he died, the victim of a local fever.

Among his important books are *Logic* (1843), *The Principles of Political Economy* (1848), *On Liberty* (1859), *Utilitarianism* (1863), *Examination of Sir William Hamilton's Philosophy* (1865), and *Autobiography* (published after his death, in 1873).

Utilitarianism

WHAT UTILITARIANISM IS

A passing remark is all that needs be given to the ignorant blunder of supposing that those who stand up for utility as the test of right and wrong use the term in that restricted and merely colloquial sense in which utility is opposed to pleasure. An apology is due to the philosophical opponents of utilitarianism, for even the momentary appearance of confounding them with anyone capable of so absurd a misconception; which is the more extraordinary, inasmuch as the contrary accusation, of referring everything to pleasure, and that, too, in its grossest form, is another of the common charges against utilitarianism: and, as has been pointedly remarked by an able writer, the same sort of persons, and often the very same persons, denounce the theory "as impracticably dry when the word 'utility' precedes the word 'pleasure,' and as too practicably voluptuous when the word 'pleasure' precedes the word 'utility'." Those who know anything about the matter are aware that every writer, from Epicurus to Bentham, who maintained the theory of utility, meant by it, not something to be contradistinguished from pleasure, but pleasure itself, together with exemption from pain; and instead of opposing the useful to the agreeable

or the ornamental, have always declared that the useful means these, among other things. Yet the common herd, including the herd of writers, not only in newspapers and periodicals, but in books of weight and pretension, are perpetually falling into this shallow mistake. Having caught up the word "utilitarian," while knowing nothing whatever about it but its sound, they habitually express by it the rejection or the neglect of pleasure in some of its forms: of beauty, of ornament, or of amusement. Nor is the term thus ignorantly misapplied solely in disparagement, but occasionally in compliment, as though it implied superiority to frivolity and the mere pleasures of the moment. And this perverted use is the only one in which the word is popularly known, and the one from which the new generation are acquiring their sole notion of its meaning. Those who introduced the word, but who had for many years discontinued it as a distinctive appellation, may well feel themselves called upon to resume it if by doing so they can hope to contribute anything towards rescuing it from this utter degradation.

The creed which accepts as the foundation of morals "utility" or the "greatest happiness principle" holds that actions are right in proportion as they tend to promote happiness, wrong as they tend to produce the reverse of happiness. By happiness is intended pleasure, and the absence of pain; by unhappiness, pain, and the privation of

---

From *Utilitarianism*, published serially in *Fraser's Magazine* in 1861 and in book form, London, 1863.

pleasure. To give a clear view of the moral standard set up by the theory, much more requires to be said; in particular, what things it includes in the ideas of pain and pleasure; and to what extent this is left an open question. But these supplementary explanations do not affect the theory of life on which this theory of morality is grounded — namely, that pleasure and freedom from pain are the only things desirable as ends; and that all desirable things (which are as numerous in the utilitarian as in any other scheme) are desirable either for the pleasure inherent in themselves, or as means to the promotion of pleasure and the prevention of pain.

Now such a theory of life excites in many minds, and among them in some of the most estimable in feeling and purpose, inveterate dislike. To suppose that life has (as they express it) no higher end than pleasure — no better and nobler object of desire and pursuit — they designate as utterly mean and groveling; as a doctrine worthy only of swine, to whom the followers of Epicurus were, at a very early period, contemptuously likened; and modern holders of the doctrine are occasionally made the subject of equally polite comparisons by its German, French, and English assailants.

When thus attacked, the Epicureans have always answered that it is not they, but their accusers, who represent human nature in a degrading light, since the accusation supposes human beings to be capable of no pleasures except those of which swine are capable. If this supposition were true, the charge could not be gainsaid, but would then be no longer an imputation; for if the sources of pleasure were precisely the same to human beings and to swine, the rule of life which is good enough for the one would be good enough for the other. The comparison of the Epicurean life to that of beasts is felt as degrading, precisely because a beast's pleasures do not satisfy a human being's conceptions of happiness. Human beings have faculties more elevated than the animal appetites and, when once made conscious of them, do not regard anything as happiness which does not include their gratification. I do not, indeed, consider the Epicureans to have been by any means faultless in drawing out their scheme of consequences from the utilitarian principle. To do this in any sufficient manner, many Stoic, as well as Christian, elements require to be included. But there is no known Epicurean theory of life which does not assign to the pleasures of the intellect, of the feelings and imagination, and of the moral sentiments, a much higher value as pleasures than to those of mere sensation. It must be admitted, however, that utilitarian writers in general have placed the superiority of mental over bodily pleasures chiefly in the greater permanency, safety, uncostliness, etc., of the former — that is, in their circumstantial advantages rather than in their intrinsic nature. And on all these points utilitarians have fully proved their case; but they might have taken the other and, as it may be called, higher ground with entire consistency. It is quite compatible with the principle of utility to recognize the fact that some kinds of pleasure are more desirable and more valuable than others. It would be absurd that, while, in estimating all other things, quality is considered as well as quantity, the estimation of pleasures should be supposed to depend on quantity alone.

If I am asked what I mean by difference of quality in pleasures, or what makes one pleasure more valuable than another, merely as a pleasure, except its being greater in amount, there is but one possible answer. Of two pleasures, if there be one to which all or almost all who have experience of both give a decided preference, irrespective of any feeling of moral obligation to prefer it, that is the more desirable pleasure. If one of the two is, by those who are competently acquainted with both, placed so far above the other that they prefer it, even though knowing it to be attended with a greater amount of discontent, and would not resign it for any quantity of the other pleasure which their nature is capable of, we are justified in ascribing to the preferred enjoyment a superiority in quality so far outweighing quantity as to render it, in comparison, of small account.

Now it is an unquestionable fact that those who are equally acquainted with and equally capable of appreciating and enjoying both, do give a most marked preference to the manner of existence which employs their higher faculties. Few human creatures would consent to be changed into any of the lower animals for a promise of the fullest allowance of a beast's pleasures; no intelligent human being would consent to be a fool, no instructed person would be an ignoramus, no person of feeling and conscience would be selfish and base, even though they should be persuaded that the fool, the dunce, or the rascal is better satisfied with his lot than they are with theirs. They would not resign what they possess more than he for the most complete satisfaction of all the desires which they have in common with him. If they ever fancy they would, it is only in cases of unhappiness so extreme that to escape from it they would exchange their lot for almost any other, however undesirable in their own eyes. A being of higher faculties requires more to make him happy, is capable probably of more acute suffering, and certainly accessible to it at more points, than one of an inferior type; but in spite of these liabilities, he can never really wish to sink into what he feels to be a lower grade of existence. We may give what explanation we please of this unwillingness; we may attribute it to pride, a name which is given indiscriminately to some of the most and to some of the least estimable feelings of which mankind are capable: we may refer it to the love of liberty and personal independence, an appeal to which was with the Stoics one of the most effective means for the inculcation of it; to the love of power or to the love of excitement, both of which do really enter into and contribute to it; but its most appropriate appellation is a sense of dignity, which all human beings possess in one form or other, and in some, though by no means in exact, proportion to their higher faculties, and which is so essential a part of the happiness of those in whom it is strong that nothing which conflicts with it could be otherwise than momentarily an object of desire to them.

Whoever supposes that this preference takes place at a sacrifice of happiness—that the superior being, in anything like equal circumstances, is not happier than the inferior—confounds the two very different ideas of happiness and content. It is undisputable that the being whose capacities of enjoyment are low has the greatest chance of having them fully satisfied; and a highly endowed being will always feel that any happiness which he can look for, as the world is constituted, is imperfect. But he can learn to bear its imperfections, if they are at all bearable; and they will not make him envy the being who is indeed unconscious of the imperfections, but only because he feels not at all the good which those imperfections qualify. It is better to be a human being dissatisfied than a pig satisfied; better to be Socrates dissatisfied than a fool satisfied. And if the fool, or the pig, are of a different opinion, it is because they only know their own side of the question. The other party to the comparison knows both sides.

It may be objected that many who are capable of the higher pleasures occasionally, under the influence of temptation, postpone them to the lower. But that is quite compatible with a full appreciation of the intrinsic superiority of the higher. Men often, from infirmity of character, make their election for the nearer good, though they know it to be the less valuable; and this no less when the choice is between two bodily pleasures than when it is between bodily and mental. They pursue sensual indulgences to the injury of health, though perfectly aware that health is the greater good. It may be

further objected that many who begin with youthful enthusiasm for everything noble, as they advance in years, sink into indolence and selfishness. But I do not believe that those who undergo this very common change voluntarily choose the lower description of pleasures in preference to the higher. I believe that, before they devote themselves exclusively to the one, they have already become incapable of the other. Capacity for the nobler feelings is in most natures a very tender plant, easily killed, not only by hostile influences, but by mere want of sustenance; and in the majority of young persons it speedily dies away if the occupations to which their position in life has devoted them, and the society into which it has thrown them, are not favorable to keeping that higher capacity in exercise. Men lose their high aspirations as they lose their intellectual tastes, because they have not time or opportunity for indulging them; and they addict themselves to inferior pleasures, not because they deliberately prefer them, but because they are either the only ones to which they have access, or the only ones which they are any longer capable of enjoying. It may be questioned whether any one who has remained equally susceptible to both classes of pleasures, every knowingly and calmly preferred the lower, though many, in all ages, have broken down in an ineffectual attempt to combine both.

From this verdict of the only competent judges, I apprehend there can be no appeal. On a question which is the best worth having of two pleasures, or which of two modes of existence is the most grateful to the feelings, apart from its moral attributes and from its consequences, the judgment of those who are qualified by knowledge of both, or, if they differ, that of the majority of them, must be admitted as final. And there needs be the less hesitation to accept this judgment respecting the quality of pleasures, since there is no other tribunal to be referred to even on the question of quantity. What means are there of determining which is the acutest of two pains, or the intensest of two pleasurable sensations, except the general suffrage of those who are familiar with both? Neither pains nor pleasures are homogeneous, and pain is always heterogeneous with pleasure. What is there to decide whether a particular pleasure is worth purchasing at the cost of a particular pain, except the feelings and judgment of the experienced? When, therefore, those feelings and judgment declare the pleasures derived from the higher faculties to be preferable *in kind*, apart from the question of intensity, to those of which the animal nature, disjointed from the higher faculties, is susceptible, they are entitled on this subject to the same regard.

I have dwelt on this point, as being a necessary part of a perfectly just conception of utility or happiness considered as the directive rule of human conduct. But it is by no means an indispensable condition to the acceptance of the utilitarian standard; for that standard is not the agent's own greatest happiness, but the greatest amount of happiness altogether; and if it may possibly be doubted whether a noble character is always the happier for its nobleness, there can be no doubt that it makes other people happier, and that the world in general is immensely a gainer by it. Utilitarianism, therefore, could only attain its end by the general cultivation of nobleness of character, even if each individual were only benefited by the nobleness of others, and his own, so far as happiness is concerned, were a sheer deduction from the benefit. But the bare enunciation of such an absurdity as this last renders refutation superfluous.

According to the greatest happiness principle, as above explained, the ultimate end, with reference to and for the sake of which all other things are desirable — whether we are considering our own good or that of other people — is an existence exempt as far as possible from pain, and as rich as possible in enjoyments, both in point of quantity and quality; the test of quality and the rule for measuring it against quantity being the preference felt by those who, in their opportunities of experience, to which must be added their habits of self-consciousness and self-observation, are best furnished with the means of comparison. This, being, according to the utilitarian opinion, the end of human action, is necessarily also the standard of morality, which may accordingly be defined "the rules and precepts for human conduct," by the observance of which an existence such as has been described might be, to the greatest extent possible, secured to all mankind; and not to them only, but, so far as the nature of things admits, to the whole sentient creation. . . .

[The remainder of the chapter is devoted to Mill's answer to objections. Some of these objections, for example,

that happiness is unobtainable, that utilitarianism is a "godless doctrine," that the doctrine is "worthy only of swine," would no longer be advanced by reputable philosophers, and can here be omitted. But a few of the objections and Mill's answers to them are worthy of attention. We shall begin with his reply to the objection that we should learn to do without happiness, since self-sacrifice is a duty.]

. . . The utilitarian morality does recognize in human beings the power of sacrificing their own greatest good for the good of others. It only refuses to admit that the sacrifice is itself a good. A sacrifice which does not increase or tend to increase the sum total of happiness, it considers as wasted. The only self-renunciation which it applauds is devotion to the happiness, or to some of the means of happiness, of others, either of mankind collectively or of individuals within the limits imposed by the collective interests of mankind.

I must again repeat what the assailants of utilitarianism seldom have the justice to acknowledge, that the happiness which forms the utilitarian standard of what is right in conduct is not the agent's own happiness but that of all concerned. As between his own happiness and that of others, utilitarianism requires him to be as strictly impartial as a disinterested and benevolent spectator. In the golden rule of Jesus of Nazareth, we read the complete spirit of the ethics of utility. "To do as you would be done by," and "to love your neighbor as yourself," constitute the ideal perfection of utilitarian morality. As the means of making the nearest approach to this ideal, utility would en-

join, first, that laws and social arrangements should place the happiness or (as, speaking practically, it may be called) the interest of every individual as nearly as possible in harmony with the interest of the whole; and, secondly, that education and opinion, which have so vast a power over human character, should so use that power as to establish in the mind of every individual an indissoluble association between his own happiness and the good of the whole, especially between his own happiness and the practice of such modes of conduct, negative and positive, as regard for the universal happiness prescribes; so that not only he may be unable to conceive the possibility of happiness to himself, consistently with conduct opposed to the general good, but also that a direct impulse to promote the general good may be in every individual one of the habitual motives of action, and the sentiments connected therewith may fill a large and prominent place in every human being's sentient existence. If the impugners of the utilitarian morality represented it to their own minds in this its true character, I know not what recommendation possessed by any other morality they could possibly affirm to be wanting to it; what more beautiful or more exalted developments of human nature any other ethical system can be supposed to foster, or what springs of action, not accessible to the utilitarian, such systems rely on for giving effect to their mandates.

The objectors to utilitarianism cannot always be charged with representing it in a discreditable light. On the contrary, those among them who entertain anything like a just idea of its disinterested character sometimes find fault with its standard as being too high for humanity. They say it is exacting too much to require that people shall always act from the inducement of promoting the general interests of society. But this is to mistake the very meaning of a standard of morals, and confound the rule of action with the motive of it. It is the business of ethics to tell us what are our duties, or by what test we may know them; but no system of ethics requires that the sole motive of all we do shall be a feeling of duty; on the contrary, ninety-nine hundredths of all our actions are done from other motives, and rightly so done if the rule of duty does not condemn them. It is the more unjust to utilitarianism that this particular misapprehension should be made a ground of objection to it, inasmuch as utilitarian moralists have gone beyond almost all others in affirming that the motive has nothing to do with the morality of the action, though much with the worth of the agent. He who saves a fellow creature from drowning does what is morally right, whether his motive be duty or the hope of being paid for his trouble; he who betrays the friend that trusts him is guilty of a crime, even if his object be to serve another friend to whom he is under greater obligations. But to speak only of actions done from the motive of duty, and in direct obedience to principle: it is a misapprehension to the utilitarian mode of thought to conceive it as implying that people should fix their minds upon so wide a generality as the world, or society at large. The great majority of good actions are intended not for the benefit of the world, but for that of individuals, of which the good of the world is made up; and the thoughts of the most virtuous man need not on these occasions travel beyond the particular persons concerned, except so far as is necessary to assure himself that in benefiting them he is not violating the rights, that is, the legitimate and authorized expectations, of any one else. The multiplication of happiness is, according to the utilitarian ethics, the object of virtue: the occasions on which any person (except one in a thousand) has it in his power to do this on an extended scale, in other words, to be a public benefactor, are but exceptional; and on these occasions alone is he called on to consider public utility; in every other case, private utility, the interest or happiness of some few persons, is all he has to attend to. Those alone the influence of whose actions extends to society in general need concern themselves habitually about so large an object. In the case of abstinences indeed — of things which people forbear to do from moral considerations, though the consequences in the particular case might be beneficial — it would be unworthy of an intelligent agent not to be consciously aware that the action is of a class which, if practiced generally, would be generally injurious, and that this is the ground of the obligation to abstain from it. The amount of regard for the public interest implied in this recognition is no greater than is demanded by every system of morals, for they all enjoin to abstain from whatever is manifestly pernicious to society.

The same considerations dispose of another reproach against the doctrine of utility, founded on a still grosser misconception of the purpose of a standard of morality, and of the very meaning of the words "right" and "wrong." It is often affirmed that utilitarianism renders men cold and unsympathizing; that it chills their moral feelings towards individuals; that it makes them regard only the dry and hard consideration of the consequences of actions, not taking into their moral estimate the qualities from which those actions emanate. If the assertion means that they do not allow their judgment respecting the rightness or wrongness of an action to be influenced by their opinion of the qualities of the person who does it, this is a complaint not against utilitarianism, but against any standard of morality at all; for certainly no known ethical standard decides an action to be good or bad because it is done by a good or a bad man, still less because done by an amiable, a brave, or a benevolent man, or the contrary. These considerations are relevant, not to the estimation of actions, but of persons; and there is nothing in the utilitarian theory inconsistent with the fact that there are other things which interest us in persons besides the rightness and wrongness of their actions. The Stoics, indeed, with the paradoxical misuse of language which was part of their system, and by which they strove to raise themselves above all concern about anything but virtue, were fond of saying that he who has that has everything; that he, and only he, is rich, is beautiful, is a king. But no claim of this description is made for the virtuous man by the utilitarian doctrine. Utilitarians are quite aware that there are other desirable possessions and qualities besides virtue, and are perfectly willing to allow to all of them their full worth. They are also aware that a right action does not necessarily indicate a virtuous character, and that actions which are blamable often proceed from qualities entitled to praise. When this is apparent in any particular case, it modifies their estimation, not certainly of the act, but of the agent. . . .

Again, utility is often summarily stigmatized as an immoral doctrine by giving it the name of "expediency," and taking advantage of the popular use of that term to contrast it with principle. But the expedient, in the sense in which it is opposed to the right, generally means that which is expedient for the particular interest of the agent himself; as when a minister sacrifices the interests of his country to keep himself in place. When it means anything better than this, it means that which is expedient for some immediate object, some temporary purpose, but which violates a rule whose observance is expedient in a much higher degree. The expedient, in this sense, instead of being the same thing with the useful, is a branch of the hurtful. Thus it would often be expedient, for the purpose of getting over some momentary embarrassment, or attaining some object immediately useful to ourselves or others, to tell a lie. But inasmuch as the cultivation in ourselves of a sensitive feeling on the subject of veracity is one of the most useful, and the enfeeblement of that feeling one of the most hurtful, things to which our conduct can be instrumental; and inasmuch as any, even unintentional, deviation from truth does that much towards weakening the trustworthiness of human assertion, which is not only the principal support of all present social well-being, but the insufficiency of which does more than any one thing that can be named to keep back civilization, virtue, everything on which human happiness on the largest scale depends — we feel that the violation, for a present advantage, of a rule of such transcendent expediency is not expedient, and that he who, for the sake of convenience to himself or to some other individual, does what depends on him to deprive mankind of the good, and inflict upon them the evil, involved in the greater or less reliance which they can place in each other's word, acts the part of one of their worst enemies. Yet that even this rule, sacred as it is, admits of possible exceptions is acknowledged by all moralists; the chief of which is when the withholding of some fact (as of information from a malefactor, or of bad news from a person dangerously ill) would save an individual (especially an individual other than oneself) from great and unmerited evil, and when the withholding can only be effected by denial. But in order that the exception may not extend itself beyond the need, and may have the least possible effect in weakening reliance on veracity, it ought to be recognized and, if possible, its limits defined; and, if the principle of utility is good for anything, it must be good for weighing these conflicting utilities against one another, and marking out the region within which one or the other preponderates.

Again, defenders of utility often find themselves called upon to reply to such objections as this — that there is not time, previous to action, for calculating and weighing the effects of any line of conduct on the general happiness. This is exactly as if any one were to say that it is impossible to guide our conduct by Christianity because there is no time, on every occasion on which anything has to be done, to read through the Old and New Testaments. The answer to the objection is that there has been ample time, namely, the whole past duration of the human species. During all that time, mankind have been learning by experience the tendencies of actions; on which experience all the prudence, as well as all the morality, of life are dependent. People talk as if the commencement of this course of experience had hitherto been put off, and as if, at the moment when some man feels tempted to meddle with the property or life of another, he had to begin considering for the first time whether murder and theft are injurious to human happiness. Even then I do not think that he would find the question very puzzling; but, at all events, the matter is now done to his hand. It is truly a whimsical supposition that, if mankind were agreed in considering utility to be the test of morality, they would remain without any agreement as to what *is* useful, and would take no measures for having their notions on the subject taught to the young, and enforced by law and opinion. There is no difficulty in proving any ethical standard whatever to work ill if we suppose universal idiocy to be conjoined with it; but on any hypothesis short of that, mankind must by this time have acquired positive beliefs as to the effects of some actions on their happiness; and the beliefs which have thus come down are the rules of morality for the multitude, and for the philosopher until he has succeeded in finding better. That philosophers might easily do this, even now, on many subjects; that the received code of ethics is by no means of divine right; and that mankind have still much to learn as to the effects of actions on the general happiness, I admit or rather earnestly maintain. The corollaries from the principle of utility, like the precepts of every practical art, admit of indefinite improvement, and, in a progressive state of the human mind, their improvement is perpetually going on. But to consider the rules of morality as improvable is one thing; to pass over the intermediate generalization entirely and endeavor to test each individual action directly by the first principle is another. It is a strange notion that the acknowledgment of a first principle is inconsistent with the admission of secondary ones. To inform a traveler respecting the place of his ultimate destination is not to forbid the use of landmarks and direction-posts on the way. The proposition that happiness is the end and aim of morality does not mean that no road ought to be laid down to that goal, or that persons going thither should not be advised to take one direction rather than another. Men really ought to leave off talking a kind of nonsense on this subject, which they would neither talk nor listen to on other matters of practical concernment. Nobody argues that the art of navigation is not founded on astronomy because sailors cannot wait to calculate the nautical almanac. Being rational creatures, they go to sea with it ready calculated; and all rational creatures go out upon the sea of life with their minds made up on the common questions of right and wrong, as well as on many of the far more difficult questions of wise and foolish. And this, as long as foresight is a human quality, it is to be presumed they will continue to do. Whatever we adopt as the fundamental principle of morality, we require subordinate principles to apply it by; the impossibility of doing without them, being common to all systems, can afford no argument against any one in particular; but gravely to argue as if no such secondary principles could be had, and as if mankind had remained till now, and always must remain, without drawing any general conclusions from the experience of human life, is as high a pitch, I think, as absurdity has ever reached in philosophical controversy. . . .

We are told that a utilitarian will be apt to make his own particular case an exception to moral rules, and, when under temptation, will see a utility in the breach of a rule, greater than he will see in its observance. But is utility the only creed which is able to furnish us with excuses for evil doing, and means of cheating our own conscience? They are afforded in abundance by all doctrines which recognize as a fact in morals the existence of conflicting considerations, which all doctrines do that have been believed by sane persons. It is not the fault of any creed, but of the complicated nature of human affairs, that rules of conduct cannot be so framed as to require no exceptions, and that hardly any kind of action can safely be laid down as either always obligatory or always condemnable. There is no ethical creed which does not temper the rigidity of its laws by giving a certain latitude, under the moral responsibility of the agent, for accommodation to peculiarities of circumstance; and under every creed, at the opening thus made, self-deception and dishonest casuistry get in. There exists no moral system under which there do not arise unequivocal cases of conflicting obligation. These are the real difficulties, the knotty points both in the theory of ethics and in the conscientious guidance of personal conduct. They are overcome practically, with greater or with less success, according to the intellect and virtue of the individual; but it can hardly be pretended that anyone will be the less qualified for dealing with them, from possessing an ultimate standard to which conflicting rights and duties can be referred. If utility is the ultimate source of moral obligations, utility may be invoked to decide between them when their demands are incompatible. Though the application of the standard may be difficult, it is better than none at all; while in other systems, the moral laws all claiming independent authority, there is no common umpire entitled to interfere between them; their claims to precedence one over another rest on little better than sophistry, and, unless determined, as they generally are, by the unacknowledged influence of considerations of utility, afford a free scope for the action of personal desires and partialities. We must remember that only in these cases of conflict between secondary principles is it requisite that first principles should be appealed to.

There is no case of moral obligation in which some secondary principle is not involved; and if only one, there can seldom be any real doubt which one it is, in the mind of any person by whom the principle itself is recognized.

Of What Sort of Proof the Principle of Utility Is Susceptible

It has already been remarked that questions of ultimate ends do not admit of proof, in the ordinary acceptation of the term. To be incapable of proof by reasoning is common to all first principles, to the first premises of our knowledge, as well as to those of our conduct. But the former, being matters of fact, may be the subject of a direct appeal to the faculties which judge of fact—namely, our senses and our internal consciousness. Can an appeal be made to the same faculties on questions of practical ends? Or by what other faculty is cognizance taken of them?

Questions about ends are, in other words, questions what things are desirable. The utilitarian doctrine is that happiness is desirable, and the only thing desirable, as an end; all other things being only desirable as means to that end. What ought to be required of this doctrine, what conditions is it requisite that the doctrine should fulfill—to make good its claim to be believed?

The only proof capable of being given that an object is visible is that people actually see it. The only proof that a sound is audible is that people hear it; and so of the other sources of our experience. In like manner, I apprehend, the sole evidence it is possible to produce that anything is desirable is that people do actually desire it. If the end which the utilitarian doctrine proposes to itself were not, in theory and in practice, acknowledged to be an end, nothing could ever convince any person that it was so. No reason can be given why the general happiness is desirable, except that each person, so far as he believes it to be attainable, desires his own happiness. This, however, being a fact, we have not only all the proof which the case admits of, but all which it is possible to require, that happiness is a good; that each person's happiness is a good to that person, and the general happiness, therefore, a good to the aggregate of all persons. Happiness has made out its title as *one* of the ends of conduct, and consequently one of the criteria of morality.

But it has not, by this alone, proved itself to be the sole criterion. To do that, it would seem, by the same rule, necessary to show, not only that people desire happiness, but that they never desire anything else. Now it is palpable that they do desire things which, in common language, are decidedly distinguished from happiness. They desire, for example, virtue and the absence of vice, no less really than pleasure and the absence of pain. The desire of virtue is not as universal, but it is as authentic a fact as the desire of happiness. And hence the opponents of the utilitarian standard deem that they have a right to infer that there are other ends of human action besides happiness, and that happiness is not the standard of approbation and disapprobation.

But does the utilitarian doctrine deny that people desire virtue, or maintain that virtue is not a thing to be desired? The very reverse. It maintains not only that virtue is to be desired, but that it is to be desired disinterestedly, for itself. Whatever may be the opinion of utilitarian moralists as to the original conditions by which virtue is made virtue, however they may believe (as they do) that actions and dispositions are only virtuous because they promote another end than virtue, yet this being granted, and it having been decided, from considerations of this description, what *is* virtuous, they not only place virtue at the very head of the things which are good as means to the ultimate end, but they also recognize as a psychological fact the possibility of its being, to the individual, a good in itself, without looking to any end beyond it; and hold that the mind is not in a right state, nor in a state conformable to utility, not in the state most conducive to the general happiness, unless it does love virtue in this manner — as a thing desirable in itself, even although, in the individual instance, it should not produce those other desirable consequences which it tends to produce, and on account of which it is held to be virtue. This opinion is not, in the smallest degree, a departure from the happiness principle. The ingredients of happiness are very various, and each of them is desirable in itself, and not merely when considered as swelling an aggregate. The principle of utility does not mean that any given pleasure, as music, for instance, or any given exemption from pain, as for example health, is to be looked upon as means to a collective something termed happiness, and to be desired on that account.

They are desired and desirable in and for themselves; besides being means, they are a part of the end. Virtue, according to the utilitarian doctrine, is not naturally and originally part of the end, but it is capable of becoming so; and in those who love it disinterestedly it has become so, and is desired and cherished, not as a means to happiness, but as a part of their happiness.

To illustrate this further, we may remember that virtue is not the only thing originally a means, and which if it were not a means to anything else would be and remain indifferent, but which by association with what it is a means to comes to be desired for itself, and that too with the utmost intensity. What, for example, shall we say of the love of money? There is nothing originally more desirable about money than about any heap of glittering pebbles. Its worth is solely that of the things which it will buy; the desires for other things than itself, which it is a means of gratifying. Yet the love of money is not only one of the strongest moving forces of human life, but money is, in many cases, desired in and for itself; the desire to possess it is often stronger than the desire to use it, and goes on increasing when all the desires which point to ends beyond it, to be compassed by it, are falling off. It may, then, be said truly that money is desired not for the sake of an end, but as part of the end. From being a means to happiness, it has come to be itself a principal ingredient of the individual's conception of happiness. The same may be said of the majority of the great objects of human life: power, for example, or fame, except that to each of these there is a certain amount of immediate pleasure annexed, which has at least the semblance of being naturally inherent in them — a thing which cannot be said of money. Still, however, the strongest natural attraction, both of power and of fame, is the immense aid they give to the attainment of our other wishes; and it is the strong association thus generated between them and all our objects of desire which gives to the direct desire of them the intensity it often assumes, so as in some characters to surpass in strength all other desires. In these cases the means have become a part of the end, and a more important part of it than any of the things which they are means to. What was once desired as an instrument for the attainment of happiness has come to be desired for its own sake. In being desired for its own sake it is, however, desired as *part* of happiness. The person is made, or thinks he would be made, happy by its mere possession; and is made unhappy by failure to obtain it. The desire of it is not a different thing from the desire of happiness any more than the love of music or the desire of health. They are included in happiness. They are some of the elements of which the desire of happiness is made up. Happiness is not an abstract idea but a concrete whole; and these are some of its parts. And the utilitarian standard sanctions and approves their being so. Life would be a poor thing, very ill provided with sources of happiness, if there were not this provision of nature by which things originally indifferent, but conducive to, or otherwise associated with, the satisfaction of our primitive desires, become in themselves sources of pleasure more valuable than the primitive pleasures, both in permanency, in the space of human existence that they are capable of covering, and even in intensity.

Virtue, according to the utilitarian conception, is a good of this description. There was no original desire of it, or motive to it, save its conduciveness to pleasure, and especially to protection from pain. But through the association thus formed it may be felt a good in itself, and desired as such with as great intensity as any other good; and with this difference between it and the love of money, of power, or of fame, that all of these may, and often do, render the individual noxious to the other members of the society to which he belongs, whereas there is nothing which makes him so much a blessing to them as the cultivation of the disinterested love of virtue. And consequently, the utilitarian standard, while it tolerates and approves those other acquired desires, up to the point beyond which they would be more injurious to the general happiness than promotive of it, enjoins and requires the cultivation of the love of virtue up to the greatest strength possible, as being above all things important to the general happiness.

It results from the preceding considerations that there is in reality nothing desired except happiness. Whatever is desired otherwise than as a means to some end beyond itself, and ultimately to happiness, is desired as itself a part of happiness, and is not desired for itself until it has become so. Those who desire virtue for its own sake desire it either because the consciousness of it is a pleasure, or because the consciousness of being without it is a pain, or for

both reasons united; as in truth the pleasure and pain seldom exist separately, but almost always together — the same person feeling pleasure in the degree of virtue attained, and pain in not having attained more. If one of these gave him no pleasure, and the other no pain, he would not love or desire virtue, or would desire it only for the other benefits which it might produce to himself or to persons whom he cared for.

We have now, then, an answer to the question, of what sort of proof the principle of utility is susceptible. If the opinion which I have now stated is psychologically true — if human nature is so constituted as to desire nothing which is not either a part of happiness or a means of happiness, we can have no other proof, and we require no other, that these are the only things desirable. If so, happiness is the sole end of human action, and the promotion of it the test by which to judge of all human conduct; from whence it necessarily follows that it must be the criterion of morality, since a part is included in the whole.

And now to decide whether this is really so, whether mankind do desire nothing for itself but that which is a pleasure to them, or of which the absence is a pain, we have evidently arrived at a question of fact and experience, dependent, like all similar questions, upon evidence. It can only be determined by practised self-consciousness and self-observation, assisted by observation of others. I believe that these sources of evidence, impartially consulted, will declare that desiring a thing and finding it pleasant, aversion to it and thinking of it as painful, are phenomena entirely inseparable or rather two parts of the same phenomenon; in strictness of language, two different modes of naming the same psychological fact; that to think of an object as desirable (unless for the sake of its consequences) and to think of it as pleasant are one and the same thing; and that to desire anything except in proportion as the idea of it is pleasant, is a physical and metaphysical impossibility.

So obvious does this appear to me that I expect it will hardly be disputed; and the objection made will be, not that desire can possibly be directed to anything ultimately except pleasure and exemption from pain, but that the will is a different thing from desire; that a person of confirmed virtue or any other person whose purposes are fixed carries out his purposes without any thought of the pleasure he has in contemplating them or expects to derive from their fulfilment, and persists in acting on them, even though these pleasures are much diminished by changes in his character or decay of his passive sensibilities, or are outweighed by the pains which the pursuit of the purposes may bring upon him. All this I fully admit and have stated it elsewhere as positively and emphatically as anyone. Will, the active phenomenon, is a different thing from desire, the state of passive sensibility, and, though originally an offshoot from it, may in time take root and detach itself from the parent stock, so much so that in the case of an habitual purpose, instead of willing the thing because we desire it, we often desire it only because we will it. This,

however, is but an instance of that familiar fact, the power of habit, and is nowise confined to the case of virtuous actions. Many indifferent things which men originally did from a motive of some sort, they continue to do from habit. Sometimes this is done unconsciously; the consciousness coming only after the action; at other times with conscious volition, but volition which has become habitual and is put in operation by the force of habit, in opposition perhaps to the deliberate preference, as often happens with those who have contracted habits of vicious or hurtful indulgence. Third and last comes the case in which the habitual act of will in the individual instance is not in contradiction to the general intention prevailing at other times, but in fulfilment of it; as in the case of the person of confirmed virtue and of all who pursue deliberately and consistently any determinate end. The distinction between will and desire thus understood is an authentic and highly important psychological fact; but the fact consists solely in this — that will, like all other parts of our constitution, is amenable to habit, and that we may will from habit what we no longer desire for itself, or desire only because we will it. It is not the less true that will, in the beginning, is entirely produced by desire; including in that term the repelling influence of pain as well as the attractive one of pleasure. Let us take into consideration no longer the person who has a confirmed will to do right, but him in whom that virtuous will is still feeble, conquerable by temptation, and not to be fully relied on; by what means can it be strengthened? How can the will to be virtuous, where it does not exist in sufficient force, be implanted or awakened? Only by making the person *desire* virtue — by making him think of it in a pleasurable light, or of its absence in a painful one. It is by associating the doing right with pleasure, or the doing wrong with pain, or by eliciting and impressing and bringing home to the person's experience the pleasure naturally involved in the one or the pain in the other, that it is possible to call forth that will to be virtuous which, when confirmed, acts without any thought of either pleasure or pain. Will is the child of desire, and passes out of the dominion of its parent only to come under that of habit. That which is the result of habit affords no presumption of being intrinsically good; and there would be no reason for wishing that the purpose of virtue should become independent of pleasure and pain were it not that the influence of the pleasurable and painful associations which prompt to virtue is not sufficiently to be depended on for unerring constancy of action until it has acquired the support of habit. Both in feeling and in conduct, habit is the only thing which imparts certainty; and it is because of the importance to others of being able to rely absolutely on one's feelings and conduct, and to oneself of being able to rely on one's own, that the will to do right ought to be cultivated into this habitual independence. In other words, this state of the will is a means to good, not intrinsically a good; and does not contradict the doctrine that nothing is a good to human beings but in so far as it is either itself pleasurable or a means of attaining pleasure or averting pain.

But if this doctrine be true, the principle of utility is proved. Whether it is so or not, must now be left to the consideration of the thoughtful reader.

COMMENT

Bentham and Mill

"What good is happiness? It won't buy money." This witticism reverses the true relation between means and ends. Money is a means, and happiness is an end. Money is important because it contributes to happiness, and happiness is good for its own sake. It is illogical — and hence amusing — to speak as if money were the end and happiness only the means.

The ethical theory known as utilitarianism maintains that right action, like money, is valuable essentially as a means. Unlike Kant, the utilitarians make *consequences* the test of right and wrong. An action is right if it brings about the best results.

But what are the *best results*? "The greatest happiness of the greatest number," declared Jeremy Bentham. By happiness he meant the surplus of pleasure over pain; and the proper end of moral action, he maintained, is to bring about this surplus in the lives of as many people as possible. Acts should be judged right in proportion as they tend to increase pleasure or decrease pain among the maximum number of people. The intrinsic value of the pleasure or disvalue of the pain is to be judged quantitatively, not qualitatively. What matters is that we get as much pleasure as possible, not that we get a certain kind. "Quantity of pleasure being equal," Bentham taught, "pushpin [a very simple game] is as good as poetry." The quantity has two dimensions — intensity and duration. The *more* intense and durable a pleasure is, and the *less* intense and durable a pain, the better — apart from future consequences. The pain of a toothache, for example, is worse the longer and more intense it is; the pleasure of a happy friendship is better the more intense and prolonged it is.

Bentham did not deny that there are, in a sense, *bad* pleasures and *good* pains. The pleasures of cruelty or intemperance produce, in the long run, an overbalance of pain — they are good in themselves but bad in their consequences, and their instrumental badness outweighs their intrinsic goodness. Similarly, there are pains with pleasant consequences. But nothing but pleasure is *intrinsically* good, and nothing but pain is *intrinsically* bad. The art of living well is to calculate the worth of actions in terms of all the plus values of pleasure and the minus values of pain, subtracting the latter from the former. Bentham exercised a great deal of ingenuity in working out the details of this "moral arithmetic."

So far he was expressing an *ethical* theory. In addition, he advanced the *psychological* doctrine that every person is naturally selfish and hence almost invariably seeks pleasure or the avoidance of pain for oneself. This egoistic doctrine is inconsistent with the contention that everyone ought to seek "the greatest happiness of the greatest number." What sense is there in saying that people ought to aim at the greatest social good if their nature is inescapably selfish? Bentham tried to avoid contradiction by arguing that governments should establish a system of rewards and punishments that would induce individuals, on the very basis of their egoism, to further the maximum social happiness.

When Mill undertook the composition of *Utilitarianism*, he was trying to defend the ethical philosophy of his father and Bentham from the attacks made on it, but he was too divided in mind to make a good defense. The conflict between his loyalty to Bentham and his deep independent convictions produced many strains and inconsistencies. His book is, nevertheless, worth very careful study because even his confusions and errors are highly instructive.

Although Mill begins his discussion of utilitarianism with remarks that appear to be in perfect agreement with Bentham's theory, he soon exhibits his independence. This divergence gives rise to some of the most fundamental issues in the whole field of ethics. Let us now consider some of these issues.

The Question of Qualities of Pleasure

In estimating the intrinsic value of pleasures, Mill subordinates Bentham's quantitative standards — intensity and duration — to a standard of quality. The pleasures of the cultivated life, he maintains, are superior in *kind* to the pleasures of the uncultivated. Hence the pleasures of a human being are qualitatively superior to the pleasures of a pig, and the pleasures of a Socrates are qualitatively superior to the pleasures of an uncultivated fool. This is a radical break with Bentham's quantitative hedonism, which maintains that the pleasure of a dolt is no better or worse intrinsically than the quantitatively equal pleasure of a highly developed person.

Is Mill correct in supposing that there are different kinds of pleasure? At first glance, the facts seem to bear out his view. The pleasure of reading a good philosophical book, for example, apparently differs qualitatively from the pleasure of playing a brisk game of handball. But is the qualitative difference in the *pleasures*, or is it in the differing *accompaniments* of the pleasures? If we consider pleasant *experiences*, and not bare pleasures, there *are* genuine qualitative differences; but these differences may be not in the pleasures but in the very different *contents* of experience that have the common property of pleasing. In the case of reading, the experience is quiet, meditative, and relaxed; in the case of playing handball, it is exciting, kinesthetic, and strenuous. Some psychologists, such as Edward Titchener in his *Textbook on Psychology*, have maintained that the pleasures in such diverse experiences differ only in intensity and duration and that the only qualitative differences are in such accompaniments as we have just pointed out. Mill inadvertently lends support to this interpretation since he speaks of the "nobility," "dignity," "intellectuality," and so on, of the "pleasures" that he prefers. It would seem that he is talking not about bare pleasures, abstracted from any content, but rather about *experiences*, which contain not only pleasure but also various intellectual, moral, and esthetic qualities.

It is theoretically possible to maintain that there are qualitative differences in pure pleasures and that these differences are ethically important. Just as there are different kinds of colors — red, blue, green, and so on — so there might be different kinds of pleasures. And just as one might hold that warm colors, let us say, are qualitatively superior to cool colors, so one might content that certain kinds of pleasures are qualitatively superior to others. One difficulty with this view is that we do not find such indisputable qualitative differences in pleasures. Even if we did, we might still be unable to tell whether some kinds of pleasure are really better than others.

This sort of qualitative hedonism, in any event, is not Mill's view. He *appears* to be advocating hedonism, but he is really maintaining, albeit unclearly and inconsistently, that the good is the pleasant *development* of the personality. This is a kind of synthesis of hedonism and self-realizationism rather than hedonism pure and simple.

The Question of Moral Arithmetic

Bentham maintained that the business of the legislator or moralist is to calculate the probable effects of alternative acts with a view to maximizing pleasure and minimizing pain. This entails the quantitative assessment of pleasures and pains. That there are great difficulties in comparing intensities with durations, adding up pleasures and pains, and subtracting pains from pleasures has often been pointed out. Bentham might reply that such calculation, although difficult, should be carried out as best we can and that at least a rough estimation of the hedonic consequences of acts is indispensable to any rational direction of our lives.

By introducing questions of quality, Mill greatly restricts the applicability of Bentham's moral arithmetic. His qualitative test is *preference* — not the preference of the average man but that of the moral connoisseur. He tells us that wise persons, such as Socrates, are more competent than the unwise to compare pleasures, to judge which are qualitatively superior, and to decide whether, in a particular instance, considerations of quantity should be sacrificed to considerations of quality. "From this verdict of the only competent judges," he declares, "I apprehend there can be no appeal."

The difference between the approaches of Bentham and of Mill gives rise to a number of questions: To what extent does utilitarianism entail the measurement of pleasures and pains? Are intensities commensurable with durations, and pains with pleasures? Is the preference of the wise a better guide than quantitative assessment? Is the concept of a moral connoisseur sound?

The Question of the Social Distribution of Good

Bentham proposes that the morality of acts be determined by their contribution to "the greatest happiness of the greatest number" — and Mill, at times, employs the same phrase. But does this formula mean the greatest amount of happiness among men, or the greatest number of men who are happy? And supposing that there is a conflict between greatest happiness and greatest number, should we sacrifice the greatest number to the greatest happiness, or the greatest happiness to the greatest number? Mill's ambiguous formula provides no answer.

There are indications, however, that Bentham is more democratic and equalitarian in his approach to the problem of distribution than Mill.

Each person, he declared, should count for one, and no one for more than one. This tenet could be interpreted as meaning that the pleasure of any person is as intrinsically good as the quantitatively equal pleasure of any other person. But it could also be interpreted to mean that a smaller amount of pleasure *equally* distributed is morally preferable (at least on occasion) to a greater amount *unequally* distributed. If this was Bentham's real conviction, he was not a strict utilitarian and hedonist — for the principle of equality so interpreted is based on a sense of distributive justice rather than on the utilitarian principle of maximizing pleasure and minimizing pain.

Mill's position, in any event, is comparatively aristocratic. Although he verbally subscribes to Bentham's phrases, his emphasis on quality, wisdom, and self-cultivation implies a very different standard than the greatest possible pleasure of the greatest possible number. The word *greatest* indicates a quantitative criterion — whether it be number of people or amount of pleasure. Mill's criterion, on the other hand, is qualitative. In effect, he favors an intellectual aristocracy — though it is worth noting that he does not identify the intellectually superior with the rich and powerful of the earth.

The differences between Bentham and Mill again serve to emphasize an important set of problems. What is a fair and just distribution of good? Can it be reconciled with a quantitative hedonism? Should the controlling consideration be the number of people receiving the good, or the amount of the good? Or should both amount and number be subordinated, as in Mill, to considerations of quality?

The Question of Ultimate Principles

The ethical philosophy of Mill, like that of Bentham, falls into two main parts. The first part is a theory about the nature of right — the doctrine that the proper standard for judging right is best results. This theory is logically independent of hedonism, or of any other particular interpretation of goodness. It simply states that the right must be determined in the light of good consequences — whatever the good may be. The good might be pleasure or satisfaction of desire or actualization of potentialities — or almost anything else. Bentham and Mill speak as if the test of consequences is necessarily linked to one and only one end — namely, "happiness" as each conceives it. But this is manifestly not the case.

The question of the validity of utilitarianism — in the wide sense of the term — turns largely on whether it can satisfactorily explain our many and varied duties. The nonutilitarian will argue that there are kinds of moral rectitude that cannot be interpreted as utilitarian rightness. He would say, for example, that having made a solemn promise, we have a duty to keep it *even if no more good is thereby to be achieved*. The utilitarian, in contrast, would maintain that there is no valid test of right and wrong except best results. Our duty is to help people and not to hurt them — and the more we help them and the less we hurt them, the better. If it becomes clear that in the long run, keeping a promise will have bad rather than good results, or results less good than some other alternative, our moral obligation is not to keep the promise but to choose whatever alternative yields the best results. This clash between the utilitarians and the nonutilitarians is one of the crucial issues in ethics — and the reader of this book should consider very carefully where the truth lies.

The second part of the ethical philosophy of Bentham and the two Mills is a theory about the nature of ultimate good and evil. Here again, as we have seen, there is disagreement between John Stuart Mill, who embraced a kind of hedonic self-realizationism, and Bentham, who clung to pure quantitative hedonism. The issue is extremely important, but it is not one that can be decided by any conclusive proof. Mill (not realizing the extent of his divergence from Bentham) undertook to "prove" that pleasure alone is ultimately good, but his so-called proof (he admits that *strict* or *conclusive* proof is impossible) contains some of the most widely advertised fallacies in the history of philosophy. We shall refrain from pointing out these fallacies, leaving to the reader the exercise of discovering them. Whether the fallacies are apparent only, being due to carelessness in the use of language, or whether they are *real* fallacies resulting from mental confusion is a question of interpretation.

To decide the question of what is ultimately good, we must summon up whatever insight we can muster. If we imagine a world of human beings and a world of lower animals, *equal in the amount of pleasure they contain*, it would not follow that the two worlds are equal in ultimate goodness — because the humans, in addition to experiencing pleasure, have insight into truth, love, imagination, excellence of character, enjoyment of beauty, and so forth. The reply of the hedonist, that all these things are good as means because they *give* pleasure, would not seem to the antihedonist an adequate answer. The latter would say that it is important not merely to feel pleasure but to feel pleasure in certain ways, with certain accompaniments rather than others. *Real* happiness embraces the great goods of beauty and truth and nobility of character as having intrinsic and not merely instrumental value. To decide who is right, the hedonist or the antihedonist, is a very important question for the reader to answer.

18

The Way of Freedom

"The noble human being honors himself as one who is powerful, also as one who has power over himself, who knows how to speak and be silent, who delights in being severe and hard on himself and respects all severity and hardness."

Friedrich Nietzsche

FRIEDRICH NIETZSCHE (1844–1900)

Nietzsche was born in Rocken, near Leipzig. His father was the son and his mother the daughter of Lutheran ministers. The father died of softening of the brain when Nietzsche was four years old, and a younger brother died in infancy. In consequence, the boy was reared in a household of women — mother, sister, grandmother, and two unmarried aunts. In 1858 he was sent for six years to a boarding school, where he studied Greek classics with great success and mathematics with no success at all. The medical records of the school contain this entry: ". . . short-sighted and often plagued by migraine headaches."

He disliked being called "the little minister" by his classmates, and when he attended the University of Bonn, he broke completely with the Christianity of his ancestors. Moving on to the University of Leipzig, he fell under the spell of Erwin Rohde, a great classical scholar, and became absorbed in the history of culture. He also became personally acquainted with Richard Wagner and fell in love with Wagner's operas. After years of friendship, the two split when Nietzsche became convinced that Wagner was sacrificing his intellectual and artistic integrity to the glorification of Christianity and the German state.

After unfortunate experiences in military service in the Austro-German and Franco-Prussian wars, he finished his studies and became a university professor of classical philology in Basel, Switzerland, at the unheard-of age of twenty-four. His health was never good, and after a decade of teaching, he was forced to resign his professorship in 1879. Living on a small academic pension for the next ten years, he spent a very lonely life at health resorts in Switzerland, northern Italy, and the French Riviera. Although this was a period of great philosophical productivity, his emotional conflicts were unendurable, and in 1888 he became insane, never to recover. The tragic character of his life is epitomized in the words of one of his interpreters: "He was ill (often violently ill) more days than he was well. He was nearly blind at the age of thirty-five: he was lonely, unpopular, unsuccessful, poor: no one understood him, and no one was interested in his work: he had every reason to believe that he had completely failed: finally he went mad."[1]

---

[1] A. H. J. Knight, *Some Aspects of the Life and Work of Nietzsche, and Particularly of His Connection with Greek Literature and Thought* (Cambridge: Cambridge University Press, 1933), p. 165.

Beyond Good and Evil

WHAT IS NOBLE[1]

257

Every enhancement of the type "man" has so far been the work of an aristocratic society—and it will be so again and again—a society that believes in the long ladder of an order of rank[2] and differences in value between man and man, and that needs slavery in some sense or other. Without that *pathos of distance* which grows out of the ingrained difference between strata —when the ruling caste constantly looks afar and looks down upon subjects and instruments and just as constantly practices obedience and command, keeping down and keeping at a distance—that other, more mysterious pathos could not have grown up either —the craving for an ever new widening of distances within the soul itself, the development of ever higher, rarer, more remote, further-stretching, more

---

From Friedrich Nietzsche, *Beyond Good and Evil: Prelude to a Philosophy of the Future.* Translated, with commentary, by Walter Kaufman. © Copyright, 1966, by Random House, Inc. Reprinted by permission of the publisher.
[1] *Vornehm.* [See Section 212 of *Beyond Good and Evil.*]
[2] *Stände: Stand* can mean—apart from position, state, condition—class, rank, profession, and *Stände* can mean the estates of the realm. Asked to indicate her *Stand* on a questionnaire, a German woman might write, even after World War II: *Strassenbahnschaffnerswitwe*, that is, "widow of a streetcar conductor."

comprehensive states—in brief, simply the enhancement of the type "man," the continual "self-overcoming of man," to use a moral formula in a supra-moral sense.

To be sure, one should not yield to humanitarian illusions about the origins of an aristocratic society (and thus of the presupposition of this enhancement of the type "man"): truth is hard. Let us admit to ourselves, without trying to be considerate, how every higher culture on earth so far has *begun.* Human beings whose nature was still natural, barbarians in every terrible sense of the word, men of prey who were still in possession of unbroken strength of will and lust for power, hurled themselves upon weaker, more civilized, more peaceful races, perhaps traders or cattle raisers or, upon mellow old cultures whose last vitality was even then flaring up in splendid fireworks of spirit and corruption. In the beginning, the noble caste was always the barbarian caste: their predominance did not lie mainly in physical strength but in strength of the soul—they were more *whole* human beings (which also means, at every level, "more whole beasts").

258

Corruption as the expression of a threatening anarchy among the instincts and of the fact that the foundation of the affects, which is called "life," has been shaken: corruption is something totally different depending on the organism in which it appears. When, for example, an aristocracy, like that of France at the beginning of the Revolution, throws away its privileges with a sublime disgust and sacrifices itself to an extravagance of its own moral feelings, that is corruption; it was really only the last act of that centuries-old corruption which had led them to surrender, step by step, their governmental prerogatives, demoting themselves to a mere *function* of the monarchy (finally even to a mere ornament and showpiece). The essential characteristic of a good and healthy aristocracy, however, is that it experiences itself *not* as a function (whether of the monarchy or the commonwealth) but as their *meaning* and highest justification — that it therefore accepts with a good conscience the sacrifice of untold human beings who, *for its sake*, must be reduced and lowered to incomplete human beings, to slaves, to instruments. Their fundamental faith simply has to be that society must *not* exist for society's sake but only as the foundation and scaffolding on which a choice type of being is able to raise itself to its higher task and to a higher state of *being*[3] — comparable to those sun-seeking vines of Java — they are called *Sipo Matador* — that so long and so often enclasp an oak tree with their tendrils until eventually, high above it but supported by it, they can unfold their crowns in the open light and display their happiness.

[3]Cf. the outlook of the heroes of the *Iliad*.

259

Refraining mutually from injury, violence, and exploitation and placing one's will on a par with that of someone else — this may become, in a certain rough sense, good manners among individuals if the appropriate conditions are present (namely, if these men are actually similar in strength and value standards and belong together in *one* body). But as soon as this principle is extended, and possibly even accepted as the *fundamental principle of society*, it immediately proves to be what it really is — a will to the *denial* of life, a principle of disintegration and decay.

Here we must beware of superficiality and get to the bottom of the matter, resisting all sentimental weak-life itself is *essentially* appropriation, injury, overpowering of what is alien and weaker; suppression, hardness, imposition of one's own forms, incorporation and at least, at its mildest, exploitation — but why should one always use those words in which a slanderous intent has been imprinted for ages?

Even the body within which individuals treat each other as equals, as suggested before — and this happens in every healthy aristocracy — if it is a living and not a dying body, has to do to other bodies what the individuals within it refrain from doing to each other: it will have to be an incarnate will to power, it will strive to grow, spread, seize, become predominant — not from any morality or immorality but because it is *living* and because life simply *is* will to power. But there is no point on which the ordinary consciousness of Europeans resists instruction as on this: everywhere people are now raving, even under scientific disguises, about coming conditions of society in which "the exploitative aspect" will be removed—which sounds to me as if they promised to invent a way of life that would dispense with all organic functions. "Exploitation" does not belong to a corrupt or imperfect and primitive society: it belongs to the *essence* of what lives, as a basic organic function; it is a consequence of the will to power, which is after all the will of life.

If this should be an innovation as a theory—as a reality it is the *primordial fact* of all history: people ought to be honest with themselves at least that far.

260

Wandering through the many subtler and coarser moralities which have so far been prevalent on earth, or still are prevalent, I found that certain features recurred regularly together and were closely associated—until I finally discovered two basic types and one basic difference.

There are *master morality* and *slave morality*[4]—I add immediately that in all the higher and more mixed cultures there also appear attempts at mediation between these two moralities, and yet

more often the interpenetration and mutual misunderstanding of both, and at times they occur directly alongside each other—even in the same human being, within a *single* soul.[5] The moral discrimination of values has originated either among a ruling group whose consciousness of its difference from the ruled group was accompanied by delight—or among the ruled, the slaves and dependents of every degree.

In the first case, when the ruling group determines what is "good," the exalted, proud states of the soul are experienced as conferring distinction and determining the order of rank. The noble human being separates from himself those in whom the opposite of such exalted, proud states finds expression: he depises them. It should be noted immediately that in this first type of morality the opposition of "good" and *"bad"* means approximately the same as "noble" and "contemptible." (The opposition of "good" and *"evil"* has a different origin.) One feels contempt for the cowardly, the anxious, the petty, those intent on narrow utility; also for the suspicious with their unfree glances, those who humble themselves, the doglike people who allow themselves to be maltreated, the begging flatterers, above all the liars: it is part of the fundamental faith of all aristocrats that the common people lie. "We truthful ones"—thus the nobility of ancient Greece referred to itself.

[4]While the ideas developed here, and explicated at greater length a year later in the first part of the *Genealogy of Morals*, had been expressed by Nietzsche in 1878 in section 45 of *Human, All-Too-Human*, this is the passage in which his famous terms "master morality" and "slave morality" are introduced.

[5]These crucial qualifications, though added immediately, have often been overlooked. "Modern" moralities are clearly mixtures; hence their manifold tensions, hypocrisies, and contradictions.

It is obvious that moral designations were everywhere first applied to *human beings* and only later, derivatively to actions. Therefore, it is a gross mistake when historians of morality start from such questions as: why was the compassionate act praised? The noble type of man experiences *itself* as determining values; it does not need approval; it judges, "what is harmful to me is harmful in itself"; it knows itself to be that which first accords honor to things; it is *value-creating*. Everything it knows as part of itself it honors: such a morality is self-glorification. In the foreground there is the feeling of fullness, of power that seeks to overflow, the happiness of high tension, the consciousness of wealth that would give and bestow: the noble human being, too, helps the unfortunate, but not, or almost not, from pity, but prompted more by an urge begotten by excess of power. The noble human being honors himself as one who is powerful, also as one who has power over himself, who knows how to speak and be silent, who delights in being severe and hard with himself and respects all severity and hardness. "A hard heart Wotan put into my breast," says an old Scandinavian saga: a fitting poetic expression, seeing that it comes from the soul of a proud Viking. Such a type of man is actually proud of the fact that he is *not* made for pity, and the hero of the saga therefore adds as a warning: "If the heart is not hard in youth it will never harden." Noble and courageous human beings who think that way are furthest removed from that morality which finds the distinction of morality precisely in pity, or in acting for others, or in *désintéressement*; faith in oneself, pride in

oneself, a fundamental hostility and irony against "selflessness" belong just as definitely to noble morality as does a slight disdain and caution regarding compassionate feelings and a "warm heart."

It is the powerful who *understand* how to honor; this is their art, their realm of invention. The profound reverence for age and tradition — all law rests on this double reverence — the faith and prejudice in favor of ancestors and disfavor of those yet to come are typical of the morality of the powerful; and when the men of "modern ideas," conversely, believe almost instinctively in "progress" and "the future" and more and more lack respect for age, this in itself would sufficiently betray the ignoble origin of these "ideas."

A morality of the ruling group, however, is most alien and embarrassing to the present taste in the severity of its principle that one has duties only to one's peers; that against beings of a lower rank, against everything alien, one may behave as one pleases or "as the heart desires," and in any case "beyond good and evil" — here pity and like feelings may find their place.[6] The capacity for, and the duty of, long gratitude and long revenge — both only

---

[6] The final clause that follows the dash, omitted in the Cowan translation, is crucial and qualifies the first part of the sentence: a noble person has no *duties* to animals but treats them in accordance with his feelings, which means, if he is noble, with pity.

The ruling masters, of course, are not always noble in this sense, and this is recognized by Nietzsche in *Twilight of the Idols*, in the chapter "The 'Improvers' of Mankind," in which he gives strong expression to his distaste for Manu's laws concerning outcastes (*Portable Nietzsche*, pp. 503–

among one's peers — refinement in repaying, the sophisticated concept of friendship, a certain necessity for having enemies (as it were, as drainage ditches for the affects of envy, quarrelsomeness, exuberance — at bottom, in order to be capable of being good *friends*): all these are typical characteristics of noble morality which, as suggested, is not the morality of "modern ideas" and therefore is hard to empathize with today, also hard to dig up and uncover.[7]

It is different with the second type of morality, *slave morality*. Suppose the violated, oppressed, suffering, unfree, who are uncertain of themselves and weary, moralize: what will their moral valuations have in common? Probably, a pessimistic suspicion about the whole condition of man will find expression, perhaps a condemnation of man along with his condition. The slave's eye is not favorable to the virtues of the powerful: he is skeptical and suspicious, *subtly* suspicious, of all the "good" that is honored there — he would like to persuade himself that even their happiness is not genuine. Conversely, those qualities are brought out and flooded with light which serve to ease existence for those who suffer: here pity, the complaisant and obliging hand, the warm heart, patience, industry, humility, and friendliness are honored — for here these are the most useful qualities and almost the only means for enduring the pressure of existence. Slave morality is essentially a morality of utility.

Here is the place for the origin of that famous opposition of "good" and "evil": into evil one's feelings project power and dangerousness, a certain terribleness, subtlety, and strength that does not permit contempt to develop. According to slave morality, those who are "evil" thus inspire fear; according to master morality it is precisely those who are "good" that inspire, and wish to inspire, fear, while the "bad" are felt to be contemptible.

The opposition reaches its climax when, as a logical consequence of slave morality, a touch of disdain is associated also with the "good" of this morality — this may be slight and benevolent — because the good human being has to be *undangerous* in the slaves' way of thinking: he is good-natured, easy to deceive, a little stupid perhaps, *un bonhomme*.[8] Wherever slave morality becomes preponderant, language tends to bring the words "good" and "stupid" closer together.

---

505); also in *The Will to Power* (ed. W. Kaufmann, New York, Random House, 1967), section 142. Indeed, in *The Antichrist*, section 57, Nietzsche contradicts outright his formulation above: "When the exceptional human being treats the mediocre more tenderly than himself and his peers, this is not mere courtesy of the heart — it is simply his *duty*."

More important: Nietzsche's obvious distaste for slave morality and the fact that he makes a point of liking master morality better does not imply that he endorses master morality. Cf. the text for note 5 above.

[7] Clearly, master morality cannot be discovered by introspection nor by the observation of individuals who are "masters" rather than "slaves." Both of these misunderstandings are widespread. What is called for is rather a rereading of, say, the *Iliad* and, to illustrate "slave morality," the New Testament.

[8] Literally "a good human being," the term is used for precisely the type described here.

One last fundamental difference: the longing for *freedom*, the instinct for happiness and the subtleties of the feeling of freedom belong just as necessarily to slave morality and morals as artful and enthusiastic reverence and devotion are the regular symptom of an aristocratic way of thinking and evaluating.

This makes plain why love *as passion* — which is our European specialty — simply must be of noble origin: as is well known, its invention must be credited to the Provençal knight-poets, those magnificent and inventive human beings of the *"gai saber"*[9] to whom Europe owes so many things and almost owes itself. —

261

Among the things that may be hardest to understand for a noble human being is vanity: he will be tempted to deny it, where another type of human being could not find it more palpable. The problem for him is to imagine people who seek to create a good opinion of themselves which they do not have of themselves — and thus also do not "deserve" — and who nevertheless end up *believing* this good opinion themselves. This strikes him half as such bad taste and lack of self-respect, and half as so baroquely irrational, that he would like to consider vanity as exceptional, and in most cases when it is spoken of he doubts it.

He will say, for example: "I may be mistaken about my value and nevertheless demand that my value, exactly as I define it, should be acknowledged by others as well — but this is no vanity (but conceit or, more frequently, what is called 'humility' or 'modesty')." Or: "For many reasons I may take pleasure in the good opinion of others: perhaps because I honor and love them and all their pleasures give me pleasure; perhaps also because their good opinion confirms and strengthens my faith in my own good opinion; perhaps because the good opinion of others, even in cases where I do not share it, is still useful to me or promises to become so — but all that is not vanity."

The noble human being must force himself, with the aid of history, to recognize that, since time immemorial, in all somehow dependent social strata the common man *was* only what he was *considered*: not at all used to positing values himself, he also attached no other value to himself than his masters attached to him (it is the characteristic *right of masters* to create values).

It may be understood as the consequence of an immense atavism that even now the ordinary man still always *waits* for an opinion about himself and then instinctively submits to that — but by no means only a "good" opinion; also a bad and unfair one (consider, for example, the great majority of the self-estimates and self-underestimates that believing women accept

---

[9] "Gay science": in the early fourteenth century the term was used to designate the art of the troubadours, codified in *Leys d'amors*. Nietzsche subtitled his own *Fröhliche Wissenschaft* (1882), "*la gaya scienza*," placed a quatrain on the title page, began the book with a fifteen-page "Prelude in German Rhymes," and in the second edition (1887) added, besides a Preface and Book V, an "Appendix" of further verses.

from their father-confessors, and believing Christians quite generally from their church).

In accordance with the slowly arising democratic order of things (and its cause, the intermarriage of masters and slaves), the originally noble and rare urge to ascribe value to oneself on one's own and to "think well" of oneself will actually be encouraged and spread more and more now; but it is always opposed by an older, ampler, and more deeply ingrained propensity — and in the phenomenon of "vanity" this older propensity masters the younger one. The vain person is delighted by *every* good opinion he hears of himself (quite apart from all considerations of its utility, and also apart from truth or falsehood), just as every bad opinion of him pains him: for he submits to both, he *feels* subjected to them in accordance with that oldest instinct of submission that breaks out in him.

It is "the slave" in the blood of the vain person, a residue of the slave's craftiness — and how much "slave" is still residual in woman, for example! — that seeks to *seduce* him to good opinions about himself; it is also the slave who afterwards immediately prostrates himself before these opinions as if he had not called them forth.

And to say it once more: vanity is an atavism.

262

A *species*[10] comes to be, a type becomes fixed and strong, through the long fight with essentially constant *unfavorable* conditions. Conversely, we know from the experience of breeders[11] that species accorded superabundant nourishment and quite generally extra protection and care soon tend most strongly toward variations of the type and become rich in marvels and monstrosities (including monstrous vices).

Now look for once at an aristocratic commonwealth — say, an ancient Greek *polis*,[12] or Venice — as an arrangement, whether voluntary or involuntary, for *breeding*:[13] human beings are together there who are dependent on themselves and want their species to prevail, most often because they *have to* prevail or run the terrible risk of being exterminated. Here that boon, that excess, and that protection which favor variations are lacking; the species needs itself as a species, as something that can prevail and make itself durable by virtue of its very hardness, uniformity, and simplicity of form, in a constant fight with its neighbors or with the oppressed who are rebellious or threaten rebellion. Manifold experience teaches them to which qualities above all they owe the fact that, despite all gods and men, they are still there, that they have always triumphed: these qualities they call virtues, these virtues alone they cultivate.[14] They do this with hardness, indeed they want hardness; every aristocratic morality is intolerant — in the education of youth, in their arrangements for women, in

---

[10] Throughout this section *Art* is rendered as species, and *Typus* as type. Elsewhere, *Art* is often translated as type.

[11] *Züchter.*
[12] City-state.
[13] *Züchtung.*
[14] *Züchtet sie gross.*

their marriage customs, in the relations of old and young, in their penal laws (which take into account deviants only) —they consider intolerance itself a virtue, calling it "justice."

In this way a type with few but very strong traits, a species of severe, warlike, prudently taciturn men, close-mouthed and closely linked (and as such possessed of the subtlest feeling for the charms and *nuances* of association), is fixed beyond the changing generations; the continual fight against ever constant *unfavorable* conditions is, as mentioned previously, the cause that fixes and hardens a type.

Eventually, however, a day arrives when conditions become more fortunate and the tremendous tension decreases; perhaps there are no longer any enemies among one's neighbors, and the means of life, even for the enjoyment of life, are superabundant. At one stroke the bond and constraint of the old discipline[15] are torn: it no longer seems necessary, a condition of existence — if it persisted it would only be a form of *luxury*, an archaizing *taste*. Variation, whether as deviation (to something higher, subtler, rarer) or as degeneration and monstrosity, suddenly appears on the scene in the greatest abundance and magnificence; the individual dares to be individual and different.

At these turning points of history we behold beside one another, and often mutually involved and entangled, a splendid, manifold, junglelike growth and upward striving, a kind of *tropical* tempo in the competition to grow, and a tremendous ruin and self-ruination, as the savage egoisms that have turned, almost exploded, against one another wrestle "for sun and light" and can no longer derive any limit, restraint, or consideration from their previous[16] morality. It was the morality itself that dammed up such enormous strength and bent the bow in such a threatening manner; now it is "outlived." The dangerous and uncanny point has been reached where the greater, more manifold, more comprehensive life transcends and *lives beyond* the old morality; the "individual" appears, obliged to give himself laws and to develop his own arts and wiles for self-preservation, self-enhancement, self-redemption.

All sorts of new what-fors and wherewithals; no shared formulas any longer; misunderstanding allied with disrespect; decay, corruption, and the highest desires gruesomely entangled; the genius of the race overflowing from all cornucopias of good and bad; a calamitous simultaneity of spring and fall, full of new charms and veils that characterize young, still unexhausted, still unwearied corruption. Again danger is there, the mother of morals, great danger, this time transposed into the individual, into the neighbor and friend, into the alley, into one's own child, into one's own heart, into the most personal and secret recesses of wish and will: what may the moral philosophers emerging in this age have to preach now?

---

[15] *Zucht.*

[16] *Bisherigen*: elsewhere *bisher* has always been rendered as "so far"; see Preface, note 1.

These acute observers and loiterers discover that the end is approaching fast, that everything around them is corrupted and corrupts, that nothing will stand the day after tomorrow, except *one* type of man, the incurably *mediocre*. The mediocre alone have a chance of continuing their type and propagating — they are the men of the future, the only survivors: "Be like them! Become mediocre" is now the only morality that still makes sense, that still gets a hearing.

But this morality of mediocrity is hard to preach: after all, it may never admit what it is and what it wants. It must speak of measure and dignity and duty and neighbor love — it will find it difficult *to conceal its irony.* —

263

There is an *instinct for rank* which, more than anything else, is a sign of a *high* rank; there is a delight in the nuances of reverence that allows us to infer noble origin and habits. The refinement, graciousness, and height of a soul is tested dangerously when something of the first rank passes by without being as yet protected by the shudders of authority against obtrusive efforts and ineptitudes — something that goes its way unmarked, undiscovered, tempting, perhaps capriciously concealed and disguised, like a living touchstone. Anyone to whose task and practice it belongs to search out souls will employ this very art in many forms in order to determine the ultimate value of a soul and the unalterable, innate order of rank to which it belongs: he will test it for its *instinct of reverence.*

Différence engendre haine[17]: The baseness of some people suddenly spurts up like dirty water when some holy vessel, some precious thing from a locked shrine, some book with the marks of a great destiny, is carried past; and on the other hand there is a reflex of silence, a hesitation of the eye, a cessation of all gestures that express how a soul *feels* the proximity of the most venerable. The way in which reverence for the *Bible* has on the whole been maintained so far in Europe is perhaps the best bit of discipline and refinement of manners that Europe owes to Christianity: such books of profundity and ultimate significance require some external tyranny of authority for their protection in order to gain those millennia of *persistence* which are necessary to exhaust them and figure them out.

Much is gained once the feeling has finally been cultivated in the masses (among the shallow and in the high-speed intestines of every kind) that they are not to touch everything; that there are holy experiences before which they have to take off their shoes and keep away their unclean hands — this is almost their greatest advance toward humanity. Conversely, perhaps there is nothing about so-called educated people and believers in "modern ideas" that is as nauseous as their lack of modesty and the comfortable insolence of their eyes and hands with which they touch, lick, and finger everything; and it is possible that even among the common people, among the less educated, especially among peasants, one finds

---

[17] Difference engenders hatred.

today more *relative* nobility of taste and tactful reverence than among the newspaper-reading *demi-monde* of the spirit, the educated.

264

One cannot erase from the soul of a human being what his ancestors liked most to do and did most constantly: whether they were, for example, assiduous savers and appurtenances of a desk and cash box, modest and bourgeois in their desires, modest also in their virtues; or whether they lived accustomed to commanding from dawn to dusk, fond of rough amusements and also perhaps of even rougher duties and responsibilities; or whether, finally, at some point they sacrificed ancient prerogatives of birth and possessions in order to live entirely for their faith — their "god" — as men of an inexorable and delicate conscience which blushes at every compromise. It is simply not possible that a human being should *not* have the qualities and preferences of his parents and ancestors in his body, whatever appearances may suggest to the contrary. This is the problem of race.[18]

[18] Here, as elsewhere, Nietzsche gives expression to his Lamarckian belief in the heredity of acquired characteristics, shared by Samuel Butler and Bernard Shaw but anathema to Nazi racists and almost universally rejected by geneticists. His Lamarckism is not just an odd fact about Nietzsche but symptomatic of his conception of body and spirit: he ridiculed belief in "pure" spirit but believed just as little in any "pure" body; he claimed that neither could be understood without the other. For a detailed discussion see Kaufmann, *Nietzsche*, Chapter 10.

If one knows something about the parents, an inference about the child is permissible: any disgusting incontinence, any sordid envy, a clumsy insistence that one is always right — these three things together have always constituted the characteristic type of the plebeian — that sort of thing must as surely be transferred to the child as corrupted blood; and with the aid of the best education one will at best *deceive* with regard to such a heredity.

And what else is the aim of education and "culture" today? In our very popularity-minded — that is, plebeian —age, "education" and "culture" *have* to be essentially the art of deceiving — about one's origins, the inherited plebs in one's body and soul. An educator who today preached truthfulness above all and constantly challenged his students, "be true! be natural! do not pretend!" — even such a virtuous and guileless ass would learn after a while to reach for that *furca* of Horace to *naturam expellere*: with what success? "Plebs" *usque recurret.*[19] —

265

At the risk of displeasing innocent ears I propose: egoism belongs to the nature of a noble soul — I mean that unshakable faith that to a being such as "we are" other beings must be subordinate by nature and have to sacrifice themselves. The noble soul accepts this fact of its egoism without any question mark, also without any feeling that it

[19] Horace's *Epistles*, I. 10, 24: "Try with a pitchfork to drive out nature, she always returns."

might contain hardness, constraint, or caprice, rather as something that may be founded in the primordial law of things: if it sought a name for this fact it would say, "it is justice itself." Perhaps it admits under certain circumstances that at first make it hesitate that there are some who have rights equal to its own; as soon as this matter of rank is settled it moves among these equals with their equal privileges, showing the same sureness of modesty and delicate reverence that characterize its relations with itself — in accordance with an innate heavenly mechanism understood by all stars. It is merely another aspect of its egoism, this refinement and self-limitation in its relations with its equals — every star is such an egoist – it honors *itself* in them and in the rights it cedes to them; it does not doubt that the exchange of honors and rights is of the nature of all social relations and thus also belongs to the natural condition of things.

The noble soul gives as it takes, from that passionate and irritable instinct of repayment that lies in its depth. The concept "grace"[20] has no meaning or good odor *inter pares*;[21] there may be a sublime way of letting presents from above happen to one, as it were, and to drink them up thirstily like drops — but for this art and gesture the noble soul has no aptitude. Its egoism hinders it: quite generally it does not like to look "up" — but either *ahead*, horizontally and slowly, or down: *it knows itself to be at a height.*

[20] "*Gnade.*"
[21] Among equals.

COMMENT

The Will to Power

"Out of my will to be in good health, out of my will to live, I have made my philosophy," wrote Nietzsche. His approach to philosophy was intensely personal, like that of Kierkegaard. However much they might differ in other respects, Kierkegaard and Nietzsche can be considered existentialists. The problems that excited their concern were not separate and distinct from their lives; they were problems that arose out of the struggle and task of existing as a human being.

"The will to live" is the phrase used by Arthur Schopenhauer, the famous pessimist, to characterize the basic drive of all living things. While still in his early twenties, Nietzsche discovered Schopenhauer's book *The World as Will and Idea* in a secondhand bookstore. Although he was greatly influenced by Schopenhauer, he more often used the phrase "the will to power" than "the will to live." A living thing, he said, seeks above all to discharge its strength and master its environment. Evolution — a concept that was much discussed in Nietzsche's lifetime — seemed to him the triumph of strength over weakness. On the basis of an anti-Darwinian theory of evolution, Nietzsche extolled might and power. But by "power" he meant much more than physical dominance—he meant intellectual and spiritual mastery as well.

What does it mean to say that will is basic? In a general way, desire or will is the active element in consciousness. It shows itself in unrest and seeking, leading finally to action, which brings the unrest to a close. We might define it as a drive or impulse toward a goal. If the drive succeeds, the result is a "state of satisfaction."

According to Nietzsche, it is impossible sharply to separate desire from feeling. The unrest of desire involves pain and the appeasement of desire involves joy or pleasure; these are phases of volition.

Schopenhauer believed that frustration and pain far outweigh satisfaction and pleasure. To a certain extent, Nietzsche agreed. The world, if unsubdued by the will to power, is a thoroughly nasty place. But Nietzsche's philosophy is a paradoxical combination of pessimism and optimism. By the triumph of the will to power, an existence otherwise terrible becomes profoundly satisfying. As a creature of volition, a person *must* will to change one's world. The will to power makes possible "the transvaluation of values" and the emergence of higher types of life.

Nietzsche exalted, above all other types, the strong, proud, self-assertive, "great-souled" aristocrat. Fulfillment for the aristocrats is achieved through exploitation and subjugation of their inferiors. From this concept of the aristocrat Nietzsche derived his distinction between master and slave morality. The master morality is a discipline that the noble impose on themselves in order to maintain their superiority. It is characterized by a reverence for the higher gradations of value, as set off against the baseness of the lower class. Even among the "slaves" (a term that Nietzsche uses to denote the masses of inferior people), the virtues of humility and meekness have mainly extrinsic worth; they are weapons of the weak in the struggle for power. The pity and charity of the slaves, no less than the pride and courage of the masters, are useful for survival. The weak, individually incapable of defense, can defend themselves against the masters only by banding together as a herd. Nietzsche detected attitudes of petty envy and resentment under the slaves' show of altruism. In modern life he saw a leveling tendency—a sheepish predisposition toward mediocrity and conformity. Defending the intrepid individual against mass tyranny and vulgarity, he maintained that a new aristocratic morality is required to scale the heights.

Some Critical Questions

This interpretation of morality is at the opposite pole from Kant's categorical imperative. Nietzsche rejected the whole doctrine of the universalizability of the moral law. Power cannot be universalized—when some dominate, others must submit. Hence Nietzsche's ethics fails to meet Kant's formula of universal generalization. Who has the better moral creed, Kant or Nietzsche?

The Nietzschean ideal of aristocracy is just as sharply opposed to the democratic ideal. Whether Nietzsche is justified in this opposition depends in part on the meaning of democracy. Does it mean that whatever varies from the average should be crushed by the herd? If so, Nietzsche is justified in rejecting it. Does it mean that all men and women should have equal and abundant opportunity to develop their unequal abilities? If so, we wonder if Nietzsche was justified in his antidemocratic stand. Democracy in this latter sense, its defenders can argue, is fully compatible with aristocratic standards of excellence. The very fact of psychological inequality is all the more reason for equal opportunity because without it, able persons will often be handicapped by lack of opportunity, and the less gifted but fortunately situated will be preferred to their natural betters.

In both Schopenhauer and Nietzsche — though they differ greatly in other respects — we find an ethics based on the primacy of the will. Is this kind of ethics one-sided? Does it underplay the values of feeling and intellect? In contrast to Nietzsche, Bertrand Russell has asserted, "The good life is one motivated by love and guided by knowledge."[1] Is this a sounder interpretation than Nietzsche's?

Russell has also said,

> I dislike Nietzsche because he likes the contemplation of pain, because he erects conceit into a duty, because the men whom he most admires are conquerors, whose glory is cleverness in causing men to die. But I think the ultimate argument against his philosophy, as against any unpleasant but internally self-consistent ethic, lies not in an appeal to facts, but in an appeal to emotions.[2]

Is this a fair characterization of Nietzsche's ethics? Is Russell's "ultimate argument" an adequate alternative? His appeal is to emotion; Nietzsche's appeal is to will. But both reject ethical objectivism and deny the appeal to facts. In this respect they differ from John Dewey, who inveighs against the "dualism" of fact and value. They also differ from Aristotle, with his emphasis on reason, and from Cicero and Marcus Aurelius, with their emphasis on natural law. Here is an issue that goes to the foundation of ethics.

A comparison of Nietzsche and Marx is illuminating. Both were in revolt against the dominant values of their age, and both took their stand

---

[1] *What I Believe* (New York: Dutton, 1925), p. 20.
[2] *A History of Western Philosophy* (New York: Simon & Schuster, 1945), pp. 772–773.

"beyond good and evil" as conceived by Christian and bourgeois. They looked to the future for their values: a future represented for Marx by the triumph of the proletariat, for Nietzsche by the emergence of the Overman. The contrast reaches its peak in the clash between an egalitarian and an elitist morality. For Marx the ultimate reliance is on the solidarity of the many, for Nietzsche on the creativity of the few. Marx is concerned with the material needs of the downtrodden, Nietzsche with the artistic and cultural values of the "noble." The Marxian ideal is a classless humanism; the Nietzschean ideal is a power elite. Who has the sounder ideals, Marx or Nietzsche?

19

The Way of Experiment

"But the experimental logic when carried into morals makes every quality that is judged to be good according as it contributes to amelioration of existing ills. And in so doing, it enforces the moral meaning of natural science."

John Dewey

JOHN DEWEY (1859–1952)

For a biographical note, see pages 195–196.

Reconstruction in Moral Conceptions

The impact of the alteration in methods of scientific thinking upon moral ideas is, in general, obvious. Goods, ends are multiplied. Rules are softened into principles, and principles are modified into methods of understanding. Ethical theory began among the Greeks as an attempt to find a regulation for the conduct of life which should have a rational basis and purpose instead of being derived from custom. But reason as a substitute for custom was under the obligation of supplying objects and laws as fixed as those of custom had been. Ethical theory ever since has been singularly hypnotized by the notion

From *Reconstruction in Philosophy* (originally given as lectures in Japan) (New York: Henry Holt and Company, 1920; enlarged edition, Boston: Beacon Press, 1948). Reprinted by permission of the Beacon Press.

that its business is to discover some final end or good or some ultimate and supreme law. This is the common element among the diversity of theories. Some have held that the end is loyalty or obedience to a higher power or authority; and they have variously found this higher principle in Divine Will, the will of the secular ruler, the maintenance of institutions in which the purpose of superiors is embodied, and the rational consciousness of duty. But they have differed from one another because there was one point in which they were agreed: a single and final source of law. Others have asserted that it is impossible to locate morality in conformity to law-giving power, and that it must be sought in ends that are goods. And some have sought the good in self-realization, some in holiness, some in happiness, some in the greatest possible aggregate of pleasures. And yet these schools have agreed in the assumption that there is a single, fixed and final good. They have been able to dispute with one another only because of their common premise.

The question arises whether the way out of the confusion and conflict is not to go to the root of the matter by questioning this common element. Is not the belief in the single, final and ultimate (whether conceived as good or as authoritative law) an intellectual product of that feudal organization which is disappearing historically and of that belief in a bounded, ordered cosmos, wherein rest is higher than motion, which has disappeared from natural science? It has been repeatedly suggested that the present limit of intellectual reconstruction lies in the fact that

it has not as yet been seriously applied in the moral and social disciplines. Would not this further application demand precisely that we advance to a belief in a plurality of changing, moving, individualized goods and ends, and to a belief that principles, criteria, laws are intellectual instruments for analyzing individual or unique situations?

The blunt assertion that every moral situation is a unique situation having its own irreplaceable good may seem not merely blunt but preposterous. For the established tradition teaches that it is precisely the irregularity of special cases which makes necessary the guidance of conduct by universals, and that the essence of the virtuous disposition is willingness to subordinate every particular case to adjudication by a fixed principle. It would then follow that submission of a generic end and law to determination by the concrete situation entails complete confusion and unrestrained licentiousness. Let us, however, follow the pragmatic rule, and in order to discover the meaning of the idea ask for its consequences. Then it surprisingly turns out that the primary significance of the unique and morally ultimate character of the concrete situation is to transfer the weight and burden of morality to intelligence. It does not destroy responsibility; it only locates it. A moral situation is one in which judgment and choice are required antecedently to overt action. The practical meaning of the situation —that is to say the action needed to satisfy it — is not self-evident. It has to be searched for. There are conflicting desires and alternative apparent goods. What is needed is to find the right course of action, the right good. Hence, inquiry is exacted: observation of the detailed makeup of the situation; analysis into its diverse factors; clarification of what is obscure; discounting the more insistent and vivid traits; tracing the consequences of the various modes of action that suggest themselves; regarding the decision reached as hypothetical and tentative until the anticipated or supposed consequences which led to its adoption have been squared with actual consequences. This inquiry is intelligence. Our moral failures go back to some weakness of disposition, some absence of sympathy, some one-sided bias that makes us perform the judgment of the concrete case carelessly or perversely. Wide sympathy, keen sensitiveness, persistence in the face of the disagreeable, balance of interests enabling us to undertake the work of analysis and decision intelligently are the distinctively moral traits — the virtues or moral excellencies.

It is worth noting once more that the underlying issue is, after all, only the same as that which has been already threshed out in physical inquiry. There too it long seemed as if rational assurance and demonstration could be attained only if we began with universal conceptions and subsumed particular cases under them. The men who initiated the methods of inquiry that are now everywhere adopted were denounced in their day (and sincerely) as subverters of truth and foes of science. If they have won in the end, it is because, as has already been pointed out, the method of universals confirmed prejudices and sanctioned ideas that had gained currency irrespective of evidence for them; while placing the initial and final weight upon the individual case, stimulated painstaking inquiry into facts and examination of principles. In the end, loss of eternal truths was more than compensated for in the accession of quotidian facts. The loss of the system of superior and fixed definitions and kinds was more than made up for by the growing system of hypotheses and laws used in classifying facts. After all, then, we are only pleading for the adoption in moral reflection of the logic that has been proved to make for security, stringency and fertility in passing judgment upon physical phenomena. And the reason is the same. The old method in spite of its nominal and esthetic worship of reason discouraged reason, because it hindered the operation of scrupulous and unremitting inquiry.

More definitely, the transfer of the burden of the moral life from following rules or pursuing fixed ends over to the detection of the ills that need remedy in a special case and the formation of plans and methods for dealing with them, eliminates the causes which have kept moral theory controversial, and which have also kept it remote from helpful contact with the exigencies of practice. The theory of fixed ends inevitably leads thought into the bog of disputes that cannot be settled. If there is one *summum bonum*, one supreme end, what is it? To consider this problem is to place ourselves in the midst of controversies that are as acute now as they were two thousand years ago. Suppose we take a seemingly more empirical view, and say that while there is not a single end, there also are not as many

as there are specific situations that require amelioration; but there are a
number of such natural goods as health,
wealth, honor or good name, friendship, esthetic appreciation, learning
and such moral goods as justice, temperance, benevolence, etc. What or who
is to decide the right of way when these
ends conflict with one another, as they
are sure to do? Shall we resort to the
method that once brought such disre-
pute upon the whole business of ethics:
Casuistry? Or shall we have recourse to
what Bentham well called the *ipse dixit*
method: the arbitrary preference of this
or that person for this or that end? Or
shall we be forced to arrange them all in
an order of degrees from the highest
good down to the least precious? Again
we find ourselves in the middle of
unreconciled disputes with no indication of the way out.

Meantime, the special moral perplexities where the aid of intelligence is
required go unenlightened. We cannot
seek or attain health, wealth, learning,
justice or kindness in general. Action is
always specific, concrete, individualized, unique. And consequently judgments as to acts to be performed must
be similarly specific. To say that a man
seeks health or justice is only to say
that he seeks to live healthily or justly.
These things, like truth, are adverbial.
They are modifiers of action in special
cases. How to live healthily or justly is
a matter which differs with every person. It varies with his past experience,
his opportunities, his temperamental
and acquired weaknesses and abilities.
Not man in general but a particular
man suffering from some particular
disability aims to live healthily, and

consequently health cannot mean for
him exactly what it means for any other
mortal. Healthy living is not something
to be attained by itself apart from other
ways of living. A man needs to be
health *in* his life, not apart from it, and
what does life mean except the aggregate of his pursuits and activities? A
man who aims at health as a distinct
end becomes a valetudinarian, or a fa-
natic, or a mechanical performer of exercises, or an athlete so onesided that
his pursuit of bodily development in-
jures his heart. When the endeavor to
realize a so-called end does not temper
and color all other activities, life is por-
tioned out into strips and fractions.
Certain acts and times are devoted to
getting health, others to cultivating religion, others to seeking learning, to
being a good citizen, a devotee of fine
art and so on. This is the only logical
alternative to subordinating all aims to
the accomplishment of one alone —
fanaticism. This is out of fashion at
present, but who can say how much of
distraction and dissipation in life, and
how much of its hard and narrow rigidity is the outcome of men's failure to
realize that each situation has its own
unique end and that the whole personality should be concerned with it?
Surely, once more, what a man needs is
to live healthily, and this result so affects all the activities of his life that it
cannot be set up as a separate and independent good.

Nevertheless the general notions of
health, disease, justice, artistic culture
are of great importance: Not, however,
because this or that case may be
brought exhaustively under a single
head and its specific traits shut out, but

because generalized science provides a man as physician and artist and citizen, with questions to ask, investigations to make, and enables him to understand the meaning of what he sees. Just in the degree in which a physician is an artist in his work he uses his science, no matter how extensive and accurate, to furnish him with tools of inquiry into the individual case, and with methods of forecasting a method of dealing with it. Just in the degree in which, no matter how great his learning, he subordinates the individual case to some classification of diseases and some generic rule of treatment, he sinks to the level of the routine mechanic. His intelligence and his action become rigid, dogmatic, instead of free and flexible.

Moral goods and ends exist only when something has to be done. The fact that something has to be done proves that there are deficiencies, evils in the existent situation. This ill is just the specific ill that it is. It never is an exact duplicate of anything else. Consequently the good of the situation has to be discovered, projected and attained on the basis of the exact defect and trouble to be rectified. It cannot intelligently be injected into the situation from without. Yet it is the part of wisdom to compare different cases, to gather together the ills from which humanity suffers, and to generalize the corresponding goods into classes. Health, wealth, industry, temperance, amiability, courtesy, learning, esthetic capacity, initiative, courage, patience, enterprise, thoroughness and a multitude of other generalized ends are acknowledged as goods. But the *value* of this systematization is intellectual or analytic. Classifications *suggest* possible traits to be on the lookout for in studying a particular case; they suggest methods of action to be tried in removing the inferred causes of ill. They are tools of insight; their value is in promoting an individualized response in the individual situation.

Morals is not a catalogue of acts nor a set of rules to be applied like drugstore prescriptions or cook-book recipes. The need in morals is for specific methods of inquiry and of contrivance: Methods of inquiry to locate difficulties and evils; methods of contrivance to form plans to be used as working hypotheses in dealing with them. And the pragmatic import of the logic of individualized situations, each having its own irreplaceable good and principle, is to transfer the attention of theory from preoccupation with general conceptions to the problem of developing effective methods of inquiry.

Two ethical consequences of great moment should be remarked. The belief in fixed values has bred a division of ends into intrinsic and instrumental, of those that are really worth while in themselves and those that are of importance only as means to intrinsic goods. Indeed, it is often thought to be the very beginning of wisdom, of moral discrimination, to make this distinction. Dialectically, the distinction is interesting and seems harmless. But carried into practice it has an import that is tragic. Historically, it has been the source and justification of a hard and fast difference between ideal goods on one side and material goods on the other. At present those who would be liberal conceive intrinsic goods as esthetic in nature rather than as exclusively religious or as intellectually contemplative. But the effect is the same. So-called intrinsic goods, whether religious or esthetic, are divorced from those interests of daily life which because of their constancy and urgency form the preoccupation of the great mass. Aristotle used this distinction to declare that slaves and the working class though they are necessary *for* the state — the commonweal — are not constituents *of* it. That which is regarded as *merely* instrumental must approach drudgery; it cannot command either intellectual, artistic or moral attention and respect. Anything becomes *unworthy* whenever it is thought of as intrinsically lacking worth. So men of "ideal" interests have chosen for the most part the way of neglect and escape. The urgency and pressure of "lower" ends have been covered up by polite conventions. Or, they have been relegated to a baser class of mortals in order that the few might be free to attend to the goods that are really or intrinsically worth while. This withdrawal, in the name of higher ends, has left, for mankind at large and especially for energetic "practical" people, the lower activities in complete command.

No one can possibly estimate how much of the obnoxious materialism and brutality of our economic life is due to the fact that economic ends have been regarded as *merely* instrumental. When they are recognized to be as intrinsic and final in their place as any others, then it will be seen that they are capable of idealization, and that if life is to be worth while, they must acquire ideal and intrinsic value. Esthetic, religious

and other "ideal" ends are now thin and meager or else idle and luxurious because of the separation from "instrumental" or economic ends. Only in connection with the latter can they be woven into the texture of daily life and made substantial and pervasive. The vanity and irresponsibility of values that are merely final and not also in turn means to the enrichment of other occupations of life ought to be obvious. But now the doctrine of "higher" ends gives aid, comfort and support to every socially isolated and socially irresponsible scholar, specialist, esthete and religionist. It protects the vanity and irresponsibility of his calling from observation by others and by himself. The moral deficiency of the calling is transformed into a cause of admiration and gratulation.

The other generic change lies in doing away once for all with the traditional distinction between moral goods, like the virtues, and natural goods like health, economic security, art, science and the like. The point of view under discussion is not the only one which has deplored this rigid distinction and endeavored to abolish it. Some schools have even gone so far as to regard moral excellencies, qualities of character as of value only because they promote natural goods. But the experimental logic when carried into morals makes every quality that is judged to be good according as it contributes to amelioration of existing ills. And in so doing, it enforces the moral meaning of natural science. When all is said and done in criticism of present social deficiencies, one may well wonder whether the root difficulty does not lie in the separation of natural and moral science. When physics, chemistry, biology, medicine, contribute to the detection of concrete human woes and to the development of plans for remedying them and relieving the human estate, they become moral; they become part of the apparatus of moral inquiry or science. The latter then loses its peculiar flavor of the didactic and pedantic; its ultra-moralistic and hortatory tone. It loses its thinness and shrillness as well as its vagueness. It gains agencies that are efficacious. But the gain is not confined to the side of moral science. Natural science loses its divorce from humanity; it becomes itself humanistic in quality. It is something to be pursued not in a technical and specialized way for what is called truth for its own sake, but with the sense of its social bearing, its intellectual indispensableness. It is technical only in the sense that it provides the technique of social and moral engineering.

When the consciousness of science is fully impregnated with the consciousness of human value, the greatest dualism which now weighs humanity down, the split between the material, the mechanical, the scientific and the moral and ideal will be destroyed. Human forces that now waver because of this division will be unified and reinforced. As long as ends are not thought of as individualized according to specific needs and opportunities, the mind will be content with abstractions, and the adequate stimulus to the moral or social use of natural science and historical data will be lacking. But when attention is concentrated upon the diversified concretes, recourse to all intellectual materials needed to clear up the special cases will be imperative. At the same time that morals are made to focus in intelligence, things intellectual are moralized. The vexatious and wasteful conflict between naturalism and humanism is terminated.

These general considerations may be amplified. First: Inquiry, discovery take the same place in morals that they have come to occupy in sciences of nature. Validation, demonstration become experimental, a matter of consequences. Reason, always an honorific term in ethics, becomes actualized in the methods by which the needs and conditions, the obstacles and resources, of situations are scrutinized in detail, and intelligent plans of improvement are worked out. Remote and abstract generalities promote jumping at conclusions, "anticipations of nature." Bad consequences are then deplored as due to natural perversity and untoward fate. But shifting the issue to analysis of a specific situation makes inquiry obligatory and alert observation of consequences imperative. No past decision nor old principle can ever be wholly relied upon to justify a course of action. No amount of pains taken in forming a purpose in a definite case is final; the consequences of its adoption must be carefully noted, and a purpose held only as a working hypothesis until results confirm its rightness. Mistakes are no longer either mere unavoidable accidents to be mourned or moral sins to be expiated and forgiven. They are lessons in wrong methods of using intelligence and instructions as to a better course in the future. They are indications of the need of revision, development, readjustment. Ends grow, standards of judgment are improved. Man is under just as much obligation to develop his most advanced standards and ideals as to use conscientiously those which he already possesses. Moral life is protected from falling into formalism and rigid repetition. It is rendered flexible, vital, growing.

In the second place, every case where moral action is required becomes of equal moral importance and urgency with every other. If the need and deficiencies of a specific situation indicate improvement of health as the end and good, then for the situation health is the ultimate and supreme good. It is no means to something else. It is a final and intrinsic value. The same thing is true of improvement of economic status, of making a living, of attending to business and family demands — all of the things which under the sanction of fixed ends have been rendered of secondary and merely instrumental value, and so relatively base and unimportant. Anything that in a given situation is an end and good at all is of equal worth, rank and dignity with every other good of any other situation, and deserves the same intelligent attention.

We note thirdly the effect in destroying the roots of Phariseeism. We are so accustomed to thinking of this as deliberate hypocrisy that we overlook its intellectual premises. The conception which looks for the end of action within the circumstances of the actual situation will not have the same measure of judgment for all cases. When one factor of the situation is a person of trained mind and large resources, more will be expected than with a person of backward mind and uncultured experience. The absurdity of applying the same standard of moral judgment to savage peoples that is used with civilized will be apparent. No individual or group will be judged by whether they come up to or fall short of some fixed result, but by the direction in which they are moving. The bad man is the man who no matter how good he *has* been is beginning to deteriorate, to grow less good. The good man is the man who no matter how morally unworthy he *has* been is moving to become better. Such a conception makes one severe in judging himself and humane in judging others. It excludes that arrogance which always accompanies judgment based on degree of approximation to fixed ends.

In the fourth place, the process of growth, of improvement and progress, rather than the static outcome and result, becomes the significant thing. Not health as an end fixed once and for all, but the needed improvement in health —a continual process— is the end and good. The end is no longer a terminus or limit to be reached. It is the active process of transforming the existent situation. Not perfection as a final goal, but the ever-enduring process of perfecting, maturing, refining is the aim in living. Honesty, industry, temperance, justice, like health, wealth and learning, are not goods to be possessed as they would be if they expressed fixed ends to be attained. They are directions of change in the quality of experience. Growth itself is the only moral "end."

Although the bearing of this idea upon the problem of evil and the controversy between optimism and pessimism is too vast to be here discussed, it may be worth while to touch upon it superficially. The problem of evil ceases to be a theological and metaphysical one, and is perceived to be the practical problem of reducing, alleviating, as far as may be removing, the evils of life. Philosophy is no longer under obligation to find ingenious methods of proving that evils are only apparent, not real, or to elaborate schemes for explaining them away or, worse yet, for justifying them. It assumes another obligation: — That of contributing in however humble a way to methods that will assist us in discovering the causes of humanity's ills. Pessimism is a paralyzing doctrine. In declaring that the world is evil wholesale, it makes futile all efforts to discover the remedial causes of specific evils and thereby destroys at the root every attempt to make the world better and happier. Wholesale optimism, which has been the consequence of the attempt to explain evil away, is, however, equally an incubus.

After all, the optimism that says that the world is already the best possible of all worlds might be regarded as the most cynical of pessimisms. If this is the best possible, what would a world which was fundamentally bad be like? Meliorism is the belief that the specific conditions which exist at one moment, be they comparatively bad or comparatively good, in any event may be bettered. It encourages intelligence to study the positive means of good and the obstructions to their realization, and to put forth endeavor for the improvement of conditions. It arouses confidence and a reasonable hopeful-

ness as optimism does not. For the latter in declaring that good is already realized in ultimate reality tends to make us gloss over the evils that concretely exist. It becomes too readily the creed of those who live at ease, in comfort, of those who have been successful in obtaining this world's rewards. Too readily optimism makes the men who hold it callous and blind to the sufferings of the less fortunate, or ready to find the cause of troubles of others in their personal viciousness. It thus cooperates with pessimism, in spite of the extreme nominal differences between the two, in benumbing sympathetic insight and intelligent effort in reform. It beckons men away from the world of relativity and change into the calm of the absolute and eternal.

The import of many of these changes in moral attitude focuses in the idea of happiness. Happiness has often been made the object of the moralists' contempt. Yet the most ascetic moralist has usually restored the idea of happiness under some other name, such as bliss. Goodness without happiness, valor and virtue without satisfaction, ends without conscious enjoyment — these things are as intolerable practically as they are self-contradictory in conception. Happiness is not, however, a bare possession; it is not a fixed attainment. Such a happiness is either the unworthy selfishness which moralists have so bitterly condemned, or it is, even if labeled bliss, an insipid tedium, a millennium of ease in relief from all struggle and labor. It could satisfy only the most delicate of mollycoddles. Happiness is found only in success; but success means succeeding, getting forward, moving in advance. It is an active process, not a passive outcome. Accordingly it includes the overcoming of obstacles, the elimination of sources of defect and ill. Esthetic sensitiveness and enjoyment are a large constituent in any worthy happiness. But the esthetic appreciation which is totally separated from renewal of spirit, from recreation of mind and purification of emotion is a weak and sickly thing, destined to speedy death from starvation. That the renewal and re-creation come unconsciously, not by set intention, but makes them the more genuine.

Upon the whole, utilitarianism has marked the best in the transition from the classic theory of ends and goods to that which is now possible. It had definite merits. It insisted upon getting away from vague generalities, and down to the specific and concrete. It subordinated law to human achievement instead of subordinating humanity to external law. It taught that institutions are made for man and not man for institutions; it actively promoted all issues of reform. It made moral good natural, humane, in touch with the natural goods of life. It opposed unearthly and other-worldly morality. Above all, it acclimatized in human imagination the idea of social welfare as a supreme test. But it was still profoundly affected in fundamental points by old ways of thinking. It never questioned the idea of a fixed, final and supreme end. It only questioned the current notions as to the nature of this end; and then inserted pleasure and the greatest possible aggregate of pleasures in the position of the fixed end.

Such a point of view treats concrete activities and specific interests not as worth while in themselves, or as constituents of happiness, but as mere external means to getting pleasures. The upholders of the old tradition could therefore easily accuse utilitarianism of making not only virtue but art, poetry, religion and the state into mere servile means of attaining sensuous enjoyment. Since pleasure was an outcome, a result valuable on its own account independently of the active processes that achieve it, happiness was a thing to be possessed and held onto. The acquisitive instincts of man were exaggerated at the expense of the creative. Production was of importance not because of the intrinsic worth of invention and re-shaping the world, but because its external results feed pleasure. Like every theory that sets up fixed and final aims, in making the end passive and possessive, it made all active operations *mere* tools. Labor was an unavoidable evil to be minimized. Security in possession was the chief thing practically. Material comfort and ease was magnified in contrast with the pains and risk of experimental creation. . . . The idea of a fixed and single end lying beyond the diversity of human needs and acts rendered utilitarianism incapable of being an adequate representative of the modern spirit. It has to be reconstructed through emancipation from its inherited elements.

If a few words are added upon the topic of education, it is only for the sake of suggesting that the educative process is all one with the moral process, since the latter is a continuous passage of experience from worse to better. Education has been traditionally thought of as preparation: as learning, acquiring certain things because they will later be useful. The end is remote, and education is getting ready, is a preliminary to something more important to happen later on. Childhood is only a preparation for adult life, and adult life for another life. Always the future, not the present, has been the significant thing in education: acquisition of knowledge and skill for future use and enjoyment; formation of habits required later in life in business, good citizenship and pursuit of science. Education is thought of also as something needed by some human beings merely because of their dependence upon others. We are born ignorant, unversed, unskilled, immature, and consequently in a state of social dependence. Instruction, training, moral discipline are processes by which the mature, the adult, gradually raise the helpless to the point where they can look out for themselves. The business of childhood is to grow into the independence of adulthood by means of the guidance of those who have already attained it. Thus the process of education as the main business of life ends when the young have arrived at emancipation from social dependence.

These two ideas, generally assumed but rarely explicitly reasoned out, contravene the conception that growing, or the continuous reconstruction of experience, is the only end. If at whatever period we choose to take a person, he is still in process of growth, then education is not, save as a by-product, a preparation for something coming later. Getting from the present the degree

and kind of growth there is in it is education. This is a constant function, independent of age. The best thing that can be said about any special process of education, like that of the formal school period, is that it renders its subject capable of further education: more sensitive to conditions of growth and more able to take advantage of them. Acquisition of skill, possession of knowledge, attainment of culture are not ends: they are marks of growth and means to its continuing.

The contrast usually assumed between the period of education as one of social dependence and of maturity as one of social independence does harm. We repeat over and over that man is a social animal, and then confine the significance of this statement to the sphere in which sociality usually seems least evident, politics. The heart of the sociality of man is in education. The idea of education as preparation and of adulthood as a fixed limit of growth are two sides of the same obnoxious untruth. If the moral business of the adult as well as the young is a growing and developing experience, then the instruction that comes from social dependencies and interdependencies is as important for the adult as for the child. Moral independence for the adult means arrest of growth, isolation means induration. We exaggerate the intellectual dependence of childhood so that children are too much kept in leading strings, and then we exaggerate the independence of adult life from intimacy of contacts and communication with others. When the identity of the moral process with the processes of specific growth is realized, the more conscious and formal education of childhood will be seen to be the most economical and efficient means of social advance and reorganization, and it will also be evident that the test of all the institutions of adult life is their effect in furthering continued education. Government, business, art, religion, all social institutions have a meaning, a purpose. That purpose is to set free and to develop the capacities of human individuals without respect to race, sex, class or economic status. And this is all one with saying that the test of their value is the extent to which they educate every individual into the full stature of his possibility. Democracy has many meanings, but if it has a moral meaning, it is found in resolving that the supreme test of all political institutions and industrial arrangements shall be the contribution they make to the all-around growth of every member of society.

COMMENT

Main Emphases in Dewey's Ethics

Dewey shifts the emphasis in ethical theory from *value* to *valuation*, being more concerned with the process of appraisal than with the qualities appraised. Valuation, he maintains, should be in accordance with the methods of experimental logic. No one has insisted more strenuously than Dewey on scientific study of the actual needs of human beings and the concrete, experimental means of satisfying these needs. "Not all who say Ideals, Ideals," he remarks, "shall enter into the kingdom of the ideal, but those who know and respect the roads that conduct to the kingdom."[1] His main contribution to ethical theory has been to explore the roads rather than to describe the destination. Indeed, he does not believe in a fixed destination but rather in a never-ending and exploratory journey. Since conditions are constantly changing, rules cannot be made nor goals ascertained in advance. Living well is an experiment, and there should be flexible reappraisal and reorientation as the experiment progresses.

Valuation is stimulated by tension, conflict, and unsatisfactoriness; and successful valuation points to ways of resolving the tensions and releasing the pent-up energies. In regard to ethics, as in pragmatist theory in general, inquiry is conceived to be instrumentalist — a tool for controlling experience. Values are not passively "given," without intelligent effort, but are actively constructed. There is a fundamental difference between what is merely "liked" and what is genuinely "likable," merely "desired" and really "desirable," merely "admired" and truly "admirable," merely

---

[1] "The Pragmatic Acquiescence," *New Republic*, Vol. 49 (Jan. 5, 1927), 189.

"satisfying" and dependably "satisfactory." Only the latter are *values* in the sense that they have been *validated*. They can be achieved only if we know the conditions and consequences of our desires, affections, and enjoyments and if we learn intelligently to coordinate and control them. The idea of a *good* should be treated as a hypothesis, to be tested like any other.

In the testing, we must see ends and means as "continuous" — the ends as means to future satisfactions, and the means as not merely instrumentally but also intrinsically valuable or disvaluable. Kant, for example, was fundamentally mistaken in exalting virtue as an end apart from being a means, for the very qualities that make it good as end make it good as means also. Dewey believed that experience is most satisfactory when the instrumental and the consummatory are closely linked — when action and contemplation fructify each other. We should neither subordinate growth and spontaneity to static contemplation nor concentrate merely on activity to the neglect of rational goals. Life should combine both repose and stimulation — the sense of achievement and the sense of adventure. In thus insisting on "the continuity of means and ends," Dewey is exhibiting the antidualistic tendency that pervades his entire philosophy. He protests strongly against the inveterate tendency to think in terms of hard-and-fast distinctions between, for example, facts and values, experience and nature, freedom and organization, learning and doing; and he seeks to resolve all such sharp dualisms by insisting on the continuity and interpenetration of "opposites." Values are to be studied as natural facts, and facts are to be evaluated; experience is to be regarded as inseparable from nature, and nature is to be interpreted in terms of experience; freedom is to be secured by organization, and organization is to be liberalized by freedom; learning is to be achieved by doing, and doing is to be directed by learning. His whole philosophy can thus be regarded as a "revolt against dualism." In this respect he has much in common with Whitehead.

There is no sense, according to Dewey, in talking about *the* end of life — as if there were a single end or final consummation. Life is simply an ongoing process, with a plurality of ends that function also as means. His stress is on the dynamic rather than the static, the specific rather than the general, the concrete and plural rather than the abstract and monistic. "Faith in the varied possibilities of diversified experience," he declares, "is attended with the joy of constant discovery and constant growing."[2] Growth provides its own sufficient criterion, and it is a mistake to seek anything more fixed and constant.

---

[2] "What I Believe," *Forum*, March 1930, p. 179.

On the Distinction Between Science, Technology, and Morals

According to some critics, Dewey's ethical philosophy is strong in method but weak in vision; strong in delineating the variety of experience but weak in revealing the unity of life; strong in its awareness of novelty but weak in its blindness to universal and enduring values; strong in opposing static absolutism but weak in yielding to mercurial relativism; strong in realizing the need for growth but weak in criticizing the direction of growth; strong in relating science, technology, and morals, but weak in failing to distinguish them. Whether this estimate is justified we shall leave to the readers of this book to decide. The last point of criticism, however, calls for more detailed comment.

The heart of Dewey's ethical philosophy is the attempt to link science, technology, and morals, and it is therefore important to consider their interrelations. We can begin by noting three realms of discourse, as illustrated by the following sentences:

> "That is a strong poison."
> "You ought to use a strong poison" (said to a would-be murderer).
> "You ought not to murder."

The first sentence is *descriptive*, it simply indicates a matter of fact, with no commendation or disparagement. The second sentence is *evaluative*, but in what Kant would call a *hypothetical* rather than a categorical sense. The "ought" here simply means that *if* you want to murder this man, you ought to use a poison strong enough to accomplish your purpose. It does not express a *duty* to use a strong poison. The third sentence is also *evaluative*, but in what Kant would call a *categorical* rather than a hypothetical sense. It expresses a duty to refrain from murdering. Sentences of the first type are characteristic of pure science; sentences of the second type are characteristic of technology; and sentences of the third type are characteristic of morals. (To accept these distinctions, we would not have to agree with Kant's formulas for determining categorical imperatives. If we were utilitarians, for example, our formula might read, "So act that in every case there shall be no better results." If our duty is to achieve the best results possible, it is still our *duty*.)

The charge that can be made against Dewey is that he has failed to distinguish clearly between science, technology, and morals. In his laudable effort to relate them, he has obscured their differences. We shall not discuss the adequacy of his distinction between pure science and technology — this question is relevant to the issues presented in Chapter 5 and might well be debated in that connection. At present, we are concerned only with the relation between morals and science and between morals and technology.

1. MORALS AND SCIENCE. "Experience," Dewey notes, "actually presents esthetic and moral traits."[3] These stand on "the same level" as the redness of a rose or the absentmindedness of a professor—they are matters of fact, which can be studied like any other. There is a valid point here that should not be denied. Human beings do exhibit esthetic and moral traits and experience satisfactions and enjoyments. These can be described like any other natural facts. Moral theories that try to exclude consideration of human nature and its environment are hopelessly unrealistic. If this is all that Dewey means, we need not disagree with him. But it is still the case that a psychologist bent on *describing* human nature has a different task than the moralist bent on *evaluating* moral alternatives. Such words as *good, right, ought*, as used by the moralist, are nouns and adjectives of commendation, not of description. How can we make the leap from description to evaluation? How can we get, for example, from *desired* to *ethically desirable*? The latter does not mean *psychologically desirable*, in the sense that someone *can* desire it. It means *worth* desiring —desiring in the sense that it *ought* to be desired. A naturalistic theory of ethics, such as that of Dewey, seems to overlook the nondescriptive, purely ethical character of the moral *ought*.

Dewey could reply that *desirable* means that which one desires *after* one has seen all its conditions and consequences. But this does not solve the problem because it is perfectly possible for a malevolent person to desire something that is morally evil after that person has thoroughly understood its connections with other things. Dewey could also reply that the ethically desirable is that which is desired by a fair and impartial judge. But this definition is circular; it amounts to saying that something is ethically desirable (good or right) when it is approved by somebody who approves only what *is* ethically desirable. The only solution, Dewey's critics would say, is to admit a clear-cut distinction between facts and norms, morals and science—and this he fails to do. So runs the criticism that could be directed against Dewey. The reader should weigh this criticism carefully and decide whether it is valid.

2. MORALS AND TECHNOLOGY. Dewey often appears to be identifying morality with technology, or to be thinking of it as a kind of supertechnology. There would seem to be much to support this point of view. The language of technological discourse, as we have already noted, is distin-

---

[3] *Experience and Nature* (Chicago: Open Court, 1929), p. 2.

guished by normative terms, such as *ought* or *ought not*, or by imperatives, such as *do this* or *do not do that*. Such language is intended to direct
choice among alternative possibilities. There are different kinds of norms
and normative statements belonging to different levels of technological
discourse. Many technological imperatives are mere counsels of skill, as
when a carpenter says to his helper, "You ought to sharpen the teeth of
that saw." He means, *"If* you want to use your saw effectively for the
purpose at hand, you ought to sharpen its teeth." At a somewhat higher
and more general level, the norms have a quasi-ethical or esthetic character, as in the case of the artistic norm of "beauty," the legal norm of
"justice," the medical norm of "health," and the economic norm of "prosperity." Finally, there are highest-level norms that pertain to a total economy of values. They are invoked when there is a conflict between lower-
level oughts, and may be thought of as decidedly ethical. Morality will
then be conceived as a technology of technologies, the function of which
is to coordinate all the various techniques that a society has at its disposal.

This view of morality is by no means new. Aristotle had a similar
conception of the art of arts, the technology of technologies. In the opening paragraphs of his *Ethics*, as we have seen, he pointed out that the arts
are to be distinguished by the ends that they serve. Health is the aim of
medicine, vessels of shipbuilding, victory of military strategy, and wealth
of economics. The ends and the corresponding arts form a hierarchy, some
being subservient to others. Bridle-making is subservient to horsemanship, horsemanship to strategy, and so on. Finally we arrive at some
ultimate end and the art corresponding to it. This is the art of arts — the
art whose function it is to harmonize and control all the other arts and
whose end, therefore, is not this or that particular good but the good for
humanity. Aristotle calls this highest art the art of politics, of which
ethics, since it defines the ultimate good, is an integral part. Here the
word *art* is being used in the same sense as that which we intend
by *technology*, and Aristotle's conception of politics as an "art of arts"
is analogous to the conception of morality as a "technology of technologies."

Up to a point, this way of looking at morality seems sound, but it is
important to recognize that morality, as a kind of supreme technology, is
fundamentally different from ordinary technology — so different, indeed,
that we should perhaps not call it a technology at all. An ordinary technological norm is an *instrument* of a decision maker, not a *control*; and
therefore, to interpret moral norms as ordinary technological norms
would imply that technology needs no control or is somehow self-regulat-
ing. Such a view is exceedingly mischievous, especially in this age of
nuclear fission. Consequently, there must be norms controlling the decision maker rather than norms that are merely his or her instruments. The

right use of instrumental norms presupposes some noninstrumental criteria.

In the case of ordinary technology, in other words, it is not the right motivation of the agent that is in question but the skill to be used in carrying out a motivation that is taken for granted. In the case of morality, on the other hand, it is precisely the motivation that is most in question, and the problem of finding the right means is secondary. The norms of ordinary technology usually prescribe how to perform some action. The moral question, on the other hand, is not simply *how* to do something but *what* to do.

Here, then, is a possible ground for criticism. Pragmatists such as Dewey, the critics might say, are prone to exaggerate the similarity between ordinary technology and morality. They are so intent on the fluidity and instrumentality of norms that they neglect or even deny the question of *ultimate* motivation. They are inclined to take "the problematic situation" as it arises and to interpret right action as "problem solving" within the context of this situation. The problem, as they see it, is "solved" when the diverse competing interests in the situation are brought into some kind of moving equilibrium, which leads to new "problematic situations" and thus to new and revised norms. So understood, morality is closely akin to ordinary technology. But morality cannot afford merely to implement and reconcile interests that are taken for granted. Its task is more radical. It criticizes interests in the light of ultimate norms; and in exercising this sort of stubborn and very radical criticism, it differentiates itself from technology.

The question that we have posed is whether Dewey has sufficiently realized this fact, and whether he has also realized the clear-cut difference between morality (or ethics, as its theoretical basis) and natural science.

PART

IV

SOCIAL
IDEALS

Social philosophy is not a sharply distinct and separate field. The fundamental issues that divide social philosophers are ultimately metaphysical, epistemological, or ethical. Among the questions debated are the following: What is the basis of political obligation? What is the nature of good social order? What is right social action? Is the state an organism? Are the actions of government to be justified by reference to the ends of the individual or of society? Does history have a pattern that can be known and predicted? All these questions involve metaphysical, epistemological, or ethical issues.

An example may help to make clear the nature of social philosophy. In his *Discourse on Political Economy*, Rousseau declares,

> The body politic . . . is also a moral being possessed of a will; and this general will, which tends always to the preservation and welfare of the whole and of every part, and is the source of the laws, constitutes for all the members of the State, in their relations to one another and to it, the rule of what is just or unjust.[1]

[1] *The Social Contract*, Everyman's Edition (New York: Dutton, 1913), p. 253.

This sentence is replete with philosophical notions: that the body politic is a moral being; that it possesses a "general will" distinct from the individual wills of its members; that the general will is a *good* will; and that it defines, through the medium of law, what is just and what is unjust in the relations of citizens to one another and to the state. Philosophers, and not social scientists, are best fitted to clarify and criticize ideas.

The philosophers represented in the following chapters discuss questions of great interest to all students of human affairs. Other important social philosophers, such as Aristotle, Rousseau, and Hegel, are omitted for lack of space. Each of the philosophers chosen represents a social ideal.

It may be helpful to indicate in advance some of the issues that will arise in studying these thinkers:

1. Plato maintains that values are absolute, not relative; that genuine knowledge — especially the knowledge of absolute values — is restricted to the few; that these few, when thoroughly educated, should rule the state; that the choice goods are to be preferred to the common goods; and that the foremost virtue, in the state or in the individual, is wisdom.

2. Hobbes contends that values are relative, not absolute; that people, being naturally egoistic, tend to prey upon one another; that the state is brought into existence to eliminate this anarchy and to attain peace and security; and that it is rational for citizens to obey their sovereign so long as they are protected.

3. Mill believes that the ultimate good is the happiness and self-realization of individuals; that actions are right to the extent that they promote individual welfare; that virtually all opinions are liable to error; that it is wrong to suppress dissident opinions; and that the progress of society depends upon the cultivation of a rich variety among individuals.

4. Locke affirms the necessity of a social contract between those governed and the state which is based in constitutional law and guarantees individual rights to life, property, and liberty, through democracy.

5. Marx argues that it is possible to know and to predict accurately the course of history; that the most fundamental factor in determining the history of any society is economic development; that human rights and values are relative to the stages of historical evolution; that conflict, especially class struggle, is the basic mode of revolutionary change; that humankind, after passing through various stages of class society — slavery, feudalism, capitalism — will finally attain a free, just, and classless social order; and that it is right and rational to assist the historical process by whatever means — even violent and dictatorial — that may be found necessary.

6. Skinner urges human control of human behavior while Rogers worries about the social and psychological dangers of such control. Buber

emphasizes the importance of relational inter-subjectivity as the ground of positive community.

To some extent these theories involve questions of fact, which social scientists are best prepared to answer, but to a great extent they involve questions of ethics, epistemology, or metaphysics, which philosophers are best qualified to discuss. Such questions are too momentous, however, to be left to experts, whether philosophers or social scientists. All of us should ponder them.

20

Aristocracy

*"Since the philosophers are those who can appre-
hend the eternal and unchanging, while those who
cannot do so, but are left in the mazes of multiplicity and change, are not philosophers, which of the
two ought to be in control of the state?"*

Plato

PLATO (428/7 – 348/7 B.C.)

For a biographical note, see pages 51 – 52

The Ideal Republic

THE RING OF GYGES

Good, said Glaucon. Listen then, and I
will begin with my first point: the nature and origin of justice.

Translated with introduction and notes by
Francis MacDonald Cornford Oxford University Press, London, 1941; some of Cornford's footnotes have been omitted. The
italisized glosses are his except for those
supplied by the editor and marked by the
initials "M.R.".

What people say is that to do wrong
is, in itself, a desirable thing; on the
other hand, it is not at all desirable to
suffer wrong, and the harm to the suf-
ferer outweighs the advantage to the
doer. Consequently, when men have
had a taste of both, those who have not
the power to seize the advantage and
escape the harm decide that they would
be better off if they made a compact
neither to do wrong nor to suffer it.

Hence they began to make laws and covenants with one another; and whatever the law prescribed they called lawful and right. That is what right or justice is and how it came into existence; it stands half-way between the best thing of all — to do wrong with impunity — and the worst, which is to suffer wrong without the power to retaliate. So justice is accepted as a compromise, and valued, not as good in itself, but for lack of power to do wrong; no man worthy of the name, who had that power, would ever enter into such a compact with anyone; he would be mad if he did. That, Socrates, is the nature of justice according to this account, and such the circumstances in which it arose.

The next point is that men practise it against the grain, for lack of power to do wrong. How true that is, we shall best see if we imagine two men, one just, the other unjust, given full licence to do whatever they like, and then follow them to observe where each will be led by his desires. We shall catch the just man taking the same road as the unjust; he will be moved by self-interest, the end which it is natural to every creature to pursue as good, until forcibly turned aside by law and custom to respect the principle of equality.

Now, the easiest way to give them that complete liberty of action would be to imagine them possessed of the talisman found by Gyges, the ancestor of the famous Lydian. The story tells how he was a shepherd in the King's service. One day there was a great storm, and the ground where his flock was feeding was rent by an earthquake. Astonished at the sight, he went down into the chasm and saw, among other wonders of which the story tells, a brazen horse, hollow, with windows in its sides. Peering in, he saw a dead body, which seemed to be of more than human size. It was naked save for a gold ring, which he took from the finger and made his way out. When the shepherds met, as they did every month, to send an account to the King of the state of his flocks, Gyges came wearing the ring. As he was sitting with the others, he happened to turn the bezel of the ring inside his hand. At once he became invisible, and his companions, to his surprise, began to speak of him as if he had left them. Then, as he was fingering the ring, he turned the bezel outwards and became visible again. With that, he set about testing the ring to see if it really had this power, and always with the same result: according as he turned the bezel inside or out he vanished and reappeared. After this discovery he contrived to be one of the messengers sent to the court. There he seduced the Queen, and with her help murdered the King and seized the throne.

Now suppose there were two such magic rings, and one were given to the just man, the other to the unjust. No one, it is commonly believed, would have such iron strength of mind as to stand fast in doing right or keep his hands off other men's goods, when he could go to the market-place and fearlessly help himself to anything he wanted, enter houses and sleep with any woman he chose, set prisoners free and kill men at his pleasure, and in a word go about among men with the powers of a god. He would behave no better than the other; both would take the same course. Surely this would be strong proof that men do right only under compulsion; no individual thinks of it as good for him personally, since he does wrong whenever he finds he has the power. Every man believes that wrongdoing pays him personally much better, and, according to this theory, that is the truth. Granted full licence to do as he liked, people would think him a miserable fool if they found him refusing to wrong his neighbours or to touch their belongings, though in public they would keep up a pretence of praising his conduct, for fear of being wronged themselves. So much for that.

Finally, if we are really to judge between the two lives, the only way is to contrast the extremes of justice and injustice. We can best do that by imagining our two men to be perfect types, and crediting both to the full with the qualities they need for their respective ways of life. To begin with the unjust man: he must be like any consummate master of a craft, a physician or a captain, who, knowing just what his art can do, never tries to do more, and can always retrieve a false step. The unjust man, if he is to reach perfection, must be equally discreet in his criminal attempts, and he must not be found out, or we shall think him a bungler; for the highest pitch of injustice is to seem just when you are not. So we must endow our man with the full complement of injustice; we must allow him to have secured a spotless reputation for virtue while committing the blackest crimes; he must be able to retrieve any mistake, to defend himself with convincing eloquence if his misdeeds are denounced,

and, when force is required, to bear down all opposition by his courage and strength and by his command of friends and money.

Now set beside this paragon the just man in his simplicity and nobleness, one who, in Aeschylus' words, "would be, not seem, the best." There must, indeed, be no such seeming; for if his character were apparent, his reputation would bring him honours and rewards, and then we should not know whether it was for their sake that he was just or for justice's sake alone. He must be stripped of everything but justice, and denied every advantage the other enjoyed. Doing no wrong, he must have the worst reputation for wrong-doing, to test whether his virtue is proof against all that comes of having a bad name; and under this lifelong imputation of wickedness, let him hold on his course of justice unwavering to the point of death. And so, when the two men have carried their justice and injustice to the last extreme, we may judge which is the happier.

My dear Glaucon, I exclaimed, how vigorously you scour these two characters clean for inspection, as if you were burnishing a couple of statues![1]

I am doing my best, he answered. Well, given two such characters, it is not hard, I fancy, to describe the sort of life that each of them may expect; and if the description sounds rather coarse,

[1] At Elis and Athens officials called *phaidryntai*, 'burnishers,' had the duty of cleaning cult statues (A. B. Cook, *Zeus*, iii. 967). At 612 c, where this passage is recalled, it is admitted to be an extravagant supposition, that the just and unjust should exchange reputations.

take it as coming from those who cry up the merits of injustice rather than from me. They will tell you that our just man will be thrown into prison, scourged and racked, will have his eyes burnt out, and, after every kind of torment, be impaled. That will teach him how much better it is to seem virtuous than to be so. In fact those lines of Aeschylus I quoted are more fitly applied to the unjust man, who, they say, is a realist and does not live for appearances: "he would be, not seem" unjust,

> . . . reaping the harvest sown
> In those deep furrows of the
>   thoughtful heart
> Whence wisdom springs.

With his reputation for virtue, he will hold offices of state, ally himself by marriage to any family he may choose, become a partner in any business, and, having no scruples about being dishonest, turn all these advantages to profit. If he is involved in a lawsuit, public or private, he will get the better of his opponents, grow rich on the proceeds, and be able to help his friends and harm his enemies. Finally, he can make sacrifices to the gods and dedicate offerings with due magnificence, and, being in a much better position than the just man to serve the gods as well as his chosen friends, he may reasonably hope to stand higher in the favour of heaven. So much better, they say, Socrates, is the life prepared for the unjust by gods and men [*Socrates sees no way of immediately refuting the theory advanced by Glaucon and suggests that an answer can best be found if the argument is projected from the level of the individ-*

ual to that of the community. He proposes to study the origin and nature of the state, in the hope of thereby discovering the nature of justice and other virtues. — M.R.]

THE VIRTUES IN THE STATE

[*Plato's original aim in constructing an ideal state was to find in it justice exemplified on a larger scale than in the individual. Assuming that four cardinal qualities make up the whole of virtue, he now asks wherein consist the wisdom, courage, temperance, and justice of the state, or, in other words, of the individuals composing the state in their public capacity as citizens.*

Wisdom in the conduct of state affairs will be the practical prudence or good counsel of the deliberative body. Only the philosophic Rulers will possess the necessary insight into what is good for the community as a whole. They will have "right belief" grounded on immediate knowledge of the meaning of goodness in all its forms. The Auxiliaries will have only a right belief accepted on the authority of the Rulers. Their functions will be executive, not deliberative.

The Courage of the state will obviously be manifested in the fighting force. Socrates had defined courage as knowledge of what really is, or is not, to be feared, and he had regarded it as an inseparable part of all virtue, which consists in knowing what things are really good or evil. If the only real evil is moral evil, then poverty, suffering, and all the so-called evils that others can inflict on us, including death itself, are not to be feared, since, if they are

*met in the right spirit, they cannot
make us worse men. This knowledge
only the philosophic Rulers will possess to the full. The courage of the Auxiliaries will consist in the power of
holding fast to the conviction implanted by their education.*

*Temperance is not, as we might ex-
pect, the peculiar virtue of the lowest
order in the state. As self-mastery, it
means the subordination of the lower
elements to the higher; but government
must be with the willing consent of the
governed, and temperance will include
the unanimous agreement of all classes
as to who should rule and who obey.[2] It
is consequently like a harmony pervading and uniting all parts of the whole, a
principle of solidarity. In the Laws,
which stresses the harmonious union
of different and complementary elements, this virtue overshadows even
Justice.*

*Justice is the complementary princi-
ple of differentiation, keeping the parts
distinct. It has been before us all
through the construction of the state
since it first appeared on the economic
level as the division of labor based on
natural aptitudes. "Doing one's own
work" now has the larger sense of a
concentration on one's peculiar duty or
function in the community. This conception of "doing and possessing what
properly belongs to one" is wide
enough to cover the justice of the law-
courts, assuring to each man his due
rights. Injustice will mean invasion*

*and encroachment upon the rights and
duties of others.*

*The virtue described in this chapter
is what Plato calls "civic" or "popular"
virtue. Except in the Rulers, it is not
directly based on that ultimate knowledge of good and evil which is wisdom,
to be attained only at the end of the
higher education of the philosopher.]*

So now at last, son of Ariston, said I,
your commonwealth is established.
The next thing is to bring to bear upon
it all the light you can get from any
quarter, with the help of your brother
and Polemarchus and all the rest, in the
hope that we may see where justice is to
be found in it and where injustice, how
they differ, and which of the two will
bring happiness to its possessor, no
matter whether gods and men see that
he has it or not.

Nonsense, said Glaucon; you promised to conduct the search yourself, because it would be a sin not to uphold
justice by every means in your power.

That is true; I must do as you say,
but you must all help.

We will.

I suspect, then, we may find what we
are looking for in this way. I take it that
our state, having been founded and
built up on the right lines, is good in
the complete sense of the word.

It must be.

Obviously, then, it is wise, brave,
temperate, and just.

Obviously.

Then if we find some of these qualities in it, the remainder will be the one
we have not found. It is as if we were
looking somewhere for one of any four
things: if we detected that one immedi-

---

[2] At *Statesman* 276 E the true king is distinguished from the despot by the voluntary
submission of his subjects to his rule.

ately, we should be satisfied; whereas if we recognized the other three first, that would be enough to indicate the thing we wanted; it could only be the remaining one. So here we have four qualities. Had we not better follow that method in looking for the one we want?

Surely.

To begin then: the first quality to come into view in our state seems to be its wisdom; and there appears to be something odd about this quality.[3]

What is there odd about it?

I think the state we have described really has wisdom; for it will be prudent in counsel, won't it?

Yes.

And prudence in counsel is clearly a form of knowledge; good counsel cannot be due to ignorance and stupidity.

Clearly.

But there are many and various kinds of knowledge in our commonwealth. There is the knowledge possessed by the carpenters or the smiths, and the knowledge how to raise crops. Are we to call the state wise and prudent on the strength of these forms of skill?

No; they would only make it good at furniture-making or working in copper or agriculture.

Well then, is there any form of knowledge, possessed by some among the citizens of our new-founded commonwealth, which will enable it to take thought, not for some particular interest, but for the best possible conduct of the state as a whole in its internal and external relations?

Yes, there is.

What is it, and where does it reside?

It is precisely that art of guardianship which resides in those Rulers whom we just now called Guardians in the full sense.

And what would you call the state on the strength of that knowledge?

Prudent and truly wise.

And do you think there will be more or fewer of these genuine Guardians in our state than there will be smiths?

Far fewer.

Fewer, in fact, than any of those other groups who are called after the kind of skill they possess?

Much fewer.

So, if a state is constituted on natural principles, the wisdom it possesses as a whole will be due to the knowledge residing in the smallest part, the one which takes the lead and governs the rest. Such knowledge is the only kind that deserves the name of wisdom, and it appears to be ordained by nature that the class privileged to possess it should be the smallest of all.

Quite true.

Here then we have more or less made out one of our four qualities and its seat in the structure of the commonwealth.

To my satisfaction, at any rate.

Next there is courage. It is not hard to discern that quality or the part of the community in which it resides so as to entitle the whole to be called brave.

Why do you say so?

Because anyone who speaks of a state as either brave or cowardly can only be thinking of that part of it which

---

[3] Because the wisdom of the whole resides in the smallest part, as explained below.

takes the field and fights in its defence; the reason being, I imagine, that the character of the state is not determined by the bravery or cowardice of the other parts.

No.

Courage, then, is another quality which a community owes to a certain part of itself. And its being brave will mean that, in this part, it possesses the power of preserving, in all circumstances, a conviction about the sort of things that it is right to be afraid of — the conviction implanted by the education which the law-giver has established. Is not that what you mean by courage?

I do not quite understand. Will you say it again?

I am saying that courage means preserving something.

Yes, but what?

The conviction, inculcated by lawfully established education, about the sort of things which may rightly be feared. When I added "in all circumstances," I meant preserving it always and never abandoning it, whether under the influence of pain or of pleasure, or desire or of fear. If you like, I will give an illustration.

Please do.

You know how dyers who want wool to take a purple dye, first select the white wool from among all the other colors, next treat it very carefully to make it take the dye in its full brilliance, and only then dip it in the vat. Dyed in that way, wool gets a fast color, which no washing, even with soap, will rob of its brilliance; whereas if they choose wool of any color but white, or if they neglect to prepare it, you know what happens.

Yes, it looks washed-out and ridiculous.

That illustrates the result we were doing our best to achieve when we were choosing our fighting men and training their minds and bodies. Our only purpose was to contrive influences whereby they might take the color of our institutions like a dye, so that, in virtue of having both the right temperament and the right education, their convictions about what ought to be feared and on all other subjects might be indelibly fixed, never to be washed out by pleasure and pain, desire and fear, solvents more terribly effective than all the soap and fuller's earth in the world. Such a power of constantly preserving, in accordance with our institutions, the right conviction about the things which ought, or ought not, to be feared, is what I call courage. That is my position, unless you have some objection to make.

None at all, he replied; if the belief were such as might be found in a slave or an animal — correct, but not produced by education — you would hardly describe it as in accordance with our institutions, and you would give it some other name than courage.

Quite true.

Then I accept your account of courage.

You will do well to accept it, at any rate as applying to the courage of the ordinary citizen;[4] if you like we will go

[4]As distinct from the perfect courage of the philosophic Ruler, based on immediate knowledge of values.

into it more fully some other time. At present we are in search of justice, rather than of courage; and for that purpose we have said enough.

I quite agree.

Two qualities, I went on, still remain to be made out in our state, temperance and the object of our whole inquiry, justice. Can we discover justice without troubling ourselves further about temperance?

I do not know, and I would rather not have justice come to light first, if that means that we should not go on to consider temperance. So if you want to please me, take temperance first.

Of course I have every wish to please you.

Do go on then.

I will. At first sight, temperance seems more like some sort of concord or harmony than the other qualities did.

How so?

Temperance surely means a kind of orderliness, a control of certain pleasures and appetites. People use the expression, "master of oneself," whatever that means, and various other phrases that point the same way.

Quite true.

Is not "master of oneself" an absurd expression? A man who was master of himself would presumably be also subject to himself, and the subject would be master; for all these terms apply to the same person.

No doubt.

I think, however, the phrase means that within the man himself, in his soul, there is a better part and a worse; and that he is his own master when the

part which is better by nature has the worse under its control. It is certainly a term of praise; whereas it is considered a disgrace, when, through bad breeding or bad company, the better part is overwhelmed by the worse, like a small force outnumbered by a multitude. A man in that condition is called a slave to himself and intemperate.

Probably that is what is meant.

Then now look at our newly founded state and you will find one of these two conditions realized there. You will agree that it deserves to be called master of itself, if temperance and self-mastery exist where the better part rules the worse.

Yes, I can see that is true.

It is also true that the great mass of multifarious appetites and pleasures and pains will be found to occur chiefly in children and women and slaves, and, among free men so called, in the inferior multitude; whereas the simple and moderate desires which, with the aid of reason and right belief, are guided by reflection, you will find only in a few, and those with the best inborn dispositions and the best educated.

Yes, certainly.

Do you see that this state of things will exist in your commonwealth, where the desires of the inferior multitude will be controlled by the desires and wisdom of the superior few? Hence, if any society can be called master of itself and in control of pleasures and desires, it will be ours.

Quite so.

On all these grounds, then, we may describe it as temperate. Furthermore, in our state, if anywhere, the governors and the governed will share the same conviction on the question who ought to rule.[5] Don't you think so?

I am quite sure of it.

Then, if that is their state of mind, in which of the two classes of citizens will temperance reside—in the governors or in the governed?

In both, I suppose.

So we were not wrong in divining a resemblance between temperance and some kind of harmony. Temperance is not like courage and wisdom, which made the state wise and brave by residing each in one particular part. Temperance works in a different way; it extends throughout the whole gamut of the state, producing a consonance of all its elements from the weakest to the strongest as measured by any standard you like to take—wisdom, bodily strength, numbers, or wealth. So we are entirely justified in identifying with temperance this unanimity or harmonious agreement between the naturally superior and inferior elements on the question which of the two should govern, whether in the state or in the individual.

I fully agree.

Good, said I. We have discovered in our commonwealth three out of our four qualities, to the best of our present judgment. What is the remaining one, required to make up its full complement of goodness? For clearly this will be justice.

[5] This principle of freedom—government with consent of the governed—is thus recognized. The "democratic" freedom to "do whatever you like" is condemned in later chapters.

Clearly.

Now is the moment, then, Glaucon, for us to keep the closest watch, like huntsmen standing round a covert, to make sure that justice does not slip through and vanish undetected. It must certainly be somewhere hereabouts; so keep your eyes open for a view of the quarry, and if you see it first, give me the alert.

I wish I could, he answered; but you will do better to give me a lead and not count on me for more than eyes to see what you show me.

Pray for luck, then, and follow me.

The thicket looks rather impenetrable, said I; too dark for it to be easy to start up the game. However, we must push on.

Of course we must.

Here I gave the view halloo. Glaucon, I exclaimed, I believe we are on the track and the quarry is not going to escape us altogether.

That is good news.

Really, I said, we have been extremely stupid. All this time the thing has been under our very noses from the start, and we never saw it. We have been as absurd as a person who hunts for something he has all the time got in his hand. Instead of looking at the thing, we have been staring into the distance. No doubt that is why it escaped us.

What do you mean?

I believe we have been talking about the thing all this while without ever understanding that we were giving some sort of account of it.

Do come to the point. I am all ears.

Listen, then, and judge whether I am right. You remember how, when we first began to establish our commonwealth and several times since, we have laid down, as a universal principle, that everyone ought to perform the one function in the community for which his nature best suited him. Well, I believe that that principle, or some form of it, is justice.

We certainly laid that down.

Yes, and surely we have often heard people say that justice means minding one's own business and not meddling with other men's concerns; and we have often said so ourselves.

We have.

Well, my friend, it may be that this minding of one's own business, when it takes a certain form, is actually the same thing as justice. Do you know what makes me think so?

No, tell me.

I think that this quality which makes it possible for the three we have already considered, wisdom, courage, and temperance, to take their place in the commonwealth, and so long as it remains present secures their continuance, must be the remaining one. And we said that, when three of the four were found, the one left over would be justice.

It must be so.

Well now, if we had to decide which of these qualities will contribute most to the excellence of our commonwealth, it would be hard to say whether it was the unanimity of rules and subjects, or the soldier's fidelity to the established conviction about what is, or is not, to be feared, or the watchful intelligence of the Rulers; or whether its excellence were not above all due to the observance by everyone, child or woman, slave or freeman or artisan,

ruler or ruled, of this principle that one should do his own proper work without interfering with others.

It would be hard to decide, no doubt.

It seems, then, that this principle can at any rate claim to rival wisdom, temperance, and courage as conducing to the excellence of a state. And would you not say that the only possible competitor of these qualities must be justice?

Yes, undoubtedly.

Here is another thing which points to the same conclusion. The judging of law-suits is a duty that you will lay upon your Rulers, isn't it?

Of course.

And the chief aim of their decisions will be that neither party shall have what belongs to another or be deprived of what is his own.

Yes.

Because that is just?

Yes.

So here again justice admittedly means that a man should possess and concern himself with what properly belongs to him.[6]

True.

Again, do you agree with me that no great harm would be done to the community by a general interchange of most forms of work, the carpenter and the cobbler exchanging their positions and their tools and taking on each other's jobs, or even the same man undertaking both?

Yes, there would not be much harm in that.

But I think you will also agree that

---

[6] Here the legal conception of justice is connected with its moral significance.

another kind of interchange would be disastrous. Suppose, for instance, someone whom nature designed to be an artisan or tradesman should be emboldened by some advantage, such as wealth or command of votes or bodily strength, to try to enter the order of fighting men; or some member of that order should aspire, beyond his merits, to a seat in the council-chamber of the Guardians. Such interference and exchange of social positions and tools, or the attempt to combine all these forms of work in the same person, would be fatal to the commonwealth.

Most certainly.

Where there are three orders, then, any plurality of functions or shifting from one order to another is not merely utterly harmful to the community, but one might fairly call it the extreme of wrongdoing. And you will agree that to do the greatest of wrongs to one's own community is injustice.

Surely.

This, then, is injustice, And, conversely, let us repeat that when each order — tradesman, Auxiliary, Guardian—keeps to its own proper business in the commonwealth and does its own work, that is justice and what makes a just society.

I entirely agree.

THE THREE PARTS OF THE SOUL

[*It has been shown that justice in the state means that the three chief social functions—deliberative and governing, executive, and productive—are kept distinct and rightly performed. Since the qualities of a community are those of the component individuals, we may expect to find three corresponding elements in the individual soul. All three will be present in every soul; but the structure of society is based on the fact that they are developed to different degrees in different types of character.*

The existence of three elements or "parts" of the soul is established by an analysis of the conflict of motives. A simple case is the thirsty man's appetite for drink, held in check by the rational reflection that to drink will be bad for him. That two distinct elements must be at work here follows from the general principle that the same thing cannot act or be affected in two opposite ways at the same time. By "thirst" is meant simply the bare craving for drink; it must not be confused with a desire for some good (e.g., health or pleasure) expected as a consequence of drinking. This simple craving says, "Drink"; Reason says, "Do not drink": the contradiction shows that two elements are at work.

A third factor is the "spirited" element, akin to our "sense of honor," manifested in indignation, which takes the side of reason against appetite, but cannot be identified with reason, since it is found in children and animals and it may be rebuked by reason.

This analysis is not intended as a complete outline of psychology; that could be reached only by following "a longer road." It is concerned with the factors involved in moral behavior. . . .]

THE VIRTUES IN THE INDIVIDUAL

[*The virtues in the state were the qualities of the citizen, as such, considered as playing the special part in society for which he was qualified by the predominance in his nature of the philosophic, the pugnacious, or the commercial spirit. But all three elements exist in every individual, who is thus a replica of society in miniature. In the perfect man reason will rule, with the spirited element as its auxiliary, over the bodily appetites. Self-control or temperance will be a condition of internal harmony, all the parts being content with their legitimate satisfactions. Justice finally appears, no longer only as a matter of external behavior toward others, but as an internal order of the soul, from which right behavior will necessarily follow. Injustice is the opposite state of internal discord and faction. To ask whether justice or injustice pays the better is now seen to be as absurd as to ask whether health is preferable to disease.]*

And so, after a stormy passage, we have reached the land. We are fairly agreed that the same three elements exist alike in the state and in the individual soul.

That is so.

Does it not follow at once that state and individual will be wise or brave by virtue of the same element in each and in the same way? Both will possess in the same manner any quality that makes for excellence.

That must be true.

Then it applies to justice: We shall conclude that a man is just in the same way that a state was just. And we have surely not forgotten that justice in the state meant that each of the three orders in it was doing its own proper work. So we may henceforth bear in mind that each one of us likewise will be a just person, fulfilling his proper function, only if the several parts of our nature fulfill theirs.

Certainly.

And it will be the business of reason to rule with wisdom and forethought on behalf of the entire soul; while the spirited element ought to act as its subordinate and ally. The two will be brought into accord, as we said earlier, by that combination of mental and bodily training which will tune up one string of the instrument and relax the other, nourishing the reasoning part on the study of noble literature and allaying the other's wildness by harmony and rhythm. When both have been thus nurtured and trained to know their own true functions, they must be set in command over the appetites, which form the greater part of each man's soul and are by nature insatiably covetous. They must keep watch lest this part, by battening on the pleasures that are called bodily, should grow so great and powerful that it will no longer keep to its own work, but will try to enslave the others and usurp a dominion to which it has no right, thus turning the whole of life upside down. At the same time, those two together will be the best of guardians for the entire soul and for the body against all enemies from without: the one will take counsel, while the other will do battle, following its ruler's commands and by its own bravery giving effect to the ruler's designs.

Yes, that is all true.

And so we call an individual brave in virtue of this spirited part of his nature, when, in spite of pain or pleasure, it holds fast to the injunctions of reason about what he ought or ought not to be afraid of.

True.

And wise in virtue of that small part which rules and issues these injunctions, possessing as it does the knowledge of what is good for each of the three elements and for all of them in common.

Certainly.

And, again, temperate by reason of the unanimity and concord of all three, when there is no internal conflict between the ruling element and its two subjects, but all are agreed that reason should be ruler.

Yes, that is an exact account of temperance, whether in the state or in the individual.

Finally, a man will be just by observing the principle we have so often stated.

Necessarily.

Now is there any indistinctness in our vision of justice, that might make it seem somehow different from what found it to be in the state?

I don't think so.

Because, if we have any lingering doubt, we might make sure by comparing it with some commonplace notions. Suppose, for instance, that a sum of money were entrusted to our state or to an individual of corresponding character and training, would anyone imagine that such a person would be specially likely to embezzle it?

No.

And would he not be incapable of sacrilege and theft, or of treachery to friend or country; never false to an oath or any other compact; the last to be guilty of adultery or of neglecting parents or the due service of the gods?

Yes.

And the reason for all this is that each part of his nature is exercising its proper function, of ruling or of being ruled.

Yes, exactly.

Are you satisfied, then, that justice is the power which produces states or individuals of whom that is true, or must we look further?

There is no need; I am quite satisfied.

And so our dream has come true — I mean the inkling we had that, by some happy chance, we had lighted upon a rudimentary form of justice from the very moment when we set about founding our commonwealth. Our principle that the born shoemaker or carpenter had better stick to his trade turns out to have been an adumbration of justice; and that is why it has helped us. But in reality justice, though evidently analogous to this principle, is not a matter of external behavior, but of the inward self and of attending to all that is, in the fullest sense, a man's proper concern. The just man does not allow the several elements in his soul to usurp one another's functions; he is indeed one who sets his house in order, by self-mastery and discipline coming to be at peace with himself, and bringing into tune those three parts, like the terms in the proportion of a musical scale, the highest and lowest notes and the mean between them, with all the intermediate intervals. Only when he has linked these parts together in well-tempered harmony and has made himself one man instead of many, will he be ready to go about whatever he may have to do, whether it be making money and satisfying bodily wants, or business transactions, or the affairs of state. In all these fields when he speaks of just and honorable conduct, he will mean the behavior that helps to produce and to preserve this habit of mind; and by wisdom he will mean the knowledge which presides over such conduct. Any action which tends to break down this habit will be for him unjust; and the notions governing it he will call ignorance and folly.

That is perfectly true, Socrates.

Good, said I. I believe we should not be thought altogether mistaken, if we claimed to have discovered the just man and the just state, and wherein their justice consists.

Indeed we should not.

Shall we make that claim, then?

Yes, we will.

So be it, said I. Next, I suppose, we have to consider injustice.

Evidently.

This must surely be a sort of civil strife among the three elements, whereby they usurp and encroach upon one another's functions and some one part of the soul rises up in rebellion against the whole, claiming a supremacy to which it has no right because its nature fits it only to be the servant of the ruling principle. Such turmoil and aberration we shall, I think, identify with injustice, intemperance, cowardice, ignorance, and in a word with all wickedness.

Exactly.

And now that we know the nature of justice and injustice, we can be equally clear about what is meant by acting justly and again by unjust action and wrong-doing.

How do you mean?

Plainly, they are exactly analogous to those wholesome and unwholesome activities which respectively produce a healthy or unhealthy condition in the body; in the same way just and unjust conduct produce a just or unjust character. Justice is produced in the soul, like health in the body, by establishing the elements concerned in their natural relations of control and subordination, whereas injustice is like disease and means that this natural order is inverted.

Quite so.

It appears, then, that virtue is as it were the health and comeliness and well-being of the soul, as wickedness is disease, deformity, and weakness.

True.

And also that virtue and wickedness are brought about by one's way of life, honorable or disgraceful.

That follows.

So now it only remains to consider which is the more profitable course: to do right and live honorably and be just, whether or not anyone knows what manner of man you are, or to do wrong and be unjust, provided that you can escape the chastisement which might make you a better man.

But really, Socrates, it seems to me ridiculous to ask that question now that the nature of justice and injustice has been brought to light. People think that all the luxury and wealth and power in the world cannot make life worth living when the bodily constitution is going to rack and ruin; and are we to believe that, when the very principle whereby we live is deranged and corrupted, life will be worth living so long as a man can do as he will, and wills to do anything rather than to free himself from vice and wrongdoing and to win justice and virtue?

Yes, I replied, it is a ridiculous question. . . .

THE PARADOX: PHILOSOPHERS MUST BE KINGS

[*Challenged to show that the ideal state can exist, Socrates first claims that an idea is none the worse for not being realizable on earth. The assertion that theory comes closer than practice to truth or reality is characteristically Platonic. The ideal state or man is the true state or man; for if men, who are in fact always imperfect, could reach perfection, they would only be realizing all that their nature aims at being and might conceivably be. Further, the realm of ideals is the real world, unchanging and eternal, which can be known by thought. The visible and tangible things commonly called real are only a realm of fleeting appearance, where the ideal is imperfectly manifested in various degrees of approximation. . . .*

An ideal has an indispensable value for practice, in that thought thereby gives to action its right aim. So, instead of proving that the ideal state or man can exist here, it is enough to discover the least change, within the bounds of possibility, that would bring the actual state nearest to the ideal. This change would be the union, in the same persons, of political power and the love of wisdom, so as to close the gulf, which had been growing wider since the age of Pericles, between the men of thought and the men of action. The corresponding change in the individual is the supremacy of the reason, the divine element in man, over the rest of our nature.]

But really, Socrates, Glaucon continued, if you are allowed to go on like this, I am afraid you will forget all about the question you thrust aside some time ago: whether a society so constituted can ever come into existence, and if so, how. No doubt, if it did exist, all manner of good things would come about. I can even add some that you have passed over. Men who acknowledged one another as fathers, sons, or brothers and always used those names among themselves would never desert one another; so they would fight with unequalled bravery. And if their womenfolk went out with them to war, either in the ranks or drawn up in the rear to intimidate the enemy and act as a reserve in case of need, I am sure all this would make them invincible. At home, too, I can see many advantages you have not mentioned. But, since I admit that our commonwealth would have all these merits and any number more, if once it came into existence, you need not describe it in further detail. All we have now to do is to convince ourselves that it can be brought into being and how.

This is a very sudden onslaught, said I; you have no mercy on my shillyshallying. Perhaps you do not realize that, after I have barely escaped the first two waves,[7] the third, which you are now bringing down upon me, is the most formidable of all. When you have seen what it is like and heard my reply, you will be ready to excuse the very natural fears which made me shrink

---

[7] The equality of women and the abolition of the family. [These concepts have been spoken of as waves, and the wave metaphor is now continued.]

from putting forward such a paradox for discussion.

The more you talk like that, he said, the less we shall be willing to let you off from telling us how this constitution can come into existence; so you had better waste no more time.

Well, said I, let me begin by reminding you that what brought us to this point was our inquiry into the nature of justice and injustice.

True; but what of that?

Merely this: suppose we do find out what justice is,[8] are we going to demand that a man who is just shall have a character which exactly corresponds in every respect to the ideal of justice? Or shall we be satisfied if he comes as near to the ideal as possible and has in him a larger measure of that quality than the rest of the world?

That will satisfy me.

If so, when we set out to discover the essential nature of justice and injustice and what a perfectly just and a perfectly unjust man would be like, supposing them to exist, our purpose was to use them as ideal patterns: we were to observe the degree of happiness or unhappiness that each exhibited, and to draw the necessary inference that our own destiny would be like that of the one we most resembled. We did not set out to show that these ideals could exist in fact.

That is true.

Then suppose a painter had drawn an ideally beautiful figure complete to the last touch, would you think any the worse of him, if he could not show that

a person as beautiful as that could exist?

No, I should not.

Well, we have been constructing in discourse the pattern of an ideal state. Is our theory any the worse, if we cannot prove it possible that a state so organized should be actually founded?

Surely not.

That, then, is the truth of the matter. But if, for your satisfaction, I am to do my best to show under what conditions our ideal would have the best chance of being realized, I must ask you once more to admit that the same principle applies here. Can theory every be fully realized in practice? Is it not in the nature of things that action should come less close to truth than thought? People may not think so; but do you agree or not?

I do.

Then you must not insist upon my showing that this construction we have traced in thought could be reproduced in fact down to the last detail. You must admit that we shall have found a way to meet your demand for realization, if we can discover how a state might be constituted in the closest accordance with our description. Will not that content you? It would be enough for me.

And for me too.

Then our next attempt, it seems, must be to point out what defect in the working of existing states prevents them from being so organized, and what is the least change that would effect a transformation into this type of government — a single change if possible, or perhaps two; at any rate let us make the changes as few and insignificant as may be.

---

[8] Justice, as a "civic" virtue, has been defined . . . but the wise man's virtue, based on knowledge, has still to be described.

By all means.

Well, there is one change which, as I believe we can show, would bring about this revolution—not a small change, certainly, nor an easy one, but possible.

What is it?

I have now to confront what we called the third and greatest wave. But I must state my paradox, even though the wave should break in laughter over my head and drown me in ignominy. Now mark what I am going to say.

Go on.

Unless either philosophers become kings in their countries or those who are now called kings and rulers come to be sufficiently inspired with a genuine desire for wisdom; unless, that is to say, political power and philosophy meet together, while the many natures who now go their several ways in the one or the other direction are forcibly debarred from doing so, there can be no rest from troubles, my dear Glaucon, for states, nor yet, as I believe, for all mankind; nor can this commonwealth which we have imagined ever till then see the light of day and grow to its full stature. This it was that I have so long hung back from saying; I knew what a paradox it would be, because it is hard to see that there is no other way of happiness either for the state or for the individual. . . .

DEFINITION OF
THE PHILOSOPHER:
THE TWO WORLDS

[The word "philosophy" originally meant curiosity, the desire for fresh experience, such as led Solon to travel and see the world (Herod. i. 30), or the pursuit of intellectual culture, as in Pericles' speech: "We cultivate the mind (φιλοσοφοῦμεν) without loss of manliness" (Thuc, ii. 40). This sense has to be excluded: the Rulers are not to be dilettanti or mere amateurs of the arts. They are to desire knowledge of the whole of truth and reality, and hence of the world of essential Forms, in contrast with the world of appearances.

The doctrine of Forms is here more explicitly invoked. Corresponding to the two worlds, the mind has two faculties: Knowledge of the real and Belief in appearances (doxa). Faculties can be distinguished only by (1) the states of mind they produce, and (2) their fields of objects. By both tests Knowledge and Belief differ. (1) Knowledge is infallible (there is no false knowledge); Belief may be true or false. (2) Knowledge, by definition, is of unique, unchanging objects. Just in this respect the Forms resemble the laws of nature sought by modern natural science: a law is an unseen intelligible principle, a unity underlying an unlimited multiplicity of similar phenomena, and supposed to be unalterable. The Forms, however, are not laws of the sequence or coexistence of phenomena, but ideals or patterns, which have a real existence independent of our minds[9] and of which the many individual things called by their names in the world of appearances are like

[9] Hence most modern critics avoid the term 'Idea,' though this is Plato's word, because it now suggests a thought existing only 'in our minds.'

*images or reflections. If we are dis-
posed, with Aristotle, to deny that Platonic Forms or ideals exist apart from
individual things in the visible world,
we should remember that the essence
of the doctrine is the conviction that
the differences between good and evil,
right and wrong, true and false, beautiful and ugly, are absolute, not 'relative'
to the customs or tastes or desires of
individual men or social groups. We
can know them or (as is commonly the
case) not know them; they cannot
change or vary from place to place or
from time to time. This conviction has
been, and is, held by many who cannot
accept, at its face value, Plato's mode of
expressing it.*

*A Form, such as Beauty itself, ex-
cludes its opposite, Ugliness: it can
never be or become ugly. But any particular beautiful thing may be also ugly
in some aspects or situations: it may
cease to be beautiful and become ugly;
it may seem beautiful to me, ugly to
you; and it must begin and cease to
exist in time. Such things cannot be objects of knowledge. Our apprehension
of these many changing things is here
called doxa and compared to dream experience, which is neither wholly real
nor utterly non-existent. Doxa is usually rendered by "Opinion." Here 'Belief' is preferred as having a corresponding verb which, unlike 'opine,' is
in common use. But both terms are inadequate. Doxa and its cognates denote
our apprehension of anything that
'seems': (1) what seems to exist, sensible appearances, phenomena; (2) what
seems true, opinions, beliefs, whether
really true or false; (3) what seems
right, legal and deliberative decisions,*
*and the "many conventional notions"
of current morality (479 D), which vary
from place to place and from time to
time. The amateur of the arts and the
politician live in the twilight realm of
these fluctuating beliefs.]*

Now, I continued, if we are to elude
those assailants you have described, we
must, I think, define for them whom
we mean by these lovers of wisdom
who, we have dared to assert, ought to
be our rulers. Once we have a clear
view of their character, we shall be able
to defend our position by pointing to
some who are naturally fitted to combine philosophic study with political
leadership, while the rest of the world
should accept their guidance and let
philosophy alone.

Yes, this is the moment for a
definition.

Here, then, is a line of thought
which may lead to a satisfactory explanation. Need I remind you that a man
will deserve to be called a lover of this
or that, only if it is clear that he loves
that thing as a whole, not merely in
parts?

You must remind me, it seems; for I
do not see what you mean.

That answer would have come better
from someone less susceptible to love
than yourself, Glaucon. You ought not
to have forgotten that any boy in the
bloom of youth will arouse some sting
of passion in a man of your amorous
temperament and seem worthy of his
attentions. Is not this your way with
your favourites? You will praise a snub
nose as piquant and a hooked one as
giving a regal air, while you call a
straight nose perfectly proportioned;

the swarthy, you say, have a manly look, the fair are children of the gods; and what do you think is that word 'honey-pale,' if not the euphemism of some lover who had no fault to find with sallowness on the cheek of youth? In a word, you will carry pretence and extravagance to any length sooner than reject a single one that is in the flower of his prime.

If you insist on taking me as an example of how lovers behave, I will agree for the sake of argument.

Again, do you not see the same behaviour in people with a passion for wine? They are glad of any excuse to drink wine of any sort. And there are the men who covet honour, who, if they cannot lead an army, will command a company, and if they cannot win the respect of important people, are glad to be looked up to by nobodies, because they must have someone to esteem them.

Quite true.

Do you agree, then, that when we speak of a man as having a passion for a certain kind of thing, we mean that he has an appetite for everything of that kind without discrimination?

Yes.

So the philosopher, with his passion for wisdom, will be one who desires all wisdom, not only some part of it. If a student is particular about his studies, especially while he is too young to know which are useful and which are not, we shall say he is no lover of learning or of wisdom; just as, if he were dainty about his food, we should say he was not hungry or fond of eating, but had a poor appetite. Only the man who has a taste for every sort of knowledge and throws himself into acquiring it with an insatiable curiosity will deserve to be called a philosopher. Am I not right?

That description, Glaucon replied, would include a large and ill-assorted company. It is curiosity, I suppose, and a delight in fresh experience that gives some people a passion for all that is to be seen and heard at theatrical and musical performances. But they are a queer set to reckon among philosophers, considering that they would never go near anything like a philosophical discussion, though they run round at all the Dionysiac festivals in town or country as if they were under contract to listen to every company of performers without fail. Will curiosity entitle all these enthusiasts, not to mention amateurs of the minor arts, to be called philosophers?

Certainly not; though they have a certain counterfeit resemblance?

And whom do you mean by the genuine philosophers?

Those whose passion it is to see the truth.

That must be so; but will you explain?

It would not be easy to explain to everyone; but you, I believe, will grant my premiss.

Which is—?

That since beauty and ugliness are opposite, they are two things; and consequently each of them is one. The same holds of justice and injustice, good and bad, and all the essential Forms: each in itself is one; but they manifest themselves in a great variety of combinations, with actions, with material things, and with one another, and so each seems to be many.[10]

That is true.

On the strength of this premiss, then, I can distinguish your amateurs of the arts and men of action from the philosophers we are concerned with, who are alone worthy of the name.

What is your distinction?

Your lovers of sights and sounds delight in beautiful tones and colours and shapes and in all the works of art into which these enter; but they have not the power of thought to behold and to take delight in the nature of Beauty itself. That power to approach Beauty and behold it as it is in itself, is rare indeed.

Quite true.

Now if a man believes in the existence of beautiful things, but not of Beauty itself, and cannot follow a guide who would lead him to a knowledge of it, is he not living in a dream? Consider: does not dreaming, whether one is awake or asleep, consist in mistaking a semblance for the reality it resembles?

I should certainly call that dreaming.

Contrast with him the man who holds that there is such a thing as Beauty itself and can discern that essence as well as the things that partake of its character, without ever confusing the one with the other — is he a dreamer or living in a waking state?

He is very much awake.

---

[10] At 523 A ff., it is explained how confused impressions of opposite qualities in sense-perception provoke reflection to isolate and define the corresponding universals or Forms.

So may we say that he knows, while the other has only a belief in appearances; and might we call their states of mind knowledge and belief?

Certainly.

But this person who, we say, has only belief without knowledge may be aggrieved and challenge our statement. Is there any means of soothing his resentment and converting him gently, without telling him plainly that he is not in his right mind?

We surely ought to try.

Come then, consider what we are to say to him. Or shall we ask him a question, assuring him that, far from grudging him any knowledge he may have, we shall be only too glad to find that there is something he knows? But, we shall say, tell us this: When a man knows, must there not be something that he knows? Will you answer for him, Glaucon?

My answer will be, that there must.

Something real or unreal?

Something real; how could a thing that is unreal ever be known?

Are we satisfied, then, on this point, from however many points of view we might examine it: that the perfectly real is perfectly knowable, and the utterly unreal is entirely unknowable?

Quite satisfied.

Good. Now if there is something so constituted that it both *is* and *is not*, will it not lie between the purely real and the utterly unreal?

It will.

Well then, as knowledge corresponds to the real, and absence of knowledge necessarily to the unreal, so, to correspond to this intermediate thing, we must look for something between ignorance and knowledge, if such a thing there be.

Certainly.

Is there not a thing we call belief?

Surely.

A different power from knowledge, or the same?

Different.

Knowledge and belief, then, must have different objects, answering to their respective powers.

Yes.

And knowledge has for its natural object the real — to know the truth about reality. However, before going further, I think we need a definition. Shall we distinguish under the general name of "faculties"[11] those powers which enable us — or anything else — to do what we can do? Sight and hearing, for instance, are what I call faculties, if that will help you to see the class of things I have in mind.

Yes, I understand.

Then let me tell you what view I take of them. In a faculty I cannot find any of those qualities, such as colour or shape, which, in the case of many other things, enable me to distinguish one thing from another. I can only look to its field of objects and the state of mind it produces, and regard these as sufficient to identify it and to distinguish it from faculties which have different fields and produce different states. Is that how you would go to work?

Yes.

Let us go back, then, to knowledge. Would you class that as a faculty?

Yes; and I should call it the most powerful of all.

And is belief also a faculty?

It can be nothing else, since it is what gives us the power of believing.

But a little while ago you agreed that knowledge and belief are not the same thing.

Yes; there could be no sense in identifying the infallible with the fallible.[12]

Good. So we are quite clear that knowledge and belief are different things?

They are.

If so, each of them, having a different power, must have a different field of objects.

Necessarily.

The field of knowledge being the real; and its power, the power of knowing the real as it is.

Yes.

Whereas belief, we say, is the power of believing. Is its object the same as that which knowledge knows? Can the same things be possible objects of knowledge and of belief?[13]

Not if we hold to the principles we

---

[11] The Greek here uses only the common word for "power" (dynamis), but Plato is defining the special sense we express by "faculty."

[12] This marks one distinction between the two states of mind. Further, even if true, belief, unlike knowledge, is (1) produced by persuasion, not by instruction; (2) cannot "give an account" of itself; and (3) can be shaken by persuasion (Timaeus 51 E).

[13] If "belief" bore its common meaning, we might answer, yes. But in this context it is essentially belief in appearances. It includes perception by the senses, and these can never perceive objects of thought, such as Beauty itself.

agreed upon. If it is of the nature of a different faculty to have a different field, and if both knowledge and belief are faculties and, as we assert, different ones, it follows that the same things cannot be possible objects of both.

So if the real is the object of knowledge, the object of belief must be something other than the real.

Yes.

Can it be the unreal? Or is that an impossible object even for belief? Consider: if a man has a belief, there must be something before his mind; he cannot be believing nothing, can he?

No.

He is believing something, then; whereas the unreal could only be called nothing at all.

Certainly.

Now we said that ignorance must correspond to the unreal, knowledge to the real. So what he is believing cannot be real nor yet unreal.

True.

Belief, then, cannot be either ignorance or knowledge.

It appears not.

Then does it lie outside and beyond these two? Is it either more clear and certain than knowledge or less clear and certain than ignorance?

No, it is neither.

It rather seems to you to be something more obscure than knowledge, but not so dark as ignorance, and so to lie between the two extremes?

Quite so.

Well, we said earlier that if some object could be found such that it both *is* and at the same time *is not*, that object would lie between the perfectly real and the utterly unreal; and that the corresponding faculty would be neither knowledge nor ignorance, but a faculty to be found situated between the two.

Yes.

And now what we have found between the two is the faculty we call belief.

True.

It seems, then, that what remains to be discovered is that object which can be said both to be and not to be and cannot properly be called either purely real or purely unreal. If that can be found, we may justly call the object of belief, and so give the intermediate faculty the intermediate object, while the two extreme objects will fall to the extreme faculties.

Yes.

On these assumptions, then, I shall call for an answer from our friend who denies the existence of Beauty itself or of anything that can be called an essential Form of Beauty remaining unchangeably in the same state for ever, though he does recognize the existence of beautiful things as a plurality — that lover of things seen who will not listen to anyone who says that Beauty is one, Justice is one, and so on. I shall say to him, Be so good as to tell us: of all these many beautiful things is there one which will not appear ugly? Or of these many just or righteous actions, is there one that will not appear unjust or unrighteous?

No, replied Glaucon, they must inevitably appear to be in some way both beautiful and ugly; and so with all the other terms your question refers to.

And again the many things which

are doubles are just as much halves as they are doubles. And the things we call large or heavy have just as much right to be called small or light.

Yes; any such thing will always have a claim to both opposite designations.

Then, whatever any one of these many things may be said to be, can you say that it absolutely *is* that, any more than that it *is not* that?

They remind me of those punning riddles people ask at dinner parties, or the child's puzzle about what the eunuch threw at the bat and what the bat was perched on.[14] These things have the same ambiguous character, and one cannot form any stable conception of them either as being or as not being, or as both being and not being, or as neither.

Can you think of any better way of disposing of them than by placing them between reality and unreality? For I suppose they will not appear more obscure and so less real than unreality, or clearer and so more real than reality.

Quite true.

It seems, then, we have discovered that the many conventional notions of the mass of mankind about what is beautiful or honourable or just and so on are adrift in a sort of twilight between pure reality and pure unreality.

We have.

And we agreed earlier that, if any

[14] A man who was not a man (eunuch), seeing and not seeing (seeing imperfectly) a bird that was not a bird (bat) perched on a bough that was not a bough (a reed), pelted and did not pelt it (aimed at it and missed) with a stone that was not a stone (pumice-stone).

such object were discovered, it should be called the object of belief and not of knowledge. Fluctuating in that halfway region, it would be seized upon by the intermediate faculty.

Yes.

So when people have an eye for the multitude of beautiful things or of just actions or whatever it may be, but can neither behold Beauty or Justice itself nor follow a guide who would lead them to it, we shall say that all they have is beliefs, without any real knowledge of the objects of their belief.

That follows.

But what of those who contemplate the realities themselves as they are for ever in the same unchangeable state? Shall we not say that they have, not mere belief, but knowledge?

That too follows.

And, further, that their affection goes out to the objects of knowledge, whereas the others set their affections on the objects of belief; for it was they, you remember, who had a passion for the spectacle of beautiful colours and sounds, but would not hear of Beauty itself being a real thing.

I remember.

So we may fairly call them lovers of belief rather than of wisdom — not philosophical, in fact, but philodoxical. Will they be seriously annoyed by that description?

Not if they will listen to my advice. No one ought to take offence at the truth.

The name of philosopher, then, will be reserved for those whose affections are set, in every case, on the reality.

By all means.

THE PHILOSOPHER'S
FITNESS TO RULE

[*The above definition of the philosopher might suggest an unpractical head-in-air, unfit to control life in the state. But the qualities most valuable in a ruler will follow naturally from the master passion for truth in a nature of the type described earlier, when it is perfected by time and education.*]

So at last, Glaucon, after this long and weary way, we have come to see who are the philosophers and who are not.

I doubt if the way could have been shortened.

Apparently not. I think, however, that we might have gained a still clearer view if this had been the only topic to be discussed; but there are so many others awaiting us, if we mean to discover in what ways the just life is better than the unjust.

Which are we to take up now?

Surely the one that follows next in order. Since the philosophers are those who can apprehend the eternal and unchanging, while those who cannot do so, but are lost in the mazes of multiplicity and change, are not philosophers, which of the two ought to be in control of a state?

I wonder what would be a reasonable solution.

To establish as Guardians whichever of the two appear competent to guard the laws and ways of life in society.

True.

Well, there can be no question whether a guardian who is to keep watch over anything needs to be keen-sighted or blind. And is not blindness precisely the condition of men who are entirely cut off from knowledge of any reality, and have in their soul no clear pattern of perfect truth, which they might study in every detail and constantly refer to, as a painter looks at his model, before they proceed to embody notions of justice, honour, and goodness in earthly institutions or, in their character of Guardians, to preserve such institutions as already exist?

Certainly such a condition is very like blindness.

Shall we, then, make such as these our Guardians in preference to men who, besides their knowledge of realities, are in no way inferior to them in experience and in every excellence of character?

It would be absurd not to choose the philosophers, whose knowledge is perhaps their greatest point of superiority, provided they do not lack those other qualifications.

What we have to explain, then, is how those qualifications can be combined in the same persons with philosophy.

Certainly.

The first thing, as we said at the outset, is to get a clear view of their inborn disposition.[15] When we are satisfied on that head, I think we shall agree that such a combination of qualities is possible and that we need look no further for men fit to be in control of a com-

---

[15] The subject of the present chapter. The next will explain why the other qualifications, of experience and character, are too often lacking.

monwealth. One trait of the philosophic nature we may take as already granted: a constant passion for any knowledge that will reveal to them something of that reality which endures for ever and is not always passing into and out of existence. And, we may add, their desire is to know the whole of that reality; they will not willingly renounce any part of it as relatively small and insignificant, as we said before when we compared them to the lover and to the man who covets honour.

True.

Is there not another trait which the nature we are seeking cannot fail to possess — truthfulness, a love of truth and a hatred of falsehood that will not tolerate untruth in any form?

Yes, it is natural to expect that.

It is not merely natural, but entirely necessary that an instinctive passion for any object should extend to all that is closely akin to it; and there is nothing more closely akin to wisdom than truth. So the same nature cannot love wisdom and falsehood; the genuine lover of knowledge cannot fail, from his youth up, to strive after the whole of truth.

I perfectly agree.

Now we surely know that when a man's desires set strongly in one direction, in every other channel they flow more feebly, like a stream diverted into another bed. So when the current has set towards knowledge and all that goes with it, desire will abandon those pleasures of which the body is the instrument and be concerned only with the pleasure which the soul enjoys independently — if, that is to say, the love of wisdom is more than a mere pretence. Accordingly, such a one will be temperate and no lover of money; for he will be the last person to care about the things for the sake of which money is eagerly sought and lavishly spent.

That is true.

Again, in seeking to distinguish the philosophic nature, you must not overlook the least touch of meanness. Nothing could be more contrary than pettiness to a mind constantly bent on grasping the whole of things, both divine and human.

Quite true.

And do you suppose that one who is so high-minded and whose thought can contemplate all time and all existence will count this life of man a matter of such concern?

No, he could not.

So for such a man death will have no terrors.

None.

A mean and cowardly nature, then, can have no part in the genuine pursuit of wisdom.

I think not.

And if a man is temperate and free from the love of money, meanness, pretentiousness, and cowardice, he will not be hard to deal with or dishonest. So, as another indication of the philosophic temper, you will observe whether, from youth up, he is fairminded, gentle, and sociable.

Certainly.

Also you will not fail to notice whether he is quick or slow to learn. No one can be expected to take a reasonable delight in a task in which much painful effort makes little headway.

And if he cannot retain what he learns, his forgetfulness will leave no room in his head for knowledge; and so, having all his toil for nothing, he can only end by hating himself as well as his fruitless occupation. We must not, then, count a forgetful mind as competent to pursue wisdom; we must require a good memory.

By all means.

Further, there is in some natures a crudity and awkwardness that can only tend to a lack of measure and proportion; and there is a close affinity between proportion and truth. Hence, besides our other requirements, we shall look for a mind endowed with measure and grace, which will be instinctively drawn to see every reality in its true light.

Yes.

Well then, now that we have enumerated the qualities of a mind destined to take its full part in the apprehension of reality, have you any doubt about their being indispensable and all necessarily going together?

None whatever.

Then have you any fault to find with a pursuit which none can worthily follow who is not by nature quick to learn and to remember, magnanimous and gracious, the friend and kinsman of truth, justice, courage, temperance?

No; Momus[16] himself could find no flaw in it.

Well then, when time and education have brought such characters as these to maturity, would you entrust the care

of your commonwealth to anyone else? . . .

FOUR STAGES OF COGNITION: THE LINE

[*Socrates has contrasted the realm of sensible appearances and shifting beliefs with the realm of eternal and unchanging Forms, dominated (as we now know) by the Good. The philosopher was he whose affections were set on knowledge of that real world. The Guardians' primary education in literature and art was mainly confined to the world of appearance and belief, though it culminated in the perception of "images" of the moral ideals, the beauty of which would excite love for the individual person in whose soul they dwelt (402). The higher intellectual training now to be described is to detach the mind from appearances and individuals and to carry it across the boundary between the two worlds and all the way beyond to the vision of the Good. It thus corresponds to the "greater mysteries" of which Diotima speaks in the Symposium (210), where Eros, detached from its individual object, advances to the vision of Beauty itself (the Good considered as the object of desire). The next chapter will give an allegorical picture of this progress.*

The allegory is here prefaced by a diagram. A line is divided into two parts, whose inequality symbolizes that the visible world has a lower degree of reality and truth than the intelligible. Each part is then subdivided in the same proportion as the whole line, (thus $A + B : C + D = A : B = C : D$). The

---

[16] The spirit of faultfinding, one of the children of Night in Hesiod's *Theogony*.

four sections correspond to *four states of mind or modes of cognition, each clearer and more certain than the one below.*

The lower part (A + B) is at first called "the Visible," but elsewhere the field of doxa in the wide sense explained above (p. 689); and so it includes the "many conventional notions of the multitude" about morality (479 D). It is the physical and moral world as apprehended by those "lovers of appearance" who do not recognize the absolute ideals which Plato calls real.

(A) The lowest form of cognition is called eikasia. The word defies translation, being one of those current terms to which Plato gives a peculiar sense, to be inferred from the context. It is etymologically connected with eikon = image, likeness, and with eikos = likely, and it can mean either likeness (representation) or likening (comparison) or estimation of likelihood (conjecture). Perhaps "imagining" is the least unsatisfactory rendering. It seems to be the wholly unenlightened state of mind which takes sensible appearances and current moral notions at their face value — the condition of the unreleased prisoners in the Cave allegory below, who see only images of images.

(B) The higher section stands for common-sense belief (pistis) in the reality of the visible and tangible things commonly called substantial. In the moral sphere it would include "correct beliefs without knowledge" (506 C), such as the young Guardians were taught to hold. True beliefs are sufficient guides for action, but are insecure until based on knowledge of the reasons for them (Meno 97).

Higher education is to effect an escape from the prison of appearances by training the intellect, first in mathematics, and then in moral philosophy. (C) The lower section of the intelligible contains the subject-matter of the mathematical sciences (511 B).[17] *Two characteristics of mathematical procedure are mentioned: (a) the use of visible diagrams and models as imperfect illustrations of the objects and truths of pure thought. Here is a sort of bridge carrying the mind across from the visible thing to the intelligible reality, which it must learn to distinguish. (b) Each branch of mathematics starts from unquestioned assumptions (postulates, axioms, definitions) and reasons from them deductively. The premisses may be true and the conclusions may follow, but the whole structure hangs in the air until the assumptions themselves shall have been shown to depend on an unconditional principle. (This may be conjectured to be Unity itself, an aspect of the Good.) Meanwhile the state of mind is dianoia, the ordinary word for "thought" or "thinking," here implying a degree of understanding which falls short of perfect knowledge (533 D). Dianoia suggests discursive thinking or reasoning from premiss to conclusion, whereas noesis is constantly compared to the immediate act of vision and suggests rather the direct intuition or apprehension of its object.*

(D) The higher method is called Dialectic, a word which since Hegel has

---

[17] The interpretation of the higher part of the Line is the subject of a long controversy which cannot be pursued here.

acquired misleading associations. In the Republic it simply means the technique of philosophic conversation (dialogue) carried on by question and answer and seeking to render, or to receive from a respondent, an "account" (logos) of some Form, usually a moral Form such as Justice in this dialogue. At this stage visible illustrations are no longer available, and the movement at first is not downward, deducing conclusions from premisses, but upward, examining the premisses themselves and seeking the ultimate principle on which they all depend. It is suggested that, if the mind could ever rise to grasp the supreme Form, it might then descend by a deduction confirming the whole structure of moral and mathematical knowledge. The state of mind is called intelligence or rational intuition (noesis) and knowledge (episteme, 533 E) in the full sense. . . .]

CONCEIVE, then, that there are these two powers I speak of, the Good reigning over the domain of all that is intelligible, the Sun over the visible world —or the heaven as I might call it; only you would think I was showing off my skill in etymology.[18] At any rate you have these two orders of things clearly before your mind: the visible and the intelligible?

I have.

Now take a line divided into two unequal parts, one to represent the visible order, the other the intelligible; and divide each part again in the same pro-

portion, symbolizing degrees of comparative clearness or obscurity. Then (A) one of the two sections in the visible world will stand for images. By images I mean first shadows, and then reflections in water or in close-grained, polished surfaces, and everything of that kind, if you understand.

Yes, I understand.

Let the second section (B) stand for the actual things of which the first are likenesses, the living creatures about us and all the works of nature or of human hands.

So be it.

Will you also take the proportion in which the visible world has been divided as corresponding to degrees of reality and truth, so that the likeness shall stand to the original in the same ratio as the sphere of appearances and belief to the sphere of knowledge?

Certainly.

Now consider how we are to divide the part which stands for the intelligible world. There are two sections. In the first (C) the mind uses as images those actual things which themselves had images in the visible world; and it is compelled to pursue its inquiry by starting from assumptions and travelling, not up to a principle, but down to a conclusion. In the second (D) the mind moves in the other direction, from an assumption up towards a principle which is not hypothetical; and it makes no use of the images employed in the other section, but only of Forms, and conducts its inquiry solely by their means.

I don't quite understand what you mean.

Then we will try again; what I have

---

[18] Some connected the word for heaven (οὐρανός) with ὁρᾶν 'to see' (*Cratylus*, 396 B). It is sometimes used for the whole of the visible universe.

just said will help you to understand. (C) You know, of course, how students of subjects like geometry and arithmetic begin by postulating odd and even numbers, or the various figures and the three kinds of angle, and other such data in each subject. These data they take as known; and, having adopted them as assumptions, they do not feel called upon to give any account of them to themselves or to anyone else, but treat them as self-evident. Then, starting from these assumptions, they go on until they arrive, by a series of consistent steps, at all the conclusions they set out to investigate.

Yes, I know that.

You also know how they make use of visible figures and discourse about them, though what they really have in mind is the originals of which these figures are images: they are not reasoning, for instance, about this particular square and diagonal which they have drawn, but about *the* Square and *the* Diagonal; and so in all cases. The diagrams they draw and the models they make are actual things, which may have their shadows or images in water; but now they serve in their turn as images, while the student is seeking to behold those realities which only thought can apprehend.[19]

True.

This, then, is the class of things that I spoke of as intelligible, but with two

[19]Conversely, the fact that the mathematician can use visible objects as illustrations indicates that the realities and truths of mathematics are embodied, though imperfectly, in the world of visible and tangible things; whereas the counterparts of the moral Forms can only be beheld by thought.

qualifications: first, that the mind, in studying them, is compelled to employ assumptions, and, because it cannot rise above these, does not travel upwards to a first principle; and second, that it uses as images those actual things which have images of their own in the section below them and which, in comparison with those shadows and reflections, are reputed to be more palpable and valued accordingly.

I understand: you mean the subject-matter of geometry and of the kindred arts.

(D) Then by the second section of the intelligible world you may understand me to mean all that unaided reasoning apprehends by the power of dialectic, when it treats its assumptions, not as first principles, but as *hypotheses* in the literal sense, things 'laid down' like a flight of steps up which it may mount all the way to something that is not hypothetical, the first principle of all; and having grasped this, may turn back and, holding on to the consequences which depend upon it, descend at last to a conclusion, never making use of any sensible object, but only of Forms, moving through Forms from one to another, and ending with Forms.

I understand, he said, though not perfectly; for the procedure you describe sounds like an enormous undertaking. But I see that you mean to distinguish the field of intelligible reality studied by dialectic as having a greater certainty and truth than the subject-matter of the 'arts,' as they are called, which treat their assumptions as first principles. The students of these arts are, it is true, compelled to exercise thought in contemplating objects which the senses cannot perceive; but because they start from assumptions without going back to a first principle, you do not regard them as gaining true understanding about those objects, although the objects themselves, when connected with a first principle, are intelligible. And I think you would call the state of mind of the students of geometry and other such arts, not intelligence, but thinking, as being something between intelligence and mere acceptance of appearances.

You have understood me quite well enough, I replied. And now you may take, as corresponding to the four sections, these four states of mind: *intelligence* for the highest, *thinking* for the second, *belief* for the third, and for the last *imagining*.[20] These you may arrange as the terms in a proportion, assigning to each a degree of clearness and certainty corresponding to the measure in which their objects possess truth and reality.

I understand and agree with you. I will arrange them as you say.

THE ALLEGORY OF THE CAVE

[*The progress of the mind from the lowest state of unenlightenment to knowledge of the Good is now illustrated by the famous parable comparing the world of appearance to an underground Cave. In Empedocles' religious poem the powers which conduct the soul to its incarnation say, "We have come under this cavern's roof." The image was probably taken from mysteries held in caves or dark chambers representing the underworld, through which the candidates for initiation were led to the revelation of sacred objects in a blaze of light. The idea that the body is a prison-house, to which the soul is condemned for past misdeeds, is attributed by Plato to the Orphics.*

One moral of the allegory is drawn from the distress caused by a too sudden passage from darkness to light. The earlier warning against plunging untrained minds into the discussion of moral problems (498 A), as the Sophists and Socrates himself had done, is reinforced by the picture of the dazed prisoner dragged out into the sunlight. Plato's ten years' course of pure mathematics is to habituate the intellect to abstract reasoning before moral ides are called in question (537 E, ff.).]

Next, said I, here is a parable to illustrate the degrees in which our nature may be enlightened or unenlightened. Imagine the condition of men living in a sort of cavernous chamber underground, with an entrance open to the light and a long passage all down the cave.[21] Here they have been from childhood, chained by the leg and also by the neck, so that they cannot move and can see only what is in front of them, because the chains will not let them turn their heads. At some distance higher up is the light of a fire burning behind them; and between the prisoners and

---

[20] Plato never uses hard and fast technical terms. The four here proposed are not defined or strictly employed in the sequel.

[21] The *length* of the "way in" (*eisodos*) to the chamber where the prisoners sit is an essential feature, explaining why no daylight reaches them.

the fire is a track[22] with a parapet built along it, like the screen at a puppet-show, which hides the performers while they show their puppets over the top.

I see, said he.

Now behind this parapet imagine persons carrying along various artificial objects, including figures of men and animals in wood or stone or other materials, which project above the parapet. Naturally, some of these persons will be talking, others silent.[23]

It is a strange picture, he said, and a strange sort of prisoners.

Like ourselves, I replied; for in the first place prisoners so confined would have seen nothing of themselves or of one another, except the shadows thrown by the fire-light on the wall of the Cave facing them, would they?

Not if all their lives they had been prevented from moving their heads.

And they would have seen as little of the objects carried past.

Of course.

Now, if they could talk to one an-other, would they not suppose that their words referred only to those passing shadows which they saw?[24]

Necessarily.

And suppose their prison had an echo from the wall facing them? When one of the people crossing behind them spoke, they could only suppose that the sound came from the shadow passing before their eyes.

No doubt.

In every way, then, such prisoners would recognize as reality nothing but the shadows of those artificial objects.[25]

Inevitably.

Now consider what would happen if their release from the chains and the healing of their unwisdom should come about in this way. Suppose one of them set free and forced suddenly to stand up, turn his head, and walk with eyes lifted to the light; all these movements would be painful, and he would be too dazzled to make out the objects whose shadows he had been used to see. What do you think he would say, if someone told him that what he had formerly seen was meaningless illusion, but now, being somewhat nearer to reality and turned towards more real objects, he was getting a truer view? Suppose further that he were shown the various objects being carried by and were made to say, in reply to questions, what each of them was. Would he not be perplexed and believe the objects now

[22] The track crosses the passage into the cave at right angles, and is *above* the parapet built along it.

[23] A modern Plato would compare his Cave to an underground cinema, where the audience watch the play of shadows thrown by the film passing before a light at their backs. The film itself is only an image of "real" things and events in the world outside the cinema. For the film Plato has to substitute the clumsier apparatus of a procession of artificial objects carried on their heads by persons who are merely part of the machinery, providing for the movement of the objects and the sounds whose echo the prisoners hear. The parapet prevents these persons' shadows from being cast on the wall of the Cave.

[24] Adam's text and interpretation. The prisoners, having seen nothing but shadows, cannot think their words refer to the objects carried past behind their backs. For them shadows (images) are the only realities.

[25] The state of mind called *eikasia* in the previous chapter.

shown him to be not so real as what he formerly saw?[26]

Yes, not nearly so real.

And if he were forced to look at the fire-light itself, would not his eyes ache, so that he would try to escape and turn back to the things which he could see distinctly, convinced that they really were clearer than these other objects now being shown to him?

Yes.

And suppose someone were to drag him away forcibly up the steep and rugged ascent and not let him go until he had hauled him out into the sunlight, would he not suffer pain and vexation at such treatment, and, when he had come out into the light, find his eyes so full of its radiance that he could not see a single one of the things that he was now told were real?

Certainly he would not see them all at once.

He would need, then, to grow accustomed before he could see things in that upper world.[27] At first it would be easiest to make out shadows, and then the images of men and things reflected in water, and later on the things themselves. After that, it would be easier to watch the heavenly bodies and the sky itself by night, looking at the light of the moon and stars rather than the Sun and the Sun's light in the day-time.

Yes, surely.

Last of all, he would be able to look at the Sun and contemplate its nature,

not as it appears when reflected in water or any alien medium, but as it is in itself in its own domain.

No doubt.

And now he would begin to draw the conclusion that it is the Sun that produces the seasons and the course of the year and controls everything in the visible world, and moreover is in a way the cause of all that he and his companions used to see.

Clearly he would come at last to that conclusion.

Then if he called to mind his fellow prisoners and what passed for wisdom in his former dwelling-place, he would surely think himself happy in the change and be sorry for them. They may have had a practice of honouring and commending one another, with prizes for the man who had the keenest eye for the passing shadows and the best memory for the order in which they followed or accompanied one another, so that he could make a good guess as to which was going to come next.[28] Would our released prisoner be likely to covet those prizes or to envy the men exalted to honour and power in the Cave? Would he not feel like Homer's Achilles, that he would far sooner "be on earth as a hired servant in the house of a landless man"[29] or endure anything rather than go back to his old beliefs and live in the old way?

---

[26] The first effect of Socratic questioning is perplexity.

[27] Here is the moral—the need of habituation by mathematical study before discussing moral ideas and ascending through them to the Form of the Good.

[28] The empirical politician, with no philosophic insight, but only a "knack of remembering what usually happens" (*Gorg.* 501 A). He has *eikasia* = conjecture as to what is likely (*eikos*).

[29] This verse (already quoted at 386 C), being spoken by the ghost of Achilles, suggests that the Cave is comparable with Hades.

Yes, he would prefer any fate to such a life.

Now imagine what would happen if he went down again to take his former seat in the Cave. Coming suddenly out of the sunlight, his eyes would be filled with darkness. He might be required once more to deliver his opinion on those shadows, in competition with the prisoners who had never been released, while his eyesight was still dim and unsteady; and it might take some time to become used to the darkness. They would laugh at him and say that he had gone up only to come back with his sight ruined; it was worth no one's while even to attempt the ascent. If they could lay hands on the man who was trying to set them free and lead them up, they would kill him.[30]

Yes, they would.

Every feature in this parable, my dear Glaucon, is meant to fit our earlier analysis. The prison dwelling corresponds to the region revealed to us through the sense of sight, and the firelight within it to the power of the Sun. The ascent to see the things in the upper world you may take as standing for the upward journey of the soul into the region of the intelligible; then you will be in possession of what I surmise, since that is what you wish to be told. Heaven knows whether it is true; but this, at any rate, is how it appears to me. In the world of knowledge, the last thing to be perceived and only with great difficulty is the essential Form of Goodness. Once it is perceived, the conclusion must follow that, for all things, this is the cause of whatever is

right and good; in the visible world it gives birth to light and to the lord of light, while it is itself sovereign in the intelligible world and the parent of intelligence and truth. Without having had a vision of this Form no one can act with wisdom, either in his own life or in matters of state.

So far as I can understand, I share your belief.

Then you may also agree that it is no wonder if those who have reached this height are reluctant to manage the affairs of men. Their souls long to spend all their time in that upper world — naturally enough, if here once more our parable holds true. Nor, again, is it at all strange that one who comes from the contemplation of divine things to the miseries of human life should appear awkward and ridiculous when, with eyes still dazed and not yet accustomed to the darkness, he is compelled, in a law-court or elsewhere, to dispute about the shadows of justice or the images that cast those shadows, and to wrangle over the notions of what is right in the minds of men who have never beheld Justice itself.[31]

It is not at all strange.

No; a sensible man will remember that the eyes may be confused in two ways — by a change from light to darkness or from darkness to light; and he will recognize that the same thing happens to the soul. When he sees it troubled and unable to discern anything clearly, instead of laughing thought-

[30] An allusion to the fate of Socrates.

[31] In the *Gorgias* 486 A, Callicles, forecasting the trial of Socrates, taunts him with the philosopher's inability to defend himself in a court.

lessly, he will ask whether, coming from a brighter existence, its unaccustomed vision is obscured by the darkness, in which case he will think its condition enviable and its life a happy one; or whether, emerging from the depths of ignorance, it is dazzled by excess of light. If so, he will rather feel sorry for it; or, if he were inclined to laugh, that would be less ridiculous than to laugh at the soul which has come down from the light.

That is a fair statement.

If this is true, then, we must conclude that education is not what it is said to be by some, who profess to put knowledge into a soul which does not possess it, as if they could put sight into blind eyes. On the contrary, our own account signifies that the soul of every man does possess the power of learning the truth and the organ to see it with; and that, just as one might have to turn the whole body round in order that the eye should see light instead of darkness, so the entire soul must be turned away from this changing world, until its eye can bear to contemplate reality and that supreme splendour which we have called the Good. Hence there may well be an art whose aim would be to effect this very thing, the conversion of the soul, in the readiest way; not to put the power of sight into the soul's eye, which already has it, but to ensure that, instead of looking in the wrong direction, it is turned the way it ought to be.

Yes, it may well be so.

It looks, then, as though wisdom were different from those ordinary virtues, as they are called, which are not far removed from bodily qualities, in that they can be produced by habituation and exercise in a soul which has not possessed them from the first. Wisdom, it seems, is certainly the virtue of some diviner faculty, which never loses its power, though its use for good or harm depends on the direction towards which it is turned. You must have noticed in dishonest men with a reputation for sagacity the shrewd glance of a narrow intelligence piercing the objects to which it is directed. There is nothing wrong with their power of vision, but it has been forced into the service of evil, so that the keener its sight, the more harm it works.

Quite true.

And yet if the growth of a nature like this had been pruned from earliest childhood, cleared of those clinging overgrowths which come of gluttony and all luxurious pleasure and, like leaden weights charged with affinity to this mortal world, hang upon the soul, bending its vision downwards; if, freed from these, the soul were turned round towards true reality, then this same power in these very men would see the truth as keenly as the objects it is turned to now.

Yes, very likely.

Is it not also likely, or indeed certain after what has been said, that a state can never be properly governed either by the uneducated who know nothing of truth or by men who are allowed to spend all their days in the pursuit of culture? The ignorant have no single mark before their eyes at which they must aim in all the conduct of their own lives and of affairs of state; and the others will not engage in action if they can help it, dreaming that, while still alive, they have been translated to the Islands of the Blest.

Quite true.

It is for us, then, as founders of a commonwealth, to bring compulsion to bear on the noblest natures. They must be made to climb the ascent to the vision of Goodness, which we called the highest object of knowledge; and, when they have looked upon it long enough, they must not be allowed, as they now are, to remain on the heights, refusing to come down again to the prisoners or to take any part in their labours and rewards, however much or little these may be worth.

Shall we not be doing them an injustice, if we force on them a worse life than they might have?

You have forgotten again, my friend, that the law is not concerned to make any one class specially happy, but to ensure the welfare of the commonwealth as a whole. By persuasion or constraint it will unite the citizens in harmony, making them share whatever benefits each class can contribute to the common good; and its purpose in forming men of that spirit was not that each should be left to go his own way, but that they should be instrumental in binding the community into one.

You will see, then, Glaucon, that there will be no real injustice in compelling our philosophers to watch over and care for the other citizens. We can fairly tell them that their compeers in other states may quite reasonably refuse to collaborate: there they have sprung up, like a self-sown plant, in despite of their country's institutions; no one has fostered their growth, and they cannot be expected to show gratitude for a care they have never received. "But," we shall say, "it is not so with you. We have brought you into existence for your country's sake as well as for your own, to be like leaders and king-bees in a hive; you have been better and more thoroughly educated than those others and hence you are more capable of playing your part both as men of thought and as men of action. You must go down, then, each in his turn, to live with the rest and let your eyes grow accustomed to the darkness. You will then see a thousand times better than those who live there always; you will recognize every image for what it is and know what it represents, because you have seen justice, beauty, and goodness in their reality; and so you and we shall find life in our commonwealth no mere dream, as it is in most existing states, where men live fighting one another about shadows and quarrelling for power, as if that were a great prize; whereas in truth government can be at its best and free from dissension only where the destined rulers are least desirous of holding office."

Quite true.

Then will our pupils refuse to listen and to take their turns at sharing in the work of the community, though they may live together for most of their time in a purer air?

No; it is a fair demand, and they are fair-minded men. No doubt, unlike any ruler of the present day, they will think of holding power as an unavoidable necessity.

Yes, my friend; for the truth is that you can have a well-governed society only if you can discover for your future rulers a better way of life than being in office; then only will power be in the hands of men who are rich, not in gold, but in the wealth that brings happiness, a good and wise life. All goes wrong when, starved for lack of anything good in their lives, men turn to public affairs hoping to snatch from thence the happiness they hunger for. They set about fighting for power, and this internecine conflict ruins them and their country. The life of true philosophy is the only one that looks down upon offices of state; and access to power must be confined to men who are not in love with it; otherwise rivals will start fighting. So whom else can you compel to undertake the guardianship of the commonwealth, if not those who, besides understanding best the principles of government, enjoy a nobler life than the politician's and look for rewards of a different kind?

There is indeed no other choice.

COMMENT

The Means of Achieving the Ideal

Since the foregoing excerpts from the *Republic* state Plato's ideal as well as his philosophical premises, I need to add, to complete the exposition, only a few remarks about the way in which he believed the idea could be implemented.

If the Guardians are to be wise, they must be very carefully bred, selected, reared, and educated. The biological fitness of the ruling class should be guaranteed by a comprehensive program of eugenics; the most select parents should be induced to have the greatest number of children. Even more important is education, which Plato regards as the main foundation of the state.

He conceives education as a journey of the mind from the concrete practicalities of sensory experience to the external and abstract realities of the intellect. It begins with the arts and gymnastics and mounts upward through mathematics, astronomy, and harmonics (the mathematical theory of musical form) to philosophy. The preliminary education continues until about the age of eighteen; then follows two years of military training, for males and females alike. The Guardians are then provisionally selected by "ordeals of toil and pain," and only those who manifest the proper character and intelligence will receive the highest training. The program of mathematical and scientific training will occupy the prospective Guardians from the age of twenty to thirty, and they will then have intensive training in philosophy ("dialectics") for five additional years, or until they have "grasped by pure intelligence the very nature of Goodness itself." The students who have distinguished themselves throughout this long and arduous training will serve a political apprenticeship for about fifteen years, discharging the subordinate functions "suitable to the young." Finally, those who have fully proved their mettle, both men and women, will be selected at the age of fifty to fulfill the high function of philosopher-kings. Others, fit to be soldiers but incapable of the highest intellectual flights, remain Auxiliaries; and the great mass of the people, as members of the producing class, receive the lesser education appropriate to their station.

Every precaution should be taken to ward off temptations and keep the Guardians and Auxiliaries faithful to the state. The chief temptations arise from private interests. The competitive struggle for property, Plato believes, is incompatible with full devotion to the social good. Hence he proposes that the Guardians and Auxiliaries should have no private possessions or acquisitive occupations and that they should receive their maintenance from the state. This proposal is not the same as modern communism since it applies only to the Auxiliaries and Guardians and not to the producers, who constitute the bulk of the population.

Plato also believes that normal marriage and family life are incompatible with wholehearted devotion to the state since there is always a temptation to prefer family interests to community welfare. Hence he proposes to abolish private homes and monogamous marriage among the Guardians and Auxiliaries. They should live and share their meals together, realizing the principle that "friends have all things in common." Sexual intercourse should be strictly controlled in the interests of the eugenics program.

Such is the pattern of the aristocratic state. But even the "best" of states may decay, and Plato imaginatively sketches, in a section here omitted, the decline of the state through successive stages of timocracy — the rule of the military class; oligarchy — the rule of the wealthy; democracy — the rule of the many; and tyranny — the rule of the irresponsible dictator. Finally, he discusses art and rewards and punishments after death, but these topics do not now concern us.

Some Main Issues

No one will agree with all of the details of Plato's argument, but even when we least agree we can find his ides challenging. Among the principal issues that he presents are the following:

1. FORCE VERSUS MORALITY. In Books I and II of the *Republic*, Plato raises one of the basic issues in political philosophy — the question of whether force or morality is the foundation of the state. Against Thrasymachus, Socrates (as a character in the dialogue) argues that the authority of the ruler is morally based on right rather than might. In reply to

Glaucon and Adeimantus, he maintains that social obligation is based on duty rather than selfish expediency. The policies of the state, he insists, should conform to the pattern of the Good, which wise persons, long disciplined by education, can alone discern. He distinguishes between *opinion* and *knowledge* about goodness and maintains that genuine knowledge requires an intellectual grasp of *forms*. The form is the universal essence that is somehow exemplified in particular instances. All beautiful things, for example, exemplify the form of beauty, and all just acts and institutions exemplify the form of justice.

According to Plato, these forms or universals are real, but they exist in their full and essential reality apart from particular things. The perfection, unity, and eternality of the forms separate them from the imperfection, multiplicity, and impermanence of particular things. The sensible nature of the thing declares itself as relative and contingent and points to the imperishable essence that is connected with it and yet independent of it—a form free from limitation, change, defilement. The nature of this superreality is hard to define—Plato appears to have struggled with the problem throughout his whole philosophical career. In the *Phaedo*, the particulars are said to "participate" in the forms, or the forms are said to be "present" in the particulars. Elsewhere in Plato's dialogues the individual things are said to "imitate" the forms or to be related as an imperfect "copy" to a pattern or archetype. But all such language is metaphorical, and the essential truth is that the universal somehow transcends the particulars. In the *Republic*, this is taken to mean that the pattern of the ideal state is eternal and hence exempt from the relativities of power politics and shifting expediency.

Whether Plato's theory—or any doctrine of eternal and objective universals—is sound has been one of the principal questions of philosophy from his day until the present. It is possible to agree with him that universals are real and yet to differ from him in holding that they are immanent in particulars rather than separate and transcendent. "Justice" really exists, but in particular instances—not in "a heaven above the heavens" or as a separate, eternal essence. The "form," in this sense, is simply the characteristic common to all members of the class of things (in this case, the class of just things). The human mind has the power to notice resemblances and to abstract (that is, mentally to extricate) the common characteristics. Thus, universals can be said to consist, on the one hand, of common properties in things, and on the other hand, of concepts that represent these properties. This theory of real but immanent universals is the doctrine of Aristotle, and it serves as well as Plato's theory as an alternative to moral relativism. What is required is that moral concepts must conform to real, objective distinctions, and on this point Plato and Aristotle agree.

2.   THE "CLOSED" VERSUS THE "OPEN" SOCIETY. With his vision fixed on eternal forms, Plato wishes, after a fundamental revolution in human affairs, to arrest history and preserve the ideal state in its static perfection. As means to this end, he proposes rigorous censorship of the arts and religion; the use of myths and "noble lies" to reconcile the lower classes to their subordinate status; and the regulation of all details of social life, including marriage and the ownership of property, among the Guardians and Auxiliaries. In effect, he insists on a tight, "closed" unity of the body politic.

This emphasis on a static unity is related to his organic theory of the state. Plato maintains that the state is the human soul writ large, just as the soul is the state writ small. There is some question of how literally we should understand this doctrine, but it seems to imply that the state, like the individual personality, is an organism — that is, a living being with a life and worth of its own. Individuals appear mainly to derive their character and value from their relation to this organic whole. This sort of ethical organicism receives its most express and elaborate expression in the social philosophy of Hegel, but it is foreshadowed in the *Republic*.

The contrasting ideal of an "open" society — in which the freedom and intrinsic value of the individual are primarily emphasized — was eloquently formulated by John Stuart Mill in *On Liberty* (see Chapter 23). Both Mill and Plato, in a sense, maintain an ethics of self-realization, but Plato contends that the private interest of the individual is at one with the interest of the state, whereas Mill is distrustful of the state and believes that self-realization lies in the cultivation of individuality.

We can roughly divide political philosophers into two schools of thought corresponding to their positions on this issue. In one camp are the organic theorists — Plato, Rousseau, Hegel, and Marx — who stress the importance of the general will and the value and significance of collective processes. In the other group are the individualistic theorists — Hume, Bentham, Mill, and Jefferson — who disbelieve in the organic nature of society and regard social institutions as means to the happiness of individuals. The dispute between these two schools of thought is perhaps the most important conflict in the whole of political philosophy.

3.   ARISTOCRACY VERSUS DEMOCRACY. The basic tenet of Plato's social philosophy, as we have seen, is that philosopher-kings should rule. This conviction is consistent with his general attitude toward life: He habitually prefers the choice goods to the common goods. Hence he ranks democracy, whose slogan is "equality," as fourth in his classification of five types of government, superior only to tyranny and inferior to aristocracy, timocracy, and oligarchy. The typical democrat seems to him an

ill-educated and superficial fellow who wishes to drag all excellent things down to the mediocre level of the average.

The democrat might reply that philosopher-kings are difficult to find or to produce and that a government *of* the few is almost certain to be a government *for* the few. No one can be trusted with irresponsible power, not even the so-called wise. It is the wearer of the shoe who knows where it pinches, and consequently we cannot allow the few aristocrats to choose our shoes for us. If the state exacts duties of its citizens, moreover, it should grant them rights — for responsibility implies freedom. It is only by living as free people — by participating in government and exercising self-rule — that we cease to be mere imitators and become fully developed human beings. With such arguments, the democrat might answer Plato.

If we democrats and liberals are sensible, however, we will not indiscriminately reject the whole of Plato's social philosophy. We need experts in our government and wisdom in our lives. We should adapt to our own ends Plato's great ideal of a state based on education, and we should seek to reconcile the aristocratic ideal of excellence with the democratic ideal of sharing. Our goal should be a culture both high in attainment and broad in terms of democratic participation.

21

Peace and Security

"The essence of the commonwealth . . . is one person, of whose acts a great multitude, by mutual covenants one with another, have made themselves every one the author, to the end he may use the strength and means of them all, as he shall think expedient, for their peace and common defence."

Thomas Hobbes

THOMAS HOBBES (1588–1679)

Hobbes was the son of a poor and ignorant country parson who could scarcely read the church prayers. A precocious lad, he attracted the attention of his schoolmaster by translating the Greek text of Euripides' *Medea* into Latin verse. At fifteen he entered Oxford, the cost of his education being paid by his uncle, a prosperous tradesman. He found the university instruction still dominated by medieval logic and Aristotelian philosophy, and most of the students "debauched to drunkenness, wantonness, gaming, and other vices." After taking his degree, he became tutor and then secretary to William Cavendish, later the second Earl of Devonshire. This connection with the influential Cavendish family was to last, with some interruptions, for the remainder of his life. It opened the door to cultivated society, and Hobbes became acquainted with Bacon, Harvey, and other distinguished men. His secretarial duties were light, and he found ample leisure for scholarly pursuits, which included a translation of Thucydides, published in 1628. He also accompanied his master on trips to the Continent, where he met Galileo in Florence and Mersenne, Gassendi, and other French philosophers in Paris.

In 1637 he returned to England, resolved to write philosophy and study politics. At the ripe age of fifty-two he published he first original book, a volume entitled *The Elements of Law Natural and Politic*. Meanwhile the civil wars were brewing, and Hobbes, finding his ideas sharply attacked, took alarm and fled to France. He spent the next eleven years in Paris, while insurrection and civil war raged in England. During this period he engaged in controversy with Descartes; wrote a second political treatise, *De Cive*; and served briefly as tutor to the Prince of Wales, later Charles II. In 1651 he published his greatest work, *Leviathan*, a plea for materialism and political absolutism. This book offended the Republicans for its defense of absolutism, the Royalists for its scorn of the divine right of kings, and the clergy for its championship of the state over the Church. Finding himself unpopular among the exiles in Paris, Hobbes returned to England and submitted to Cromwell.

Hobbes now devoted himself to philosophy, expounding his materialistic metaphysics in *De Corpore* (1655). He also engaged in furious controversy with his critics, not always creditably. In 1660 the Stuarts were restored, with Hobbes' former student and friend, now Charles II, on the throne. Despite his friendship with the king, however, his public reputation was that of an atheist and blasphemer, and the House of Commons considered the advisability of ordering a public burning of his books. Since he could not obtain leave in England to publish works on controversial subjects, his *Behemoth: The History of the Causes of the Civil Wars of England* (1688) had to be published abroad. By this time he was old in years but indefatigable in spirit, singing by night and playing tennis by day, as intellectually keen as he was physically vigorous. At eighty-four he wrote an autobiography in Latin verse, and in the next few years translated the whole of Homer's *Iliad* and *Odyssey*. He died in his boots at the age of ninety-one, struck by apoplexy.

From *Leviathan*

CHAPTER XIII

Of the Natural Condition of Mankind as Concerning Their Felicity, and Misery

Nature hath made men so equal, in the faculties of the body and mind; as that, though there be found one man sometimes manifestly stronger in body or of quicker mind than another, yet when all is reckoned together, the difference between man and man is not so considerable, as that one man can thereupon claim to himself any benefit, to which another may not pretend as well as he. For as to the strength of body, the weakest has strength enough to kill the strongest, either by secret machination, or by confederacy with others that are in the same danger with himself.

And as to the faculties of the mind —setting aside the arts grounded upon words, and especially that skill of proceeding upon general and infallible rules, called science; which very few have, and but in few things; as being not a native faculty, born with us; nor attained, as prudence, while we look after somewhat else—I find yet a greater equality amongst men, than that of strength. For prudence is but experience, which equal time equally bestows on all men, in those things they equally apply themselves unto. That which may perhaps make such equality incredible, is but a vain conceit of one's own wisdom, which almost all men think they have in a greater degree than the vulgar; that is, than all men but themselves, and a few others, whom by fame, or for concurring with themselves, they approve. For such is the nature of men, that howsoever they may acknowledge many others to be more witty, or more eloquent, or more learned, yet they will hardly believe there be many so wise as themselves; for they see their own wit at hand, and other men's at a distance. But this proveth rather than men are in that point equal, than unequal. For there is not ordinarily a greater sign of the equal distribution of anything, than that every man is contented with his share.

From this equality of ability, ariseth equality of hope in the attaining of our ends. And therefore if any two men desire the same thing, which nevertheless they cannot both enjoy, they become enemies; and in the way to their end, which is principally their own conservation, and sometimes their delectation only, endeavor to destroy, or subdue one another. And from hence it comes to pass that where an invader hath no more to fear than another man's single power; if one plant, sow, build, or possess a convenient seat, others may probably be expected to come prepared with forces united, to dispossess and deprive him, not only of the fruit of his labor, but also of his life or liberty. And the invader again is in the like danger of another.

And from this diffidence of one another, there is no way for any man to secure himself so reasonable as anticipation; that is, by force or wiles to master the persons of all men he can, so long, till he see no other power great enough to endanger him: and this is no more than his own conservation requireth, and is generally allowed. Also because there be some, that taking pleasure in contemplating their own power in the acts of conquest, which they pursue farther than their security requires; if others, that otherwise would be glad to be at ease within modest bounds, should not by invasion increase their power, they would not be able long time, by standing only on their defence, to subsist. And by consequence, such augmentation of dominion over men being necessary to a man's conservation, it ought to be allowed him.

Again, men have no pleasure, but on the contrary a great deal of grief, in keeping company, where there is no power able to overawe them all. For every man looketh that his companion should value him at the same rate he sets upon himself; and upon all signs of contempt, or undervaluing, naturally endeavors, as far as he dares (which amongst them that have no common power to keep them in quiet, is far enough to make them destroy each other), to extort a greater value from his contemners by damage, and from others by the example.

So that in the nature of man, we find three principal causes of quarrel. First, competition; second, diffidence; thirdly, glory.

The first maketh men invade for gain; the second, for safety; and the third, for reputation. The first use violence to make themselves masters of other men's persons, wives, children, and cattle; the second, to defend them; the third, for trifles, as a word, a smile, a different opinion, and any other sign of undervalue, either direct in their persons, or by reflection in their kindred, their friends, their nation, their profession, or their name.

Hereby it is manifest that during the time men live without a common power to keep them all in awe, they are in that condition which is called war; and such a war as is of every man against every man. For *war* consisteth not in battle only, or the act of fighting, but in a tract of time wherein the will to contend by battle is sufficiently known, and therefore the notion of *time* is to be considered in the nature of war, as it is in the nature of weather. For as the nature of foul weather lieth not in a shower or two of rain, but in an inclination thereto of many days together; so the nature of war consisteth not in actual fighting, but in the known disposition thereto, during all the time there is no assurance to the contrary. All other time is *peace*.

Whatsoever therefore is consequent to a time of war, where every man is enemy to every man; the same is consequent to the time, wherein men live without other security than what their own strength and their own invention shall furnish them withal. In such condition there is no place for industry, because the fruit thereof is uncertain: and consequently no culture of the earth; no navigation, nor use of the commodities that may be imported by sea; no commodious building; no instruments of moving, and removing, such things as require much force; no knowledge of the face of the earth; no account of time; no arts; no letters; no society; and which is worst of all, continual fear, and danger of violent death; and the life of man, solitary, poor, nasty, brutish, and short.

It may seem strange to some man that has not well weighed these things, that nature should thus dissociate, and render men apt to invade and destroy one another; and he may therefore, not trusting to this inference, made from the passions, desire perhaps to have the same confirmed by experience. Let him therefore consider with himself, when taking a journey, he arms himself and seeks to go well accompanied; when going to sleep, he locks his doors; when even in his house he locks his chests; and this when he knows there be laws, and public officers, armed, to revenge all injuries shall be done him: what opinion he has of his fellow-subjects, when he rides armed; of his fellow citizens, when he locks his doors; and of his children, and servants, when he locks his chests. Does he not there as much accuse mankind by his actions, as I do by my words? But neither of us accuse man's nature in it. The desires, and other passions of man, are in themselves no sin. No more are the actions that proceed from those passions, till they know a law that forbids them: which till laws be made they cannot know; nor can any law be made, till they have agreed upon the person that shall make it.

It may preadventure be thought, there was never such a time nor condition of war as this; and I believe it was never generally so, over all the world: but there are many places where they live so now. For the savage people in many places of America, except the government of small families, the concord whereof dependeth on natural lust, have no government at all; and live at this day in that brutish manner, as I said before. Howsoever, it may be perceived what manner of life there would be, where there were no common power to fear; by the manner of life which men that have formerly lived under a peaceful government, use to degenerate into in a civil war.

But though there had never been any time wherein particular men were in a condition of war one against another; yet in all times kings and persons of sovereign authority, because of their independency, are in continual jealousies, and in the state and posture of gladiators; having their weapons pointing, and their eyes fixed on one another; that is, their forts, garrisons, and guns upon the frontiers of their kingdoms; and continual spies upon their neighbors; which is a posture of war. But because they uphold thereby the industry of their subjects, there does not follow from it that misery which accompanies the liberty of particular men.

To this war of every man against every man, this also is consequent: *that nothing can be unjust*. The notions of right and wrong, justice and injustice, have there no place. Where there is no common power, there is no law; where no law, no injustice. Force and fraud are in war the two cardinal virtues. Justice and injustice are none of the faculties neither of the body nor mind. If they were, they might be in a man that were alone in the world, as well as his senses and passions. They are qualities that relate to men in society, not in solitude. It is consequent also to the same condition, that there be no propriety, no dominion, no *mine* and *thine* distinct; but only that to be every man's, that he can get; and for so long as he can keep it. And thus much for the ill condition which man by mere nature is actually placed in; though with a possibility to come out of it, consisting partly in the passions, partly in his reason.

The passions that incline man to peace are fear of death, desire of such things as are necessary to commodious living, and a hope by their industry to obtain them. And reason suggesteth convenient articles of peace, upon which men may be drawn to agreement. These articles are they which otherwise are called the Laws of Nature; whereof I shall speak more particularly in the two following chapters.

CHAPTER XIV

Of the First and Second Natural Laws, and of Contracts

The right of nature, which writers commonly call *jus naturale*, is the liberty each man hath to use his own power, as he will himself, for the preservation of his own nature; that is to say, of his own life; and consequently, of doing anything, which in his own judgment and reason, he shall conceive to be the aptest means thereunto.

By *liberty*, is understood, according to the proper signification of the word, the absence of external impediments:

which impediments, may oft take away part of a man's power to do what he would; but cannot hinder him from using the power left him, according as his judgment, and reason shall dictate to him.

A *law of nature, lex naturalis*, is a precept or general rule, found out by reason, by which a man is forbidden to do that which is destructive of his life, or taketh away the means of preserving the same; and to omit that by which he thinketh it may be best preserved. For though they that speak of this subject, use to confound *jus* and *lex*, *right* and *law*; yet they ought to be distinguished: because *right* consisteth in liberty to do or to forbear, whereas *law* determineth and bindeth to one of them; so that law, and right differ as much as obligation and liberty; which in one and the same matter are inconsistent.

And because the condition of man, as hath been declared in the precedent chapter, is a condition of war of everyone against everyone; in which case everyone is governed by his own reason, and there is nothing he can make use of that may not be a help unto him in preserving his life against his enemies: it followeth, that in such a condition every man has a right to everything; even to one another's body. And therefore, as long as this natural right of every man to everything endureth, there can be no security to any man, how strong or wise soever he be, of living out the time which nature ordinarily alloweth men to live. And consequently it is a precept, or general rule of reason, *that every man ought to endeavor peace, as far as he has hope of obtaining it; and when he cannot ob-*

tain it, *that he may seek and use all helps and advantages of war*. The first branch of which rule containeth the first and fundamental law of nature; which is, *to seek peace and follow it*. The second, the sum of the right of nature; which is, *by all means we can, to defend ourselves*.

From this fundamental law of nature, by which men are commanded to endeavor peace, is derived this second law: *that a man be willing, when others are so too, as far forth as for peace and defence of himself he shall think it necessary, to lay down this right to all things; and be contented with so much liberty against other men, as he would allow other men against himself*. For as long as every man holdeth this right, of doing anything he liketh, so long are all men in the condition of war. But if other men will not lay down their right, as well as he, then there is no reason for anyone to divest himself of his: for that were to expose himself to prey, which no man is bound to, rather than to dispose himself to peace. . . .

Whensoever a man transferreth his right, or renounceth it; it is either in consideration of some right reciprocally transferred to himself, or for some other good he hopeth for thereby. For it is a voluntary act; and of the voluntary acts of every man, the object is some *good to himself*. And therefore there be some rights which no man can be understood by any words, or other signs, to have abandoned or transferred. As first a man cannot lay down the right of resisting them that assault him by force, to take away his life; because he cannot be understood to aim thereby, at any good to himself. The same may be said of wounds, and chains, and imprisonment: both because there is no benefit consequent to such patience, as there is to the patience of suffering another to be wounded or imprisoned; as also because a man cannot tell, when he seeth men proceed against him by violence, whether they intend his death or not. And lastly the motive, an end for which this renouncing and transferring of right is introduced, is nothing else but the security of a man's person, in his life, and in the means of so preserving life as not to be weary of it. And therefore if a man by words, or other signs, seem to despoil himself of the end for which those signs were intended, he is not to be understood as if he meant it, or that it was his will, but that he was ignorant of how such words and actions were to be interpreted.

The mutual transferring of right, is that which men call *contract*.

CHAPTER XV

Of Other Laws of Nature

From that law of nature by which we are obliged to transfer to another such rights as, being retained, hinder the peace of mankind, there followeth a third; which is this, *that men perform their covenants made*: without which, covenants are in vain, and but empty words; and the right of all men to all things remaining, we are still in the condition of war.

And in this law of nature, consisteth the fountain and original of *justice*. For where no covenant hath preceded, there hath no right been transferred, and every man has right to everything; and consequently, no action can be unjust. But when a covenant is made, then to break it is *unjust;* and the definition of *injustice* is no other than *the not performance of covenant.* And whatsoever is not unjust, is *just.*

But because covenants of mutual trust, where there is a fear of not performance on either part, as hath been said in the former chapter, are invalid; though the original of justice be the making of covenants; yet injustice actually there can be none, till the cause of such fear be taken away; which while man are in the natural condition of war, cannot be done. Therefore before the names of just and unjust can have place, there must be some coercive power, to compel men equally to the performance of their covenants, by the terror of some punishment greater than the benefit they expect by the breach of their covenant; and to make good that propriety which by mutual contract men acquire, in recompense of the universal right they abandon: and such power there is none before the erection of a commonwealth. And this is also to be gathered out of the ordinary definition of justice in the Schools; for they say, that *justice is the constant will of giving to every man his own.* And therefore where there is no *own* that is no propriety, there is no injustice; and where is no coercive power erected, that is, where there is no commonwealth, there is no propriety; all men having right to all things: therefore where there is no commonwealth, there nothing is unjust. So that the nature of justice consisteth in keeping of valid covenants; but the validity of covenants begins not but with the constitu-

tion of a civil power sufficient to compel men to keep them, and then it is also that propriety begins. . . .

CHAPTER XVII

Of the Causes, Generation, and Definition of a Commonwealth

The final cause, end, or design of men who naturally love liberty and dominion over others, in the introduction of that restraint upon themselves in which we see them live in commonwealths, is the foresight of their own preservation, and of a more contented life thereby; that is to say, of getting themselves out from that miserable condition of war, which is necessarily consequent, as hath been shown in Chapter XIII, to the natural passions of men, when there is no visible power to keep them in awe, and tie them by fear of punishment to the performance of their covenants and observation of those laws of nature set down in the fourteenth and fifteenth chapters.

For the laws of nature, as justice, equity, modesty, mercy, and, in sum, *doing to others as we would be done to,* of themselves, without the terror of some power to cause them to be observed, are contrary to our natural passions, that carry us to partiality, pride, revenge, and the like. And covenants, without the sword, are but words, and of no strength to secure a man at all. Therefore notwithstanding the laws of nature, which everyone hath then kept, when he has the will to keep them when he can do it safely; if there be no power erected, or not great enough for our security, every man will, and may, lawfully rely on his own strength and art, for caution against all other men. And in all places where men have lived by small families, to rob and spoil one another has been a trade, and so far from being reputed against the law of nature, that the greater spoils they gained, the greater was their honor; and men observed no other laws therein but the laws of honor; that is, to abstain from cruelty, leaving to men their lives, and instruments of husbandry. And as small families did then; so now do cities and kingdoms, which are but greater families, for their own security enlarge their dominions, upon all pretences of danger and fear of invasion, or assistance that may be given to invaders, and endeavor as much as they can to subdue or weaken their neighbors, by open force and secret arts, for want of other caution, justly; and are remembered for it in after ages with honor.

Nor is it the joining together of a small number of men, that gives them this security; because in small numbers, small additions on the one side or the other make the advantage of strength so great, as is sufficient to carry the victory, and therefore gives encouragement to an invasion. The multitude sufficient to confide in for our security, is not determined by any certain number, but by comparison with the enemy we fear; and is then sufficient, when the odds of the enemy is not of so visible and conspicuous moment, to determine the event of war, as to move him to attempt.

And be there never so great a multitude, yet if their actions be directed according to their particular judgments and particular appetites, they can expect thereby no defence nor protection, neither against a common enemy nor against the injuries of one another. For being distracted in opinions concerning the best use and application of their strength, they do not help but hinder one another; and reduce their strength by mutual opposition to nothing: whereby they are easily, not only subdued by a very few that agree together; but also when there is no common enemy, they make war upon each other, for their particular interests. For if we could suppose a great multitude of men to consent in the observation of justice, and other laws of nature, without a common power to keep them all in awe, we might as well suppose all mankind to do the same; and then there neither would be, nor need to be any civil government or commonwealth at all, because there would be peace without subjection.

Nor is it enough for the security, which men desire should last all the time of their life, that they be governed and directed by one judgment for a limited time, as in one battle or one war. For though they obtain a victory by their unanimous endeavor against a foreign enemy; yet afterwards, when either they have no common enemy, or he that by one part is held for an enemy, is by another part held for a friend, they must needs by the difference of their interests dissolve, and fall again into a war amongst themselves.

It is true that certain living creatures, as bees and ants, live sociably one with another, which are therefore by Aristotle numbered amongst political creatures; and yet have no other direction than their particular judgments and appetites; nor speech, whereby one of them can signify to another what he thinks expedient for the common benefit: and therefore some man may perhaps desire to know why mankind cannot do the same. To which I answer:

First, that men are continually in competition for honor and dignity, which these creatures are not; and consequently amongst men there ariseth on that ground, envy and hatred, and finally war; but amongst these not so.

Secondly, that amongst these creatures, the common good differeth not from the private; and being by nature inclined to their private, they procure thereby the common benefit. But man, whose joy consisteth in comparing himself with other men, can relish nothing but what is eminent.

Thirdly, that these creatures, having not, as man, the use of reason, do not see, nor think they see, any fault in the administration of their common business; whereas amongst men, there are very many that think themselves wiser, and able to govern the public better, than the rest; and these strive to reform and innovate, one this way, another that way; and thereby bring it into distraction and civil war.

Fourthly, that these creatures, though they have some use of voice in making known to one another their desires and other affections; yet they want that art of words by which some men can represent to others, that which is good in the likeness of evil, and evil in the likeness of good, and augment or diminish the apparent greatness of good and evil; discontenting men and troubling their peace at their pleasure.

Fifthly, irrational creatures cannot distinguish between *injury* and *damage*; and therefore as long as they be at ease, they are not offended with their fellows: whereas man is then most troublesome when he is most at ease; for then it is that he loves to show his wisdom, and control the actions of them that govern the commonwealth.

Lastly, the agreement of these creatures is natural; that of men is by covenant only, which is artificial: and therefore it is no wonder if there be somewhat else required, besides covenant, to make their agreement constant and lasting; which is a common power, to keep them in awe, and to direct their actions to the common benefit.

The only way to erect such a common power, as may be able to defend them from the invasion of foreigners and the injuries of one another, and thereby to secure them in such sort as that, by their own industry, and by the fruits of the earth, they may nourish themselves and live contentedly; is, to confer all their power and strength upon one man, or upon one assembly of men, that may reduce all their wills, by plurality of voices, unto one will: which is as much as to say, to appoint one man, or assembly of men, to bear their person; and everyone to own and acknowledge himself to be author of whatsoever he that so beareth their person, shall act or cause to be acted in those things which concern the common peace and safety; and therein to submit their wills, everyone to his will, and their judgments, to his judgment. This is more than consent, or concord; it is a real unity of them all, in one and the same person, made by covenant of every man with every man, in such manner as if every man should say to every man, *"I authorize and give up my right of governing myself to this man, or to this assembly of men, on this condition, that thou give up thy right to him, and authorize all his actions in like manner."* This done, the multitude so united in one person, is called a *commonwealth*, in Latin *civitas*. This is the generation of that great LEVIATHAN, or rather, to speak more reverently, of that *mortal god*, to which we owe under the *immortal God*, our peace and defence. For by this authority, given him by every particular man in the commonwealth, he hath the use of so much power and strength conferred on him, that by terror thereof he is enabled to perform the wills of them all, to peace at home and mutual aid against their enemies abroad. And in him consisteth the essence of the commonwealth; which, to define it, is *one person, of whose acts a great multitude, by mutual covenants one with another, have made themselves every one the author, to the end he may use the strength and means of them all, as he shall think expedient, for their peace and common defence.*

And he that carrieth this person, is called *sovereign*, and said to have sovereign power; and everyone besides, his *subject*. . . .

COMMENT

The Premises of Hobbes' Argument

Hobbes was born prematurely, as the story goes, because his mother took fright at the near approach of the Spanish Armada. In commenting on the circumstances of his birth, he said, "Fear and I were twins." This remark, made in his old age, expresses his realization that fear had been a dominant motive in his life. His social philosophy is concerned primarily with the need for security.

He lived during the most unstable period of English history. Among the shifts and disturbances that occurred during his lifetime were the First Civil War between King and Parliament (1642–1645), the Second Civil War (1648), the rule of the "Rump Parliament" (1649–1653), Cromwell's dictatorship (1654–1658), and the Restoration of the Stuarts (1660). Hobbes' emphasis on security was a natural reaction to a period so unsettled.

This emphasis rested on several premises: (1) an interpretation of human nature, (2) an analysis of moral experience, and (3) a conception of the precivil condition of man.

1. *An interpretation of human nature.* Hobbes believed that a person is a kind of elaborate machine, whose "vital motions" are determined by

outward stimuli. If a stimulus is favorable to the machine's operations, it evokes *desire* or motion toward; if unfavorable, it evokes *aversion* or motion away from. More complex motives and emotions are all derived from these elementary reactions of advance or retreat. The emotions springing from desire, such as love and hope, are generally pleasant; the emotions springing from aversion, such as hate and fear, are unpleasant. If the effect is pleasant, the organism seeks to continue or renew the stimulus; if unpleasant, to avoid it. "The object of man's desire is not to enjoy once only, and for one instant of time; but to assure for ever the way of his future desire."[1] There is no lasting repose, no final breathing space, but only ceaseless pursuit of power. Power is defined as the "present means to obtain future, apparent good." Since the means are precarious, there is no limit to the power that men seek. "I put for a general inclination of all mankind," declares Hobbes, "a perpetual and restless desire of power after power, which ceases only in death."[2]

Motivated by egoistic concern for one's own power, each person tends to conflict with others. "If any two men desire the same thing, which they nevertheless cannot both enjoy, they become enemies and . . . endeavor to destroy or subdue one another."[3] The result would be a constant and intolerable war of each against all if it were not for the faculty of reason. By means of this faculty, we "acquire the knowledge of consequences, and dependence of one fact upon another."[4] Reason does not select the ends of action — these are determined by desire and aversion — but it reflects on the consequences of acts and judges how the ends can be most fully achieved. By its means, we escape from the suicidal anarchy that our predatory natures would force on us.

2. *An analysis of moral experience.* At the most primitive and pre-social level of human life, *good* simply means "whatsoever is the object of any man's appetite or desire," and *evil* means "the object of his hate and aversion."[5] Values are derived from human drives, and since the drives are invariably egoistic, good and evil are always relative to the individual.

> These words of good, evil, and contemptible are ever used with relation to the person that useth them: there being nothing simply and absolutely so; nor any common rule of good and evil to be taken from the nature of the objects themselves; but from the person of the man, where there is no commonwealth; or, in

[1]*Leviathan, XI.*
[2]Ibid.
[3]Ibid., XIII.
[4]Ibid., V.
[5]Ibid., VI.

> a commonwealth, from the person that representeth it; or from
> an arbitrator or judge, whom men disagreeing shall by consent
> set up, and make his sentence rule thereof.[6]

This quotation points to two levels of moral experience: the level *before* and the level *after* the creation of the commonwealth. *Before* there is no moral authority except the desires and aversions of the individual, whoever he or she be. But *after* the creation of the state, the ultimate moral authority is the sovereign or judicial arbitrator. The social concepts of law and justice arise only within the state.

In speaking of a precivil level of morality, Hobbes did not mean that he actually *finds* individuals at this level. He was pointing out the kind of morality they would have if they lacked civil institutions, and he was saying that the second or higher level of morality requires an organized political state.

3. *The precivil condition of humankind.* That "the state of nature" is a nasty condition of anarchy follows from Hobbes' analysis of human nature. Since everyone naturally preys upon one's fellows, the consequence is "such a war as is of every man against every man." It is easy to misunderstand Hobbes' meaning. "The state of nature" may never have existed; and whether it did or not does not really affect his argument. This is the state that *would* exist if people were wholly dominated by passions, without the restraint of reason and civil society. It is an analytical, not a historical, concept. Hobbes, in effect, was saying that we must permanently be on guard because the brutish state of nature would be our lot if we should abandon reason and destroy political sovereignty. It is an emphatic way of saying that the civil state is extremely necessary.

Natural Law and the Social Contract

The state of nature is haunted by "continual fear and danger of violent death," and reason therefore impels human beings to set up the coercive power of a central government, which alone can establish peace and security. The contrast between the condition of humankind *outside* and *in* a duly constituted state is sharply drawn.

> Out of it, any man may rightly spoil or kill another; in it, none
> but one. Out of it, we are protected by our own forces; in it, by
> the power of all. Out of it, no man is sure of the fruit of his
> labors; in it, all men are. Lastly, out of it, there is a dominion of
> passions, war, fear, poverty, slovenliness, solitude, barbarism,

[6]Ibid.

ignorance, cruelty; in it, the dominion of reason, peace, security, riches, decency, society, elegancy, sciences and benevolence.[7]

What is required to pass from the natural to the civil state is determined by "the laws of nature." These laws are the dictates of reason defining what needs to be done to safeguard life. They are "natural" in the sense that they are based on the instinct of self-preservation aided by reason. In substance these laws state that peace, cooperation, and the keeping of covenants are essential to survival, but that if these be lacking, it is rational to defend oneself with the most effective means available.

In conformity to natural law, reason impels individuals to escape from the lethal anarchy of the state of nature, and to set up, by mutual agreement, the civil state. Every individual must agree to live in peace in consideration of the like agreement of others. But human nature being what it is, mere agreement to live peaceably together is insufficient. For this reason, people must form a contract with one another to set up a common power "to keep them in awe, and to direct their actions to the Common Benefit."[8]

The idea of a "social contract" was not original with Hobbes. Its roots are to be found in ancient Greek philosophy, and it had become a commonplace in political theory by the time Hobbes wrote *Leviathan*. His account is distinguished by its sharp insistence that the conferring of absolute power on a sovereign is the only refuge from chronic war, which would break out again if ever the civil power should crumble. The power of the sovereign *is* absolute since no limiting conditions were stipulated when he or she received power. Indeed, no effective condition could have been stipulated since covenants are only words without the power of enforcement until the sovereign is established. According to this interpretation, the contract is not between citizen and ruler but between citizen and citizen — every citizen covenanting with every other to form a civil society *and to obey the government.*

The government is not necessarily a monarchy. Hobbes personally thought monarchy the safest and best type of government, but he recognized that the sovereign *might* be an assembly. There is nothing in his theory that presupposes a king or single ruler, provided that the sovereign group is sufficiently united to maintain authority.

It is sometimes said that the power conferred on the sovereign is irrevocable. This is a misinterpretation of Hobbes' theory. He insisted that the sovereign power must be undisputed as long as it is effective in keeping

[7] *De Cive*, ed. Sterling P. Lamprecht (New York: Appleton-Century-Crofts, 1949), p. 114.
[8] Op. cit., XVII.

the peace; but if the government does not in fact govern, if anarchy breaks out afresh, there is no longer reason for submission. The citizens are then thrown back on their natural resources for self-preservation and may rightly set up a new sovereign who can protect them.

The social contract, like the state of nature, should not be interpreted historically. Only in special circumstances do states originate by deliberate contract. The "social contract" is the *logical* basis of the state, which, as far as people are governed by reason, remains operative as a continuing tacit agreement. The function of this type of theory is to emphasize the activity of reason in devising, and the activity of will in instituting, the political community. Among democratic theorists, such as Locke, it is a way of insisting that legitimate government rests on the consent of the governed.

Application to International Politics

The clearest example of "the state of nature" is the relation of sovereign states to one another:

> . . . In all times, kings, and persons of sovereign authority, because of their independency, are in continual jealousies, and in the state and posture of gladiators; having their weapons pointing, and their eyes fixed on one another; that is, their forts, garrisons, and guns upon the frontiers of their kingdoms; and continual spies upon their neighbors; which is a posture of war.[9]

Hobbes remarked that this international anarchy does not occasion as much misery as anarchy among individuals.

Living in the seventeenth century, Hobbes could not foresee how powerfully his social philosophy would apply to international affairs in the second half of the twentieth century. We now know that a hydrogen bomb can obliterate a city like Moscow or New York in a trice, and that the fallout from such a bomb can destroy life over a vastly wider area. Competent authorities have declared that an atomic world war might so poison the earth's atmosphere as to cause universal death. Here is danger on a scale that Hobbes never even dreamed of.

The remedy for anarchy, as he clearly perceived, is the creation of government with power to enforce its decisions. It is not sufficient for nations to promise not to go to war with one another, for "covenants, without the sword, are but words."[10] A binding covenant must be a

[9] Ibid., XIII.
[10] Ibid., XVII.

surrender of sovereignty, whether of individuals or of nations, to some effective central authority.

The establishment of the United Nations was a step toward world government. The supreme question is whether this beginning can be transformed into an international authority with power to enforce the peace. The human race has now reached the point at which it must either abandon war and the dogma of unlimited national sovereignty or accept the possibility of universal annihilation. Hobbes' argument that we should obey the dictates of self-preservation applies today with terrific force.

Some Critical Remarks

The main defect of Hobbes' social philosophy is fairly obvious. His insistence on the necessity of coercive government is excessive because his account of human nature is too grim. Having described human beings as essentially selfish and predatory, he concluded that only fear and coercion could hold them in check. There is a vein of realism in this argument that should not be overlooked, but it does scant justice to the fraternal aspects of human life. The impulse to cooperate is as real as the impulse to compete; sympathy is as real as selfishness. Hobbes speaks as if rational self-interest alone impels individuals to unite in a political order, but it is at least as true to say, with Aristotle, that a human being is naturally a political animal.

Hobbes' one-sided characterization of human nature leads to a paradoxical theory of the state. At the same time that he demands unlimited power for his sovereign, he virtually limits the sovereign's functions to the safeguarding of life and limb. Thus his state is maximal in powers but minimal in functions. It may be instructive to compare Hobbes' view with that of Lincoln, who also lived during a period of civil strife. "The legitimate object of government," declared Lincoln, "is 'to do for the people what needs to be done, but which they cannot, by individual effort, do at all, or do so well, for themselves.'"[11] The emphasis is positive rather than negative — on the promotion of welfare rather than the suppression of antisocial impulses. Lincoln would limit the powers of the state but not its functions; Hobbes would limits its functions but not its powers.

He was so insistent on the unfettered power of the sovereign that he had no sympathy for a bill of rights or a system of constitutional checks. He did not recognize, as did Locke and Jefferson, that irresponsible absolute power corrupts absolutely or that the social contract should be a democratic instrument, based on the will and participation of the gov-

[11] Michael D. Oakeshott, *The Social and Political Doctrines of Contemporary Europe* (Cambridge: Cambridge University Press, 1939), p. 19.

erned. He conceived of law as the mere command of the rulers rather than as a body of principles limiting their arbitrary power and applying to sovereign and subjects alike.

The social-contract theory, as he developed it, is inadequate to explain the inner cohesion of society. Purely selfish interests, even though enlightened by reason, cannot provide social unity or generate a binding social contract. In opposition to Hobbes, Rousseau pointed out that there is a great difference between a real community of interests and a mere sum of selfish interests. He maintained that society must be "a moral, collective body," which essentially binds people together, their wills merged and transformed in a corporate will. His theory has defects of its own, but it lacks the particular defects of Hobbes' egoistic theory.

The strength of Hobbes' argument is most evident when we consider its application to international affairs. In the atomic age, the simple dictates of self-preservation demand an international authority with power to maintain peace. But even here the argument can easily be oversimplified — there are many causes of war besides political anarchy among nations. Poverty, imperialism, racial antagonism, and the conflict of ideologies — to mention only a few factors — are also productive of international strife. There is no single cause of war and no single remedy. We must act in many fields at once — political, economic, moral, religious, and philosophical — creating a real world community to give force and substance to international peace.

22

Social Contract

"Wherever, therefore, any number of men so unite into one society, as to quit every one his executive power of the law of nature, and to resign it to the public, there, and there only, is a political, or civil society . . . For thereby he authorizes the society . . . to make laws for him, as the public good of the society may require.

John Locke

JOHN LOCKE (1632–1704)

John Locke was born in England and raised according to strict Puritan discipline. In 1656 he completed his degree in Oxford and became a teacher of Latin and Greek. After his father's death in 1661, he took up the study of medicine as a result of his growing interest in the sciences. In 1667 Locke began an impressive career in politics, though for some years he was forced to live in exile in Holland. In addition to his very influential *Essay Concerning Human Understanding*, which is often regarded as the first work in psychology, Locke wrote a number of political essays and *Treatise on Civil Government*, from which the following pages have been selected. Locke's work in epistemology lay the foundations for the empiricism of Hume, even as his political writings provided much of the inspiration for the beliefs of Thomas Jefferson.

The Basis of Civil Society*

Of the State of Nature

To understand political power aright, and derive it from its original, we must consider what state all men are naturally in, and that is a state of perfect freedom to order their actions and dispose of their possessions and persons as they think fit, within the bounds of the law of nature, without asking leave, or depending upon the will of any other man.

A state also of equality, wherein all the power and jurisdiction is reciprocal, no one having more than another; there being nothing more evident than that creatures of the same species and rank, promiscuously born to all the same advantages of nature, and the use of the same faculties, should also be equal one amongst another without subordination or subjection, unless the Lord and Master of them all should by any manifest declaration of His will set one above another, and confer on him by an evident and clear appointment an undoubted right to dominion and sovereignty.

This quality of men by nature the judicious Hooker looks upon as so evident in itself and beyond all question, that he makes it the foundation of that obligation to mutual love amongst men on which he builds the duties they owe

Reprinted by permission of the publishers from *Treatise on Civil Government*, edited by C. K. Sherman (New York: Appleton-Century-Crofts, 1937).

on another, and from whence he derives the great maxims of justice and charity. His words are: —

"The like natural inducement hath brought men to know that it is no less their duty to love others than themselves; for seeing those things which are equal must needs all have one measure, if I cannot but wish to receive good, even as much at every man's hands as any man can wish unto his own soul, how should I look to have any part of my desire herein satisfied, unless myself be careful to satisfy the like desire, which is undoubtedly in other men weak, being of one and the same nature? To have anything offered them repugnant to this desire, must needs in all respects grieve them as much as me, so that, if I do harm, I must look to suffer, there being no reason that others should show greater measures of love to me than they have by me showed unto them. My desire, therefore, to be loved of my equals in nature as much as possible may be, imposeth upon me a natural duty of bearing to themward fully the like affection; from which relation of equality between ourselves and them that are as ourselves, what several rules and canons natural reason hath drawn for direction of life no man is ignorant." — "Eccl. Pol.," lib. I.

But though this be a state of liberty, yet it is not a state of licence; though man in that state have an uncontrollable liberty to dispose of his person or possessions, yet he has not liberty to destroy himself, or so much as any creature in his possession, but where some nobler use than its bare preservation calls for it. The state of nature has a law of nature to govern it, which obliges every one; and reason, which is that law, teaches all mankind who will but consult it, that, being all equal and independent, no one ought to harm another in his life, health, liberty, or possessions. For men being all the workmanship of one omnipotent and infinitely wise Maker — all the servants of one sovereign Master, sent into the world by His order, and about His business — they are His property, whose workmanship they are, made to last during His, not one another's pleasure; and being furnished with like faculties, sharing all in one community of nature, there cannot be supposed any such subordination among us, that may authorise us to destroy one another, as if we were made for one another's uses, as the inferior ranks of creatures are for ours. Every one, as he is bound to preserve himself, and not to quit his station wilfully, so, by the like reason, when his own preservation comes not in competition, ought he, as much as he can, to preserve the rest of mankind, and not, unless it be to do justice on an offender, take away or impair the life, or what tends to the preservation of the life, the liberty, health, limb, or goods of another.

And that all men may be restrained from invading others' rights, and from doing hurt to one another, and the law of nature be observed, which willeth the peace and preservation of all mankind, the execution of the law of nature is in that state put into every man's hand, whereby every one has a right to punish the transgressors of that law to such a degree as may hinder its violation. For the law of nature would, as all other laws that concern men in this world, be in vain if there were nobody that, in the state of nature, had a power to execute that law, and thereby preserve the innocent and restrain offenders. And if any one in the state of nature may punish another for any evil he has done, every one may do so. For in that state of perfect equality, where naturally there is no superiority or jurisdiction of one over another, what any may do in prosecution of that law, every one must needs have a right to do.

And thus in the state of nature one man comes by a power over another; but yet no absolute or arbitrary power, to use a criminal, when he has got him in his hands, according to the passionate heats or boundless extravagance of his own will; but only to retribute to him so far as calm reason and conscience dictate what is proportionate to his transgression, which is so much as may serve for reparation and restraint. For these two are the only reasons why one man may lawfully do harm to another, which is that we call punishment. In transgressing the law of nature, the offender declares himself to live by another rule than that of common reason and equity, which is that measure God has set to the actions of men, for their mutual security; and so he becomes dangerous to mankind, the tie which is to secure them from injury and violence being slighted and broken by him. Which, being a trespass against the whole species, and the peace and safety of it, provided for by the law of nature, every man upon this score, by the right he hath to preserve mankind in general, may restrain, or, where it is necessary, destroy things noxious to them, and so may bring such evil on any one who hath transgressed that law, as may make him repent the doing of it, and there-by deter him, and by his example others, from doing the like mischief. And in this case, and upon this ground, every man hath a right to punish the offender, and be executioner of the law of nature.

I doubt not but this will seem a very strange doctrine to some men; but before they condemn it, I desire them to resolve me by what right any prince or State can put to death or punish an alien, for any crime he commits in their country. 'Tis certain their laws, by virtue of any sanction they receive from the promulgated will of the legislature, reach not a stranger: they speak not to him, nor, if they did, is he bound to hearken to them. The Legislative authority, by which they are in force over the subjects of that commonwealth, hath no power over him. Those who have the supreme power of making laws in England, France, or Holland, are to an Indian but like the rest of the world—men without authority. And, therefore, if by the law of nature every man hath not a power to punish offences against it, as he soberly judges the case to require, I see not how the magistrates of any community can punish an alien of another country; since in reference to him they can have no more power than what every man naturally may have over another.

Besides the crime which consists in violating the law, and varying from the right rule of reason, whereby a man so far becomes degenerate, and declares himself to quit the principles of human nature, and to be a noxious creature, there is commonly injury done, and some person or other, some other man receives damage by his transgression, in which case he who hath received any damage, has, besides the right of punishment common to him with other men, a particular right to seek reparation from him that has done it. And any other person who finds it just, may also join with him that is injured, and assist him in recovering from the offender so much as may make satisfaction for the harm he has suffered.

From those two distinct rights—the one of punishing the crime, for restraint and preventing the like offence, which right of punishing is in everybody; the other of taking reparation, which belongs only to the injured party —comes it to pass that the magistrate, who by being magistrate hath the common right of punishing put into his hands, can often, where the public good demands not the execution of the law, remit the punishment of criminal offences by his own authority, but yet cannot remit the satisfaction due to any private man for the damage he has received. That he who has suffered the damage has a right to demand in his own name, and he alone can remit. The damnified person has this power of approaching to himself the goods or service of the offender, by right of self-preservation, as every man has a power to punish the crime, to prevent its being committed again, by the right he has of preserving all mankind, and doing all reasonable things he can in order to that end. And thus it is that every man in the state of nature has a power to kill a murderer, both to deter others from doing the like injury, which no reparation can compensate, by the example of the punishment that attends it from everybody, and also to secure men from the attempts of a criminal who having renounced reason, the common rule and measure God hath given to mankind, hath by the unjust violence and slaughter he hath committed upon one, declared war against all mankind, and therefore may be destroyed as a lion or a tiger, one of those wild savage beasts with whom men can have no society nor security. And upon this is grounded that great law of nature. "Whoso sheddeth man's blood, by man shall his blood be shed." And Cain was so fully convinced that every one had a right to destroy such a criminal, that after the murder of his brother he cries out, "Every one that findeth me shall slay me;" so plain was it writ in the hearts of mankind.

By the same reason may a man in the state of nature punish the lesser breaches of that law. It will perhaps be demanded, With death? I answer, each transgression may be punished to that degree, and with so much severity, as will suffice to make it an ill bargain to the offender, give him cause to repent, and terrify others from doing the like. Every offence that can be committed in the state of nature, may in the state of nature be also punished equally, and as far forth as it may, in a commonwealth. For though it would be beside my present purpose to enter here into the particulars of the law of nature, or its measures of punishment, yet it is certain there is such a law, and that, too, as intelligible and plain to a rational creature and a studier of that law as the positive laws of commonwealths; nay, possibly plainer, as much as reason is easier to be understood than the fancies and intricate contrivances of men, following contrary and hidden interests put into words; for truly so are a great part of the municipal laws of countries, which are only so far right as they are founded on the law of nature, by which they are to be regulated and interpreted.

To this strange doctrine — viz, That in the state of nature every one has the executive power of the law of nature — I doubt not but it will be objected that it is unreasonable for men to be judges in their own cases, that self-love will make men partial to themselves and their friends. And on the other side, that ill-nature, passion, and revenge will carry them too far in punishing others; and hence nothing but confusion and disorder will follow; and that therefore God hath certainly appointed government to restrain the partiality and violence of men. I easily grant that civil government is the proper remedy for the inconveniences of the state of nature, which must certainly be great where men may be judges in their own case, since 'tis easy to be imagined that he who was so unjust as to do his brother an injury, will scarce be so just as to condemn himself for it. But I shall desire those who make this objection, to remember that absolute monarchs are but men, and if government is to be the remedy of those evils which necessarily follow from men's being judges in their own cases, and the state of nature is therefore not to be endured, I desire to know what kind of government that is, and how much better it is than the state of nature, where one man commanding a multitude, has the liberty to be judge in his own case, and may do to all his subjects whatever he pleases, without the least question or control of those who execute his pleasure; and in whatsoever he doth, whether led by reason, mistake, or passion, must be submitted to, which men in the state of nature are not bound to do one to another? And if he that judges, judges amiss in his own or any other case, he is answerable for it to the rest of mankind.

'Tis often asked as a mighty objection, Where are, or ever were there, any men in such a state of nature? To which it may suffice as an answer at present: That since all princes and rulers of independent governments all through the world are in a state of nature, 'tis plain the world never was, nor ever will be, without numbers of men in that state. I have named all governors of independent communities, whether they are or are not in league with others. For 'tis not every compact that puts an end to the state of nature between men, but only this one of agreeing together mutually to enter into one community, and make one body politic; other promises and compacts men may make one with another, and yet still be in the state of nature. The promises and bargains for truck, etc., between the two men in Soldania, in or between a Swiss and an Indian, in the woods of America, are binding to them, though they are perfectly in a state of nature in reference to one another. For truth and

keeping of faith belong to men as men, and not as members of society.

To those that say there were never any men in the state of nature, I will not only oppose the authority of the judicious Hooker—"Eccl. Pol.," lib. i, sec. 10, where he says, "The laws which have been hitherto mentioned," *i.e.*, the laws of nature, "do bind men absolutely, even as they are men, although they have never any settled fellowship, and never any solemn agreement amongst themselves what to do or not to do; but forasmuch as we are not by ourselves sufficient to furnish ourselves with competent store of things needful for such a life as our nature doth desire—a life fit for the dignity of man—therefore to supply those defects and imperfections which are in us, as living single and solely by ourselves, we are naturally induced to seek communion and fellowship with others; this was the cause of men's uniting themselves at first in politic societies"—but I moreover affirm that all men are naturally in that state, and remain so, till by their own consents they make themselves members of some politic society; and I doubt not, in the sequel of this discourse, to make it very clear. . . .

Of Property . . .

God, who hath given the world to men in common, hath also given them reason to make use of it to the best advantage of life and convenience. The earth and all that is therein is given to men for the support and comfort of their being. And though all the fruits it naturally produces, and beasts it feeds, belong to mankind in common, as they are produced by the spontaneous hand of nature; and nobody has originally a private dominion exclusive of the rest of mankind in any of them as they are thus in their natural state; yet being given for the use of men, there must of necessity be a means to appropriate them some way or other before they can be of any use or at all beneficial to any particular man. The fruit or venison which nourishes the wild Indian, who knows no enclosure, and is still a tenant in common, must be his, and so his, *i.e.*, a part of him, that another can no longer have any right to it, before it can do any good for the support of his life.

Though the earth and all inferior creatures be common to all men, yet every man has a property in his own person; this nobody has any right to but himself. The labour of his body and the work of his hands we may say are properly his. Whatsoever, then, he removes out of the state that nature hath provided and left it in, he hath mixed his labour with, and joined to it something that is his own, and thereby makes it his property. It being by him removed from the common state nature placed it in, it hath by this labour something annexed to it that excludes the common right of other men. For this labour being the unquestionable property of the labourer, no man but he can have a right to what that is once joined to, at least where there is enough, and as good left in common for others. . . .

Of Political or Civil Society . . .

Man being born, as has been proved, with a title to perfect freedom, and an uncontrolled enjoyment of all the rights and privileges of the law of nature equally with any other man or number of men in the world, hath by nature a power not only to preserve his property—that is, his life, liberty, and estate—against the injuries and attempts of other men, but to judge of and punish the breaches of that law in others as he is persuaded the offence deserves, even with death itself, in crimes where the heinousness of the fact in his opinion requires it. But because no political society can be nor subsist without having in itself the power to preserve the property, and, in order thereunto, punish the offences of all those of that society, there, and there only, is political society, where every one of the members hath quitted this natural power, resigned it up into the hands of the community in all cases that exclude him not from appealing for protection to the law established by it; and thus all private judgment of every particular member being excluded, the community comes to be umpire; and by understanding indifferent rules and men authorized by the community for their execution, decides all the differences that may happen between any members of that society concerning any matter of right, and punishes those offences which any member hath committed against the society with such penalties as the law has established; whereby it is easy to discern who are and who are not in political society together. Those who are united into one body, and have a common established law and judicature to appeal to, with authority to decide controversies between them and punish offenders, are in civil society one with another; but those who have no such common appeal—I mean on earth—are still in the state of nature, each being, where there is no other, judge for himself and executioner, which is, as I have before shown it, the perfect state of nature.

And thus the commonwealth comes by a power to set down what punishment shall belong to the several transgressions which they think worthy of it committed amongst the members of that society, which is the power of making laws, as well as it has the power to punish any injury done unto any of its members by any one that is not of it, which is the power of war and peace; and all this for the preservation of the property of all the members of that society as far as is possible. But though every man entered into civil society, has acquitted his power to punish offences against the law of nature in prosecution of his own private judgment, yet with the judgment of offences, which he has given up to the legislature in all cases where he can appeal to the magistrate, he has given a right to the commonwealth to employ his force for the execution of the judgments of the commonwealth whenever he shall be called to it; which, indeed, are his own judgments, they being made by himself or his representative. And herein we have the original of the legislative and executive power of civil society, which is to judge by standing laws how far offences are to be punished when committed within the commonwealth, and also by occasional judgments founded on the present circumstances of the fact, how far injuries from without are to be vindicated; and in both these to employ all the force of all the members when there shall be need.

Wherever, therefore, any number of men so unite into one society, as to quit every one his executive power of the law of nature, and to resign it to the public, there, and there only, is a political, or civil society. And this is done wherever any number of men, in the state of nature, enter into society to make one people, one body politic, under one supreme government, or else when any one joins himself to, and incorporates with, any government already made. For thereby he authorises the society, or, which is all one, the legislative thereof, to make laws for him, as the public good of the society shall require, to the execution whereof his own assistance (as to his own decrees) is due. And this puts men out of a state of nature into that of a commonwealth, by setting up a judge on earth with authority to determine all the controversies and redress the injuries that may happen to any member of the commonwealth; which judge is the legislative, or magistrates appointed by it. And wherever there are any number of men, however associated, that have no such decisive power to appeal to, there they are still in the state of nature.

Hence it is evident that absolute monarchy, which by some men is counted the only government in the world, is indeed inconsistent with civil society, and so can be no form of civil government at all. For the end of civil society being to avoid and remedy those inconveniences of the state of nature which necessarily follow from every man's being judge in his own case, by setting up a known authority to which every one of that society may appeal upon any injury received or controversy that may arise, and which every one of the society ought to obey; wherever any persons are who have not such an authority to appeal to and decide any difference between them there, those persons are still in the state of nature. And so is every absolute prince, in respect of those who are under his dominion.

For he being supposed to have all, both legislative and executive power in himself alone, there is no judge to be found; no appeal lies open to any one who may fairly and indifferently and with authority decide, and from whence relief and redress may be expected of any injury or inconvenience that may be suffered from or by his order; so that such a man, however entitled — Czar, or Grand Seignior, or how you please — is as much in the state of nature, with all under his dominion, as he is with the rest of mankind. For wherever any two men are, who have no standing rule and common judge to appeal to on earth for the determination of controversies of right betwixt them, there they are still in the state of nature, and under all the inconveniences of it, with only this woeful difference to the subject, or rather slave, of an absolute prince: that, whereas in the ordinary state of nature he has a liberty to judge of his right, and according to the best of his power to maintain it, now, whenever his property is invaded by the will and order of his monarch, he has not only no appeal, as those in the society ought to have, but, as if he were degraded from the common state of rational creatures, is denied a liberty to judge of or to defend his right; and so is exposed to all the misery and inconveniences that a man can fear from one who, being in the unrestrained state of nature, is yet corrupted with flattery, and armed with power. . . .

Of the Ends of Political Society and Government . . .

The great and chief end, therefore, of men's uniting into commonwealths, and putting themselves under government, is the preservation of their property; to which in the state of nature there are many things wanting.

First, There wants an established, settled, known law, received and allowed by common consent to be the standard of right and wrong, and the common measure to decide all controversies between them. For though the law of nature be plain and intelligible to all rational creatures; yet men, being biased by their interest, as well as ignorant for want to study of it, are not apt to allow of it as a law binding to them in the application of it to their particular cases.

Secondly, In the state of nature there wants a known and indifferent judge, with authority to determine all differences according to the established law. For every one in that state, being both judge and executioner of the law of nature, men being partial to themselves, passion and revenge is very apt to carry them too far, and with too much heat in their own cases, as well as negligence and unconcernedness, to make them too remiss in other men's.

Thirdly, In the state of nature there often wants power to back and support the sentence when right, and to give it due execution. They who by any injustice offend, will seldom fail, where they are able by force to make good their injustice; such resistance many times makes the punishment dangerous, and frequently destructive to those who attempt it.

Thus mankind, notwithstanding all the privileges of the state of nature, being but in an ill condition, while they remain in it, are quickly driven into society. Hence it comes to pass that we seldom find any number of men live any time together in this state. . . .

Of the Extent of the Legislative Power

The great end of men's entering into society being the enjoyment of their properties in peace and safety, and the great instrument and means of that being the laws established in that society: the first and fundamental positive law of all commonwealths, is the establishing of the legislative power; as the first and fundamental natural law, which is to govern even the legislative itself, is the preservation of the society, and (as far as will consist with the public good) of every person in it. This legislative is not only the supreme power of the commonwealth, but sacred and unalterable in the hands where the community have once place it; nor can any edict of anybody else, in what form soever conceived, or by what power soever backed, have the force and obligation of a law, which has not its sanction from that legislative which the public has chosen and appointed. For without this the law could not have that, which is absolutely necessary to its being a law, the consent of the society over whom nobody can have a power to make laws; but by their own consent, and by authority received from them; and therefore all the obedience, which by the most solemn ties any one can be obliged to pay, ultimately terminates in this supreme power, and is directed by those laws which it enacts; nor can any oaths to any foreign power whatsoever, or any domestic subordinate power discharge any member of the society from his obedience to the legislative, acting pursuant to their trust; nor oblige him to any obedience contrary to the laws so enacted, or farther than they do allow; it being ridiculous to imagine one can be tied ultimately to obey any power in the society which is not the supreme.

Though the legislative, whether placed in one or more, whether it be always in being, or only by intervals, though it be the supreme power in every commonwealth, yet,

First, It is not nor can possibly be absolutely arbitrary over the lives and fortunes of the people. For it being but the joint power of every member of the society given up to that person, or assembly, which is legislator; it can be no more than those persons had in a state of nature before they entered into society, and gave it up to the community. For nobody can transfer to another more power than he has in himself; and nobody has an absolute arbitrary power over himself, or over any other to destroy his own life, or take away the life or property of another. A man as has been proved cannot subject himself to the arbitrary power of another; and having in the state of nature no arbitrary power over the life, liberty, or possession of another, but only so much as the law of nature gave him for the preservation of himself, and the rest of mankind; this is all he doth, or can give up to the commonwealth, and by it to the legislative power, so that the legislative can have no more than this. Their power in the utmost bounds of it, is limited to the public good of the society. It is a power that hath no other end but preservation, and therefore can never have a right to destroy, enslave, or designedly to impoverish the subjects. The obligations of the law of nature cease not in society, but only in many cases are drawn closer, and have by human laws known penalties annexed to them to enforce their observation. Thus the law of nature stands as an eternal rule to all men, legislators as well as others. The rules that they make for other men's actions must, as well as their own, and other men's actions be conformable to the law of nature, *i.e.* to the will of God, of which that is a declaration, and the fundamental law of nature being the preservation of mankind, no human sanction can be good or valid against it.

Secondly, The legislative, or supreme authority, cannot assume to itself a power to rule by extemporary arbitrary decrees, but is bound to dispense justice, and decide the rights of the subject by promulgated standing laws, and known authorised judges. For the law of nature being unwritten, and so nowhere to be found but in the minds of men, they who through passion or interest shall miscite or misapply it, cannot so easily be convinced of their mistake where there is no established judge. And so it serves not, as it ought, to determine the rights, and fence the properties of those that live under it, especially where every one is

judge, interpreter, and executioner of it too, and in his own case; and he that has right on his side, having ordinarily but his own single strength hath not force enough to defend himself from injuries, or punish delinquents. To avoid these inconveniences, which disorder men's properties in the state of nature, men unite into societies that they may have the united strength of the whole society to secure and defend their properties, and may have standing rules to bound it, by which every one may know what is his. To this end it is that men give up all their natural power to the society which they enter into, and the community put the legislative power into such hands as they think fit, with this trust, that they shall be governed by declared laws, or else their peace, quiet, and property, will still be at the same uncertainty as it was in the state of nature.

Absolute arbitrary power, or governing without settled standing laws, can neither of them consist with the ends of society and government, which men would not quit the freedom of the state of nature for, and tie themselves up under, were it not to preserve their lives, liberties, and fortunes; and by stated rules of right and property to secure their peace and quiet. It cannot be supposed that they should intend, had they a power so to do, to give to any one, or more, an absolute arbitrary power over their persons and estates, and put a force into the magistrate's hand to execute his unlimited will arbitrarily upon them. This were to put themselves into a worse condition than the state of nature, wherein they had a liberty to defend their right against the injuries of others, and were upon equal terms of force to maintain it, whether invaded by a single man or many in combination. Whereas, by supposing they have given up themselves to the absolute arbitrary power and will of a legislator, they have disarmed themselves, and armed him, to make prey of them when he pleases. He being in a much worse condition that is exposed to the arbitrary power of one man who has the command of 100,000 than he that is exposed to the arbitrary power of 100,000 single men; nobody being secure that his will, who hath such a command, is better than that of other men, though his force be 100,000 times stronger. And, therefore, whatever form the commonwealth is under, the ruling power ought to govern by declared and received laws, and not by extemporary dictates and undetermined resolutions. For then mankind will be in a far worse condition than in the state of nature, if they shall have armed one, or a few men, with the joint power of a multitude to force them to obey at pleasure the exorbitant and unlimited decrees of their sudden thoughts, or unrestrained, and, till that moment, unknown wills, without having any measures set down which may guide and justify their actions. For all the power the government has, being only for the good of the society, as it ought not to be arbitrary and at pleasure, so it ought to be exercised by established and promulgated laws; that both the people may know their duty and be safe and secure within the limits of the law; and the rules too kept within their due bounds, and not be tempted by the power they have in their hands to employ it to such purposes, and by such measures as they would not have known, and own not willingly.

Thirdly, The supreme power cannot take from any man any part of his property without his own consent. For the preservation of property being the end of government, and that for which men enter into society, it necessarily supposes and requires that the people should have property, without which they must be supposed to lose that by entering into society, which was the end for which they entered into it, too gross an absurdity for any man to own. Men, therefore, in society having property, they have such a right to the goods which by the law of the community are theirs, that nobody hath a right to take them or any part of them from them, without their own consent; without this they have no property at all. For I have truly no property in that which another can by right take from me when he pleases, against my consent. Hence it is a mistake to think that the supreme or legislative power of any commonwealth can do what it will, and dispose of the estates of the subjects arbitrarily, or take any part of them at pleasure. This is not much to be feared in government where the legislative consists wholly, or in part, in assemblies which are variable, whose members, upon the dissolution of the assembly, are subjects under the common laws of their country, equally with the rest. But in governments where the legislative is in one lasting assembly, always in being, or in one man, as in absolute monarchies, there is danger still, that they will think themselves to have a distinct interest from the rest of the community, and so will be apt to increase their own riches and power by taking what they think fit from the people. For a man's property is not at all secure, though there be good and equitable laws to see the bounds of it between him and his fellow subjects, if he who commands those subjects have power to take from any private man what part he pleases of his property, and use and dispose of it as he thinks good.

But government, into whosesoever hands it is put, being, as I have before shown, entrusted with this condition, and for this end, that men might have and secure their properties, the prince, or senate, however it may have power to make laws for the regulating of property between the subjects one amongst another, yet can never have a power to take to themselves the whole or any part of the subject's property without their own consent. For this would be in effect to leave them no property at all. And to let us see that even absolute power, where it is necessary, is not arbitrary by being absolute, but is still limited by that reason, and confined to those ends which required it in some cases to be absolute, we need look no farther than the common practice of martial discipline. For the preservation of the army, and in it the whole commonwealth, requires an absolute obedience to the command of every superior officer, and it is justly death to disobey or dispute the most dangerous or unreasonable of them; but yet we see that neither the sergeant, that could command a soldier to march up to the mouth of a cannon, or stand in a breach, where he is almost sure to perish, can command that soldier to give him one penny of his money; nor the general that can condemn him to death for deserting his post, or not obeying the most desperate orders, cannot yet, with all his absolute power of life and death, dispose of one farthing of that soldier's estate, or seize one jot of his goods, whom yet he can command anything, and hang for the least disobedience. Because such a blind obedience is necessary to that end for which the commander has his power, viz., the preservation of the rest; but the disposing of his goods has nothing to do with it.

'Tis true governments cannot be supported without great charge, and it is fit every one who enjoys a share of the protection should pay out of his estate his proportion for the maintenance of it. But still it must be with his own consent, *i.e.*, the consent of the majority giving it either by themselves or their representatives chosen by them. For if any one shall claim a power to lay and levy taxes on the people, by his own authority, and without such consent of the people, he thereby invades the fundamental law of property, and subverts the end of government. For what property have I in that which another may by right take when he pleases to himself?

Fourthly, The legislative cannot transfer the power of making laws to any other hands; for it being but a delegated power from the people, they who have it cannot pass it over to others. The people alone can appoint the form of the commonwealth, which is by constituting the legislative, and appointing in whose hands that shall be. And when the people have said we will submit to rules, and be governed by laws made by such men, and in such forms, nobody else can say other men shall make laws for them; nor can the people be bound by any laws but such as are enacted by those whom they have chosen and authorised to make laws for them.

These are the bounds which the trust that is put in them by society, and the law of God and Nature, have set to the legislative power of every commonwealth, in all forms of government.

First, They are to govern by promulgated established laws, not to be varied in particular cases, but to have one rule for rich and poor, for the favourite at court and the countryman at plough.

Secondly, These laws also ought to be designed for no other end ultimately but the good of the people.

Thirdly, They must not raise taxes on the property of the people without the consent of the people, given by themselves or their deputies. And this properly concerns only such governments where the legislative is always in being, or at least where the people have not reserved any part of the legislative to deputies, to be from time to time chosen by themselves.

Fourthly, The legislative neither must nor can transfer the power of making laws to anybody else, or place it anywhere but where the people have.

COMMENT

Like Hobbes, Locke believed that apart from civil society, human beings would live in a "state of nature," enjoying an existence little better than that of animals, or what they termed "savages." Unlike Hobbes, however, Locke believed that the "social contract" on which civil society is based is itself grounded, not in fear and power, but in a mutual desire to sustain and improve human life. Whereas Hobbes thought that the chief goal of political organization and authority is to provide peace and security, Locke thought that these provisions are the necessary means to the greater end of a free and productive life. Thus for Locke, civil society has a positive function, whereas for Hobbes its function is primarily negative.

Another crucial difference between Locke and Hobbes is that the former maintained that since the state exists to facilitate the "rights and privileges" of its citizens, its power can never be used to deprive its citizens of these basic rights and privileges. The social contract, for Locke, is subject to adjudication, as it were, by a higher authority; either side, including the state, can be guilty of breaking the contract and thus be found deserving of punishment and recompense. For Hobbes, on the other hand, the only way to ensure peace and security is to give the state absolute power over the needs and wishes of its individual citizens. The law, in Locke's view, stands above both the state and the individual, and either can call the other to task for breaking the social contract between them.

To put these points in a slightly different manner, for Hobbes once the original contract is made, the state holds and executes sole authority. For Locke, the authority of the state is subject to systematic review by means of the democratic process under constitutional law. Exactly how Locke viewed the democratic process and how it was to be connected to the concept of private property is too complex to go into at this juncture. It is sufficient to say that Locke's notions of social contract and private property have had a profound influence upon the planning and development of Western political and economic life, as well as upon democracy and capitalism as the pillars of "the American way." The chapter on the philosophy of Marxism will return to these issues.

Another way of understanding Locke's idea of the social contract is to compare it to that of Jean-Jacques Rousseau. Locke saw government as providing the foundation for civil society by means of a conscious agreement between the state and its citizens to abide by law. Rousseau, on the other hand, saw society itself, in all of its natural and unspoken interrelationships, as the foundation for civil government and the state. For Rousseau, the real social contract exists at the society or cultural level, and the state is at best a necessary evil. In other words, where Hobbes and Locke saw the human "state of nature" negatively, and civil government positively, Rousseau saw things just the other way around. Rousseau's point of view is similar to that of Thoreau as presented in the next chapter.

In addition to the potential criticisms of Locke's position implied by the foregoing comparisons with those of Hobbes and Rousseau, there remain several other issues that bear mentioning. There is, of course, serious question as to whether human beings ever have existed in a "state of nature." Perhaps social and political life are actually coextensive with the very definition of human nature. Also, there are those thinkers who, from a Marxist perspective, suggest that far from being a natural right, private property is actually a form of robbery. Surely many primal peoples know nothing of this way of life. For most, the world is considered a "home" in which people dwell and share its resources. Socialists would suggest that only when resources and capital are held in common can democracy actually work. The Scandinavian countries, which practice democratic socialism, have the world's highest standard of living.

Finally, questions can be raised as to whether Locke's perspective does not presuppose some form of "Divine" or "Natural" law upon which civil law is to be based. Apart from some such grounding, one is hard pressed to see how the notion of social contract can work since for Locke it is not based on an earthly Sovereign. Many modern philosophers have objected to the idea that there is something inherent within nature itself which grounds human-made laws; even more have doubted the rationality of a belief in a heavenly sovereign. The big question would appear to be: Is it possible to provide an adequate basis for the state without appealing either to God, Natural Law, or to the power of a dictator?

23

Liberal Democracy

> "The only purpose for which power can be rightly exercised over any member of a civilized community, against his will, is to prevent harm to others . . . Over himself, the individual is sovereign."
>
> John Stuart Mill

JOHN STUART MILL (1806–1873)

For a biographical note, see page 455.

On Liberty

CHAPTER I

Introductory

. . . The object of this Essay is to assert one very simple principle, as entitled to govern absolutely the dealings of society with the individual in

On Liberty was first published in London in 1859.

the way of compulsion and control, whether the means used be physical force in the form of legal penalties, or the moral coercion of public opinion. That principle is, that the sole end for which mankind are warranted, individually or collectively, in interfering with the liberty of action of any of their number, is self-protection. That the only purpose for which power can be rightfully exercised over any member

586

of a civilized community, against his will, is to prevent harm to others. His own good, either physical or moral, is not a sufficient warrant. He cannot rightfully be compelled to do or forbear because it will be better for him to do so, because it will make him happier, because, in the opinions of others, to do so would be wise, or even right. These are good reasons for remonstrating with him, or reasoning with him, or persuading him, or entreating him, but not for compelling him, or visiting him with any evil in case he do otherwise. To justify that, the conduct from which it is desired to deter him must be calculated to produce evil to some one else. The only part of the conduct of anyone, for which he is amenable to society, is that which concerns others. In the part which merely concerns himself, his independence is, of right, absolute. Over himself, over his own body and mind, the individual is sovereign.

It is perhaps hardly necessary to say that this doctrine is meant to apply only to human beings in the maturity of their faculties. We are not speaking of children, or of young persons below the age which the law may fix as that of manhood or womanhood. Those who are still in a state to require being taken care of by others, must be protected against their own actions as well as against external injury. For the same reason, we may leave out of consideration those backward states of society in which the race itself may be considered as in its nonage. The early difficulties in the way of spontaneous progress are so great, and there is seldom any choice of means for overcoming them; and a ruler full of the spirit of improvement

is warranted in the use of any expedients that will attain an end, perhaps otherwise unattainable. Despotism is a legitimate mode of government in dealing with barbarians, provided the end be their improvement, and the means justified by actually effecting that end. Liberty, as a principle, has no application to any state of things anterior to the time when mankind have become capable of being improved by free and equal discussion. Until then, there is nothing for them but implicit obedience to an Akbar or a Charlemagne, if they are so fortunate as to find one. But as soon as mankind have attained the capacity of being guided to their own improvement by conviction or persuasion (a period long since reached in all nations with whom we need here concern ourselves), compulsion, either in the direct form or in that of pains and penalties for noncompliance, is no longer admissible as a means to their own good, and justifiable only for the security of others.

It is proper to state that I forego any advantage which could be derived to my argument from the idea of abstract right, as a thing independent of utility. I regard utility as the ultimate appeal on all ethical questions; but it must be utility in the largest sense, grounded on the permanent interests of a man as a progressive being. Those interests, I contend, authorized the subjection of individual spontaneity to external control, only in respect to those actions of each which concern the interest of other people. If anyone does an act hurtful to others, there is a *prima facie* case for punishing him, by law, or, where legal penalties are not safely applicable, by general disapprobation. There are also many positive acts for the benefit of others, which he may rightfully be compelled to perform: such as to give evidence in a court of justice; to bear his fair share in the common defense, or in any other joint work necessary to the interest of the society of which he enjoys the protection; and to perform certain acts of individual beneficence, such as saving a fellow-creature's life, or interposing to protect the defenseless against ill-usage, things which wherever it is obviously a man's duty to do, he may rightfully be made responsible to society for not doing. A person may cause evil to others not only by his actions but by his inaction, and in either case he is justly accountable to them for the injury. The latter case, it is true, requires a much more cautious exercise of compulsion than the former. To make anyone answerable for doing evil to others is the rule; to make him answerable for not preventing evil is, comparatively speaking, the exception. Yet there are many cases clear enough and grave enough to justify that exception. In all things which regard the external relations of the individual, he is *de jure* amenable to those whose interests are concerned, and, if need be, to society as their protector. There are often good reasons for not holding him to the responsibility; but these reasons must arise from the special expediencies of the case: either because it is a kind of case in which he is on the whole likely to act better, when left to his own discretion, than when controlled in any way in which society have it in their power to control him; or because the attempt to exercise control would produce other evils, greater than those which it would prevent. When such reasons as these preclude the enforcement of responsibility, the conscience of the agent himself should step into the vacant judgment seat, and protect those interests of others which have no external protection; judging himself all the more rigidly, because the case does not admit of his being made accountable to the judgment of his fellow-creatures.

But there is a sphere of action in which society, as distinguished from the individual, has, if any, only an indirect interest; comprehending all that portion of a person's life and conduct which affects only himself, or if it also affects others, only with their free, voluntary, and undeceived consent and participation. When I say only himself, I mean directly, and in the first instance; for whatever affects himself, may affect others through himself; and the objection which may be grounded on this contingency, will receive consideration in the sequel. This, then, is the appropriate region of human liberty. It comprises, *first*, the inward domain of consciousness; demanding liberty of conscience in the most comprehensive sense; liberty of thought and feeling; absolute freedom of opinion and sentiment on all subjects, practical or speculative, scientific, moral or theological. The liberty of expressing and publishing opinions may seem to fall under a different principle, since it belongs to that part of the conduct of an individual which concerns other people; but, being almost of as much importance as the liberty of thought itself, and resting in great part on the same reasons, is practically inseparable from it. *Secondly*, the principle requires liberty of tastes and pursuits; of framing the plan of our life to suit our own character; of doing as we like, subject to such consequences as may follow: without impediment from our fellow-creatures, so long as what we do does not harm them, even though they should think our conduct foolish, perverse, or wrong. *Thirdly*, from this liberty of each individual, follows the liberty, within the same limits, of combination among individuals; freedom to unite, for any purpose not involving harm to others: the persons combining being supposed to be of full age, and not forced or deceived.

No society in which these liberties are not, on the whole, respected, is free, whatever may be its form of government; and none is completely free in which they do not exist absolute and unqualified. The only freedom which deserves the name, is that of pursuing our own good in our own way, so long as we do not attempt to deprive others of theirs, or impede their efforts to obtain it. Each is the proper guardian of his own health, whether bodily, or mental and spiritual. Mankind are greater gainers by suffering each other to live as seems good to themselves, than by compelling each to live as seems good to the rest.

Though this doctrine is anything but new, and, to some persons, may have the air of a truism, there is no doctrine which stands more directly opposed to the general tendency of existing opinion and practice. . . . There is . . . an inclination to stretch un-

duly the powers of society over the individual, both by the force of opinion and even by that of legislation; and as the tendency of all the changes taking place in the world is to strengthen society, and diminish the power of the individual, this encroachment is not one of the evils which tend spontaneously to disappear, but, on the contrary, to grow more and more formidable. The disposition of mankind, whether as rulers or as fellow-citizens, to impose their own opinions and inclinations as a rule of conduct on others, is so energetically supported by some of the best and by some of the worst feelings incident to human nature, that it is hardly ever kept under restraint by anything but want of power; and as the power is not declining, but growing, unless a strong barrier of moral conviction can be raised against the mischief, we must expect, in the present circumstances of the world, to see it increase. . . .

CHAPTER II

Of the Liberty of Thought and Discussion

The time, it is to be hoped, is gone by, when any defence would be necessary of the "liberty of the press" as one of the securities against corrupt or tyrannical government. . . . Speaking generally, it is not, in constitutional countries, to be apprehended that the government, whether completely responsible to the people or not, will often attempt to control the expression of opinion, except when in doing so it makes itself the organ of the general intolerance of the public. Let us suppose, therefore, that the government is entirely at one with the people, and never thinks of exerting any power of coercion unless in agreement with what it conceives to be their voice. But I deny the right of the people to exercise such coercion, either by themselves or by their government. The power itself is illegitimate. The best government has no more title to it than the worst. It is as noxious, or more noxious, when exerted in accordance with public opinion, than when in opposition to it. If all mankind minus one were of one opinion, and only one person were of the contrary opinion, mankind would be no more justified in silencing that one person, than he, if he had the power, would be justified in silencing mankind. Were an opinion a personal possession of no value except to the owner; if to be obstructed in the enjoyment of it were simply a private injury, it would make some difference whether the injury was inflicted only on a few persons or on many. But the peculiar evil of silencing the expression of an opinion is, that it is robbing the human race: posterity as well as the existing generation; those who dissent from the opinion, still more than those who hold it. If the opinion is right, they are deprived of the opportunity of exchanging error for truth; if wrong, they lose, what is almost as great a benefit, the clearer perception and livelier impression of truth, produced by its collision with error.

It is necessary to consider separately these two hypotheses, each of which has a distinct branch of the argument corresponding to it. We can never be sure that the opinion we are endeavoring to stifle is a false opinion; and if we were sure, stifling it would be an evil still.

First: the opinion which it is attempted to suppress by authority may possibly be true. Those who desire to suppress it, of course deny its truth; but they are not infallible. They have no authority to decide the question for all mankind, and exclude every other person from the means of judging. To refuse a hearing to an opinion, because they are sure that it is false, is to assume that *their* certainty is the same thing as *absolute* certainty. All silencing of discussion is an assumption of infallibility. Its condemnation may be allowed to rest on this common argument, not the worse for being common.

Unfortunately for the good sense of mankind, the fact of their fallibility is far from carrying the weight in their practical judgment which is always allowed to it in theory; for while everyone well knows himself to be fallible, few think it necessary to take any precautions against their own fallibility, or admit the supposition that any opinion of which they feel very certain, may be one of the examples of the error to which they acknowledge themselves to be liable. Absolute princes, or others who are accustomed to unlimited deference, usually feel this complete confidence in their own opinions on nearly all subjects. People more happily situated, who sometimes hear their opinions disputed, and are not wholly unused to be set right when they are wrong, place the same unbounded reliance only on such of their opinions as are shared by all who surround them, or to whom they habitually defer; for in proportion to a man's want of confidence in his own solitary judgment, does he usually repose, with implicit trust, on the infallibility of "the world" in general. And the world, to each individual, means the part of it with which he comes in contact—his party, his sect, his church, his class of society; the man may be called, by comparison, almost liberal and large-minded to whom it means anything so comprehensive as his own country or his own age. Nor is his faith in this collective authority at all shaken by his being aware that other ages, countries, sects, churches, classes, and parties have thought, and even now think, the exact reverse. He devolves upon his own world the responsibility of being in the right against the dissentient worlds of other people; and it never troubles him that mere accident has decided which of these numerous worlds is the object of his reliance, and that the same causes which make him a Churchman in London, would have made him a Buddhist or a Confucian in Peking. Yet it is as evident in itself as any amount of argument can make it, that ages are no more infallible than individuals; every age having held many opinions which subsequent ages have deemed not only false but absurd; and it is as certain that many opinions now general will be rejected by future ages, as it is that many, once general, are rejected by the present.

The objection likely to be made to this argument would probably take some such form as the following. There is no greater assumption of infallibility in forbidding the propagation of error, than in any other thing which is done by public authority on its own judgment and responsibility. Judgment is given to men that they may use it. Because it may be used erroneously, are men to be told that they ought not to use it at all? To prohibit what they think pernicious, is not claiming exemption from error, but fulfilling the duty incumbent on them, although fallible, of acting on their conscientious conviction. If we were never to act on our opinions, because those opinions may be wrong, we should leave all our interests uncared for, and all our duties unperformed. An objection which applies to all conduct can be no valid objection to any conduct in particular. It is the duty of governments, and of individuals, to form the truest opinions they can; to form them carefully, and never impose them upon others unless they are quite sure of being right. But when they are sure (such reasoners may say), it is not conscientiousness but cowardice to shrink from acting on their opinions, and allow doctrines which they honestly think dangerous to the welfare of mankind, either in this life or in another, to be scattered abroad without restraint, because other people, in less enlightened times, have persecuted opinions now believed to be true. Let us take care, it may be said, not to make the same mistake; but governments and nations have made mistakes in other things, which are not denied to be fit subjects for the exercise of authority: they have laid on bad taxes, made unjust wars. Ought we therefore to lay on no taxes, and, under whatever provocation, make no wars? Men, and governments, must act to the best of their ability. There is no such thing as absolute certainty, but there is assurance sufficient for the purposes of human life. We may, and must, assume our opinion to be true for the guidance of our own conduct: and it is assuming no more when we forbid bad men to pervert society by the propagation of opinions which we regard as false and pernicious.

I answer that it is assuming very much more. There is the greatest difference between presuming an opinion to be true because, with every opportunity for contesting it, it has not been refuted, and assuming its truth for the purpose of not permitting its refutation. Complete liberty of contradicting and disproving our opinion is the very condition which justifies us in assuming its truth for purposes of action; and on no other terms can a being with human faculties have any rational assurance of being right.

When we consider either the history of opinion, or the ordinary conduct of human life, to what is it to be ascribed that the one and the other are no worse than they are? Not certainly to the inherent force of the human understanding; for, on any matter not self-evident, there are ninety-nine persons totally incapable of judging of it for one who is capable; and the capacity of the hundredth person is only comparative: for the majority of the eminent men of every past generation held many opinions now known to be erroneous, and did or approved numerous things which no one will now justify. Why is it, then, that there is on the whole a preponderance among mankind of rational opinions and rational conduct? If there really is this preponderance — which there must be unless human af-

fairs are, and have always been, in an almost desperate state — it is owing to a quality of the human mind, the source of everything respectable in man either as an intellectual or as a moral being, namely, that his errors are corrigible. He is capable of rectifying his mistakes, by discussion and experience. Not by experience alone. There must be discussion, to show how experience is to be interpreted. Wrong opinions and practices gradually yield to fact and argument; but facts and arguments, to produce any effect on the mind, must be brought before it. Very few facts are able to tell their own story, without comments to bring out their meaning. The whole strength and value, then, of human judgment, depending on the one property, that it can be set right when it is wrong, reliance can be placed on it only when the means of setting it right are kept constantly at hand. In the case of any person whose judgment is really deserving of confidence, how has it become so? Because he has kept his mind open to criticism of his opinions and conduct. Because it has been his practice to listen to all that could be said against him; to profit by as much of it as was just, and expound to himself, and upon occasion to others, the fallacy of what was fallacious. Because he has felt that the only way in which a human being can make some approach to knowing the whole of a subject, is by hearing what can be said about it by persons of every variety of opinion, and studying all modes in which it can be looked at by every character of mind. No wise man ever acquired his wisdom in any mode but this; nor is it in the nature of human intellect to become wise in any other manner. The steady habit of correcting and completing his own opinion by collating it with those of others, so far from causing doubt and hesitation in carrying it into practice, is the only stable foundation for a just reliance on it: for, being cognizant of all that can, at least obviously, be said against him, and having taken up his position against all gainsayers — knowing that he has sought for objections and difficulties, instead of avoiding them, and has shut out no light which can be thrown upon the subject from any quarter — he has a right to think his judgment better than that of any person, or any multitude, who have not gone through a similar process.

It is not too much to require that what the wisest of mankind, those who are best entitled to trust their own judgment, find necessary to warrant their relying on it, should be submitted to by that miscellaneous collection of a few wise and many foolish individuals, called the public. The most intolerant of churches, the Roman Catholic Church, even at the canonization of a saint, admits, and listens patiently to, a "devil's advocate." The holiest of men, it appears, cannot be admitted to posthumous honors, until all that the devil could say against him is known and weighed. If even the Newtonian philosophy were not permitted to be questioned, mankind could not feel as complete assurance of its truth as they now do. The beliefs which we have most warrant for, have no safeguard to rest on but a standing invitation to the whole world to prove them unfounded. If the challenge is not accepted, or is accepted and the attempt fails, we are far enough from certainty still; but we have done the best that the existing state of human reason admits of; we have neglected nothing that could give the truth a chance of reaching us: if the lists are kept open, we may hope that if there be a better truth, it will be found when the human mind is capable of receiving it; and in the meantime we may rely on having attained such approach to truth as is possible in our own day. This is the amount of certainty attainable by a fallible being, and this the sole way of attaining it.

Strange it is that men should admit the validity of the arguments for free discussion, but object to their being "pushed to an extreme"; not seeing that unless the reasons are good for an extreme case, they are not good for any case. Strange that they should imagine that they are not assuming infallibility, when they acknowledge that there should be free discussion on all subjects which can possibly be *doubtful*, but think that some particular principle or doctrine should be forbidden to be questioned because it is so *certain*, that is, because *they are certain* that it is certain. To call any proposition certain while there is anyone who would deny its certainty if permitted, but who is not permitted, is to assume that we ourselves, and those who agree with us, are the judges of certainty, and judges without hearing the other side.

In the present age — which has been described as "destitute of faith, but terrified at scepticism" — in which people feel sure, not so much that their opinions are true, as that they should not know what to do without them — the claims of an opinion to be protected from public attack are rested not so much on its truth, as on its importance to society. There are, it is alleged, certain beliefs so useful, not to say indispensable, to well-being that it is as much the duty of governments to uphold those beliefs, as to protect any other of the interests of society. In a case of such necessity, and so directly in the line of their duty, something less than infallibility may, it is maintained, warrant, and even bind, governments to act on their own opinion, confirmed by the general opinion of mankind. It is also often argued, and still oftener thought, that none but bad men would desire to weaken these salutary beliefs; and there can be nothing wrong, it is thought, in restraining bad men, and prohibiting what only such men would wish to practice. This mode of thinking makes the justification of restraints on discussion not a question of the truth of doctrines, but of their usefulness; and flatters itself by that means to escape the responsibility of claiming to be an infallible judge of opinions. But those who thus satisfy themselves, do not perceive that the assumption of infallibility is merely shifted from one point to another. The usefulness of an opinion is itself matter of opinion: as disputable, as open to discussion, and requiring discussion as much as the opinion itself. There is the same need of an infallible judge of opinions to decide an opinion to be noxious, as to decide it to be false, unless the opinion condemned has full opportunity of defending itself. And it will not do to say that the heretic may be allowed to maintain the utility or harmlessness of his opinion, though forbidden to maintain its truth. The truth of an opinion is part of its utility. If we would know whether or not it is desirable that a proposition should be believed, is it possible to exclude the consideration of whether or not it is true? In the opinion, not of bad men, but of the best men, no belief which is contrary to truth can be really useful; and can you prevent such men from urging that plea, when they are charged with culpability for denying some doctrine which they are told is useful, but which they believe to be false? Those who are on the side of received opinions never fail to take all possible advantages of this plea: you do not find *them* handling the question of utility as if it could be completely abstracted from that of truth; on the contrary, it is, above all, because their doctrine is "the truth," that the knowledge or the belief of it is held to be so indispensable. There can be no fair discussion of the question of usefulness when an argument so vital may be employed on one side, but not on the other. And in point of fact, when law or public feeling do not permit the truth of an opinion to be disputed, they are just as little tolerant of a denial of its usefulness. The utmost they allow is an extenuation of its absolute necessity, or of the positive guilt of rejecting it.

In order more fully to illustrate the mischief of denying a hearing to opinions because we, in our own judgment, have condemned them, it will be desirable to fix down the discussion to a concrete case; and I choose, by preference, the cases which are least favorable to me — in which the argument against freedom of opinion, both on the score of truth and on that of utility, is considered the strongest. Let the opinions impugned be the belief in a God and in a future state, or any of the commonly received doctrines of morality. To fight the battle on such ground gives a great advantage to an unfair antagonist; since he will be sure to say (and many who have no desire to be unfair will say it internally), "Are these the doctrines which you do not deem sufficiently certain to be taken under the protection of laws? Is the belief in a God one of the opinions to feel sure of which you hold to be assuming infallibility?" But I must be permitted to observe that it is not the feeling sure of a doctrine (be it what it may) which I call an assumption of infallibility. It is the undertaking to decide that question *for others*, without allowing them to hear what can be said on the contrary side. And I denounce and reprobate this pretension not the less if put forth on the side of my most solemn convictions. However positive anyone's persuasion may be, not only of the falsity but of the pernicious consequences—not only of the pernicious consequences, but (to adopt expressions which I altogether condemn) the immorality and impiety of an opinion; yet if, in pursuance of that private judgment, though backed by the public judgment of his country or his contemporaries, he prevents the opinion from being heard in its defense, he assumes infallibility. And so far from the assumption being less objectionable or less dangerous because the opinion is called immoral or impious, this is the case of all others in which it is most fatal. These are exactly the occasions on which the men of one generation commit those dreadful mistakes which ex-

cite the astonishment and horror of posterity. It is among such that we find the instances memorable in history, when the arm of the law has been employed to root out the best men and the noblest doctrines; with deplorable success as to the men, though some of the doctrines have survived to be (as if in mockery) invoked in defense of similar conduct toward those who dissent from *them*, or from their received interpretation.

Mankind can hardly be too often reminded, that there was once a man named Socrates, between whom and the legal authorities and public opinion of his time there took place a memorable collision. Born in an age and country abounding in individual greatness, this man has been handed down to us by those who best knew both him and the age, as the most virtuous man in it; while *we* know him as the head and prototype of all subsequent teachers of virtue, the source equally of the lofty inspiration of Plato and the judicious utilitarianism of Aristotle . . . the two head-springs of ethical as of all other philosophy. This acknowledged master of all the eminent thinkers who have since lived—whose fame, still growing after more than two thousand years, all but outweighs the whole remainder of the names which make his native city illustrious—was put to death by his countrymen, after a judicial conviction, for impiety and immorality. Impiety, in denying the gods recognized by the State; indeed his accuser asserted (see the *Apologia*) that he believed in no gods at all. Immorality, in being, by his doctrines and instructions, a "corruptor of youth." Of these charges the tribunal, there is every ground for believing, honestly found him guilty, and condemned the man who probably of all then born had deserved best of mankind to be put to death as a criminal.

To pass from this to the only other instance of judicial iniquity, the mention of which, after the condemnation of Socrates, would not be an anti-climax: the event which took place on Calvary rather more than eighteen hundred years ago. The man who left on the memory of those who witnessed his life and conversation such an impression of his moral grandeur that eighteen subsequent centuries have done homage to him as the Almighty in person, was ignominiously put to death, as what? As a blasphemer. Men did not merely mistake their benefactor; they mistook him for the exact contrary of what he was, and treated him as that prodigy of impiety which they themselves are now held to be for their treatment of him. The feelings with which mankind now regard these lamentable transactions, especially the later of the two, render them extremely unjust in their judgment of the unhappy actors. These were, to all appearance, not bad men — not worse than men commonly are, but rather the contrary; men who possessed in a full, or somewhat more than a full measure, the religious, moral, and patriotic feelings of their time and people: the very kind of men who, in all times, our own included, have every chance of passing through life blameless and respected. The high-priest who rent his garments when the words were pronounced which, according to all the ideas of his country, constituted the blackest guilt, was in all probability quite as sincere in his horror and indignation as the generality of respectable and pious men now are in the religious and moral sentiments they profess; and most of those who now shudder at his conduct, if they had lived in his time, and been born Jews, would have acted precisely as he did. Orthodox Christians who are tempted to think that those who stoned to death the first martyrs must have been worse men than they themselves are, ought to remember that one of those persecutors was Saint Paul.

Let us add one more example, the most striking of all, if the impressiveness of an error is measured by the wisdom and virtue of him who falls into it. If ever anyone possessed of power had grounds for thinking himself the best and most enlightened among his contemporaries, it was the Emperor Marcus Aurelius. Absolute monarch of the whole civilized world, he preserved through life not only the most unblemished justice, but what was less to be expected from his Stoical breeding, the tenderest heart. The few failings which are attributed to him were all on the side of indulgence; while his writings, the highest ethical product of the ancient mind, differ scarcely perceptibly, if they differ at all, from the most characteristic teachings of Christ. This man, a better Christian in all but the dogmatic sense of the word than almost any of the ostensibly Christian sovereigns who have since reigned, persecuted Christianity. Placed at the summit of all the previous attainments of humanity, with an open, unfettered intellect, and a character which led him of himself to embody in his moral writings the Christian ideal, he yet failed to see that Christianity was to be a good and not an evil to the world, with his duties to which he was so deeply penetrated. Existing society he knew to be in a deplorable state. But such as it was, he saw, or thought he saw, that it was held together, and prevented from being worse, by belief and reverence of the received divinities. As a ruler of mankind, he deemed it his duty not to suffer society to fall in pieces; and saw not how, if its existing ties were removed, any others could be formed which could again knit it together. The new religion openly aimed at dissolving these ties: unless, therefore, it was his duty to adopt that religion, it seemed to be his duty to put it down. Inasmuch then as the theology of Christianity did not appear to him true or of divine origin; inasmuch as this strange history of a crucified God was not credible to him, and a system which purported to rest entirely upon a foundation to him so wholly unbelievable, could not be foreseen by him to be that renovating agency which, after all abatements, it has in fact proved to be; the gentlest and most amiable of philosophers and rulers, under a solemn sense of duty, authorized the persecution of Christianity. To my mind this is one of the most tragical facts in all history. It is a bitter thought, how different a thing the Christianity of the world might have been, if the Christian faith had been adopted as the religion of the empire under the auspices of Marcus Aurelius instead of those of Constantine. But it would be equally unjust to him and false to truth to deny that no one plea which can be urged for punishing anti-Christian teaching was wanting to Marcus Aurelius for punishing as he did the propagation of Christianity. No Christian more firmly believes that atheism is false, and tends to the dissolution of society, than Marcus Aurelius believed the same things of Christianity; he who, of all men then living, might have been thought the most capable of appreciating it. Unless anyone who approves of punishment for the promulgation of opinions, flatters himself that he is a wiser and better man than Marcus Aurelius—more deeply versed in the wisdom of his time, more elevated in his intellect above it— more earnest in his search for truth, or more single-minded in his devotion to it when found; let him abstain from that assumption of the joint infallibility of himself and the multitude, which the great Antoninus made with so unfortunate a result.

Aware of the impossibility of defending the use of punishment for restraining irreligious opinions by any argument which will not justify Marcus Antoninus, the enemies of religious freedom, when hard pressed, occasionally accept this consequence, and say, with Dr. Johnson, that the persecutors of Christianity were in the right; that persecution is an ordeal through which truth ought to pass, and always passes successfully, legal penalties being, in the end, powerless against truth, though sometimes beneficially effective against mischievous errors. This is a form of the argument for religious intolerance sufficiently remarkable not to be passed without notice.

A theory which maintains that truth may justifiably be persecuted because persecution cannot possibly do it any harm, cannot be charged with being intentionally hostile to the reception of new truths; but we cannot commend the generosity of its dealing with the persons to whom mankind are indebted for them. To discover to the world something which deeply concerns it, and of which it was previously ignorant; to prove to it that it had been mistaken on some vital point of temporal or spiritual interest, is as important a service as a human being can render to his fellow-creatures, and in certain cases, as in those of the early Christians and of the Reformers, those who think with Dr. Johnson believe it to have been the most precious gift which could be bestowed on mankind. That the authors of such splendid benefits should be requited by martyrdom, that their reward should be to be dealt with as the vilest of criminals, is not, upon this theory, a deplorable error and misfortune, for which humanity should mourn in sackcloth and ashes, but the normal and justifiable state of things. The propounder of a new truth, according to this doctrine, should stand, as stood, in the legislation of the Locrians, the proposer of a new law, with a halter round his neck to be instantly tightened if the public assembly did not, on hearing his reasons, then and there adopt his proposition. People who defend this mode of treating benefactors cannot be supposed to set much value on the benefit; and I believe this view of the subject is mostly confined to the sort of persons who think that new truths may have been desirable once, but that we have had enough of them now.

But, indeed, the dictum that truth always triumphs over persecution is one of those pleasant falsehoods which men repeat after one another till they pass into commonplaces, but which all experience refutes. History teems with instances of truth put down by persecution. If not suppressed forever, it may be thrown back for centuries. To speak only of religious opinions: the Reformation broke out at least twenty times before Luther, and was put down. Arnold of Brescia was put down. Fra Dolcino was put down. Savonarola was put down. The Albigeois were put down. The Vaudois were put down. The Lollards were put down. The Hussites were put down. Even after the era of Luther, wherever persecution was persisted in, it was successful. In Spain, Italy, Flanders, the Austrian Empire, Protestantism was rooted out; and, most likely, would have been so in England, had Queen Mary lived, or Queen Elizabeth died. Persecution has always succeeded, save where the heretics were too strong a party to be effectually persecuted. No reasonable person can doubt that Christianity might have been extirpated in the Roman Empire. It spread, and became predominant, because the persecutions were only occasional, lasting but a short time, and separated by long intervals of almost undisturbed propagandism. It is a piece of idle sentimentality that truth, merely as truth, has any inherent power denied to error of prevailing against the dungeon and the stake. Men are not more zealous for truth than they often are for error, and a sufficient application of legal or even of social penalties will generally succeed in stopping the propagation of either. The real advantage which truth has, consists in this, that when an opinion is true, it may be extinguished once, twice, or many times, but in the course of ages there will generally be found persons to rediscover it, until some one of its reappearances falls on a time when from favorable circumstances it escapes persecution until it has made such head as to withstand all subsequent attempts to suppress it.

It will be said that we do not now put to death the introducers of new opinions: we are not like our fathers who slew the prophets, we even build sepulchres to them. It is true we no longer put heretics to death; and the amount of penal infliction which modern feeling would probably tolerate, even against the most obnoxious opinions, is not sufficient to extirpate them. . . . But though we do not now inflict so much evil on those who think differently from us as it was formerly our custom to do, it may be that we do ourselves as much evil as ever by our treatment of them. Socrates was put to death, but the Socratic philosophy rose like the sun in heaven, and spread its illumination over the whole intellectual firmament. Christians were cast to the lions, but the Christian church grew up a stately and spreading tree, overtopping the older and less vigorous growths, and stifling them by its shade. Our merely social intolerance kills no one, roots out no opinions, but induces men to disguise them, or to abstain from any active effort for their diffusion. With us, heretical opinions do not perceptibly gain, or even lose, ground in each decade or generation; they

never blaze out far and wide, but continue to smolder in the narrow circles of thinking and studious persons among whom they originate, without ever lighting up the general affairs of mankind with either a true or a deceptive light. And thus is kept up a state of things very satisfactory to some minds, because, without the unpleasant process of fining or imprisoning anybody, it maintains all prevailing opinions outwardly undisturbed, while it does not absolutely interdict the exercise of reason by dissentients afflicted with the malady of thought. A convenient plan for having peace in the intellectual world, and keeping all things going on therein very much as they do already! But the price paid for this sort of intellectual pacification is the sacrifice of the entire moral courage of the human mind. A state of things in which a large portion of the most active and inquiring intellects find it advisable to keep the general principles and grounds of their convictions within their own breasts, and attempt, in what they address to the public, to fit as much as they can of their own conclusions to premises which they have internally renounced, cannot send forth the open, fearless characters, and logical, consistent intellects who once adorned the thinking world. The sort of men who can be looked for under it, are either mere conformers to common-place, or time-servers for truth, whose arguments on all great subjects are meant for their hearers, and are not those which have convinced themselves. Those who avoid this alternative, do so by narrowing their thoughts and interest to things which can be spoken of without venturing within the region of principles — that is, to small practical matters which would come right of themselves if but the minds of mankind were strengthened and enlarged, and which will never be made effectually right until then; while that which would strengthen and enlarge men's minds, free and daring speculation on the highest subjects, is abandoned.

Those in whose eyes this reticence on the part of heretics is no evil should consider, in the first place, that in consequence of it there is never any fair and thorough discussion of heretical opinions; and that such of them as could not stand such a discussion, though they may be prevented from spreading, do not disappear. But it is not the minds of heretics that are deteriorated most by the ban placed on all inquiry which does not end in the orthodox conclusions. The greatest harm done is to those who are not heretics, and whose whole mental development is cramped, and their reason cowed, by the fear of heresy. Who can compute what the world loses in the multitude of promising intellects combined with timid characters, who dare not follow out any bold, vigorous, independent train of thought, lest it should land them in something which would admit of being considered irreligious or immoral? Among them we may occasionally see some man of deep conscientiousness, and subtle and refined understanding, who spends a life in sophisticating with an intellect which he cannot silence, and exhausts the resources of ingenuity in attempting to reconcile the promptings of his conscience and reason with orthodoxy, which he does not, perhaps, to the end succeed in doing. No one can be a great thinker who does not recognize that as a thinker it is his first duty to follow his intellect to whatever conclusions it may lead. Truth gains more even by the errors of one who, with due study and preparation, thinks for himself, than by the true opinions of those who only hold them because they do not suffer themselves to think. Not that it is solely, or chiefly, to form great thinkers, that freedom of thinking is required. On the contrary, it is as much and even more indispensable to enable average human beings to attain the mental stature which they are capable of. There have been, and may again be, great individual thinkers in a general atmosphere of mental slavery. But there never has been, nor ever will be, in that atmosphere an intellectually active people. Where any people has made a temporary approach to such a character, it has been because the dread of heterodox speculation was for a time suspended. Where there is a tacit convention that principles are not to be disputed; where the discussion of the greatest questions which can occupy humanity is considered to be closed, we cannot hope to find that generally high scale of mental activity which has made some periods of history so remarkable. Never when controversy avoided the subjects which are large and important enough to kindle enthusiasm, was the mind of a people stirred up from its foundations, and the impulse given which raised even persons of the most ordinary intellect to something of the dignity of thinking beings. Of such we have had an example in the condition of

Europe during the times immediately following the Reformation; another, though limited to the Continent and to a more cultivated class, in the speculative movement of the latter half of the eighteenth century; and a third, of still briefer duration, in the intellectual fermentation of Germany during the Goethean and Fichtean period. These periods differed widely in the particular opinions which they developed; but were alike in this, that during all three the yoke of authority was broken. In each, an old mental despotism had been thrown off, and no new one had yet taken its place. The impulse given at these three periods has made Europe what it now is. Every single improvement which has taken place either in the human mind or in institutions, may be traced distinctly to one or other of them. Appearances have for some time indicated that all three impulses are well nigh spent; and we can expect no fresh start until we again assert our mental freedom.

Let us now pass to the second division of the argument, and dismissing the supposition that any of the received opinions may be false, let us assume them to be true, and examine into the worth of the manner in which they are likely to be held, when their truth is not freely and openly canvassed. However unwilling a person who has a strong opinion may admit the possibility that his opinion may be false, he ought to be moved by the consideration that, however true it may be, if it is not fully, frequently, and fearlessly discussed, it will be held as a dead dogma, not a living truth.

There is a class of persons (happily not quite so numerous as formerly) who think it enough if a person assents undoubtingly to what they think true, though he has no knowledge whatever of the grounds of the opinion, and could not make a tenable defense of it against the most superficial objections. Such persons, if they can once get their creed taught from authority, naturally think that no good, and some harm, comes of its being allowed to be questioned. Where their influence prevails, they make it nearly impossible for the received opinion to be rejected wisely and considerately, though it may still be rejected rashly and ignorantly; for to shut out discussion entirely is seldom possible, and when it once gets in, beliefs not grounded on conviction are apt to give way before the slightest semblance of an argument. Waiving, however, this possibility — assuming that the true opinion abides in the mind, but abides as a prejudice, a belief independent of, and proof against, argument — this is not the way in which truth ought to be held by a rational being. This is not knowing the truth. Truth, thus held, is but one superstition the more, accidentally clinging to the words which enunciate a truth.

If the intellect and judgment of mankind ought to be cultivated, a thing which Protestants at least do not deny, on what can these faculties be more appropriately exercised by anyone, than on the things which concern him so much that it is considered necessary for him to hold opinions on them? If the cultivation of the understanding consists in one thing more than in another, it is surely in learning the grounds of one's own opinions. Whatever people believe, on subjects on which it is of the first importance to believe rightly, they ought to be able to defend against at least the common objections. But, some one may say, "Let them be *taught* the grounds of their opinions. It does not follow that opinions must be merely parroted because they are never heard controverted. Persons who learn geometry do not simply commit the theorems to memory, but understand and learn likewise the demonstrations; and it would be absurd to say that they remain ignorant of the grounds of geometrical truths, because they never hear any one deny, and attempt to disprove them." Undoubtedly: and such teaching suffices on a subject like mathematics, where there is nothing at all to be said on the wrong side of the question. The peculiarity of the evidence of mathematical truths is that all the argument is on one side. There are no objections, and no answers to objections. But on every subject on which difference of opinion is possible, the truth depends on a balance to be struck between two sets of conflicting reasons. Even in natural philosophy, there is always some other explanation possible of the same facts — some geocentric theory instead of heliocentric, some phlogiston instead of oxygen — and it has to be shown why that other theory cannot be the true one; and until this is show, and until we know how it is show, we do not understand the grounds of our opinion. But when we turn to subjects infinitely more complicated, to morals, religion, politics, social relations, and the business of life, three-fourths of the arguments for every disputed opinion consist in dispelling the appearances which favor some opinion different from it. The greatest orator, save one, of antiquity, has left it on record that he always studied his adversary's case with as great, if not still greater, intensity than even his own. What Cicero practiced as the means of forensic success requires to be imitated by all who study any subject in order to arrive at the truth. He who knows only his own side of the case, knows little of that. His reasons may be good, and no one may have been able to refute them. But if he is equally unable to refute the reasons on the opposite side; if he does not so much as know what they are, he has no ground for preferring either opinion. The rational position for him would be suspension of judgment, and unless he contents himself with that, he is either led by authority, or adopts, like the generality of the world, the side to which he feels most inclination. Nor is it enough that he should hear the arguments of adversaries from his own teachers, presented as they state them, and accompanied by what they offer as refutations. That is not the way to do justice to the arguments, or bring them into real contact with his own mind. He must be able to hear them from persons who actually believe them; who defend them in earnest, and do their very utmost for them. He must know them in their most plausible and persuasive form; he must feel the whole force of the difficulty which the true view of the subject has to encounter and dispose of; else he will never really possess himself of the portion of truth which meets and removes that difficulty. Ninety-nine in a hundred of what are called educated men are in this condition; even of those who can argue fluently for their opinions. Their conclusion may be true, but it might be false for anything they know: they have never thrown themselves into the mental position of those who think differently from them, and considered what such persons may have to say; and consequently they do not, in any proper sense of the word, know the doctrine which they themselves profess. They do not know those parts of it which explain and justify the remainder; the considerations which show that a fact which seemingly conflicts with another is reconcilable with it, or that, of two apparently strong reasons, one and not the other ought to be preferred. All that part of the truth which turns the scale, and decides the judgment of a completely informed mind, they are strangers to; nor is it ever really known but to those who have attended equally and impartially to both sides, and endeavored to see the reasons of both in the strongest light. So essential is this discipline to a real understanding of moral and human subjects, that if opponents of all important truths do not exist, it is indispensable to imagine them, and supply them with the strongest arguments which the most skilful devil's advocate can conjure up. . . .

If, however, the mischievous operation of the absence of free discussion, when the received opinions are true, were confined to leaving men ignorant of the grounds of those opinions, it might be thought that this, if an intellectual, is no moral evil, and does not affect the worth of the opinions, re-

garded in their influence on the character. The fact, however, is that not only the grounds of the opinion are forgotten in the absence of discussion, but too often the meaning of the opinion itself. The words which convey it cease to suggest ideas, or suggest only a small portion of those they were originally employed to communicate. Instead of a vivid conception and a living belief, there remain only a few phrases retained by rote; or, if any part, the shell and husk only of the meaning is retained, the finer essence being lost. The great chapter in human history which this fact occupies and fills, cannot be too earnestly studied and meditated on.

It is illustrated in the experience of almost all ethical doctrines and religious creeds. They are full of meaning and vitality to those who originate them, and to the direct disciples of the originators. Their meaning continues to be felt in undiminished strength, and is perhaps brought out into even fuller consciousness, so long as the struggle lasts to give the doctrine or creed an ascendancy over other creeds. At last it either prevails, and becomes the general opinion, or its progress stops; it keeps possession of the ground it has gained, but ceases to spread further. When either of these results has become apparent, controversy on the subject flags, and gradually dies away. The doctrine has taken its place, if not as a received opinion, as one of the admitted sects or divisions of opinion: those who hold it have generally inherited, not adopted it; and conversion from one of these doctrines to another, being now an exceptional fact, occupies little place in the thoughts of their professors. Instead of being, as at first, constantly on the alert either to defend themselves against the world, or to bring the world over to them, they have subsided into acquiescence, and neither listen, when they can help it, to arguments against their creed, nor trouble dissentients (if there be such) with arguments in its favor. From this time may usually be dated the decline in the living power of the doctrine. We often hear the teachers of all creeds lamenting the difficulty of keeping up in the minds of believers a lively apprehension of the truth which they nominally recognize, so that it may penetrate the feelings, and acquire a real mastery over the conduct. No such difficulty is complained of while the creed is still fighting for its existence: even the weaker combatants then know and feel what they are fighting for, and the difference between it and other doctrines; and in that period of every creed's existence, not a few persons may be found, who have realized its fundamental principles in all the forms of thought, have weighed and considered them in all their important bearings, and have experienced the full effect on the character which belief in that creed ought to produce in a mind thoroughly imbued with it. But when it has come to be an hereditary creed, and to be received passively, not actively; when the mind is no longer compelled, in the same degree as at first, to exercise its vital powers on the questions which its belief presents to it: there is a progressive tendency to forget all of the belief except the formularies, or to give it a dull and torpid assent, as if accepting it on trust dispensed with the necessity of re-

alizing it in consciousness, or testing it by personal experience, until it almost ceases to connect itself at all with the inner life of the human being. Then are seen the cases, so frequent in this age of the world as almost to form the majority, in which the creed remains as it were outside the mind, incrusting and petrifying it against all other influences addressed to the higher parts of our nature; manifesting its power by not suffering any fresh and living conviction to get in, but itself doing nothing for the mind or heart, except standing sentinel over them to keep them vacant.

To what an extent doctrines intrinsically fitted to make the deepest impression upon the mind may remain in it as dead beliefs, without being ever realized in the imagination, the feelings, or the understanding, is exemplified by the manner in which the majority of believers hold the doctrines of Christianity. By Christianity I here mean what is accounted such by all churches and sects — the maxims and precepts contained in the New Testament. These are considered sacred, and accepted as laws, by all professing Christians. Yet it is scarcely too much to say that not one Christian in a thousand guides or tests his individual conduct by reference to those laws. The standard to which he does refer it, is the custom of his nation, his class, or his religious profession. He has thus, on the one hand, a collection of ethical maxims, which he believes to have been vouchsafed to him by infallible wisdom as rules for his government; and on the other a set of every-day judgments and practices, which go a certain length with some of those maxims, not so great a length with others, stand in direct opposition to some, and are, on the whole, a compromise between the Christian creed and the interests and suggestions of worldly life. To the first of these standards he gives his homage; to the other his real allegiance. . . .

The same thing holds true, generally speaking, of all traditional doctrines — those of prudence and knowledge of life, as well as of morals or religion. All languages and literatures are full of general observations on life, both as to what it is, and how to conduct oneself in it; observations which everybody knows, which everybody repeats, or hears with acquiescence, which are received as truisms, yet of which most people first truly learn the meaning when experience, generally of a painful kind, has made it a reality to them. How often, when smarting under some unforeseen misfortune or disappointment, does a person call to mind some proverb or common saying, familiar to him all his life, the meaning of which, if he had ever before felt it as he does now, would have saved him from the calamity. There are indeed reasons for this, other than the absence of discussion; there are many truths of which the full meaning *cannot* be realized until personal experience has brought it home. But much more of the meaning even of these would have been understood, and what was understood would have been far more deeply impressed on the mind, if the man had been accustomed to hear it argued *pro* and *con* by people who did understand it. The fatal tendency of mankind to leave off thinking about a thing when it is no longer doubtful, is the cause of half

their errors. A contemporary author has well spoken of "the deep slumber of a decided opinion."

But what! (it may be asked) Is the absence of unanimity an indispensable condition of true knowledge? Is it necessary that some part of mankind should persist in error to enable any to realize the truth? Does a belief cease to be real and vital as soon as it is generally received; and is a proposition never thoroughly understood and felt unless some doubt of it remains? As soon as mankind have unanimously accepted a truth, does the truth perish within them? The highest aim and best result of improved intelligence, it has hitherto been thought, is to unite mankind more and more in the acknowledgment of all important truths; and does the intelligence only last as long as it has not achieved its object? Do the fruits of conquest perish by the very completeness of the victory?

I affirm no such thing. As mankind improve, the number of doctrines which are no longer disputed or doubted will be constantly on the increase: and the well-being of mankind may almost be measured by the number and gravity of the truths which have reached the point of being uncontested. The cessation, on one question after another, of serious controversy, is one of the necessary incidents of the consolidation of opinion; a consolidation as salutary in the case of true opinions, as it is dangerous and noxious when the opinions are erroneous. But though this gradual narrowing of the bounds of diversity of opinion is necessary in both senses of the term, being at once inevitable and indispensable, we are not therefore obliged to conclude that all its consequences must be beneficial. The loss of so important an aid to the intelligent and living apprehension of a truth, as is afforded by the necessity of explaining it to, or defending it against, opponents, though not sufficient to outweigh, is no trifling drawback from, the benefit of its universal recognition. Where this advantage can no longer be had, I confess I should like to see the teachers of mankind endeavoring to provide a substitute for it; some contrivance for making the difficulties of the question as present to the learner's consciousness, as if they were pressed upon him by a dissentient champion, eager for his conversion. . . .

It is the fashion of the present time to disparage negative logic — that which points out weaknesses in theory or errors in practice, without establishing positive truths. Such negative criticism would indeed be poor enough as an ultimate result; but as a means to attaining any positive knowledge or conviction worthy the name, it cannot be valued too highly; and until people are again systematically trained to it, there will be few great thinkers, and a low general average of intellect, in any but the mathematical and physical departments of speculation. On any other subject no one's opinions deserve the name of knowledge, except so far as he has either had forced upon him by others, or gone through of himself, the same mental process which would have been required of him in carrying on an active controversy with opponents. That, therefore, which when absent, it is so indispensable, but so difficult, to create, how worse than absurd it is to

forego, when spontaneously offering itself! If there are any persons who contest a received opinion, or who will do so if law or opinion will let them, let us thank them for it, open our minds to listen to them, and rejoice that there is some one to do for us what we otherwise ought, if we have any regard for either the certainty or the vitality of our convictions, to do with much greater labor for ourselves.

It still remains to speak of one of the principal causes which make diversity of opinion advantageous, and will continue to do so until mankind shall have entered a stage of intellectual advancement which at present seems at an incalculable distance. We have hitherto considered only two possibilities: that the received opinion may be false, and some other opinion consequently true; out: or that, the received opinion being true, a conflict with the opposite error is essential to a clear apprehension and deep feeling of its truth. But there is a commoner case than either of these: when the conflicting doctrines, instead of being one true and the other false, share the truth between them; and the nonconforming opinion is needed to supply the remainder of the truth, of which the received doctrine embodies only a part. Popular opinions, on subjects not palpable to sense, are often true, but seldom or never the whole truth. They are a part of the truth; sometimes a greater, sometimes a smaller part, but exaggerated, distorted, and disjointed from the truths by which they ought to be accompanied and limited. Heretical opinions, on the other hand, are generally some of these suppressed and neglected truths, bursting the bonds which kept them down, and neither seeking reconciliation with the truth contained in the common opinion, or fronting it as enemies, and setting themselves up, with similar exclusiveness, as the whole truth. The latter case is hitherto the most frequent, as, in the human mind, one-sidedness has always been the rule, and many-sidedness the exception. Hence, even in revolutions of opinion, one part of the truth usually sets while another rises. Even progress, which ought to super-add, for the most part only substitutes, one partial and incomplete truth for another; improvement consisting chiefly in this, that the new fragment of truth is more wanted, more adapted to the needs of the time, than that which it displaces. Such being the partial character of prevailing opinions, even when resting on a true foundation, every opinion which embodies somewhat of the portion of truth which the common opinion omits, ought to be considered precious, with whatever amount of error and confusion that truth may be blended. No sober judge of human affairs will feel bound to be indignant because those who force on our notice truths which we should otherwise have overlooked, overlook some of those which we see. Rather, he will think that so long as popular truth is one-sided, it is more desirable than otherwise that unpopular truth should have one-sided assertors too; such being usually the most energetic, and the most likely to compel reluctant attention to the fragment of wisdom which they proclaim as if it were the whole.

Thus, in the eighteenth century, when nearly all the instructed, and all those of the uninstructed who were led by them, were lost in admiration of what is called civilization, and of the marvels of modern science, literature, and philosophy, and while greatly overrating the amount of unlikeness between the men of modern and those of ancient times, indulged the belief that the whole of the difference was in their own favor; with what a salutary shock did the paradoxes of Rousseau explode like bombshells in the midst, dislocating the compact mass of one-sided opinion, and forcing its elements to recombine in a better form and with additional ingredients. Not that the current opinions were on the whole farther from the truth than Rousseau's were: on the contrary, they were nearer to it: they contained more of positive truth, and very much less of error. Nevertheless there lay in Rousseau's doctrine, and has floated down the stream of opinion along with it, a considerable amount of exactly those truths which the popular opinion wanted; and these are the deposit which was left behind when the flood subsided. The superior worth of simplicity of life, the enervating and demoralizing effect of the trammels and hypocrisies of artificial society, are ideas which have never been entirely absent from cultivated minds since Rousseau wrote; and they will in time produce their due effect, though at present needing to be asserted as much as ever, and to be asserted by deeds, for words, on this subject, have nearly exhausted their power.

In politics, again, it is almost a commonplace, that a party of order or stability, and a party of progress or reform, are both necessary elements of a healthy state of political life; until the one or the other shall have so enlarged its mental grasp as to be a party equally of order and of progress, knowing and distinguishing what is fit to be preserved from what ought to be swept away. Each of these modes of thinking derives its utility from the deficiencies of the other; but it is in a great measure the opposition of the other that keeps each within the limits of reason and sanity. Unless opinions favorable to democracy and to aristocracy, to property and to equality, to coöperation and to competition, to luxury and to abstinence, to sociality and individuality, to liberty and discipline, and all the other standing antagonisms of practical life, are expressed with equal freedom, and enforced and defended with equal talent and energy, there is no chance of both elements obtaining their due: one scale is sure to go up, and the other down. Truth, in the great practical concerns of life, is so much a question of the reconciling and combining of opposites, that very few have minds sufficiently capacious and impartial to make the adjustment with an approach to correctness, and it has to be made by the rough process of a struggle between combatants fighting under hostile banners. On any of the great open questions just enumerated, if either of the two opinions has a better claim than the other, not merely to be tolerated, but to be encouraged and countenanced, it is the one which happens at the particular time and place to be in a minority. That is the opinion which, for the time being, represents the neglected interests, the side of human well-being which is in danger of obtaining less than its share. I am aware that there is not, in this country, any intolerance of differences of opinion on most of these topics. They are adduced to show, by admitted and multiplied examples, the universality of the fact that only through diversity of opinion is there, in the existing state of human intellect, a chance of fair play to all sides of the truth. When there are persons to be found who form an exception to the apparent unanimity of the world on any subject, even if the world is in the right, it is always probable that dissentients have something worth hearing to say for themselves, and that truth would lose something by their silence. . . .

We have now recognized the necessity to the mental well-being of mankind (on which all their other well-being depends) of freedom of opinion, and freedom of the expression of opinion, on four distinct grounds; which we will now briefly recapitulate.

First, if any opinion is compelled to silence, that opinion may, for aught we can certainly know, be true. To deny this is to assume our own infallibility.

Secondly, though the silenced opinion be an error, it may, and very commonly does, contain a portion of truth; and since the general or prevailing opinion on any subject is rarely or never the whole truth, it is only by the collision of adverse opinions that the remainder of the truth has any chance of being supplied.

Thirdly, even if the received opinion be not only true, but the whole truth; unless it is suffered to be, and actually is, vigorously and earnestly contested, it will, by most of those who receive it, be held in the manner of a prejudice, with little comprehension or feeling of its rational grounds. And not only this, but, fourthly, the meaning of the doctrine itself will be in danger of being lost, or enfeebled, and deprived of its vital effect on the character and conduct: the dogma becoming a mere formal procession, inefficacious for good, but cumbering the ground, and preventing the growth of any real and heartfelt conviction, from reason or personal experience. . . .

CHAPTER III

Of Individuality, As One of the Elements of Well-being

Such being the reasons which make it imperative that human beings should be free to form opinions, and to express their opinions without reserve; and such the baneful consequences to the intellectual, and through that to the moral nature of man, unless this liberty is either conceded, or asserted in spite of prohibition; let us next examine whether the same reasons do not require that men should be free to act upon their opinions—to carry these out in their lives, without hindrance, either physical or moral, from their fellow-men, so long as it is at their own risk and peril. This last proviso is of course indispensable. No one pretends that actions should be as free as opinions. On the contrary, even opinions lose their immunity when the circumstances in which they are expressed are such as to constitute their expression a positive instigation to some mischievous act. An opinion that corn-dealers are starvers of the poor, or that private property is robbery, ought to be unmolested when simply circulated through the press, but may justly incur punishment when delivered orally to an excited mob assembled before the house of a corn-dealer, or when handed about among the same mob in the form of a placard. Acts, of whatever kind, which without justifiable cause do harm to others, may be, and in the more important cases absolutely require to be, controlled by the unfavorable sentiments, and, when needful, by the active interference of mankind. The liberty of the individual must be thus far limited; he must not make himself a nuisance to other people. But if he refrains from molesting others in what concerns them, and merely acts according to his own inclination and judgment in things which concern himself, the same reasons which show that opinion should be free, prove also that he should be allowed, without molestation, to carry his opinions into practice at his own cost. That mankind are not infallible; that their truths, for the most part, are only half-truths; that unity of opinion, unless resulting from the fullest and freest comparison of opposite opinions, is not desirable, and diversity not an evil, but a good, until mankind are much more capable than at present of recognizing all sides of the truth, are principles applicable to men's modes of action, not less than to their opinions. As it is useful that while mankind are imperfect there should be different opinions, so it is that there should be different experiments of living; that free scope should be given to varieties of character, short of injury to others;

and that the worth of different modes of life should be proved practically, when any one thinks fit to try them. It is desirable, in short, that in things which do not primarily concern others, individuality should assert itself. Where not the person's own character, but the traditions or customs of other people are the rule of conduct, there is wanting one of the principal ingredients of human happiness, and quite the chief ingredient of individual and social progress.

In maintaining this principle, the greatest difficulty to be encountered does not lie in the appreciation of means toward an acknowledged end, but in the indifference of persons in general to the end in itself. If it were felt that the free development of individuality is one of the leading essentials of well-being; that it is not only a coördinate element with all that is designated by the terms civilization, instruction, education, culture, but is itself a necessary part and condition of all those things; there would be no danger that liberty should be under-valued, and the adjustment of the boundaries between it and social control would present no extraordinary difficulty. But the evil is, that individual spontaneity is hardly recognized by the common modes of thinking as having any intrinsic worth, or deserving any regard on its own account. The majority, being satisfied with the ways of mankind as they now are (for it is they who make them what they are), cannot comprehend why those ways should not be good enough for everybody; and what is more, spontaneity forms no part of the ideal of the majority of moral and social reformers, but is rather looked on with jealousy, as a troublesome and perhaps rebellious obstruction to the general acceptance of what these reformers, in their own judgment, think would be best for mankind. Few persons, out of Germany, even comprehend the meaning of the doctrine which Wilhelm von Humboldt, so eminent both as a *savant* and as a politician, made the text of a treatise — that "the end of man, or that which is prescribed by the eternal or immutable dictates of reason, and not suggested by vague and transient desires, is the highest and most harmonious development of his powers to a complete and consistent whole"; that, therefore, the object "towards which every human being must ceaselessly direct his efforts, and on which especially those who design to influence their fellow-men must ever keep their eyes, is the individuality of power and development"; that for this there are two requisites, "freedom, and variety of situations"; and that from the union of these arise "individual vigor and manifold diversity," which combine themselves in "originality."[1]

Little, however, as people are accustomed to a doctrine like that of Von Humboldt, and surprising as it may be to them to find so high a value attached to individuality, the question, one must nevertheless think, can only be one of degree. No one's idea of excellence in conduct is that people should do absolutely nothing but copy one another. No one would assert that people ought

[1] *The Sphere and Duties of Government,* from the German of Baron Wilhelm von Humboldt, pp. 11–13.

not to put into their mode of life, and into the conduct of their concerns, any impress whatever of their own judgment, or of their own individual character. On the other hand, it would be absurd to pretend that people ought to live as if nothing whatever had been known in the world before they came into it; as if experience had as yet done nothing toward showing that one mode of existence, or of conduct, is preferable to another. Nobody denies that people should be so taught and trained in youth as to know and benefit by the ascertained results of human experience. But it is the privilege and proper condition of a human being, arrived at the maturity of his faculties, to use and interpret experience in his own way. It is for him to find out what part of recorded experience is properly applicable to his own circumstances and character. The traditions and customs of other people are to a certain extent, evidence of what their experience has taught *them*: presumptive evidence, and as such, have a claim to his deference. But in the first place, their experience may be too narrow, or they may not have interpreted it rightly. Secondly, their interpretation of experience may be correct, but unsuitable to him. Customs are made for customary circumstances and customary characters, and his circumstances or his character may be uncustomary. Thirdly, though the customs be both good as customs, and suitable to him, yet to conform to custom, merely *as* custom, does not educate or develop in him any of the qualities which are the distinctive endowment of a human being. The human faculties of perception, judgment, discriminative feeling, mental activity, and even moral preference, are exercised only in making a choice. He who does anything because it is the custom makes no choice. He gains no practice either in discerning or in desiring what is best. The mental and moral, like the muscular powers, are improved only by being used. The faculties are called into no exercise by doing a thing merely because others do it, no more than by believing a thing only because others believe it. If the grounds of an opinion are not conclusive to the person's own reason, his reason cannot be strengthened, but is likely to be weakened, by his adopting it; and if the inducements to an act are not such as are consentaneous to his own feelings and character (where affection, or the rights of others, are not concerned) it is so much done toward rendering his feelings and character inert and torpid, instead of active and energetic.

He who lets the world, or his own portion of it, choose his plan of life for him, has no need of any other faculty than the ape-like one of imitation. He who chooses his plan for himself, employs all his faculties. He must use observation to see, reasoning and judgment to foresee, activity to gather materials for decision, discrimination to decide, and when he has decided, firmness and self-control to hold to his deliberate decision. And these qualities he requires and exercises exactly in proportion as the part of his conduct which he determines according to his own judgment and feelings is a large one. It is possible that he might be guided in some good path, and kept out of harm's way, without any of these things. But what will be his comparative worth as a human being? It really is of importance, not only what men do, but also what manner of men they are that do it. Among the works of man which human life is rightly employed in perfecting and beautifying, the first in importance surely is man himself. Supposing it were possible to get houses built, corn grown, battles fought, causes tried, and even churches erected and prayers said, by machinery—by automatons in human form—it would be a considerable loss to exchange for these automatons even the men and women who at present inhabit the more civilized parts of the world, and who assuredly are but starved specimens of what nature can and will produce. Human nature is not a machine to be built after a model, and set to do exactly the work prescribed for it, but a tree, which requires to grow and develop itself on all sides, according to the tendency of the inward forces which make it a living thing.

It will probably be conceded that it is desirable people shall exercise their understandings, and that an intelligent following of custom, or even occasionally an intelligent deviation from custom, is better than a blind and simple mechanical adhesion to it. To a certain extent it is admitted that our understanding should be our own: but there is not the same willingness to admit that our desires and impulses should be our own likewise; or that to possess impulses of our own, and of any strength, is anything but a peril and a snare. Yet desires and impulses are as much a part of a perfect human being as beliefs and restraints; and strong impulses are only perilous when not properly balanced—

when one set of aims and inclinations is developed into strength, while others, which ought to coexist with them, remain weak and inactive. It is not because men's desires are strong that they act ill; it is because their consciences are weak. There is no natural connection between strong impulses and a weak conscience. The natural connection is the other way. To say that one person's desires and feelings are stronger and more various than those of another, is merely to say that he has more of the raw material of human nature, and is therefore capable, perhaps of more evil, but certainly of more good. Strong impulses are but another name for energy. Energy may be turned to bad uses; but more good may always be made of an energetic nature than of an indolent and impassive one. Those who have most natural feeling are always those whose cultivated feelings may be made the strongest. The same strong susceptibilities which make the personal impulses vivid and powerful, are also the source from whence are generated the most passionate love of virtue, and the sternest self-control. It is through the cultivation of these that society both does its duty and protects its interests; not by rejecting the stuff of which heroes are made because it knows not how to make them. A person whose desires and impulses are his own—are the expression of his own nature, as it has been developed and modified by his own culture—is said to have a character. One whose desires and impulses are not his own, has no character, no more than a steam-engine has a character. If, in addition to being his own, his impulses are strong, and are under the government of a strong will, he has an energetic character. Whoever thinks that individuality of desires and impulses should not be encouraged to unfold itself, must maintain that society has no need of strong natures — is not the better for containing many persons who have much character — and that a high general average of energy is not desirable. . . .

It is not by wearing down into uniformity all that is individual in themselves, but by cultivating it, and calling it forth, within the limits imposed by the rights and interests of others, that human beings become a noble and beautiful object of contemplation; and as the works partake the character of those who do them, by the same process human life also becomes rich, diversified, and animating, furnishing more abundant aliment to high thoughts and elevating feelings, and strengthening the tie which binds every individual to the race, by making the race infinitely better worth belonging to. In proportion to the development of his individuality, each person becomes more valuable to himself, and is therefore capable of being more valuable to others. There is a greater fullness of life about his own existence, and when there is more life in the units there is more in the mass which is composed of them. As much compression as is necessary to prevent the stronger specimens of human nature from encroaching on the rights of others cannot be dispensed with; but for this there is ample compensation even in the point of view of human development. The means of development which the individual loses by being prevented from gratifying his inclinations to the injury of others, are chiefly obtained at the expense of the development of other people. And even to himself there is a full equivalent in the better development of the social part of his nature, rendered possible by the restraint put upon the selfish part. To be held to rigid rules of justice for the sake of others, develops the feelings and capacities which have the good of others for their object. But to be restrained in things not affecting their good, by their mere displeasure, develops nothing valuable, except such force of character as may unfold itself in resisting the restraint. If acquiesced in, it dulls and blunts the whole nature. To give any fair play to the nature of each, it is essential that different persons should be allowed to lead different lives. In proportion as this latitude has been exercised in any age, has that age been noteworthy to posterity. Even despotism does not produce its worst effects, so long as individuality exists under it; and whatever crushes individuality is despotism, by whatever name it may be called, and whether it professes to be enforcing the will of God or the injunctions of men.

Having said that the individuality is the same thing with development, and that it is only the cultivation of individuality which produces, or can produce, well-developed human beings, I might here close the argument: for what more or better can be said of any condition of human affairs than that it brings human beings themselves nearer to the best thing they can be? or what worse can be said of any obstruction to good than that it prevents this? Doubtless, however, these considerations will not suffice to convince those who most need convincing; and it is necessary further to show that these developed human beings are of some use to the undeveloped — to point out to those who do not desire liberty, and would not avail themselves of it, that they may be in some intelligible manner rewarded for allowing other people to make use of it without hindrance.

In the first place, then, I would suggest that they might possibly learn something from them. It will not be denied by anybody that originality is a valuable element in human affairs. There is always need of persons not only to discover new truths, and point out when what were once truths are true no longer, but also to commence new practices, and set the example of more enlightened conduct, and better taste and sense in human life. This cannot well be gainsaid by anybody who does not believe that the world has already attained perfection in all its ways and practices. It is true that this benefit is not capable of being rendered by everybody alike: there are but few persons, in comparison with the whole of mankind, whose experiments, if adopted by others, would be likely to be any improvement on established practice. But these few are the salt of the earth; without them, human life would become a stagnant pool. Not only is it they who introduce good things which did not before exist; it is they who keep the life in those which already exist. If there were nothing new to be done, would human intellect cease to be necessary? Would it be a reason why those who do the old things

should forget why they are done, and do them like cattle, nor like human beings? There is only too great a tendency in the best beliefs and practices to degenerate into the mechanical; and unless there were a succession of persons whose over-recurring originality prevents the grounds of those beliefs and practices from becoming merely traditional, such dead matter would not resist the smallest shock from anything really alive, and there would be no reason why civilization should not die out, as in the Byzantine Empire. Persons of genius, it is true, are, and are always likely to be, a small minority; but in order to have them, it is necessary to preserve the soil in which they grow. Genius can only breathe freely in an *atmosphere* of freedom. Person of genius are, *ex vi termini* [by the force of the phraseology], more individual than any other people — less capable, consequently, of fitting themselves, without hurtful compression, into any of the small number of molds which society provides in order to save its members the trouble of forming their own character. If from timidity they consent to be forced into one of these molds, and to let all that part of themselves which cannot expand under the pressure remain unexpanded, society will be little the better for their genius. If they are of a strong character, and break their fetters, they become a mark for the society which has not succeeded in reducing them to commonplace, to point out with solemn warning as "wild," "erratic," and the like; much as if one should complain of the Niagara river for not flowing smoothly between its banks like a Dutch canal.

I insist thus emphatically on the importance of genius, and the necessity of allowing it to unfold itself freely both in thought and in practice, being well aware that no one will deny the position in theory, but knowing also that almost everyone, in reality, is totally indifferent to it. People think genius a fine thing if it enables a man to write an exciting poem, or paint a picture. But in its true sense, that of originality in thought and action, though no one says that it is not a thing to be admired, nearly all, at heart, think that they can do very well without it. Unhappily this is too natural to be wondered at. Originality is the one thing which unoriginal minds cannot feel the use of. They cannot see what it is to do for them: how should they? If they could see what it would do for them, it would not be originality. The first service which originality has to render them, is that of opening their eyes: which being once fully done, they would have a chance of being themselves original. Meanwhile, recollecting that nothing was ever yet done which someone was not the first to do, and that all good things which exist are the fruits of originality, let them be modest enough to believe that there is something still left for it to accomplish, and assure themselves that they are more in need of originality, the less they are conscious of the want.

In sober truth, whatever homage may be professed, or even paid, to real or supposed mental superiority, the general tendency of things throughout the world is to render mediocrity the ascendant power among mankind. In ancient history, in the Middle Ages, and in a diminishing degree through the long transition from feudality to the present time, the individual was a power in himself; and if he had either great talents or a high social position, he was a considerable power. At present individuals are lost in the crowd. In politics it is almost a triviality to say that public opinion now rules the world. The only power deserving the name is that of masses, and of governments while they make themselves the organ of the tendencies and instincts of masses. This is as true in the moral and social relations of private life as in public transactions. Those whose opinions go by the name of public opinion are not always the same sort of public: in America they are the whole white population; in England, chiefly the middle class. But they are always a mass, that is to say, collective mediocrity. And what is a still greater novelty, the mass do not now take their opinions from dignitaries in Church or State, from ostensible leaders, or from books. Their thinking is done for them by men much like themselves, addressing them or speaking in their name, on the spur of the moment, through the newspapers. I am not complaining of all this. I do not assert that anything better is compatible, as a general rule, with the present low state of the human mind. But that does not hinder the government of mediocrity from being mediocre government. No government by a democracy or a numerous aristocracy, either in its political acts or in the opinions, qualities, and tone of mind which it fosters, ever did or could rise above mediocrity, except in so far as the sovereign Many have let themselves be guided (which in their best times they always have done) by the counsels and influence of a more highly gifted and instructed One or Few. The initiation of all wise or noble things comes and must come from individuals; generally at first from some one individual. The honor and glory of the average man is that he is capable of following that initiative; that he can respond internally to wise and noble things, and be led to them with his eyes open. I am not countenancing the sort of "hero-worship" which applauds the strong man of genius for forcibly seizing on the government of the world and making it do his bidding in spite of itself. All he can claim is, freedom to point out the way. The power of compelling others into it is not only inconsistent with the freedom and development of all the rest, but corrupting to the strong man himself. It does seem, however, that when the opinions of masses of merely average men are everywhere become or becoming the dominant power, the counterpoise and corrective to that tendency would be the more and more pronounced individuality of those who stand on the higher eminences of thought. It is in these circumstances most especially, that exceptional individuals, instead of being deterred, should be encouraged in acting differently from the mass. In other times there was no advantage in their doing so, unless they acted not only differently but better. In this age, the mere example of nonconformity, the mere refusal to bend the knee to custom, is itself a service. Precisely because the tyranny of opinion is such as to make eccentricity a reproach, it is desirable, in order to break through that tyranny, that people should be

eccentric. Eccentricity has always abounded when and where strength of character has abounded; and the amount of eccentricity in a society has generally been proportional to the amount of genius, mental vigor, and moral courage it contained. That so few now dare to be eccentric marks the chief danger of the time.

I have said that it is important to give the freest scope possible to uncustomary things, in order that it may in time appear which of these are fit to be converted into customs. But independence of action, and disregard of custom, are not solely deserving of encouragement for the chance they afford that better modes of action, and customs more worthy of general adoption, may be struck out; nor is it only persons of decided mental superiority who have a just claim to carry on their lives in their own way. There is no reason that all human existence should be constructed on some one or some small number of patterns. If a person possesses any tolerable amount of common sense and experience, his own mode of laying out his existence is the best, not because it is the best in itself, but because it is his own mode. Human beings are not like sheep; and even sheep are not undistinguishably alike. A man cannot get a coat or a pair of boots to fit him unless they are either made to his measure, or he has a whole warehouseful to choose from: and is it easier to fit him with a life than with a coat, or are human beings more like one another in their whole physical and spiritual conformation than in the shape of their feet? If it were only that people have diversities of taste, that is reason enough for not attempting to shape them all after one model. But different persons also require different conditions for their spiritual development; and can no more exist healthily in the same moral, than all the variety of plants can in the same physical, atmosphere and climate. The same things which are helps to one person towards the cultivation of his higher nature are hindrances to another. The same mode of life is a healthy excitement to one, keeping all his faculties of action and enjoyment in their best order, while to another it is a distracting burthen, which suspends or crushes all internal life. Such are the differences among human beings in their sources of pleasure, their susceptibilities of pain, and the operation on them of different physical and moral agencies, that unless there is a corresponding diversity in their modes of life, they neither obtain their fair share of happiness, nor grow up to the mental, moral, and aesthetic stature of which their nature is capable. . . .

There is one characteristic of the present direction of public opinion peculiarly calculated to make it intolerant of any marked demonstration of individuality. The general average of mankind are not only moderate in intellect, but also moderate in inclinations: they have no tastes or wishes strong enough to incline them to do anything unusual, and they consequently do not understand those who have, and class all such with the wild and intemperate whom they are accustomed to look down upon. Now, in addition to this fact which is general, we have only to suppose that a strong movement has set in towards the improvement of morals,

and it is evident what we have to expect. In these days such a movement has set in; much has actually been effected in the way of increased regularity of conduct and discouragement of excesses; and there is a philanthropic spirit abroad, for the exercise of which there is no more inviting field than the moral and prudential improvement of our fellow-creatures. These tendencies of the times cause the public to be more disposed than at most former periods to prescribe general rules of conduct, and endeavor to make every one conform to the approved standard. And that standard, express or tacit, is to desire nothing strongly. Its ideal of character is to be without any marked character; to maim by compression, like a Chinese lady's foot, every part of human nature which stands out prominently, and tends to make the person markedly dissimilar in outline to commonplace humanity.

As is usually the case with ideals which exclude one-half of what is desirable, the present standard of approbation produces only an inferior imitation of the other half. Instead of great energies guided by vigorous reason, and strong feelings strongly controlled by a conscientious will, its result is weak feelings, and weak energies, which therefore can be kept in outward conformity to rule without any strength either of will or of reason. Already energetic characters on any large scale are becoming merely traditional. There is now scarcely any outlet for energy in this country except business. The energy expended in this may still be regarded as considerable. What little is left from that employment is expended on some hobby; which may be a useful, even a philanthropic hobby, but is always some one thing, and generally a thing of small dimensions. The greatness of England is now all collective; individually small, we only appear capable of anything great by our habit of combining; and with this our moral and religious philanthropists are perfectly contented. But it was men of another stamp than this that made England what it has been; and men of another stamp will be needed to prevent its decline.

The despotism of custom is everywhere the standing hindrance to human advancement, being in unceasing antagonism to that disposition to aim at something better than customary, which is called, according to circumstances, the spirit of liberty, or that of progress or improvement. The spirit of improvement is not always a spirit of liberty, for it may aim at forcing improvements on an unwilling people; and the spirit of liberty, in so far as it resists such attempts, may ally itself locally and temporarily with the opponents of improvement; but the only unfailing and permanent source of improvement is liberty, since by it there are as many possible independent centers of improvement as there are individuals. The progressive principle, however, in either shape, whether as the love of liberty or of improvement, is antagonistic to the sway of custom, involving at least emancipation from that yoke; and the contest between the two constitutes the chief interest of the history of mankind. . . .

What has made the European family of nations an improving, instead of a stationary portion of mankind? Not any superior excellence in them, which, when it exists, exists as the effect not as the cause; but their remarkable diversity of character and culture. Individuals, classes, nations, have been extremely unlike one another: they have struck out a great variety of paths, each leading to something valuable; and although at every period those who traveled in different paths have been intolerant of one another, and each would have thought it an excellent thing if all the rest could have been compelled to travel his road, their attempts to thwart each other's development have rarely had any permanent success, and each has in time endured to receive the good which the others have offered. Europe is, in my judgment, wholly indebted to this plurality of paths for its progressive and many-sided development. But it already begins to possess this benefit in a considerably less degree. M. de Tocqueville, in his last important work, remarks how much more the Frenchmen of the present day resemble one another than did those even of the last generation. The same remark might be made of Englishmen in a far greater degree. In a passage already quoted from Wilhelm von Humboldt, he points out two things as necessary conditions of human development, because necessary to render people unlike one another: namely, freedom, and variety of situations. The second of these two conditions is in this country every day diminishing. The circumstances which surround different classes and individuals, and shape their characters, are daily becoming more assimilated. Formerly, different ranks, different neighborhoods, different trades and professions, lived in what might be called different worlds; at present to a great degree in the same. Comparatively speaking, they now read the same things, listen to the same things, see the same things, go to the same places, have their hopes and fears directed to the same objects, have the same rights and liberties, and the same means of asserting them. Great as are the differences of position which remain, they are nothing to those which have ceased. And the assimilation is still proceeding. All the political changes of the age promote it, since they all tend to raise the low and to lower the high. Every extension of education promotes it, because education brings people under common influences, and gives them access to the general stock of facts and sentiments. Improvement in the means of communication promotes it, by bringing the inhabitants of distant places into personal contact, and keeping up a rapid flow of changes of residence between one place and another. The increase of commerce and manufactures promotes it, by diffusing more widely the advantages of easy circumstances, and opening all objects of ambition, even the highest, to general competition, whereby the desire of rising becomes no longer the character of a particular class, but of all classes. A more powerful agency than even all these, in bringing about a general similarity among mankind, is the complete establishment, in this and other free countries, of the ascendancy of public opinion in the State. As the various social eminences which enabled persons en-

trenched on them to disregard the opinion of the multitude gradually become leveled; as the very idea of resisting the will of the public, when it is positively known that they have a will, disappears more and more from the minds of practical politicians: there ceases to be any social support for nonconformity— any substantive power in society which, itself opposed to the ascendancy of numbers, is interested in taking under its protection opinions and tendencies at variance with those of the public.

The combination of all these causes forms so great a mass of influences hostile to individuality, that it is not easy to see how it can stand its ground. It will do so with increasing difficulty, unless the intelligent part of the public can be made to feel its value—to see that it is good there should be differences, even though not for the better, even though, as it may appear to them, some should be for the worse. If the claims of individuality are ever to be asserted, the time is now, while much is still wanting to complete the enforced assimilation. It is only in the earlier stages that any stand can be successfully made against the encroachment. The demand that all other people shall resemble ourselves grows by what it feeds on. If resistance waits till life is reduced *nearly* to one uniform type, all deviations from that type will come to be considered impious, immoral, even monstrous and contrary to nature. Mankind speedily become unable to conceive diversity, when they have been for some time unaccustomed to see it.

COMMENT

The Basis of Mill's Argument

The older liberals, especially Locke and Jefferson, espoused liberty as an inalienable natural right. Mill, in contrast, avowedly based his argument on "utility, in the largest sense." Progress, he maintained, is desirable for human welfare, and free thought and action are necessary for that end. The ultimate standard for judging social institutions is their contribution to happiness. Mill thus began by running up the banner of utilitarianism.

The real premise of his argument, however, is not the calculation of pleasure and pain but the inner value of character and unhampered individuality. In Chapter III of *On Liberty*, he mentions with approval the doctrine of "self-realization" advocated by Wilhelm von Humboldt. "The end of man," according to this German writer, "is the highest and most harmonious development of his powers to a complete and consistent whole," and for this there are two requisites, "freedom and variety of situations." This theory of self-realization is the focus of Mill's teaching. It underlies his decided preference for highly developed individuals rather than "ape-like imitators." Liberty enables a person to be a person — to attain the full use and development of one's powers. To live freely is to unfold one's individual human capacities; to live servilely — by custom, imitation, social pressure, or repressive political rule — is to be less than a human being. Liberty is the acknowledgment of the peculiar dignity of a person as a person — and of *each* person's matchless individuality. There is slight trace in this essay of the earlier teaching of the utilitarians that it does not matter what people are like provided that they have as much pleasure and as little pain as possible.

Mill had become convinced that the modern enemy of liberty is the tyranny of the majority. No longer is the problem that of overthrowing a tyrannical king or the oligarchy of a few. It is the much more difficult problem of freeing dissident individuals and minorities from the pressure of a mass society. Mill had been shocked by Alexis de Tocqueville's classic study, *Democracy in America* (1835–1840), which maintained that the ultimate triumph of democracy is inevitable and that its tendency is to reduce all people to a level of equal mediocrity. Sharing de Tocqueville's alarm, Mill believed that a truly liberal society must be created as a safeguard against mass illiberalism. Such a society would be deeply respectful of human freedom. His argument, therefore, is primarily a defense of individuality against the conventionalities of society, the despotism of social custom, and the overweening powers of government.

Individual and Social Standards of Human Fulfillment

The traditional theory of democracy is the doctrine of natural rights. The language of the American Declaration of Independence and the French Declaration of the Rights of Man, for example, is largely derived from this tradition. Mill believed that his doctrine of the supreme importance of individuality contradicts the natural rights tradition, but his standard of self-realization is not so far removed from that of natural rights as might be supposed at first glance. What distinguishes his doctrine from most theories of natural right is the strong emphasis on the diversity of human nature. To live freely is to unfold one's *individual* human capacities. His theory in this sense is complementary rather than contradictory to the natural rights theory. It calls attention to the individual, and not merely the generic, elements in human nature.

More than the older natural rights theorists, such as Locke and Rousseau, Mill was aware that society must adapt itself to changing historical circumstances. Similarly Dewey, in his version of democratic liberalism, was keenly aware of the tides of historical change and their relevance to democratic ideals. This is also the characteristic approach of Marxists who insist that "democracy," "socialism," and "communism" are historical concepts with changing meaning and content. Typical is Marx's remark in *The Critique of the Gotha Program* that "right can never be higher than the economic structure of the society and the cultural development conditioned by it." But Mill, more than Marx, insisted on the autonomy and self-fulfillment of the individual.

The contrast between the more individualistic emphasis of Mill and the more social emphasis of Marx should incite lively discussion. While thinking about these differences, however, we should not overlook the similarities. Mill became increasingly convinced as he grew older that real freedom requires the resources and opportunities that enable people to fulfill their potentialities and effectuate their choices. In his essay on Coleridge, he contended that "a State ought to be considered a great benefit society, or mutual insurance company, for helping (under the necessary regulations for preventing abuse) that large proportion of its members who cannot help themselves." He was inclined to favor cooperative ownership and management of industry by the workers instead of either capitalistic or state-socialistic operation. "There can be little doubt," he said in *Principles of Political Economy*, "that the relation of masters and workpeople will be gradually superseded by partnership in one of two forms: in some cases, association of the labourers with the capitalist; in others, and perhaps finally in all, association of labourers among themselves." In his *Autobiography*, he declared that "the social problem of the future" is "how to unite the greatest individual liberty of action with a common ownership of the raw materials of the globe, and an equal participation of all in the benefits of combined labour." He was nevertheless opposed to state intervention "to chain up the free agency of individuals."

Conclusion

So far we have examined the ideas of four major figures in social philosophy — Plato, Hobbes, Marx, and Mill. They differ in many respects, and not least in their attitudes toward democracy. Plato believed in the cultivation of excellence by the rule of the wise — he rejected democracy because its leaders are neither wise nor devoted to excellence. Marx regarded democracy in a capitalist society as a façade for the rule of wealth and privilege, and he predicted that it would be superseded by a socialist state. Socialism, in turn, will develop into a cooperative anarchism, and the state, as a coercive organization, will "wither away." Mill regarded representative democracy as the best form of government for a modern civilized society, but he warned against the tyranny of the majority and he defended the liberties of the dissident individual. If we add to these characterizations other relevant ideas, such as the concept of natural rights, we have a wide and rich gamut of theories.

HENRY DAVID THOREAU (1817 – 1861)

Born in Concord, Massachusetts, as the son of a pencil maker, Thoreau graduated from Harvard College, after which he made pencils, taught school, did surveying and manual labor. He simplified his life so that he could spend most of his time rambling over the countryside and doing as he pleased. For a period of two years he dwelt in a cabin in the woods where he read, wrote, meditated, and lived as far as possible off the bounty of nature. "I went to the woods," he explained, "because I wished to live deliberately, to front only the essential facts of life, and to see if I could learn what it had to teach, and not, when I came to die, discover that I had not lived." The record of this search for a sound scale of values is to be found in *Walden*, his most famous book.

Like his literary friends in the "Concord group," which included Emerson and Hawthorne, he was a bitter foe of slavery. He was jailed for refusing to pay his poll tax to a state which countenanced both slavery and war with Mexico, and later he delivered the lecture on *Civil Disobedience* as explanation of his defiance. This lecture has had a worldwide influence.

Contracting bronchitis which turned into tuberculosis, he died at the early age of forty-four.

Civil Disobedience

I heartily accept the motto, — "That government is best which governs least"; and I should like to see it acted up to more rapidly and systematically. Carried out, it finally amounts to this, which also I believe, — "That government is best which governs not at all"; and when men are prepared for it, that will be the kind of government which they will have. Government is at best but an expedient; but most governments are usually, and all governments are sometimes, inexpedient. The objections which have been brought against a standing army, and they are many and weighty, and deserve to prevail, may also at last be brought against a standing government. The standing army is only an arm of the standing government. The government itself, which is only the mode which the people have chosen to execute their will, is equally liable to be abused and perverted before the people can act through it. Witness the present Mexican war, the work of comparatively a few individuals using the standing government as their tool; for, in the outset, the people would not have consented to this measure.

This American government, — what is it but a tradition, though a recent one, endeavoring to transmit itself unimpaired to posterity, but each instant losing some of its integrity? It has not the vitality and force of a single living man; for a single man can bend it to his will. It is a sort of wooden gun to the people themselves. But it is not the less necessary for this; for the people must have some complicated machinery or other, and hear its din, to satisfy that idea of government which they have. Governments show thus how successfully men can be imposed on, even impose on themselves, for their own advantage. It is excellent, we must all allow. Yet this government never of itself furthered any enterprise, but by the alacrity with which it got out of its way. *It* does not keep the country free. *It* does not settle the West. *It* does not educate. The character inherent in the American people has done all that has been accomplished; and it would have done somewhat more, if the government had not sometimes got in its way. For government is an expedient by which men would fain succeed in letting one another alone; and, as has been said, when it is most expedient, the governed are most let alone by it. Trade and commerce, if they were not made of India-rubber, would never manage to bounce over the obstacles which legislators are continually putting in their way; and, if one were to judge these men wholly by the effects of their actions and not partly by their intentions, they would deserve to be classed and punished with those mischievous persons who put obstructions on the railroads.

Delivered by Thoreau as a lecture before the Concord Lyceum on January 26, 1848. The present version was first published in Thoreau's *A Yankee in Canada, with Anti-Slavery and Reform Papers* (Boston: Tichnor & Fields, 1866).

But, to speak practically and as a citizen, unlike those who call themselves no-government men, I ask for, not at once no government, but *at once* a better government. Let every man make known what kind of government would command his respect, and that will be one step toward obtaining it.

After all, the practical reason why, when the power is once in the hands of the people, a majority are permitted, and for a long period continue, to rule, is not because they are most likely to be in the right, nor because this seems fairest to the minority, but because they are physically the strongest. But a government in which the majority rule in all cases cannot be based on justice, even as far as men understand it. Can there not be a government in which majorities do not virtually decide right and wrong, but conscience? — in which majorities decide only those questions to which the rule of expediency is applicable? Must the citizen ever for a moment, or in the least degree, resign his conscience to the legislator? Why has every man a conscience, then? I think that we should be men first, and subjects afterward. It is not desirable to cultivate a respect for the law, so much as for the right. The only obligation which I have a right to assume, is to do at any time what I think right. It is truly enough said, that a corporation has no conscience; but a corporation of conscientious men is a corporation *with* a conscience. Law never made men a whit more just; and, by means of their respect for it, even the well-disposed are daily made the agents of injustice. A common and natural result of an undue respect for law is, that you may see a file of soldiers, colonel, captain, corporal, privates, powder-monkeys, and all, marching against their wills, ay, against their common sense and consciences, which makes it very steep marching indeed, and produces a palpitation of the heart. They have no doubt that it is a damnable business in which they are concerned; they are all peaceably inclined. Now, what are they? Men at all? or small movable forts and magazines, at the service of some unscrupulous man in power? Visit the Navy-Yard, and behold a marine, such a man as an American government can make, or such as it can make a man with its black arts, — a mere shadow and reminiscent of humanity, a man laid out alive and standing, and already, as one may say, buried under arms with funeral accompaniments, though it may be, —

Not a drum was heard, not a funeral
    note,
    As his corse to the rampart we
        hurried;
Not a soldier discharged his farewell
    shot
    O'er the grave where our hero we
        buried.[1]

The mass of men serve the state thus, not as men mainly, but as machines, with their bodies. They are the standing army, and the militia, jailers, constables, posse comitatus,[2] &c. In most cases there is no free exercise

[1]"Burial of Sir John Moore at Corunna," by Charles Wolfe (1791–1823).
[2]The body of men that the sheriff is empowered to call into service in case of a riot or similar disturbance.

whatever of the judgment or of the moral sense; but they put themselves on a level with wood and earth and stones; and wooden men can perhaps be manufactured that will serve the purpose as well. Such command no more respect than men of straw or a lump of dirt. They have the same sort of worth only as horses and dogs. Yet such as these even are commonly esteemed good citizens. Others, — as most legislators, politicians, lawyers, ministers, and office-holders, — serve the state chiefly with their heads; and, as they rarely make any moral distinctions, they are as likely to serve the Devil, without *intending* it, as God. A very few, as heroes, patriots, martyrs, reformers in the great sense, and *men*, serve the state with their consciences also, and so necessarily resist it for the most part; and they are commonly treated as enemies by it. A wise man will only be useful as a man, and will not submit to be "clay," and "stop a hole to keep the wind away,"[3] but leave that office to his dust at least: —

I am too high-born to be propertied,
To be a secondary at control,
Or useful serving-man and instru-
*   ment*
To any sovereign state throughout
*   the world.*[4]

He who gives himself entirely to his fellow-men appears to them useless and selfish; but he who gives himself partially to them is pronounced a benefactor and philanthropist.

How does it become a man to behave toward this American government today? I answer, that he cannot without disgrace be associated with it. I cannot for an instant recognize that political organization as *my* government which is the *slave's* government also.

All men recognize the right of revolution; that is, the right to refuse allegiance to, and to resist, the government, when its tyranny or its inefficiency are great and unendurable. But almost all say that such is not the case now. But such was the case, they think, in the Revolution of '75. If one were to tell me that this was a bad government because it taxed certain foreign commodities brought to its ports, it is most probable that I should not make an ado about it, for I can do without them. All machines have their friction; and possibly this does enough good to counterbalance the evil. At any rate, it is a great evil to make a stir about it. But when the friction comes to have its machine, and oppression and robbery are organized, I say, let us not have such a machine any longer. In other words, when a sixth of the population of a nation which has undertaken to be the refuge of liberty are slaves, and a whole country is unjustly overrun and conquered by a foreign army, and subjected to military law, I think that it is not too soon for honest men to rebel and revolutionize. What makes this duty the more urgent is the fact, that the country so overrun is not our own, but ours is the invading army.

Paley,[5] a common authority with

---

[3]"Imperious Caesar, dead and turn'd to clay, Might stop a hole to keep the wind away." —Shakespeare, *Hamlet*, V. i. 236–237.
[4]Shakespeare, *King John*, V. ii. 79–82.

[5]William Paley (1743–1805), *Moral and Political Philosophy*.

many on moral questions, in his chapter on the "Duty of Submission to Civil Government," resolves all civil obligation into expediency; and he proceeds to say, "that so long as the interest of the whole society requires it, that is, so long as the established government cannot be resisted or changed without public inconveniency, it is the will of God that the established government be obeyed, and no longer. . . . This principle being admitted, the justice of every particular case of resistance is reduced to a computation of the quantity of the danger and grievance on the one side, and of the probability and expense of redressing it on the other." Of this, he says, every man shall judge for himself. But Paley appears never to have contemplated those cases to which the rule of expediency does not apply, in which a people, as well as an individual, must do justice, cost what it may. If I have unjustly wrested a plank from a drowning man, I must restore it to him though I drown myself. This, according to Paley, would be inconvenient. But he that would save his life, in such a case, shall lose it. This people must cease to hold slaves, and to make war on Mexico, though it cost them their existence as a people.

In their practice, nations agree with Paley; but does any one think that Massachusetts does exactly what is right at the present crisis?

A drab of state, a cloth-o'-silver slut,
To have her train borne up, and her
soul trail in the dirt.[6]

[6]Cyril Tourneur, *The Revengers Tragaedie* (1608), IV. iv.

Practically speaking, the opponents to a reform in Massachusetts are not a hundred thousand politicians at the South, but a hundred thousand merchants and farmers here, who are more interested in commerce and agriculture than they are in humanity, and are not prepared to do justice to the slave and to Mexico, *cost what it may.* I quarrel not with far-off foes, but with those who, near at home, co-operate with, and do the bidding of, those far away, and without whom the latter would be harmless. We are accustomed to say, that the mass of men are unprepared; but improvement is slow, because the few are not materially wiser or better than the many. It is not so important that many should be as good as you, as that there be some absolute goodness somewhere; for that will leaven the whole lump. There are thousands who are *in opinion* opposed to slavery and to the war, who yet in effect do nothing to put an end to them; who, esteeming themselves children of Washington and Franklin, sit down with their hands in their pockets, and say that they know not what to do, and do nothing; who even postpone the question of freedom to the question of free-trade, and quietly read the prices-current along with the latest advices from Mexico, after dinner, and, it may be, fall asleep over them both. What is the price-current of an honest man and patriot today? They hesitate, and they regret, and sometimes they petition; but they do nothing in earnest and with effect. They will wait, well disposed, for others to remedy the evil, that they may no longer have it to regret. At most, they give only a cheap vote, and a feeble countenance and God-speed, to the right, as it goes by them. There are nine hundred and ninety-nine patrons of virtue to one virtuous man. But it is easier to deal with the real possessor of a thing than with the temporary guardian of it.

All voting is a sort of gaming, like checkers or backgammon, with a slight moral tinge to it, a playing with right and wrong, with moral questions; and betting naturally accompanies it. The character of the voters is not staked. I cast my vote, perchance, as I think right; but I am not vitally concerned that that right should prevail. I am willing to leave it to the majority. Its obligation, therefore, never exceeds that of expediency. Even voting *for the right* is *doing* nothing for it. It is only expressing to men feebly your desire that it should prevail. A wise man will not leave the right to the mercy of chance, nor wish it to prevail through the power of the majority. There is but little virtue in the action of masses of men. When the majority shall at length vote for the abolition of slavery, it will be because they are indifferent to slavery, or because there is but little slavery left to be abolished by their vote. *They* will then be the only slaves. Only *his* vote can hasten the abolition of slavery who asserts his own freedom by his vote.

I hear of a convention to be held at Baltimore,[7] or elsewhere, for the selection of a candidate for the Presidency, made up chiefly of editors, and men who are politicians by profession; but I think, what is it to any independent, intelligent, and respectable man what decision they may come to? Shall we not have the advantage of his wisdom and honesty, nevertheless? Can we not count upon some independent votes? Are there not many individuals in the country who do not attend conventions? But no: I find that the respectable man, so called, has immediately drifted from his position, and despairs of his country, when his country has more reason to despair of him. He forthwith adopts one of the candidates thus selected as the only *available* one, thus proving that he is himself *available* for any purposes of the demagogue. His vote is of no more worth than that of any unprincipled foreigner or hireling native, who may have been bought. O for a man who is a *man*, and, as my neighbor says, has a bone in his back which you cannot pass your hand through! Our statistics are at fault: the population has been returned too large. How many *men* are there to a square thousand miles in this country? Hardly one.

It is not a man's duty, as a matter of course, to devote himself to the eradication of any, even the most enormous wrong; he may still properly have other concerns to engage him; but it is his duty, at least, to wash his hands of it, and, if he gives it no thought longer, not to give it practically his support. If I devote myself to other pursuits and contemplations, I must first see, at least, that I do not pursue them sitting upon another man's shoulders. I must get off him first, that he may pursue his contemplations too. See what gross in-

---

[7] The Democratic Party, holding its 1848 convention in Baltimore, straddled the fence by avoiding any discussion of slavery.

consistency is tolerated. I have heard some of my townsmen say, "I should like to have them order me out to help put down an insurrection of the slaves, or to march to Mexico;—see if I would go"; and yet these very men have each, directly by their allegiance, and so indirectly, at least, by their money, furnished a substitute. The soldier is applauded who refuses to serve in an unjust war by those who do not refuse to sustain the unjust government which makes the war; is applauded by those whose own act and authority he disregards and sets at naught; as if the State were penitent to that degree that it hired one to scourge it while it sinned, but not to that degree that it left off sinning for a moment. Thus, under the name of Order and Civil Government, we are all made at last to pay homage to and support our own meanness. After the first blush of sin comes its indifference; and from immoral it becomes, as it were, unmoral, and not quite unnecessary to that life which we have made. . . .

Unjust laws exist: shall we be content to obey them, or shall we endeavor to amend them, and obey them until we have succeeded, or shall we transgress them at once? Men generally, under such a government as this, think that they ought to wait until they have persuaded the majority to alter them. They think that, if they should resist, the remedy would be worse than the evil. But it is the fault of the government itself that the remedy *is* worse than the evil. *It* makes it worse. Why is it not more apt to anticipate and provide for reform? Why does it not cherish its wise minority? Why does it cry and re-sist before it is hurt? Why does it not encourage its citizens to be on the alert to point out its faults, and *do* better than it would have them? Why does it always crucify Christ, and excommunicate Copernicus and Luther, and pronounce Washington and Franklin rebels? . . .

If the injustice is part of the necessary friction of the machine of government, let it go, let it go: perchance it will wear smooth,—certainly the machine will wear out. If the injustice has a spring, or a pulley, or a rope, or a crank, exclusively for itself, then perhaps you may consider whether the remedy will not be worse than the evil; but if it is of such a nature that it requires you to be the agent of injustice to another, then, I say, break the law. Let your life be a counter friction to stop the machine. What I have to do is to see, at any rate, that I do not lend myself to the wrong which I condemn. . . .

Under a government which imprisons any unjustly, the true place for a just man is also a prison. The proper place to-day, the only place which Massachusetts has provided for her freer and less desponding spirits, is in her prisons, to be put out and locked out of the State by her own act, as they have already put themselves out by their principles. It is there that the fugitive slave, and the Mexican prisoner on parole, and the Indian come to plead the wrongs of his race, should find them; on that separate, but more free and honorable ground, where the State places those who are not *with* her, but *against* her,—the only house in a slave State in which a free man can abide with honor. If any think that their influence would be lost there, and their voices no longer afflict the ear of the State, that they would not be as an enemy within its walls, they do not know by how much truth is stronger than error, nor how much more eloquently and effectively he can combat injustice who has experienced a little in his own person. Cast your whole vote, not a strip of paper merely, but your whole influence. A minority is powerless while it conforms to the majority; it is not even a minority then; but it is irresistible when it clogs by its whole weight. If the alternative is to keep all just men in prison, or give up war and slavery, the State will not hesitate which to choose. If a thousand men were not to pay their tax-bills this year, that would not be a violent and bloody measure, as it would be to pay them, and enable the State to commit violence and shed innocent blood. This is, in fact, the definition of a peaceable revolution, if any such is possible. If the tax-gatherer, or any other public officer, asks me, as one has done, "But what shall I do?" my answer is, "If you really wish to do anything, resign your office." When the subject has refused allegiance, and the officer has resigned his office, then the revolution is accomplished. But even suppose blood should flow. Is there not a sort of blood shed when the conscience is wounded? Through this wound a man's real manhood and immortality flow out, and he bleeds to an everlasting death. I see this blood flowing now. . . .

I have paid no poll-tax for six years. I was put into a jail once on this account, for one night; and, as I stood considering the walls of solid stone, two or three feet thick, the door of wood and iron, a foot thick, and the iron grating which strained the light, I could not help being struck with the foolishness of that institution which treated me as if I were mere flesh and blood and bones, to be locked up. I wondered that it should have concluded at length that this was the best use it could put me to, and had never thought to avail itself of my services in some way. I saw that, if there was a wall of stone between me and my townsmen, there was a still more difficult one to climb or break through, before they could get to be as free as I was. I did not for a moment feel confined, and the walls seemed a great waste of stone and mortar. I felt as if I alone of all my townsmen had paid my tax. They plainly did not know how to treat me, but behaved like persons who are underbred. In every threat and in every compliment there was a blunder; for they thought that my chief desire was to stand the other side of that stone wall. I could not but smile to see how industriously they locked the door on my meditations, which followed them out again without let or hindrance, and *they* were really all that was dangerous. As they could not reach me, they had resolved to punish my body; just as boys, if they cannot come at some person against whom they have a spite, will abuse his dog. I saw that the State was half-witted, that it was timid as a lone woman with her silver spoons, and that it did not know its friends from its foes, and I lost all my remaining respect for it, and pitied it.

Thus the State never intentionally confronts a man's sense, intellectual or moral, but only his body, his senses. It is not armed with superior wit or honesty, but with superior physical strength. I was not born to be forced. I will breathe after my own fashion. Let us see who is the strongest. What force has a multitude? They only can force me who obey a higher law[8] than I. They force me to become like themselves. I do not hear of *men* being *forced* to live this way or that by masses of men. What sort of life were that to live? When I meet a government which says to me, "Your money or your life," why should I be in haste to give it my money? It may be in a great strait, and not know what to do: I cannot help that. It must help itself; do as I do. It is not worth the while to snivel about it. I am not responsible for the successful working of the machinery of society. I am not the son of the engineer. I perceive that, when an acorn and a chestnut fall side by side, the one does not remain inert to make way for the other, but both obey their own laws and spring and grow and flourish as best they can, till one, perchance, overshadows and destroys the other. If a plant cannot live according to its nature, it dies; and so a man. . . .

The authority of government, even such as I am willing to submit to, — for I will cheerfully obey those who know and can do better than I, and in many

[8] The law of one's conscience regarded as higher than that of the State.

things even those who neither know nor can do so well, — is still an impure one: to be strictly just, it must have the sanction and consent of the governed. It can have no pure right over my person and property but what I concede to it. The progress from an absolute to a limited monarchy, from a limited monarchy to a democracy, is a progress toward a true respect for the individual. Even the Chinese philosopher [Confucius] was wise enough to regard the individual as the basis of the empire. Is a democracy, such as we know it, the last improvement possible in government? Is it not possible to take a step further towards recognizing and organizing the rights of man? There will never be a really free and enlightened State, until the State comes to recognize the individual as a higher and independent power, from which all its own power and authority are derived, and treats him accordingly. I please myself with imagining a State at last which can afford to be just to all men, and to treat the individual with respect as a neighbor; which even would not think it inconsistent with its own repose, if a few were to live aloof from it, not meddling with it, nor embraced by it, who fulfilled all the duties of neighbors and fellow-men. A State which bore this kind of fruit, and suffered it to drop off as fast as it ripened, would prepare the way for a still more perfect and glorious State, which also I have imagined, but not yet anywhere seen.

COMMENT

The defense of civil disobedience by Thoreau is even more sharply individualistic than is Mill's argument for liberty. His argument is based on the premise that individual conscience is the only valid criterion of what is politically right and just.

We have already confronted the question of civil disobedience in Chapter 1. The position of Socrates in Plato's *Apology* is as uncompromising as that of Thoreau. He declares that if the Athenian state should spare his life on condition that he will no longer teach he would not obey. His own judgment as to what is good and right takes precedence over the decision of the jury. He is determined to obey God and his own conscience, come what may. Superficially regarded, the *Crito* seems to contradict this stand. Here Socrates replies to the arguments of his old friend Crito in favor of escaping from prison. Thus to break the law and defy the state, Socrates argues, would be to violate one's faith with the civic community that has acted, in effect, as parent and teacher. What makes the two dialogues consistent is that in both Socrates is following the dictates of his conscience. In the *Apology* he recognizes that being true to his philosophical mission represents the highest duty. In the *Crito* he contends that escape by bribery and ruse is dishonorable, and that he will not really be doing himself, his friends, his family, or the state any good by becoming an outlaw and going into exile. If Thoreau's *Civil Disobedience* is compared with Plato's two dialogues, they will provide rich source material for the discussion of the nature and limits of duty to the state.

Thoreau's attitude toward civil disobedience is also related to Cicero's defense of "the law of nature" as higher and more binding than the law of the state. In effect Thoreau is proclaiming a one-man Declaration of Independence, which, like Jefferson's Declaration, has its roots in the ancient tradition of natural law and natural rights.

Although Thoreau had his spiritual roots in the past, he appealed most deeply not to his own contemporaries but to men in the twentieth century. Translated by Mahatma Gandhi, his lecture became a manual for the civil disobedience movement in India against British imperialism. In Denmark it was used as a text by the anti-Nazi resistance during World War II. In America in the 1960s, Dr. Martin Luther King and other civil rights leaders took it to heart, and it helped to inspire conscientious objection to the war in Viet Nam. These are a few of the uses to which Thoreau's ideas have been put.

His lecture was delivered a long time ago but it retains its perennial appeal. He has reminded all of us — and we in this age of mass-civilization need to be reminded — that it is the toughness, the intransigence, and the spiritual vitality of the individual that gives edge to democracy. "Men

have become the tools of their tools," he said, and many will sympathize
with this protest against the mechanization of life. His conviction that
every man should find his own integrity in whatever fashion seems best to
him, fits in with the mood of the younger generation.

Both Thoreau and Mill, it should be noted, were intense individualists.
Thoreau was at least half serious when he said, "That government is best
which governs not at all." Although less the philosophical anarchist, Mill
defended the *uncommon* man in his independence, even in his eccentricity, as against government, public opinion, and "collective mediocrity."
His essay, as George H. Sabine has said, "is in a sense a defense of liberty
against democracy."[1]

Communism

> *"In a higher phase of communist society, when the enslaving subordination of the individual to the division of labour . . . has vanished; when labour is no longer a means of life but has become life's principle need; . . . and all the springs of co-operative wealth flow more abundantly . . . only then will society be able to inscribe on its banners: From each according to his ability, to each according to his need."*
>
> KARL MARX

KARL MARX (1818-1883)

Born in Treves in the German Rhineland, Marx was the son of well-to-do Jewish parents who had been converted to Christianity. He studied law, history, and philosophy at the universities of Bonn, Berlin, and Jena, imbibing the doctrines of Hegel, then at the height of his fame. His doctoral thesis was on the materialism of Democritus and Epicurus. In 1842-1843 he edited a newspaper at Cologne, which was suppressed by the Prussian government because of its advanced ideas. After marrying Jennie von Westphalen, a beautiful young woman of aristocratic lineage, he went to Paris, where he studied the socialist movement. There he met Friedrich Engels, a young German who worked in the family business of Ermen and Engels, cotton spinners in Manchester, first as clerk, eventually as manager and part owner. On the basis of the socialist convictions that they shared, the two young men formed a friendship that endured throughout their lives.

In 1845 the Prussian government, incensed by Marx's continued attacks, persuaded the French authorities to deport him. He then went with Engels to live in Brussels, where he continued his political and journalistic activities. During this period he wrote, singly or in collaboration with Engels, a number of socialist works, the most famous of which is the *Communist Manifesto*, published on the eve of the revolutionary disturbances of 1848. Expelled in turn from Belgium, Marx returned to Cologne, where he founded a radical newspaper and participated in the revolutionary uprisings of 1848-1849. The ensuing political reaction compelled him to seek refuge in England.

With his family, he spent the remainder of his life in London, There he worked for years in the British Museum, accumulating the research materials for his indictment of capitalist society. Having only a small income as a correspondent for the New York *Tribune*, he lived with his wife and children in a squalid attic, often without sufficient food, decent clothing, or other basic necessities. His later years were saddened by ill health and the death of three of his children, but nothing could divert him from unremitting service to his ideals. In 1864 he helped to organize the First International, a radical political organization, which continued under his direction until 1872. His major work is *Capital*, a detailed historical and economic analysis of capitalist society, which he referred to as "the task to which I have sacrificed my health, my happiness in life, and my family." Volume One was published in 1867 and the two remaining volumes after his death.

Communism and History

I. The Materialist Conception of History

I was led by my studies to the conclusion that legal relations as well as forms of state could neither be understood by themselves, nor explained by the so-called general progress of the human mind, but that they are rooted in the

summed up by Hegel after the fashion of the English and French writers of the eighteenth century under the name *civil society*, and the anatomy of civil society is to be sought in political economy. The study of the latter which I had begun in Paris, I continued in Brussels where I had emigrated on account of an expulsion order issued by M. Guizot. The general conclusion at which I arrived and which, once reached, continued to serve as the guiding thread in my studies, may be formulated briefly as follows: In the social production which men carry on they enter into definite relations that are indispensable and independent of their will; these relations of production correspond to a

---

All passages except the speech at the Anniversary of the *People's Paper* are taken from *Karl Marx: Selected Writings in Sociology and Social Philosophy*, ed. T. B. Bottomore and M. Rubel (London: C. A. Watts & Co. Ltd., 1956), or *Karl Marx: Early Writings*, ed. T. B. Bottomore (London: C. A. Watts & Co. Ltd., 1963). Translations are by Bottomore. Reprinted by permission of the publisher. Each passage is followed by a reference to its original source.

definite stage of development of their material powers of production. The totality of these relations of production constitutes the economic structure of society—the real foundation, on which legal and political superstructures arise and to which definite forms of social consciousness correspond. The mode of production of material life determines the general character of the social, political and spiritual processes of life. It is not the consciousness of men that determines their being, but, on the contrary, their social being determines their consciousness. At a certain stage of their development, the material forces of production in society come in conflict with the existing relations of production, or—what is but a legal expression for the same thing—with the property relations within which they had been at work before. From forms of development of the forces of production these relations turn into their fetters. Then occurs a period of social revolution. With the change of the economic foundation the entire immense superstructure is more or less rapidly transformed. In considering such transformations the distinction should always be made between the material transformation of the economic conditions of production which can be determined with the precision of natural science, and the legal, political, religious, aesthetic or philosophical— in short ideological, forms in which men become conscious of this conflict and fight it out. Just as our opinion of an individual is not based on what he thinks of himself, so can we not judge of such a period of transformation by its own consciousness; on the contrary, this consciousness must rather be explained from the contradictions of material life, from the existing conflict between the social forces of production and the relations of production. No social order ever disappears before all the productive forces for which there is room in it have been developed; and new, higher relations of production never appear before the material conditions of their existence have matured in the womb of the old society. Therefore, mankind always sets itself only such problems as it can solve; since, on closer examination, it will always be found that the problem itself arises only when the material conditions necessary for its solution already exist or are at least in the process of formation. In broad outline we can designate the Asiatic, the ancient, the feudal, and the modern bourgeois modes of production as progressive epochs in the economic formation of society. The bourgeois relations of production are the last antagonistic form of the social process of production; not in the sense of individual antagonisms, but of conflict arising from conditions surrounding the life of individuals in society. At the same time the productive forces developing in the womb of bourgeois society create the material conditions for the solution of that antagonism. With this social formation, therefore, the prehistory of human society comes to an end.

Preface to A Contribution to the Critique of Political Economy (1859)

The premises from which we begin are not arbitrary ones, not dogmas, but real premises from which abstraction can be made only in the imagination. They are the real individuals, their activity and their material conditions of life, including those which they find already in existence and those produced by their activity. These premises can thus be established in a purely empirical way.

The first premise of all human history is, of course, the existence of living human individuals. The first fact to be established, therefore, is the physical constitution of these individuals and their consequent relation to the rest of Nature. Of course we cannot here investigate the actual physical nature of man or the natural conditions in which man finds himself — geological, orohydrographical, climatic and so on. All historiography must begin from these natural bases and their modification in the course of history by men's activity.

Men can be distinguished from animals by consciousness, by religion, or by anything one likes. They themselves begin to distinguish themselves from animals as soon as they begin to *produce* their means of subsistence, a step which is determined by their physical constitution. In producing their means of subsistence men indirectly produce their actual material life.

The way in which men produce their means of subsistence depends in the first place on the nature of the existing means which they have to reproduce. This mode of production should not be regarded simply as the reproduction of the physical existence of individuals. It is already a definite form of activity of these individuals, a definite way of expressing their life, a definite *mode of life*. As individuals express their life, so they are. What they are, therefore, coincides with their production, with *what* they produce and with *how* they produce it. What individuals are, therefore, depends on the material conditions of their production. . . .

This conception of history, therefore, rests on the exposition of the real process of production, starting out from the simple material production of life, and on the comprehension of the form of intercourse connected with and created by this mode of production, i.e. of civil society in its various stages as the basis of all history, and also in its action as the State. From this starting point, it explains all the different theoretical productions and forms of consciousness, religion, philosophy, ethics, etc., and traces their origins and growth, by which means the matter can of course be displayed as a whole (and consequently, also the reciprocal action of these various sides on one another). Unlike the idealist view of history, it . . . remains constantly on the real ground of history; it does not explain practice from the idea but explains the formation of ideas from material practice, and accordingly comes to the conclusion that all the forms of and products of consciousness can be dissolved, not by intellectual criticism . . . but only by the practical overthrow of the actual relations . . . that not criticism but revolution is the driving force of history, as well as of religion, philosophy, and all other types of theory. It

shows that history does not end by being resolved into "self-consciousness," as "spirit of the spirit," but that at each stage of history there is found a material result, a sum of productive forces, a historically created relation of individuals to Nature and to one another, which is handed down to each generation from its predecessors, a mass of productive forces, capital, and circumstances, which is indeed modified by the new generation but which also prescribes for it its conditions of life and gives it a definite development, a special character. It shows that circumstances make men just as much as men make circumstances. . . .

The fact is, therefore, that determinate individuals, who are productively active in a definite way, enter into these determinate social and political relations. Empirical observation must, in each particular case, show empirically, and without any mystification or speculation, the connection of the social and political structure with production. The social structure and the State are continually evolving out of the life-process of determinate individuals, of individuals not as they may appear in their own or other people's imagination, but as they really are: i.e. as they act, produce their material life, and are occupied within determinate material limits, presuppositions and conditions, which are independent of their will.

The production of ideas, conceptions and consciousness is at first directly interwoven with the material activity and the material intercourse of men, the language of real life. Representation and thought, the mental intercourse of men, still appear at this stage as the direct emanation of their material behaviour. The same applies to mental production as it is expressed in the political, legal, moral, religious and metaphysical language of a people. Men are the producers of their conceptions, ideas, etc., — real, active men, as they are conditioned by a determinate development of their productive forces, and of the intercourse which corresponds to these, up to its most extensive forms. Consciousness can never be anything else than conscious existence, and the existence of men is their actual life process. If in all idealogy men and their circumstances appear upside down as in a *camera obscura*, this phenomenon arises from their historical life process just as the inversion of objects on the retina does from their physical life-process.

In direct contrast to German philosophy, which descends from heaven to earth, here we ascend from earth to heaven. That is to say, we do not set out from what men say, imagine, or conceive, nor from what has been said, thought, imagined, or conceived of men, in order to arrive at men in the flesh. We begin with real, active men, and from their real life-process show the development of the ideological reflexes and echoes of this life-process. The phantoms of the human brain also are necessary sublimates of men's material life-process, which can be empirically established and which is bound to material preconditions. Morality, religion, metaphysics, and other ideologies, and their corresponding forms of consciousness, no longer retain therefore their appearance of autonomous existence. They have no history, no development; it is men, who, in developing their material production and their material intercourse, change, along with this their real existence, their thinking and the products of their thinking. Life is not determined by consciousness, but consciousness by life. Those who adopt the first method of approach begin with consciousness, regarded as the living individual; those who adopt the second, which corresponds with real life, begin with the real living individuals themselves, and consider consciousness only as *their* consciousness. . . .

The ideas of the ruling class are, in every age, the ruling ideas: i.e. the class which is the dominant *material* force in society is at the same time its dominant *intellectual* force. The class which has the means of material production at its disposal, has control at the same time over the means of mental production, so that in consequence the ideas of those who lack the means of mental production are, in general, subject to it. The dominant ideas are nothing more than the ideal expression of the dominant material relationships, the dominant material relationships grasped as ideas, and thus of the relationships which make one class the ruling one; they are consequently the ideas of its dominance. The individuals composing the ruling class possess among other things consciousness, and therefore think. In so far, therefore, as they rule as a class and determine the whole extent of an epoch, it is self-evident that they do this in their whole range and thus, among other things, rule also as thinkers, as producers of ideas, and regulate the production and distribution of the ideas of their age. Consequently their ideas are the ruling ideas of the age. For instance, in an age and in a country where royal power, aristocracy and the bourgeoisie are contending for domination and where, therefore, domination is shared, the doctrine of the separation of powers appears as the dominant idea and is enunciated as an "eternal law." The division of labour, which we saw earlier as one of the principal forces of history up to the present time, manifests itself also in the ruling class, as the division of mental and material labour, so that within this class one part appears as the thinkers of the class (its active conceptualizing ideologists, who make it their chief source of livelihood to develop and perfect the illusions of the class about itself), while the others have a more passive and receptive attitude to these ideas and illusions, because they are in reality the active members of this class and have less time to make up ideas and illusions about themselves. This cleavage within the ruling class may even develop into a certain opposition and hostility between the two parts, but in the event of a practical collision in which the class itself is endangered, it disappears of its own accord and with it also the illusion that the ruling ideas were not the ideas of the ruling class and had a power distinct from the power of this class. The existence of revolutionary ideas in a particular age presupposes the existence of a revolutionary class. . . .

If, in considering the course of history, we detach the ideas of the ruling class from the ruling class itself and attribute to them an independent exis-tence, if we confine ourselves to saying that in a particular age these or those ideas were dominant, without paying attention to the conditions of production and the world conditions which are the source of the ideas, it is possible to say, for instance, that during the time that the aristocracy was dominant the concepts honour, loyalty, etc., were dominant; during the dominance of the bourgeoisie the concepts freedom, equality, etc. The ruling class itself in general imagines this to be the case. This conception of history which is common to all historians, particularly since the eighteenth century, will necessarily come up against the phenomenon that increasingly abstract ideas hold sway, i.e. ideas which increasingly take on the form of universality. For each new class which puts itself in the place of the one ruling before it, is compelled, simply in order to achieve its aims, to represent its interest as the common interest of all members of society, i.e. employing an ideal formula, to give its ideas the form of universality and to represent them as the only rational and universally valid ones. The class which makes a revolution appears from the beginning not as a class but as the representative of the whole of society, simply because it is opposed to a *class*. It appears as the whole mass of society confronting the single ruling class. It can do this because at the beginning its interest really is more closely connected with the common interest of all other non-ruling classes and has been unable under the constraint of the previously existing conditions to develop as the particular interest of a particular class. Its victory, therefore, also benefits many individuals of the other classes which are not achieving a dominant position, but only in so far as it now puts these individuals in a position to raise themselves into the ruling class. When the French bourgeoisie overthrew the rule of the aristocracy it thereby made it possible for many proletarians to raise themselves above the proletariat, but only in so far as they became bourgeois. Every new class, therefore, achieves its domination only on a broader basis than that of the previous ruling class. On the other hand, the opposition of the non-ruling class to the new ruling class later develops all the more sharply and profoundly. These two characteristics entail that the struggle to be waged against this new ruling class has as its object a more decisive and radical negation of the previous conditions of society than could have been accomplished by all previous classes which aspired to rule.

The German Ideology
(with Engels, 1845-1846)

II. Alienation

We shall begin from a *contemporary* economic fact. The worker becomes poorer the more wealth he produces and the more his production increases in power and extent. The worker becomes an ever cheaper commodity the more goods he creates. The *devaluation* of the human world increases in direct relation with the *increase in value* of the world of things. Labor does not only create goods; it also produces itself and the worker as a *commodity*, and indeed in the same proportion as it produces goods.

This fact simply implies that the object produced by labor, its product, now stands opposed to it as an *alien being*, as a *power independent* of the producer. The product of labor is labor which has been embodied in an object and turned into a physical thing; this product is an *objectification* of labor. The performance of work is at the same time its objectification. The performance of work appears in the sphere of political economy as a *vitiation* of the worker, objectification as a *loss* and as *servitude to the object*, and appropriation as *alienation*.

So much does the performance of work appear as vitiation that the worker is vitiated to the point of starvation. So much does objectification appear as loss of the object that the worker is deprived of the most essential things not only of life but also of work. Labor itself becomes an object which he can acquire only by the greatest effort and with unpredictable interruptions. So much does the appropriation of the object appear as alienation that the more objects the worker produces the fewer he can possess and the more he falls under the domination of his product, of capital.

All these consequences follow from the fact that the worker is related to the *product of his labor* as to an *alien* object. For it is clear on this presupposition that the more the worker expends himself in work the more powerful becomes the world of objects which he creates in face of himself, the poorer he becomes in his inner life, and the less he belongs to himself. It is just the same as in religion. The more of himself man attributes to God the less he has left in himself. The worker puts his life into the object, and his life then belongs no longer to himself but to the object. The greater his activity, therefore, the less he possesses. What is embodied in the product of his labor is no longer his own. The greater this product is, therefore, the more he is diminished. The *alienation* of the worker in his product means not only that his labor becomes an object, assumes an external existence, but that it exists independently, *outside himself*, and alien to him, and that it stands opposed to him as an autonomous power. The life which he has given to the object sets itself against him as an alien and hostile force.

Let us now examine more closely the phenomenon of *objectification*, the worker's production and the *alienation* and *loss* of the object it produces, which is involved in it. The worker can create nothing without *nature*, without the *sensuous external world*. The latter is the material in which his labor is realized, in which it is active, out of which and through which it produces things.

But just as nature affords the *means of existence* of labor in the sense that labor cannot *live* without objects upon which it can be exercised, so also it provides the *means of existence* in a narrower sense; namely the means of physical existence for the *worker* himself. Thus, the more the worker *appropriates* the external world of sensuous nature by his labor the more he deprives himself of *means of existence*, in two respects: first, that the sensuous external world becomes progressively less an object belonging to his labor or a means of existence of his labor, and secondly, that it becomes progressively less a means of existence in the direct sense, a means for the physical subsistence of the worker.

In both respects, therefore, the worker becomes a slave of the object; first, in that he receives an *object of work*, i.e., receives *work*, and secondly that he receives *means of subsistence*. Thus the object enables him to exist, first as a *worker* and secondly, as a *physical subject*. The culmination of this enslavement is that he can only maintain himself as a *physical subject* so far as he is worker, and that it is only as a *physical subject* that he is a worker.

(The alienation of the worker in his object is expressed as follows in the laws of political economy: the more the worker produces the less he has to consume; the more value he creates the more worthless he becomes; the more refined his product the more crude and misshapen the worker; the more civilized the product the more barbarous the worker; the more powerful the work the more feeble the worker; the more the work manifests intelligence the more the worker declines in intelligence and becomes a slave of nature.)

Political economy conceals the alienation in the nature of labor insofar as it does not examine the direct relationship between the worker (work) and production. Labor certainly produces marvels for the rich but it produces privation for the worker. It produces palaces, but hovels for the worker. It produces beauty, but deformity for the worker. It replaces labor by machinery, but it casts some of the workers back into a barbarous kind of work and turns the others into machines. It produces intelligence, but also stupidity and cretinism for the workers.

The direct relationship of labor to its products is the relationship of the worker to the objects of his production. The relationship of property owners to the objects of production and to production itself is merely a *consequence* of this first relationship and confirms it. We shall consider this second aspect later.

Thus, when we ask what is the important relationship of labor, we are concerned with the relationship of the *worker* to production.

So far we have considered the alienation of the worker only from one aspect; namely, *his relationship with the products of his labor.* However, alienation appears not only in the result, but also in the *process*, of *production, within productive activity* itself. How could the worker stand in an alien relationship to the product of his activity if he did not alienate himself in the act of production itself? The product is indeed only the *résumé* of activity, of production. Consequently, if the product of labor is alienation, production itself must be active alienation — the alienation of activity and the activity of alienation. The alienation of the object of labor merely summarizes the alienation in the work activity itself.

What constitutes the alienation of labor? First, that the work is *external* to the worker, that it is not part of his nature; and that, consequently, he does not fulfill himself in his work but denies himself, has a feeling of misery rather than well being, does not develop freely his mental and physical energies but is physically exhausted and mentally debased. The worker therefore feels himself at home only during his leisure time, whereas at work he feels homeless. His work is not voluntary but imposed, *forced labor.* It is not the satisfaction of a need, but only a *means* for satisfying other needs. Its alien character is clearly shown by the fact that as soon as there is no physical or other compulsion it is avoided like the plague. External labor, labor in which man alienates himself, is a labor of self-sacrifice, of mortification. Finally, the external character of work for the worker is shown by the fact that it is not his own work but work for someone else, that in work he does not belong to himself but to another person.

Just as in religion the spontaneous activity of human fantasy, of the human brain and heart, reacts independently as an alien activity of gods or devils upon the individual, so the activity of the worker is not his own spontaneous activity. It is another's activity and a loss of his own spontaneity.

We arrive at the result that man (the worker) feels himself to be freely active only in his animal functions — eating, drinking and procreating, or at most also in his dwelling and in personal adornment — while in his human functions he is reduced to an animal. The animal becomes human and the human becomes animal.

Eating, drinking and procreating are of course also genuine human functions. But abstractly considered, apart from the environment of other human activities, and turned into final and sole ends, they are animal functions.

We have now considered the act of alienation of practical human activity, labor, from two aspects: (1) the relationship of the worker to the *product of labor* as an alien object which dominates him. This relationship is at the same time the relationship to the sensuous external world, to natural objects, as an alien and hostile world; (2) the relationship of labor to the *act of production* within *labor*. This is the relationship of the worker to his own activity as something alien and not belonging to him, activity as suffering (passivity), strength as powerlessness, creation as emasculation, the *personal* physical and mental energy of the worker, his personal life (for what is life but activity?) as an activity which is directed against himself, independent of him and not belonging to him. This is *self-alienation* as against the above-mentioned alienation of the *thing*.

We have now to infer a third characteristic of *alienated labor* from the two we have considered.

Man is a species-being[1] not only in the sense that he makes the community (his own as well as those of other things) his objects both practically and theoretically, but also (and this is simply another expression for the same thing) in the sense that he treats himself as the present, living species, as a *universal* and consequently free being.

Species-life, for man as for animals, has its physical basis in the fact that man (like animals) lives from inorganic nature, and since man is more universal than an animal so the range of inorganic nature from which he lives is more universal. Plants, animals, minerals, air, light, etc. constitute, from the theoretical aspect, a part of human consciousness as objects of natural science and art; they are man's spiritual inorganic nature, his intellectual means of life, which he must first prepare for enjoyment and perpetuation. So also, from the practical aspect they form a part of human life and activity. In practice man lives only from these natural products, whether in the form of food, heating, clothing, housing, etc. The universality of man appears in practice in the universality which makes the whole of nature into his inorganic body: (1) as a direct means of life; and equally (2) as the material object and instrument of his life activity. Nature is the *inorganic body* of man; that is to say, nature excluding the human body itself. To say that man *lives* from nature means that nature is his *body* with which he must remain in a continuous interchange in order not to die. The statement that the physical and mental life of man, and nature, are interdependent means simply that nature is interdependent with itself, for man is a part of nature.

Since alienated labor: (1) alienates nature from man; and (2) alienates man from himself, from his own active function, his life activity; so it alienates him from the species. It makes *species-life* into a means of individual life. In the first place it alienates species-life and individual life, and secondly, it turns the latter, as an abstraction, into

---

[1]The term 'species-being' is taken from Feuerbach's *Das Wesen des Christentums* (The Essence of Christianity). Feuerbach used the notion in making a distinction between consciousness in man and in animals. Man is conscious not merely of himself as an individual but of the human species or 'human essence.' — *Tr. Note*

the purpose of the former, also in its abstract and alienated form.

For labor, *life activity, productive life*, now appear to man only as *means* for the satisfaction of a need, the need to maintain his physical existence. Productive life is, however, species-life. It is life creating life. In the type of life activity resides the whole character of a species, its species-character; and free, conscious activity is the species-character of human beings. Life itself appears only as *means of life*.

The animal is one with its life activity. It does not distinguish the activity from itself. It is *its activity*. But man makes his life activity itself an object of his will and consciousness. He has a conscious life activity. It is not a determination with which he is completely identified. Conscious life activity distinguishes man from the life activity of animals. Only for this reason is he a species-being. Or rather, he is only a self-conscious being, i.e. his own life is an object for him, because he is a species-being. Only for this reason is his activity free activity. Alienated labor reverses the relationship, in that man because he is a self-conscious being makes his life activity, his *being*, only a means for his *existence*.

The practical construction of an *objective world*, the *manipulation* of inorganic nature, is the confirmation of man as a conscious species-being, i.e. a being who treats the species as his own being or himself as a species-being. Of course, animals also produce. They construct nests, dwellings, as in the case of bees, beavers, ants, etc. But they only produce what is strictly necessary for themselves or their young. They produce only in a single direction, while man produces universally. They produce only under the compulsion of direct physical need, while man produces when he is free from physical need and only truly produces in freedom from such need. Animals produce only themselves, while man reproduces the whole of nature. The products of animal production belong directly to their physical bodies, while man is free in face of his product. Animals construct only in accordance with the standards and needs of the species to which they belong, while man knows how to produce in accordance with the standards of every species and knows how to apply the appropriate standard to the object. Thus man constructs also in accordance with the laws of beauty.

It is just in his work upon the objective world that man really proves himself as a *species-being*. This production is his active species life. By means of it nature appears as *his* work and his reality. The object of labor is, therefore, the *objectification of man's species life*; for he no longer reproduces himself merely intellectually, as in consciousness, but actively and in a real sense, and he sees his own reflection in a world which he has constructed. While, therefore, alienated labor takes away the object of production from man, it also takes away his *species life*, his real objectivity as a species-being, and changes his advantage over animals into a disadvantage in so far as his inorganic body, nature, is taken from him.

Just as alienated labor transforms free and self-directed activity into a means, so it transforms the species life of man into a means of physical existence.

Consciousness, which man has from

his species, is transformed through alienation so that species life becomes only a means for him.

(3) Thus alienated labor turns the *species life of man*, and also nature as his mental species-property, into an *alien* being and into a *means* for his *individual existence*. It alienates from man his own body, external nature, his mental life and his *human* life.

(4) A direct consequence of the alienation of man from the product of his activity and from his species life is that *man is alienated* from other *men*. When man confronts himself he also confronts *other* men. What is true of man's relationship to his work, to the product of his work and to himself, is also true of his relationship to other men, to their labor and to the objects of their labor.

In general, the statement that man is alienated from his species life means that each man is alienated from others, and that each of the others is likewise alienated from human life.

Human alienation, and above all the relation of man to himself, is first realized and expressed in the relationship between each man and other men. Thus in the relationship of alienated labor every man regards other men according to the standards and relationships in which he finds himself placed as a worker.

We began with an economic fact, the alienation of the worker and his production. We have expressed this fact in conceptual terms as *alienated labor*, and in analyzing the concept we have merely analyzed an economic fact.

Let us now examine further how this concept of alienated labor must express and reveal itself in reality. If the product of labor is alien to me and confronts me as an alien power, to whom does it belong? If my own activity does not belong to me but is an alien, forced activity, to whom does it belong? To a being *other* than myself. And who is this being? The *gods*? It is apparent in the earliest stages of advanced production, e.g., temple building, etc. in Egypt, India, Mexico, and in the service rendered to gods, that the product belonged to the gods. But the gods alone were never the lords of labor. And no more was *nature*. What a contradiction it would be if the more man subjugates nature by his labor, and the more the marvels of the gods are rendered superfluous by the marvels of industry, he should abstain from his joy in producing and his enjoyment of the product for love of these powers.

The *alien* being to whom labor and the product of labor belong, to whose service labor is devoted, and to whose enjoyment the product of labor goes, can only be *man* himself. If the product of labor does not belong to the worker, but confronts him as an alien power, this can only be because it belongs to *a man other than the worker*. If his activity is a torment to him it must be a source of enjoyment and pleasure to another. Not the gods, nor nature, but only man himself can be this alien power over men.

Economic and Philosophical Manuscripts (1844)

The so-called Revolutions of 1848 were but poor incidents — small fractures and fissures in the dry crust of European society. However, they denounced the abyss. Beneath the apparently solid surface, they betrayed oceans of liquid matter, only needing expansion to rend into fragments continents of hard rock. Noisedly and confusedly they proclaimed the emancipation of the proletarian, *i.e.*, the secret of the nineteenth century, and of the revolution of that century. That social revolution, it is true, was no novelty invented in 1848. Steam, electricity, and the self-acting mule were revolutionists of a rather more dangerous character than even citizens Barbès, Raspail and Blanqui. But, although the atmosphere in which we live weighs upon everyone with a 20,000 pound force, do you feel it? No more than European society before 1848 felt the revolutionary atmosphere enveloping and pressing it from all sides.

There is one great fact, characteristic of this, our nineteenth century, a fact which no party dares deny. On the one hand, there have started into life industrial and scientific forces, which no epoch of the former human history had ever suspected. On the other hand, there exist symptoms of decay, far surpassing the horrors recorded of the latter times of the Roman empire. In our days everything seems pregnant with its contrary; machinery gifted with the wonderful power of shortening and fructifying human labor, we behold starving and overworking it. The new-fangled sources of wealth, by some strange weird spell, are turned into sources of want. The victories of art seem bought by the loss of character. At the same pace that mankind masters nature, man seems to become enslaved to other men or to his own infamy. Even the pure light of science seems unable to shine but on the dark background of ignorance. All our inventions and progress seem to result in endowing material forces with intellectual life, and in stultifying human life into a material force. This antagonism between modern industry and science on the one hand, modern misery and dissolution on the other hand; this antagonism between the productive powers and the social relations of our epoch, is a fact, palpable, overwhelming, and not to be controverted. Some parties may wail over it; others may wish to get rid of modern arts in order to get rid of modern conflicts. Or they may imagine that so signal a progress in industry wants to be completed by as signal a regress in politics.

On our part, we do not mistake the shape of the shrewd spirit that continues to mark all these contradictions. We know that to work well the new-fangled forces of society, they only want to be mastered by new-fangled men—and such are the working men. They are as much the invention of modern times as machinery itself. In the signs that bewilder the middle class, the aristocracy and the poor prophets of regression, we do recognize our brave friend, Robin Goodfellow, the old mole that can work in the earth so fast, that worthy pioneer—the revolution. The English working men are the first born sons of modern industry. They will then, certainly, not be the last in aiding the social revolution produced by that industry, a revolution, which means the emancipation of their own class all over the world, which is as universal as capital-rule and wages-slavery. I know the heroic struggles the English working class have gone through since the middle of the last century — struggles less glorious because they are shrouded in obscurity and burked by the middle class historians to revenge the misdeeds of the ruling class.

There existed in the middle ages in Germany a secret tribunal, called the "Vehmgericht." If a red cross was seen marked on a house people knew that its owner was doomed by the "Vehm." All the houses of Europe are now marked with the mysterious red cross. History is the judge — its executioner, the proletarian.

> *Speech by Marx at the anniversary celebration of the* People's Paper, *a Chartist publication, in April 1856.*

III. Communist Revolution and Future Society

(1) In the development of the productive forces a stage is reached where productive forces and means of intercourse are called into being which, under the existing relations, can only work mischief, and which are, therefore, no longer productive, but destructive, forces (machinery and money). Associated with this is the emergence of a class which has to bear all the burdens of society without enjoying its advantages, which is excluded from society and is forced into the most resolute opposition to all other classes; a class which comprises the majority of the members of society and in which there develops a consciousness of the need for a fundamental revolution, the communist consciousness. This consciousness can, of course, also arise in other classes from the observation of the situation of this class.

(2) The conditions under which determinate productive forces can be used are also the conditions for the dominance of a determinate social class, whose social power, derived from its property ownership, invariably finds its *practical* and ideal expression in a particular form of the State. Consequently, every revolutionary struggle is directed against the class which has so far been dominant.

(3) In all former revolutions the form of activity was always left unaltered and it was only a question of redistributing this activity among different people, of introducing a new division of labour. The communist revolution, however, is directed against the former *mode* of activity, does away with *labour*, and abolishes all class rule along with the classes themselves, because it is effected by the class which no longer counts as a class in society, which is not recognized as a class, and which is the expression of the dissolution of all classes, nationalities, etc., within contemporary society.

(4) For the creation on a mass scale of this communist consciousness, as well as for the success of the cause itself, it is necessary for men themselves to be changed on a large scale, and this change can only occur in a practical movement, in a *revolution*. Revolution is necessary not only because the *ruling* class cannot be overthrown in any other way, but also because only in a revolution can *the class which overthrows it* rid itself of the accumulated rubbish of the past and become capable of reconstructing society. . . .

The transformation of personal powers (relationships) into material powers through the division of labour cannot be undone again merely by dismissing the idea of it from one's mind, but only by the action of individuals who reestablish their control over these material powers and abolish the division of labour. This is not possible without a community. Only in association with others has each individual the means of cultivating his talents in all directions. Only in a community therefore is personal freedom possible. In the previous substitutes for community, in the State, etc., personal freedom existed only for those individuals who grew up in the ruling class and only in so far as they were members of this class. The illusory community in which, up to the present, individuals have combined, always acquired an independent existence apart from them, and since it was a union of one class against another it represented for the dominated class not only a completely illusory community but also a new shackle. In a genuine community individuals gain their freedom in and through their association.

The German Ideology (1845-1846)

The possessing class and the proletarian class express the same human alienation. But the former is satisfied with its situation, feels itself well established in it, recognizes this self-alienation as *its own* power, and thus has the appearance of a human existence. The latter feels itself crushed by this self-alienation, sees in it its own impotence and the reality of an inhuman situation. It is, to use an expression of Hegel's, "in the midst of degradation the *revolt* against degradation,"

a revolt to which it is forced by the contradiction between its *humanity* and its situation, which is an open, clear and absolute negation of its humanity.

Within the framework of alienation, therefore, the property owners are the *conservative* and the proletarians the *destructive* party.

It is true that, in its economic development, private property advances towards its own dissolution; but it only does this through a development which is independent of itself, unconscious and achieved against its will — solely because it produces the proletariat *as* proletariat, poverty conscious of its moral and physical poverty, degradation conscious of its degradation, and for this reason trying to abolish itself. The proletariat carries out the sentence which private property, by creating the proletariat, passes upon itself, just as it carries out the sentence which wage-labour, by creating wealth for others and poverty for itself, passes upon itself. If the proletariat triumphs this does not mean that it becomes the absolute form of society, for it is only victorious by abolishing itself as well as its opposite. Thus the proletariat disappears along with the opposite which conditions it, private property.

If socialist writers attribute this world-historical role to the proletariat this is not at all . . . because they regard the proletarians as *gods*. On the contrary, in the fully developed proletariat, everything human is taken away, even the *appearance* of humanity. In the conditions of existence of the proletariat are condensed, in their most inhuman form, all the conditions of existence of present-day society. Man has lost himself, but he has not only acquired, at the same time, a theoretical consciousness of his loss, he has been forced, by an ineluctable and imperious *distress* — by practical *necessity* — to revolt against this inhumanity. It is for these reasons that the proletariat can and must emancipate itself. But it can only emancipate itself by destroying its own conditions of existence. It can only destroy its own conditions of existence by destroying *all* the inhuman conditions of existence of present-day society, conditions which are epitomized in its situation. It is not in vain that it passes through the rough but stimulating school of *labour*. It is not a matter of knowing what this or that proletarian, or even the proletariat as a whole, *conceives* as its aims at any particular moment. It is a question of knowing *what* the proletariat *is*, and what it must historically accomplish in accordance with its *nature*. Its aim and its historical activity are ordained for it, in a tangible and irrevocable way, by its own situation as well as by the whole organization of present-day civil society. It is unnecessary to show here that a large part of the English and French proletariat has already become *aware* of its historic mission, and works incessantly to clarify this awareness.

The Holy Family (1845)

The realm of freedom only begins, in fact, where that labour which is determined by need and external purposes, ceases; it is therefore, by its very nature, outside the sphere of material production proper. Just as the savage must wrestle with Nature in order to satisfy his wants, to maintain and reproduce his life, so also must civilized man, and he must do it in all forms of society and under any possible mode of production. With his development the realm of natural necessity expands, because his wants increase, but at the same time the forces of production, by which these wants are satisfied, also increase. Freedom in this field cannot consist of anything else but the fact that socialized mankind, the associated producers, regulate their interchange with Nature rationally, bring it under their common control, instead of being ruled by it as by some blind power, and accomplish their task with the least expenditure of energy and under such conditions as are proper and worthy for human beings. Nevertheless, this always remains a realm of necessity. Beyond it begins that development of human potentiality for its own sake, the true realm of freedom, which however can only flourish upon that realm of necessity as its basis. The shortening of the working day is its fundamental prerequisite.

Capital, Vol. III (published posthumously)

What we have to deal with here is a communist society, not as it has *developed* on its own foundation, but, on the contrary, just as it *emerges* from capitalist society; and which is thus in every respect, economically, morally and intellectually, still stamped with the birth-marks of the old society from whose womb it emerges. Accordingly, the individual producer receives back from society — after the deductions have been made — exactly what he contributes to it. What he has contributed to it is his individual quantum of labour. For example, the social working day consists of the sum of the individual hours of work; the individual labour-time of the individual producer is the part of the social working day contributed by him, his share in it. He receives a certificate from society that he has furnished such and such an amount of labour (after deducting his labour for the common funds), and with this certificate he draws from the social stock of means of consumption as much as costs the same amount of labour. The same amount of labour which he has given to society in one form he receives back in another.

Here obviously the same principle prevails as that which regulates the exchange of commodities, as far as this is exchange of equal values. Content and form are changed, because under the altered conditions no one can give anything except his labour, and because, on the other hand, nothing can pass into the ownership of individuals except individual means of consumption. But, as far as the distribution of the latter among the individual producers is concerned, the same principle prevails as in the exchange of commodity-equivalents: a given amount of labour in another form.

Hence, *equal right* here is still in principle — *bourgeois right*, although principle and practice are no longer at loggerheads, whereas the exchange of equivalents in commodity exchange only exists *on the average* and not in the individual case.

In spite of this advance, *equal right* is still burdened with bourgeois limitations. The right of the producers is *proportional* to the labour they supply; the equality consists in the fact that measurement is made with an *equal standard, labour.*

But one man is superior to another physically or mentally and so supplies more labour in the same time, or can labour for a longer time; and labour, to serve as a measure, must be defined by its duration or intensity, otherwise it ceases to be a standard of measurement. The *equal* right is an unequal right for unequal labour. It recognizes no class differences, because everyone is only a worker like everyone else; but it tacitly recognizes unequal individual endowment, and thus natural privileges in respect of productive capacity. *It is, therefore, in its content, a right of inequality, like every right.* Right by its very nature can consist only in the application of an equal standard; but unequal individuals (and they would not be different individuals if they were not unequal) can only be assessed by an equal standard in so far as they are regarded from a single aspect, from one particular side only, as for instance, in the present case, they are regarded *only as workers,* and nothing more is seen in them, everything else being ignored. Further, one worker is married, another not; one has more children than another, and so on. Thus, with an equal performance of labour, and hence an equal share in the social consumption fund, one individual will in fact receive more than another, one will be richer than another, and so on. To avoid all these defects, right instead of being equal would have to be unequal.

But these defects are inevitable in

the first phase of communist society as it is when it has just emerged after prolonged birth-pangs from capitalist society. Right can never be higher than the economic structure of society and the cultural development conditioned by it.

In a higher phase of communist society, when the enslaving subordination of the individual to the division of labour, and with it the antithesis between mental and physical labour, has vanished; when labour is no longer merely a means of life but has become life's principal need; when the productive forces have also increased with the all-round development of the individual, and all the springs of co-operative wealth flow more abundantly—only then will it be possible completely to transcend the narrow outlook of bourgeois right and only then will society be able to inscribe on its banners: From each according to his ability, to each according to his needs!

Critique of the Gotha Program (1875)

COMMENT

In this chapter we are dealing with an extremely complex thinker whose ideas were not only ambiguous but subject to change and development. Marx once even remarked, "One thing I know and that is that I am not a Marxist."[1] He was aware of the common tendency among "Marxists" to reduce and distort his ideas, being perhaps as misinterpreted by friends as by foes.

Despite some unguarded statements, his theory was not a simpleminded economic determinism nor a rigid scheme of historical development. He maintained that the economic system primarily determines the history of a social order, but he believed that all sorts of other forces enter into the very complex interaction of causal factors. Contrary to the usual interpretation of his doctrine, he did not suppose that all history can be arranged in a definite series of stages, beginning with primitive communism and going on to slavery, feudalism, capitalism, socialism, and finally advanced communism. He pointed out that the historical development in India and China, and to a considerable extent in Russia, deviated greatly from the pattern in western Europe, and he recognized that the future is somewhat uncertain. In 1844, in his *Economic and Philosophical Manuscripts*, he said that communism may appear in a democratic or an autocratic form, and in his famous speech at The Hague in 1872 he declared that the "emancipation of the workers" may be achieved peacefully in the more democratic countries. Thus he advocated—not always consistently

[1]Karl Marx and Friedrich Engels, *Selected Correspondence* (New York: International Publishers, 1936), p. 472.

—a complex, multilinear theory of history rather than the very simple unilinear theory that is usually attributed to him.[2]

He also foresaw that communism may take the form of a raw and repressive system. "This entirely crude and unreflective communism," he declared, "would negate the personality of man in every sphere. . . . It would be a system in which universal envy sets itself up as a power, and . . . in this form of envy, it would reduce everything to a common level." "Crude communism," he went on to say, "is only the culmination of such envy and levelling down to a preconceived minimum." He spoke of it as "the negation of the whole world of culture and civilization."[3]

These remarks were made in 1844, but in his later works, Marx occasionally recognized the dangers of collectivism and bureaucracy. In the 1850s he wrote articles for the New York *Daily Tribune* in which he characterized "Oriental despotism," the state managerialism of the old Asiatic societies, as dooming the masses to a kind of "general [state] slavery."[4] In his comments of 1871 on the Paris Commune, he emphasized the need for popular control of the revolutionary government, warning against bureaucracy and militarism. His ultimate ideal was to abolish the coercive state and to organize society on a decentralized basis. His works contain an impassioned protest against the dehumanizing process of mass industry, with its tendency toward the depersonalization of life. Although expressed most fully in the early *Economic and Philosophical Manuscripts*, his theory of "alienation" remains basic in the later works, but more often implicit than explicit. For example, Marx's speech at the anniversary celebration of the *People's Paper* (1856) mentions two basic sides of the process of alienation: first, material forces taking on "life" and dominating human beings ("objectification"), and second, human life being stultified into a material force ("self-alienation"). Although Marx seldom used the *word* "alienation" in these later works, he still thought of human beings as estranged from themselves, from other people, from their work, from their products, from their society, from nature. He also clung to the ideal of dealienation, demanding that human beings be treated as human beings, and things as things. A nonalienated person would be *really* a person, a free, creative, well-rounded being, no longer the victim of impersonal forces.

No well-informed liberal would deny that there are totalitarian trends in the writings of Marx. In his criticism of the Gotha Program of the

[2]See Melvin Rader, *Ethics and the Human Community* (New York: Holt, Rinehart and Winston, 1964), Ch. 12, for a fuller discussion.
[3]*Economic and Philosophical Manuscripts*, in T. B. Bottomore, *Karl Marx: Early Writings* (London: C. A. Watts & Co., 1963), pp 153-154.
[4]See Karl Wittfogel, *Oriental Despotism* (New Haven, CT: Yale University Press, 1959).

German Social-Democrats, he insisted on the dictatorship of the proletariat as a necessary step in the transition from capitalism to socialism. In the *Communist Manifesto*, he proposed "to centralize all instruments of production in the hands of the state." The more orthodox Marxists have selected and elaborated such features of the original Marxist creed, whereas the revisionists have seized on the more liberal elements. Both sides can point to authentic Marxist texts.

In various respects we can question and debate the validity of Marx's ideas, but I shall leave this task to the readers of this book. If, in conclusion, I should venture some opinions of my own, I would say this: We need to be sensitive, as Marx was sensitive, to the enormous burden of human suffering. His humanitarian concern does honor to him as a man. If we were as sincerely concerned it would be very much to our credit. But Marx, even though his ideas are far from the caricature that is so often presented, was too sure about the way history would go, too one-sided in his emphasis on economic forces, and too ready to accept dictatorship in his eagerness for revolutionary change. With our different tradition of civil liberties and human rights, we need to cherish the free, humane values of our civilization — and so we have to revise Marx. But insofar as his moral passion is concerned, we have to heed him.

Behaviorism and Humanism

"The dilemma 'individualism or collectivism,' no longer appears inescapable . . . Neither one can provide the genuine freedom and realization that each promises, and there is a third alternative . . . The essential human reality is neither one of individual nor of collective existence, but lies in the relation between man and man, and is a matter between me and you."

MARTIN BUBER

We now come to a symposium in which two famous psychologists, B. F. Skinner and Carl Rogers, debate the philosophical issues involved in the educational and political molding of human beings. In a discussion highly pertinent to our scientific and technological age, some of the most crucial issues that have been raised in preceding chapters are brought to a sharp focus. Faced by "the spectre of predictable man," we are forced to reconsider our most basic concepts and ideals.

BURRHUS FREDERIC SKINNER (1904–) and CARL RANSOM ROGERS (1902–)

B. F. Skinner studied English and Greek classics at Hamilton College in Clinton, New York. Turning from literature to psychology, he received his Master's degree in 1930 and Doctor's degree in 1931 at Harvard, where he has taught since 1947. During World War II he worked for the Office of Scientific Research and Development, training pigeons to pilot bombs and torpedoes through a guidance system activated by the birds' pecking in response to radar. His other remarkable exploits include teaching pigeons how to play ping-pong, and the invention of mechanical baby-tenders and teaching machines. The machines, combined with his theory of "programmed instruction," could revolutionize teaching methods. His novel, *Walden Two* (1948), depicts a Utopian community run on the principles of behavioral psychology. In other widely read books, *Science and Human Behavior* (1953) and *Cumulative Record* (revised, 1961), he applies his theory to the full range of human phenomena.

Carl Rogers received his M.A. in 1928 and Ph.D. in 1931 from Teachers' College, Columbia University. He has worked as a clinical psychologist in Rochester, New York, and at the Universities of Ohio and Chicago. In 1957 he became Professor of Psychology and Psychiatry at the University of Wisconsin, and since 1964 he has been a resident fellow at the Western Behavioral Sciences Institute at La Jolla, California. He is best known for his "client-centered" theory of psychotherapy, which prescribes a person-to-person relationship between therapist and patient and encourages the patient, within wide limits, to control the course, pace, and length of his treatment. Rogers and his wife Helen love isolated spots in Mexico and the Caribean, where they paint, take color photographs, swim and lie on the beach. In these spots, he has said, his most important ideas have come to him. Like Skinner, he is deeply interested in the philosophical implications of psychology.

Some Issues Concerning the Control of Human Behavior: A Symposium

I [SKINNER]

Science is steadily increasing our power to influence, change, mold — in a word, control — human behavior. It has ex-

From *Science*, Vol. 124, November 30, 1956. Copyright 1956 by the American Association for the Advancement of Science. Reprinted by permission of *Science* and the authors.

tended our "understanding" (whatever that may be) so that we deal more successfully with people in nonscientific ways, but it has also identified conditions or variables which can be used to predict and control behavior in a new, and increasingly rigorous, technology. The broad disciplines of government and economics offer examples of this, but there is special cogency in those contributions of anthropology, sociology, and psychology which deal with individual behavior. Carl Rogers has listed some of the achievements to date in a recent paper.[1] Those of his examples which show or imply the control of the single organism are primarily due, as we should expect, to psychology. It is the experimental study of behavior which carries us beyond awkward or inaccessible "principles," "factors," and so on, to variables which can be directly manipulated.

It is also, and for more or less the same reasons, the conception of human behavior emerging from an experimental analysis which most directly challenges traditional views. Psychologists themselves often do not seem to be aware of how far they have moved in this direction. But the change is not passing unnoticed by others. Until only recently it was customary to deny the possibility of a rigorous science of human behavior by arguing, either that a lawful science was impossible because man was a free agent, or that merely statistical predictions would always leave room for personal freedom. But those who used to take this line have become most vociferous in expressing their alarm at the way these obstacles are being surmounted.

Now, the control of human behavior has always been unpopular. Any undisguised effort to control usually arouses emotional reactions. We hesitate to admit, even to ourselves, that we are engaged in control, and we may refuse to control, even when this would be

helpful, for fear of criticism. Those who have explicitly avowed an interest in control have been roughly treated by history. Machiavelli is the great prototype. As Macaulay said of him, "Out of his surname they coined an epithet for a knave and out of his Christian name a synonym for the devil." There were obvious reasons. The control that Machiavelli analyzed and recommended, like most political control, used techniques that were aversive to the controllee. The threats and punishments of the bully, like those of the government operating on the same plan, are not designed — whatever their success — to endear themselves to those who are controlled. Even when the techniques themselves are not aversive, control is usually exercised for the selfish purposes of the controller and, hence, has indirectly punishing effects upon others.

Man's natural inclination to revolt against selfish control has been exploited to good purpose in what we call the philosophy and literature of democracy. The doctrine of the rights of man has been effective in arousing individuals to concerted action against governmental and religious tyranny. The literature which has had this effect has greatly extended the number of terms in our language which express reactions to the control of men. But the ubiquity and ease of expression of this attitude spells trouble for any science which may give birth to a powerful technology of behavior. Intelligent men and women, dominated by the humanistic philosophy of the past two centuries, cannot view with equanimity what Andrew Hacker has called "the specter of

[1] Carl Rogers, *Teachers College Record*, Vol. 57 (1956), p. 316.

predictable man."[2] Even the statistical or actuarial prediction of human events, such as the number of fatalities to be expected on a holiday weekend, strikes many people as uncanny and evil, while the prediction and control of individual behavior is regarded as little less than the work of the devil. I am not so much concerned here with the political or economic consequences for psychology, although research following certain channels may well suffer harmful effects. We ourselves, as intelligent men and women, and as exponents of Western thought, share these attitudes. They have already interfered with the free exercise of a scientific analysis, and their influence threatens to assume more serious proportions. . . .

EDUCATION

The techniques of education were once frankly aversive. The teacher was usually older and stronger than his pupils and was able to "make them learn." This meant that they were not actually taught but were surrounded by a threatening world from which they could escape only by learning. Usually they were left to their own resources in discovering how to do so. Claude Coleman has published a grimly amusing reminder of these older practices. He tells of a schoolteacher who published a careful account of his services during 51 years of teaching, during which he administered: ". . . 911,527 blows with a cane; 124,010 with a rod; 20,989 with a ruler; 136,715 with the hand;

10,295 over the mouth; 7,905 boxes on the ear; [and] 1,115,800 slaps on the head. . . ."[3]

Progressive education was a humanitarian effort to substitute positive reinforcement for such aversive measures, but in the search for useful human values in the classroom it has never fully replaced the variables it abandoned. Viewed as a branch of behavioral technology, education remains relatively inefficient. We supplement it, and rationalize it, by admiring the pupil who learns *for himself*; and we often attribute the learning process, or knowledge itself, to something *inside* the individual. We admire behavior which seems to have inner sources. Thus we admire one who *recites* a poem more than one who simply *reads* it. We admire one who *knows* the answer more than one who *knows where to look it up*. We admire the *writer* rather than the reader. We admire the arithmetician who can do a problem in his head rather than with a slide rule or calculating machine, or in "original" ways rather than by a strict application of rules. In general we feel that any aid or "crutch"—except those aids to which we are now thoroughly accustomed—reduces the credit due. In Plato's *Phaedrus*, Thamus, the king, attacks the invention of the alphabet on similar grounds! He is afraid "it will produce forgetfulness in the minds of those who learn to use it, because they will not practice their memories. . . ." In other words, he holds it more admi-

[2]Andrew Hacker, *Antioch Review*, Vol. 14 (1954), p. 195.

[3]Claude Coleman, *Bulletin of the American Association of University Professors*, Vol. 39 (1953), p. 457.

rable to remember than to use a memorandum. He also objects that pupils "will read many things without instruction . . . [and] will therefore seem to know many things when they are for the most part ignorant." In the same vein we are today sometimes contemptuous of book learning, but, as educators, we can scarcely afford to adopt this view without reservation.

By admiring the student for knowledge and blaming him for ignorance, we escape some of the responsibility of teaching him. We resist any analysis of the educational process which threatens the notion of inner wisdom or questions the contention that the fault of ignorance lies with the student. More powerful techniques which bring about the same changes in behavior by manipulating *external* variables are decried as brainwashing or thought control. We are quite unprepared to judge *effective* educational measures. As long as only a few pupils learn much of what is taught, we do not worry about uniformity or regimentation. We do not fear the feeble technique; but we should view with dismay a system under which every student learned everything listed in a syllabus — although such a condition is far from unthinkable. Similarly, we do not fear a system which is so defective that the student must *work* for an education; but we are loath to give credit for anything learned without effort — although this could well be taken as an ideal result — and we flatly refuse to give credit if the student already knows what a school teaches.

A world in which people are wise and good without trying, without "having to be," without "choosing to be," could conceivably be a far better world for everyone. In such a world we should not have to "give anyone credit"—we should not need to admire anyone—for being wise and good. From our present point of view we cannot believe that such a world would be admirable. We do not even permit ourselves to imagine what it would be like.

Government

Government has always been the special field of aversive control. The state is frequently defined in terms of the power to punish, and jurisprudence leans heavily upon the associated notion of personal responsibility. Yet it is becoming increasingly difficult to reconcile current practice and theory with these earlier views. In criminology, for example, there is a strong tendency to drop the notion of responsibility in favor of some such alternative as capacity or controllability. But no matter how strongly the facts, or even practical expedience, support such a change, it is difficult to make the change in a legal system designed on a different plan. When governments resort to other techniques (for example, positive reinforcement), the concept of responsibility is no longer relevant and the theory of government is no longer applicable.

The conflict is illustrated by two decisions of the Supreme Court in the 1930's which dealt with, and disagreed on, the definition of control or coercion.[4] The Agricultural Adjustment Act

[4]P. A. Freund and others, *Constitutional Law: Cases and Other Problems* (Boston: Little, Brown, 1954), p. 233.

proposed that the Secretary of Agriculture make "rental or benefit payments" to those farmers who agreed to reduce production. The government agreed that the Act would be unconstitutional if the farmer had been *compelled* to reduce production but was not, since he was merely *invited* to do so. Justice Roberts expressed the contrary majority view of the court that "The power to confer or withhold unlimited benefits is the power to coerce or destroy." This recognition of positive reinforcement was withdrawn a few years later in another case in which Justice Cardozo wrote "To hold that motive or temptation is equivalent to coercion is to plunge the law in endless difficulties."[5] We may agree with him, without implying that the proposition is therefore wrong. Sooner or later the law must be prepared to deal with all possible techniques of governmental control.

The uneasiness with which we view government (in the broadest possible sense) when it does not use punishment is shown by the reception of my utopian novel, *Walden Two*. This was essentially a proposal to apply a behavioral technology to the construction of a workable, effective, and productive pattern of government. It was greeted with wrathful violence. *Life* magazine called it "a travesty on the good life," and "a menace . . . a triumph of mortmain or the dead hand not envisaged since the days of Sparta . . . a slur upon a name, a corruption of an impulse." Joseph Wood Krutch devoted a substantial part of his book, *The Mea-*

sure of Man, to attacking my views and those of the protagonist, Frazier, in the same vein, and Morris Viteles has recently criticized the book in a similar manner in *Science*.[6] Perhaps the reaction is best expressed in a quotation from *The Quest for Utopia* by Negley and Patrick:

"Halfway through this contemporary utopia, the reader may feel sure, as we did, that this is a beautifully ironic satire on what has been called 'behavioral engineering.' The longer one stays in this better world of the psychologist, however, the plainer it becomes that the inspiration is not satiric, but messianic. This is indeed the behaviorally engineered society, and while it was to be expected that sooner or later the principle of psychological conditioning would be made the basis of a serious construction of utopia — Brown anticipated it in *Limanora* — yet not even the effective satire of Huxley is adequate preparation for the shocking horror of the idea when positively presented. Of all the dictatorships espoused by utopists, this is the most profound, and incipient dictators might well find in this utopia a guidebook of political practice."[7]

One would scarcely guess that the authors are talking about a world in which there is food, clothing, and shelter for all, where everyone chooses his own work and works on the average only 4 hours a day, where music and the arts flourish, where personal rela-

[5] Freund: *Constitutional Law*, p. 244.

[6] M. Viteles, *Science*, Vol. 122 (1955), p. 1167.

[7] Glenn Negley and J. M. Patrick, *The Quest for Utopia* (New York: Schuman, 1952).

tionships develop under the most favorable circumstances, where education prepares every child for the social and intellectual life which lies before him, where — in short — people are truly happy, secure, productive, creative, and forward-looking. What is wrong with it? Only one thing: someone "planned it that way." If these critics had come upon a society in some remote corner of the world which boasted similar advantages, they would undoubtedly have hailed it as providing a pattern we all might well follow — provided that it was clearly the result of a natural process of cultural evolution. Any evidence that intelligence had been used in arriving at this version of the good life would, in their eyes, be a serious flaw. No matter if the planner of *Walden Two* diverts none of the proceeds of the community to his own use, no matter if he has no current control or is, indeed, unknown to most of the other members of the community (he planned that, too), somewhere back of it all he occupies the position of prime mover. And this, to the child of the democratic tradition, spoils it all.

The dangers inherent in the control of human behavior are very real. The possibility of the misuse of scientific knowledge must always be faced. We cannot escape by denying the power of a science of behavior or arresting its development. It is no help to cling to familiar philosophies of human behavior simply because they are more reassuring. As I have pointed out elsewhere,[8] the new techniques emerging

[8]B. F. Skinner, *Transactions of the New York Academy of Sciences*, Vol. 17 (1955), p. 547.

from a science of behavior must be subject to the explicit countercontrol which has already been applied to earlier and cruder forms. Brute force and deception, for example, are now fairly generally suppressed by ethical practices and by explicit governmental and religious agencies. A similar countercontrol of scientific knowledge in the interests of the group is a feasible and promising possibility. Although we cannot say how devious the course of its evolution may be, a cultural pattern of control and countercontrol will presumably emerge which will be most widely supported because it is most widely reinforcing.

If we cannot forsee all the details of this (as we obviously cannot), it is important to remember that this is true of the critics of science as well. The dire consequences of new techniques of control, the hidden menace in original cultural designs — these need some proof. It is only another example of my present point that the need for proof is so often overlooked. Man has got himself into some pretty fixes, and it is easy to believe that he will do so again. But there is a more optimistic possibility. The slow growth of the methods of science, now for the first time being applied to human affairs, *may* mean a new and exciting phase of human life to which historical analogies will not apply and in which earlier political slogans will not be appropriate. If we are to use the knowledge that a science of behavior is now making available with any hope of success, we must look at human nature as it is brought into focus through the methods of science rather than as it has been presented to us in a series of historical accidents.

If the advent of a powerful science of behavior causes trouble, it will not be because science itself is inimical to human welfare but because older conceptions have not yielded easily or gracefully. We expect resistance to new techniques of control from those who have heavy investments in the old, but we have no reason to help them preserve a series of principles that are not ends in themselves but rather outmoded means to an end. What is needed is a new conception of human behavior which is compatible with the implications of a scientific analysis. All men control and are controlled. The question of government in the broadest possible sense is not how freedom is to be preserved but what kinds of control are to be used and to what ends. Control must be analyzed and considered in its proper proportions. No one, I am sure, wishes to develop new master-slave relationships to bend the will of the people to despotic rulers in new ways. These are patterns of control appropriate to a world without science. They may well be the first to go when the experimental analysis of behavior comes into its own in the design of cultural practices.

II [ROGERS]

There are, I believe, a number of matters in connection with this important topic on which the authors of this article, and probably a large majority of psychologists, are in agreement. These matters then are not issues as far as we are concerned, and I should like to mention them briefly in order to put them to one side.

Points of Agreement

I am sure we agree that men — as individuals and as societies — have always endeavored to understand, predict, influence, and control human behavior — their own behavior and that of others.

I believe we agree that the behavioral sciences are making and will continue to make increasingly rapid progress in the understanding of behavior, and that as a consequence the capacity to predict and to control behavior is developing with equal rapidity.

I believe we agree that to deny these advances, or to claim that man's behavior cannot be a field of science, is unrealistic. Even though this is not an issue for us, we should recognize that many intelligent men still hold strongly to the view that the actions of men are free in some sense such that scientific knowledge of man's behavior is impossible. Thus Reinhold Niebuhr, the noted theologian, heaps scorn on the concept of psychology as a science of man's behavior and even says, "In any event, no scientific investigation of past behavior can become the basis of predictions of future behavior."[9] So, while this is not an issue for psychologists, we should at least notice in passing that it is an issue for many people.

I believe we are in agreement that the tremendous potential power of a science which permits the prediction

[9]Reinhold Niebuhr, *The Self and the Dramas of History* (New York: Scribner's, 1955), p. 47.

and control of behavior may be misused, and that the possibility of such misuse constitutes a serious threat.

Consequently Skinner and I are in agreement that the whole question of the scientific control of human behavior is a matter with which psychologists and the general public should concern themselves. As Robert Oppenheimer told the American Psychological Association last year[10] the problems that psychologists will pose for society by their growing ability to control behavior will be much more grave than the problems posed by the ability of physicists to control the reactions of matter. I am not sure whether psychologists generally recognize this. My impression is that by and large they hold a laissez-faire attitude. Obviously Skinner and I do not hold this laissez-faire view, or we would not have written this article.

Points at Issue

With these several points of basic and important agreement, are there then any issues that remain on which there are differences? I believe there are. They can be stated very briefly: Who will be controlled? Who will exercise control? What type of control will be exercised? Most important of all, toward what end or what purpose, or in the pursuit of what value, will control be exercised?

It is on questions of this sort that there exist ambiguities, misunderstandings, and probably deep differences.

[10]Robert Oppenheimer, *American Psychologist*, Vol. 11 (1956), p. 127.

These differences exist among psychologists, among members of the general public in this country, and among various world cultures. Without any hope of achieving a final resolution of these questions, we can, I believe, put these issues in clearer form.

Some Meanings

To avoid ambiguity and faulty communication, I would like to clarify the meanings of some of the terms we are using.

Behavioral science is a term that might be defined from several angles but in the context of this discussion it refers primarily to knowledge that the existence of certain describable conditions in the human being and/or in his environment is followed by certain describable consequences in his actions.

Prediction means the prior identification of behaviors which then occur. Because it is important in some things I wish to say later, I would point out that one may predict a highly specific behavior, such as an eye blink, or one may predict a class of behaviors. One might correctly predict "avoidant behavior," for example, without being able to specify whether the individual will run away or simply close his eyes.

The word *control* is a very slippery one, which can be used with any one of several meanings. I would like to specify three that seem most important for our present purposes. *Control* may mean: (i) The setting of conditions by B for A, A having no voice in the matter, such that certain predictable behaviors then occur in A. I refer to this as external control. (ii) The setting of conditions by *B* for *A*, *A* giving some degree of consent to these conditions, such that certain predictable behaviors then occur in *A*. I refer to this as the influence of *B* on *A*. (iii) The setting of conditions by *A* such that certain predictable behaviors then occur in himself. I refer to this as internal control. It will be noted that Skinner lumps together the first two meanings, external control and influence, under the concept of control. I find this confusing.

Usual Concept of Control of Human Behavior

With the underbrush thus cleared away (I hope), let us review very briefly the various elements that are involved in the usual concept of the control of human behavior as mediated by the behavioral sciences. I am drawing here on the previous writings of Skinner, on his present statements, on the writings of others who have considered in either friendly or antagonistic fashion the meanings that would be involved in such control. I have not excluded the science fiction writers, as reported recently by Vandenburg,[11] since they often show an awareness of the issues involved, even though the methods described are as yet fictional. These then are the elements that seem common to these different concepts of the application of science to human behavior.

1. There must first be some sort of decision about goals. Usually desirable goals are assumed, but sometimes, as in George Orwell's book *1984*, the goal that is selected is an aggrandizement of individual power with which most of us would disagree. In a recent paper Skinner suggests that one possible set of goals to be assigned to the behavioral technology is this: "Let men be happy, informed, skillful, well-behaved and productive."[12] In the first draft of his part of this article, which he was kind enough to show me, he did not mention such definite goals as these, but desired "improved" education practices, "wiser" use of knowledge in government, and the like. In the final version of his article he avoids even these value-laden terms, and his implicit goal is the very general one that scientific control of behavior is desirable, because it would perhaps bring "a far better world for everyone."

Thus the first step in thinking about the control of human behavior is the choice of goals, whether specific or general. It is necessary to come to terms in some way with the issue, "For what purpose?"

2. A second element is that, whether the end selected is highly specific or is a very general one such as wanting "a better world," we proceed by the methods of science to discover the means to these ends. We continue through further experimentation and investigation to discover more effective means. The method of science is self-correcting in thus arriving at increasingly effective ways of achieving the purpose we have in mind.

3. The third aspect of such control

---

[11]S. G. Vandenberg, *American Psychologist*, Vol. 11 (1956), p. 339.

[12]B. F. Skinner, *American Scholar*, Vol. 25 (1955–1956), p. 47.

is that as the conditions or methods are discovered by which to reach the goals, some person or some group establishes these conditions and uses these methods, having in one way or another obtained the power to do so.

4.   The fourth element is the exposure of individuals to the prescribed conditions, and this leads, with a high degree of probability, to behavior which is in line with the goals desired. Individuals are now happy, if that has been the goal, or well-behaved, or submissive, or whatever it has been decided to make them.

5.   The fifth element is that if the process I have described is put in motion then there is a continuing social organization which will continue to produce the types of behavior that have been valued.

Some Flaws

Are there any flaws in this way of viewing the control of human behavior? I believe there are. In fact the only element in this description with which I find myself in agreement is the second. It seems to me quite incontrovertibly true that the scientific method is an excellent way to discover the means by which to achieve our goals. Beyond that, I feel many sharp differences, which I will try to spell out.

I believe that in Skinner's presentation here and in his previous writings, there is a serious underestimation of the problem of power. To hope that the power which is being made available by the behavioral sciences will be exercised by the scientists, or by a benevolent group, seems to me a hope little

supported by either recent or distant history. It seems far more likely that behavioral scientists, holding their present attitudes, will be in the position of the German rocket scientists specializing in guided missiles. First they worked devotedly for Hitler to destroy the U.S.S.R. and the United States. Now, depending on who captured them, they work devotedly for the U.S.S.R. in the interest of destroying the United States, or devotedly for the United States in the interest of destroying the U.S.S.R. If behavioral scientists are concerned solely with advancing their science, it seems most probable that they will serve the purposes of whatever individual or group has the power.

But the major flaw I see in this review of what is involved in the scientific control of human behavior is the denial, misunderstanding, or gross underestimation of the place of ends, goals or values in their relationship to science. This error (as it seems to me) has so many implications that I would like to devote some space to it.

Ends and Values in Relation to Science

In sharp contradiction to some views that have been advanced, I would like to propose a two-pronged thesis: (i) In any scientific endeavor — whether "pure" or applied science — there is a prior subjective choice of the purpose or value which that scientific work is perceived as serving. (ii) This subjective value choice which brings the scientific endeavor into being must always lie outside of that endeavor and can never become a part of the science involved in that endeavor.

Let me illustrate the first point from Skinner himself. It is clear that in his earlier writing it is recognized that a prior value choice is necessary, and it is specified as the goal that men are to become happy, well-behaved, productive, and so on. I am pleased that Skinner has retreated from the goals he then chose, because to me they seem to be stultifying values. I can only feel that he was choosing these goals for others, not for himself. I would hate to see Skinner become "well-behaved," as that term would be defined for him by behavioral scientists. His recent article in the *American Psychologist*[13] shows that he certainly does not want to be "productive" as that value is defined by most psychologists. And the most awful fate I can imagine for him would be to have him constantly "happy." It is the fact that he is very unhappy about many things which makes me prize him.

In the first draft of his part of this article, he also included such prior value choices, saying for example, "We must decide how we are to use the knowledge which a science of human behavior is now making available." Now he has dropped all mention of such choices, and if I understand him correctly, he believes that science can proceed without them. He has suggested this view in another recent paper, stating that "We must continue to experiment in cultural design . . . testing the consequences as we go. Eventually the practices which make for the greatest biological and psychological strength of the group will presumably survive."[14]

I would point out, however, that to choose to experiment is a value choice. Even to move in the direction of perfectly random experimentation is a value choice. To test the consequences of an experiment is possible only if we have first made a subjective choice of a criterion value. And implicit in his statement is a valuing of biological and psychological strength. So even when trying to avoid such choice, it seems inescapable that a prior subjective value choice is necessary for any scientific endeavor, or for any application of scientific knowledge. . . .

Is the Situation Hopeless?

The thoughtful reader may recognize that, although my remarks up to this point have introduced some modifications in the conception of the processes by which human behavior will be controlled, these remarks may have made such control seem, if anything, even more inevitable. We might sum it up this way: Behavioral science is clearly moving forward; the increasing power for control which it gives will be held by someone or some group; such an individual or group will surely choose the values or goals to be achieved; and most of us will then be increasingly controlled by means so subtle that we will not even be aware of them as controls.

[13]B. F. Skinner, *American Psychologist*, Vol. 11 (1956), p. 221.

[14]B. F. Skinner, *Transactions of the New York Academy of Sciences*, Vol. 17 (1955), p. 549.

Thus, whether a council of wise psychologists (if this is not a contradiction in terms), or a Stalin, or a Big Brother has the power, and whether the goal is happiness, or productivity, or resolution of the Oedipus complex, or submission, or love of Big Brother, we will inevitably find ourselves moving toward the chosen goal and probably thinking that we ourselves desire it. Thus, if this line of reasoning is correct, it appears that some form of *Walden Two* or of *1984* (and at a deep philosophic level they seem indistinguishable) is coming. The fact that it would surely arrive piecemeal, rather than all at once, does not greatly change the fundamental issues. In any event, as Skinner has indicated in his writings, we would then look back upon the concepts of human freedom, the capacity for choice, the responsibility for choice, and the worth of the human individual as historical curiosities which once existed by cultural accident as values in a prescientific civilization.

I believe that any person observant of trends must regard something like the foregoing sequence as a real possibility. It is not simply a fantasy. Something of that sort may even be the most likely future. But is it an inevitable future? I want to devote the remainder of my remarks to an alternative possibility.

Alternative Set of Values

Suppose we start with a set of ends, values, purposes, quite different from the type of goals we have been considering. Suppose we do this quite openly, setting them forth as a possible value choice to be accepted or rejected. Suppose we select a set of values that focuses on fluid elements of process rather than static attributes. We might then value: man as a process of becoming, as a process of achieving worth and dignity through the development of his potentialities; the individual human being as a self-actualizing process, moving on to more challenging and enriching experiences; the process by which the individual creatively adapts to an ever-new and changing world; the process by which knowledge transcends itself, as, for example, the theory of relativity transcended Newtonian physics, itself to be transcended in some future day by a new perception.

If we select values such as these we turn to our science and technology of behavior with a very different set of questions. We will want to know such things as these: Can science aid in the discovery of new modes of richly rewarding living? more meaningful and satisfying modes of interpersonal relationships? Can science inform us on how the human race can become a more intelligent participant in its own evolution — its physical, psychological and social evolution? Can science inform us on ways of releasing the creative capacity of individuals, which seem so necessary if we are to survive in this fantastically expanding atomic age? Oppenheimer has pointed out[15] that knowledge, which used to double in millenia or centuries, now doubles in a generation or a decade. It appears that

[15]Robert Oppenheimer, *Roosevelt University Occasional Papers*, Vol. 2 (1956).

we must discover the utmost in release of creativity if we are to be able to adapt effectively. In short, can science discover the methods by which man can most readily become a continually developing and self-transcending process, in his behavior, his thinking, his knowledge? Can science predict and release an essentially "unpredictable" freedom?

It is one of the virtues of science as a method that it is as able to advance and implement goals and purposes of this sort as it is to serve static values, such as states of being well-informed, happy, obedient. Indeed we have some evidence of this. . . .

Possible Concept of the Control of Human Behavior

It is quite clear that the point of view I am expressing is in sharp contrast to the usual conception of the relationship of the behavioral sciences to the control of human behavior. In order to make this contrast even more blunt, I will state this possibility in paragraphs parallel to those used before.

1. It is possible for us to choose to value man as a self-actualizing process of becoming; to value creativity, and the process by which knowledge becomes self-transcending.

2. We can proceed, by the methods of science, to discover the conditions which necessarily precede these processes and, through continuing experimentation, to discover better means of achieving these purposes.

3. It is possible for individuals or groups to set these conditions, with a minimum of power or control. According to present knowledge, the only authority necessary is the authority to establish certain qualities of interpersonal relationships.

4. Exposed to these conditions, present knowledge suggests that individuals become more self-responsible, make progress in self-actualization, become more flexible, and become more creatively adaptive.

5. Thus such an initial choice would inaugurate the beginnings of a social system or subsystem in which values, knowledge, adaptive skills, and even the concept of science would be continually changing and self-transcending. The emphasis would be upon man as a process of becoming.

I believe it is clear that such a view as I have been describing does not lead to any definable utopia. It would be impossible to predict its final outcome. It involves a step-by-step development, based on a continuing subjective choice of purposes, which are implemented by the behavioral sciences. It is in the direction of the "open society," as that term has been defined by Popper,[16] where individuals carry responsibility for personal decisions. It is at the opposite pole from his concept of the closed society, of which *Walden Two* would be an example.

I trust it is also evident that the whole emphasis is on process, not on end-states of being. I am suggesting that it is by choosing to value certain

[16]Karl R. Popper, *The Open Society and Its Enemies* (London: Routledge and Kegan Paul, 1945).

qualitative elements of the process of becoming that we can find a pathway toward the open society.

The Choice

It is my hope that we have helped to clarify the range of choice which will lie before us and our children in regard to the behavioral sciences. We can choose to use our growing knowledge to enslave people in ways never dreamed of before, depersonalizing them, controlling them by means so carefully selected that they will perhaps never be aware of their loss of personhood. We can choose to utilize our scientific knowledge to make men happy, well-behaved, and productive, as Skinner earlier suggested. Or we can insure that each person learns all the syllabus which we select and set before him, as Skinner now suggests. Or at the other end of the spectrum of choice we can choose to use the behavioral sciences in ways which will free, not control; which will bring about constructive variability, not conformity; which will develop creativity, not contentment; which will facilitate each person in his self-directed process of becoming; which will aid individuals, groups, and even the concept of science to become self-transcending in freshly adaptive ways of meeting life and its problems. The choice is up to us, and, the human race being what it is, we are likely to stumble about, making at times some nearly disastrous value choices and at other times highly constructive ones.

I am aware that to some, this setting forth of a choice is unrealistic, because a choice of values is regarded as not possible. Skinner has stated: "Man's vaunted creative powers . . . his capacity to choose and our right to hold him responsible for his choice—none of these is conspicuous in this new self-portrait (provided by science). Man, we once believed, was free to express himself in art, music, and literature, to inquire into nature, to seek salvation in his own way. He could initiate action and make spontaneous and capricious changes of course. . . . But science insists that action is initiated by forces impinging upon the individual, and that caprice is only another name for behavior for which we have not yet found a cause."[17]

I can understand this point of view, but I believe that it avoids looking at the great paradox of behavioral science. Behavior, when it is examined scientifically, is surely best understood as determined by prior causation. This is one great fact of science. But responsible personal choice, which is the most essential element in being a person, which is the core experience in psychotherapy, which exists prior to any scientific endeavor, is an equally prominent fact in our lives. To deny the experience of responsible choice is, to me, as restricted a view as to deny the possibility of a behavioral science. That these two important elements of our experience appear to be in contradiction has perhaps the same significance as the contradiction between the wave theory and the corpuscular theory of light, both of which can be shown to be true,

[17]B. F. Skinner, *American Scholar*, Vol. 25 (1955–1956), p. 47.

even though incompatible. We cannot profitably deny our subjective life, any more than we can deny the objective description of that life.

In conclusion then, it is my contention that science cannot come into being without a personal choice of the values we wish to achieve. And these values we choose to implement will forever lie outside of the science which implements them; the goals we select, the purposes we wish to follow, must always be outside of the science which achieves them. To me this has the encouraging meaning that the human person, with his capacity of subjective choice, can and will always exist, separate from and prior to any of his scientific undertakings. Unless as individuals and groups we choose to relinquish our capacity of subjective choice, we will always remain persons, not simply pawns of a self-created science.

III [SKINNER]

. . . The values I have occasionally recommended (and Rogers has not led me to recant) are transitional. Other things being equal, I am betting on the group whose practices make for healthy, happy, secure, productive, and creative people. And I insist that the values recommended by Rogers are transitional, too, for I can ask him the same kind of question. Man as a process of becoming—*what*? Self-actualization— for what? Inner control is no more a goal than external.

What Rogers seems to me to be proposing, both here and elsewhere, is this: Let us use our increasing power of control to create individuals who will not need and perhaps will no longer respond to control. Let us solve the problem of our power by renouncing it. At first blush this seems as implausible as a benevolent despot. Yet power has occasionally been foresworn. A nation has burned its Reichstag, rich men have given away their wealth, beautiful women have become ugly hermits in the desert, and psychotherapists have become nondirective. When this happens, I look to other possible reinforcements for a plausible explanation. A people relinquish democratic power when a tyrant promises them the earth. Rich men give away wealth to escape the accusing finger of their fellowmen. A woman destroys her beauty in the hope of salvation. And a psychotherapist relinquishes control because he can thus help his client more effectively.

The solution that Rogers is suggesting is thus understandable. But is he correctly interpreting the result? What evidence is there that a client ever becomes truly *self*-directing? What evidence is there that he ever makes a truly *inner* choice of ideal or goal? Even though the therapist does not do the choosing, even though he encourages "self-actualization"—he is not out of control as long as he holds himself ready to step in when occasion demands—when, for example, the client chooses the goal of becoming a more accomplished liar or murdering his boss. But supposing the therapist does withdraw completely or is no longer necessary—what about all the other forces acting upon the client? Is the self-chosen goal independent of his early ethical and religious training? of the folk-wisdom of his group? of the opinions and attitudes of others who are important to him? Surely not. The therapeutic situation is only a small part of the world of the client. From the therapist's point of view it may appear to be possible to relinquish control. But the control passes, not to a "self," but to forces in other parts of the client's world. The solution of the therapist's problem of power cannot be *our* solution, for we must consider *all* the forces acting upon the individual.

The child who must be prodded and nagged is something less than a fully developed human being. We want to see him hurrying to his appointment, not because each step is taken in response to verbal reminders from his mother, but because certain temporal contingencies, in which dawdling has been punished and hurrying reinforced, have worked a change in his behavior. Call this a state of better organization, a greater sensitivity to reality, or what you will. The plain fact is that the child passes from a temporary verbal control exercised by his parents to control by certain inexorable features of the environment. I should suppose that something of the same sort happens in successful psychotherapy. Rogers seems to me to be saying this: Let us put an end, as quickly as possible, to any pattern of master-and-slave, to any direct obedience to command, to the submissive following of suggestions. Let the individual be free to adjust himself to more rewarding features of the world about him. In the end, let his teachers and counselors "wither away," like the Marxist state. I not only agree with this as a useful ideal, I have constructed a fanciful world to demonstrate its ad-

vantages. It saddens me to hear Rogers say that "at a deep philosophic level" *Walden Two* and George Orwell's *1984* "seem indistinguishable." They could scarcely be more unlike—at any level. The book *1984* is a picture of immediate aversive control for vicious selfish purposes. The founder of *Walden Two*, on the other hand, has built a community in which neither he nor any other person exerts any *current* control. His achievement lay in his original *plan*, and when he boasts of this ("It is enough to satisfy the thirstiest tyrant") we do not fear him but only pity him for his weakness.

Another critic of *Walden Two*, Andrew Hacker,[18] has discussed this point in considering the bearing of mass conditioning upon the liberal notion of autonomous man. In drawing certain parallels between the Grand Inquisition passage in Dostoevsky's *Brothers Karamazov*, Huxley's *Brave New World*, and *Walden Two*, he attempts to set up a distinction to be drawn in any society between conditioners and conditioned. He assumes that "the conditioner can be said to be autonomous in the traditional liberal sense." But then he notes: "Of course the conditioner has been conditioned. But he has not been conditioned by the conscious manipulation of another *person*." But how does this affect the resulting behavior? Can we not soon forget the origins of the "artificial" diamond which is identical with the real thing? Whether it is an "accidental" cultural pattern, such as is said to have produced the founder of *Wal-*

[18]Andrew Hacker, *Journal of Politics*, Vol. 17 (1955), p. 17.

den Two, or the engineered environment which is about to produce his successors, we are dealing with sets of conditions generating human behavior which will ultimately be measured by their contribution to the strength of the group. We look to the future, not the past, for the test of "goodness" or acceptability.

If we are worthy of our democratic heritage we shall, of course, be ready to resist any tyrannical use of science for immediate or selfish purposes. But if we value the achievements and goals of democracy we must not refuse to apply science to the design and construction of cultural patterns, even though we may then find ourselves in some sense in the position of controllers. Fear of control, generalized beyond any warrant, has led to a misinterpretation of valid practices and the blind rejection of intelligent planning for a better way of life. In terms which I trust Rogers will approve, in conquering this fear we shall become more mature and better organized and shall, thus, more fully actualize ourselves as human beings.

COMMENT

The discussion between Skinner and Rogers is a fitting conclusion to this book. It surveys "the enduring questions" from a fresh and contemporary perspective. Among these questions are the following:

1. WHAT IS THE CORRECT METHOD OF INQUIRY? Skinner, as a brilliant experimentalist, operates in the tradition of empiricists such as Locke, Hume, and Peirce. He rejects the introspective method and traces knowledge back to experience rather than to innate mental factors. Scientific method as he interprets it is based upon sensory and, therefore, public observation. The study of human activities, he insists, should concentrate upon the forms of external behavior, exhibited with various regularities and probabilities. He thinks that there is no great difference in method between animal and human psychology.

Rogers, as a clinical psychologist and psychotherapist, seeks to understand the unfolding development of inner needs and purposes. Although he could not be called a rationalist, he agrees with Descartes in recognizing an innate structure to the mind and in distinguishing rather sharply between the human and animal levels of behavior. For him, man is to be studied at his own level and each man is to be understood in his own terms. Like the existentialists, Kierkegaard and Buber, he seeks to penetrate behind all masks and false fronts to "that self which one truly is." Using language identical with Buber's, he has said that the deepest and most satisfying interpersonal contact is "a real I-Thou relationship, not an I-It relationship."[1]

2. WHAT IS THE RELATION BETWEEN MIND AND BODY? Skinner sides with Gilbert Ryle against Descartes. In renouncing "the dogma of the ghost in the machine," he rejects the "ghost" more emphatically than the "machine." Although he is too sophisticated to deny that there are thoughts and feelings, he declares that a scientific psychology must wholly abandon the conception of psychic causes. He has defined such mental factors as "intentions" in terms of observable relations that refer exclusively to antecedent stimulus conditions and motions of bodies. Everything that a psychologist legitimately wants to say about mental events, he believes, can be said in purely behavioral terms.

Although Rogers does not accept so sharp a dualism as that of Descartes, he insists that the inner life is causally important and nonreducible. Man is a psychophysiological organism, and it is a mistake to slight or disregard the mental side of his nature.

3. DO PEOPLE HAVE FREE WILL? Skinner agrees with Spinoza in rejecting the possibility of undetermined choices and final causes. He has said that a scientific theory of human behavior "must abolish the conception of the individual as a doer, as an originator of action."[2] Explaining behavior in terms of stimuli impinging on the individual, he is skeptical that a person "ever becomes truly *self*-directing," or "that he ever makes a truly *inner* choice of ideal or goal." Although, like Hume, he speaks of freedom of action, it is within the context of a deterministic theory.

Rogers aligns himself with free-will advocates such as William James. He is as insistent on the importance and reality of "subjective value choice" as Skinner is on "conditioning." His aim as a therapist is to liberate the individual from both inner and outer blocks to permit more freedom and self-direction. Granted that there are limits to our environmental opportunities and our given and potential nature, we are free within these limits to guide our growth by reflective goals.

4. WHAT IS THE NATURAL BASIS OF ETHICS? Skinner tends toward an "evolutionary ethics" based on the principle of "the survival of the fittest." When pressed for justification of his ethical preferences, he falls back on the criterion of "the strength of the group" and "the survival of mankind." He is much more inclined than Rogers to think that science can supply the norms for the control of human behavior.

---

[1]For Rogers' sympathy with Kierkegaard, see Clark E. Moustakes (ed.), *The Self* (New York: Harper & Row, 1956), pp. 197 – 198; and for his relation to Buber, see Maurice S. Friedman, *Martin Buber: The Life of Dialogue* (New York: Harper & Row, 1960), pp. 191 – 195. Also see the dialogue between Buber and Rogers in Martin Buber, *The Knowledge of Man* (New York: Harper & Row, 1965), pp. 166 – 184.

[2]B. F. Skinner, *Cumulative Record* (New York: Appleton-Century-Crofts, 1959), p. 236.

Rogers believes that human beings, by nature, are loaded and cocked to develop in certain ways, and that it is good to realize this potential. The ethical goal is fulfillment of what is deepest in a person's nature. He thus approximates the humanism of the natural-law tradition that stems from Aristotle and Cicero, but he differs in putting greater emphasis on the freedom and uniqueness of the individual person. "Basic human nature," he has said, "is something that is really to be *trusted*. . . . It's been very much my experience in therapy that one does not need to supply motivation toward the positive or toward the constructive. That exists in the individual. . . . If we can release what is most basic in the individual . . . it will be constructive."[3] To pursue this goal calls for a "subjective value choice" that lies outside the scope of science.

5. HOW SHOULD HUMAN BEHAVIOR BE CONTROLLED?   In view of the contrasting answers of Skinner and Rogers to the foregoing questions, we should not be surprised that they differ radically in their educational and political ideals.

Skinner approaches education as a technological problem, believing that the art of teaching should be based on the science of learning. He puts great stress on "what are called contingencies of reinforcement — the relations which prevail between behavior on the one hand and the consequences of that behavior on the other."[4] These consequences he proposes to manipulate by rewards ("positive reinforcement") more than punishments ("aversive control" or "negative reinforcement"). He advocates "programmed instruction" with the aid of ingenious teaching machines. The sad thing, he declares, is that we are not making use of a tenth of the knowledge about learning that we have at our disposal.

In sketching his Utopia in *Walden Two*, he applies the same basic principle as in his educational theory — namely, control over positive and negative reinforcements (the carrot and stick approach, with emphasis on the carrot). His proposal for social reconstruction resembles Plato's in the *Republic*, except that psychological-engineers replace philosopher-kings. Having found that he can do amazing things with rats and pigeons, he believes that equally amazing results can be achieved by the scientific and technological reshaping of human beings within an "engineered environment." For him, the viable choice is not between freedom and control but between scientific control, on the one hand, and caprice and unscientific control, on the other. He is convinced that we gain freedom *through* control and not otherwise. Although he recognizes that authoritarian figures may shape people the wrong way, he thinks that countercontrols can be devised that will minimize this danger.

[3]Martin Buber, *The Knowledge of Man*, pp. 179–180.
[4]B. F. Skinner, *The Technology of Teaching* (New York: Appleton-Century-Crofts, 1968), p. 9.

For Rogers the idea of manipulating human beings, whether in school or in society, is highly distasteful. He draws a sharper distinction than does Skinner between the training of animals and the education of human beings. For the latter he advocates something like the "Socratic method" when liberally interpreted. This method was described by Ralph Cudworth, the seventeenth-century Platonist, as based on the belief that "knowledge was not to be poured into the soul like liquor, but rather to be invited and gently drawn forth from it; nor the mind so much to be filled therewith from without, like a vessel, as to be kindled and awaked."[5] Rogers, I think, would put more emphasis than Cudworth on environmental factors in the teaching process, but he too wishes to release inner potentialities and to awaken and kindle the mind.

Because he dislikes the manipulation of human beings even by "positive reinforcement," he sees a deeper affinity between *Walden Two* and Orwell's *1984* than Skinner is willing to admit. He is convinced that the freedom of persons ought categorically to be respected and that the goal of happiness by contrived reinforcement should not override the demands of freedom. In the tradition of Mill and Dewey he proposes a liberal set of values to guide us politically as well as educationally. "We can choose the behavioral sciences," he says, "in ways which will free, not control." He warns against the danger that science will be used, as in Hitler's Germany or Stalin's Russia, for vicious or totalitarian ends. There is nothing in science itself, in the absence of "subjective value choice," that can prevent such abuse. In this clash of opinion between Rogers and Skinner there are exciting grounds for debate and discussion. In the following and final selection, Martin Buber explores the notion of dialog as the necessary basis for this discussion.

MARTIN BUBER (1878–1965)

Born in Vienna of Jewish parentage, Martin Buber studied philosophy and the history of art at the Universities of Vienna and Berlin. From his youth he was active in the Zionist movement, especially in its cultural and religious aspects, and in 1901 he became editor of the Zionist journal *Die Welt*. He also edited for eight years (1916–1924) the influential German periodical *Der Jude*, devoted to the renascence of Jewish life and culture. For a decade (1923–1933) he taught philosophy and religion at the University of Frankfurt. He escaped from Hitler's Germany in 1938 and became, at the age of sixty, professor of philosophy at Hebrew University

---

[5]Ralph Cudworth, *Treatise Concerning Eternal and Immutable Morality*, American ed. of *Works*, ed. T. Birch, 1838, p. 427. I am indebted to Noam Chomsky, *Cartesian Linguistics*, for this reference.

in Jerusalem, continuing in this post for fifteen years. In Israel he worked to bring about understanding between the Jews and Arabs and advocated a binational state. He also supported, as an alternative to both individualism and collectivism, experiments in communal living within small, autonomous groups. His book *I and Thou*, more than any other of his numerous publications, established his worldwide fame as a moral and religious existentialist.

Elements of the Interhuman

THE SOCIAL AND THE INTERHUMAN

It is usual to ascribe what takes place between men to the social realm, thereby blurring a basically important line of division between two essentially different areas of human life. I myself, when I began nearly fifty years ago to find my own bearings in the knowledge of society, making use of the then unknown concept of the interhuman, made the same error. From that time it became increasingly clear to me that we have to do here with a separate category of our existence, even a separate dimension, to use a mathematical term, and one with which we are so familiar that its peculiarity has hitherto almost escaped us. Yet insight into its peculiarity is extremely important not only for our thinking, but also for our living.

We may speak of social phenomena wherever the life of a number of men,

From *The Knowledge of Man*, edited by Maurice Friedman. Translated by Robert Gregor Smith. Copyright © 1965 by Martin Buber and Maurice Friedman. Reprinted by permission of Harper & Row, Publishers.

lived with one another, bound up together, brings in its train shared experiences and reactions. But to be thus bound up together means only that each individual existence is enclosed and contained in a group existence. It does not mean that between one member and another of the group there exists any kind of personal relation. They do feel that they belong together in a way that is, so to speak, fundamentally different from every possible belonging together with someone outside the group. And there do arise, especially in the life of smaller groups, contacts which frequently favour the birth of individual relations, but, on the other hand, frequently make it more difficult. In no case, however, does membership in a group necessarily involve an existential relation between one member and another. It is true that there have been groups in history which included highly intensive and intimate relations between two of their members — as, for instance, in the homosexual relations among the Japanese Samurai or among Doric warriors — and these were countenanced for the sake of the stricter cohesion of the group. But in general it must be said that the leading elements in groups, especially in the later course of human history, have rather been inclined to suppress the personal relation in favour of the purely collective element. Where this latter element reigns alone or is predominant, men feel themselves to be carried by the collectivity, which lifts them out of loneliness and fear of the world and lostness. When this happens—and for modern man it is an essential happening—the life between person and person seems to retreat more and more before the advance of the collective. The collective aims at holding in check the inclination to personal life. It is as though those who are bound together in groups should in the main be concerned only with the work of the group and should turn to the personal partners, who are tolerated by the group, only in secondary meetings.

The difference between the two realms became very palpable to me on one occasion when I had joined the procession through a large town of a movement to which I did not belong. I did it out of sympathy for the tragic development which I sensed was at hand in the destiny of a friend who was one of the leaders of the movement. While the procession was forming, I conversed with him and with another, a good-hearted 'wild man,' who also had the mark of death upon him. At that moment I still felt that the two men really were there, over against me, each of them a man near to me, near even in what was most remote from me; so different from me that my soul continually suffered from this difference, yet

by virtue of this very difference confronting me with authentic being. Then the formations started off, and after a short time I was lifted out of all confrontation, drawn into the procession, falling in with its aimless step; and it was obviously the very same for the two with whom I had just exchanged human words. After a while we passed a café where I had been sitting the previous day with a musician whom I knew only slightly. The very moment we passed it the door opened, the musician stood on the threshold, saw me, apparently saw me alone, and waved to me. Straightway it seemed to me as though I were taken out of the procession and of the presence of my marching friends, and set there, confronting the musician. I forgot that I was walking along with the same step; I felt that I was standing over there by the man who had called out to me, and without a word, with a smile of understanding, was answering him. When consciousness of the facts returned to me, the procession, with my companions and myself at its head, had left the café behind.

The realm of the interhuman goes far beyond that of sympathy. Such simple happenings can be part of it as, for instance, when two strangers exchange glances in a crowded streetcar, at once to sink back again into the convenient state of wishing to know nothing about each other. But also every casual encounter between opponents belongs to this realm, when it affects the opponent's attitude—that is, when something, however imperceptible, happens between the two, no matter whether it is marked at the time by any feeling or not. The only thing that matters is that for each of the two men the other happens as the particular other, that each becomes aware of the other and is thus related to him in such a way that he does not regard and use him as his object, but as his partner in a living event, even if it is no more than a boxing match. It is well known that some existentialists assert that the basic factor between men is that one is an object for the other. But so far as this is actually the case, the special reality of the interhuman, the fact of the contact, has been largely eliminated. It cannot indeed be entirely eliminated. As a crude example, take two men who are observing one another. The essential thing is not that the one makes the other his object, but the fact that he is not fully able to do so and the reason for his failure. We have in common with all existing beings that we can be made objects of observation. But it is my privilege as man that by the hidden activity of my being I can establish an impassable barrier to objectification. Only in partnership can my being be perceived as an existing whole.

The sociologist may object to any separation of the social and the interhuman on the ground that society is actually built upon human relations, and the theory of these relations is therefore to be regarded as the very foundation of sociology. But here an ambiguity in the concept 'relation' becomes evident. We speak, for instance, of a comradely relation between two men in their work, and do not merely mean what happens between them as comrades, but also a lasting disposition which is actualized in those happenings and which even includes purely psychological events such as the recollection of the absent comrade. But by the sphere of the interhuman I mean solely actual happenings between men, whether wholly mutual or tending to grow into mutual relations. For the participation of both partners is in principle indispensable. The sphere of the interhuman is one in which a person is confronted by the other. We call its unfolding the dialogical.

In accordance with this, it is basically erroneous to try to understand the interhuman phenomena as psychological. When two men converse together, the psychological is certainly an important part of the situation, as each listens and each prepares to speak. Yet this is only the hidden accompaniment to the conversation itself, the phonetic event fraught with meaning, whose meaning is to be found neither in one of the two partners nor in both together, but only in their dialogue itself, in this 'between' which they live together.

BEING AND SEEMING

The essential problem of the sphere of the interhuman is the duality of being and seeming.

Although it is a familiar fact that men are often troubled about the impression they make on others, this has been much more discussed in moral philosophy than in anthropology. Yet this is one of the most important subjects for anthropological study.

We may distinguish between two different types of human existence. The one proceeds from what one really is, the other from what one wishes to seem. In general, the two are found mixed together. There have probably been few men who were entirely independent of the impression they made on others, while there has scarcely existed one who was exclusively determined by the impression made by him. We must be content to distinguish between men in whose essential attitude the one or the other predominates.

This distinction is most powerfully at work, as its nature indicates, in the interhuman realm—that is, in men's personal dealings with one another.

Take as the simplest and yet quite clear example the situation in which two persons look at one another—the first belonging to the first type, the second to the second. The one who lives from his being looks at the other just as one looks at someone with whom he has personal dealings. His look is 'spontaneous', 'without reserve'; of course he is not uninfluenced by the desire to make himself understood by the other, but he is uninfluenced by any thought of the idea of himself which he can or should awaken in the person whom he is looking at. His opposite is different. Since he is concerned with the image which his appearance, and especially his look or glance, produces in the other, he 'makes' this look. With the help of the capacity, in greater or lesser degree peculiar to man, to make a definite element of his being appear in his look, he produces a look which is meant to have, and often enough does have, the effect of a spontaneous utterance—not only the utterance of a psychical event supposed to be taking place at that very moment, but also, as

it were, the reflection of a personal life of such-and-such a kind.

This must, however, be carefully distinguished from another area of seeming whose ontological legitimacy cannot be doubted. I mean the realm of 'genuine seeming', where a lad, for instance, imitates his heroic model and while he is doing so is seized by the actuality of heroism, or a man plays the part of a destiny and conjures up authentic destiny. In this situation there is nothing false; the imitation is genuine imitation and the part played is genuine; the mask, too, is a mask and no deceit. But where the semblance originates from the lie and is permeated by it, the interhuman is threatened in its very existence. It is not that someone utters a lie, falsifies some account. The lie I mean does not take place in relation to particular facts, but in relation to existence itself, and it attacks interhuman existence as such. There are times when a man, to satisfy some stale conceit, forfeits the great chance of a true happening between I and Thou.

Let us now imagine two men, whose life is dominated by appearance, sitting and talking together. Call them Peter and Paul. Let us list the different configurations which are involved. First, there is Peter as he wishes to appear to Paul, and Paul as he wishes to appear to Peter. Then there is Peter as he really appears to Paul, that is, Paul's image of Peter, which in general does not in the least coincide with what Peter wishes Paul to see; and similarly there is the reverse situation. Further, there is Peter as he appears to himself, and Paul as he appears to himself. Lastly, there are the bodily Peter and the bodily Paul. Two living beings and six ghostly appearances, which mingle in many ways in the conversation between the two. Where is there room for any genuine interhuman life?

Whatever the meaning of the word 'truth' may be in other realms, in the interhuman realm it means that men communicate themselves to one another as what they are. It does not depend on one saying to the other everything that occurs to him, but only on his letting no seeming creep in between himself and the other. It does not depend on one letting himself go before another, but on his granting to the man to whom he communicates himself a share in his being. This is a question of the authenticity of the interhuman, and where this is not to be found, neither is the human element itself authentic.

Therefore, as we begin to recognize the crisis of man as the crisis of what is between man and man, we must free the concept of uprightness from the thin moralistic tones which cling to it, and let it take its tone from the concept of bodily uprightness. If a presupposition of human life in primeval times is given in man's walking upright, the fulfilment of human life can only come through the soul's walking upright, through the great uprightness which is not tempted by any seeming because it has conquered all semblance.

But, one may ask, what if a man by his nature makes his life subservient to the images which he produces in others? Can he, in such a case, still become a man living from his being, can he escape from his nature?

The widespread tendency to live from the recurrent impression one makes instead of from the steadiness of one's being is not a 'nature'. It originates, in fact, on the other side of interhuman life itself, in men's dependence upon one another. It is no light thing to be confirmed in one's being by others, and seeming deceptively offers itself as a help in this. To yield to seeming is man's essential cowardice, to resist it is his essential courage. But this is not an inexorable state of affairs which is as it is and must so remain. One can struggle to come to oneself — that is, to come to confidence in being. One struggles, now more successfully, now less, but never in vain, even when one thinks he is defeated. One must at times pay dearly for life lived from the being; but it is never too dear. Yet is there not bad being, do weeds not grow everywhere? I have never known a young person who seemed to me irretrievably bad. Later indeed it becomes more and more difficult to penetrate the increasingly tough layer which has settled down on a man's being. Thus there arises the false perspective of the seemingly fixed 'nature' which cannot be overcome. It is false; the foreground is deceitful; man as man can be redeemed.

Again we see Peter and Paul before us surrounded by the ghost of the semblances. A ghost can be exorcized. Let us imagine that these two find it more and more repellent to be represented by ghosts. In each of them the will is stirred and strengthened to be confirmed in their being as what they really are and nothing else. We see the forces of real life at work as they drive out the ghost, till the semblance vanishes and the depths of personal life call to one another.

PERSONAL MAKING PRESENT

By far the greater part of what is today called conversation among men would be more properly and precisely described as speechifying. In general, people do not really speak to one another, but each, although turned to the other, really speaks to a fictitious court of appeal whose life consists of nothing but listening to him. Chekhov has given poetic expression to this state of affairs in *The Cherry Orchard*, where the only use the members of a family make of their being together is to talk past one another. But it is Sartre who has raised to a principle of existence what in Chekhov still appears as the deficiency of a person who is shut up in himself. Sartre regards the walls between the partners in a conversation as simply impassable. For him it is inevitable human destiny that a man has directly to do only with himself and his own affairs. The inner existence of the other is his own concern, not mine; there is no direct relation with the other, nor can there be. This is perhaps the clearest expression of the wretched fatalism of modern man, which regards degeneration as the unchangeable nature of *Homo sapiens* and the misfortune of having run into a blind alley as his primal fate, and which brands every thought of a breakthrough as reactionary romanticism. He who really knows how far our generation has lost the way of true freedom, of free giving between I and Thou, must himself, by virtue of

the demand implicit in every great knowledge of this kind, practise directness — even if he were the only man on earth who did it — and not depart from it until scoffers are struck with fear, and hear in his voice the voice of their own suppressed longing.

The chief presupposition for the rise of genuine dialogue is that each should regard his partner as the very one he is. I become aware of him, aware that he is different, essentially different from myself, in the definite, unique way which is peculiar to him, and I accept whom I thus see, so that in full earnestness I can direct what I say to him as the person he is. Perhaps from time to time I must offer strict opposition to his view about the subject of our conversation. But I accept this person, the personal bearer of a conviction, in his definite being out of which his conviction has grown — even though I must try to show, bit by bit, the wrongness of this very conviction. I affirm the person I struggle with: I struggle with him as his partner, I confirm him as creature and as creation, I confirm him who is opposed to me as him who is over against me. It is true that it now depends on the other whether genuine dialogue, mutuality in speech arises between us. But if I thus give to the other who confronts me his legitimate standing as a man with whom I am ready to enter into dialogue, then I may trust him and suppose him to be also ready to deal with me as his partner.

But what does it mean to be 'aware' of a man in the exact sense in which I use the word? To be aware of a thing or a being means, in quite general terms, to experience it as a whole and yet at the same time without reduction or abstraction, in all its concreteness. But a man, although he exists as a living being among living beings and even as a thing among things, is nevertheless something categorically different from all things and all beings. A man cannot really be grasped except on the basis of the gift of the spirit which belongs to man alone among all things, the spirit as sharing decisively in the personal life of the living man, that is, the spirit which determines the person. To be aware of a man, therefore, means in particular to perceive his wholeness as a person determined by the spirit; it means to perceive the dynamic centre which stamps his every utterance, action, and attitude with the recognizable sign of uniqueness. Such an awareness is impossible, however, if and so long as the other is the separated object of my contemplation or even observation, for this wholeness and its centre do not let themselves be known to contemplation or observation. It is only possible when I step into an elemental relation with the other, that is, when he becomes present to me. Hence I designate awareness in this special sense as 'personal making present'.

The perception of one's fellow man as a whole, as a unity, and as unique — even if his wholeness, unity, and uniqueness are only partly developed, as is usually the case — is opposed in our time by almost everything that is commonly understood as specifically modern. In our time there predominates an analytical, reductive, and deriving look between man and man. This look is analytical, or rather pseudo analytical, since it treats the whole being as put together and therefore able to be taken apart — not only the so-called unconscious which is accessible to relative objectification, but also the psychic stream itself, which can never, in fact, be grasped as an object. This look is a reductive one because it tries to contract the manifold person, who is nourished by the microcosmic richness of the possible, to some schematically surveyable and recurrent structures. And this look is a deriving one because it supposes it can grasp what a man has become, or even is becoming, in genetic formulae, and it thinks that even the dynamic central principle of the individual in this becoming can be represented by a general concept. An effort is being made today radically to destroy the mystery between man and man. The personal life, the ever near mystery, once the source of the stillest enthusiasms, is levelled down.

What I have just said is not an attack on the analytical method of the human sciences, a method which is indispensable wherever it furthers knowledge of a phenomenon without impairing the essentially different knowledge of its uniqueness that transcends the valid circle of the method. The science of man that makes use of the analytical method must accordingly always keep in view the boundary of such a contemplation, which stretches like a horizon around it. This duty makes the transposition of the method into life dubious; for it is excessively difficult to see where the boundary is in life.

If we want to do today's work and prepare tomorrow's with clear sight, then we must develop in ourselves and in the next generation a gift which lives in man's inwardness as a Cinderella, one day to be a princess. Some call it intuition, but that is not a wholly unambiguous concept. I prefer the name 'imagining the real', for in its essential being this gift is not a looking at the other, but a bold swinging — demanding the most intensive stirring of one's being — into the life of the other. This is the nature of all genuine imagining, only that here the real of my action is not the all-possible, but the particular real person who confronts me, whom I can attempt to make present to myself just in this way, and not otherwise, in his wholeness, unity, and uniqueness, and with his dynamic center which realizes all these things ever anew.

Let it be said again that all this can only take place in a living partnership, that is, when I stand in a common situation with the other and expose myself vitally to his share in the situation as really his share. It is true that my basic attitude can remain unanswered, and the dialogue can die in seed. But if mutuality stirs, then the interhuman blossoms into genuine dialogue.

IMPOSITION AND UNFOLDING

I have referred to two things which impede the growth of life between men: the invasion of seeming, and the inadequacy of perception. We are now faced with a third, plainer than the others, and in this critical hour more powerful and more dangerous than ever.

There are two basic ways of affecting men in their views and their attitude to life. In the first a man tries to impose himself, his opinion and his attitude, on the other in such a way that the latter feels the psychical result of the action to be his own insight, which has only been freed by the influence. In the second basic way of affecting others, a man wishes to find and to further in the soul of the other the disposition toward what he has recognized in himself as the right. Because it is the right, it must also be alive in the microcosm of the other, as one possibility. The other need only be opened out in this potentiality of his; moreover, this opening out takes place not essentially by teaching, but by meeting, by existential communication between someone that is in actual being and someone that is in a process of becoming. The first way has been most powerfully developed in the realm of propaganda, the second in that of education.

The propagandist I have in mind, who imposes himself, is not in the least concerned with the person whom he desires to influence, as a person; various individual qualities are of importance only is so far as he can exploit them to win the other and must get to know them for this purpose. In his indifference to everything personal the propagandist goes a substantial distance beyond the party for which he works. For the party, persons in their difference are of significance because each can be used according to his special qualities in a particular function. It is true that the personal is considered only in respect of the specific use to which it can be put, but within these limits it is recognized in practice. To propaganda as such, on the other hand, individual qualities are rather looked on as a burden, for propaganda is concerned simply with *more* — more members, more adherents, an increasing extent of support. Political methods, where they rule in an extreme form, as here, simply mean winning power over the other by depersonalizing him. This kind of propaganda enters upon different relations with force; it supplements it or replaces it, according to the need or the prospects, but it is in the last analysis nothing but sublimated violence, which has become imperceptible as such. It places men's souls under a pressure which allows the illusion of autonomy. Political methods at their height mean the effective abolition of the human factor.

The educator whom I have in mind lives in a world of individuals, a certain number of whom are always at any one time committed to his care. He sees each of these individuals as in a position to become a unique, single person, and thus the bearer of a special task of existence which can be fulfilled through him and through him alone. He sees every personal life as engaged in such a process of actualization, and he knows from his own experience that the forces making for actualization are all the time involved in a microcosmic struggle with counterforces. He has come to see himself as a helper of the actualizing forces. He knows these forces; they have shaped and they still shape him. Now he puts this person shaped by them at their disposal for a new struggle and a new work. He cannot wish to impose himself, for he believes in the effect of the actualizing forces, that is, he believes that in every man what is right is established in a single and uniquely personal way. No

other way may be imposed on a man, but another way, that of the educator, may and must unfold what is right, as in this case it struggles for achievement, and help it to develop.

The propagandist, who imposes himself, does not really believe even in his own cause, for he does not trust it to attain its effect of its own power without his special methods, whose symbols are the loudspeaker and the television advertisement. The educator who unfolds what is there believes in the primal power which has scattered itself, and still scatters itself, in all human beings in order that it may grow up in each man in the special form of that man. He is confident that this growth needs at each moment only that help which is given in meeting, and that he is called to supply that help.

I have illustrated the character of the two basic attitudes and their relation to one another by means of two extremely antithetical examples. But wherever men have dealings with one another, one or the other attitude is to be found in more or less degree.

These two principles of imposing oneself on someone and helping someone to unfold should not be confused with concepts such as arrogance and humility. A man can be arrogant without wishing to impose himself on others, and it is not enough to be humble in order to help another unfold. Arrogance and humility are dispositions of the soul, psychological facts with a moral accent, while imposition and helping to unfold are events between men, anthropological facts which point to an ontology, the ontology of the interhuman.

In the moral realm Kant expressed the essential principle that one's fellow man must never be thought of and treated merely as a means, but always at the same time as an independent end. The principle is expressed as on 'ought' which is sustained by the idea of human dignity. My point of view, which is near to Kant's in its essential features, has another source and goal. It is concerned with the presuppositions of the interhuman. Man exists anthropologically not in his isolation, but in the completeness of the relation between man and man; what humanity is can be properly grasped only in vital reciprocity. For the proper existence of the interhuman it is necessary, as I have shown, that the semblance not intervene to spoil the relation of personal being to personal being. It is further necessary, as I have also shown, that each one means and makes present the other in his personal being. That neither should wish to impose himself on the other is the third basic presupposition of the interhuman. These presuppositions do not include the demand that one should influence the other in his unfolding; this is, however, an element that is suited to lead to a higher stage of the interhuman.

That there resides in every man the possibility of attaining authentic human existence in the special way peculiar to him can be grasped in the Aristotelian image of entelechy, innate self-realization; but one must note that it is an entelechy of the work of creation. It would be mistaken to speak here of individuation alone. Individuation is only the indispensable personal stamp of all realization of human exis-

tence. The self as such is not ultimately the essential, but the meaning of human existence given in creation again and again fulfils itself as self. The help that men give each other in becoming a self leads the life between men to its height. The dynamic glory of the being of man is first bodily present in the relation between two men each of whom in meaning the other also means the highest to which this person is called, and serves the self-realization of this human life as one true to creation without wishing to impose on the other anything of his own realization.

GENUINE DIALOGUE

We must now summarize and clarify the marks of genuine dialogue.

In genuine dialogue the turning to the partner takes place in all truth, that is, it is a turning of the being. Every speaker 'means' the partner or partners to whom he turns as this personal existence. To 'mean' someone in this connection is at the same time to exercise that degree of making present which is possible to the speaker at that moment. The experiencing senses and the imagining of the real which completes the findings of the senses work together to make the other present as a whole and as a unique being, as the person that he is. But the speaker does not merely perceive the one who is present to him in this way; he receives him as his partner, and that means that he confirms this other being, so far as it is for him to confirm. The true turning of his person to the other includes this confirmation, this acceptance. Of course, such a confirmation does not mean approval; but no matter in what I am against the other, by accepting him as my partner in genuine dialogue I have affirmed him as a person.

Further, if genuine dialogue is to arise, everyone who takes part in it must be willing on each occasion to say what is really in his mind about the subject of the conversation. And that means further that on each occasion he makes the contribution of his spirit without reduction and without shifting his ground. Even men of great integrity are under the illusion that they are not bound to say everything 'they have to say'. But in the great faithfulness which is the climate of genuine dialogue, what I have to say at any one time already has in me the character of something that wishes to be uttered, and I must not keep it back, keep it in myself. It bears for me the unmistakable sign which indicates that it belongs to the common life of the word. Where the dialogical word genuinely exists, it must be given its right by keeping nothing back. To keep nothing back is the exact opposite of unreserved speech. Everything depends on the legitimacy of 'what I have to say'. And of course I must also be intent to raise into an inner word and then into a spoken word what I have to say at this moment but do not yet possess as speech. To speak is both nature and work, something that grows and something that is made, and where it appears dialogically, in the climate of great faithfulness, it has to fulfill ever anew the unity of the two.

Associated with this is that overcoming of semblance to which I have referred. In the atmosphere of genuine

dialogue, he who is ruled by the thought of his own effect as the speaker of what he has to speak, has a destructive effect. If instead of what has to be said, I try to bring attention to my *I*, I have irrevocably miscarried what I had to say; it enters the dialogue as a failure, and the dialogue is a failure. Because genuine dialogue is an ontological sphere which is constituted by the authenticity of being, every invasion of semblance must damage it.

But where the dialogue is fulfilled in its being, between partners who have turned to one another in truth, who express themselves without reserve and are free of the desire for semblance, there is brought into being a memorable common fruitfulness which is to be found nowhere else. At such times, at each such time, the word arises in a substantial way between men who have been seized in their depths and opened out by the dynamic of an elemental togetherness. The interhuman opens out what otherwise remains unopened.

This phenomenon is indeed well known in dialogue between two persons; but I have also sometimes experienced it in a dialogue in which several have taken part.

About Easter of 1914 there met a group consisting of representatives of several European nations for a three-day discussion that was intended to be preliminary to further talks.[1] We wanted to discuss together how the catastrophe, which we all believed was imminent, could be avoided. Without

[1] I have set down elsewhere an episode from this meeting. See my essay 'Dialogue' in *Between Man and Man*, especially pp. 4–6.

our having agreed beforehand on any sort of modalities for our talk, all the presuppositions of genuine dialogue were fulfilled. From the first hour immediacy reigned between all of us, some of whom had just got to know one another; everyone spoke with an unheard-of unreserve, and clearly not a single one of the participants was in bondage to semblance. In respect of its purpose the meeting must be described as a failure (though even now in my heart it is still not a certainty that it had to be a failure); the irony of the situation was that we arranged the final discussion for the middle of August, and in the course of events the group was soon broken up. Nevertheless, in the time that followed, not one of the participants doubted that he shared in a triumph of the interhuman.

One more point must be noted. Of course it is not necessary for all who are joined in a genuine dialogue actually to speak; those who keep silent can on occasion be especially important. But each must be determined not to withdraw when the course of the conversation makes it proper for him to say what he has to say. No one, of course, can know in advance what it is that he has to say; genuine dialogue cannot be arranged beforehand. It has indeed its basic order in itself from the beginning, but nothing can be determined, the course is of the spirit, and some discover what they have to say only when they catch the call of the spirit.

But it is also a matter of course that all the participants, without exception, must be of such nature that they are capable of satisfying the presuppositions of genuine dialogue and are ready to do so. The genuineness of the dialogue is called in question as soon as even a small number of those present are felt by themselves and by the others as not being expected to take any active part. Such a state of affairs can lead to very serious problems.

I had a friend whom I account one of the most considerable men of our age. He was a master of conversation, and he loved it: his genuineness as a speaker was evident. But once it happened that he was sitting with two friends and with the three wives, and a conversation arose in which by its nature the women were clearly not joining, although their presence in fact had a great influence. The conversation among the men soon developed into a duel between two of them (I was the third). The other 'duelist', also a friend of mine, was of a noble nature; he too was a man of true conversation, but given more to objective fairness than to the play of the intellect, and a stranger to any controversy. The friend whom I have called a master of conversation did not speak with his usual composure and strength, but he scintillated, he fought, he triumphed. The dialogue was destroyed.

COMMENT

The Doctrine of I and Thou

Martin Buber represents the third of those great watchwords of the French Revolution, "Liberty, Equality, Fraternity." His basic theory, as set forth in *I and Thou*, is a poetic and rather cryptic statement of his "communitarian" creed. Since this book is difficult in style, I have reproduced instead his essay "Elements of the Interhuman." But it will be helpful in understanding the latter to review some of the central concepts of *I and Thou*.

Basic to his thought is the distinction between two types of relation. He states this distinction in enigmatic language:

> To man the world is twofold, in accordance with his twofold attitude. The attitude of man is twofold, in accordance with the twofold nature of the primary words which he speaks. The primary words are not isolated words, but combined words. The one primary word is the combination *I-Thou*. The other primary word is the combination *I-It*; wherein, without a change in the primary word, one of the words *He* and *She* can replace *it*. Hence the *I* of man is also twofold. For the *I* of the primary word *I-Thou* is a different *I* from that of the primary word *I-It*.[1]

Buber's meaning is this: One adopts a twofold interpretation of one's world, according to the "primary word" that one speaks. To speak the word is not to use one's vocal cords but to stand before existence and to comport oneself in a certain way. In the I-It relation, I regard the object, even if it be a He or a She, as if it were a mere thing. I stand apart from it in order coldly to scrutinize and exploit it: to observe, measure, categorize, and manipulate it — to bend it to my advantage. In this relation there is no reciprocity: The relation is that of master to instrument. If I treat someone as an *It*, I do not acknowledge *his* or *her* right to treat me as an *It* in return. In the I-Thou relation, on the other hand, one's essential being is in direct and sympathetic contact with another essential being. The Thou is cherished for what one is in one's "singleness" — not as an *object* but as a *presence*, not as a *type* but as an *individual*, not as a *means* but as an *end*. The I-Thou relation is reciprocal: I-Thou implies Thou-I. I not only give but also receive; I not only speak but also listen; I not only respond but also invite response. "My *Thou* affects me, as I affect it."[2]

---

[1]*I and Thou* (New York: Charles Scribner's Sons, 1937), p. 3.
[2]Ibid., p. 15.

The *I* is constituted and remade in this act of meeting: "Through the *Thou* a man becomes *I*."[3]

Not only does the *Thou* differ from the *it*, but also the *I* in the first relation differs fundamentally from the *I* in the second. The first *I* is a real person in a world of persons; the second is a depersonalized individual in a world of things. A person is fully a person only in relation to other persons. One is not a real person as far as one regards others as things, as mere objects or implements. The real meeting between person and person comes about only when each regards the other as an end. This is not always possible. To live, we need to use things, and what is more to the point, to use human beings. But in a real community, the means-relation between individuals, the *I-it* relation, is subordinated to the ends-relation between persons, the "I-Thou" relation. "Only men who are capable of truly saying *Thou* to one another can truly say *We* with one another."[4]

The world of the I-Thou and the world of the I-It are not sharply separated. "Every *Thou* in our world must become an *It*."[5] There is nothing wrong with such impersonal relations so long as they remain subordinate to the personal. But "in our age the I-It relation, gigantically swollen, has usurped, practically uncontested, the mastery and the rule. The I of this relation, an I that . . . is unable to say Thou, unable to meet a being essentially, is the lord of the hour."[6]

The essay "Elements of the Interhuman" develops some of the implications of *I and Thou*. In particular Buber delineates "the sphere of the between." He means by this phrase "the relation between man and man" —a person-to-person relation of genuine mutuality. It stands in sharp contrast to the depersonalization of relations in massive, bureaucratic organizations. The "interhuman" is the I-Thou relation as embodied in the "dialogue" between man and man. To achieve this kind of authentic relationship a person must *be* and not *seem*. The significance of this duality between being and seeming is discussed in the essay.

"INTERHUMAN": ITS POLITICAL AND RELIGIOUS IMPLICATIONS

The question can be asked whether Buber's ideal of the "interhuman" represents a viable alternative to the social rootlessness of individualism and the mass anonymity of collectivism. He contends that the dilemma,

---

[3]*I and Thou*, p. 28.
[4]Ibid., p. 176.
[5]Ibid., p. 16.
[6]*Eclipse of God* (New York: Harper and Brothers, 1952), p. 166.

"individualism or collectivism," no longer appears inescapable, and that the choice it presents no longer appears attractive. Neither horn of the dilemma can provide the genuine freedom and realization that each promises, and there is a *third* alternative that avoids the extremes and distortions of the other two. "The essential human reality is neither one of individual nor of collective existence," he declares, "but lies in the relation between man and man, and is a matter between me and you."[7] Here, then, is the ideal of a fraternity whose roots are personal rather than abstract and impersonal. It is based upon free mutuality rather than like-mindedness. It excludes any relation of dominance or exploitation, and it heals the homelessness of the alienated individual. Clearly, modern civilization is desperately in need of reorientation. The student might well consider whether this reorientation should be around Buber's concept of the "interhuman."

A second question is whether the basis of the reorientation should be theistic or purely humanistic. Ludwig used the language of "I and Thou," contending that fellowship should be the basis of life. Buber has hailed this doctrine as "the Copernican revolution of modern thought," declaring: "I myself in my youth was given a decisive impetus by Feuerbach."[8] Buber, however, clings to theism, as opposed to atheistic humanism. The love of man for man and the love of man for God, he insists, are interdependent. "I-Thou finds its highest intensity and transfiguration in religious reality, in which unlimited Being becomes, as absolute person, my partner."[9] Human beings relate themselves most deeply to each other by thus relating themselves to an eternal Thou. But "real relationship with God cannot be achieved on earth if real relationship to the world and mankind are lacking."[10] The meeting with God is direct and mutual; it is a totality act of personality; it requires that we meet human beings and the world in the same total way. "Meet the world with the fullness of your being, and you shall meet God. . . . If you wish to believe, love!"[11]

Thus both Feuerbach and Buber developed an ethics of love, but the one was a humanist and the other a theist. The question is whether Buber or Feuerbach has provided the sounder basis for ethics.

[7]From Martin Buber's foreword to E. A. Gutkind, *Community and Environment* (London: C. A. Watts & Co., 1953), p. viii.
[8]*Between Man and Man* (Boston: Beacon Press, 1955), p. 148.
[9]*Eclipse of God*, p. 61.
[10]*At the Turning* (New York: Farrar, Straus, and Cudahy, 1952), p. 39.
[11]*At the Turning*, p. 44.

Bibliography

Titles marked by an asterisk are recommended for beginners; those with a dagger are available in paperback. Publishers in parentheses refer to the paperback edition.

INTRODUCTION

The Nature of Philosophy

*Blanshard, Brand. *On Philosophical Style*. Bloomington: Indiana University Press, 1967.

Bronstein, Daniel J., Krikorian, Yervant H., and Wiener, Philip P. *Basic Problems of Philosophy*, 3rd ed., Ch. 9. Englewood Cliffs, NJ: Prentice-Hall, 1964.

Cohen, Morris R. *The Faith of a Liberal*, Chs. 42–46. New York: Holt, Rinehart & Winston, 1946.

Collingwood, R. G. *Speculum Mentis*. Oxford: Clarendon Press, 1924.

Ducasse, C. J. *Philosophy as a Science*. New York: Piest, 1941.

Edman, Irwin. *Four Ways of Philosophy*. New York: Holt, Rinehart & Winston, 1937.

Edwards, Paul, Ed. *The Encyclopedia of Philosophy*, 8 vols. New York: Macmillan and Free Press, 1967. An invaluable reference work with extensive bibliographies.

*James, William. *Some Problems of Philosophy*, Ch. 1. New York: Longmans, Green, 1911.

Jaspers, Karl. *The Perennial Scope of Philosophy*. New York: Philosophical Library, 1949.

Merleau-Ponty, M. *In Praise of Philosophy*. Evanston, IL: Northwestern University Press, 1963.

*Montague, William P. *Great Visions of Philosophy*, Prologue. La Salle, IL: Open Court, 1950.

690

Newell, R. W. *The Concept of Philosophy*. London: Methuen, 1967.
*Perry, Ralph Barton. *A Defence of Philosophy*. Cambridge, MA: Harvard University Press, 1931.
†*Russell, Bertrand. *The Problems of Philosophy*, Ch. 15. London: Oxford University Press, 1912.

The Socratic Quest

†Cornford, F. M. *Before and After Socrates*. Cambridge: Cambridge University Press, 1932.
Field, G. C. *Plato and His Contemporaries*. London: Methuen, 1930.
†*Guardini, Romanom. *The Death of Socrates: An Interpretation of the Platonic Dialogues: Euthyphro, Apology, Crito and Phaedo*. New York: Sheed & Ward, 1948 (Meridian).
Hackforth, Reginald. *Composition of Plato's Apology*. Cambridge: Cambridge University Press, 1933.
*Jaeger, Werner. *Paideia: The Idea of Greek Culture*, Vol. II. Oxford: Blackwell, 1946–1947.
†*Taylor, A. E. *Socrates*. New York: Appleton, 1933 (Doubleday).

CHAPTER 1. RATIONALISM

Beck, Leslie J. *The Method of Descartes: A Study of the Regulae*. Oxford: Clarendon Press, 1952.
Chomsky, Noam. *Cartesian Linguistics*. New York: Harper & Row, 1966.
Joachim, H. H. *Descartes' Rules for the Direction of the Mind*. London: Allen & Unwin, 1957.
Malcolm, Norman. *Knowledge and Certainty*. Englewood Cliffs, NJ: Prentice-Hall, 1963.
*Mellone, Sydney. *The Dawn of Modern Thought: Descartes, Spinoza, Leibniz*. New York: Oxford University Press, 1930.
Montegue, W. P. *The Ways of Knowing*, Ch. 3. London: Allen & Unwin, 1925.
Roth L. *Descartes' Discourse on Method*. Oxford: Clarendon Press, 1937.

CHAPTER 2. EMPIRICISM AND ITS LIMITS

Hume

Anderson, R. F. *Hume's First Principles*. Lincoln: University of Nebraska Press, 1966.
†*Basson, Anthony H. *David Hume*. Harmondsworth Eng.: Penguin, 1958.
Church, R. W. *Hume's Theory of the Understanding*. Ithaca, NY: Cornell University Press, 1935.
Flew, Anthony G. *Hume's Philosophy of Belief*. New York: Humanities Press, 1961.

Hendel, C. W. *Studies in the Philosophy of David Hume*, rev. ed. Indianapolis: Bobbs-Merrill, 1963.

Laird, John. *Hume's Philosophy of Human Nature*. London: Methuen, 1932.

Macnabb, D. G. C. *David Hume*. London: Hutchinson, 1951.

Price, H. H. *Hume's Theory of the External World*. Oxford: Clarendon Press, 1940.

†Smith, Norman Kemp. *The Philosophy of David Hume*. London: Macmillan, 1941 (St. Martin's).

Kant

*Blakney, Raymond B. *An Immanuel Kant Reader*. New York: Harper & Row, 1960. Readings and commentary.

†Ewing, A. C. *A Short Commentary on Kant's Critique of Pure Reason*. London: Methuen, 1938 (Phoenix).

Korner, S. *Kant*. Harmondsworth Eng.: Penguin, 1955.

Paton, H. J. *Kant's Metaphysic of Experience*, 2 vols. London: Macmillan, 1936. Difficult.

Smith, Norman Kemp. *A Commentary on Kant's Critique of Pure Reason*, 2nd ed. New York: Macmillan, 1962. Difficult.

Strawson, P. F. *The Bounds of Sense*. London: Methuen, 1966.

Weldon, T. D. *Kant's Critique of Pure Reason*, 2nd ed. London: Oxford University Press, 1958.

†Wolff, R. P., Ed. *Kant*, Part One. New York: Doubleday, 1967.

———. *Kant's Theory of Mental Activity*. Cambridge, MA: Harvard University Press, 1963.

CHAPTER 3. COMMON SENSE

Barker, Stephen F., and Beauchamp, Tom L., Eds. "Thomas Reid: Critical Interpretations." *Philosophical Monographs*, 3 (1976).

Ellos, William J. *Thomas Reid's Newtonian Realism*. Lanham, MD: University Press of America, 1981.

Grave, S. A. *The Scottish Philosophy of Common Sense*. Oxford: Oxford University Press, 1960.

Jones, O. M. *Empiricism and Intuitionism in Reid's Common Sense Philosophy*. Princeton, NJ: Princeton University Press, 1927.

Kuklick, Bruce. *The Rise of American Philosophy: Cambridge, Massachusetts, 1860–1930*. New Haven, CT: Yale University Press, 1977.

Marcil-LaCoste, Louise. *Claude Buffer and Thomas Reid: Two Common-Sense Philosophers*. Kingston, Ont.: McGill-Queens University Press, 1982.

———. "The Philosophy of Thomas Reid." *The Monist*, 61 (April 1978).

CHAPTER 4. INTUITION AND ACQUAINTANCE

Bergson

Bergson, Henri. *Creative Evolution*, especially p 1 – 7, 135 – 187. New York: Holt, Rinehart & Winston, 1911.

†———. *The Creative Mind.* New York: Philosophical Library, 1946.

Hanna, Thomas, Ed. *The Bergsonian Heritage.* New York: Columbia University Press, 1962.

*Hocking, W. E. *Types of Philosophy*, Chs. 11 – 15. New York: Scribner's, 1929.

†Hulme, T. E. *Speculations.* New York: Harcourt, Brace, 1924.

Lindsay, A. D. *The Philosophy of Bergson.* London: Dent, 1911.

Luce, A. A. *Bergson's Doctrine of Intuition.* London: Society for Promoting Christian Knowledge, 1922.

Russell

Russell, Bertrand. *A History of Western Philosophy*, Ch. 28. New York: Simon & Schuster, 1945.

†———. *Our Knowledge of the External World*, Ch. 1. London: Allen & Unwin, 1960. (Mentor).

Schlipp, P. A., Ed. *The Philosophy of Bertrand Russell.* Evanston, IL: Northwestern University Press, 1944.

CHAPTER 5. PRAGMATISM

Peirce

Buchler, Justus. *Charles Peirce's Empiricism.* New York: Harcourt, Brace & World, 1939.

†Buchler, Justus, Ed. *Philosophical Writings of Peirce.* New York: Harcourt, Brace & World 1940 (Dover).

†Gallie, W. B. *Peirce and Pragmatism.* Harmondsworth, Eng.: Penguin, 1952.

Gouge,Thomas A. *The Thought of C. S. Peirce.* Toronto: University of Toronto Press, 1950.

Murphey, Murray G. *The Development of Peirce's Philosophy.* Cambridge, MA: Harvard University Press, 1961.

†*Thompson, Manley. *The Pragmatic Philosophy of C. S. Peirce.* Chicago: University of Chicago Press, 1953.

Wiener, Philip P., and Young, Frederick H., Eds. *Studies in the Philosophy of Charles Sanders Peirce.* Cambridge, MA: Harvard University Press, 1952.

James

†Bergson, Henri. "On the Pragmatism of William James." In *The Creative Mind.* New York: Philosophical Library, 1946.

James, William. *The Meaning of Truth.* New York: Longmans, Green, 1914.

†*————. *Pragmatism.* New York: Longmans, Green, 1907 (Meridian).

Mead, George H. "The Philosophies of Royce, James and Dewey in their American Setting." *International Journal of Ethics,* Vol. 40 (1929–1930).

Moore, G. E. "William James' 'Pragmatism.'" In *Philosophical Studies.* London: Kegan Paul, 1922.

*Perry, Ralph Barton. *The Thought and Character of William James,* 2 vols. Cambridge, MA: Harvard University Press, 1948. The most important work of James.

Reck, Andrew J. *Introduction to William James: An Essay and Selected Texts.* Bloomington: University Press, 1967.

Russell, Bertrand. "William James' Conception of Truth." In *Philosophical Essays.* London: Longmans, Green, 1910.

Dewey

Bernstein, Richard J. *John Dewey.* New York: Washington Square Press, 1966.

†Dewey, John. *Experience and Nature,* rev. ed. New York: Norton, 1929 (Dover).

————. *How We Think.* Boston: Heath, 1933.

†————. *The Quest for Certainty.* New York: Minton, Balch, 1929 (Putnam).

†*————. *Reconstruction in Philosophy.* Boston: Beacon Press, 1957.

*Geiger, George R. *John Dewey in Perspective.* New York: Oxford University Press, 1958.

Hook, Sidney. *John Dewey.* New York: John Day, 1939.

Schlipp, P. A., Ed. *The Philosophy of John Dewey.* Evanston, IL: Northwestern University Press, 1939.

Thomas, M. H. *John Dewey: A Centennial Bibliography.* Chicago: University of Chicago Press, 1962.

CHAPTER 6. EXISTENTIALISM

†*Barrett, William. *Irrational Man.* New York: Doubleday, 1958.

†Blackham, H. J. *Six Existential Thinkers.* London: Routledge & Kegan Paul, 1952 (Bantam).

*Bretall, Robert. *A Kierkegaard Anthology.* Princeton, NJ: Princeton University Press, 1946.

†Camus, Albert. *The Myth of Sisyphus.* New York: Random House, 1955.

Collins, James. *The Existentialists: A Critical Study.* Chicago: Regnery, 1952.

†Grene, Marjorie. *Introduction to Existentialism.* Chicago: University of Chicago Press, 1959.

*Hanna, Thomas. *The Lyrical Existentialists.* New York: Atheneum, 1962.

†Heidegger, Martin. *Existence and Being.* Chicago: Regnery, 1949.

†Heinemann, F. H. *Existentialism and the Modern Predicament.* New York: Harper & Row, 1958.

Jaspers, Karl. *Reason and Existenz.* London: Routledge & Kegan Paul, 1956.

†*Kaufmann, Walter, Ed. *Existentialism from Dostoevsky to Sartre.* New York: Harcourt, Brace & World, 1956.

Kuhn, Helmut. *Encounter with Nothingness.* London: Methuen, 1951.

Lee, Edward N., and Mandelbaum, Maurice. *Phenomenology and Existentialism.* Baltimore: Johns Hopkins University Press, 1967.

Marcel, Gabriel. *The Philosophy of Existence.* New York: Philosophical Library, 1949.

Molina, Fernando. *Existentialism as Philosophy.* Englewood Cliffs, NJ: Prentice-Hall, 1962.

Murphy, Arthur E. "On Kierkegaard's Claim That Truth Is Subjectivity." In *Reason and the Common Good* Englewood Cliffs, NJ: Prentice-Hall, 1963. Recommended.

Olafson, Frederick A. *Principles and Persons: An Ethical Interpretation of Existentialism.* Baltimore: Johns Hopkins University Press, 1967.

†Olson, R. G. *An Introduction to Existentialism.* New York: Dover, 1962.

Sartre, Jean-Paul. *Being and Nothingness.* New York: Philosophical Library, 1956.

———. *Existentialism and Humanism.* London: Methuen, 1948.

†*Tillich, Paul. *The Courage to Be.* New Haven, CT: Yale University Press, 1952.

Warnock, Mary. *Existentialist Ethics.* New York: St. Martin's Press, 1967.

*Wild, John. *The Challenge of Existentialism.* Bloomington: Indiana University Press, 1955.

†Wilde, Jean T., and Kimmel, Walter, Eds. *The Search for Being.* New York: Noonday Press, 1962.

CHAPTER 7. THE EXISTENCE OF GOD

Alexander, Samuel. *Space, Time and Diety.* New York: Macmillan, 1920. See especially Vol. 2.

Broad, C. D. "Arguments for the Existence of God." In *Religion, Philosophy and Psychical Research.* New York: Harcourt, Brace & World, 1953.

†*Copleston, F. C. *Aquinas,* Ch. 3. Harmondsworth, Eng.: Penguin, 1955.

Flew, Anthony. *Hume's Philosophy of Belief.* New York: Humanities Press, 1961.

Garrigou-Lagrange, R. *God, His Existence and His Nature,* 2 vols. St. Louis: Herter, 1934, 1936.

*Gilson, Etienne. *The Philosophy of Thomas Aquinas.* Cambridge: Heffer, 1929.

———. *God and Philosophy.* New Haven, CT: Yale University Press, 1941.

Hartshorne, Charles. *The Logic of Perfection.* La Salle, IL: Open Court, 1962. On the ontological argument.

Hick, John. *Evil and the God of Love.* London: Macmillan, 1966.

Hicks, G. Dawes. *The Philosophical Bases of Theism.* London: Allen & Unwin, 1937.

†Hocking, William E. *The Meaning of God in Human Experience.* New Haven, CT: Yale University Press, 1912.

Hume, David. *Dialogues Concerning Natural Religion,* ed. Norman Kemp Smith. New York: Nelson, 1947. Contains detailed analysis of Hume's arguments and important background material.

James, E. O. *The Concept of Diety.* London: Hutchinson, 1950.

Malcom, Norman. "Anselm's Ontological Arguments." *Philosophical Review,* Vol. 69 (1960).

Matson, Wallace. *The Existence of God.* Ithaca, NY: Cornell University Press, 1965.

*Mill, John Stuart. *Three Essays on Religion.* London: Longmans, Green, 1885.

†Plantinga, Alvin, Ed. *The Ontological Argument: From Anselm to Contemporary Philosphers.* New York: Doubleday, 1967.

Smith, John E. *Reason and God.* New Haven, CT: Yale University Press, 1961.

Smith, Norman Kemp. *The Credibility of Divine Existence.* New York: St. Martin's Press, 1967.

Stace, W. T. *Religion and the Modern Mind.* Philadelphia: Lippincott, 1952.

*Taylor, A. E. *Does God Exist?* New York: Macmillan, 1947.

Temple, William. *Nature, Man and God.* London: Macmillan, 1934.

Tennant, F. R. *Philosophical Theology,* 2 vols. Cambridge: Cambridge University Press, 1928, 1930.

*Whitehead, Alfred North. *Religion in the Making.* New York: Macmillan, 1926.

Wisdom, John. "Gods" In *Philosophy and Psycho-Analysis.* New York: Philosophical Library, 1953.

CHAPTER 8. MATERIALISM

†Anderson, Alan Ross, Ed. *Minds and Machines.* Englewood Cliffs, NJ: Prentice-Hall, 1964.

Eliot, Hugh. *Modern Science and Materialism.* London: Longmans, Green, 1919.

Epicurus. *The Extant Remains,* trans. Cyril Bailey. Oxford: Clarendon Press, 1926.

Hobbes, Thomas. *De Corpore.* Various editions.

†*Hook, Sidney, Ed. *Dimensions of Mind.* New York: Macmillan, 1961.

Krikorian, Y. H., Ed. *Naturalism and the Human Spirit.* New York: Columbia University Press, 1944.

La Mattrie, Julien. *Man a Machine.* La Salle, IL.: Open Court, 1912.

Lange, F. A. *The History of Materialism.* New York: Harcourt, Brace & World, 1925.

Laslett, P., Ed. *The Physical Basis of Mind.* Oxford: Blackwell, 1951.

Santayana, George. *Reason in Science.* New York: Scribner's, 1948.

Smart, J. J. C. *Philosophy and Scientific Realism.* London: Routledge & Kegan Paul, 1963.

Winspear, Alban D. *Lucretius and Scientific Thought.* Montreal: Harvest House, 1963.

†Woddbridge, F. J. E. *An Essay on Nature.* New York: Columbia University Press, 1940. Naturalism rather than mere materialism.

CHAPTER 9. IDEALISM

*Adams, George P. *Idealism and the Modern Age.* New Haven, CT: Yale University Press, 1919.

Blanshard, Brand. *The Nature of Thought*, 2 vols. New York: Macmillan, 1940.
Bradley, F. H. *Appearance and Reality*. Oxford: Clarendon Press, 1930.
Cunningham, G. W. *The Idealistic Argument in Recent British and American Philiosophy*. New York: Century, 1933.
Ewing, A. C. *Idealism: A Critical Survey*. London: Methuen, 1934.
Ewing, A. C., Ed. *The Idealist Tradition from Berkeley to Blanshard*. New York: Free Press, 1957.
*Hocking, Williiam E. *Types of Philosophy*, 3rd ed., Chs. 19–26. New York: Scribner's, 1959.
*Hoernle, R. F. A. *Idealism as a Philosophy*. New York: Doran, 1927.
†Moore, G. E. "The Refutation of Idealism." In *Philosophical Studies*. London: Kegan Paul, 1922 (Littlefield).

CHAPTER 10. PANTHEISM

Curley, E. M. *Spinoza's Metaphysics*. Cambridge, MA: Harvard University Press, 1969.
Freeman, Eugene, & Mandelbaum, Maurice, Eds. *Spinoza: Essays in Interpretation*. La Salle, IL: Open Court, 1975.
Grene, Marjorie, Ed. *Spinoza: A Collection of Critical Essays*. New York: Doubleday, 1973.
Hall, Roland. "Monoism and Pluralism." In Paul Edwards, Ed., *The Encyclopedia of Philosophy*, Bibliography. New York: Macmillan and Free Press, 1967.
Hallett, H. F. *Benedict Spinoza*. London: Athlone, 1957.
Hampshire, Stuart. *Spinoza*. Harmondsworth, Eng.: Penguin, 1951.
Jaspers, Karl. *Spinoza*. New York: Harcourt Brace Jovanovich, 1974.
Kashap, S. Paul, Ed. *Studies in Spinoza*. Berkeley: University of California Press, 1972.
Parkinson, G. H. R. *Spinoza's Theory of Knowledge*. Oxford: Clarendon Press, 1964.
Quinton, A. M. "Pluralism and Monism." *Encyclopedia Britannica*, Vol. 18, (1971) 66–68.
Shahan, Robert W., and Biro, J. I., Eds. *Spinoza: New Perspectives*. Norman: University of Oklahoma Press, 1978.
Sullivan, Celestine. *Critical and Historical Reflections on Spinoza's "Ethics."* Berkeley: University of California Press, 1958.

CHAPTER 11. DUALISM

Balz, A. G. A. *Descartes and the Modern Mind*. New Haven, CT: Yale University Press, 1952.
Beck, Leslie. *The Metaphysica of Descartes*. Oxford: Clarendon Press, 1965.
Bouwsma, O. K. *Philosophical Essays*. Lincoln: University of Nebraska Press, 1965.
Butler, R. J., Ed. *Cartesian Studies*. Oxford: Blackwell, 1972.

Curley, Edwin M. *Descartes Against the Sceptics.* Cambridge, MA: Harvard University Press, 1978.

Doney, Willis, Ed. *Descartes.* New York: Doubleday, 1968.

Gibson, A. Boyce. *The Philosophy of Descartes.* London: Russell & Russell, 1967.

Grayeff, Felix. *Descartes.* London: Philip Goodall, 1977.

Hooker, Michael, Ed. *Descartes: Critical and Interpretive Essays.* Baltimore: Johns Hopkins University Press, 1978.

Keeling, Stanley V. *Descartes,* 2nd ed. New York: Oxford University Press, 1968.

Kenny, Anthony. *Descartes.* New York: Random House, 1968.

Malcolm, Norman. *Problems of Mind: Descartes to Wittgenstein.* New York: Harper & Row, 1971.

Popkin, Richard H. *The History of Skepticism from Erasmus to Descartes.* New York: Harper & Row, 1968.

Sesonske, Alexander, and Fleming, Noel, Eds. *Meta-Meditations.* Belmont, CA: Wadsworth, 1965.

Smith, Norman Kemp. *New Studies in the Philosophy of Descartes.* New York: Russell & Russell, 1963.

Vrooman, Jack R. *Rene Descartes: A Biography.* New York: Putnam, 1970.

Williams, Bernard. *Descartes.* Atlantic Highlands, NJ: Humanities Press, 1978.

Wilson, Margaret D. *Descartes.* London: Routledge & Kegan Paul, 1978.

CHAPTER 12. RELATIONALISM

Blythe, John W. *Whitehead's Theory of Knowledge.* Providence, RI: Brown University Press, 1941.

Christian, William A. *An Interpretation of Whitehead's Metaphysics.* New Haven, CT: Yale University Press, 1959.

Das, R. *The Philosophy of Whitehead.* London: J. Clarke, 1938.

Emmet, Dorothy M. *Whitehead's Philosophy of Organism.* London: Macmillan, 1932.

Johnson, A. H. *Whitehead's Theory of Reality.* Boston: Beacon Press, 1952.

LeClerc, I., Ed. *The Relevance of Whitehead.* London: Allen & Unwin, 1961.

Lowe, Victor. *Understanding Whitehead.* Baltimore: Johns Hopkins University Press, 1962.

Miller, D. L., and Gentry, G. V. *The Philosophy of A. N. Whitehead.* Minneapolis: Burgess Publ., 1938.

Palter, R. M. *Whitehead's Philosophy of Science.* Chicago: University of Chicago Press, 1960.

Price, Lucien. *Dialogues of Alfred North Whitehead.* Boston: Little, Brown, 1954.

Schilpp, Paul Arthur, Ed. *The Philosophy of Alfred North Whitehead.* Evanston and Chicago: Northwestern University Press, 1941.

Whitehead, Alfred North. *Alfred North Whitehead: An Anthology,* ed. F. S. C. Northrop and Mason W. Gross. New York: Macmillan, 1953.

CHAPTER 13. THE WAY OF REASON

Blanshard, Brand. *Reason and Goodness.* London: Allen & Unwin, 1961.

Kemp, G. *Reason, Action and Morality.* London: Routledge & Kegan Paul, 1964.

†Mure, G. R. G. *Aristotle*, Ch. 7. New York: Oxford University Press, 1939.

Oates, Whitney J. *Aristotle and the Problem of Value.* Princeton, NJ: Princeton University Press, 1961.

Ross, W. D. *Aristotle*, 2nd ed, Ch. 7. London: Methuen, 1930.

Santayana, George. *Reason in Science*, Chs. 8–10. New York: Scribner's, 1928.

Toulmen, Stephen. *The Place of Reason in Ethics.* Cambridge: Cambridge University Press, 1950.

†*Walsh, J. J., and Shapiro, H. L., Eds. *Aristotle's Ethics.* Belmont, CA.: Wadsworth, 1967.

Wild, John. *Introduction to Realistic Philosophy*, Part I. New York: Harper & Row, 1948.

Wilson, J. *Reason and Morals.* Cambridge: Cambridge University Press, 1961.

CHAPTER 14. THE WAY OF PLEASURE

Bailey, C. *Epicurus: The Extant Remains.* Oxford: Clarendon Press, 1926.

———. *The Greek Atomists and Epicurus.* New York: Russell & Russell, 1964.

DeWitt, N. W. *Epicurus and His Philosophy.* Minneapolis: University of Minnesota Press, 1954.

Farrington, B. *The Faith of Epicurus.* London: Weidenfeld & Nicolson, 1967.

Festugiere, A. *Epicurus and His Gods*, trans C. W. Chilton. Cambridge, MA: Harvard University Press, 1956.

Oates, W. J. *The Stoic and Epicurean Philosophers: Complete Extant Writings of Epicurus, Epictetus, Lucretius, Marcus Aurelius.* Trans. C. Baily, P. E. Matheson, H. A. J. Munro, and G. Long. New York: Random House, 1940.

CHAPTER 15. THE WAY OF NATURE

*Huxley, Thomas Henry, and Huxley, Julien. *Touchstone for Ethics.* New York: Harper & Row, 1947.

†Lippman, Walter. *The Public Philosophy.* Boston: Little, Brown, 1956 (Mentor).

Maritain, Jacques. *The Rights of Man and Natural Law.* New York: Scribner's, 1945.

†*Mill, John Stuart. "Nature" In *Three Essays on Religion.* London: Longmans, Green, 1885 (Liberal Arts).

Needham, Joseph. *Human Law and the Laws of Nature in China and the West.* New York: Oxford University Press, 1951.

Ritchie, David G. *Natural Rights.* London: Allen, 1916.

Simon, Yves. *The Tradition of Natural Law.* New York: Fordham University Press, 1964.

Stammler, Rudolf. *The Theory of Justice.* New York: Macmillan, 1925.
*Wild, John. *Plato's Modern Enemies and the Theory of Natural Law.* Chicago: University of Chicago Press, 1953.

CHAPTER 16. THE WAY OF DUTY

†Beck, L. W. *Commentary on Kant's Critique of Practical Reason.* Chicago: University of Chicago Press, 1960.
Broad, C. D. *Five Types of Ethical Theory.* New York: Harcourt, Brace & World, 1930.
Carritt, E. F. *Ethical and Political Thinking.* New York: Oxford University Press, 1947.
———. *The Theory of Morals.* New York: Oxford University Press, 1947.
†*Ewing, A. D. *Ethics,* Ch. 4. London: English Universities Press, 1953.
———. "What Would Happen if Everybody Acted Like Me?" *Philosophy,* Vol. 28 (1953).
Frankena, William. *Ethics.* Englewood Cliffs, NJ: Prentice-Hall, 1963.
Hare, R. M. "Universalizability." *Proceedings of the Aristotelian Society,* 1954–1955.
†Paton, H. J. *The Categorical Imperative.* London: Hutchinson, 1947 (Harper).
Prichard, H. A. *Duty and Interest.* New York: Oxford University Press, 1928.
———. *Moral Obligation.* New York: Oxford University Press, 1950.
Ross, W. D. *Foundations of Ethics.* New York: Oxford University Press, 1939.
*———. *Kant's Ethical Theory.* New York: Oxford University Press, 1954.
———. *The Right and the Good.* New York: Oxford University Press, 1930.
Sidgwick, Henry. *The Methods of Ethics,* Book III. London: Macmillan, 1922.
Singer, Marcus G. *Generalization in Ethics.* New York: Knopf, 1961.
———. "Moral Rules and Principles." In A. I. Melden, Ed. *Essays in Moral Philosophy.* Seattle: University of Washington Press, 1958.
Teale, Alfred E. *Kantian Ethics.* New York: Oxford University Press, 1951.
†*Wolff, Robert Paul, Ed. *Kant,* Part Two. New York: Doubleday, 1967.

CHAPTER 17. THE WAY OF UTILITY

Anschutz, Richard P. *The Philosophy of John Stuart Mill.* Oxford: Clarendon Press, 1953.
†Ayer, A. J. "The Principal of Utility." In *Philosophical Essays.* London: Macmillan, 1953 (St. Martin's).
Baumgardt, R. B. *Bentham and the Ethics of Today.* Princeton, NJ: Princeton University Press, 1952.
†*Britton, Karl. *John Stuart Mill.* Harmondsworth, Eng.: Penguin, 1953.
†Foot, Phillipa, Ed. *Theories of Ethics,* Chs. 9–12. London: Oxford University Press, 1967.
Hodgson, D. H. *Consequences of Utilitarianism.* Oxford: Clarendon Press, 1967.

Lyons, D. *Forms and Limits of Utilitarianism.* Oxford: Clarendon Press, 1965.
†Moore, G. E. *Ethica Principia.* Cambridge: Cambridge University Press, 1903. Ideal utilitarianism.
Narveson, Jan. *Morality and Utility.* Baltimore: Johns Hopkins University Press, 1966.
*Plamenatz, John. *The English Utilitarians.* Oxford: Blackwell, 1958.
Rawls, John B. "Two Concepts of Rules." *Philosophical Review*, Vol. 64 (1955).
Rescher, Nicholas. *Distributive Justice: A Constructive Critique of the Utilitarian Theory of Distribution.* Indianapolis: Bobbs, Merrill, 1966.
Schlick, Moritz. *The Problems of Ethics.* Englewood Cliffs, NJ: Prentice-Hall, 1938.
Sidgwick, Henry. *The Methods of Ethics.* London: Macmillan, 1922.
Smart, J. J. C. *An Outline of a System of Utilitarian Ethics.* Melbourne, Aust.: University of Melbourne Press, 1961.

CHAPTER 18. THE WAY OF FREEDOM

Brinton, Crane. *Nietzsche.* Cambridge, MA.: Harvard University Press, 1941.
Hubben, William. *Four Prophets of Our Destiny.* New York: Macmillan, 1952.
Lea, F. A. *The Tragic Philosopher.* New York: Philosophical Library, 1957.
Kaufmann, Walter. *Nietzsche: Philosopher, Psychologist, Antichrist.* New York: Meridian Books, 1956 (a reprint of the first edition by the Princeton University Press, 1947).
Knight, A. H. J. *Some Aspects of the Life and Work of Nietzsche.* Cambridge: Cambridge University Press, 1933.
Mann, Thomas. "Nietzsche's Philosophy in the Light of Comtemporary Events," Address, Library of Congress. Washington, DC: Library of Congress, 1947.

CHAPTER 19. THE WAY OF EXPERIMENT

Dewey, John. *Human Nature and Conduct.* New York: Holt, Rinehart & Winston, 1922.
———. *The Quest for Certainty*, Ch. 10. New York: Minton, Balch, 1929. (Putnam).
———. "Theory of Valuation." *International Encyclopaidia Unified Science*, Vol. II, No. 4. Chicago: University of Chicago Press, 1939.
Dewey, John, and Tufts, J. H. *Ethics*, rev. ed. New York: Holt, Rinehart & Winston, 1932.
[See also Chapter 5.]

CHAPTER 20. ARTISTOCRACY

†Barker, Ernest. *Greek Political Theory: Plato and His Predecessors.* London: Methuen, 1918 (Barnes & Noble).

Brumbaugh, R. S. *Plato for the Modern Age.* New York: Crowell-Collier and Macmillan, 1962.

*Cross, R. C., and Woozley, A. D. *Plato's Republic.* New York: St. Martin's Press, 1964.

Crossman, R. H. S. *Plato Today*, 2nd ed. London: Allen & Unwin, 1959.

Gould, John. *The Development of Plato's Ethics.* New York: Cambridge University Press, 1955.

Jaeger, Werner. *Paideia*, Vol. II. Oxford: Blackwell, 1946–1947.

†*Koyre, Alexander. *Discovering Plato.* New York: Columbia University Press, 1945.

Levinson, Ronald. *In Defense of Plato.* Cambridge, MA: Harvard University Press, 1953.

Murphy, N. R. *The Interpretation of Plato's Republic.* Oxford: Clarendon Press, 1951.

Popper, Karl R. *The Open Society and Its Enemies.* Princeton, NJ: Princeton University Press, 1950 (Harper).

Ryle, Gilbert. *Plato's Progress.* Cambridge: Cambridge University Press, 1966.

Sesonske, Alexander, Ed, *Plato's Republic.* Belmont, CA: Wadsworth, 1966.

Strauss, Leo. *The City and Man.* Chicago: University of Chicago Press, 1964.

Thorson, T. L. *Plato: Totalitarian or Democrat.* Englewood Cliffs, NJ: Prentice-Hall, 1963.

CHAPTER 21. SECURITY

Bowle, John. *Hobbes and His Critics: A Study in Seventeenth Century Constitutionalism.* New York: Oxford University Press, 1952.

Brandt, Frithiof. *Thomas Hobbes' Mechanical Conception of Nature.* London: Levin & Munksgaard, 1928.

Catlin, George E. G. *Thomas Hobbes as Philosopher, Publicist and Man of Letters.* Oxford: Blackwell, 1922.

Hearnshaw, F. J. C., Ed. *The Social and Political Ideas of Some Great Thinkers of the Sixteenth and Seventeenth Centuries*, Ch. 7. London: Barnes & Noble NY, 1926.

Laird, John. *Hobbes.* London: Oxford University Press, 1926.

Peters, Richard. *Hobbes.* Baltimore: Penguin Books, 1956.

Stephen, Sir Leslie. *Hobbes.* London: 1904.

Strauss, Leo. *The Political Philosophy of Hobbes, Its Basis and Its Genesis.* Trans. Elsa M. Sinclair. Oxford: The Clarendon Press, 1936.

Warrender, Howard. *The Political Philosophy of Hobbes: His Theory of Obligation.* Oxford: The Clarendon Press, 1957.

CHAPTER 22. SOCIAL CONTRACT

Gough, J. W. *John Locke's Political Philosophy.* Oxford: The Clarendon Press, 1950.

————. *The Social Contract*, 2nd ed., Ch. 9. Oxford: Oxford University Press, 1957.

Hearnshaw, F. J. C., Ed. *The Social and Political Ideas of Some English Thinkers of the Augustan Age, A.D. 1650–1750*. Chs. 3, 4. London: Harrap & Company, 1928.

Kendall, Willmoore. *John Locke and the Doctrine of Majority-rule*. Urbana, IL.: The University of Illinois Press, 1941.

Lamprecht, Sterling P. *The Moral and Political Philosophy of John Locke*. New York. 1918.

Laski, Harold J. *Political Thought in England from Locke to Bentham*. London: Oxford University Press, 1920.

von Leyden, W., Ed. *John Locke: Essays on the Law of Nature*. Oxford: The Clarendon Press, 1954.

O'Conner, John D. *John Locke, A Critical Introduction*. Baltimore: Penguin Books, 1952.

Pollock, Sir Frederick. "Locke's Theory of the State." In *Essays in the Law*, Ch. 3. London: Macmillan and Co., Ltd., 1922.

Vaughn, C. E. *Studies in the History of Political Philosophy before and after Rousseau*, Vol. I, Ch. 4. Manchester: The University Press, 1925.

Yolton, John W. *John Locke and the Way of Ideas*. London: Oxford University Press, 1956.

————, "Locke on the Law of Nature" In *The Philosophical Review*, Vol. 67. New York: Cornell University Press, (1959), pp. 477–498.

CHAPTER 23. LIBERAL DEMOCRACY

Aiken, Henry D. "Utilitarianism and Liberty: John Stuart Mill's Defense of Freedom." In *Reason and Conduct*. New York: Knopf, 1962.

Anschutz, R. P. *The Philosophy of J. S. Mill*. Oxford: Clarendon Press, 1953.

Bay, Christian. *The Structure of Freedom*. Palo Alton, CA.: Stanford University Press, 1958. Recommended.

Berlin, Isaiah. *Two Concepts of Liberty*. London: Oxford University Press, 1958.

Britton, Karl. *John Stuart Mill*. London: Penguin, 1953.

Dewey, John. *Freedom and Culture*. New York: Minton, Balch, 1939 (Putnam).

*————. *Individualism, Old and New*. New York: Minton, Balch, 1939 (Putnam).

*————. *Liberalism and Social Action*. New York: Putnam's, 1939.

Green, Thomas Hill. *Lectures on the Principles of Political Obligation* (1882). New York: McKay, 1942 (University of Michigan Press).

Hand, Learned. *The Spirit of Liberty*. New York, Random House, 1959.

Hobhouse, Leonard T. *Liberalism*. New York: Holt, Rinehart and Winston, 1911 (Oxford).

Laski, Harold. *The Rise of Liberalism*. New York: Harper, 1936.

Madden, Edward H. *Civil Disobedience and Moral Law*. Seattle: University of Washington Press, 1968.

*Meiklejohn, Alexander. *Free Speech and Its Relation to Self-Government*. New York: Harper & Row, 1948.

Packe, Michael St. John. *The Life of John Stuart Mill.* New York: Macmillan, 1954.

†*Radcliff, Peter. *Limits of Liberty: Studies of Mill's on Liberty.* Belmont, CA: Wadsworth, 1966. Contains bibliography.

*Russell, Bertrand. *Authority and the Individual.* New York: Simon & Schuster, 1949.

———. *Freedom Versus Organization, 1814–1914.* New York: Norton, 1914.

CHAPTER 24. COMMUNISM

Adams, H. P. *Karl Marx in His Earlier Writings.* London: Allen & Unwin, 1940.

†*Berlin, Isaiah. *Karl Marx: His Life and Environment.* New York: Oxford University Press, 1959.

†*Buber, Martin. *Paths in Utopia.* London: Routledge & Kegan Paul, 1949 (Beacon).

†Dupre, Louis. *The Philosophical Foundations of Marxism.* New York: Harcourt, Brace & World, 1966.

Federn, Karl. *The Materialistic Interpretation of History.* London: Macmillan, 1939.

†Fromm, Erich. *Beyond the Chains of Illusion.* New York: Simon & Schuster, 1962 (Pocket Books).

†*———. *Marx's Concept of Man.* New York: Ungar, 1961.

†Fromm, Erich., Ed. *Socialist Humanism.* New York: Doubleday, 1967.

Gregor, A. James. *A Survey of Marxism.* New York: Random House, 1965.

†Hook, Sidney. *From Hegel to Marx.* New York: Reynal and Hitchcock, 1963 (University of Michigan Press).

———. *Towards the Understanding of Karl Marx.* New York: John Day, 1933.

Kamenka, Eugene. *The Ethical Foundations of Marxism.* London: Routledge & Kegan Paul, 1949.

Lachs, John. *Marxist Philosophy: A Bibliographical Guide.* Chapel Hill: University of North Carolina Press, 1967.

†Lichtheim, G. *Marxism.* New York: Praeger, 1961.

†Marcuse, Herbert. *Reason and Revolution,* 2nd ed. New York: Humanities Press, 1954 (Beacon).

———. *Soviet Communism.* New York: Columbia University Press, 1958.

†Mehring, Franz. *Karl Marx: The Story of His Life.* Ann Arbor: University of Michigan Press, 1962.

Pappenheim, Fritz. *The Alienation of Modern Man.* New York: Monthly Review Press, 1959.

†Petrovic, Gajo. *Marx in the Mid-Twentieth Century.* New York: Doubleday, 1967.

†Popper, Karl R. *The Open Society and Its Enemies.* Princeton, NJ: Princeton University Press, 1950 (Harper).

CHAPTER 25. BEHAVIORISM AND HUMANISM

†Allport, Gordon W. *Personality and Social Encounter.* Boston: Beacon Press, 1960.

Bertocci, Peter A., and Millard, Richard M. *Personality and the Good.* New York: David McKay, 1963.

Chomsky, Noam. *Cartesian Linguistics.* New York: Harper & Row, 1966. Based on an antibehaviorist theory of learning.

———. *Current Issues in Linguistic Theory.* The Hague: Mouton, 1964 (Humanities Press).

———. *Language and Mind.* New York: Harcourt, Brace & World, 1968.

———. "Review of B. F. Skinner, *Verbal Behavior.*" *Language,* Vol. 35 (1959). Sharply critical.

Estes, William, and others. *Modern Learning Theory.* New York: Appleton-Century-Crofts, 1954.

†*Freud, Sigmund. *Civilization and Its Discontents.* New York: Norton, 1962.

†Hook, Sidney, Ed. *Dimensions of Mind.* New York: Collier, 1961.

Lewin, Kurt. *Resolving Social Conflicts.* New York: Harper & Row, 1948.

†Marcuse, Herbert. *One Dimensional Man.* Boston: Beacon Press, 1964.

†*Rogers, Carl R. *On Becoming a Person.* Boston: Houghton Mifflin, 1961.

*———. *Client-Centered Therapy.* Boston: Houghton Mifflin, 1951.

Rothblatt, R., Ed. *Changing Perspectives on Man.* Chicago: University of Chicago Press, 1968.

Skinner, B. F. *Cumulative Record,* rev. ed. New York: Appleton-Century-Crofts, 1961.

†*———. *Science and Human Behavior.* New York: Macmillan, 1953.

†*———. *The Technology of Teaching.* New York: Appleton-Century-Crofts, 1968.

———. *Verbal Behavior.* New York: Appleton-Century-Crofts, 1957.

†*———. *Walden Two.* New York: Macmillan, 1948.

†Tolman, E. C. *Purposive Behavior in Animals and Men.* New York: Appleton-Century-Crofts, 1932.

Wann, T. W., Ed. *Behaviorism and Phenomenology.* Chicago: University of Chicago Press, 1964. See especially the essays by B. F. Skinner and Normal Malcolm.

Index